FIGURES		EVENTS AND PUBLICATIONS	
Ptolemy	c. 90–168	Domitian banishes philosophers from Rome	c. 89
Marcus Aurelius	121–180		
Sextus Empiricus	c. 200	*Confessions* (Augustine)	c. 397–401
Diogenes Läertius	c. 200	*On the City of God* (Augustine)	c. 413–427
Ambrose	339–397		
Aurelius Augustine	354–430	Fall of the Roman Empire	c. 476
Boethius	c. 480–524	*Consolation of Philosophy* (Boethius)	523
Anselm	1033–1109	Ontological argument appears in the *Proslogion* (Anselm)	1088
Abu Hamid al-Ghazali	1058–1111		
Albertus Magnus	c. 1200–1280	Formal charter of the University of Paris	1215
Thomas Aquinas	1225–1274	Renaissance begins in Italy	c. 1300
Nicolaus Copernicus	1473–1543		
Martin Luther	1483–1546	Protestant Reformation begins	1517
Francis Bacon	1561–1626	Copernican Revolution begins	1543
Galileo Galilei	1564–1642		
Thomas Hobbes	1588–1679		
René Descartes	1596–1650		
Baruch de Spinoza	1632–1677	Galileo tried by the Inquisition	1632
John Locke	1632–1704	*Discourse on Method* (Descartes)	1637
Nicolas Malebranche	1638–1715		
Isaac Newton	1642–1727	The Enlightenment begins with the publication of Descartes' *Meditations on First Philosophy*	1641
George Berkeley	1685–1753	*An Essay Concerning Human Understanding* (Locke)	*1690*
		A Treatise Concerning the Principles of Human Knowledge (Berkeley)	*1710*
David Hume	1711–1776	*Three Dialogues between Hylas and Philonous* (Berkeley)	1713
Adam Smith	1723–1790		
Immanuel Kant	1724–1804	*Treatise of Human Nature* (Hume)	1737
Jeremy Bentham	1748–1832	*An Enquiry Concerning Human Understanding* (Hume)	1748
Comte de Saint-Simon	1760–1825		
Thomas Malthus	1766–1834		
G. W. F. Hegel	1770–1831	American Revolution	1775–1783
		Dialogues Concerning Natural Religion (Hume)	1779
		Industrial Revolution begins in England	c. 1780
		Critique of Pure Reason (Kant)	1781
		Foundations of the Metaphysics of Morals (Kant)	1785
Arthur Schopenhauer	1788–1860	French Revolution	1789–1791
		Introduction to the Principles of Morals and Legislation (Bentham)	1789
		Reign of Terror and Defeat of Reason	1793–1794
		Essay on the Principles of Population (Malthus)	1798

ARCHETYPES OF WISDOM

An Introduction to Philosophy

ARCHETYPES OF WISDOM

An Introduction to Philosophy

Seventh Edition

Douglas J. Soccio

WADSWORTH
CENGAGE Learning™

Australia • Brazil • Japan • Korea • Mexico • Singapore • Spain • United Kingdom • United States

Archetypes of Wisdom, Seventh Edition
Douglas J. Soccio

Senior Sponsoring Editor: Joann Kozyrev

Assistant Editor: Nathan Gamache

Editorial Assistant: Michaela Henry

Media Editor: Diane Akerman

Marketing Manager: Mark Haynes

Marketing Assistant: Josh Hendrick

Marketing Communications Manager: Elizabeth Rodio

Project Manager, Editorial Production: Matt Ballantyne

Creative Director: Bruce Bond

Art Director: Faith Brosnan

Print Buyer: Marcia Locke

Rights Acquisitions Account Manager, Text: Roberta Broyer

Rights Acquisitions Account Manager, Image: Deanna Ettinger

Production Service: Robin Calkins

Text Designer: Marsha Cohen

Copy Editor: Jennifer Gordon

Photo Researcher: Billie Porter

Cover Designer: RHDG

Cover Image: © Jupiter Images

Compositor: Macmillan Publishing Solutions

For product information and technology assistance, contact us at **Cengage Learning Customer & Sales Support, 1-800-354-9706.**

For permission to use material from this text or product, submit all requests online at **www.cengage.com/permissions.** Further permissions questions can be e-mailed to **permissionrequest@cengage.com.**

Library of Congress Control Number: 2008942303

Student Edition:
ISBN-13: 978-0-495-60382-5

ISBN-10: 0-495-60382-1

Wadsworth
10 Davis Drive
Belmont, CA 94002-3098
USA

Cengage Learning is a leading provider of customized learning solutions with office locations around the globe, including Singapore, the United Kingdom, Australia, Mexico, Brazil, and Japan. Locate your local office at **www.cengage.com/international.**

Cengage Learning products are represented in Canada by Nelson Education, Ltd.

To learn more about Wadsworth or imprint, visit **www.cengage.com/ wadsworth**

Purchase any of our products at your local college store or at our preferred online store **www.ichapters.com.**

Printed in the United States of America
1 2 3 4 5 6 7 13 12 11 10 09

WE ARE ALL PHILOSOPHERS BECAUSE OUR CONDITION DEMANDS IT. WE LIVE EVERY MOMENT IN A UNIVERSE OF SEEMINGLY ETERNAL THOUGHTS AND IDEAS, YET SIMULTANEOUSLY IN THE CONSTANTLY CHURNING AND DECAYING WORLD OF OUR BODIES AND THEIR HUMBLE SITUATIONS. . . . THE RESULT IS A NAGGING NEED TO FIND MEANING. —RUSSELL SHORTO

FOR MARGARET,
WHO HAS SHOWN ME THAT GREATNESS OF SOUL
IS MORE THAN A PHILOSOPHER'S FANTASY.
THANK YOU DOES NOT BEGIN
TO COVER IT.

AND FOR FAVORITE FUTURE PHILOSOPHERS:
JAMES
JAKE
ABBY
MICHAEL
EMMA
RAYMOND

BRIEF CONTENTS

CONTENTS

PREFACE

All Seventh Edition modifications to *Archetypes of Wisdom* have been made with an eye to preserving that which makes it unique among introductory philosophy textbooks, namely, the respect it pays to the common expectation that philosophy has something to do with living issues, with the search for wisdom. Changes have not been made just for the sake of change. This revision enhances and refreshes the search-for-wisdom motif without impairing the presentation of core philosophical issues. This classroom-proven approach respects what some philosophers have unfortunately, in my opinion, characterized as a naive notion that needs to be corrected. I prefer to think of our meaning needs as common ground that unites us in a common desire to live meaningful lives.

Archetypes of Wisdom is designed to demonstrate to even moderately interested readers that philosophy—as both popularly and professionally conceived—is interesting and worthwhile for its own sake. To the extent that it succeeds, students discover naturally and for themselves that philosophy and philosophical questions play a role in their lives, even if they have not been aware of it.

Beginning with the Second Edition, each revision of *Archetypes of Wisdom* has benefited from an ongoing collaboration with readers ranging from highly specialized philosophers and philosophy teachers to students and individuals who read philosophy for pleasure and out of curiosity. In this light, the Seventh Edition of *Archetypes of Wisdom* sports a number of changes that will be obvious to readers familiar with earlier incarnations.

- ■ *Chapter 3:* "The Sophist: Protagoras" now includes a streamlined survey of the Presocratic Sophos. Setting the stage for the emergence of professional philosophers in the context of Presocratic questions and themes gets the philosophical show on the road with a bang, as it were, and shows how philosophical disagreements have practical consequences. By selectively alluding to current questions and controversies in metaphysics, education, ethics, and politics, this approach to the development of sophistry introduces readers to the origins of Western philosophy via a compelling narrative that allows them to recognize the philosophical nature of so many present-day concerns about fairness, the difference between knowledge and opinion, about the roles power, charm, and attractiveness play in getting ahead in the "real world," and other questions that recur again and again in the history of philosophy.

■ *Chapter 17:* "The Twentieth-Century: Ludwig Wittgenstein and Martin Heidegger" expands the presentation of Heidegger's critique of technology and the human condition and does so in less technical language. In an extensively revised style, Heidegger's sensitivity to what he saw as the "spiritual crisis" of our era is rendered in language that informs and engages readers by highlighting the existential dimension of what too often comes across as merely strange and forbidding. Heidegger's concern over the condition of humanity in a world seduced by idle talk, gossip, technology, inauthenticity, and the opinions of others neatly brings our story back to the big questions that so many students innately and genuinely care about, questions that they often expect to encounter in a philosophy course. These are precisely the sorts of questions today's busy culture tends to simplify, trivialize, or ignore: What does it mean to be a human being? Is there such a thing as wisdom? Does life, in general and in my particular case, have a meaning? Will modern technology save us, and if so from what? Or will it diminish or destroy us?

■ *Chapter 18:* "Philosophy As a Way of Life is back!" I am delighted to report that—after many, many requests, this capstone chapter, which was cut from the Sixth Edition to make room for Wittgenstein and Heidegger, has been reinstated, revised, updated and, I think, improved. As the title suggests, Philosophy As a Way of Life is a look at contemporary public philosophers and philosophical advocates—Carol Gilligan, Pierre Hadot, Martha Nussbaum, and Peter Singer—who see philosophy as more than an academic or theoretical practice. *New to this edition* are a discussion of the under representation of black women among academic philosophers and an expansion of Nussbaum's "capabilities approach" to philosophy. Sharing a big, open-hearted, and humane view of philosophy, the philosophers highlighted in Chapter 18 invite us, collectively and individually, to examine our lives in particular and as part of something larger than ourselves—to make philosophy our friend.

■ **For Your Reflection** questions have been placed at both the *beginning* and *end* of each chapter. Broken down into pre- and post-reading prompts, previous editions' end-of-chapter reflections have been reformulated into pedagogically improved learning objectives of varying degrees of sophistication that instructors can assign without modification or easily customize to suit their individual teaching styles and course objectives.

■ **For Deeper Reflection** are two new critical thinking/analysis questions placed at the front of each chapter to encourage students to look for more than information as they read. Without intruding on the joy of discovering new ideas for themselves, these front-of-chapter questions nurture students' critical thinking habits by giving them some important and interesting things to think about as they study—to read for more than mere information.

■ New and Continuing ■ Pedagogical Strengths

As in previous revisions, the entire text has been edited and modified with an emphasis on precision, historical flow, and useful cross-references. Here are some of the features that students, instructors, and general readers have consistently identified as contributing to *Archetypes of Wisdom*'s effectiveness and readability.

Multiple levels of sophistication The philosophical material presented here varies in degree of difficulty. Sophisticated philosophical arguments are always presented as part of a cultural context. Philosophical passages are explained in an unobtrusive way that shows students how to read critically and carefully by asking them pointed questions and by connecting philosophical issues to students' current interests in a natural, unforced, and nontrivializing way.

Inviting, visually appealing format encourages readers of many levels *Archetypes of Wisdom*'s large format makes possible the illustrations, margin quotes, margin glossary, and boxed passages that draw readers of various levels in "just to look around." Responses from students and instructors consistently indicate that many readers begin looking at pictures and reading margin quotes and boxed material out of curiosity and for pleasure only to find that they are also learning something about philosophy. Without a doubt, the most rewarding and touching comments I receive about *Archetypes of Wisdom* refer to the combined effects of these inviting features and take the form of "I never thought I would be able to understand philosophy, but this book has helped me to see that I can."

Integrated margin quotes and boxed passages From its inception, the carefully chosen and positioned margin quotes have been a particularly popular feature of *Archetypes of Wisdom*, cited by students and general readers alike as "fun" and "intriguing." Many readers indicate that they learn a great deal just by reading margin quotes. Margin quotes come from the central figures in each chapter, other philosophers, and a variety of other sources. Margin quotes and boxed passages enrich the content of the main text and make excellent discussion material. Reading them first can provide a painless overview of a philosopher's interests and related philosophical themes.

The pull of stories Even the most uninterested and resistant students respond to personal anecdotes about philosophers. With the exception of the first chapter, every chapter contains a brief but engaging philosophical biography of one or two main figures. These biographies provide cultural and historical context for the philosophical ideas covered in the chapter by *showing* students how philosophers respond to important concerns of their times.

Accessible depth *Archetypes of Wisdom* solves the problem of choosing between accessibility and depth by covering selected philosophers and philosophical ideas on a fundamental level. Careful juxtaposition of secondary commentary with primary source material of varying length and difficulty helps students learn how to read philosophical literature.

Cultural breadth *Archetypes of Wisdom* blends traditional Western philosophy, non-Western and nontraditional philosophy, and contemporary issues. Whenever appropriate, the figure of the *sophos* (sage) is used to link traditional and academic philosophical concerns with "everyday meaning needs." Nontraditional and non-Western selections include Asian humanism (philosophical Taoism, Confucianism, and Buddhism), existential iconoclasm (Søren Kierkegaard and Friedrich Nietzsche), public philosophy (Martha Nussbaum, and Peter Singer), philosophical feminism (Susan Bordo, Susan Moller Okin, and Carol Gilligan), philosophy of religion (Augustine, Abu Hamid Muhammad al-Ghazali, Thomas Aquinas, David Hume, Søren Kierkegaard, William James, Friedrich Nietzsche), and postmodern philosophy (Friedrich Nietzsche, Ludwig Wittgenstein, Martin Heidegger).

A *wide range of contemporary sources* *Archetypes of Wisdom* contains a variety of contemporary sources that address philosophical issues from beyond academic philosophy. These show—rather than merely tell—students that philosophy occurs outside of philosophy class and under other guises.

Flexible structure Each chapter is a self-contained unit. It is not necessary to cover sections in chronological order nor is it necessary to cover every chapter to have an effective class. Material not covered by the instructor can be used for independent writing assignments, group presentations, and the like.

Overviews of philosophical themes Summaries of classical and modern philosophical themes give students a story-like preview of key philosophical issues and a sense of historical context and continuity.

Philosophical Queries Philosophical Queries are topical questions that directly address the reader, prompting him or her to react critically to specific passages of text. They range from the personal to the controversial and can be readily modified for use as essay questions or to focus class discussion.

Chapter Commentaries Chapters conclude with clearly identified brief commentaries that include general evaluations or personal reflections concerning the philosophical ideas covered in the chapter; often they connect chapter ideas to contemporary issues.

Summary of Main Points Highlights of key ideas can be used as a handy preview, review, and discussion aid for each chapter.

Learning Objectives As previously noted, each chapter opens and concludes with questions keyed to the text. These range from specific to general and can function as review questions and as test or essay questions. Individual questions can be taken as they are or easily modified for use as reading quizzes, essay assignments or paper topics.

Sources A Notes section documents all sources for primary source extracts.

Two Glossaries In addition to a handy margin glossary, which defines key terms in the margins, highlighting their importance and facilitating text reviews, an alphabetical glossary with chapter and page references makes it easy to locate key terms in the text.

Bibliography of Philosophical Delights This collection of books (and a movie) contains some overlooked gems, as well as the more usual philosophy texts.

Index of Margin Quote Authors This popular feature helps students locate authors of margin quotes featured throughout the text.

Student-oriented Index Geared toward novice philosophers, the Index is extensively cross-referenced to help budding researchers and readers unfamiliar with philosophy find what they are looking for—and what they did not know they were looking for until they found it (serendipity).

Ancillary materials include

Companion Website This free Web site (www.cengage.com/philosophy/soccio/7e) contains overviews of key concepts, quizzes, flashcards, a pronunciation guide, and lecture containing overviews of each chapter in PowerPoint®, all presented in an engaging interactive format that encourages active studying.

Archetypes of Wisdom Resource Center This website contains tutorials, homework, and other tools to help students succeed in your Introductory Philosophy course. The resource center offers video and audio, and additional resources to help student's master course content and optimize study time.

Online Pronunciation Guide and Glossary This *valuable feature* combines an easily searchable online glossary with a handy pronunciation guide. In addition, easy-to-use flashcards provide students with an opportunity to see how well they know the terms.

Online Instructor's Manual with Tests In addition to the usual sections containing over 1200 true/false, multiple-choice, and essay questions, this unique manual includes a section on the philosophy of testing (how to prepare tests), lecture and discussion tips for all chapters, tips for new philosophy teachers (which are useful for all teachers), and a discussion of the special pedagogical features of *Archetypes of Wisdom,* and an updated list of 106 "philosophical films." Few, if any, instructor aids are as practical or complete; this is not a cursory job, but a truly useful compendium of tips, timesaving *classroom-tested* test questions, and flexible lecture guides.

Powerlecture with Examview and Joinin This easy-to-use lecture preparation and presentation tool allows you to assemble, edit, and present custom lectures for your course using Microsoft® PowerPoint®. The CD-ROM contains ExamView® computerized testing, PowerPoint presentations, and slides for use with the JoinIn Student Response System featuring TurningPoint®. There are also example syllabi, resource integration guides, an electronic version of the Instructor's Manual, video clips, and a link to the Book Companion Website.

How to Get the Most Out of Philosophy More than just a handbook for philosophy students, this success surprise of the first edition of *Archetypes of Wisdom* has grown in popularity with each revision. Today, thousands of instructors, counselors, and students use *How to Get the Most Out of Philosophy* as a general "student success" manual. *How to Get the Most Out of Philosophy* is available as a bundled supplement at a significantly reduced cost for adopters of *Archetypes of Wisdom* or as an independent text.

■ Acknowledgments ■

I am grateful to Tama Weisman, Quincy University; David M. Turner, National Park Community College; Christina M. Tomczak, Cedar Valley College; Terry Sader, Butler Community College; Paul Giaimo, Highland Community College; Dennis R. Cooley, North Dakota State University; Thomas Baker, Jefferson Community College; Alexander M. Izrailevsky, Salt Lake Community College; and Thomas A. Baker, Jefferson Community College for their advice and insight regarding this revision. Thank you for the generosity of spirit with which you conveyed your thoughtful and helpful responses to this text and your excellent suggestions for improving it. With so much good advice, I had to make some pretty tough decisions. Had I taken all of them, *Archetypes of Wisdom* would look like the hardback, multi-volume edition of the *Oxford English Dictionary*!

At Cengage/Wadsworth Publishing Company, this revision began under the superb stewardship of Worth Hawes and ended under the guidance of a new sponsoring editor, Joann Kozyrev. Worth and Joann are supportive, enthusiastic, and kind. They make working with them more an act of friendship than business.

Archetypes of Wisdom is a complicated book to put together, and once again I have been the beneficiary of a great team, including one of my favorite collaborators, production manager Robin Calkins. Robin is a joy to work with as she bears the brunt of coordinating artwork, text elements, and printing with aplomb and care. For this edition, Robin introduced me to Jennifer Gordon, a delightful, wise, and thorough copy editor. Jennifer has polished the text, caught errors of grammar and inconsistency, and saved me from many an embarrassing "uh-oh." As I have reviewed and reviewed and reviewed the manuscript, I have become increasingly impressed with Jennifer's skill and judgment.

I am also lucky enough to have Billie Porter as my photo researcher. Billie's expertise, energy, experience, and good-humor have, once again, helped me find new photographs and art to reflect and enhance my vision of *Archetypes of Wisdom* as a philosophy book with a heart, a book that speaks to our minds, hearts, and eyes.

Lastly, Siddhartha Ghosh of ICCORP has proven to be a careful, caring, and talented steward of the book I think of as one of my "children."

In the past, I have made fun of what, in my darker moods, I see as an academic obsession with "collaboration." But there is *pro forma* collaboration and then there is the real thing. This revision is a product of the latter, for which I am truly thankful.

A Brief Personal Note

Most importantly, I want to thank my wife, Margaret Malone, without whom, this book and my life would be much the poorer. When I am tempted to cut corners, Margaret says, in effect, "Okay, if *that's* good enough for you. Okay, if you don't mind putting your name to *that*." And, of course, it is not really okay. But more than being an editorial conscience when I need one, Margaret is a student advocate and a lover of philosophy. It matters to her that all readers and especially students get true, fair value from *Archetypes of Wisdom*. So she reads and rereads and re-rereads every jot and tittle, patiently, carefully, lovingly. I am her grateful and willing debtor.

This Preface was written during the last weeks of the very contentious 2008 Presidential Election. Like so many others, I got tangled in the frenzy of demonizing one candidate while beatifying the other. I fretted, moaning along with millions of others: "Woe are we if you-know-who wins!" By the time you read this, that which some dreaded so direly—and to which others looked with such hope— has come upon us and yet . . .

Our daily duties, our joys, our fundamental concerns, our life's meaning— whatever that means—do not depend on who the President is or on how many people agree with us about politics or religion or about anything else. As interesting or uninteresting as such things may be, they are not primary matters. Why, then, do we devote so much energy to such things and to things like them?

Because we are prone to forgetting what matters, maybe not in Plato's sense of forgetting, but, forgetting nonetheless. We routinely indulge in periods of philosophical amnesia, the alternative to which is not navel-gazing or logic-chopping, but philosophical conversation and reflection.

There is, of course, nothing new in this realization. Just the opposite, in fact. Philosophy's role in living a full, rich, life has been recognized and acknowledged throughout human history—and simultaneously mocked and denied as well. Philosophical concerns are found in the earliest reflections of our ancestors, in the record of their longings to belong, to matter, and to linger a while, to exist, to know themselves, to know God, to be free of God's shadow, to find a philosophy that worked for them or discover the one true philosophy that would endure for all time, to do our duty or to be as happy as possible, to seek power or strive to achieve serenity.

And so my final note of gratitude is for the existence of a deep, rich philosophical record reaching from the archaic sages down through the turbulent present. This is a record of profound, consoling human accomplishment, not because it is a record of linear progress, but because it is a record of seekers, a record of universal themes and questions, a record of controversies and changing philosophical fashions, but underneath the particulars, always a record of taking life seriously, a record of thinking about thinking, a record of *wonder*.

Archetypes of Wisdom is my antidote to forgetting philosophy. I hope that, in some small way, I have done right by the philosophers whom I have been able to include in it. They are superb company and it is a privilege to share them with you.

PHILOSOPHY AND THE SEARCH FOR WISDOM

GREY-EYED ATHENA SENT THEM A FAVORABLE BREEZE,
A FRESH WIND, SINGING OVER THE WINE-DARK SEA.

Homer

FOR YOUR REFLECTION

KEEP THESE QUESTIONS IN MIND AS YOU LEARN ABOUT PHILOSOPHY AND THE SEARCH FOR WISDOM.

1. *What is philosophy?*
2. *What are the primary areas of philosophy?*
3. *What is an archetype?*
4. *How does an archetype differ from a stereotype?*
5. *What is wisdom?*
6. *What is knowledge?*
7. *What is belief?*

FOR DEEPER CONSIDERATION

A. Analyze your own education up to this point. In what ways has it hindered, and in what ways has it supported, a love of wisdom?

B. To what extent do you think gender and ethnic background should be considered in evaluating an individual's philosophical beliefs? Do gender, ethnic background, and other factors (age, income, and so on) control what we think? Is your response to this question dependent on such factors? How would—or could—you find out without being unduly influenced by the very factors under scrutiny?

Philosophy is already an important part of your life, whether you know it or not. The word **philosophy** comes from Greek roots meaning "the love of wisdom." The earliest philosophers were considered wise men and women, or sages, because they devoted themselves to asking "big questions": What is the meaning of life? Where did everything come from? What is the nature of reality? For a long time, most philosophers were wisdom-seeking amateurs. That is, philosophy was a way of living for them, not a way of making a living. (The original meaning of *amateur* is one who is motivated by love, rather than by profit.)

We use the term *philosophy* in a similar sense when we think of a person's basic philosophy as the code of values and beliefs by which someone lives. Sometimes we talk about Abby's philosophy of cooking or Mikey's philosophy of betting on the horses. In such instances, we are thinking of philosophy as involving general principles or guidelines. Technically, that's known as *having a philosophy;* it is not the same thing as *being a philosopher.*

You don't have to be a philosopher to ask philosophical questions, you just have to be a naturally curious and thoughtful person. Here's just a sampling of the kinds of questions philosophers study:

▦ Does God exist?

▦ What's the meaning of life?

▦ Why do innocent people suffer?

▦ Is everything a matter of opinion?

▦ Are all people really equal, and if so, in what sense?

▦ What is the best form of government?

▦ Is it better to try to make the majority happy at the expense of the few, or make the few happy at the expense of the many?

▦ How are minds connected to bodies?

▦ Is there one standard of right and wrong for everyone, or are moral standards relative?

▦ Is beauty in the eye of the beholder?

▦ Does might make right?

▦ Is objectivity possible? Desirable?

▦ WHAT TO EXPECT ▦ FROM THIS BOOK

Although the idea of studying selected highlights of nearly three thousand years of (mostly) Western philosophizing may seem *exhausting*, this is not meant to be an *exhaustive* history of philosophy or survey of philosophical topics. That is, *Archetypes of Wisdom* is not meant to be "complete," covering every significant philosopher or every significant contribution made by the philosophers it does include. Rather, it's meant to be a *representative* and

philosophy
From Greek roots meaning "the love of wisdom."

First learn, then form opinions.
THE TALMUD

Beggars get handouts before philosophers because people have some idea of what it's like to be blind and lame.
DIOGENES

It is said that when Empedocles told Xenophanes that it was impossible to find a wise man, Xenophanes replied: "Naturally, for it takes a wise man to recognize a wise man."

"Surely, Life Is Not Merely a Job"

Why do we go through the struggle to be educated? Is it merely in order to pass some examinations and get a job? Or is it the function of education to prepare us while we are young to understand the whole process of life? Having a job and earning one's livelihood is necessary—but is that all? Are we being educated only for that? Surely, life is not merely a job, an occupation; life is wide and profound, it is a great mystery, a vast realm in which we function as human beings. If we merely prepare ourselves to earn a livelihood, we shall miss the whole point of life; and to understand life is much more important than merely to prepare for examinations and become very proficient in mathematics, physics, or what you will.

Jiddu Krishnamurti, from "The Function of Education," quoted in Daniel Kolak and Raymond Martin, *The Experience of Philosophy* (Belmont, Calif.: Wadsworth, 1990), pp. 20–21.

The effect of life in society is to complicate our existence, making us forget who we really are by causing us to become obsessed with what we are not.

CHUANG-TZU

---

inviting introduction to interesting and important questions of value, meaning, and knowledge and the cultural conditions that gave rise to them.

If you're reading this book as part of an academic course, I recommend treating your introduction to philosophy as an opportunity to distinguish between saying philosophical-sounding things and actually philosophizing. Perhaps the chief difference between just talking about philosophical ideas and actually philosophizing about them involves the degree of rigor and discipline you apply to your reflections.

We can say, then, that, generally, philosophy consists of careful reasoning about certain kinds of issues. Philosophical thinking includes careful assessment of terms, evaluation of logical reasoning, willingness to make refined distinctions, and so forth. Philosophers are especially interested in the arguments (reasons) offered to support our ideas.

Philosophical issues concern ultimate values, general principles, the nature of reality, knowledge, justice, happiness, truth, God, beauty, and morality. Philosophy addresses questions that other subjects do not address at all, and it addresses them in a more thorough way.

That's not to say, however, that we can tell whether or not a person is a philosopher just by their job description. Physicists, psychologists, physicians, literary critics, artists, poets, novelists, soldiers, housewives—all sorts of folks—engage in philosophical reflection without necessarily being labeled as philosophers. The quality of philosophical reasoning should concern us most, rather than the label "philosopher."

FRANK & ERNEST® by Bob Thaves

Frank and Ernest reprinted by permission of Bob Thaves.

Because of their nature, philosophical questions cannot be answered in the way that a mathematical or factual question can be answered with "4" or "the year 1066." Certain questions must be asked and answered anew by each culture and by any person who awakens to what Plato and Aristotle called the *philosophical sense of wonder*. Indeed, thoughtful individuals wrestle with philosophical questions all their lives.

• • • • • •

So what do you think? If you had the choice of being happy and blissfully ignorant or philosophically concerned but not always happy, which would you choose? Why?

PHILOSOPHICAL

QUERY

Of what use is a philosopher who doesn't hurt anybody's feelings?

DIOGENES

■ AREAS OF PHILOSOPHY ■

In practice, philosophy consists of the systematic, comprehensive study of certain questions that center on meaning, interpretation, evaluation, and logical or rational consistency. The primary areas of philosophy are listed here:

- *Metaphysics* encompasses the study of what is sometimes termed "ultimate reality." As such, metaphysics raises questions about reality that go beyond sense experience, beyond ordinary science. Metaphysical questions involve free will, the mind–body relationship, supernatural existence, personal immortality, and the nature of being. Some philosophers (see Chapters 10, 11, 13, and 15–17) question the very possibility of a reality beyond human experience, while others (see Chapters 2, 3, 5, 7, 8, and 9) base their philosophies on metaphysical notions.

- *Epistemology,* from the Greek for "knowledge," is the branch of philosophy that asks questions about knowledge, its nature and origins, and whether or not it is even possible. Epistemological questions involve standards of evidence, truth, belief, sources of knowledge, gradations of knowledge, memory, and perception. Epistemological issues cut across all other branches of philosophy. (See, in particular, Chapters 2–6, 8–11, and 13–17.)

- *Ethics,* from the Greek word *ethos,* encompasses the study of moral problems, practical reasoning, right and wrong, good and bad, virtues and vices, character, moral duty, and related issues involving the nature, origins, and scope of moral values. Today, it is not uncommon for ethicists to specialize in medical ethics, business ethics, environmental ethics, academic ethics, issues of ethnicity and gender, and the nature of the good life. Ethical issues include truth-telling, relativism, and universality. (See Chapters 2–7, 10–13, 16, and 17.)

- *Social and political philosophy* are concerned with the nature and origins of the state (government), sovereignty, the exercise of power, the effects of social institutions on individuals, ethnicity, gender, social status, and the strengths and weaknesses of different types of societies. (See Chapters 2, 4, 5, 7, 12, 13, 16, and 17.)

Without philosophy we would be little above the animals.

VOLTAIRE

Can we not understand that all the outward tinkerings and improvements do not touch man's inner nature, and that everything ultimately depends upon whether the man who wields the science and the techniques is capable of responsibility or not?

C. G. JUNG

Specialization is the price we pay for the advancement of knowledge. A price, because the path of specialization leads away from the ordinary and concrete acts of understanding in terms of which man actually lives his day-to-day life.

WILLIAM BARRETT

Other important areas of philosophy include logic, the study of the rules of correct reasoning; axiology, the study of values; aesthetics, the study of perceptions, feelings, judgments, and ideas associated with the appreciation of beauty, art, and objects in general; and ontology, the study of being and what it means to "Exist."

Philosophers sometimes concentrate on only one of these primary areas. Today some philosophers go so far as to reject whole areas of philosophy as unfit for study. For example, a logician might view metaphysics as overly abstract and confused; a moral philosopher might see the study of symbolic logic as belonging to mathematics, rather than philosophy. Whenever philosophers concern themselves with the meaning of life or the general search for wisdom, however, all of these primary areas are involved, even if some are not dealt with explicitly.

Contemporary academic philosophers tend to specialize even within these areas, concentrating on historical periods; certain philosophers; the philosophy of music, religion, or law; or particular philosophical issues, such as What is justice? Is objectivity possible? More than two hundred areas of specialization are currently listed by the Philosophical Documentation Center, a professional organization dedicated to compiling and disseminating research data and articles about philosophy.

■ PHILOSOPHICAL ARCHETYPES ■

In the ancient world, the wise person was known as the sage; in parts of Asia, a bodhisattva, yogi, or guru; in parts of Africa, a witch doctor; among Native Americans and the nomadic tribes of Asia, a shaman. In the Bible, the prophets were people of wisdom. In many cultures, the "grandmother" or "grandfather" or some other elder represents the basic image of the wise person. In the West, the wise person is often depicted as a male, but not always. In cartoons, the "wise man" is often caricatured as an oddball or hermit wearing a robe of some sort, maybe carrying a staff, and sporting a long white beard. Why do you suppose that is? Because even cartoonists tap into this nearly universal image—and we recognize it.

This kind of basic image is sometimes referred to as an *archetype*. According to psychologist C. G. Jung (1875–1961), an **archetype** is an image that has been shared by the whole human race from the earliest times. In its more traditional sense, an archetype represents our conception of the essence of a certain kind of person. An archetype is a fundamental, original model of some type: mother, warrior, trickster, cynic, saint, pessimist, optimist, atheist, rationalist, idealist, and so on. A **philosophical archetype** is a philosopher who expresses an original or influential point of view in a way that significantly affects subsequent philosophers and nonphilosophers.

The difference between an archetype and an *ideal* is that the archetype need not be good or perfect. The difference between an archetype and a *stereotype* is in their depth. A stereotype is a simplistic distortion of a type of person. An archetype, by contrast, is a powerful representation of a fundamental response to universal experiences. Archetypes exemplify essential ways of coping with the universal aspects of life (suffering, death, loss, society, wealth, knowledge, love, purpose) in uncommonly pure ways. There are archetypes of evil as well as good and of fools as well as of wise people.

archetype

Basic image that represents our conception of the essence of a certain type of person; according to psychologist C. G. Jung, some of the images have been shared by the whole human race from the earliest times.

archetype (philosophical)

A philosopher who represents an original or influential point of view in a way that significantly affects philosophers and nonphilosophers: cynic, saint, pessimist, optimist, atheist, rationalist, idealist, and so on.

©Erich Lessing/Art Resource, NY

© Leonard Freed/Magnum Photos

Archetypes of wisdom appear in many forms, from the rational Greek *sophos* (left) to the whirling Sufi dervish (right).

This introduction to philosophy is organized around philosophical archetypes. Even people who have not studied philosophy recognize the basic qualities of many philosophical archetypes. Most likely you have already encountered individuals who resemble some of them. Two brief examples will show you what I mean.

One philosophical archetype is the *skeptic* (Chapter 10). Skeptics believe that any claim to knowledge must be personally verified by their own sensory experience. They want to see, touch, taste, or measure everything. The New Testament contains an excellent example of this archetype in the person of "Doubting" Thomas, the disciple who would not believe that Jesus had risen from the grave until he carefully examined Jesus' wounds for himself.

Another philosophical archetype is the *utilitarian* (Chapter 12). Utilitarians believe that pain is inherently bad, that pleasure is inherently good, and that all creatures strive to be as happy as possible. Thus, utilitarians argue that our private and communal behavior should always maximize pleasure and minimize pain. You might recognize their famous formula: Always act to produce the greatest possible happiness for the greatest number of people. You probably also recognize utilitarian thinking in all sorts of "majority rules" reasoning.

The philosophers we will study include these two archetypes as well as exemplars of other significant philosophical schools and orientations. Philosophical archetypes are often the founders of the schools they represent, but not always. Sometimes the archetypal representatives of a philosophy are individuals who refine and develop others' ideas. In addition to their significance in the history of philosophy, archetypes confront universally important philosophical questions in ways that continue to be interesting and engaging.

A special virtue of archetypal figures is the intensity and purity of their belief in their philosophies. Philosophical archetypes are strict advocates of a philosophical worldview or philosophical method. The intensity with which they hold to their views, combined with exceptional philosophical depth and rigor, almost

It is no use at all to learn a list of archetypes by heart. Archetypes are complexes of experience that come upon us like fate, and their effects are felt most in our personal life.

C. G. JUNG

The only important problem of philosophy, the only problem which concerns us and our fellow men, is the problem of the wisdom of living. Wisdom is not wisdom unless it knows its own subject and scope.

LIN YUTANG

"It Is a Shameful Question"

The idea that devoting time to philosophy distracts us from "practical" concerns is an old one. And, of course, the very suggestion that philosophy is not as useful or practical as other subjects or activities is itself a philosophical idea that requires justification. In the following passage, the prolific philosophical historian Will Durant challenges the notion that being useful is supremely important:

The busy reader will ask, is all this philosophy useful? It is a shameful question: We do not ask it of poetry, which is also an imaginative construction of a world incompletely known. If poetry reveals to us the beauty our untaught eyes have missed, and philosophy gives us the wisdom to understand and forgive, it is enough, and more than the world's wealth. Philosophy will not fatten our purses, nor lift us to dizzy dignities in a democratic state; it may even make us

a little careless of these things. For what if we should fatten our purses, or rise to high office, and yet all the while remain ignorantly naive, coarsely unfurnished in the mind, brutal in behavior, unstable in character, chaotic in desire, and blindly miserable?

. . . Perhaps philosophy will give us, if we are faithful to it, a healing unity of soul. We are so slovenly and self-contradictory in our thinking; it may be that we shall clarify ourselves, and pull ourselves together into consistency, and be ashamed to harbor contradictory desires or beliefs. And through unity of mind may come that unity of purpose and character which makes a personality, and lends some order and dignity to our existence.

Will Durant, *The Mansions of Philosophy* (New York: Simon & Schuster, 1929), p. x.

---

always challenges our own, often unclarified, beliefs—whether we want to be challenged or not. Never fear. You alone always remain responsible for what you choose to believe, reject, or modify.

Learning about philosophical archetypes is a good way to get an initial picture of a philosophical orientation and the kinds of philosophers who are drawn to it. Learning about philosophical archetypes may also give you a better sense of your own present philosophy of life, or at least some aspects of it.

■ ARE PHILOSOPHERS ALWAYS MEN? ■

The history of Western philosophy contains mostly male representatives, most of them of European ancestry. This has led to the sarcastic but important charge that Western philosophy is nothing but the study of "dead white males." Even though increasing numbers of women are entering the ranks of professional philosophy today, men still outnumber women among professional philosophers.

Although throughout history individual women were recognized for their insight and brilliance, most of them remained—or were kept—outside of the formal history of philosophy. In our own times, the recognition of women philosophers is improving: Susanne Langer, L. Susan Stebbing, Simone de Beauvoir, Simone Weil, Ayn Rand, Christina Hoff Sommers, Alison Jaggar, Susan Moller Okin, and Martha Nussbaum, among many others, have achieved renown as philosophers. Women philosophers are still generally not as well known, however, as women in fields such as psychology. (The fact that women are still

I see many people die because they judge that life is not worth living. I see others paradoxically getting killed for the ideas and illusions that give them a reason for living (what is called a reason for living is also an excellent reason for dying). I therefore conclude that the meaning of life is the most urgent of questions.

ALBERT CAMUS

"The Prejudices of Practical Men"

If we are not to fail in our endeavour to determine the value of philosophy, we must first free our minds from the prejudices of what are wrongly called "practical" men. The "practical" man, as this word is often used, is one who recognizes only material needs, who realizes that men must have food for the body, but is oblivious of the necessity of providing food for the mind. If all men were well off, if poverty and disease had been reduced to their lowest possible point, there would still remain much to be done to produce a valuable society; and even in the existing world the goods of the mind are at least as important as the goods of the body. It is exclusively among the goods of the mind that the value of philosophy is to be found; and only those who are not indifferent to these goods can be persuaded that the study of philosophy is not a waste of time.

. . . Philosophy is to be studied, not for the sake of any definite answers to its questions, since no definite answers can, as a rule, be known to be true, but rather for the sake of the questions themselves; because these questions enlarge our conception of what is possible, enrich our intellectual imagination and diminish the dogmatic assurance which closes the mind against speculation; but above all because, through the greatness of the universe which philosophy contemplates, the mind also is rendered great, and becomes capable of that union with the universe which constitutes its highest good.

Bertrand Russell, *The Problems of Philosophy* (Oxford: Oxford University Press, 1912), selections from Chapters 1, 14, and 15.

underrepresented in many fields underscores the serious consequences that pervasive cultural prejudices have on the search for truth.)

Because, until recently, Western philosophy has been dominated by an emphasis on logical reasoning and written argument, other expressions of philosophical insight have been given less attention. Until the eighteenth century, most Western philosophers represented a small class of highly educated men, able to support themselves independently or associated with the Church or some other source of income. Only with the emergence of great public universities were higher education and philosophy open to people from other backgrounds. And even then, philosophers tended to remain members of an educated male elite.

In the following passage, Mary Ellen Waithe, the head of a team of scholars that has compiled a valuable series called *A History of Women Philosophers*, notes firsthand the difficulty of filling in some of the gaps in the history of philosophy:

> On a sweltering October afternoon in 1980 . . . I sought comfort in the basement library of City University of New York's Graduate Center. I came upon a reference to a work by Aegidius Menagius [on the history of women philosophers] published in 1690 and 1692. I had never heard of any women philosophers prior to the 20th century with the exceptions of Queen Christina of Sweden, known as Descartes' student, and Hildegard von Bingen, who lived in the 12th century. . . . It took sixteen months to obtain a copy of Menagius' book. . . .
>
> As it turns out, many of the women he listed as philosophers were astronomers, astrologers, gynecologists, or simply relatives of male philosophers. Nevertheless, the list of women alleged to have been philosophers was impressive.

One may view the history of philosophy as a history of heresy.

WALTER KAUFMANN

I do not know how to teach philosophy without becoming a disturber of the peace.

BARUCH SPINOZA

. . . By the end of 1981 I had concluded that the accomplishments of some one hundred or more women philosophers had been omitted from the standard philosophic reference works and histories of philosophy. Just check sources such as *The Encyclopedia of Philosophy,* Copleston, Zeller, Bury, Grote and others. If the women are mentioned at all, it is in passing, in a footnote.[1]

There is no escaping the fact that Western philosophy has been predominantly male-influenced throughout its history, shaped by a strong preference for rational and objective evidence rather than by more holistic and intuitive approaches to problems. The pervasiveness of this orientation makes it imperative that we acknowledge this problem. Chapters 9, 11, and 13–17 include some intriguing critiques of rationalism and universalism.

▪ PHILOSOPHY AND THE SEARCH FOR TRUTH ▪

Even with its cultural limits and biases, philosophy is perhaps the most open of all subjects. Its primary goals are clarity of expression and thought, and its chief components are reason, insight, contemplation, and experience. No question or point of view is off-limits.

The best philosophers—no matter what their personal beliefs—defer to the most compelling arguments regardless of their origins. Such important philosophers as Plato, Augustine, Thomas Aquinas, John Stuart Mill, Søren Kierkegaard, Friedrich Nietzsche, and Martin Heidegger, to name but a few, radically questioned and revised their own thinking over the course of their lives, reacting to what they saw as more compelling evidence.

Today, the philosophical arguments raised by women and other philosophical "outsiders" have expanded the ever-growing philosophical community. The history of philosophy is, in the words of Walter Kaufmann, the history of heresy.

There has always been a powerful philosophical tradition that challenges the status quo and confronts social institutions. In recent times, this tradition has found effective and powerful expression among philosophers concerned with the environment, animal rights, family structure, racism, and sexism.

Because archetypal figures exert such far-reaching influence, it is hard to predict who they will be with any certainty. That's understandable—we cannot merely assign archetypal status to a person, no matter how tempting that seems. In this regard, philosophy is no different from other fields. History teaches us that most of any given era's significant and popular figures don't usually retain their significance much beyond their own lifetimes. So predicting the emergence of archetypal philosophers must be approached with caution. In Chapters 17 and 18, we will look at some important twentieth-century philosophers and reflect on the persistence of philosophical questions.

The history of philosophy is a living thing. It is still being written. Perhaps you will contribute to it. Eventually all facets of wisdom may be equally welcome—and future textbooks will not have sections like this one. And as you will quickly see, the ultimate issue is not who said something or who said it first, but whether it

Philosophy's first promise is a sense of participation, of belonging to mankind, being a member of society.
SENECA

The most important thing that we can learn to do today is think for ourselves.
MALCOLM X

Reason or a halter.
DIOGENES

is true and worthwhile. Wisdom, it seems, transcends color, gender, social class, and ethnicity.

■ "Isn't All This Just a Matter of Opinion?" ■

Does it ever occur to you that there's no way to settle the kinds of philosophical issues we have been discussing because they are only about beliefs and opinions? Perhaps you believe that "What's right for someone else might not be right for me. It's best to just let others believe whatever they want, and I'll believe whatever I want." This kind of thinking is a form of "mellow" relativism. **Relativism** is the belief that knowledge is determined by specific qualities of the observer. In other words, absolute (universal) knowledge of the truth is impossible—one opinion is as good as another.

People who see themselves as sophisticated sometimes adopt a relativistic attitude toward such "philosophical" questions as What is the meaning of life? or Is democracy the best form of government? They reason that there are nearly as many answers to such questions as there are lifestyles, religions, cultures, and individuals.

Then, too, relativists can also point to the seemingly endless differences of opinion about abortion, the right to die, capital punishment, the existence and nature of God, affirmative action, immigration policies, the president's moral character, or the greatest rock and roll singer or basketball player in history. We haven't even gotten to evolution versus intelligent design, alien autopsies, whether men are from Mars and women are from Venus, whether one ethnicity or gender is superior to another, or whether homosexuals are fit to raise children. With all this diversity of opinion, the relativist wonders how we can ever agree on who is really wise.

Amateur relativists can be heard saying things like, "Well, there's no way to decide if this particular affirmative action policy is better than that one. African Americans, women, and members of other protected classes favor it because they'll get first crack at all the good jobs, government grants, and scholarships. Middle-aged white males don't like it because now it's their turn to ride in the back of the social bus. It's always a matter of *perspective*." Relativists say things like, "Professor, I think my essay grade is unfair. It's only your *opinion*. I mean this is not like science or math. Here in philosophy class, there's no real way to determine which opinion about Plato's theory of justice is true. Just because you've got a Ph.D. doesn't mean you're right. You're still just giving your opinion."

Somewhat more sophisticated versions of this sort of relativistic reasoning are made by some social scientists, who argue that there is no way for one culture to judge another. In America, for instance, most of us think it's wrong to treat women as second-class citizens who should defer to their fathers, brothers, and husbands. But in some Middle Eastern countries, the notion that women should have social equality is viewed as absolutely wrong. Who are we, the relativist asks, to judge a completely different way of life?

relativism
Belief that knowledge is determined by specific qualities of the observer, including age, ethnicity, gender, cultural conditioning.

Knowledge is power, but only wisdom is liberty.
WILL DURANT

In the following passage, the sociologist James Q. Wilson describes his experiences with relativism in the classroom.

In my classes, college students asked to judge a distant people, practice, or event will warn one another and me not to be "judgmental" or to "impose your values on other people." These remarks are most often heard when they are discussing individual "lifestyles," the modern, "nonjudgmental" word for what used to be called character. . . . If asked to defend their admonitions against "being judgmental," the students sometimes respond by arguing that moral judgments are arbitrary, but more often they stress the importance of tolerance and fair play, which, in turn, require understanding and even compassion. Do not condemn some practice—say, drug use or unconventional sexuality—that ought to be a matter of personal choice; do not criticize some group—say, ghetto rioters—whom you do not know and whose beliefs and experiences you do not understand. . . .

These students are decent people. In most respects, their lives are exemplary. Thus it was all the more shocking when, during a class in which we were discussing people who at great risk to themselves had helped European Jews during the Holocaust, I found that there was no general agreement that those guilty of the Holocaust itself were guilty of a moral horror. "It all depends on your perspective," one said. "I'd first have to see those events through the eyes of people affected by them," another remarked. No doubt some perpetrators were caught up in that barbaric episode for reasons that we might understand and even excuse. What worried me was not that the students were prepared to accept some excuses, but that they began their moral reasoning on the subject by searching for excuses. They seemed to assume that one approaches a moral question by taking a relativist position and asking, "How, given the interests and values of another person, might we explain what happened?" . . . To . . . many of my students . . . "What counts as a decent human being is relative to historical circumstance, a matter of transient consensus about what attitudes are normal and what practices are unjust."[2]

Wilson claims that such radical relativism is "rampant" among college students (and many professors) today. That's difficult to say. Regardless of how common relativism is, the issue of relativism remains controversial. Sometimes relativism is advocated as a form of tolerance, as in the example Wilson cites.

Conflicts between relativists and nonrelativists are found throughout the history of philosophy. Indeed, the first major Western philosopher, Socrates, emerged as a public figure partly because of his struggles with early relativists, known as sophists. The struggle between relativists and nonrelativists is one of the most exciting in the history of ideas. We'll study it in Chapters 3, 4, and 5, and then again toward the end of our survey of philosophy in Chapters 11 and 14–17.

(By the way, just about every relativist I have met *argues* for his relativism or at least tries to give *reasons* why my nonrelativism is inferior, misguided, mistaken, or intolerant. As if that weren't odd enough, the relativist often gets angry when I simply point out that, according to his own relativistic claims, it is impossible for his views to be "righter" than mine. After all, relativism is "just his opinion.")

Whether or not we're relativists, let's do our best to give philosophers a chance to make their cases before we accept or reject them.

There is no such thing as a crime of thought. There are only crimes of action.

Clarence Darrow

There is a principle which is a bar against all information, which is proof against all arguments and which cannot fail to keep a man in everlasting ignorance—that principle is contempt prior to investigation.

Herbert Spencer

The recipe for perpetual ignorance is: be satisfied with your opinions and content with your knowledge.

Elbert Hubbard

■ WISDOM, KNOWLEDGE, AND BELIEF ■

The chief goal of **wisdom** is a fundamental understanding of reality as it relates to living a good life. At its core, wisdom is reasonable and practical, focusing on the true circumstances and character of each individual. We might say then, that wisdom is good judgment about complex situations. Consequently, wisdom involves reflection, insight, a capacity to learn from experience, and some plausible conception of the human condition. Unlike forms of knowledge that require formal education and specialized intelligence, wisdom has been associated with experience in a way that theoretical and intellectual knowledge have not. That may be why wisdom is so often associated with the elders of a tribe or clan. Yet, clearly, age alone cannot guarantee wisdom, nor can intelligence. Wisdom has also been associated with personal virtue far more than knowledge has.

Philosophers generally agree that **knowledge** is some form of true belief. Questions then arise as to how to distinguish true belief from mistaken belief; and, as you might expect, different philosophers give different answers involving the roles of reason, perception, experience, intuition, and social agreement in this process. Some philosophers go so far as to deny the possibility of knowledge entirely. (See Chapters 3, 5, 9, 10, 14–17.)

Philosophers also distinguish between theoretical and practical knowledge. **Theoretical knowledge** involves the accurate compilation and assessment of factual and systematic information and relationships. **Practical knowledge** consists of skills needed to do things like play the piano, use a band saw, remove a tumor, or bake a cake.

Depending on their nature, evaluating knowledge claims involves logical argumentation, scientific experiments and predictions, or the demonstration of some skillful performance. It would seem, then, that to know *X* means, first, that *X* actually is true; second, that I believe *X* to be true; and third, that I can justify or establish my belief in *X* by providing adequate evidence.

Knowledge *claims* raise some interesting and thorny questions. For example, Is a strong personal feeling adequate evidence? How much proof is enough? According to whose criteria? Philosophers demand that we provide reasons to justify our knowledge claims.

In contrast to knowledge, **belief** refers to the *subjective mental acceptance* that a claim is true. Beliefs—unlike knowledge—need not be true. Because beliefs are subjective mental states, it is possible to be firmly convinced that a belief is correct when it is not. On the other hand, sometimes our beliefs are true, but we're unable to offer adequate evidence for them.

Although beliefs can be either true or false, technically speaking, "false knowledge" is impossible. The very idea is self-contradictory. For the most part, our everyday language reflects an understanding of this important distinction. We rarely say "I had false knowledge that peach pits boost intelligence." Instead, we say something like "I had pretty good reasons to think that peach pits boost intelligence, but I've since learned that I was mistaken." Or we say "I used to believe that peach pits boost intelligence, but now I know better." In other words, sometimes what we *thought we knew* turns out to be mistaken.

wisdom
Fundamental understanding of reality as it relates to living a good life; reasonable and practical, focusing on the true circumstances and character of each individual; good judgment about complex situations involving reflection, insight, and a plausible conception of the human condition.

knowledge
True belief.

knowledge (theoretical)
The accurate compilation and assessment of factual and systematic relationships.

knowledge (practical)
The skills needed to do things like play the piano, use a band saw, remove a tumor, or bake a cake.

belief
Conviction or trust that a claim is true; an individual's subjective mental state; distinct from knowledge.

belief (mere)
A conviction that something is true for which the only evidence is the sincerity of the believer.

Some beliefs are more reasonable than others, and there's a big difference between *informed* belief and *mere* belief. **Mere belief** refers to a conviction that something is true for which the only evidence is the conviction itself. If that sounds circular, it's because it is. Mere belief validates itself—or tries to. Most philosophers and scientists believe that truth cannot be reduced to merely believing something. For example, you do not have cancer just because you believe that you do. The best way to distinguish reliable beliefs from problematic ones is to subject important ideas to careful scrutiny. To a certain extent, we can, and must, do this for ourselves.

Ignorance Is Not an Option

Since ignorance is no guarantee of security, and in fact only makes our insecurity still worse, it is probably better despite our fear to know where the danger lies. To ask the right question is already half the solution of a problem. . . . Discerning persons have realized for some time that external . . . conditions, of whatever kind, are only . . . jumping-off grounds, for the real dangers that threaten our lives.

C. G. JUNG

Because we are all limited by our experiences, abilities, and preferences, we cannot just rely on our own untested thinking. We need to consider others' ideas, and we need to subject our beliefs to the scrutiny of others. In the realm of philosophy, we would be wise to take advantage of those thinkers and ideas that have stood the test of time and significance. (Of course, we do not want to accept the arguments of philosophers just because they are considered great or important.)

Even though we need to think for ourselves, impulsively or defensively rejecting important philosophical arguments before we have really thought about them is foolish—and arrogant. It is foolish because we cannot really know what value there is in a position if we do not give it fair hearing. It is arrogant because summarily rejecting (or mocking) ideas that have influenced careful thinkers from the past and present implies that *without any background knowledge* we know more than philosophers, scientists, and theologians who have devoted years of study to these issues.

More subtly, we can shut off challenging questions by prejudging them, by being inattentive and bored when they come up, or by mocking other points of view without investigating them. When we do this, we put ourselves in the position of holding onto a belief regardless of the facts. In such a state, we become indifferent to the possibility of error or enlightenment. **Willed ignorance** is the name of this closed-minded attitude, and it is as opposite from the love of wisdom as any attitude I can think of.

willed ignorance
An attitude of indifference to the possibility of error or enlightenment that holds on to beliefs regardless of the facts.

For most of us, ignorance is not a serious option. As thoughtful people, our choices are not between philosophical indifference and philosophical inquiry, but between a life lived consciously and fully or a life that just happens. Because of its fragility and finiteness, life is just too important not to philosophize about—and we know it.

▨ SUMMARY OF MAIN POINTS ▨

● The word *philosophy* comes from Greek roots meaning "the love of wisdom." Philosophy in the archetypal sense is an activity as well as a fixed body of knowledge. A philosopher is a lover of wisdom, someone who has a compelling need to pursue wisdom. Areas of philosophy include metaphysics, epistemology, axiology, ethics, aesthetics, political philosophy, social philosophy, and logic.

- Philosophical archetypes are philosophers who express an original or influential point of view in a way that significantly affects subsequent philosophers and nonphilosophers.

- The history of Western philosophy has been dominated by males of European ancestry, but increasing interest in women philosophers is expanding the scope and nature of philosophy.

- The chief goal of wisdom is a fundamental understanding of reality as it relates to living a good life. Wisdom is reasonable and practical, focusing on the true circumstances and character of each individual; wisdom is good judgment about complex situations that involves reflection, insight, and some plausible conception of the human condition.

- Philosophers generally agree that knowledge is some form of true belief. This raises questions about distinguishing true belief from mistaken belief; and different philosophers give different weights to the roles reason, perception, experience, intuition, and social agreement play in this process. Some philosophers deny the possibility of knowledge entirely.

- Philosophers distinguish between theoretical and practical knowledge. Theoretical knowledge involves the accurate compilation and assessment of factual and systematic relationships. Practical knowledge consists of skills needed to do things like play the piano, use a band saw, remove a tumor, or bake a cake.

- Relativism is the belief that knowledge is determined by specific qualities of the observer. In other words, absolute (universal) knowledge of the truth is impossible; "one opinion is as good as another."

- Willed ignorance is indifference to the possibility of one's error or one's enlightenment; people with this attitude hold on to beliefs regardless of the facts.

▨ POST-READING REFLECTIONS ▨

Now that you have had a chance to learn about philosophy, use your new knowledge to answer these questions.

1. Is our culture suffering from a kind of philosophical illiteracy? Cite specific examples and identify patterns to support your answer.

2. If you could make only one improvement in the American educational system, what would it be and why?

3. Are there better reasons for studying philosophy than just meeting some academic requirement? If yes, what are they? If no, why not? Don't be hesitant to give your honest opinion.

4. What is the difference between knowledge and belief? How are they related?

5. Popular and historical conceptions of the wise man usually present him as an elder. Do you think this is accurate? Is the notion of a wise young person somehow flawed? Explain, citing examples.

6. How would you explain what philosophy is to someone who did not already know?

PHILOSOPHY INTERNET RESOURCES

Go to the Soccio Web page at **http://philosophy.wadsworth.com/ Soccio7e** for Web links, practice quizzes and tests, a pronunciation guide, and study tips.

Overview of Classical Themes

Empty is the philosopher's argument by which no human suffering is therapeutically treated. For just as there is no use in a medical art that does not cast out the sicknesses of the bodies, so too there is no use in philosophy, unless it casts out the suffering of the soul.

EPICURUS

There is, I assure you, a medical art for the soul. It is philosophy, whose aid need not be sought, as in bodily diseases, from outside ourselves. We must endeavor with all our strength to become capable of doctoring ourselves.

CICERO

All humanity is sick. I come therefore to you as a physician who has diagnosed this universal disease and is prepared to cure it.

BUDDHA

The unexamined life is not worth living.

SOCRATES

Western philosophy began in ancient Greece about eight hundred years before the time of Christ. At that time, the chief component of Greek culture was a powerful religious mythology. These early myths offered primitive explanations of natural phenomena, human history, and the gods. They provided standards of conduct, morality, social obligations, education, art, religious practices, and so on. The most important mythical view of life was expressed in the *Iliad* and the *Odyssey*, two epic poems attributed to the ancient Greek poet Homer (c. eighth century B.C.E.).

For the Greeks of Homer's era, everything happened through some kind of divine agency. They believed, for example, that the sun was carried around the heavens by Apollo's golden chariot, that thunder and lightning were hurled down from the top of Mount Olympus by Zeus, and that the motion of Poseidon's trident created waves. Other natural phenomena were thought to have similar divine origins. The nature of the community, victory or defeat in war, the course of love, and other human affairs were also directly tied to the gods.

The ancient Greek gods were exaggerated human beings: bigger, stronger, and faster. Like human beings, they were also jealous, sneaky, biased, lazy, promiscuous, and violent. They were not, however, morally or spiritually superior to humans. In fact, the gods were often indifferent to human affairs, including human suffering, because they were involved in complicated soap operas of their own. Occasionally the gods took an interest in an individual human being or involved themselves in wars or politics, often treating people as pieces in an elaborate chesslike game.

Although the ancient Greeks' mythological accounting of events ultimately failed, it implied two crucial principles that are still disputed by philosophers:

1. There is a difference between the way things *appear* and the way they *really* are.

2. There are unseen *causes* of events.

These principles marked a major advance beyond less analytic mythological characterizations of nature and society.

Greek mythology was not sheer fantasy; it was the product of a desire to find explanations. Science grew out of this search for explanations, and philosophy grew out of attempts to provide rational justification for these early prescientific explanations.

As ancient Greece developed, its social structure became less restrictive (though by no means democratic in the modern sense). Colonization of outlying cities and communities contributed to the rise of philosophy, as increased social and political freedom combined with an established culture to permit increasingly free inquiry and exchange of ideas. As Greek civilization grew, colonization led to increasing interaction with sophisticated nearby Eastern cultures and the mythological worldview became less effective. Explaining events with "the gods willed it" became less and less satisfying.

Presocratic Western philosophers challenged the mythological worldview by asking for rational explanations of questions that mythology could not adequately answer: "Why doesn't the earth fall out of the sky like an apple from a tree?" "What holds it up? And what holds that up?" "Why don't the stars fall out of the sky?" Or, more subtly yet, "How come if I eat fish and grain, I don't look like a fish or stalk of wheat? How does 'fish stuff' become fingernail 'stuff'? Where does the stone go that is worn away by the waterfall? I cannot see it being chipped away. What is

Homer's *Iliad* had a major impact on ancient Greek culture. This powerful tale of the Trojan war intertwined the lives of humans with the whims of Olympian gods and provided a mythical ideal of the hero.

this invisible 'stuff' that 'goes away'?" And, again: "Where did 'stuff' come from? Where does it go?" (See Chapter 3 for a fuller account of this stage of philosophical development.)

■ NATURE AND CONVENTION ■

In their efforts to provide *unified* rational explanations, these early philosophers first concentrated on the "world order" (*kosmos* in Greek) and "nature" (*phusis* or *physis* in Greek). You may recognize the roots of the English words *cosmos* and *physics* in these ancient Greek terms.

Around the fifth century, an element of specialization emerged throughout the ancient world. Actually, the word *division* is probably more accurate than *specialization* because philosophers began to distinguish between nature (*physis*) and convention (*nomos*), rather than to specialize along narrower lines. The terms *norm*, *normative*, and *normal* derive from the Greek root *nomos*. In the West, humanistic philosophers known as Sophists (Chapter 3) turned away from the study of nature and toward the study of "man." In China and Southeast Asia, humanistic sages (Chapter 2) turned away from the study of gods and spirits and toward the study of "man" and nature.

■ CONTEMPORARY LESSONS FROM THE PAST ■

You're right to wonder about the use of the word *man* here: The ancient world was socially hierarchical and chauvinistic in its divisions of people into social classes of varying status, influence, and power according to nationality, bloodlines (a crude form of "racial" thinking), gender, language and dialect, talent, and beauty.

For many—but not all—classical philosophers, women were, by nature, not capable of philosophical reasoning. Of course, in this, the philosophers were not alone; they reflected the norms of their times, as did many women. The

The Olympian god Atlas was said to support the world on his shoulders. Growing dissatisfied with such mythological accounts of natural phenomena, Presocratic philosophers sought rational explanations.

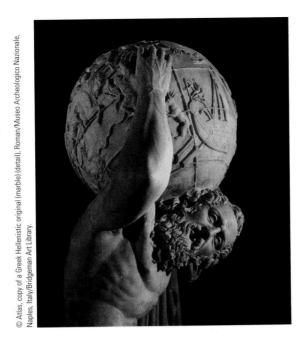

© Atlas, copy of a Greek Hellenistic original (marble) (detail). Roman/Museo Archeologico Nazionale, Naples, Italy/Bridgeman Art Library.

Asian sage Confucius (Chapter 2), for example, compared women to servants who were easily offended. Plato, arguably the single most influential Western philosopher, thought of women as "lesser men," although he also allows women in the ranks of the philosopher-kings who occupy the highest strata in his ideal state (Chapter 5). Aristotle (Chapter 6), one of the most significant thinkers in the history of Western philosophy, thought of women as "mistakes" of nature—"incomplete" or "misbegotten" men. The hedonist Epicurus, on the other hand, made no philosophical distinctions between men and women (Chapter 7).

Persons and Arguments

When we uncritically and rigidly apply contemporary values to past practices and ideas, we commit the *fallacy of anachronism*. Even though we can never be sure that our current understanding of the past is accurate, we can make good-faith efforts to understand the conditions that affected people's thinking and acting. Doing so does not commit us to some form of relativism or prevent us from evaluating ideas from other times and cultures. Rather, understanding the historical context that gives rise to a philosophical point of view allows us to cull from the richness and complexity of the entire human condition. Further, we do not need to reject an entire philosophical enterprise just because we find some aspect of it unacceptable—unless what's unacceptable is the heart of the enterprise or is entailed by essential components of it.

Just as we do not want to uncritically impose contemporary values on ancient philosophers, neither do we want to reject a philosopher's arguments because we object to that philosopher's personal habits or beliefs. When we do that, we commit what is known as the *ad hominem* fallacy. *Ad hominem* is Latin for "at the man." In this context it means "against the arguer, against the person making the argument." (Ironically, the term *ad hominem* presents us with an example of the pervasiveness and ambiguity of terms based on the root *man*: *mankind, human, chairman, humanistic,* even *woman*.)

Some of the most important and complex questions philosophers ask today concern proper attitudes toward thinkers from the past. Chapters 9, 11, 17, and 18 address this issue directly, and reference to it recurs throughout our philosophical journey. But at the beginning of this inquiry, let me encourage you to *seek empathetic understanding before passing judgment on new ideas and those who advocate them.* Practicing this principle helps avoid confusing issues and arguments with the persons who advocate them. (See the "Persons and Arguments" box on page 19.)

◼ THE SEARCH FOR EXCELLENCE ◼

One of the major themes in ancient philosophy is the search for general human excellence, or virtue. The Greek word for virtue (*arete*) means "excellence" and is associated with potency and functionality. The Chinese word for virtue (*jen*) connotes benevolence, humanity, and being a real, authentic person. Thus, something lacking in virtue fails to function in some way. Without virtue, things are dysfunctional, incomplete, not themselves, not what they are meant to be.

In the West, the philosophical search for human excellence links the Sophists (Chapter 3) to Socrates (Chapter 4), Plato (Chapter 5), Aristotle (Chapter 6), and the Stoics (Chapter 7). In Asia, the ancient sages also produced longstanding theories of virtue and well-being (Chapter 2).

◼ THE SEARCH FOR HAPPINESS ◼

As a rule, ancient philosophers did not distinguish between "being good" and "being happy" the way many of us do today. Rather, they thought of living the good life as living well, in the sense of thriving, of being healthy or "fully human."

Today, it is common to equate being happy with almost any form of personal satisfaction. If happiness is a feeling, then I cannot be wrong about being happy: If I *feel* happy, I *am* happy. This particular view of happiness defines "being happy" in purely subjective and individualistic terms.

Classical notions of happiness were more complicated. A helpful analogy here is between *being* healthy and *feeling* healthy and *being* happy and *feeling* happy. It's easy to understand that Margaret may not be well even though Margaret feels well. In other words, Margaret can be unhealthy and feel fine. Conversely, Joe can be convinced that he is dying from cancer even though he is cancer-free. Further, unhealthy individuals can—because they are unhealthy—get used to being sick. Thus, the habitual smoker "feels good" when she poisons herself with a puff on a cigar, but "feels bad" when she acts wisely and refrains from smoking.

If, however, more than subjective conditions are necessary for happiness, then the individual is not the determiner of happiness. In such a view, it is possible to think you are happy and be wrong. If that sounds crazy to you, you are not alone. But before dismissing classical notions of happiness, wait and see what sorts of reasons the ancient philosophers give for their views.

THE ASIAN SAGES

Lao-tzu, Confucius, and Buddha

WHO KNOWS WHY HEAVEN DISLIKES WHAT IT DISLIKES?
EVEN THE SAGE CONSIDERS IT A DIFFICULT QUESTION.

Lao-tzu

HE WHO LEARNS BUT DOES NOT THINK IS LOST; HE WHO
THINKS BUT DOES NOT LEARN IS IN DANGER.

Confucius

IF YOU WILL NOW AND AT ALL TIMES, WHETHER WALKING,
STANDING, SITTING, OR LYING, ONLY CONCENTRATE ON
ELIMINATING ANALYTIC THINKING, AT LONG LAST
YOU WILL INEVITABLY DISCOVER THE TRUTH.

Buddha

2

LEARNING OBJECTIVES

- WHAT ARE THE QUALITIES OF THE SAGE?
- WHAT IS *TAO*?
- WHAT ARE *YIN* AND *YANG*?
- WHAT IS THE GOLDEN MEAN?
- WHAT IS HUMANISM?
- WHAT IS *LI*?
- WHAT IS *JEN*?
- WHAT IS ASCETICISM?
- WHAT ARE THE FOUR NOBLE TRUTHS?
- WHAT IS A *BODHISATTVA*?
- WHAT IS *NIRVANA*?

FOR YOUR REFLECTION

KEEP THESE QUESTIONS IN MIND AS YOU LEARN ABOUT THE ASIAN SAGES.

1. *What are the qualities of the sage?*
2. *What is* Tao?
3. *What are* yin *and* yang?
4. *What is the Golden Mean?*
5. *What is humanism?*
6. *What is* li?
7. *What is* jen?
8. *What is asceticism?*
9. *What are the Four Noble Truths?*
10. *What is a* bodhisattva?
11. *What is* nirvana?

FOR DEEPER CONSIDERATION

A. According to ancient Chinese cosmology, the whole of nature consists of the continual interaction of two opposing forces, yin and yang. Discuss how this belief (or is it an observation?) leads Lao-tzu to the "way of inaction." What kind of action does Lao-tzu warn against? Why? Cite some current real-life examples of "action that rebounds" to support Lao-tzu. On balance, do you think the doctrine of inaction is sound? Feasible? Explain.

B. Confucius's distinction between the superior individual (*chun-tzu*) and the petty individual (*hsiao-jen*) strikes some philosophers as elitist, as does his advocacy of ceremony (ritual and manners). At first glance, it is easy to see why, given the value we place on egalitarianism and equality and given our distrust of "artificial" values. But are we, perhaps, exalting individuality at the expense of humanity and, thus, ultimately trapping the very selves we are trying to protect from repressive, "uptight" artificiality?

*O**ur survey of philosophical archetypes*** begins with a look at three of the most influential philosophical archetypes of all time, the sages Lao-tzu, Confucius, and Buddha. A therapeutic figure who combines religious inspiration with extraordinary insight into the human condition, the **sage** is the oldest of the philosophical archetypes. The English word *sage* is derived from the Latin *sapiens*, meaning "wise." The term *sage* has been used to refer to masters associated with religious traditions and to the wise elders of a group or tribe. Philosophers who address how we live and whose lives reflect noteworthy integrity, compassion, and courage are also referred to as sages. As a rule, the ancient sages focused on identifying the root causes of happiness and unhappiness. Today, the title *sage* is associated with individuals who manifest a deep, lifelong commitment to learning and teaching that extends beyond an academic or merely theoretical interest in living wisely.

THE HARMONY OF HEAVEN AND EARTH

In ancient Asian cosmologies, all events were said to be interconnected. In ancient Chinese cosmology, everything was influenced by the harmonious working together of Heaven and Earth following the *Tao* of all existence. Literally "way" or "path," **Tao** (or **Dao**) cannot be precisely defined or named. It is translated as the source of all existence, the principle of all things, the way or path of the universe, or the moral law. Tao "unfolds" and "influences" all of nature while remaining hidden from empirical (sensory) experience.

In this cosmology, Heaven and Earth constitute a single reality, a sort of Heaven-Earth, rather than two diametrically opposed and separate realities; nature consists of the continual interaction of two opposing, but not separable, forces known as *yin* (Earth, passive element) and *yang* (Heaven, active element). **Yin** is weak, negative, dark, and destructive; **yang** is strong, positive, light, and constructive. Heaven (yang) and Earth (yin) exist in a perpetually harmonious balance, actually a perpetual *balancing*, according to Tao. Yin and yang go so far back in Chinese history that we cannot be sure of their original meanings. The classic Confucian text *The Doctrine of the Mean* says, "Equilibrium is the great foundation of the world, and harmony its universal path.[1]

By the fifth century B.C.E., yin and yang were thought of as inextricably linked together. Each was viewed as an expression of the other, operating together in a never-ending cycle of coming together and falling apart, birth and death, wet and dry, day and night, good and evil, male and female, full and empty. This ceaseless interplay of opposing forces is the natural order of things. "Part" and "whole" cannot be understood—much less exist—without each other. How could they? The very essence of being a part requires a whole to be a part of, and there can be no whole without parts.

Thus, there are no firm (permanent and fixed) divisions between the spiritual and the physical or between the natural and the supernatural, nor is there a distinct division between the divine and the human, between reason and intuition.[2]

---

sage

Archetypal figure who combines religious inspiration and extraordinary insight into the human condition; the English word *sage* is derived from the Latin *sapiens*, meaning "wise."

Tao

Literally "way" or "path," Tao (or Dao) is variously translated as the source of all existence, the principle of all things, the way or path of the universe, or the moral law; key concept in Confucian and Taoist philosophy.

yin

In Ancient Chinese metaphysics, weak, negative, dark, and destructive natural force or principle; Earth; linked with yang.

yang

In Ancient Chinese metaphysics, strong, positive, light, and constructive natural force or principle; Heaven; linked with yin.

The intellect can understand any part of a thing as a part, but not as a whole.

   R. H. BLYTH

By nature men are alike. Through practice they have become far apart.

   CONFUCIUS

Therefore, Tao, the way of Heaven-Earth, cannot be understood analytically, considered piecemeal, individually.

But if life consists of some fundamental, never-ending, and harmonious exchange, why do we so often experience it as a series of apparently discrete, independent events and either-or options? We experience life, or more properly the illusion of life, as discrete events because we are unenlightened and confused. Unaware that the flow of Tao cannot be trapped, we identify with particularities; we prefer the familiar to the exclusion of all else; we cling to things for fear of losing them; we confuse words (labels) with perception (experience). It falls to the sage to identify and preserve Tao by refining the way we talk about it.[3]

So elusive is this goal that even the sages, with all their wisdom, remain susceptible to the partial view. They disagree over whether human beings are naturally good or naturally evil, over whether Tao is best realized actively through social customs and training (Confucius) or through setting aside all personal striving while spreading compassion to others (Buddha). Lao-tzu recommends passively going with the flow of Tao by abandoning social cultivation and following our natural instincts. Yet for all their apparent differences, the sages insist—if that's the word for it—that suffering, division, and strife need not be our permanent condition, for we share a common human nature from which we can learn. Religion, philosophy, culture, and politics are themselves manifestations of Tao; they interact as complementary parts of a single reality perpetually seeking balance.

■ SAGEHOOD ■

The sages' focus on achieving harmony and virtue here and now is a response to the social conditions in which they lived. For Lao-tzu and Confucius, this was a time of such widespread political and social turmoil that it came to be known as the Period of the Warring States. Although traditional Chinese history holds that the Period of the Warring States began in 453 B.C.E. and lasted for nearly 550 years, some historians push the beginning as far back as 771 B.C.E.

The Period of the Warring States was marked by fierce struggles for power waged by a succession of warring princes. The resulting civil wars became increasingly violent as armies ignored the customs and traditional rules of conduct known as *li* that had previously prevented wholesale pillage and destruction. Each atrocity was answered with an equal or greater atrocity. In one notorious incident, soldiers from one army were not paid until they showed the paymaster the severed heads of their enemies.

A. C. Graham, a leading authority on Chinese thought and grammar, describes the teachings of the ancient sages as responses to the "breakdown of the rule of Heaven" and the moral and political chaos that resulted. Instead of asking "What is the truth?" as early Western philosophers did, the Asian sages asked "Where is the Way (Tao)?" Where, they wondered, is the way back to social order and proper conduct?[4] As a result of their practical concerns, the teachings of the sages are marked by what the philosopher Michael Brannigan characterizes as "an intimate rapport between philosophy and its actualization in society."[5]

The superior man stands in awe of three things. He stands in awe of the Mandate of Heaven; he stands in awe of great men; and he stands in awe of the words of the sages. The inferior man is ignorant of the Mandate of Heaven and does not stand in awe of it. He is disrespectful of great men and is contemptuous toward the words of the sages.

CONFUCIUS

To live in the company of Men-at-their-best is the finest thing possible. How can a man be considered wise if, when he has the choice, he does not live in such surroundings?

CONFUCIUS

A "fully human" sensitivity links the three sages we'll look at in this chapter, each of whom speaks from intimate knowledge of suffering and disappointment. Offering anyone who will listen the fruits of their hard-earned "research," sages perform a complex social function: part physician of the soul, part prophet, part preacher, part philosopher, part fellow seeker. In subsequent chapters, we'll look at the Western sages Socrates (Chapter 4), Epicurus, Epictetus, and Marcus Aurelius (all Chapter 7).

Unsurprisingly, the sage has no exact equivalent today, at least not in this culture, a culture that encourages individuation and competition, seemingly perpetual social war—precisely what the sages sought to overcome. In this regard, you might find it interesting to contrast the sage with the more warlike Sophist, a might-makes-right seller of methods for getting whatever one wants, whose philosophy seems surprisingly contemporary. Sophists are discussed in Chapter 3.

If you are unfamiliar with the teachings of the ancient philosophical sages, don't be fooled into thinking that because they talk about harmony and balance sages are preachy "anti-life" figures who don't have anything practical to offer a high-tech, high-energy, individualistic, competitive society. Perhaps the high-tech, specialized (disharmonious) nature of our lives means that just the opposite is true. The lasting appeal and influence of the sages suggests that we're not completely sold on the pursuit of fame, power, riches, and prestige, even though we can't just toss our interest in them aside. In distinct but overlapping ways, these archetypal figures encourage us to achieve sagehood for ourselves.

> *When you find something that is bad or that turns out bad, drop it and leave it alone.*
> SITTING BULL

> *Only the most intelligent and the most stupid do not change.*
> CONFUCIUS

• • • • • •

Based on what you've read so far, can you think of any contemporary examples of sages? If you can, what specific qualities or teachings impress you as sagelike? If you can't, why do you suppose you can't?

PHILOSOPHICAL

QUERY

▪ THE DO-NOTHING SAGE: LAO-TZU ▪

Legend says that **Lao-tzu** (c. 575 B.C.E) was a bureaucrat in ancient China, known only by a nickname variously translated as Old Master, Old Man, Old Boy, or Old Philosopher. He may have compiled his book, the *Tao te Ching*, under a pseudonym as a form of self-preservation, since he lived during the instability of the Period of the Warring States. The scholar A. C. Graham suggests that living in a state of "perpetual fear" taught the reclusive Lao-tzu (whoever he really was) to develop a self-preserving "habit of evasive speech."[6] In fact, however, we know very little of Lao-tzu.

According to legend, when he was 160 years old Lao-tzu grew so disgusted with the hypocrisy and decay of his time that he decided to resign from his position as a bureaucrat to pursue virtue in a more natural environment. Heading west, Lao-tzu reached the Han-ku Pass, where the keeper of the pass recognized the old sage and said, "You are about to withdraw yourself from sight. I pray you compose a book for me." Lao-tzu honored the man's request by producing a little (5,000-word) book known today as the *Tao te Ching*.[7]

Lao-tzu

Next to the *Analects* of Confucius, the *Tao te Ching* is the most influential book in Chinese history. Nearly a thousand commentaries on it have been written in China and Japan alone. The *Tao te Ching,* or *The Classic of the Way and the Power (Virtue),* is second only to the Bible in the number of English translations available. Today, interpretations of Taoism are continuously emerging in popular philosophical, spiritual, and psychological literature.

What accounts for the power of this slim volume, usually divided into eighty-one "chapters" of a page or less in length? Some scholars claim that the *Tao te Ching* is so cloudy and obscure, so romantic and poetic, that the reader is free to make it mean anything. To them, the popularity of the *Tao te Ching* derives from its lack of clarity, from its ability to mean all things to all people, and from its brevity.

A more intriguing possibility is that the book credited to the secretive, perhaps fearful Old Philosopher expresses genuine, timeless wisdom. Let's see what Lao-tzu has to say to us in the twenty-first century.

■ THE WAY ■

Rather than presenting a philosophic *system,* Lao-tzu struggled to express a sense of the ultimate, underlying great principle, rule, or cause of "the way all things are."

Lao-tzu refers to Tao in poetic, suggestive terms. He appeals to our "natural instincts" and intuitions. In so doing, he hopes to render as little injustice as possible to the throbbing, rich, ever-flowing stream of the Way. Tao is, he implies, too rich, too big and too small, simply "too much" to be "trapped" by definition, description, or system. Thus, this Taoist sage often speaks in apparent contradictions, in pairs of opposites. He points out "the rest of the story" by calling our attention to overlooked, but essential, aspects of the Way. In *A Source Book in Chinese Philosophy,* Wing-Tsit Chan points out that Tao does not refer to a system or moral truth but to a way of life. Tao is

> . . . the One which is natural, eternal, spontaneous, nameless, and indescribable. . . . As a way of life, it denotes simplicity, spontaneity, tranquility, weakness, and most important of all, non-action (*wu wei*). By the latter is not meant literally "inactivity" but rather "taking no action that is contrary to Nature"—in other words, letting Nature take its own course.[8]

In the opening stanza of the *Tao te Ching,* Lao-tzu signals us that this is not an attempt to articulate Tao according to the limiting rules of rational consistency. Ever-flowing, Tao cannot be captured in systems or in words. Consider the subtle differences among the following two translations of the famous opening lines of Chapter 1 of the *Tao te Ching:*

(1) The Tao that can be told of
Is not the absolute Tao;
The Names that can be given
Are not the Absolute Names.
The Nameless is the origin of Heaven and Earth;
The Named is the Mother of All Things.[9]

(2) As for the Way, the Way that can be spoken of is not the constant Way;

As for names, the name that can be named is not the constant name.

The nameless is the beginning of the ten thousand things;

The named is the mother of the ten thousand things.[10]

Each translation *approximates* a "sense of something," circles but cannot explicitly define the Way. In Lao-tzu's phrase, words cannot "trap" Tao. The sage must find a way to "speak without speaking" and "discuss what cannot be discussed." The sage will attempt to communicate the experience of a cosmic or spiritual pattern; this is quite different from expressing a concept, idea, or principle.

People Cannot Stop Talking About It

Why doesn't Lao-tzu just come right out and tell us straightforwardly that the Way cannot be expressed in words, that it is the source of all things, and that it is only discovered by ridding ourselves of desire? Perhaps because that's not precisely what he means. "The trouble with words," Graham says, "is not that they do not fit at all but that they always fit imperfectly."[11] Just because the Way cannot be "reduced" to words or principles does not mean that nothing important and useful can be said about it. Poignantly, Lao-tzu says that although we cannot talk about Tao, "people cannot cease discussing It." And that includes, of course, Lao-tzu.

Lao-tzu's solution to the problem of expressing what cannot be trapped in words is to develop a kind of paradoxical way of communicating in which contradictory assertions and demands keep us from fixing on one "trapped" or "dead" interpretation. The sage's hope is that this kind of giving with one hand and taking with the other will "draw us in the direction which is the Way."[12]

Western philosophers as diverse as Heraclitus (Chapter 3), Søren Kierkegaard (Chapter 14), William James (Chapter 15), Friedrich Nietzsche (Chapter 16), and Martin Heidegger, Ludwig Wittgenstein, and Jacques Derrida (Chapter 17) struggle with the "problem of language" and adopt their own indirect strategies for dealing with what cannot be said, usually with more sting than the Old Boy.

In many ways, the history of philosophy is a history of struggling to say what must be said in ways that do justice to human experience. The sages are not alone in confronting the problem of language. Yet the problem of language lingers because, upon reflection, experience always seems to elude us, to defy complete verbalization. No matter what we say about life, *living itself* is always something more. It seems as if our best attempts to define or explain "the Way of life" always fall short. Yet the attempts themselves, Lao-tzu reminds us, the very failures themselves, are Tao, are part of life. It is the mark of a sage to know when to stop talking—and when not to.

When we consider all the philosophical, religious, and scientific talk—chatter—about life, virtue, and ultimate Reality with a capital R, Meaning with a capital M, and Truth with a capital T, Lao-tzu's puzzling opening lines attain the power of insight: Talk in the form of once-and-for-all, absolute, fixed systems, dogmas, objective truths, and universal theories pales beside *living itself*.

"Saying" (talk) can help, but saying can also hurt. Saying helps when it draws us to the Way, when it awakens us to something more, something beyond ordinary

What we cannot speak about we must pass over in silence.

LUDWIG WITTGENSTEIN

With coarse rice to eat, with water to drink, and with a bent arm for a pillow, there is still joy. Wealth and honor obtained through unrighteousness are but floating clouds to me.

CONFUCIUS

What can be shown, cannot be said.

LUDWIG WITTGENSTEIN

Since all things are longing for peace, why not let them alone?

CHUANG-TZU

understanding. Saying hurts when labels substitute for perception, when abstract ideas and rigid, exclusive notions of good or bad, right or wrong, true or false block feeling and intuition.

Ancient sages and prophets took "saying" or "naming" very seriously. Across cultures, names, incantations, curses, blessings, and classifications have governed our sense of who we are, who the other is, how we should live, feel, think, and even perceive the world or reality. The more "names" there are, the more things there are. Once a thing has been named (right, wrong, true, false, God, man, higher, lower), we tend to cling to its name, to one perspective. We become "dead" in Lao-tzu's scheme of things—because we lose sight of the ever-flowing range of possibilities, perspectives, and conditions that always go beyond the name. Unlike the "myriad things," "The Way is constantly nameless."[13]

And yet . . . From another point of view, it is convenient to think of the Way in words, to think of it as a thing with a name:

> As for the thing the Way is
> It is vague and dim.
> Dim! Vague!
> Within it is a model.
> Vague! Dim!
> Within it is a thing. . . .
> From the present to the past
> Its name does not depart.[14]

■ THE WAY OF REVERSAL ■

Lao-tzu often calls the "undivided" the One. Subsequent commentators sometimes refer to it as Being or Reality. Whatever Lao-tzu means, he does not *conceive* of the Way at all. That is, the Way (or the One) is not a concept to grasp cognitively or logically. Lao-tzu is not trying to discover something "more real" than what appears to the senses, but a "constant Way behind the changing and conflicting ways of life and government claimed by competing schools" as the official, one, true, way.[15]

Lao-tzu's nonrational, nonlogical approach presents difficulties for more analytically inclined Western philosophers, some of whom refuse to classify Lao-tzu among the philosophers, suggesting that he belongs with prophetic or religious figures. This is not satisfactory, however, for Asian scholars distinguish between religious Taoism, with its various rituals and beliefs, and philosophical Taoism, exemplified by the *Tao te Ching* and the *Chuang-tzu*.

Where does that leave us? How can we evaluate a "philosophy" that does not attempt to be systematic, rational, even organized in any ordinary sense? Indeed, what are we to make of a philosophy that suggests that what are often thought of as the basic tools of philosophy—systems, theories, logical reasoning, and linguistic precision—are, in fact, impediments to reality and truth? It is hardly surprising that some philosophers reject Taoism as unphilosophical babbling. Nor is it surprising that other philosophers share Taoism's discomfort with objectivity, dogmatism, rationalism, scientism, and technology. (See Chapters 14–17.)

The true man of old slept without dreaming and awakened without anxiety. . . . Living, he experienced no elation; dying, he offered no resistance; unconsciously he went, unconsciously he came, that is all.

CHUANG-TZU

If a man's lusts and desires are deep, his spring of nature is shallow.

CHUANG-TZU

● ● ● ● ● ●

PHILOSOPHICAL

QUERY

The tension between "beliefs" and "facts" recurs throughout the history of Western philosophy and explodes in our own time in the form of challenges to the very possibilities of objectivity and universality. Can you spot signs of this division in current affairs? Religion? Politics? Among your friends? Which side of the fence are you on? Do you think this problem has a solution that is fair to both sides?

We must, Lao-tzu suggests, sometimes violate our own carefully crafted rules and systems if we wish to be decent human beings responsive to the ebb and flow of *living itself. Living itself* is not a problem to be solved; consequently, it cannot be contained in any system. We must do more than understand, more than provide rules, more than explain with tightly reasoned precision. We must respond and resonate to the "ultimate something" that throbs with life just beyond the edge of understanding. Lao-tzu says:

> When the people of the world all know beauty as beauty
> > There arises the recognition of ugliness.
> When they all know the good as good,
> > There arises the recognition of evil. Therefore:
> > Being and non-being produce each other;
> > Difficult and easy complete each other;
> > Long and short contrast each other;
> > High and low distinguish each other;
> > Sound and voice harmonize with each other;
> > Front and back follow each other.[16]

But how can we turn off our need to classify, arrange, judge, and label things? How can we stop thinking (analyzing) so much and still remain conscious, alert, and intelligent? Lao-tzu suggests that we adopt an astonishing method of "getting mind out of the way" as it were.

One who really loves humanity will not place anything above it.
CONFUCIUS

One who really hates humanity will practice humanity in such a way that humanity has no chance to get at him.
CONFUCIUS

Prefer Yin to Yang

As we have seen, according to ancient Chinese cosmology, the whole of nature consists of the continual interaction of two opposing forces known as yin (passive, weak, negative, dark, and destructive) and yang (active, strong, positive, light, and constructive), inextricably linked together, each an expression of the other, operating together in a never-ending cycle of coming together and falling apart, part of one seamless cycle. According to Lao-tzu, the true sage, recognizing this, realizes that conditions call up opposite conditions and, thus, nothing is permanent.

What we call the bad "produces" the good (and the good is but the necessary other side of the bad). The reverse is also true: What we call the good "produces" the bad. The bad is but the necessary other side of the good, just as the good is necessary for the bad. Understanding this, the sage is patient, knowing that today's unfortunate circumstance will change into something good. (Nietzsche will say much the same thing in his critique of morality—only without the sage's patience. See Chapter 16.)

The sage knows himself but doesn't show himself.
LAO-TZU

Lao-tzu preaches his "doctrine without words" as a strategy for surviving in difficult times (the Period of Warring States) by turning away from common values and reversing common priorities. He repeatedly advises his readers to *prefer* (choose or lean toward) yin rather than yang. The following chains of oppositions are culled from the *Tao te Ching*:

Heaven and Earth are not humane;
They regard the people as straw dogs.
The sage is not humane;
He regards the people as straw dogs.

LAO-TZU

YANG (TO BE RESISTED)	YIN (TO BE PREFERRED)
Something	Nothing
Doing something	Doing nothing
Knowledge	Ignorance
Male	Female
Full	Empty
Above	Below
Before	After
Moving	Still
Big	Small
Strong	Weak
Hard	Soft
Straight	Bent[17]

The Union of Relative Opposites

If you're brave in being daring, you'll be killed.
If you're brave in not being daring, you'll live.

LAO-TZU

If Lao-tzu is correct, if there is one undivided Way, then neat, fixed, hard distinctions are arbitrary and misleading. Nothing is purely matter or spirit (energy). Nothing is completely male or female, wet or dry, good or bad. As the Western philosopher Heraclitus said, "All things are becoming." (See Chapter 3.)

The good and the bad exist in an everlasting exchange, and the names we give conditions depend on our circumstances and temperaments. For instance, rain is good in a time of drought; bad in a time of flood. Great size might be good on the football field; great size will be bad trying to squeeze through a tiny window opening during a fire. The good and the bad are relative opposites. Things become good or bad according to our reactions. They are not fixed.

According to Lao-tzu, we glimpse Tao in the flux of life. Chaos and disorder are only apparent. They are interpretations and judgments made from a small or fixed perspective. Things seem out of control when we focus on isolated particulars instead of looking for patterns. The sage embraces opposition and flux—yin and yang.

PHILOSOPHICAL

QUERY

• • • • • •

Stop and reflect on this point. In various forms, it recurs regularly in what is known as wisdom literature. See, for example, how Lao-tzu's position compares with what the Stoics (Chapter 7) say about our attitudes (labels) determining whether things appear to us as good or bad. What is lost if we accept Lao-tzu's teaching? What is gained?

If everything is part of one whole, why bother to resist yang and to prefer yin? To understand what Lao-tzu is doing, it helps to remember two things. First,

Lao-tzu was interested in surviving during a period of widespread corruption, intrigue, and violence. The common reaction of people in such conditions, then as now, was to meet force with counterforce. Rulers, their underlings, even the common people were constantly taking action—doing things, planning, scheming, trying to get what they wanted through force, seduction, any way they could.

The result, then as now, was continuous commotion, busy-ness, frustration, stress, and exhaustion as individuals, groups, and rulers fought to impose their wills on each other. Can you recognize the operant yang principle here? It is *control*. But, as Lao-tzu saw it, no one really has control. There is always Something Beyond, Some Process, Something that seems to have its own purposes (if we can use such a word). And that Something, as you no doubt now know, is Tao (the Way). (Compare what Lao-tzu suggests about being in control and Tao with what the Stoics Epictetus and Marcus Aurelius say about control and *Logos* in Chapter 7.)

If Lao-tzu pushed to *get people to let go of attempts at control,* then he would violate his own insight. Besides, it was (and is) only natural for push to come to shove, for force to produce counterforce. If Lao-tzu actively and forcefully argued for or promoted his doctrine, he would engender its very opposite. What to do?

Lao-tzu's (to us) odd answer is "Do nothing (and great deeds are accomplished)."

■ THE WAY OF INACTION ■

Often translated as "do nothing," the doctrine of **wu wei** is a most intriguing aspect of Taoism. The literal translation of *wu wei* is "not to act," but it is probably more accurate to think of it as a warning against unnatural or demanding action, demanding as in, I demand X! In the following passage, A. C. Graham calls our attention to the paradoxical nature of this crucial Taoist principle:

> The paradox that the way to attain a goal is to cease to aim at it deliberately is most explicit in Lao-tzu's constant appeals to "do nothing" (*wu wei*). This term, which goes back to Confucius, is often translated by such innocuous phrases as "non-action" to avoid giving the impression that Taoists recommend idleness, but it seems better to keep the paradoxical force of the Chinese expression. *Wei* is ordinary human action, deliberated for a purpose, in contrast with the spontaneous processes of nature. . . . Man takes pride in distinguishing himself from nature by his purposive action; *Lao-tzu* by a classic reversal describes the behavior of the sage as Doing Nothing.[18]

Here, "natural" does not mean common or widespread, but natural in the sense of healthy, spontaneous, and in harmony with Tao. Spontaneity stands in contrast to calculation, deliberation, and the careful (crafty) weighing of advantages and disadvantages, profit and gain, social image, and other priorities and considerations that get us out of touch with the natural order of things: Tao.

Doing Something—planning, pushing, scheming, fixing, saving the world—is exhausting because Doing Something never ends; it never completely accomplishes its goal. Doing Nothing, on the other hand,

> relaxes the body, calms the mind, loosens the grip of categories [judgments and labels] made habitual by naming, frees the current of thought for more

Everyman does what he really can do; that is all. The bird flies high to avoid the snare or dart. The mouse burrows down below the altar to avoid the danger of being smoked out or dug up.

CHUANG-TZU

wu wei

Literally "not to act"; in the *Tao te Ching;* refers to unnatural or demanding action.

The ignorant do not know that no matter how well you conceal things, smaller ones in larger ones, there will always be a chance for them to escape.

CHUANG-TZU

I have never seen one who really loves humanity or one who really hates inhumanity.

CONFUCIUS

fluid differentiations . . . and instead of pondering choices lets . . . problems solve themselves as inclination spontaneously finds its own direction, which is the Way.[19]

When Lao-tzu says that "by doing nothing great deeds are accomplished," he does not mean "by sitting like a lump, no matter what, great deeds are accomplished." He means that by taking no contrived, calculated, "controlling" action, we are most likely to contribute to improving conditions around us. Rather than set out to "save the environment," the sage spontaneously picks up trash while he takes his morning walk. Rather than agitate and argue to put an end to racism, the sage naturally and spontaneously (without calculation or ulterior motive) associates with all sorts of people—and naturally and spontaneously (and unaggressively) walks away when a co-worker tells racist jokes. Thus the sage preaches without preaching and teaches without lecturing.

Concentrating on being a cheerful, helpful, tolerant "friend of Tao," the sage is consistently nonjudgmental. He acts, to be sure, but not through his specific efforts or words, or with concern over precise results:

> I treat those who are good with goodness,
> And I also treat those who are not good with goodness.
> Thus goodness is attained.
> I am honest with those who are honest,
> And I am also honest with those who are not honest.
> Thus honesty is attained.[20]

According Lao-tzu, the best way to deal with social turmoil is "not to do anything about it." If this sounds crazy to you, you are not alone. Just think of how much time and energy we devote to "solving problems," "fixing things," "saving the environment," "winning the war on drugs," "ending racism and poverty." In today's jargon, we are encouraged to be *proactive,* not *reactive.*

Does aggressive social and political action really accomplish its goals—or does it result in contest after contest, with proliferating factions struggling against each other for control? Can social "progress" be linked directly to specific efforts, or does something more mysterious and more complex account for social and technological change? Is there such a thing as progress-pure-and-simple, or is the very notion of progress itself a judgment—a judgment with which others disagree?

For most readers of this book, I hope, circumstances are not as bad as those Lao-tzu lived through. Yet in many ways, we, too, live without guarantees of physical safety, financial security, social harmony. Sometimes it seems as if we live in our own Period of Warring Factions, a time during which almost any significant action taken to legislate or enforce one faction's notion of social order and harmony generates a counterforce from opposing factions as generations, nations, ethnic coalitions, political affiliations, and religious groups ceaselessly jump into action with grand plans to proactively fix things.

No matter what is accomplished, struggle and turmoil remain, just in different forms. Lao-tzu says

> The more taboos in the world
> The poorer the people:
> The more sharp tools among the people
> The stupider the state.
> The more men's arts and skills,
> The more oddities arise:
> The more laws and edicts are proclaimed
> The more thieves and bandits there will be.

Hence the sage says:

> If I do nothing, of themselves the people are transformed.
> If I love stillness, of themselves the people are correct.
> If I meddle in nothing, of themselves the people are rich.
> If I desire nothing, of themselves the people are unhewn.[21]

According to Lao-tzu, we would be wise to learn to live in harmony with Tao in the midst of this world, a world of overpopulation, rampant commercialism, aggressive politicians, global terrorism, environmental insult, and our own strong, willful desires to get things done, to get ahead, to hoard wealth—the whole seemingly irresistible, frustrating commotion that we know as life in the high-tech twenty-first century. In harmony with Tao, we can survive, even blossom, in stressful times. Are there any other kinds?

When the people don't respect those in power, then what they greatly fear is about to arrive.

LAO-TZU

Who am I? Why am I here?

JAMES BOND STOCKDALE

▪ THE SOCIAL SAGE: CONFUCIUS ▪

Confucius (551–479 B.C.E.) is the Latinized name of K'ung Fu-tzu or Master K'ung, the honorific name of K'ung Ch'iu of Lu, a legendary teacher who vainly sought high political office so that he could initiate a series of governmental reforms. In response to what he saw as widespread social decline, Confucius took a more active approach than Lao-tzu and promoted social order based on humanity (benevolence), custom, and personal moral cultivation.

As a teacher and would-be political reformer, Confucius tried to produce political harmony by cultivating moral harmony within each individual. "Guide the people by governmental measures," he said, "and regulate them by the threat

Confucius

of punishment, and the people will have no sense of honor and shame. Guide the people by virtue and regulate them by *li* (rules of conduct and sense of propriety) and the people will have a sense of honor and respect.[22]

One disciple characterized Confucius as "gentle but dignified, austere, yet not harsh, polite and completely at ease." When another disciple admitted that he had been unable to describe Confucius to the king, Confucius said, "Why didn't you tell him that I am a man who forgets all worries when he is happy, and who is not aware that old age is coming on?" To a disciple who liked to criticize people, Confucius said, "Ah Sze, you are very clever, aren't you? I have no time for such things." On another occasion, some young people from a village known for its mischief-making came to see Confucius, who welcomed them. This surprised his disciples. "Why be harsh with them?" the sage gently replied. "What concerns me is how they come and not what they do when they go away. When a man approaches me with pure intentions, I respect his pure intentions, although I cannot guarantee what he does afterwards."[23]

Confucius was not always so accepting, however, particularly when it came to "the inferior (or petty) man." He especially disliked hypocrites, whom he called goody-goody thieves of virtue and "rice bags"—that is, people only good for filling their bellies with rice. Confucius took good manners and proper social customs seriously because he was convinced that they are necessary for social order and individual moral cultivation. He is said to have struck an elderly man on the shin with a walking stick for singing disrespectfully at the man's mother's funeral. "As a young boy," Confucius said to the ill-mannered fellow, "you were unruly; when grown up, you have accomplished nothing; and now in your old age you refuse to die. You are a thief!"[24]

The Teacher

Confucius probably began teaching in his twenties or thirties. Legend has it that he was the first man in Chinese history to devote his whole life to teaching, teaching, even when he worked as a public official in his home province of Lu. Although today he has a reputation as a conservative wedded to tradition, in his time Confucius was a daring and radical educator who defied traditional practices by making a new form of character education—as opposed to vocational training— available to all social classes. He is said to have had as many as three thousand pupils at once. In spite of his open-door approach to education, Confucius attracted a special class of gentlemen-scholars known as *literati;* the literati dominated Chinese history and culture for thousands of years.[25]

When he was fifty-six years old, Confucius retired from civil service because his superiors were uninterested in his ideas. For the next thirteen years he wandered and taught in what Wing-Tsit Chan calls a "desperate attempt" at social reform, traveling from state to state in search of a ruler who would listen to him. He seems to have had almost no success selling his reforms, although he did manage to win audiences with at least four dukes. At sixty-eight, dejected and disappointed, Confucius returned to Lu, where he continued to teach, write, and edit until his death.

When substance exceeds refinement, one becomes rude. When refinement exceeds substance, one becomes urbane. It is only when one's substance and refinement are properly blended that he becomes a superior man.

CONFUCIUS

The superior man does what is proper to his position and does not want to go beyond this.

CONFUCIUS

Great Man demands it of himself; Petty Man, of others.

CONFUCIUS

I do not instruct the uninterested. I do not help those who fail to try. If I mention one corner of a subject and the pupil does not deduce therefrom the other three, I drop him.

CONFUCIUS

Is one not a superior man if he does not feel hurt even though he is not recognized?

CONFUCIUS

Despite his failures as a political reformer, Confucius remains one of the great teachers of all time, probably surpassing even Socrates (Chapter 4) in the subsequent influence he has had on his culture. Like Socrates, Confucius was witty, humane, complicated, confident, and modest. Like Socrates, Confucius was unimpressed by wealth and social standing. "The people who live extravagantly," he said, "are apt to be snobbish (or conceited), and the people who live simply are apt to be vulgar. I prefer the vulgar people to the snobs."[26]

Shortly before he died, Confucius wept and said, "For a long time the world has been living in moral chaos, and no ruler has been able to follow me." Leaning on a stick, he walked slowly around his door, singing, "Ah! The Mountain is crumbling down! The pillar is falling down! The Philosopher is passing out!"[27]

A collection of Confucius's conversations known as the *Analects* is the single most influential book of Asian philosophy. Two other important Confucian texts are *The Book of Mencius* and *The Hsun Tzu,* named after their authors, the Confucian philosophers Mencius (c. 372–c. 298 B.C.E.) and Hsun Tzu (c. 313–c. 238 B.C.E.).

■ CONFUCIAN HUMANISM ■ AND THE GOLDEN MEAN

If one word characterizes the overall approach of the ancient sages, it is **humanism,** the name given to any philosophy that emphasizes human welfare and dignity. In general, humanism is based on the belief that human intelligence and effort are capable of improving present conditions.

Confucius's humanistic notion that "man can make the Way (Tao) great" was a radical departure from the traditional Chinese emphasis on nature spirits.[28] In the *Analects* we are told that "The Master did not talk about marvels, feats of strength, irregularities, gods."[29] When he was asked about serving ghosts and gods, Confucius said, "Until you can serve men, how can you serve the ghosts?" When he asked about death he said, "Until you know about life how can you know about death?" In other words, we should not be distracted by nonhuman matters that do not concern us.[30] Asked about wisdom, Confucius said, "To work at doing right for the people, and to be reverent to the ghosts and gods but keep them at a distance, may be called wisdom."[31]

Confucian humanism is rooted in Confucius's vision of himself as preserver and restorer of a declining culture rather than as an inventor or creator of something new.[32] "It is in transmitting but not originating, trusting in and loving the ancient, that I would venture to compare myself," he said.[33] In contrast to contemporary educational practices, Confucius stressed social preservation over individual creation. Confucius acknowledged the need to think, but focused on the importance of learning. "I used to go without food all day, without sleep all night, to think," he said. "No use, better to learn."[34]

Learn what? Learn the way of **chung-yung,** the Golden Mean. Variously translated as the Mean, moderation, normality, and universal moral law, *chung-yung* literally means "centrality and universality." According to Wing-Tsit Chan, the Mean is the same as equilibrium or harmony. By restoring equilibrium to the individual, Confucius thought, order would be restored to the family, to other relationships, to the state, to the world, to the universe. *The Doctrine of the Mean,*

When a student asked Confucius about serving the spiritual beings, Confucius said, "If we are not yet able to serve man, how can we serve spiritual beings?" Then what about death, the student asked. Confucius said, "If we do not yet know about life, how can we know about death?"

humanism
Name given to any philosophy that emphasizes human welfare and dignity; belief that human intelligence and effort are capable of improving conditions in the here and now.

Heaven and Earth are not humane. / The sage is not humane.

LAO-TZU

chung-yung
Literally "centrality and universality," the Golden Mean of Confucius, consisting of moderation and normality; universal moral law; also equilibrium or harmony.

PHILOSOPHICAL

QUERY

a text that some ancient scholars attributed to Confucius's grandson, expresses Confucius's characterization of Tao as a universal moral Mean:

1. What Heaven (*T'ien*, Nature) imparts to man is called human nature. To follow our nature is called the Way (Tao). Cultivating the Way is called education. The Way cannot be separated from us even for a moment. What can be separated from us is not the Way. Therefore the superior man is cautious over what he does not see and apprehensive over what he does not hear. There is nothing more visible than what is hidden and nothing more manifest than what is subtle. Therefore the superior man is watchful over himself when he is alone. . . .

2. Chung-ni (Confucius) said, "The superior man [exemplifies] the Mean (*chung-yung*). The inferior man acts contrary to the Mean. The superior man [exemplifies] the Mean because, as a superior man, he can maintain the Mean at any time. The inferior man [acts contrary to] the Mean because, as an inferior man, he has no caution."

3. Confucius said, "Perfect is the Mean. For a long time few people have been able to follow it."[35]

The pity is that, if Confucius is right, the Way is not far off, yet we fail to find it, choosing instead the little by-paths of imbalance and partiality. We eat and drink too much or too little, thereby savoring less. When we do seek self-improvement for ourselves, we seek it for *ourselves;* we step away from the Mean (centrality and universality) into partiality:

4. Confucius said, "I know why the Way is not pursued. The intelligent go beyond it and the stupid do not come up to it. I know why the Way is not understood. The worthy go beyond it and the unworthy do not come up to it. There is no one who does not eat and drink, but there are few who can really know flavor." . . .

13. Confucius said, "The Way is not far from man. When a man pursues the Way and yet remains away from man, his course cannot be considered the Way. The *Book of Odes* says, 'In hewing an axe handle, in hewing an axe handle, the pattern is not far off.' If we take an axe handle to hew another axe handle and look askance from the one to the other, we may still think the pattern is far away. Therefore the superior man governs men as men, in accordance with human nature, and as soon as they change [what is wrong], he stops. Conscientiousness (*chung*) and altruism (*shu*) are not far away from the Way. What you do not wish for others, do not do unto them."[36]

• • • • • •

Interestingly, the concept of a mean serves as the basis for Aristotle's Nicomachean Ethics, *one of the most influential moral philosophies in the Western philosophical tradition. Compare Aristotle's more linear characterization of the mean with Confucius's more holistic or poetic one. Why do you suppose two of the most influential moral philosophers of all time stressed moderation and balance as the basis for human well-being and happiness? Aristotle's mean is discussed in Chapter 6.*

■ VIRTUE AND CEREMONY ■

In contrast to Lao-tzu's let-it-be sense of Tao, Confucius confines the meaning of Tao to the proper course of human conduct and the organization of government. Confucius's focus on the organic relation of Tao and human virtue (*te*) marked the first time those concepts came to philosophical prominence in Chinese philosophy.[37]

Traditionally, **te** (virtue) meant potency, the power to affect others without using physical force. In this sense, *te* is morally neutral in the way that a knife's "virtues"—strength, flexibility, sharpness—are neutral. The same knife can be used to save a life in surgery or to take a life in anger. For both good and bad purposes, strength, flexibility, and sharpness are virtues in a knife. Although Confucius sometimes uses *te* in this functional, morally neutral sense, he also expands it to mean the capacity to act according to Tao and to bring others to Tao. In that use, Tao and *te* cannot be separated.[38]

According to Confucius, producing a harmonious society based on a good government and benevolent (virtuous) human relationships can only be accomplished by mastering and honoring *li*. Literally, "ceremony," **li** encompasses rites, customs, and conventions ranging from ritual sacrifices honoring one's ancestors to everyday etiquette and good manners. If we don't master *li,* we stray from Tao and *te* and degenerate into disorder (dysfunction) and imbalance (disharmony).

By following *li,* we become gracious and well-mannered in all aspects of life, treating all people with dignity and respect. There is more at stake here than mere good manners because there is a sacred quality to *li* that transforms human relations from barbaric, not-truly-human interactions to fully human ones. This quality is independent of the particular ritual or ceremony involved, be it a religious service, a greeting or leave-taking, a shared meal, or observation of participation in a musical performance.[39]

Without mastering good manners and ceremonial forms (*li,*) even our good acts will be lacking. We will behave "insincerely," doing the right thing out of obedience rather than "with sincerity" and harmony. Without *li,* even great knowledge lacks virtue, potency, *te:* "Where things are not on course, if you harmonize by knowledge of harmony without regulating it by ceremony, they still cannot be put on course."[40]

---

te

Traditionally, morally neutral virtue; potency, the power to affect others without using physical force; expanded by Confucius to mean the capacity to act according to Tao and to bring others to Tao.

li

Literally, "ceremony"; encompasses rites, customs, and conventions ranging from ritual sacrifices honoring one's ancestors to everyday etiquette and good manners.

When there is a motive to be virtuous, there is no virtue.

LIE ZI

Great Man is always at ease; Petty Man is always on edge.

CONFUCIUS

PHILOSOPHICAL QUERY

● ● ● ● ● ●

In broad strokes, human history can almost be reduced to an ongoing struggle between two distinct approaches to managing human affairs. One advocates minimal governance—managing by not managing—and the cultivation of healthy (natural) instincts. The other calls for the inculcation of formal manners and habits of repression combined with rules and regulations covering all aspects of our lives. See if you can find examples of each approach in contemporary politics, education, parenting. Do you think one approach is (generally) superior to the other? Why? Do you agree that these two approaches to life seem to persist throughout history? Discuss.

■ THE EXAMPLE OF THE *CHUN-TZU* ■

Whereas his great contemporary Lao-tzu associated Tao and *te* with nature independent of man, and with passivity and psychological withdrawal, Confucius associated them with human conduct and social order. He believed that in addition to rules and regulations (*li*), a harmonious society requires an elaborate bureaucracy of highly cultured and learned men to provide examples of conscientiousness and altruism.

To this end, Confucius, in another move away from tradition, modified the concept of the *chun-tzu,* or superior man. Prior to Confucius, **chun-tzu,** literally the lord's son, could refer to either the sovereign himself or to a "cultivated gentleman." Although Confucius himself occasionally uses the term *chun-tzu* in these traditional ways, for the most part, and most significantly, he uses it to refer to the morally superior man, the great or noble soul. That the morally superior man is also a cultivated gentleman reflects Confucius's emphasis on the importance of *li*. So important are the nature and example of the superior man to Confucius, that the term *chun-tzu* occurs 107 times in the *Analects*.[41]

The opposite of the *chun-tzu* is the **hsiao-jen,** the small or vulgar man. The *hsiao-jen* is petty and base.[42] The *chun-tzu* thinks of humanity; the *hsiao-jen* thinks of himself and perhaps those he sees as his "kind." The *chun-tzu* does not seek to put himself above or below others but seeks to help others by becoming noble himself. The *hsiao-jen* looks to others for help and competes with them; he is, in today's vernacular, partial to himself. Consequently, he disrespects *li* and departs from the Mean. When his disciple Yen Yüan asked about this, Confucius said:

> "By conquest of self returning to ceremony one becomes noble. If by conquest of self you return to ceremony for a single day, the whole world will acknowledge you as noble. Becoming noble derives from oneself, not from others!"
>
> "I would ask you to itemize it."
>
> "What isn't according to ceremony don't look at, don't listen to, don't say, don't do."[43]

Confucius's faith in the moral power of the example of the superior man is particularly evident in an anecdote concerning a rapacious, rich official, an obviously inferior man. The greedy *hsiao-jen* told Confucius that he was worried about the high number of robbers in his province. Confucius's reply was blunt: "If you yourself don't love money, you can give the money to thieves and they won't take it."[44]

chun-tzu

Literally, "the lord's son"; originally the sovereign himself or a "cultivated gentleman"; Confucian morally superior man; a great or noble soul.

hsiao-jen

Small or vulgar man; in Confucian philosophy, the opposite of the *chun-tzu*; a petty and base individual.

Would a sick person be helped merely by reading a medical text?

SHANTIVEDA

PHILOSOPHICAL

QUERY

• • • • • •

The notion of the noble or great soul has intrigued philosophers from Confucius's time to our own. Does it have any resonance for you? Is the concept of the petty or inferior soul clearer? If it is, why do you suppose that it is easier to come up with examples of pettiness than of nobility? What do you think Confucius was really saying in his reply to the rapacious official? (Hint: Are giving and taking ambiguous?) Discuss.

Note the harmonious blending of aesthetic, moral, social, and personal qualities that constitute Confucius's characterization of the *chun-tzu* in the *Analects*. Note, too, how unappealing the character of the inferior or petty *hsiao-jen* is in contrast—that is, by way of counterexample.

▪ THE THREAD OF HUMANITY ▪

The nobility that characterizes the Confucian *chun-tzu* is not a matter of bloodline (ethnicity) or political power (social status), but of character, specifically of humanity, or *jen*. **Jen** is a general human virtue, the humane principle rooted in empathy and fellow feeling. The Chinese character for *jen* is composed of "two" and "man," signifying the relationship between men. *Jen* has been translated as human, humane, humanitarian, humanity, and benevolence. According to Chinese American philosopher Lin Yutang, *jen* can have the double meaning of humankind and kindness, as well as referring to a man or woman who is truly himself or herself, a "real person," as it were.[45] *Jen* is expressed by conscientiousness (*chung*) and altruism (*shu*), which in combination constitute the "one thread" of Confucianism.

Realization of *jen* leads to "full humanness," which we only achieve by learning how to balance the needs of self and others, the individual and society. Full humanness (nobility of soul) and harmony are the goals of Confucian moral cultivation, something to which all people are susceptible, at least to some degree. Because *jen* cannot be realized for oneself alone, good manners, proper customs, kindness, and social harmony converge:

> A man of humanity wishing to establish his own character, also establishes the character of others, and wishing to be prominent himself, also helps others to be prominent. To be able to judge others by what is near to ourselves may be called the method of realizing humanity.[46]

To be a fully human person, a real person, one "merely" has to start out by being a good son or daughter or brother or sister or citizen:

> There are five universal ways [in human relations], and the way by which they are practiced is three. The five are those governing the relationship between the ruler and the minister, between father and son, between husband and wife, between elder and younger brothers, and those in the intercourse between friends. These five are universal paths in the world. Wisdom, humanity, and courage, these three are universal virtues. The way by which they are practiced is one.
>
> Some are born with the knowledge [of these virtues]. Some learn it through study. Some learn it through hard work. But when the knowledge is acquired, it comes to the same thing. Some practice them naturally and easily. Some practice them for their advantage. Some practice them with effort and difficulty. But when achievement is made, it comes to the same thing.
>
> Confucius said, "Love of learning is akin to wisdom. To practice with vigor is akin to humanity. To know to be shameful is akin to courage. He who knows these three things knows how to cultivate his personal life. Knowing how to cultivate his personal life, he knows how to govern other men. And knowing how to govern other men, he knows how to govern the empire, its states, and the families."[47]

Formerly men studied for self-improvement; today men study for the sake of appearances.

CONFUCIUS

jen
General human virtue; translated as human, humane, humanitarian, humanity, and benevolence; can mean both humankind and kindness; also a man or woman who is truly himself or herself; a "real-person."

Tuan-mu Tz'u asked about Great Man. "First he sets the good example, then he invites others to follow it."

CONFUCIUS

Wisdom, humanity, and courage, these three are universal virtues. The way by which they are practiced is one.

CONFUCIUS

When strict with oneself one rarely fails.

CONFUCIUS

One who is not a man of humanity cannot endure adversity for long, nor can he enjoy prosperity for long. The man of humanity is naturally at ease with humanity. The man of humanity cultivates wisdom for its advantage.

CONFUCIUS

Interestingly, Confucius did not teach about *jen* directly, perhaps because *jen* itself is not susceptible to precise formulation, perhaps because humanity is not something that can be taught, or perhaps because Confucius, like so many other sages, was as aware of his own limits as he was of humanity's promise. Confucius said:

> I have never seen one who really loves humanity or one who really hates inhumanity. One who really loves humanity will not place anything above it. One who really hates humanity will practice humanity in such a way that humanity has no chance to get at him. Is there anyone who has devoted his strength to humanity for as long as a single day? I have not seen any one without sufficient strength to do so. Perhaps there is such a case, but I have never seen it.[48]

> When it comes to the practice of humanity, one should not defer even to his teacher.
>
> CONFUCIUS

■ THE BUDDHA ■

So powerful was the person and vision of **Siddhartha Gautama** (c. 560–480 B.C.E.) that he was recognized during his lifetime as an archetype unto himself. Today the archetype of the Buddha is a major source of meaning and purpose for over 2 billion people. The Buddha was a sage, yet more than a sage. Among his many names, perhaps the most enduring are the Awakened or Enlightened One (the original meaning of "the Buddha" in Sanskrit) and the Compassionate Buddha. Yet for all his influence, we have very little factual information about him; most of what we know comes from oral tradition and myth.[49]

Siddhartha Gautama

Unlike Lao-tzu and Confucius, Siddhartha Gautama was born into wealth and power as the son of a prince (rajah) in what is today Nepal. Siddhartha was intelligent and alert, a talented student and athlete. Legend says that he was a first-rate hunter and archer and enjoyed a rich and active life. An only son, Siddhartha was spoiled and indulged by his family; he became a hedonist and a womanizer. At sixteen he married his cousin, but this does not seem to have slowed his pleasure seeking.

The young prince lived in protected isolation, surrounded by servants who catered to his slightest whim. One version of his life claims that Siddhartha's parents took great pains to shield him from the ugliness of life, even surrounding him with young, attractive servants to spare him the sight of the ravages of age. His parents tried to protect him from knowing about poverty, hunger, sickness, and death by seducing him with every imaginable delight—and by trying to confine him within their palatial grounds. Siddhartha should experience only luxury and pleasure.

> The follower of the law, even if he can recite only a small portion of it but, having forsaken passion and hatred and foolishness, possesses true knowledge and serenity of mind; he is attached to nothing in this world or that to come, has indeed a share in the religious life.
>
> BUDDHA

But Siddhartha was not content. As with many young people, curiosity and rebelliousness led him away from home. During secret trips outside the palace to a nearby city, he saw three of the now-famous Four Signs that altered his life forever: a destitute and homeless beggar, a dead man being prepared for cremation by weeping mourners, a diseased and handicapped person. The seeds of the Buddha were planted when Siddhartha encountered his first sight of suffering.

Siddhartha the Seeker

Before his forbidden excursions outside the family compound, Siddhartha had no real idea of what sickness or old age could do to the body and spirit. He had no sense of the depths that poverty could reach. He was unaware of the power of grief.

The price he had paid for living in a cocoon of soft pleasures and hidden from the suffering of others was a feeling of bored unease. But ignorance could not protect him forever. Driven by the restless boredom that almost always accompanies an unproductive, self-indulgent life, Siddhartha felt compelled to stray outside. All the pleasures of his wealthy family could not quell his nagging sense of discomfort. He simply had to know more.

The young prince had no one to talk with about his troubling questions except his servant Channa, a hired companion and charioteer, who was also his guardian and bodyguard. To every question Siddhartha raised about life outside the family compound, good Channa could only reply, with great sadness and resignation, "Yes, master, there is no escape. Old age, sickness, death—such is the lot of all men."[50]

In today's language, we might say that Siddhartha "had his eyes opened." His naive unawareness was spoiled forever. No longer were his pleasures as sweet. Try as he might, Siddhartha could not shake the haunting images of old age, sickness, and death. His anxiety grew. How, he asked himself again and again, could anyone be happy if—ultimately—there is absolutely no escape from suffering, disappointment, sadness, and loss? If no one escapes, why be born at all? How could any woman want to give birth knowing what awaited her child? None of his family or servants could answer him.

Walking outside the palace grounds one day, deep in despair, Siddhartha saw a wandering monk, an ascetic. **Ascetics** turn away from pleasure and severely limit all sensual appetites in order to achieve salvation or peace of mind. Asceticism involves long hours of prayer and fasting, living on plain food, wearing simple clothes. Monks in many cultures live ascetic lives. In Western traditions, Old Testament prophets were often ascetics. When John the Baptist and Jesus went into the desert and fasted or lived on locusts, honey, and water, they were going through ascetic trials.

When Siddhartha looked closely into the face of the wandering monk he was astonished to see serenity, purpose, and detachment. This experience was the last of the Four Signs. Here, finally, was a promise of escape from suffering via self-discipline and a program of resistance to the ego's cravings and fears.

Siddhartha concluded that he must leave the security of his home and live as a monk, homeless, with only a simple robe and beggar's bowl. He would go to the wisest sages, no matter how far and difficult the journey. He would find someone to tell him the answers to life's most basic questions: Why live if suffering is inescapable? Is it possible to be happy in the face of inevitable sickness, old age, and death? What is the real meaning of life?

The Long Search

For years Siddhartha wandered with his beggar's bowl, seeking one master or guru after another. Even though many of them were wise and deeply interested in helping Siddhartha, he did not find his answer. He found only more teachers, and though he learned many clever philosophical notions, as well as techniques for meditating and disciplining the body, he found no satisfying answers to his basic, timeless questions.

Finally tiring of gurus and ordinary sages, he settled in a grove of trees on the outskirts of the village of Uruvela, India. There he formed a little community with

---

The sage is neither elated by prosperity nor depressed by adversity. His endeavor always is to rely on himself and to seek his whole satisfaction within himself.
SENECA

There are superior men who are in accord with the Mean, retire from the world unknown to their age, but do not regret. It is only a sage who can do this.
CONFUCIUS

ascetic
Individual who turns away from pleasure and severely limits all sensual appetites in order to achieve salvation or peace of mind.

The adult has to break his attachment to persons and things.
WALTER LIPPMANN

I once went a day without food and all night without sleep to enable me to think. I found no advantage in it; it's best to study.

CONFUCIUS

Great Man, being universal in his outlook, is impartial; Petty Man, being partial, is not universal in outlook.

CONFUCIUS

If a fool is associated with a wise man even all his life, he will perceive the truth as little as a spoon perceives the taste of soup.

BUDDHA

Cut out the love of self, like an autumn lotus with your hand! Cherish the road to peace. Nirvana has been shown by the Blessed One.

BUDDHA

a few other seekers. For six years he meditated, fasted, and concentrated daily on his original questions. During this time, he is said to have conquered most physical appetites and weaknesses and learned how to control "the mad monkey of the mind."[51] But still he found no answers.

In his efforts to subdue his body, Siddhartha nearly destroyed it. He is supposed to have said, "When I touched my stomach I felt my backbone." His extreme asceticism left him a wasted shell. In Buddhist art portraying him during this period, bone and muscle pushes through his skin. Ultimately, Siddhartha realized that his body was an important instrument in his search, and he realized that he must honor the spirit by honoring the body that houses it. This lesson was clear: The Way cannot be found by either indulgence or denial. We must walk a Middle Path.

Siddhartha's fellow monks were disgusted when he began to take proper nourishment. They had been impressed with his ascetic ways as signs of strength and willpower. From this Siddhartha learned another lesson: We must stop worrying about what others think of us and quit trying to impress people if we are ever to find wisdom. He realized that ascetic self-denial can be of value as a temporary corrective for indulgences or as a momentary cleansing, but it is not an adequate way of life. To subdue the appetites to show strength and willpower is a way of showing off, which prevents one from growing wise.

So Siddhartha returned to his lonely wandering. One day when he was thirty, as he sat in meditation under a fig tree, he was given a special bowl of rice milk by a young woman because he reminded her of a figure she had seen in a vision. In her vision, she had presented rice milk in a golden bowl to a single figure seated under a tree. She took this figure to be a god because of a special glow she saw around him. He was, of course, the Buddha.

Siddhartha accepted the rice milk and, according to one legend, did not eat again for forty-nine days. Another legend says that he divided the milk into numerous portions, and these sustained him during his deepening meditation. After Siddhartha had finished the rice milk, he threw the golden bowl into a nearby river, where it miraculously floated upstream. (This symbolizes the fact that the Buddha's teachings go against the currents of our ordinary, unenlightened thinking, just as Lao-tzu's do.) Siddhartha then ceremoniously bathed in the river, and, taking the lotus position, once more sat under the fig tree and said: "Here I shall remain until I am answered or dead." The tree under which the Buddha sat became known as the Bodhi Tree—the Tree of Wisdom.

Finally, the awakening came. What Buddhist tradition refers to as the "greatest event in human history" occurred during the full moon of May, c. 524 B.C.E. Refusing to be swayed from his goal, heeding some inner call despite all costs, Siddhartha Gautama had transformed himself from a spoiled, pampered young man into "the one who had awakened": the Buddha.

■ THE BODHISATTVA ■

According to Buddhist teachings, it is impossible to explain the awakening. Nonetheless, we can get a rough idea of what the Buddha "saw." Siddhartha saw himself and all life as part of an unending process of change, a great chain of being through which things come into and leave one form of existence for another. Everything is one. The whole universe is a system of interconnected, inseparable parts, rich and complex, composed of all varieties of life forever moving from one form to another.

The Buddha did not arrive at this perception intellectually. He saw it all at once, in what we in the West might call a mystical vision. The now-Buddha realized instantly how difficult it would be to teach a doctrine that could not be grasped by mere reasoning and that could not be realized by blind faith, but only by unswerving personal diligence. Only by the greatest effort could an individual achieve release from suffering. The price of wisdom is love of the whole rather than love of any one part—including, especially, ourselves.[52]

When you see a man of the highest caliber, give thought to attaining his stature. When you see one who is not, go home and conduct a self-examination.

CONFUCIUS

● ● ● ● ● ●

PHILOSOPHICAL
QUERY

Compare what Marcus Aurelius says about "the perpetual renewing of the world's youthfulness" (page 196) with Buddha's insight that the whole universe is "forever moving from one form to another." To what philosophical and personal use do Marcus and the Buddha put their notions in this regard?

Siddhartha had reached a state of bliss and utter detachment called *nirvana*. **Nirvana** is annihilation of the ego, a state of emptiness or "no-thing-ness." It is described as a state of bliss because there is only "pure consciousness" with no sense of individuality, separateness, discrimination, or intellectualizing. It cannot be explained in words because words are limiting and exist to identify similarities and differences. Nirvana is beyond even similarity. It can only be talked around or expressed in contradictions. It transcends all ordinary experience. Nirvana is release from suffering while conscious. (If you do not "understand" what nirvana is, don't feel inadequate. Nirvana must be experienced; it cannot be described or understood.)

nirvana
Annihilation of the ego; a state of emptiness or "no-thing-ness"; a state of bliss: "pure consciousness" that leads to release from suffering while remaining conscious.

Siddhartha now had to make another important choice. He could stay in nirvana, meditating and remaining uninvolved with the commotion and suffering of life. Or he could share his vision. Legend says that "the very earth trembled" while waiting for his decision. At last, the "Great Buddha Heart of Infinite Compassion prevailed."[53] Siddhartha refused ultimate release and, because he chose to stay and help others, became the Buddha, "He Who Awoke," or "He Who Became Aware." This helpful part of him is sometimes referred to as "The Walking Buddha," the man who wandered about once more, only now as a teacher rather than as a seeker.

The Buddha who chose to remain among people giving help to other lost souls is known as the Bodhisattva in some branches of Buddhism. A **bodhisattva** is an enlightened being who voluntarily postpones his own nirvana to help all other conscious life-forms find "supreme release." A bodhisattva is *not* a savior. The Buddha did not *intercede* for others; he showed them a path (a Way). A bodhisattva no longer perceives separateness on any level. A bodhisattva no longer even perceives a separate self, a being, a person.

bodhisattva
An enlightened being who voluntarily postpones his own nirvana in order to help all other conscious life-forms find "supreme release"; not a savior.

PHILOSOPHICAL
QUERY

● ● ● ● ● ●

Compare the Buddha's decision to become a bodhisattva with Plato's characterization of the enlightened figure who escapes from the Cave and then returns to help others. See Chapter 5.

The superior man is not an implement.
CONFUCIUS

His consciousness forever altered, Siddhartha was at last ready to teach personal transformation through compassion. It did not take long for the Buddha to acquire many followers. As with other great sages, who the Buddha was became as significant as what he taught. Siddhartha's once-disappointed ascetic companions even became disciples of the Buddha, as did his wife and son. To share his message with everyone, Siddhartha sent groups of his earliest disciples out as teachers. He did not seek converts, and his monks were not missionaries. Their goal was to spread information that all people could use for themselves to reduce suffering.

The Death of the Buddha

To live is to die, to be awake is to sleep, to be young is to be old, for the one flows into the other, and the process is capable of being reversed.
HERACLITUS

Throughout the ages, Buddhist monks have emulated the "Way of Siddhartha" in their attire and daily meditations.

Legend teaches that the Buddha died from either poisonous mushrooms or tainted pork. His last meal was at the humble home of a blacksmith (significantly, a person of low status in ancient Asian culture). Soon after eating, the Buddha took sick. He asked his host to bury the rest of the food so that no one else would eat it. Calling upon the discipline learned through years of meditation, he was able

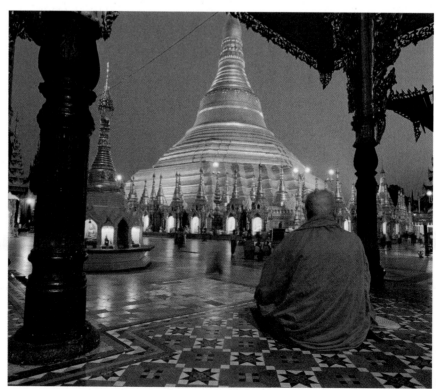

©Bob Krist/Corbis

to control his pain well enough to travel to a certain river. He bathed in the river and then lay down in a mango grove "on his right side in the attitude of a lion with one foot on the other."[54]

As he lay dying, the Buddha made a special point to tell his closest disciple, Ananda, that the blacksmith was not to blame. The Buddha also sent special word to the blacksmith thanking him for his "alms." By this the Buddha meant that the blacksmith was blessed for having been the vehicle by which the Buddha would escape "the wheel of suffering" and attain nirvana. After sending this message, the Buddha crossed the river and resumed the lion's pose in a different grove.

Just as Socrates reassured his disciples while the hemlock was being prepared for his execution (Chapter 4), Siddhartha reassured his followers that change—including death and decay—is universal, natural, and inescapable. "Do not weep, do not mourn, oh ye monks," the Buddha said.

> As a mother, even at the risk of her own life, protects and loves her child, her only child, so let a man cultivate love without measure toward the whole world, above, below, and around, unstinted, unmixed with any feeling of differing or opposing interests. Let a man remain steadfastly in this state of mind, walking, sitting or lying down. This state of mind is the best in the world.[55]

After his death, the teachings of the Buddha were handed down in the form of an oral tradition, and not until the first century B.C.E. did monks began to transcribe these discourses onto ola leaves. These teachings remained so until modern times, when the Pali Text Society took up the task of editing and printing them. They are now known collectively as the "three baskets": the *Vinaya Pitaka* (rules for monks), the *Sutta Pitaka* (basic teachings of the Buddha), and an organized later commentary known as the *Abhidhamma Pitaka*. Today, so many people produce books, journal articles, and video- and audiotaped lectures commenting on Buddhism that the diligent seeker will have trouble keeping up with a year's worth.

All humanity is sick. I come therefore to you as a physician who has diagnosed this universal disease and is prepared to cure it.

BUDDHA

Who knows why Heaven dislikes what it dislikes? Even the sage considers it a difficult question.

LAO-TZU

Only the man of humanity knows how to love people and how to hate people.

CONFUCIUS

"Three in the Morning"

Chuang-tzu (c. 399–295 B.C.E.) is the second great Taoist sage. Very little is known about his life, but the book bearing his name contains some of the richest stories in Taoist literature. The stories attributed to him reflect a generous soul, capable of great humor and great sadness. Here's an excellent example:

> On Knowing and Not Knowing the Oneness of Things. Only the truly intelligent understand this principle of the leveling of all things into One. . . . But to wear out one's intellect in an obstinate adherence to the individuality of things, not recognizing the fact that all things are One—this is called "Three in the Morning." What is "Three in the Morning"? A keeper of monkeys said that with regard to their rations of nuts each monkey was to have three in the morning and four at night. At this the monkeys were very angry. Then the keeper said they might have four in the morning and three at night, with which arrangement they were well pleased. The actual number of nuts remained the same, but there was a difference owing to (subjective evaluations of) likes and dislikes. It also derives from this (principle of subjectivity). Wherefore the true Sage brings all the contraries together and rests in the natural Balance of Heaven. This is called (the principle of following) two courses (at once).

Chuang-tzu, in *The Wisdom of Laotse*, trans. and ed. Lin Yutang (New York: Modern Library, 1976), p. 244.

"He abused me, he beat me, he defeated me, he robbed me"—in those who harbor such thoughts hatred will never cease. For hatred does not cease by hatred at any time; hatred ceases by love—this is an eternal law.

BUDDHA

We are all chained to Fortune. Some chains are golden and loose, some tight and of base metal; but what difference does it make? All of us are in custody, the binders as well as the bound—unless you suppose the left of the chain is lighter. Some of us are chained by office, some by wealth; some are weighed down by high birth, some by low; some are subject to another's tyranny, some to their own; some are confined to one spot by banishment, some by a priesthood. All life is bondage.

SENECA

I cannot discuss things with a gentleman who, while devoted to [the Way], is at the same time ashamed of poor clothes or bad food.

CONFUCIUS

karma

From the Pali *kamma;* according to Buddhist tradition, the law of moral causation (moral cause and effect); it includes past and present actions and is not to be confused with fate or predestination: good or bad karma results from our own actions.

Perhaps this is a tribute both to the profundity of the Buddha's pivotal insight and to a common human hunger for enlightenment.

Although our brief look at this great sage can be no more than a glimpse of the rich and profound legacy left by Buddha's great experiment, even reflected wisdom casts valuable light. So let us tread tentatively and respectfully through a tiny corner of one of the world's greatest wisdom traditions.

▦ KARMA ▦

Among the insights Buddha gained during his arduous search for enlightenment, three "realities" command our attention: impermanence, suffering, and egolessness. In simplistic, contemporary terms, we can sum up this part of Buddha's teaching like this: "Although nothing lasts, suffering is everywhere, and the 'me' that suffers isn't even real."

At the core of the Buddha's doctrine is the concept of the primal unsatisfactoriness (*dukkha*) generated by the perilousness of the human condition and by the inescapability of physical suffering and sickness, psychological conflict, anxiety, and anguish. As if this is not enough, Buddha reminds us that beneath our dissatisfaction lies a profounder insight: the insubstantiality of existence.[56]

Awareness of insubstantiality is related to the Buddhist doctrines of impermanence (ever-change) and egolessness. According to the Buddha, what we usually think of as "I" or "an individual" is a continuously changing combination of physical and psychological elements. Out of ignorance, we project a sense of permanence onto impermanent conditions. Because all is in flux, we are inevitably disappointed by change, destruction, and loss.[57]

Is this vision of the fundamental human condition pessimistic? Perhaps it would be, if Buddha had nothing more to teach. But Buddha promised that through a discipline of meditation, we can learn to control unruly desires and realize what happiness is possible given the *facts*—not our *projections*—of the human condition. Central to Buddha's teachings is a notion of free will, a belief that we can control our thoughts, attitudes, and behavior and that thoughts, attitudes, and behavior have consequences. These consequences, their causes, and their control are called *karma*.

The word *karma* comes from the Pali word *kamma*, a term referring to acts of the will that are expressed in thought, word, and deed. The concept of karma combines *kamma* (action-cause) with *vipaka* (reaction-effect). According to Buddhist tradition, **karma** is the law of moral causation (moral cause and effect); it includes past and present actions and is not to be confused with fate or predestination. Good or bad karma results from our own actions.[58]

Buddha did not teach that everything that happens is due to karma. In the first place, different laws govern natural change, physical phenomena, certain psychological processes, and so forth. In the second place, if karma alone accounted for the human condition, a person with good karma would always be good, and a person with bad karma would always be bad. Yet such is not the case. Indeed, self-reliance and peace of mind come only from understanding karma and living wisely in light of that understanding. "No one," said the Buddha, "can escape the wheel of suffering who does not understand the causes of suffering."

■ THE FOUR NOBLE TRUTHS ■

 The Buddha's basic teachings rest on what are called the **Four Noble Truths:**

1. No one can deny that suffering is the condition of all existence.

2. Suffering and general dissatisfaction come to human beings because they are possessive, greedy, and, above all, self-centered.

3. Egocentrism, possessiveness, and greed can, however, be understood, overcome, rooted out.

4. This rooting out, this vanquishing, can be brought about by following a simple, reasonable Eightfold Path of behavior in thought, word, and deed. Change of viewpoint will manifest itself in a new outlook and new patterns of behavior.[59]

In a nutshell, the Buddha taught that we suffer because we are partial to ourselves. For example, I cannot be bored listening to you complain about your philosophy class for the umpteenth time unless I am judging you or wishing you were talking about something interesting to *me*. It's the *me* that gets bored. I cannot be envious of the attention *my* parents give *my* brother without being greedy for more attention for *me*. If I were not greedy for *my* share, I would be delighted by his delight. The more self-conscious I am, the more *me* there is to suffer.

Contemporary Buddhist commentators and philosophers use the term *ego* differently from psychologists; they use it to refer to various self-centered, immature, and selfish tendencies. A person with too much ego thinks of himself or herself as unique and special in ways that emphasize differences. The loss or annihilation of this false *ego projection* results in the emergence of the soul or true self, the *Buddha nature*. The awakened or reborn soul/self sees similarities rather than differences, acts from love rather than fear, helps rather than judges. The bliss of nirvana comes from the annihilation of the self-consciousness, judgmentalism, greed, and fear that characterize ego.

The Buddha taught that the way to transcend the ego and see the interconnected whole of life is through loving-kindness. At the moment we feel love for others we cannot be bored or hostile with them. But it is difficult to maintain our compassion even with those we already love. Can we really alter our viewpoint to love every living thing?

Four Noble Truths
Foundation of Buddha's teachings: (1) to exist is to suffer; (2) self-centeredness is the chief cause of human suffering; (3) the cause of suffering can be understood and rooted out; (4) suffering can be alleviated by following the Eightfold Path.

Your self-partiality is the root of all your illusions. There aren't any illusions when you don't have this preference for yourself.

BANKEI

Those in the prime of their beauty are proud, those in the prime of their strength are impetuous; you cannot talk to them about Tao.

LIE ZI

• • • • • •

Think back to circumstances in which you were bored or hostile. Did "ego" play a role in your discomfort? Do you believe that all suffering comes from self-partiality? Discuss.

PHILOSOPHICAL

QUERY

■ THE EIGHTFOLD PATH ■

 According to Buddha, understanding the Four Noble Truths and following the law of karma are keys to release from suffering, but only if combined as a new way of life that combines three vital components of Buddhist

The Buddhist priest Juran's painting *Seeking the Tao in the Autumn Mountains* (c. 940–1000) reflects his vision of Tao as the fundamental natural harmony of all things.

©National Palace Museum, Taiei, Taiwan, Republic of China

Eightfold Path

Buddha's prescription for rooting out suffering: (1) right understanding; (2) right purpose; (3) right speech; (4) right conduct; (5) right livelihood; (6) right effort; (7) right mindfulness; (8) right meditation.

practice into an **Eightfold Path** of wisdom (*panna*), right conduct (*sila*), and right mental training (*samadhi*). The first two steps along the Eightfold Path are the steps of *panna;* steps three, four, and five are the steps of *sila;* and steps six, seven, and eight are the steps of *samadhi:*

1. Right understanding (or views)
2. Right purpose
3. Right speech
4. Right conduct
5. Right livelihood
6. Right effort
7. Right mindfulness (or awareness)
8. Right meditation[60]

Now let's look at a modified version. Gerald Heard, an Anglo-Irish historian and philosopher, phrased the Eightfold Path in an especially contemporary and insightful form:

1. First you must see clearly what is wrong.
2. Next you must decide that you want to be cured.

The way of the superior man may be compared to traveling to a distant place: one must start from the nearest point.

CONFUCIUS

3. You must act and

4. speak so as to aim at being cured.

5. Your livelihood must not conflict with your therapy.

6. That therapy must go forward at the "staying speed," that is, the critical velocity that can be sustained.

7. You must think about it incessantly and

8. learn how to contemplate with the *deep mind*.[61]

It is probably quite an understatement to note that the wisdom expressed in the Eightfold Path sounds so obvious, almost trivially simple. But simple is not always easy, and we often overlook the obvious. Consider: In many schools of psychology, the most important therapeutic event is the *moment of insight,* in which the client sees for the first time some important factor in his or her unhappiness. Something similar occurs in many religions, either at the moment of "rebirth" or during periods of atonement. The fallen soul sees by the grace of God its fallen nature and the way of salvation. One of the most effective treatment programs for alcoholism is Alcoholics Anonymous (AA), which is based on a list of guidelines for living called the Twelve Steps. The very first step begins, "We admitted we were powerless over alcohol and that our lives were unmanageable." The key to the first step

> *It should not be thought that the eight categories or divisions of the Path should be followed and practised one after the other in the numerical order given in the usual list. . . . But they are to be developed more or less simultaneously, as far as possible according to the capacity of each individual. They are all linked together and each helps the cultivation of the others.*
>
> WAPOLA RAHULA

"One Day"

Some of the richest Buddhist literature consists of stories that reveal the process of enlightenment indirectly. Though highly refined, these gemlike little tales leave the heart of the story unspoken. Thus they function like spiritual inkblots, drawing new insights from each listener's response. Here's a sampler of four:

One day a potential suicide was talking to a Buddhist monk, asking whether he had the right to commit suicide if he wanted to. The monk replied, "Anyone has the right to do anything. Everyone else has the right to resist it."

The student said, "Do you see suicide as a moral act?"

The monk answered, "Where there is no victim, every act is morally right, but I personally think suicide is a symptom of taking oneself too seriously."

One day the Buddhist monk Joshu fell down in the snow. He began wailing and crying for help. Seeing his distress, another monk lay down beside him and began thrashing about, crying and wailing as well. Joshu got up and left.

One day Chinso was up in a tower with some important people, and one of them saw a group of

monks approaching. "Look," he said, "holy men." "No, they aren't," Chinso said, "and I'll prove it." When the monks were directly below, Chinso leaned out of the tower window and yelled, "Hey! Holy men!" When they all looked up in response to his call, he said to his companions, "See?"

One day a rich man asked Sengai to write something ensuring the continued prosperity of his family. Sengai wrote, "Father dies, son dies, grandson dies." This angered the rich man, who said, "I asked you to write something for the happiness of my family! Why do you make such a joke as this?" "This is no joke," Sengai explained. "If your son dies before you do, you would grieve greatly. If your grandson dies before your son, both of you would be brokenhearted. If your family, generation after generation, passes away in the order I have named, it will be the natural course of life. I call this real prosperity."

The first story is from Camden Benares, *Zen Without Zen Masters* (Berkeley: And/Or Press, 1977), p. 37. The next three are paraphrased from Paul Reps, *Zen Flesh, Zen Bones: A Collection of Zen and Pre-Zen Writings* (Garden City, N.Y.: Anchor, 1973), p. 67.

is to see fully our own actual condition, whatever it involves. This "seeing" is, of course, the first step on the Eightfold Path.

It helps to remind ourselves that the Eightfold Path is designed to change us by changing our way of seeing things (consciousness), changing our behavior, and changing our emotions. It is designed to subdue our egocentric sense of identity, replacing the self-centered *me* with a compassionate heart. If I can change the way I view things, I have, in effect, changed the *world*. The difficulty of doing this is underscored by a poignant version of the Buddha's deathbed statement to his monks that ends, "Perhaps someone, somewhere will not misunderstand me."

PHILOSOPHICAL QUERY

• • • • • •

Discuss some of the difficulties you might encounter by trying to follow the Eightfold Path. What, for example, might consist of "wrong livelihoods" (or "wrong college majors")? Are there some jobs that no truly enlightened person could perform? What determines whether an occupation (or college major) is "right"? Explain.

■ THE BUDDHA'S LEGACY ■

Buddha was a perceptive psychological observer who realized that even though we all must actively work for our own enlightenment, most of us benefit from the support and guidance of regular, intimate association with others working toward a common goal.[62] What he envisioned was the free association of seekers on all levels of the path. What occurred was something else—as subsequent generations of Buddhists developed. In the twenty-five centuries since the Buddha lived, his basic message has been transformed into "schools of Buddhism," each with its own prescribed rules of dress, diet, habitation, and so on.

Buddha himself, however, did not think it mattered where one lived, what one ate, and so on. Any serious seeker following the Eightfold Path would avoid

"IN TODAY'S VIOLENT WORLD, FIGURING OUT THE SOUND OF ONE HAND CLAPPING SEEMS BESIDE THE POINT— WHAT, O WISE ONE, IS YOUR THOUGHT ON THE MATTER?"

extremes and remain in the *Middle Way*. Awareness, compassion, and helpfulness are more important than the particular clothes we wear or food we eat or place we live: "Let those who wish to dwell in the forest, dwell in the forest, and let those who wish to live in the village, live in the village."[63] Speaking ironically, Buddha said:

> If the mere wearing of a robe could banish greed, malice and other weaknesses, then as soon as a child was born his friends and kinfolk would make him wear the robe and would press him to wear it saying, "Come thou favored of fortune! Come wear the robe; for by the mere wearing of it the greedy will put from them their greed, the malicious their malice, and so on!"[64]

As happened among the followers of Socrates, Moses, Jesus, and Muhammad, Buddhist sects and divisions arose after Siddhartha's death. "Experts" in theory and ritual emerged, quarreling and competing for the title of true successor. The two main branches of Buddhism are Hinayana (or Theravada), "the Way of the Elders," and Mahayana, after its founder Mahayana, "the Greater Vehicle of Salvation." Other Buddhist sects such as Tibetan Buddhism and Japanese Zen Buddhism are usually seen as branches of the many-sided Mahayana branch.

The quarrels among Buddhists tend to take less hostile and more tolerant tones than do the quarrels among other philosophies and religions. The power of the Buddha's original vision is perhaps nowhere more clearly felt than in this restraint. Buddhists of one school tend to accept Buddhists of another, for in all cases, "the individual disciple is seen as directly, personally involved in his own salvation, a point of view which allows exceptional latitude in matters of instruction and practice."[65]

▪ WHAT THE BUDDHA DID ▪ NOT EXPLAIN

Some Western philosophers and theologians find it difficult to accept Buddha's refusal to present a theology or system of metaphysics. But Buddha's goal was existential and pragmatic. He was not a scholar or philosopher in a technical sense, but a sage, an insightful teacher who believed that questions of theology and complex philosophy confuse and distract us from our search for wisdom. Buddha believed that we are best served by dealing with the here and now in helpful, uncomplicated ways rather than fretting and quibbling over unanswerable metaphysical claims and theological doctrines.

Ultimately, Buddha calls on us to adopt a *way of life*, rather than "a philosophy," as we in the West understand "having a philosophy." Buddha insisted that to discover the truth, we must somehow set aside the kind of "analytic thinking" that leads to establishing schools of Buddhism or to quibbling over the correct interpretation of various texts. (In this, he reminds us of Lao-tzu and other Taoist sages.) Buddha says:

> If you will now and at all times, whether walking, standing, sitting, or lying, only concentrate on eliminating analytic thinking, at long last you will inevitably discover the truth. . . . [Relying on analytic thinking is] like using yellow leaves of gold to stop the crying of a child, and [is] decidedly not real. If you take it for something real, you are not one of our sect and, moreover, what

---

A man who talks much of his teaching but does not practice it himself is like a cattleman counting another man's cattle. . . . Like beautiful flowers full of color, but without scent, are the well-chosen words of the man who does not act accordingly.

BUDDHA

Do you know where to stop? Can you let unimportant things go? Can you learn not to depend on others but to seek it in yourself?

CHUANG-TZU

Nobody is normal, everybody is a little bit crazy or unbalanced, people's minds are running all the time. Their perceptions of the world are partial, incomplete. They are eaten alive by their egos. They think they see, but . . . all they do is project their madness upon the world. There is no clarity, no wisdom in that!

TAISEN DESHIMARU

Let the other man do his job without your interference.

CONFUCIUS

Abandon learning and there will be no sorrow.

LAO-TZU

The greatest eloquence seems to stutter.

LAO-TZU

"You Must Attune Your Inner Ear"

You do not like these quirky phrases? Paradoxes put you off? Ah well, no [Asian] sage ever promised you a garden of platitudes. . . . It is not cruelty that makes good gurus demanding. It is unusual kindness. In the spiritual life you become what you do . . . outer persona and inner self must come closer and closer together.

What doth it profit a person if she can assemble any stereo and never hears the music of the spheres? What doth it profit a person to place all his energies in the stock market? Stereos and the stock market have their place—all the Eastern sages allow them. What the Eastern sages do not allow them is primacy of place. . . . To hear the Tao in the morning or in the evening, to die content, one must vacate assembling and selling. The business of life is not business. The business of life is being. . . . It does not matter that many of our schools know nothing of such Eastern wisdom. The college catalogue is seldom a great book. Real learning occurs in dark nights and painful passages. Wisdom to live goes far below figures and facts.

. . . If today you would possess your soul, you must empty it of what is tawdry. If today you would hear the Tao, you must attune your inner ear.

Denise L. Carmody and John T. Carmody, *Eastern Ways to the Center: An Introduction to Religions of the East* (Belmont, Calif.: Wadsworth, 1981), pp. 201–203.

relation can it [analytic thinking] have to your real self? . . . In reality, everything is pure and glistening, neither square nor round, big nor small, long nor short; it is beyond passion and phenomena, ignorance and Enlightenment. . . .[66]

The function of a sage is to engage us, to challenge us to ask the deepest questions: Who am I? How am I to live? And it is to Buddha the sage that we shall turn as we take our leave of the Compassionate One. Perhaps we can experience a pale reflection of the power of Buddha's transforming vision by considering one of his most famous and intriguing sermons, called "On Questions Not Tending Toward Edification." Another title might be, "What You Don't Need to Know to Live Wisely and Compassionately." This sermon touches on one of the most difficult things for most of us to accept: We need to find a way of living a meaningful life in the absence of absolute answers. Here's a brief excerpt from one of the richest passages in Buddhist literature (and one my favorite passages in all wisdom literature):

It is as if . . . man had been wounded by an arrow thickly smeared with poison, and his friends and companions, his relatives and kinsfolk, were to procure for him a physician or surgeon; and the sick man were to say, "I will not have this arrow taken out until I have learnt . . . the name of the man who wounded me or whether the man who wounded me was . . . tall, or short, or of the middle height . . . whether the man who wounded me was black, or dusky, or of a yellow skin . . . whether the man who wounded me was from this or that village, or town, or city. . . ." That man would die without ever having learnt this. . . .

In exactly the same way . . . anyone who should say, "I will not lead the religious life under the Blessed One until the Blessed One shall explain to me that the world is eternal or that the world is not eternal . . . or that the saint either exists or does not exist after death";—that person would die . . . before [it was] ever explained to him.

What ought to be done is neglected, what ought not to be done is done; the desires of unruly, thoughtless people are always increasing.

BUDDHA

The religious life . . . does not depend on the dogma. . . .

Accordingly. . . bear always in mind what it is that I have not explained. . . . And what . . . have I explained? Misery . . . have I explained; the origin of misery have I explained; the cessation of misery have I explained. And why . . . have I explained this? Because . . . this does profit, has to do with the fundamentals of religion, and tends to . . . [tranquillity], knowledge, supreme wisdom, and Nirvana; therefore, I have explained it.[67]

It is my contention that in the field of morals . . . the insight of the sages into the value of disinterestedness has become the clue to otherwise insoluble perplexities.

WALTER LIPPMANN

• • • • • •

PHILOSOPHICAL
QUERY

Compare what Buddha "did not say" with what Confucius did not discuss concerning spirits (page 35). Do you think indifference to these matters is wise? Is it indifference or something else? Explain.

■ COMMENTARY ■

As we will discover in the next chapter, Western philosophy (and science) developed in the direction of objective, rational knowledge rather than the intuitive, holistic wisdom of the sages. One result is a technologically oriented Western culture that provides us with material comforts beyond our ancestors' wildest imaginings. But—as the sages remind us—the price for concentrating on this objective, rational paradigm has been alienation from nature and other rich sources of knowledge and wisdom.

The sage did not separate the human from the divine, or daily life from a sacred Way. The sage saw himself *as a part of* nature and the cosmos, not *apart from it.* In our rediscovery of the importance of nature (the environment), we move a little more in the direction of the sage. In our growing awareness of what Carol Gilligan called the "different voice" of compassion and care expressed by women and nontraditional Western philosophers, we move a little more in the direction of the sage.

In our haste to acquire sophisticated knowledge and its fruits—prestige, gadgets, the satisfaction of being "experts"—we can easily become unbalanced. Aggressive efforts (yang) to manage, analyze, and possess nature overlook the inevitability of flux (yin must follow yang). For example, using complex engineering principles, people build elaborate houses in the floodplains of the Mississippi River or crowd together in California coastal canyons (yang), only to see storms and fires bring them down (yin). To pursue sophisticated pleasures, we crowd into cities, which run short of water; we dirty the air; we pile up on freeways. Perhaps it would be wiser to pursue harmony, a Golden Mean, and live where we work and build simpler homes where nature welcomes us.

In recent years, philosophers, psychologists, ministers, environmentalists, and others have increasingly turned toward Asia to complement—as in "complete"—Western knowledge of technique and mastery. Social criticisms of elitist divisions have reawakened us to the need to see beyond differences to some kind of commonality. Perhaps these trends reflect greater sensitivity to the sacred essence the sages "stammer" about. Perhaps not.

Indeed, the saving truth has never been preached by the Buddha, seeing that one has to realize it within oneself.

SUTRALAMAKARA

These teachings are simple truth, and their power is that they can be applied immediately to our everyday life and the world we live in.

JÖSEL TENDZIN

God offers to every mind its choice between truth and repose; take which you please—you can never have both.

RALPH WALDO EMERSON

To be born when you will be born, that's good fortune. To die when you will die, that's good fortune. To be born and yet not to cherish life, that's opposing heaven. Not to want to die when it's time to die, that's opposing heaven.

LIE ZI

Though my skin, my nerves, and my bones should waste away and my lifeblood dry, I will not leave this seat until I have attained Supreme Enlightenment.

BUDDHA

Yet in acknowledging the wisdom of the sages, we must not make the mistake of elevating their teachings above Western science and philosophy—or vice versa. To do either is merely to perpetuate the chief problems the sages address: judgmentalism, partiality, alienation and division, argumentation, and "Doing Something" all the time.

The Asian sage stands between the traditional Western models of a philosopher and a saint or prophet. Saints and prophets of the major Western religious traditions differ from the sage in important ways. The most significant difference is in their relationship to "the one, true God," the Creator who is distinct from His creatures. For the sages, "all is one," and there is no equivalent to the separate God of the Bible.

For the sages, only those who actively work to achieve awareness deserve the title "sage"—and then only if they act on and live by what they have discovered to be true for themselves. No teachings, no scriptures, no theories take the place of experience. When we see clearly, we do not need teachers, scriptures, or theories. When we do not see clearly—for ourselves—nothing else matters.

"All right," you may grant, "but what about when we do see clearly?" Then, too, it seems "nothing else matters," as this delightful story from the teachings of the ninth-century Ch'an (Zen) master Hsi Yun hints:

> Stepping into the public hall [His Reverence] said: "The knowledge of many things cannot compare to giving up the search. The sage is one who puts himself outside the range of objectivity. There are not different kinds of mind, and there is no doctrine which can be taught."
>
> As there was no more to be said, everybody went away.[68]

■ SUMMARY OF MAIN POINTS ■

- The sage is an archetypal figure who combines religious inspiration with a love of wisdom. Sages understand and teach the requirements of the good life. Sages tend to be humanists who believe that human intelligence and effort are capable of improving conditions in the here and now.

- In ancient Chinese cosmology, everything was influenced by the harmonious working together of Heaven and Earth following the Tao, literally "way" or "path." Tao, which cannot be precisely defined, is translated as the source or principle of all existence, the way or path of the universe or moral law. Heaven and Earth constitute a single reality perpetually balancing between two opposing, but not separable, forces: Yin (Earth, passive element) is weak, negative, dark, and destructive; yang (Heaven, active element) is strong, positive, light, and constructive.

- According to legend, Lao-tzu (c. 575 B.C.E.) was a bureaucrat in ancient China, known only by a nickname, variously translated as the Old Master, the Old Man, the Old Boy, or the Old Philosopher. He is thought to be the author of the *Tao te Ching*, a slim classic that advocates harmony with Tao. Lao-tzu developed a nonlogical and paradoxical manner of communicating his belief that Tao is not a concept that can be grasped cognitively or logically. According to Lao-tzu, error, suffering, and unhappiness accompany all attempts to separate things, to understand the part without the whole.

- The *Tao te Ching* advocates reversing common priorities by preferring yin to yang. According to Lao-tzu's doctrine of inaction (*wu wei*), the best way to deal with social turmoil is "not to do anything about it." Although *wu wei* means "not to act," Lao-tzu uses the phrase as a warning against unnatural or demanding action. Natural action is "natural" in the sense of being spontaneous, healthy, and in harmony with Tao.

- Confucius (551–479 B.C.E.) is the Latinized name of K'ung Ch'iu of Lu, a legendary teacher who vainly sought high political office so that he could initiate a series of governmental reforms. He promoted social order based on personal moral cultivation of *jen* (humanity) and *li* (custom and ceremony). Confucian humanism, the name given to any philosophy that emphasizes human welfare and dignity, focuses on moderation according to the Golden Mean. A collection of Confucius's sayings known as the *Analects* is one of the most influential works in Asian philosophy.

- Confucius placed great emphasis on the moral example of the *chun-tzu*. Conventionally either the sovereign or a "cultivated gentleman," the Confucian *chun-tzu* is the morally superior man, a great and noble soul as well as a cultivated gentleman. His undesirable opposite is the small or vulgar *hsiao-jen*. The *chun-tzu* is a "real person" because he has realized *jen*, general human virtue rooted in empathy and fellow-feeling. Expressed through conscientiousness and altruism, *jen* is the "one thread" of Confucianism.

- Siddhartha Gautama (c. 560–480 B.C.E.) was born into wealth and power as the son of a prince in what today is Nepal. Siddhartha was so disturbed by his first encounters with old age, sickness, and death that he began a search for enlightenment that resulted in his transformation into the Buddha (the One Who Awakened).

- Rejecting the extremes of indulgence or denial, Siddhartha proposed a Middle Path. By choosing to remain among people to help other lost souls, the Buddha became a bodhisattva—an enlightened being who voluntarily postpones his own nirvana to help all other conscious life-forms find "supreme release." A bodhisattva is not a savior.

- The Buddha's basic teachings rest on what are called the Four Noble Truths: (1) Suffering is the condition of all existence. (2) Suffering comes from possessiveness, greed, and self-centeredness. (3) These traits can, however, be understood and overcome. (4) This overcoming can be accomplished by following an Eightfold Path, a practical cure for the suffering caused by being partial to ourselves: (1) right understanding, (2) right purpose, (3) right speech, (4) right conduct, (5) right livelihood, (6) right effort, (7) right mindfulness, (8) right meditation. The resultant state of emptiness or "no-thing-ness" is known as nirvana.

▪ POST-READING REFLECTIONS ▪

Now that you have had a chance to learn about the Asian Sages, use your new knowledge to answer these questions.

1. What is the relation between Heaven and Earth in ancient Chinese cosmology?

2. How did living during the Period of Warring States affect Confucius's and Lao-tzu's philosophies?

3. What is Lao-tzu trying to say about language when he claims to "say without saying"?

4. What is *chung-yung* and how does it figure into Confucius's teaching?

5. What is *te*? What is its relation to Tao?

6. What is *li*? Why is it important to Confucius?

7. How did the Buddha's protected early life contribute to his enlightenment?

8. What role did asceticism play in Buddha's search for wisdom and what did Buddha teach concerning it?

9. Identify key elements in Buddha's long search for enlightenment and explain their significance.

10. What is the relationship between nirvana and becoming a bodhisattva?

11. Did the Buddha establish a religion? Explain.

12. What is the Middle Way? What are the Four Noble Truths? What is their place in Buddha's teaching?

13. What is the Eightfold Path? What is its relationship to the Four Noble Truths?

14. What is significant about "what the Buddha did not explain"?

15. What is the lesson of "Three in the Morning"?

Philosophy Internet Resources

Go to the Soccio Web page at **http://philosophy.wadsworth.com/ Soccio7e** for Web links, practice quizzes and tests, a pronunciation guide, and study tips.

THE SOPHIST

Protagoras

MAN IS THE MEASURE OF ALL THINGS,
OF THE THINGS THAT ARE,
[HOW] THEY ARE,
AND THE THINGS THAT ARE NOT,
[HOW] THEY ARE NOT.

Protagoras of Abdera

LEARNING OBJECTIVES

- WHAT IS THE DIFFERENCE BETWEEN A *SOPHOS* AND A PHILOSOPHER?
- WHAT ROLE DID THE NEED FOR EXPLANATIONS PLAY IN THE DEVELOPMENT OF PRESOCRATIC PHILOSOPHY?
- WHAT IS RATIONAL DISCOURSE?
- WHAT IS A SOPHIST?
- WHAT IS ETHNOCENTRISM?
- HOW DID CHARGING FEES AFFECT THE TEACHINGS OF THE SOPHISTS?
- WHAT IS RELATIVISM?
- WHAT IS THE RING OF GYGES?
- WHAT IS MORAL REALISM?
- WHAT IS THE DOCTRINE OF THE SUPERIOR INDIVIDUAL?

For Your Reflection

KEEP THESE QUESTIONS IN MIND AS YOU LEARN ABOUT THE SOPHIST.

1. *What is the difference between a* sophos *and a philosopher?*
2. *What role did the need for explanations play in the development of Presocratic philosophy?*
3. *What is rational discourse?*
4. *What is a Sophist?*
5. *What is ethnocentrism?*
6. *How did charging fees affect the teachings of the Sophists?*
7. *What is relativism?*
8. *What is the Ring of Gyges?*
9. *What is moral realism?*
10. *What is the doctrine of the superior individual?*

For Deeper Consideration

A. Consider the argument that "justice is in the interest of the stronger." Is there a contradiction involved in the way Callicles makes his case? If so, what? Can you present a better version of the argument? Lastly, what do you think of the Sophists' overall assessment of the way society really operates? Are they onto something or not?

B. "That's just your opinion" is an all-too-common—and lazy—response to all sorts of arguments and assertions these days. And many scholars believe that most of our most cherished moral and political notions are culturally determined, that is, "true" for those who've been socialized to believe that they're true. But if "all opinions are true," as Protagoras claimed, why dispute them? What grounds does any relativist have for being angry or claiming that nonrelativists are wrong when they reject relativism? Does the relativist *need* any grounds? And what sorts of grounds are we talking about—logical or psychological? If we can never get beyond opinions, what follows?

The scene: A society showing signs of tension and strain, yet still exciting and important. The privileges of the establishment are being challenged by immigrants and more liberal democratic groups. Wealthy parents pay outrageous tuitions to have their children taught by prestigious educators, only to have these very same children then reject their parents' ideals and beliefs. People complain that atheistic, relativistic trends are permeating the schools and that basic values are breaking down. Traditional religions and beliefs are challenged by intellectuals, by occult practices, and by competing "foreign" religions. Scientific, mathematical, and intellectual advances compete for social control and influence with conservative, fundamentalist religious and moral tenets. Political corruption is pervasive and public. People take one another to court for a variety of real and inflated slights and transgressions. Success, prestige, and power become the overriding goals of many. Consider one commentator's description:

> It seems as if the dominant drive of more and more citizens is the objective of getting as rich as possible. . . . Meanwhile the money-makers, bent on their business, . . . continue to inject their poisoned loans wherever they can, and to demand high rates of interest, with the result that drones and beggars multiply. . . . Yet even when the evil becomes flagrant [the rulers] will do nothing to quench it. . . . This being so, won't everyone arrange his life as pleases him best? It's a wonderfully pleasant way of carrying on in the short-run, isn't it? It's an agreeable, anarchic form of society, with plenty of variety, which treats all men as equal, whether they are or not.
>
> It is a picture easy to recognize.[1]

America today? No. You have just read Plato's characterization of the "democratic" state of Athens. Because of their sophisticated, successful civilization, the Athenians had long viewed themselves as unique, special, superior to all others. The Athens of around 500–400 B.C.E. attracted aspiring entrepreneurs from all over Greece and parts of Asia. Those who considered themselves "original, true Athenians" grew uncomfortable and defensive.

Social scientists call this attitude **ethnocentrism** (from Greek roots meaning "the race or group is the center"). Ethnocentric individuals see their ways as inherently superior to all others: Their religion is the one true religion. Their science, music, tastes in all areas of life are unsurpassed. The ethnocentric person thinks, "The gods speak *our* language, look like *us*, are *our* color. *Our* family practices are *natural,* others are *deviant.*"

Yet things aren't so simple. In some Hindu cultures eating the flesh of a cow is forbidden. In other cultures, it is not. Some people get sick at the mere idea of eating a dog or monkey; to others, such culinary practices are normal. Ethnocentrism is what makes us laugh at the way other people dress or talk. We even do this to other citizens of our own country. Some Southerners make fun of people with a "New York accent," and New Yorkers in their turn mock those with "Southern accents." The ethnocentric person thinks that he or she doesn't even have an accent!

Ancients of our culture sought clarity: Plato portrays Socrates tirelessly splitting hairs to extract essential truth from the ambiguities of language and thought. Two thousand years later we are reversing that, for now we pay intellectual talent a high price to amplify ambiguities, distort thought, and bury reality. . . . One of the discoveries of the twentieth century is the enormous variety of ways of compelling language to lie.

JULES HENRY

ethnocentrism
From Greek roots meaning "the race is the center"; belief that the customs and beliefs of one's own culture are inherently superior to all others.

When Homer said he wished war might disappear from the lives of gods and men, he forgot that without opposition all things would cease to exist.

HERACLITUS

©ScienceCartoonsPlus.com

barbarian

From a rude "bar-bar" noise used to mock dialects considered crude by the ancient Athenians; originally referred to other cultures considered "less than human" or uncivilized.

The Greeks of this time were so ethnocentric that they invented the term **barbarian** to mock people who spoke in other languages. They mimicked the way foreigners talked by making a sound something like "bar, bar, bar." Today we would probably say, "blah, blah, blah." So the outsiders were bar-bar-ians (or blah-blah-ians)—people whose language sounded like noise or nonsense to the Greeks. To these Greeks, other cultures were simply "uncivilized," "less human." But what happens when a closed-off culture begins to interact with other highly civilized cultures on a regular basis?

PHILOSOPHICAL

QUERY

• • • • • •

Can you think of any ways you are ethnocentric? What are some close parallels between Athens of the fifth century B.C.E. *and America after September 11, 2001? Discuss.*

■ FROM *SOPHOS* TO PHILOSOPHER ■

As early Greek civilization grew more complex (c. 500 B.C.E.), mythology and religion began to develop into philosophy (and later into science). As part of this development, a new kind of thinker emerged known as a **sophos**, from the Greek word for "wise." These "wise men," and they were almost exclusively men, asked increasingly sophisticated questions about all sorts of things, especially natural processes and the origins and essence of life. Although mythology and religion continued to play important roles in the lives of people for centuries to come, these first philosophers were noted for their attempts to use reason and observation to figure out how the world works.

In his wonderful book *Philosophy as a Way of Life*, French philosopher Pierre Hadot describes how, in the ancient world, a true philosopher was usually viewed as someone out of step with daily life. To be a philosopher in those days was to be "different." The sorts of traits Hadot has in mind as different include lack of concern with such normal things as practicing a trade (having a regular job), pursuing wealth, or desiring fame and power.

sophos

Sage or wise man; term applied to the first philosophers; from the Greek word for "wise."

Woman as Sophos

Aesara of Lucania (c. fourth century B.C.E.–first century C.E.) was a Pythagorean philosopher who has only recently attracted any attention. In the single existing fragment of her book, *On Human Nature,* she says that through the introspection and contemplation of our own souls we can discover the "natural" foundation of all law and the structure of morality. In the following passage, Aesara wisely acknowledges the importance of reason as a guide, without overlooking the importance of emotions. Reading it, we cannot help but wonder what philosophy may have lost by overlooking the contributions of women philosophers for so long.

> By following the tracks within himself whoever seeks will make a discovery: Law is in him and justice, which is the orderly arrangement of the soul. Being threefold, it is organized in accordance with triple functions: That which effects judgment and thoughtfulness is [the mind] . . . that which effects strength and ability is [high spirit] . . . and that which effects love and kindness is desire. These are all so disposed relatively to one another that the best part is in command, the most inferior part is governed, and the one in between holds a middle place; it both governs and is governed.
>
> . . . And indeed, a certain unanimity and agreement in sentiment accompanies such an arrangement. This sort would justly be called good order, whichever, due to the better part's ruling and the inferior part's being ruled, should add the strength of virtue to itself. Friendship and love and kindliness, cognate and kindred, will sprout from these parts. For closely-inspecting mind persuades, desire loves, and high spirit is filled with strength; once seething with hatred, it becomes friendly to desire.
>
> Mind having fitted the pleasant together with the painful, mingling also the tense and robust with the slight and relaxed portion of the soul, each part is distributed in accordance with its kindred and suitable concern for each thing: mind closely inspecting and tracking out things, high spirit adding impetuosity and strength to what is closely inspected, and desire, being kin to affection, adapts to the mind, preserving the pleasant as its own and giving up [reasoning] to the thoughtful part of the soul. By virtue of these things the best life for man seems to me to be whenever the pleasant should be mixed with the earnest, and pleasure with virtue. Mind is able to fit these things to itself, becoming lovely through systematic education and virtue.

Holger Thesleff, "Pythagorean Texts of the Hellenistic Period," in Mary Ellen Waithe, ed., *Introduction to the Series, A History of Women Philosophers,* vol. 1, 600 B.C.–A.D. 500. trans. Vicki Lynn Harper (Dordrecht: Martinus Nijhoff, 1987), pp. 20–21.

Instead of living a "normal life," the *sophos* devoted himself to asking questions that so-called normal people thought had already been answered (by religion and mythology) or were unanswerable (and thus a waste of time). In respect to public perceptions, it didn't help that the *sophos* lived and spoke in ways that were interpreted as showing disregard and possibly disrespect for conventional values, and that set him or (infrequently) her apart from "regular folks" living "normal" lives.[2]

It is hardly surprising, then, that one of the earliest popular images of philosophers is the stereotype of an odd, "absent-minded," starry-eyed dreamer and asker of silly questions. For instance, **Thales** (c. 624–545 B.C.E.), traditionally said to be the first Western philosopher, was characterized as being absorbed in his speculative studies, devoting only the minimum effort necessary to his financial affairs. In one of the earliest absent-minded professor stories, Plato says that Thales fell into a well "when he was looking up to study the stars . . . being so eager to know what was happening in the sky that he could not see what lay at his feet."[3] Socrates (Chapter 4), perhaps the most-recognized example of the ancient Western *sophos*, was deemed "unclassifiable" (*atopos*) because he was a "philo-sopher" in the archetypal sense: a person in love with wisdom rather than power, prestige, pleasure, or wealth.

Hadot notes that this reputation for strangeness was not confined to fifth-century B.C.E. Greek philosophers. By the third century B.C.E., Roman law singled out "philosophers" as odd and unreliable, as "a race apart," and held that "in the litigation between professors and their debtors [students] the authorities did not need to concern themselves with philosophers, for these people [philosophers] professed to despise money."

In other words, Roman law took seriously the claims of those sages who, like some religious and spiritual figures today, claim that ideas and the soul matter more than the body, material possessions and money! Emperor Antoninus Pious went so far as to issue a decree pointing out that "if a philosopher haggles over his possessions, he shows he is no philosopher."[4] If these ancient commentators are correct, an authentic *sophos* is always a "stranger to the world."[5]

The decrees of the people are in large measure repealed by the sages.
SENECA

In Greece wise men speak and fools decide.
ANACHARSIS

The sage probes, not the fact of survival, but the reasons.
GUAN YIN

PHILOSOPHICAL

QUERY

• • • • • •

How do you think it would go over today if we treated philosophers, preachers, and anyone who professes not to value money and wealth as much as integrity, honor, God, or truth as if they mean what they say and hold them personally and legally accountable for living like they talk? Is it reasonable—or fair—to judge a person's philosophical claims in terms of behavior? Do we trivialize "being" a philosopher—or "being" a Christian or Muslim or liberal or conservative—when we make a radical distinction between persons and their beliefs?

▪ THE FIRST PHILOSOPHERS ▪

In his earliest incarnations, the Western *sophos* was predominantly a sage or wise man in the general or generic sense. He was not a professional thinker. That is, he did not charge people fees (tuition) to study with him or to accompany him. His relationships with his students were personally complex and long-lasting. In many cases his pupils were more like disciples and friends than paying students.

The very first Western thinkers identified as *philosophers* were initially concerned with questions about the nature of nature (*physis*) and of the "world order" (*kosmos*). Today, we would classify many of their concerns as scientific. It would be a mistake, however, to think that ancient philosophers "specialized" in the modern sense. Indeed, Plato and Aristotle (Chapters 5 and 6) were both interested in ethics, logic, language, art, human nature, politics, mental and physical health. Aristotle was also interested in physics, biology, botany, and anatomy.

Whereas the *sophos* (sage or wise man) was seen as a kind of prophet-priest-therapist, the *philosopher*, who is in love with wisdom but not necessarily wise, was seen as an unusual sort of thinker and truth-seeker. Thus, we notice an ambiguity in the early use of the word *philosopher* that carries over into the present day. Although initially the philosopher, like the *sophos*, was expected to live a "philosophical life," today a philosopher is not required to live a wise—"philosophical"—life, but to devote his or her energies to "thinking" about certain things in a rigorous way. In Chapters 17 and 18 we will see how the very notion of being a philosopher came under scrutiny as contemporary philosophers challenge the possibility of objectivity and universal truth.

■ PRESOCRATIC RATIONAL DISCOURSE ■

The earliest Western philosophers are referred to as the *Presocratics* because they appeared prior to Socrates, the first major figure in the Western philosophical tradition. Some of the Presocratic philosophers are described as *proto-scientists* because they initiated the transformation of mythology into rational inquiry about nature and the cosmos. In the beginning, the difference between a *sophos* who became a *philosopher* and one who became a *proto-scientist* was one of subject matter; later it became one of method. A very general characterization of the development of Presocratic philosophy is helpful for placing subsequent philosophical issues and disagreements in context. Of most interest for our purposes is the Presocratic philosophers' struggle to offer rational, "objective" arguments and explanations for their views. These concerns played a major role in the origins and historical development of Western philosophy.

The first philosophers' intense interest in *explanations* shaped the development of reason by triggering questions of logical consistency and standards of knowledge that went beyond the sorts of evidence that a craftsman could offer to back up his claims to expertise. A boatwright could prove his case by making a ship that sailed, a builder of columns by constructing columns, an armorer by fitting armor. By what comparable method could a philosopher "prove" that the universe is intelligent or that "everything is water" (Thales) or "mind" (Anaxagoras) or number (Pythagoras) or atoms (Democritus), or that everything is always changing (Heraclitus) or that change is an illusion (Parmenides and Zeno)—all claims made by the first philosophers?

Social historian Amaury de Riencourt characterizes this early history of the philosophers' radical search for explanations as a series of increasingly abstract

rational discourse
The interplay of carefully argued ideas; the use of reason to order, clarify, and identify reality and truth according to agreed-upon standards of verification.

steps shaped by a "fanatical concern" with logical consistency and rules of thinking leading ultimately to theories that, though logically consistent, did not match observed facts. The result, de Riencourt says, was "the absolute predominance of the *dissociating*, analytical . . . principle in Greek [thought] . . . its strength and its weakness."[6]

The "dissociation" that de Riencourt describes refers to a separation of theoretical knowledge from practical wisdom that developed as certain strains of philosophical speculation became increasingly alienated from common experience, and as unemotional, implacable reason (modeled after the *logos*) threatened to dominate other sources of wisdom. See the box "Zeno's Paradoxes," page 66, for an intriguing and entertaining example of what can result when a philosophical theory clashes with everyday experience.

■ CHANGE ALONE IS REAL ■

One of the most important and enigmatic of the Presocratics, **Heraclitus** (fl. 500 B.C.E., d. 510–480 B.C.E.), said that ignorance is bound to result when we try to understand the **cosmos** when we do not even comprehend the basic structure of the human **psyche** (soul) and its relationship to the *Logos*.

The complex Greek word *logos* is intriguing. It could and at times did mean all of the following: "intelligence," "speech," "discourse," "thought," "reason," "word," "meaning," "study of," "the record of," "the science of," "the fundamental principles of," "the basic principles and procedures of a particular discipline," "those features of a thing that make it intelligible to us," and "the rationale for a thing."

The Heraclitean capital L *Logos* is like God, only without the anthropomorphizing (humanizing) of the earlier philosophers and poets who attributed human qualities to the gods. According to Heraclitus's impersonal view of God, the *Logos* is a process, not an entity. As such, the *Logos* is unconcerned with individuals and human affairs, in much the same way that gravity affects us but is unconcerned with us.

More radically yet, Heraclitus asserted that even though things *appear* to remain the same, "Change alone is unchanging."[7] Traditionally, it has been held that Heraclitus went so far as to claim that *everything is always changing all the time*. But whether he really meant that everything is always changing, or that individual things are held together by energy (change), remains unclear.

Heraclitus's concept of change is not what you and I usually mean by change. Our common experience suggests that, contrary to Heraclitus, most things "stay the same" for very long periods of time and do not change all the time. In order to reconcile this common misperception of permanence with his conviction that everything is always changing, Heraclitus made a major contribution to the development of rational discourse by distinguishing between *appearance* and *reality* in a way that contrasted *apparent permanence* with *hidden reality*.[8]

The result was yet another instance of the dissociation of philosophy from common experience discussed earlier, in this case a dissociation that characterizes most of us as unwise, slumbering individuals seduced by conventional notions and appearances while remaining unaware of what is real and true. (This is a theme that recurs throughout the history of philosophy, with some notable exceptions.)

cosmos
Greek term for "ordered whole"; first used by the Pythagoreans to characterize the universe as an ordered whole consisting of harmonies of contrasting elements.

psyche
Greek for "soul"; in today's terms, combination of mind and soul, including capacity for reflective thinking.

Logos
One of the richest and most complex terms in ancient philosophy; associated meanings include: "intelligence," "speech," "discourse," "thought," "reason," "word," "meaning"; the root of "log" (record), "logo," "logic," and the "ology" suffix found in terms like *sociology* and *physiology*. According to Heraclitus, the rule according to which all things are accomplished and the law found in all things.

"The Celestial Music of the Spheres"

About 530 B.C.E., Pythagoras of Samos (sixth century B.C.E.) left Greece for the Greek colony of Crotona in southern Italy, where he established a religious community that existed in one form or another for hundreds of years. The Pythagorean community eventually developed important mathematical and philosophical ideas that grew out of efforts to purify the psyche.

Although we know that Pythagoras was a historical figure, it is difficult to determine exactly what Pythagoras himself taught. He wrote nothing, and the ideas of other members of the community were attributed to him as a sign of respect and as a way of lending weight to the ideas. Plato and Aristotle rarely assign ideas to Pythagoras himself, although Pythagorean ideas seem to have influenced Plato's philosophy.

Pythagoreans asserted that number is the first principle of all things. They were the first systematic developers of mathematics in the West and discovered that natural events could be described in mathematical terms, especially as ratios.

To the Pythagoreans, the "principle of number" accounted for everything. Number was a real thing. Somehow, numbers existed in space, not just as mental constructs. *One,* for instance, was a point, *two* a line, *three* a surface, *four* a solid, and so forth. The earth, being a solid, was associated with the cube; fire was associated with the pyramid, air the octahedron, and water the icosahedron. From this perspective, all things "follow rules" and are "ordered."

According to Pythagorean doctrine, the entire universe is an ordered whole consisting of harmonies of contrasting elements. The Greek for "ordered whole" is *cosmos.* The Pythagoreans were the first philosophers to use the term *cosmos* to refer to the universe in this way. In contrast to the nearly mystical quality of the Heraclitean *Logos,* the Pythagorean cosmos is accessible to arithmetic, geometry, and rationality on a far greater scale. Rationality and truth are both functions of number.

The "celestial music of the spheres" is the hauntingly beautiful phrase the Pythagoreans coined to describe the sound of the heavens as they rotate according to cosmic number and harmony. One point of view held that because we have been exposed to the music of the spheres from birth we do not hear it. Other Pythagoreans thought that the music of the spheres was beyond the range of human hearing. Aristotle says:

> Some thinkers [Pythagoreans] suppose that the motion of bodies of that size must produce a noise, since on our earth the motion of bodies far inferior in size and speed of movement has that effect. Also, when the sun and moon, they say, and all the stars, so great in number and in size, are moving with so rapid a motion, how should they not produce a sound immensely great? Starting from this argument and from the observation that their speeds, as measured by their distances, are in the same ratios as musical concordances, they assert that the sound given forth by the circular movement of the stars is a harmony. Since, however, it appears unaccountable that we should not hear this music, they explain this by saying that the sound is in our ears from the very moment of birth and is thus indistinguishable from its contrary silence, since sound and silence are discriminated by mutual contrast. What happens . . . then, is just what happens to coppersmiths, who are so accustomed to the noise of the smithy that it makes no difference to them.

Aristotle, *De Caelo,* trans. J. L. Stocks, B9, 290B12, in G. S. Kirk and J. E. Raven, *The Presocratic Philosophers* (Cambridge: Cambridge University Press, 1957), pp. 258–259.

■ CHANGE IS AN ILLUSION ■

Parmenides of Elea (fl. fifth century B.C.E.) radically transformed the early philosophers' interest in **cosmology**, the study of the universe as a rationally ordered system (cosmos), into **ontology**, the study of being. Parmenides was probably born around 515 B.C.E. in Elea, a Greek colony in southern Italy. His work was a major influence on Plato, who suggests that Parmenides and

cosmology
From the Greek word *kosmos,* meaning "world," "universe," or "orderly structure," the study of the universe as an ordered system or cosmos.

ontology
The study of being.

his pupil Zeno (see the box "Zeno's Paradoxes") came to Athens, where they met young Socrates.[9]

According to Parmenides, none of his predecessors adequately accounted for the *process* by which the one basic stuff of the cosmos changes into the many

Zeno's Paradoxes

Zeno of Elea (c. 490–430 B.C.E.) forcefully defended the idea that change in the form of motion is impossible. These intriguing paradoxes present one of the earliest examples of a particular method of proof known as a **reductio ad absurdum** (reduce to absurdity). In a *reductio*, an opponent's position is refuted by showing that accepting it leads to absurd, unacceptable, or contradictory conclusions. Zeno is credited with perfecting a way of revealing an idea's absurdity by (1) showing that accepting it leads to a logical contradiction or (2) showing that it leads to a logical conclusion that is somehow obviously ridiculous because it offends either our reason or common sense.

Using a form of the *reductio*, Zeno tried to show that the Heraclitean claim that everything is always changing is absurd because the very idea of change or motion is absurd. The paradoxes also reveal the ultimate inadequacy of the Presocratic notion of the continuum.

Zeno's paradoxes were admired by ancient philosophers and continue to generate lively discussions among contemporary philosophers. See what you make of his three most famous paradoxes.

The Dichotomy

The first argument is this: If movement exists, it is necessary that the mobile [moving thing] traverse an infinite number of points in a finite time; but this is impossible, hence movement does not exist. Zeno demonstrated his position affirming that whatever is moved must traverse a certain distance: but any distance is divisible to infinity, what is moved must first traverse half of the distance and then the whole of it. But first he must traverse the entire half of the distance, and the half of that and the new half of the previous half. But if the halves are infinite in number, since for every whole taken it is possible to take half, then it is impossible to traverse in a finite time an infinite number of points. . . . Then, given that every magnitude admits of infinite divisions, it is impossible to traverse any magnitude in a finite time.

Simplicius, *In Aristotle's Physics*, 1013.4ff.; quoted in Giovanni Reale, *A History of Ancient Philosophy*, vol. 1, *From the Origins to Socrates*, trans. John R. Catan (Albany: State University of New York Press, 1987), p. 91.

Achilles and the Tortoise

The second [paradox] is the so-called Achilles, and it amounts to this, that in a race the quickest runner can never overtake the slowest, since the pursuer must first reach the point whence the pursued started, so that the slower must always hold a lead. This argument is the same in principle as that which depends on bisection [cutting the distance in half], though it differs from it in that the spaces with which we successively have to deal are not divided into halves. The result of the argument is that the slower is not overtaken: but it proceeds along the same lines as the dichotomy argument (for in both, a division of the space in a certain way leads to the result that the goal is not reached, though the Achilles goes further in that it affirms that even the quickest runner in legendary tradition must fail in his pursuit of the slowest). . . .

Aristotle, *Physics*, Hardie and Gaye translation, 239B.14ff.

The Flying Arrow

The argument of Zeno, beginning from the premise that everything which occupies a space equal to itself either is in motion or is at rest, that nothing is moved in an instant, and that the mobile always occupies in each instant a space equal to itself, seems to adjust itself in this way: The flying arrow in every instant occupies a place equal to itself, and thus, for the whole time of its motion. But what occupies in an instant a place equal to itself does not move because nothing is moved in an instant. Hence the flying arrow, as long as it is in motion, does not move for the whole time of its flight.

Simplicius, in *Aristotle's Physics*, 1015.19ff.; in Reale, *A History of Ancient Philosophy*, vol. 1, *From the Origins to Socrates*, trans. John R. Catan (Albany: State University of New York Press, 1987), p. 93.

individual things we experience every day. In his search for a solution to the problem of "the one and the many," Parmenides turned to a reasoned analysis of the process of change itself.

According to Parmenides, all sensations occur in the realm of appearance. This means that reality cannot be apprehended by the senses. Change and variety (the many) are only *appearances*; they are not *real*. If this is true, then our most commonly held beliefs about reality are mere opinions. The senses cannot recognize "what is," much less can they discover—observe—it, ever. In other words, whatever we see, touch, taste, hear, or smell is not real, does not exist.

Here—again—we encounter a radical dissociation of a philosopher's explanation of reality and wisdom (knowledge and understanding) from our common experience and deepest beliefs.

Perhaps most unsettling of all, Parmenides "solved" the problem of the *appearance of change* by concluding—in direct opposition to Heraclitus's insistence that everything is always changing—that the very concept of change is self-contradictory. What we think of as change is merely an illusion. The logic runs as follows: "Change" equals transformation into something else. When a thing becomes "something else," it becomes what it is not. But since it is impossible for "nothing" (what is not) to exist, there is no "nothing" into which the old thing can disappear. (There is no "no place" for the thing to go into.) Therefore, change cannot occur.[10]

Whatever the power of Parmenides' reasoning, change and motion remain basic facts of experience for most of us. That is, regardless of the reasonableness of Parmenides' argument, we find ourselves convinced that change and movement are real. And if we cannot—or will not—be convinced otherwise, then, once again, we find ourselves at odds with philosophy (or at least with this philosophy).

The popularity or unpopularity of an opinion is not a measure of its merit, however. And Parmenides' position was the product of careful reasoning in a way that common sense rarely is. Further, Parmenides' philosophical contemporaries took his arguments seriously, and Parmenides' notion of what is real played an important part in the development of Plato's theory of forms (as we shall see in Chapter 5).

■ ATOMS OR NOTHING ■

The Parmenidean assault on the senses was countered in the middle of the fifth century B.C.E., when **Leucippus** of Miletus (c. fifth century B.C.E.) and **Democritus** of Abdera (c. 460–370 B.C.E.) argued that reality consists entirely of empty space and ultimately simple entities that combine to form objects. This materialistic view is known as **atomism**. Leucippus is credited with being the originator of atomism and Democritus with developing it.

Rather than reject Parmenides' assertion that change is an illusion, Leucippus argued that reality consists of many discrete "ones," or beings. Democritus termed these "ones" *atoms*, from the Greek *atomos*, meaning "indivisible," "having no

---

reductio ad absurdum
From the Latin for "reduce to absurdity"; form of argument that refutes an opponent's position by showing that accepting it leads to absurd, unacceptable, or contradictory conclusions because (1) accepting it leads to a logical contradiction, or (2) it leads to a logical conclusion that is somehow obviously ridiculous because it offends either our reason or common sense.

[The path] that it is not . . . is bound not to be: This I tell you is a path that cannot be explored; for you could neither recognize that which is not, nor express it.
PARMENIDES

You cannot conceive the many without the one.
PLATO

atomism
Early Greek philosophy developed by Leucippus and Democritus and later refined by Epicurus and Lucretius; materialistic view that the universe consists entirely of empty space and ultimately simple entities that combine to form objects.

atoms

From the Greek *atomos*, meaning "indivisible," "having no parts," or "uncuttable"; minute material particles; the ultimate material constituents of all things. Atoms have such properties as size, shape, position, arrangement (combination), and motion, but lack qualities like color, taste, temperature, or smell.

parts," or "uncuttable." **Atoms** are minute material particles, the ultimate material constituents of all things. According to Democritus, atoms have properties such as size, shape, position, arrangement (combination), and motion, but they do not possess sensible qualities like color, taste, temperature, or smell. However, combinations (compounds and composites) of atoms can grow large enough for us to perceive.

According to Democritus, atoms are so small that they are invisible to the naked eye. Being so small, they are "uncuttable"—thus they cannot be destroyed. In other words, atoms are eternal. Because motion is an inherent property of atoms, they are constantly moving, bumping into each other and bouncing away or quivering in one spot.

■ NATURE VERSUS CONVENTION ■

According to Democritus, we never experience (perceive) atoms directly. Shape, taste, and other sensible properties are the result of "effluences" and "images" that we sense as atoms strike the eye, ear, skin, tongue, and so on. Thus, we are "cut off from the real" because our sensations are products of our own particular condition: our sensory acuity, whether we are sick, intoxicated, dehydrated, and so on.

Not only do we never experience atoms directly, even perceptual qualities—like sweet and sour, hot and cold, smooth and rough, hard and soft—are matters of *convention*, not nature: "Sweet exists by convention, bitter by convention, color by convention; but in reality atoms and the void alone exist," according to Democritus.

Although Democritus rejected the most radical skeptical implications of this insight, later philosophers have elaborated on them with stunning effect. In the rest of this chapter (and subsequent chapters), we will look at some of the far-reaching consequences engendered by the question of what is true by nature and what is true by convention.

To many "normal" people, it was the philosophers themselves who, for all their inventiveness and cleverness, were the ones utterly out of touch with reality. To these observers, philosophical speculation was viewed as an indulgence suitable only for those not fit for real life or as a hobby for independently wealthy individuals or for those supported by friends or family. The suspicion lurked that philosophy was some how unseemly, fit only for those obsessed with pointless "intellectual squabbles." After all, nonphilosophers asked, What is the point of explanations that don't square with everyday experience? What is the point of logical consistency if the results are bizarre claims that nothing changes *and* that everything changes *and* that arrows do not fly *and* the fleet Achilles will never catch the slow tortoise?

Ultimately—and understandably—for many people philosophy developed a conflicted and confused reputation, something at once noble and somehow ridiculous.

This clouded reputation haunts philosophy to this day, as we saw in Chapter 1. "What are you philosophers good for," we are asked, "if you can hold contradictory and absurd ideas that bear no resemblance to common sense? How can the rest of us take seriously your charges that we can never experience reality, that our most cherished and widely held beliefs are merely illusions, that our thinking is muddled, that *we*, the majority, are wrong and that our unwillingness to agree with you is a symptom of our ignorance rather than your own? If even the most careful philosophical thinkers end up in such tangles, maybe it's better to think less and enjoy life more."

We are about to see how this suspicious attitude toward philosophy contributed to a philosophical and cultural revolution that occurred when the first "professional" thinkers, known as Sophists, turned from the study of the cosmos to the study of human beings and brought philosophy back down to earth. The Sophists' demands for "philosophy that pays" blew through the ancient world like a bracing wind.

■ THE ADVENT OF PROFESSIONAL ■ EDUCATORS

Ancient Athens was chauvinistic in many respects. For example, full citizenship was originally confined to males from certain aristocratic families. The ambitious, talented young immigrants from throughout the Mediterranean area who were attracted by Athens's vitality as a trading center had fewer rights and opportunities than did Athenian citizens. Regardless of their abilities, it was difficult, if not impossible, for noncitizens to achieve the same levels of success as those lucky enough to have been born into the right families.

As the number of capable immigrants settling in and around Athens grew, tension and conflict became inevitable. The Athenians' snobbery was challenged. Some Persians and Spartans and Milesians were smarter, quicker, stronger, more attractive; some of their goods were of higher quality; their traders sometimes outfoxed Athenians. Thus, the Athenians' image of themselves as unique and superior people became increasingly difficult to maintain as interaction with people from other cultures increased (as is always ultimately the case). Indeed, great deliberate effort was required to maintain a view of unquestioned superiority.

As the lively trade center flourished, the privileges of birth were challenged by the emergence of a wealthy new business class. Good business sense, personal charm and persuasiveness, the willingness to work hard, and individual ability began to be as important as having been born in the right place to the right kind of family.[11]

In this changing climate, more and more individuals were allowed both to speak before the Athenian Assembly and to sue one another over business and personal matters. The ability to think clearly and speak persuasively was a means for members of the new middle class to enter political life and to improve their social status. These conditions combined to create a demand for something unknown in the Mediterranean world before this time: formal, specialized higher education in such subjects as letters, rhetoric (persuasive speaking), science, statesmanship, and philosophy.[12]

These social changes also affected philosophy. Presocratic philosophers had inconsistently asserted various explanations of "reality" that did not conform to common experience. Each theory was flawed. Each philosopher's position was criticized logically by a newer point of view, which was in turn criticized. Even good logic and sound reasoning seemed ultimately unhelpful in sorting things out. One problem was with the characteristics of arguments themselves. All

The Ethiopians say that their gods are snub-nosed and black, the Thracians that theirs have light blue eyes and red hair.

XENOPHANES

The religion of one seems madness unto another.

SIR THOMAS BROWNE

But it is well to remember from time to time that nothing that is worth knowing can be taught.

OSCAR WILDE

There are two sides to every question.

PROTAGORAS

The sun is one foot wide.

HERACLITUS

Reality has nothing to do with reputation, reputation has nothing to do with reality. Reputation is nothing but pretense.

LIE ZI

Because my philosophy was based on reality, all of my techniques were either directly or indirectly aimed at the most important reality of all: the necessity of getting paid.

ROBERT J. RINGER

arguments consist of two aspects: their logical structure and the truth (or falsity) of their content. Sound arguments consist of good reasoning based on true premises. If one or more premises of an argument are false, the conclusion will be unreliable. Thus, if its starting point is flawed, even the most tightly reasoned argument or theory will be flawed.

Overwhelmed by so many conflicting theories, the new *sophos* of the fifth century B.C.E., now called a **Sophist,** concluded that it is impossible to discover "the Truth" because the only difference between a "good" argument and a "bad" argument is custom and individual preference. (See Chapters 14–17 for subsequent challenges to "the Truth.")

■ POWER AND EDUCATION ■

The original Sophists were wandering teachers who gravitated toward Athens during the fertile fifth century. They were also the first professional teachers, charging a fee to teach anyone who wished to study with them. They made Athenian education democratic, at least in the sense that all who could pay were equal. It was no longer necessary to belong to a certain family—as long as you had enough money to pay high tuitions. The *sophos,* in contrast to the Sophist, had followers and disciples rather than paying students.

The Sophists also differed from the *sophos* in that the Sophists turned increasingly from the study of nature to the formal study of human life and conduct. Many of them had traveled rather widely and thus were "sophist-icated," or worldly wise. (We get the word *sophisticated* from this period.) The Sophists knew firsthand about various cultures; they had witnessed a variety of religious practices and had experienced a variety of tastes in clothing, food, family patterns, legal values, and morals.

In many ways, the Sophists can be thought of as the first social scientists, combining, as it were, anthropology, psychology, and sociology to produce a particular view of social life and human nature. Their sophistication was a direct threat to the chauvinistic elite that ruled Athens. The idea that anyone with the fee could be educated was offensive to those who saw themselves as inherently superior.

The Sophists looked closely at "what worked" in various cultures and concluded that virtually nothing was good or bad by nature, but that good and bad were matters of custom and preference. Further, they noticed that although different individuals desire different things, *everyone seeks some form of power.* The Sophists argued that every living thing seeks to be happy and to survive as long as possible, so the only "natural" good is power because power increases control over the conditions of happiness and survival. For instance, getting a new car won't make you happy if you cannot keep it. Being right about something at work won't help if you lack the ability (power) to get your boss to recognize it. Based on such observations, the Sophists concluded that so-called truth is subservient to power.[13]

The Sophists remained professionals, in the sense of always demanding payment, eventually becoming infamous for their insistence on being well paid. It was widely believed that the worst of them would teach anything they could get someone to pay for. The Sophists' reputation also suffered because of their emphasis

---

Sophists

In fifth century B.C.E., teachers of rhetoric (who were paid); relativists who taught that might makes right, truth is a matter of appearance and convention, and power is the ultimate value.

To speak much is one thing, to speak well is another.

SOPHOCLES

Life may have no meaning. Or even worse, it may have a meaning of which I disapprove.

ASHLEIGH BRILLIANT

And how many legions does the Pope have?

STALIN, AT YALTA

If a man were really able to instruct mankind, to receive money for giving instruction would, in my opinion, be an honour to him.

SOCRATES

The Ring of Gyges

The technical name for the view that all morality reduces to self-interest is *egoism*. It is usually associated with moral skepticism, since it is the only source of values left for the moral skeptic. One of the earliest and most interesting presentations of the egoist's position occurs in Plato's *Republic*:

> Even those who practise justice do so against their will because they lack the power to do wrong. This we would realize if we clearly imagined ourselves granting to both the just and the unjust the freedom to do whatever they liked. We could then follow both of them and observe where their desires led them, and we would catch the just man redhanded travelling the same road as the unjust. The reason is the desire for undue gain which every organism by nature pursues as good, but the law forcibly sidetracks him to honour equality. The freedom I just mentioned would most easily occur if these men had the power which they say the ancestor of the Lydian Gyges possessed. The story is that he was a shepherd in the service of the ruler of Lydia. There was a violent rainstorm and an earthquake which broke open the ground and created a chasm at the place where he was tending sheep. Seeing this and marvelling, he went down into it. He saw, besides many other wonders of which we are told, a hollow bronze horse. There were window-like openings in it; he climbed through one of them and caught sight of a corpse which seemed of more than human stature, wearing nothing but a ring of gold on its finger. This ring the shepherd put on and came out.

> He arrived at the usual monthly meeting which reported to the king on the state of the flocks, wearing the ring. As he was sitting among the others he happened to twist the hoop of the ring towards himself, to the inside of his hand, and as he did this he became invisible to those sitting near him and they went off talking as if he had gone. He marvelled at this and, fingering the ring, turned the hoop outward again and became visible. Perceiving this he tested whether the ring had this power and so it happened: if he turned the hoop inwards he became invisible, but he was visible when he turned it outwards. When he realized this, he at once arranged to become one of the messengers of the king. He went, committed adultery with the king's wife, attacked the king with her help, killed him, and took over the kingdom.

> Now if there were two such rings, one worn by the just man, the other by the unjust, no one, as these people think, would be so incorruptible that he would stay on the path of justice or bring himself to keep away from other people's property and not touch it, when he could with impunity take whatever he wanted from the market, go into houses and have sexual relations with anyone he wanted, kill anyone, free all those he wished from prison, and do other things which would make him like a god among men.

Plato, *The Republic*, trans. G. M. A. Grube (Indianapolis: Hackett, 1974), p. 32f.

on winning debates in and out of court at all costs. Since they believed that power was the ultimate value, the key issue became not right or wrong, but getting your own way.

As the Sophists became expert debaters and advertisers, they learned to use emotional appeals, physical appearance, and clever language to sell their particular point of view. These characteristics have led to the modern meaning of "a sophistry" as an example of overly subtle, superficially plausible, but ultimately fallacious reasoning. Plato characterizes the Sophist this way:

> First, I believe he was found to be a paid hunter after the young and wealthy . . . secondly a kind of merchant in articles of knowledge for the soul . . . third did he not turn up as a retailer of these same articles of knowledge? . . . and in the fourth place we found he was a seller of his own products of knowledge . . . and

The art of the Sophist is the semblance of wisdom without the reality, and the Sophist is one who makes money from an apparent but unreal wisdom.

ARISTOTLE

in the fifth he was an athlete in contests of words, who had taken for his own the art of disputation . . . the sixth case was doubtful, but nevertheless we agreed to consider him a purger of souls, who removes opinions that obstruct learning.[14]

Socrates (Chapter 4), the first great Western philosopher, lived at the same time as the Sophists and was also a famous educator. He often had what he claimed were *discussions* with Sophists; the Sophists, however, thought they were *contests*. Many Athenians weren't sure whether Socrates was a Sophist or a *sophos*. Socrates himself, though, was clear on one thing: It is wrong to charge money for teaching philosophy. He said:

> [I believe] that it is possible to dispose of beauty or of wisdom alike honorably or dishonorably; for if a person sells his beauty for money to anyone who wishes to purchase it, men call him a male prostitute; but if anyone makes a friend of a person whom he knows to be an honorable and worthy admirer, we regard him as prudent. In like manner those who sell their wisdom for money to any that will buy, men call sophists, or, as it were, prostitutes of wisdom; but whoever makes a friend of a person whom he knows to be deserving, and teaches him all the good that he knows, we consider him to act the part which becomes a good and honorable citizen.[15]

Convention is the ruler of all.
PINDAR

The very eyes with which we see the problem are conditioned by the long habits of our own society.
RUTH BENEDICT

PHILOSOPHICAL QUERY

• • • • • •

Discuss some of the pros and cons of personal education versus commercialized education. Try to consider a variety of factors: efficiency; effects of money on pupils, teachers, and institutions; mediocrity; conformity. Do you agree that it is wrong to "sell wisdom"? Is it realistic to expect teachers (or philosophers) to teach for free, for love only? Can't any source of financial support lead to bias? Must it?

■ RELATIVISM ■

The Sophists were among the first systematic thinkers to conclude that the truth is relative. **Relativism** is the belief that knowledge is determined by specific qualities of the observer. The Sophists, for example, claimed that place of birth, family habits, personal abilities and preferences, religious training, age, and so forth control an individual's beliefs, values, and even perceptions. (Don't confuse relativism with subjectivism, the belief that we can only know our own sensations.)

Based on this tenet, the Sophists argued that we need only accept what, according to our culture, seems true at the moment. The most extreme Sophists claimed that even within the same culture, individuals have their own truths. The consequences of this position can be unsettling, to say the least. If no ultimate truth exists, no moral code is universally correct or absolutely superior to any other. The Sophists taught that each culture (or individual!) only *believes* that its ways are best, but the person who has studied many cultures *knows* better: One way is as good as another if you believe in it.

relativism
Belief that knowledge is determined by specific qualities of the observer, including age, ethnicity, gender, cultural conditioning.

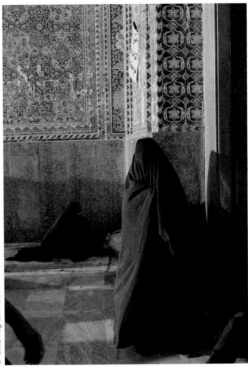

©Abbas/Magnum Photos

Comparing the lifestyles and beliefs of these contemporary Islamic women to those of contemporary American women shows how difficult it is to dispute the Sophists' claim that all values are culturally determined.

If ethical relativism is correct, it is clearly impossible for the moral beliefs of a society to be mistaken because the certainty of the majority that its beliefs were right would prove that those beliefs were right for that society at that time. The minority view would therefore be mistaken, no matter what it was. Needless to say, most people who state that "in morals everything is relative" and who proceed to call themselves ethical relativists are unaware of these implications of their theory.

JOHN HOSPERS

Concepts of gain and loss, joy and sorrow, good and bad, are all man-made. If one wants to live a life of freedom, then one must not be caught in such states of duality.

LIE ZI

There are two basic variants of relativism: cultural and individual. Cultural relativism is the belief that all values are culturally determined. Values do not reflect a divine order or a natural pattern, but merely the customs and preferences that develop in a given culture. Thus, what is right in America is not necessarily right in Saudi Arabia or Brazil. Your grandmother's sexual morality was right for a particular person at a particular time and place, but not for all people all the time and in every place. What is right for a twenty-year-old African American woman will be different from what is right for a ninety-year-old Chinese American man, and so on. Consequently, what's right for you may very well be different from what's right for people of different ages and backgrounds.

Individual relativism, simply carries the logic of cultural relativism to a more radical conclusion. It goes like this: Even in the same place and time, right and wrong are relative to the unique experiences and preferences of the individual. There is no unbiased way to say that one standard is better than another because the standard used to make that claim is itself the reflection of a preference, ad infinitum. No matter how far back we push "ultimate" reasons, they always reduce to someone's preference. Hence, moral and social values are matters of individual taste and opinion.

• • • • • •

PHILOSOPHICAL

QUERY

Today, some English teachers hesitate to impose "relative" standards of English grammar. They see all grammar—dialects, that is—as "preferences." Do you agree? Ask your English teacher about the notion of imposing standards.

Protagoras

■ PROTAGORAS THE PRAGMATIST ■

Perhaps the greatest of the Sophists was **Protagoras** of Abdera (481–411 B.C.E.). Attracted to Athens around the middle of the fifth century B.C.E., he became a famous teacher there. He was befriended by wealthy and powerful Athenians and, consequently, became rich and powerful himself. Plato even named a dialogue after him.

Protagoras was an archetypal Sophist: an active traveler and first-rate observer of other cultures who noted that although there are a variety of customs and beliefs, each culture believes unquestioningly that its own ways are right—and roundly condemns (or at least criticizes) views that differ from its own. So he asked himself, "What really makes something right or wrong? Is anything really right or wrong? What is truth? Can we know it? Can we know that we know it, or are we limited to mere beliefs?" His answers may strike you as surprisingly contemporary. And they are—as the term *Sophist* suggests—quite sophisticated.

Based on his observations and travels, Protagoras concluded that morals are nothing more than the social traditions, or mores, of a society or group. What makes the Athenian way right for someone living in Athens is that following the mores of one's place is the best way to live successfully and well—in that place. The task of the truly wise observer is to record accurately and describe without bias what works and what does not work. Hence, the famous remark quoted at the beginning of this chapter: Man is the measure of all things. Here is how Plato reported Socrates' characterization of what Protagoras meant:

> Well, is not this what [Protagoras] means, that individual things are for me such as they appear to me, and for you in turn such as they appear to you—you and I being "man"? . . . Is it not true that sometimes, when the same wind blows, one of us feels cold and the other does not? or one feels slightly and the other exceedingly cold? . . . Then in that case, shall we say that the wind is in itself cold or not cold; or shall we accept Protagoras' saying that it is cold for him who feels cold, not for him who does not?[16]

Protagoras predicted a crucial tenet of modern social science: Our values are determined by our culture, our conditioning, our experience, and our particular biopsychology. It is, according to Protagoras, utterly impossible to form a culture-free or context-free belief. For instance, philosophy students born, raised, and educated in Moscow, Russia, cannot help but "see" a different world than do those born, raised, and educated in Moscow, Idaho.

Thus, the useful issue is not what is true, since true always means "true for the believer." If Student A believes something, that alone makes it true from her perspective. The worthwhile issue is what "works" for Student A, not what is universally true or what "works" for Student B. The point of view that beliefs are to be interpreted in terms of "whether they work" (their usefulness) is called **pragmatism,** from the Greek *pragma,* "deed." Pragmatic ideas have meaning or truth value to the extent that they produce practical results and are effective in furthering our aims. (See Chapter 15.)

"What is right in one group is wrong in another," he says. *But what exactly is a group? and which group is one to select? Every person is a member of many different groups—his nation, his state, his city, his club, his school, church, fraternity, or athletic association. Suppose that most of the people in his club think that a certain kind of act is wrong and that most of the people in his nation think it is right; what then?*

JOHN HOSPERS

pragmatism
From the Greek for "deed"; ideas have meaning or truth value to the extent that they produce practical results and effectively further our aims; empirically based philosophy that defines knowledge and truth in terms of practical consequences.

© Kyodo/Landov

©Thierry Lopez/Maxppp/Landov

Protagoras's claim that "each one of us is the measure" is dramatically and tragically illustrated in the case of Isabelle Caro, who was twenty-seven years old and weighed 66 pounds when this photo was taken. In today's fat-obsessed world, anorexics see themselves as obese no matter how thin they are and, in the most extreme cases would rather die than become obese like these athletic sumo wrestlers. Do you think our culture suffers from a kind of collective anorexia nervosa, and, if so, does that mean that the individual, not the doctor or scientist, is the measure of health? Are widespread concerns about nutrition, weight, and appearance "reasonable" or just present-day trends and preferences?

Plato criticized Protagoras for—in Plato's view—reducing the concept of what is useful to whatever people *think* is useful. Of course, Protagoras could respond to Plato this way: "What is useful if not useful to some particular individual, at some particular place and time? What sense is there in talking about

It is only about things that do not interest one that one can give a really unbiased opinion, which is no doubt the reason why an unbiased opinion is always valueless.

OSCAR WILDE

We are what we think, having become what we thought.

THE DHAMMAPADA

As to the Gods I have no means of knowing that they exist or that they do not exist.

PROTAGORAS

'useful in general'? Useful always means useful for the specific purposes and desires of an individual. And even for individuals, what is useful changes."

In a speech Plato attributes to Protagoras, the Sophist makes his case that *wisdom is what works:*

> For I maintain that the truth is as I have written; each one of us is the measure of the things that are and those that are not; but each person differs immeasurably from every other in just this, that to one person some things appear and are, and to another person other things. . . . do not lay too much stress upon the words of my argument, but get a clearer understanding of my meaning from what I am going to say. Recall to your mind what was said before, that his food appears and is bitter to the sick man, but appears and is the opposite of bitter to the man in health. Now neither of these two is to be made wiser than he is—that is not possible—nor should the claim be made that the sick man is ignorant because his opinions are ignorant, or the healthy man wise because his opinions are different; but a change must be made from the one condition to the other, for the other is better. So, too, in education a change has to be made from a worse condition to a better condition; but the physician causes the change by means of drugs, and the teacher of wisdom by means of words. . . . And on the same principle the teacher who is able to train his pupils in this manner is not only wise but is also entitled to receive high pay from them when their education is finished. And in this sense it is true that some men are wiser than others, and that no one thinks falsely, and that you, whether you will or no, must . . . be a measure. Upon these positions my doctrine stands firm.[17]

PHILOSOPHICAL QUERY

• • • • • •

Analyze Protagoras's speech. Has he convinced you? Explain. See if you can identify the trick used by both Protagoras and his pupil in the Wager.

Probably most people who call themselves ethical relativists are not so at all, for they believe in one moral standard which applies in different ways to different societies because of the various conditions in which they live. One might as well talk about gravitational relativism because a stone falls and a balloon rises; yet both events are equally instances of one law of universal gravitation.

JOHN HOSPERS

Protagoras was a rather tame Sophist. He reasoned that the most intelligent thing to do is to accept the customs and beliefs of your own community. By understanding that the mores of the community are not universal absolutes, you will develop a relaxed, effective attitude about them. This in turn will allow you to use them rather than being controlled by them. Openly flouting convention is most likely to be counterproductive. With the rare exceptions of talented and charismatic individuals, *behaving in a generally conventional way affords us the most social power.*

Dress the way that will get you promoted at work or get you a date at the club. Write the kind of essay your teacher wants and you'll get a good grade; write your own creative masterpiece and you might not. Drive with the flow of traffic—neither too fast nor too slow—and you'll lower your insurance rates. If you want to get elected, go to church and keep your hair neat and conservative.

Tradition has it that Protagoras did not always follow his own advice. The story goes that at the home of a friend, Protagoras gave a reading of one of his

Protagoras's Wager

Competitiveness and boldness flourished among the Sophists as they competed for prestige and paying students. This is not surprising given their emphasis on power, winning, and relativism. Moreover, because the Sophists chose to be public figures, seeking fame and influence, they were always eager to show off their abilities. They used their speaking skills to attack one another and attract students. Whenever possible, they spoke to large audiences, whether in the Assembly or in the public square. The average Athenian found these sparring matches entertaining at first. As you will learn, however, Athenians soon regarded the Sophists as disturbing and dangerous. A famous example of sophistic sparring is the story known as *Protagoras's Wager*.

It seems that Protagoras had a pupil named Eulathus, who arranged to take Protagoras's course in rhetoric and sophistry, a kind of law school, for partial tuition. So sure was Protagoras of his abilities as a teacher that he told Eulathus he did not have to pay the balance until Eulathus won his first court case. In fact, Protagoras guaranteed that Eulathus would win his first case.

Time dragged on and Eulathus neither paid up nor argued any cases in court. Not only was Protagoras out the money, he looked bad to his students and to other Sophists. After all, if winning is what counts, and if appearance is reality, and if the pupil can outmaneuver the old master, why should anyone continue to pay his high fees? Protagoras was compelled to act.

Confronting Eulathus (probably in a public place where he could use his crowd-pleasing skills), Protagoras demanded payment in the form of this dilemma: "Eulathus, you might as well pay me, since I am going to sue you for the rest of the tuition. If I win in court, the court will rule that you owe me the money; if I lose in court, you will have won your first case, and you will owe me the money. Either I win in court or I lose, so either you owe me the money or you owe me the money."

Protagoras, alas, was a good teacher, and Eulathus was ready for him. He shot back with a counterdilemma: "No, sir, you have it backwards. If you defeat me in court, then I have lost my first case and so do not owe the money; if I defeat you, the court will rule that I do not owe you the money. Either I defeat you or you defeat me. In either case, I do not owe you the money."

Who won? The story does not tell us. And besides, Sophists being what they were, neither Eulathus nor Protagoras would have wanted to lose big in a highly publicized trial. Protagoras's Wager gives us an instructive glimpse of sophistry in action. Such encounters were common, as Sophists vied for students and reputation. To the general citizenry, these encounters were sometimes amusing entertainment. Men like Protagoras lived rather mild lives considering what they taught and the reactions their excitable pupils had to their ideas. But when the same kinds of tricks were used for high stakes—say, to convict innocent citizens, to control democracy, to wrest property away from people—no one laughed. Sophistry's reputation grew darker.

own treatises called *On the Gods*. This particular work applied the principle of relativism to religious belief, apparently holding religion to the pragmatic standard. There was no separation of church and state in Athens at this time. Failure to believe in and respect "the gods of the state" was considered a form of treason known as impiety. One of the other guests, a conservative army officer, was so offended by Protagoras's ideas that he consequently had Protagoras indicted for impiety. Protagoras was found guilty. All copies of *On the Gods* were confiscated and burned, and the authorities set out to confiscate Protagoras, too. Facing death or exile, he attempted to escape on a ship headed for Sicily. The ship was wrecked, and Protagoras drowned.

It's not what you know, it's who you know.

CONVENTIONAL WISDOM?

■ MORAL REALISM: MIGHT ■ MAKES RIGHT

moral realism
Pragmatic social philosophy unfettered by moral considerations; expressed in the formula "might makes right."

In contrast to Protagoras, the next generation of Sophists carried moral relativism to the more radical level of **moral realism,** a pragmatic social philosophy unfettered by any moral considerations.

The laws of every society, says the moral realist, turn out to reflect the interests of those in power. The U.S. Constitution, for example, places great emphasis on property rights and protections because most of its chief architects were landed gentry: persons with property. Hence their view of the "ideal" state reflected and furthered their material interests. Each new Supreme Court reflects the values of the majority of its members, now liberal, now conservative. The "right" view is the view held by those currently in power. The rest of us, says the moral realist, ultimately obey because we have to; we have no other choice: Regardless of whether we believe that what is legal is also right, the average person obeys anyway because he or she lacks sufficient power (and courage) not to obey.

From a certain perspective, history seems to support the view that might and power determine right. But what about counterexamples like the civil rights movement of the 1960s? Here "right" finally prevailed, even against centuries of custom and habit that supported racist practices. This example seems to show that moral progress is possible and that not everyone acts from limited self-interest.

When Aesop's lion was shown a painting in which a man was depicted killing a lion, he commented contemptuously, "The artist was obviously a man."

B. F. SKINNER

A contemporary Sophist could point out, however, that civil rights changes occurred in this country only after members of the powerful white middle class began to support the position of the nonwhite minorities. The view of the most powerful faction of the time won. Civil might made civil rights. The same is true of women's rights. Women's rights have increased in proportion to women's power. African Americans, Hispanic Americans, Asian Americans, and other groups have rights in direct proportion to their might. The elderly will have more rights in the future because they will outnumber members of other age groups for years to come. And so it goes. Your philosophy instructor has more power over your philosophy course than you do. Thus—ultimately—her interpretation of your test is more "right" than yours. Her answers are more "useful" than yours. Parents are "right" about many things simply because they have more power than children. Whoever has power gets to be right. Or so it seems.

• • • • • •

Is "might makes right" the only explanation for social changes like the civil rights movement? Could other factors besides self-interest account for a shift in basic social values? What factors? Is anything lost by accepting a might-makes-right interpretation? Is anything gained? Explain.

■ THE DOCTRINE OF THE ■ SUPERIOR INDIVIDUAL

Not everybody willingly submits to those in power or depends on a group for clout. Those who do not are well represented by a Sophist named Callicles (c. 435 B.C.E.). His version of moral realism goes by different names: the doctrine of the superior individual, the true man, the natural man, the superman. You may recognize foreshadowings of Nazism, racism, and religious intolerance in the doctrine of the superior individual. It is always *elitist,* but it is not always a *racial* doctrine. Indeed, in its most compelling form, it is highly individualistic, holding that a person is superior not because of ethnic or cultural background but only because of individual virtues and traits. (We will study one of the most notorious expressions of this view in Chapter 16.)

Callicles distinguished what is right by nature from what is right by convention. In the following selection from Plato's *Gorgias,* Callicles asserts that by nature the strong dominate the weak, whereas conventional morality tries to restrain the superior, strong, truly powerful individual. In nature, the survival of the fittest is the rule. This, said Sophists such as Callicles, shows that power is the ultimate value and that *the superior and powerful individual has a natural right to dominate others. All people are no more created equal than all animals are.*

> For to suffer wrong is not the part of a man at all, but that of a slave for whom it is better to be dead than alive, as it is for anyone who is unable to come either to his own assistance when he is wronged or mistreated or to that of anyone he cares about. I can quite imagine that the manufacturers of laws and conventions are the weak, the majority, in fact. It is for themselves and their own advantage that they make their laws and distribute their praises and their censures. It is to frighten men who are stronger than they and able to enforce superiority that they keep declaring, to prevent aggrandizement, that this is ugly and unjust, that injustice consists in seeking to get the better of one's neighbor. They are quite content, I suppose, to be on equal terms with others since they are themselves inferior.

The majority of just acts according to the law are prescribed contrary to nature. For there is legislation about the eyes, what they must see and what not; and about the ears, what they must hear and what not; and about the tongue, what it must speak and what not; and about the hands, what they must do and what not; and about the feet, where they must go and where not. And about the soul, what it must desire and what not.

ANTIPHON

But if a man arises endowed with a nature sufficiently strong he will, I believe, shake off these controls, burst his fetters, and break loose. And trampling upon our scraps of paper, our spells and incantations, and all our unnatural conventions, he rises up and reveals himself our master who was once our slave, and there shines forth nature's true justice.

CALLICLES

This, then, is the reason why convention declares that it is unjust and ugly to seek to get the better of the majority. But my opinion is that nature herself reveals it to be only just and proper that the better man should lord it over his inferior: It will be the stronger over the weaker. Nature, further, makes it quite clear in a great many instances that this is the true state of affairs, not only in the other animals, but also in whole states and communities. This is, in fact, how justice is determined: The stronger shall rule and have the advantage over his inferior. . . .

. . . Now, my dear friend, take my advice: Stop your [philosophy], take up the Fine Art of Business, and cultivate something that will give you a reputation for good sense. Leave all these over-subtleties to someone else. Should one call them frivolities or just plain nonsense? They'll only land you in a house where you'll be the only visitor! You must emulate, not those whose very refutations are paltry, but men of substance and high repute and everything else that is good.[18]

> *Traditions and customs are set by people. Therefore what people regard as "truth" tends to be a subjective matter.*
>
> LIE ZI

PHILOSOPHICAL QUERY

● ● ● ● ● ●

Is some part of you stirred by all this talk of power and superiority? The Sophists would say that if you can be honest, you'll answer in the affirmative. What might prevent you (in the Sophists' view) from admitting that you agree with them? Are they correct? Even if you personally reject Callicles' position, how common do you think it is? What's your evidence?

Darrow's Cigar

An apocryphal story about the legendary lawyer Clarence Darrow circulates among law students: Darrow had to defend an especially unsavory client. This was a hard case to make. As the prosecutor ranted and raved to the jury about the heinous nature of the crime and the plight of the suffering victims, Darrow paid him close and courteous attention, puffing distractedly on a large cigar. The ash grew, an eighth of an inch, a quarter, a half, an inch or more—yet did not fall. Darrow didn't seem to notice. He just politely concentrated on the prosecutor's words. But the jury noticed. Instead of paying full attention to the prosecutor, they were drawn again and again to Darrow's cigar—into which he had secretly inserted a thin piece of wire.

One sophistry used by contemporary Darrows is having their clients dress "persuasively." Wealthy defendants Erik and Lyle Menendez often wore "college boy" crewneck sweaters at their trials for killing their parents. O. J. Simpson testified that he could not pay the $30 million civil judgment against him while uncharacteristically wearing inexpensive shoes—and slacks with a hole in the backside.

Sophists were also notorious for "making the better argument appear the worse" by playing word games. Of course, what's a "word game" and what's "being precise" is itself the sort of issue sophists addressed. In 1998, then-president Bill Clinton came under scrutiny for answering a question about whether or not he was having sexual relations with Monica Lewinsky by stating that the answer "depends on what the meaning of 'is' is." Some commentators accused President Clinton of sophistry. What do you think?

▦ COMMENTARY ▦

The questions raised by the Sophists are important, not just in the dusty archives of scholarly concerns but also because of the continuing influence sophistic ideas exert on our lives and beliefs. Sophists helped free the Greeks to think on new, less restricted levels. From this beginning emerged a nonreligious (amoral) scientific method as well as a philosophic method of questioning, both of which are free to pursue knowledge for its own sake and wherever it leads. The Sophists laid the cornerstone for the scientific study of human behavior—what would become the social, psychological, political, and anthropological sciences. In other words, the Sophists helped break the shackles of dogma and superstition. For that, we remain in their debt.

The Sophists' emphasis on the individual as determiner of value and the challenges Sophists posed to the possibility of a moral absolute contributed to increased democracy in Athens. Thus, the Sophists were perceived as a direct threat by the "establishment" of privileged aristocrats.

The youth of Athens responded with gusto to these ideas, treating them as a call to unrestrained self-assertion and personal freedom. It was stimulating to challenge the stuffy, square, straight, uptight values of the establishment. The glorification of the "superior individual" or "natural man" appealed to adolescent cravings for power, fame, freedom, and identity.

Logic and the rhetorical devices refined by the Sophists were liberally applied to legal maneuvering, politics, techniques of manipulation, and control of the marketplace. By the third generation, Sophists no longer claimed to be *sophistai*, teachers of wisdom, but advertised shortcuts to guaranteed social, political, financial, and personal success. These Sophists were the forerunners of today's how-to-succeed, you-can-have-it-all books, courses, and techniques. Freed of any moral anchor, the most ruthless Sophists were often deadly and effective. They took no responsibility for the ways people might use their ideas, as the great Sophist Gorgias reminds us:

> And if a man learns rhetoric, and then does injustice through the power of his art, we shall not be right, in my opinion, in detesting and banishing his teacher. For while the teacher imparted instruction to be used rightly, the pupil made a contrary use of it. Therefore, it is only right to detest the misuser and banish and kill him, not his teacher.[19]

Although they were attacked by Plato and others on moral grounds, most Sophists were actually amoral (nonmoral) rather than immoral. Like the caricature of a mob attorney who uses all his persuasive skills to vigorously and lucratively defend known drug dealers and crime bosses, the Sophists made no moral judgments. They were concerned only with "what worked." They saw the world as hard and brutal, a jungle. Because, in their view, the restraints and inhibitions of morality weaken us, the Sophists refused to acknowledge any moral prohibitions. In contemporary terms, they were masters of "effective" thinking, communicating, and acting.

Many sophistic techniques, like Darrow's cigar, are genuinely clever and clearly effective. The Sophists of ancient Athens inspired mixed feelings of awe

There is no definite right or wrong human principle. To be able to adapt to the changing times is true wisdom.

LIE ZI

Go about with your middle finger up and people will say you're daft; go about with your little finger out, and they will cultivate your company.

DIOGENES

"Pick the right time and flourish, miss the right time and perish." Nowhere is there a principle which is right in all circumstances, or an action that is wrong in all circumstances. The method we used yesterday we may discard today and use again in the future. There is no fixed right and wrong to decide whether we use it or not.

LIE ZI

The Sophists speak in order to deceive, and they write for their own gain, and in no way to be of use to anyone.

XENOPHON

People generally quarrel because they cannot argue.

GILBERT K. CHESTERTON

and admiration, anger and disgust. They raised vital, ongoing questions: When the stakes are high, is playing fair the smart thing to do? Just how important is winning? And how should we be judged? On the conventional morals most of us profess? Or on the values we actually practice and (secretly?) admire: strength, power, daring, attractiveness, social contacts, success? Can we ever have objective knowledge or escape the limits of culture? In the absence of certainty, might it be better to allow more individual choice rather than less?

As you reflect on the archetype of the Sophist, think about its place in today's world. As you are probably realizing, the similarities between the cultural climate of ancient Athens and that of contemporary America are widespread and deeply rooted. The Sophists represent one side of the timeless struggle between "the world" and wisdom. Because we all face this struggle, we're not just learning about the past, about dead ideas, but we are also learning about living issues.

As the original Sophists grew in numbers and boldness, they attracted more and more enemies. Unable to distinguish sophistic philosophies from other forms, the citizens of Athens began to agree with each other that philosophy itself was unacceptably subversive. Philosophy's reputation for being somehow unpatriotic and dangerous was established. Into this breach stepped perhaps the single most influential and arresting philosopher of all, the first major philosopher of the West: Socrates.

It is impossible to defeat an ignorant man in argument.
WILLIAM G. MCADOO

For all their shameless accusations, my accusers have not been able in all their impudence to bring forward a single witness to say I have ever received a fee or asked for one. I, on the other hand, have a convincing witness that I speak the truth, my poverty.
SOCRATES

■ SUMMARY OF MAIN POINTS ■

● As early Greek civilization grew more complex, mythology and religion began to develop into philosophy (and later into science). As part of this development, a new kind of thinker emerged known as a *sophos*, from the Greek word for "wise." Although the ancient Greeks' mythological accounting of events ultimately failed, it established two crucial principles: (1) There is a difference between the way the things *appear* and the way *they really are*. (2) There are unseen causes of events; things happen as they do for some reason. These first philosophers were noted for their attempts to use reason and observation to "figure out" how the world works.

● The first Western philosophers, known as the Presocratics, searched for *rational* explanations to questions that mythology could not adequately answer. This interest in *explanations* played a vital role in the development of reason and rational discourse, the use of reason to order, clarify, and identify reality and truth according to agreed-upon standards of verification. This in turn triggered questions of logical consistency, rules of thinking, and standards of knowledge that led to a radical separation or

dissociation of theoretical knowledge from practical wisdom.

● As Athens grew in influence it attracted more and more people from other city-states and countries. Opportunities for a growing number of Athenians to speak before the Assembly created a demand for specialized education in subjects such as letters, rhetoric, science, statesmanship, and philosophy.

● Those who considered themselves original, true Athenians became increasingly ethnocentric. Ethnocentrism is the tendency to consider one's own customs and values as superior to all others.

● The Sophists were the first professional educators, a group of wandering teachers who charged a fee to teach anyone who wished to study with them. Sophists argued that the difference between a good argument and a bad argument is custom and individual preference.

● The Sophists believed that virtually nothing is good or bad by nature, but only by custom and preference. They argued that truth is relative and that knowledge is determined by specific qualities of the observer. Cultural relativism is the belief that all values are culturally determined. Individual relativism is the belief that even in the same place and time, right and wrong are relative to the unique experiences and preferences of the individual.

● Protagoras of Abdera was one of the most influential of the Sophists. He said that morals are nothing more than the social traditions, or mores, of a society or group and that following local mores is the best way to live successfully and well—in that place. Hence his famous remark: *Man is the measure of all things.*

● Later generations of Sophists carried moral relativism to more radical levels than Protagoras did. Moral realism is the belief that all values reflect the interests of the strong. Certain values dominate because they are the views preferred by the most powerful individual or group, not because they are in some absolute sense "right." Callicles was a Sophist associated with an aspect of moral realism known as the doctrine of the superior individual, which holds that nature dictates that the strong should dominate the weak.

▦ POST-READING REFLECTIONS ▦

Now that you have had a chance to learn about the Sophist, use your new knowledge to answer these questions.

1. Explain how the first philosophers' reliance on rational explanations contributed to the change from *sophos* to Sophist.

2. Is there any merit to the claim that modern colleges and universities are sophistic in their attempts to compete for students by teaching whatever they will pay to learn? Do you think there is a conflict of interest in charging students tuition *and* grading them honestly? That is, might schools be reluctant to flunk out paying customers—er, I mean, students?

3. Is there any way to refute the idea that "might makes right"? Why is this question more complicated than it might seem at first glance?

4. Suppose it were discovered that Protagoras secretly violated many of his teachings. Would this affect your attitude toward his philosophy? How? Why?

5. Are lawyers Sophists? Are advertisers? In what ways are these professions susceptible to sophistry? Explain.

6. Today, the terms *sophist* and *sophistry* are usually used as criticisms of those whom we distrust for having ulterior motives or a win-at-all-costs attitude. Have the Sophists been given a bad rap? Why or why not? Is sophistry always wrong? If not, when is sophistry warranted and why?

7. Does the fact that politicians carefully craft their messages, speaking styles, clothing, hair, and personae to sell themselves make them sophists—or just practical? Are there social consequences to the *perception* that politicians are sophists?

PHILOSOPHY INTERNET RESOURCES

Go to the Soccio Web page at **http://philosophy.wadsworth.com/ Soccio7e** for Web links, practice quizzes and tests, a pronunciation guide, and study tips.

THE WISE MAN

Socrates

I DO NOT SUPPOSE THAT I KNOW.

Socrates

FOR YOUR REFLECTION

KEEP THESE QUESTIONS IN MIND AS YOU LEARN ABOUT SOCRATES.

1. *What is the "Socratic problem"?*

2. *What is a paradigmatic individual?*

3. *What is the Socratic dialect?*

4. *What role did Socrates' ugliness play in his philosophy?*

5. *What role did Socrates' poverty play in his philosophy?*

6. *What role does Socrates' claim of ignorance play in his philosophy?*

7. *What is Socratic irony?*

8. *Why did some Athenians think that Socrates was a Sophist?*

9. *What is Socratic intellectualism?*

FOR DEEPER CONSIDERATION

A. Socrates said that the unexamined life is not worth living for a human being. Does that strike you as a reasonable assertion? Is there any way to know whether or not an "unexamined" life is worth living except by "examining" it? In other words, can we make any reasonable claims about the quality of an unexamined life—or an unexamined anything? Consider the possibility that Socrates has "something up his sleeve" when he talks about this.

B. As you read about Socrates, take seriously the possibility of encountering a truly wise individual—not just a "sort of wise" person or a "really smart" person, but a person who fits the description of a wise person discussed in this chapter. How do you think you would fare in such an encounter? Would it be "enjoyable"? Oh, and how can those of us who are not wise recognize and evaluate the truly wise? Is recognizing wisdom different from, say, recognizing strength, in that the recognition of strength does not require being strong, whereas the recognition of wisdom might require at least a modicum of wisdom? Be on the lookout for Socrates' solution to this puzzlement.

𝒴*ou are about to meet* **Socrates** (c. 470–399 B.C.E.), one of the most powerful, intriguing, annoying, inspiring, widely known, and yet misunderstood figures in the history of philosophy. He has been called the greatest of philosophers and also the cleverest of Sophists. Stoics, Hedonists, and Cynics (each of whom we shall study in other chapters) have all claimed him as their chief inspiration and model. He was a pagan who is seen by many Jews and Christians as a man of God. His Holiness Tenzin Gyatso, the fourteenth Dalai Lama of Tibetan Buddhism, has expressed respect for him as an enlightened individual. Socrates claimed to have devoted his life to serving his country but was executed as a traitor. He attracted faithful and adoring admirers and was idolized by many young followers, yet the second charge at his trial was "corrupting the youth of Athens." Although he wrote no philosophy himself, he taught and inspired one of the two most influential philosophers in Western history, who in turn taught the other one: Plato and Aristotle.

In his impressive book *Socrates,* the renowned classical scholar W. K. C. Guthrie says, "Any account must begin with the admission that there is, and always will be, a 'Socratic problem.' "[1] In the first place, Socrates wrote nothing. (Or at least nothing philosophical. In *Phaedo,* Plato asserted that Socrates wrote a hymn to Apollo and versified some of Aesop's fables while in prison.)[2] Our two main sources of information about Socrates are the dialogues of his most brilliant and famous pupil, Plato, and the anecdotes and memoirs of the less philosophical soldier, Xenophon. In addition, briefer references to Socrates appear in Aristotle, Aristophanes, and elsewhere. The "Socratic problem" is compounded because Socrates' philosophy was nearly inseparable from the way his whole personality was reflected in his spoken teachings and the conduct of his life. Guthrie says, "In spite of the most scientific methods, in the end we must all have to some extent our own Socrates, who will not be precisely like anyone else's."[3]

What will *your* Socrates be like? Perhaps you too will be "stung" by the man who referred to himself as a gadfly (horsefly) sent by "the god" to keep his drowsy fellows alert. Perhaps you too will give birth to a brainchild with the aid of this ancient *sophos* (wise man) who claimed to "teach nothing" but merely to act as a "kind of midwife," helping others draw out the wisdom hidden within them. Or perhaps you too will be annoyed—even angered—at the sophistic arrogance and logical tricks of a dangerous enemy of conventional morality, democracy, and religion. These are just some of the documented reactions to Socrates.

"The fact is," Guthrie says, "that no one was left indifferent by this altogether unusual character: everyone who has written about him was also reacting to him in one way or another."[4] We can still get a basic picture of Socrates, however. For example, even though Plato and Xenophon present almost completely different views of him, we can treat their accounts as honest reflections of Socrates filtered through the minds and experiences of two completely different admirers. Neither account is "inaccurate" as much as incomplete and perhaps exaggerated. By comparing and evaluating various accounts of Socrates, we can get some idea of the man as well as his philosophy. So, let me introduce you to my Socrates.

Never mind the manner, which may or may not be good, but think only of the truth of my words, and give heed to that: Let the speaker speak truly and the judge decide justly.

SOCRATES

One ought not to talk or act as if he were asleep.

HERACLITUS

It is not the knowledge of the wise we acknowledge to be special but the value they place and invite us to place on it. In some sense, the recognition of wisdom is the recognition of that which we, the unwise, not only have known but should have known all along.

STANLEY GODLOVITCH

In spite of being in sympathy with the sages, I am well aware of not having been one of them. As a person I was too self-indulgent and not heroic enough: as a writer I was too miscellaneous: as a thinker I was born at the wrong time and bred in the wrong way.

GEORGE SANTAYANA

Socrates

THE GENERAL CHARACTER
OF SOCRATES

Plato presents Socrates as an integrated, essentially unambivalent individual who stood clearly for some values and clearly against others. Then, as now, such personal clarity, strong sense of direction and purpose, were attractive to young people (or to anyone) confused about who they are or want to be. Then, as now, Socrates' consistent respect for justice, integrity, courage, temperance, decency, beauty, and balance was especially appealing in a cultural climate of dizzy excesses, crass materialism, and cutthroat competition for money, power, and prestige. In a complex, sophisticated society in which old values were under siege, the simplicity and clarity of an individual with Socrates' obvious abilities were intriguing, even when they were upsetting. Socrates' guiding motto of "Know thyself" has been challenging to people all over the world and in all historical periods. Socrates struggled with one of the great problems of our time: Who am I? How can I discover my true identity? How shall *I* live?

Against the popular notion of his time (and ours), Socrates taught that beauty and goodness should be determined by usefulness and fitness of function, rather than by mere appearance or personal feelings of delight. An interesting illustration of this can be found in his own appearance. Socrates was universally acknowledged to be "extraordinarily ugly"—so ugly, in fact, that he fascinated people. His most notable physical features were a broad, flat, turned-up nose, protruding, staring eyes, thick, fleshy lips, and a belly that he himself characterized as "a stomach rather too large for convenience,"[5] and that he elsewhere announced plans to "dance off." His friends compared him to a satyr or an electric eel, whose penetrating questions stunned his listeners, "shocked" them into higher awareness.

Socrates made his appearance serve him well. His humorous references to it reflect his good nature and modesty, as well as his hierarchy of values. If, as he taught, the true self is not the body but the soul (*psyche*), and if *virtue* implies *excellence of function,* then the appearance of the body is less important than how well it functions. True beauty is inner beauty, beauty of spirit and character. In Plato's *Gorgias,* Socrates says that we cannot know whether a person is happy just because his external condition is attractive to us. He insists that happiness, like goodness, is a matter of inner qualities:

> Then doubtless you will say, Socrates, that you do not know that even the Great King is happy.
>
> Yes, and I shall be speaking the truth; for I do not know how he stands in point of interior formation and justice.
>
> Why, does happiness entirely consist of that?
>
> Yes, by my account, Polus; for a good and honorable man or woman, I say, is happy, and an unjust and wicked one is wretched.[6]

Don't think Socrates was a prude. He was not. He was tempted by physical attractiveness, but he governed his life according to "true beauty and goodness," preferring a good and beautiful soul to a pleasing body that housed a lesser self.

Many are ruined by admirers whose heads are turned by the sight of a pretty face; many are led by their strength to attempt tasks too heavy for them, and meet serious evils; many by their wealth are corrupted, and fall victims to conspiracies; many through glory and political power have suffered great evils.

SOCRATES

This nineteenth-century sculpture of Socrates teaching in the agora shows the contrast between Socrates' inner beauty and outer ugliness.

● ● ● ● ● ●

PHILOSOPHICAL

QUERY

One of my college friends resembled Socrates. I had noticed him in the cafeteria. I thought he was one of the most unfortunate-looking persons I had ever seen. He knew some acquaintances of mine, and so I eventually met him. I initially felt uncomfortable even being around him because of his looks, I'm sorry to say. But, slowly I discovered an intelligent, funny, kind, strong, and courageous man. Over the years of our friendship, I lost the capacity to see him as ugly. Sadly, the converse has been true in my experience as well. A beautiful or handsome countenance that belongs to a slothful or self-centered or shallow or cruel person over time becomes less handsome or beautiful to me. Have you noticed this pattern in yourself? Analyze it, if you have.

An informative and humorous passage from Chapter 5 of Xenophon's *Symposium* illustrates how Socrates could incorporate philosophy into anything, even joking around with friends. Socrates is engaged in a good-natured "beauty contest" with a handsome young man named Critobulus. Critobulus has challenged Socrates to use his famous question-and-answer method (we'll look at this shortly) to prove that Socrates is "more beautiful" than Critobulus.

Critobulus: All right, but which of our noses is the more beautiful?
Socrates: Mine, I should say, if the gods give us noses to smell with, for your nostrils point to earth, but mine are spread out widely to receive odours from every quarter.
Critobulus: But how can a snub nose be more beautiful than a straight one?
Socrates: Because it does not get in the way but allows the eyes to see what they will, whereas a high bridge walls them off, as if to spite them.
Critobulus: As for the mouth, I give in, for if mouths are made for biting you could take a much larger bite than I.
Socrates: And with my thick lips don't you think I could give a softer kiss?
Critobulus: By your account I seem to have a mouth uglier than an ass's. . . . I give up. Let's put it to the vote, so that I may know as quickly as possible the forfeit I have to pay.[7]

When I think of both the wisdom and nobility of this man [Socrates], I cannot refrain from writing of him nor, in writing of him, from praising him.

Xenophon

Should not every man hold self-control to be the foundation of all virtue, and first lay this foundation firmly in his soul?

Xenophon

When the votes were counted, Socrates lost unanimously, prompting him to accuse Critobulus of bribing the judges.

Barefoot in Athens

Socrates was usually barefoot and apparently had only one tattered coat, about which his friends joked. His enemies accused him of being "unwashed," and even his friends admitted that it was a surprise to see Socrates freshly bathed. One of his most noted characteristics was hardiness, reflected in remarkable self-control, or *temperance*. *Temperance* in this sense means indifference to both the presence and absence of material pleasures; it does not mean total abstinence from pleasure or extreme asceticism. In Xenophon's *Memorabilia*, Socrates put it like this:

> You seem, Antiphon, to imagine that happiness consists in luxury and extravagance. But my belief is that *to have no wants is divine; to have as few as possible comes next to the divine;* and as that which is divine is supreme, so that which approaches nearest to its nature is nearest to supreme.[8] [emphasis added]

Socrates' self-control included indifference to fear. During a battle at Delium, he is said to have been the last Athenian soldier to give way before the advancing Spartans. In the Potidaean military campaign, Socrates is reported to have walked about barefoot on the icy winter ground of Thrace, dressed as he customarily was back home. In Plato's *Symposium*, Alcibiades claims that this irritated the other soldiers, who, bundled and muffled against the fierce winter with their feet wrapped in felt and sheepskin, thought Socrates was trying to humiliate them.

In Xenophon's *Memorabilia*, Socrates talks about self-control and self-discipline with his friend Euthydemus. He uses the term *incontinence* in its original sense to mean lack of self-control, especially concerning appetites and passions. Socrates argues that self-control—not self-indulgence and weakness of will—leads to pleasure. Lack of self-control, he asserts, prevents us from the finest expressions of pleasure in eating, drinking, resting, and making love. If we gratify every urge

The majority of just acts according to the law are prescribed contrary to nature. For there is legislation about the eyes, what they must see and what not; and about the ears, what they must hear and what not; and about the tongue, what it must speak and what not; and about the hands, what they must do and what not; and about the feet, where they must go and where not. And about the soul, what it must desire and what not.

ANTIPHON

The Sophos at Large

When Socrates prayed, he asked only for "good gifts, for the gods know best what things are good."

According to Diogenes Läertius, Socrates' style of arguing was sometimes so intense that his opponents frequently attacked him with their fists or tore his hair out, "yet he bore all this ill-usage patiently."

When Alcibiades offered Socrates a large site on which to build a house, he replied, "Suppose, then, I wanted shoes and you offered me a whole hide to make a pair, would it not be ridiculous of me to take it?"

Socrates used to say that he most enjoyed the food that was least in need of seasoning and the drink that made him feel the least desire for another drink, adding that he was as the gods because he had few wants.

When someone asked Socrates whether he should marry or not, the *sophos* replied, "Whichever you do you will repent it."

When Socrates invited some rich men to dinner, his wife Xanthippe said she was embarrassed by the meal she had prepared. "Never mind," he said. "If they are reasonable they will put up with it, if they are good for nothing, we shall not trouble ourselves about them."

When someone said, "Socrates, you are condemned by Athens to die," he responded, "So are you, by nature."

as soon as it arises, we must often settle for fast food, cheap drink, sleeping all day, and crude sexual encounters. We will be little more than animals. Without self-control, we have no hope of learning how to moderate ourselves and our lives:

> "The delights of learning something good and excellent, and of studying some of the means whereby a man knows how to regulate his body well and manage his household successfully, to be useful to his friends and city and to defeat his enemies—knowledge that yields not only very great benefits but very great pleasures—these are the delights of the self-controlled; but the incontinent have no part in them. For who should we say has less concern with these than he who has no power of cultivating them because all his serious purposes are centered in the pleasures that lie nearest?"
>
> "Socrates," said Euthydemus, "I think you mean that he who is at the mercy of the bodily pleasures has no concern whatever with virtue in any form?"
>
> "Yes, Euthydemus," said Socrates.[9]

Part of Socrates' appeal comes from the fact that he had many of the same desires as the rest of us. They may even have been more intense. So we respond to the effort he must have exerted to keep all his appetites and passions under strict control. His philosophical searching was, consequently, based on a full involvement with life. It was not the product of a withered, passionless mentality. Nor was it based on a naive goody-goody view of the human condition. Socrates knew and loved life at its fullest, wrestling with it and challenging others to join his "enduring quest."

PHILOSOPHICAL QUERY

. . . . . .

What do you think of Socrates' views on self-control? Does the current concern with healthy diets, exercise, and so on seem to be in line with what Socrates thought or are we, perhaps, overdoing it or acting from love of beauty, not self-control? Discuss.

A Most Unusual Father and Husband

Socrates was married to Xanthippe and had three sons. He was seventy years old at the time of his execution; his oldest son was not yet twenty, and the youngest was said to be a small child.[10] We know relatively little of Socrates' home life, but Xanthippe probably had aristocratic connections.

Although he was probably apprenticed as a stonecutter or sculptor by his father, Socrates worked only now and then. He lived off a modest inheritance from his father, consisting of a house and some money, which his best friend Crito invested for him.[11] And while he never took money for teaching (as the Sophists did), he occasionally accepted gifts from his wealthy friends and admirers.

Socrates' well-known contempt for indiscriminate social approval made it a simple matter for him to live comfortably without shoes and with an old coat. But what effect would Socrates' uncommon values have had on his wife and sons? Here was an obviously brilliant, physically powerful man who spent his time wandering

In the world, one cannot have it both ways. If he wants to maintain his good reputation, he must not think of pursuing status and wealth. But if he wants status and riches, he must bear in mind that it will be at the expense of his integrity.

LIE ZI

about the marketplace asking philosophical questions all day. He seems to have had ample opportunity to eat and drink and mingle with the movers and shakers of Athens, yet he refused to seek political, social, or financial influence.

The Archetypal Individual

The combined portraits of Plato and Xenophon reveal Socrates as a master teacher, a man of unusual intellectual force, possessing an integrated self, whose charisma and personal power sprang from more than either mere intellect or personality. In other words, Socrates is a genuine **archetypal individual,** or, in a term coined by philosopher and psychologist Karl Jaspers (1883–1969) a **paradigmatic individual.** Jaspers applied the term to a special class of teachers, philosophers, and religious figures whose nature becomes a standard by which a culture judges the "ideal" human being.

An archetypal or paradigmatic individual is a rare human being whose very nature represents something elemental about the human condition. "The historical reality of [the paradigmatic individual]," says Jaspers, "can be discerned only in [his] extraordinary impact on those who knew [him] and in [his] later echoes."[12] In any encounter with an archetypal individual, the power or force of the whole person is galvanic. This power does not come from a rational argument. It is an experience that almost goes beyond words and cannot be ignored. It triggers not just personal but deep philosophical and spiritual responses in others.

These human paradigms possess a timeless quality, according to Jaspers. They serve as *archetypal images* for their cultures and usually speak to other cultures as well. Although different cultures and eras produce different archetypes (Jaspers used as his examples Socrates, Confucius, Buddha, and Jesus), *the archetypal individual's very nature demands a response:* What is it to be a human being? What is most important? What is good? How should *I* live?

Jaspers says:

A radical change is experienced and demanded [by paradigmatic individuals]. They are stirred to their depths, by what we do not know. They express what there is no appropriate way of saying. They speak in parables, dialectical contradictions, conversational replies . . .

Socrates seeks himself and his relation to other men. By his extreme questioning he arouses a real, living certainty that is *not mere knowledge* of something. He transcends the world without negating it. He forges total

archetypal (paradigmatic) individual

A special class of teachers, philosophers, and religious figures whose nature becomes a standard by which a culture judges the "ideal" human being; a rare human being whose very nature represents something elemental about the human condition.

There is no doubt that in one form or another, Socrates and Buddha, Jesus and St. Paul, Plotinus and Spinoza, taught that . . . without renunciation of many of the ordinary appetites, no man can really live well.

WALTER LIPPMANN

knowledge, total judgments, contenting himself with a nonknowledge in which truth and reality are actualized.[13] [emphasis added]

In other words, Socrates continued to develop and grow as a person because of his philosophical search. He did not "fragment" himself into two parts, the thinker and the real person. He did not force himself to stick to a rigid theory. He responded anew to each experience. When Jaspers refers to "a nonknowledge," he means that Socrates always insisted that his "wisdom" lay in knowing what he did not know. (We'll look into this important concept shortly.)

Because their very natures "demand response," paradigmatic individuals provoke extreme community reactions: Love and embrace them or reject and exclude them. The paradigmatic individual is more challenging and intense than the mere sage is. We saw in Chapter 3 that the sage was considered "strange" and "alien," *atopos* in Greek. But this kind of strangeness can be trivialized or dismissed as merely odd or eccentric. The paradigmatic individual may be just as "strange" as the sage, but in a manner that is more personally disturbing, more deeply unsettling to our everyday habits and values.

Something about a paradigmatic teacher "shocks" us into a state of uncomfortable, reflective alertness. By actually or very nearly living up to principles that we, too, profess to see as worthy—and by living up to them with remarkable consistency and courage—the mere existence of a "human paradigm" provokes us into wondering how well our own lives reflect our beliefs. In other words, the life and teachings of the paradigmatic individual form a whole, a harmony that precludes the "safe distance" that exists between the lives of more ordinary teachers and their teachings. The paradigmatic figure invites us to close the gap by calling on us to live courageously and honestly according to articulated principles—without excusing ourselves.

For the most part, paradigmatic teachers stand in opposition to moral compromises to our integrity—however that is understood. But living without significant compromise is dangerous and perhaps wrong. In the first place, there is the risk that what appears to be integrity is, in fact, dogmatic rigidity, self-satisfied and self-righteous fanaticism. Then, too, by holding themselves to purportedly high standards, paradigmatic teachers step outside the "norm"—become estranged from the more modest or common standards and goals of the community. This "outsider" position is, itself, seen as a threat to conformity and group identity. This threat is amplified whenever a sage or prophet refuses to stop with mere *questioning* and throws down the gauntlet by *living* with fearless integrity.

One contemporary educational philosophy actually advises teachers to admit their failings and "share" their weaknesses with their students to make it easier for the students to "relate" to the teachers. From a certain perspective, it does seem safer (easier) to admire the *lessons* of teachers who are "just like us." The shared weaknesses of teachers who are "just like us" protect us from feeling deeply challenged: We are not confronted by the power of the kind of teacher whose teaching is completely reflected in his or her *being*. By actually "living up to" their teachings, integrated teachers deny us the safety of believing that the standard is set too high to reach, the notion that *no one really lives like that*.

Sometimes, we actually prefer the pastor who humbly admits to—and indulges in—a love of fine automobiles or sailboarding, willingly paid for out of the

Asked what was very difficult, Thales replied: "To know thyself." Asked what was very easy, he answered: "To give advice."

I found that the men in most repute were all but the most foolish; and that others less esteemed were really wiser and better.

SOCRATES

The gods help them that help themselves.

AESOP

"What an Extraordinary Effect His Words Have Had on Me"

In Plato's *Symposium*, Alcibiades notes the staggering power of Socrates:

> . . . when we listen to you, or to someone else repeating what you've said, even if he puts it ever so badly, and never mind whether the person who's listening is man, woman, or child, we're absolutely staggered and bewitched. And speaking for myself, gentlemen, if I wasn't afraid you'd tell me that I was completely bottled, I'd swear on oath what an extraordinary effect his words have had on me—and still do if it comes to that. For the moment I hear him speak I am smitten with a kind of sacred rage . . . oh, and not only me, but lots of other men.
>
> . . . He makes me admit that while I'm spending time on politics I am neglecting all the things crying for attention in myself. So I just refuse to listen to him—as if he were one of those Sirens, you know—and get out of earshot as quick as I can, for fear he will keep me sitting listening till I'm positively senile.
>
> And there's one thing I've never felt with anybody else—not the kind of thing you'd expect to find in me, either—and that is a sense of shame. Socrates is the only man in the world that can make me feel ashamed. Because there's no getting away from it, I know I ought to do the things he tells me to, and yet the moment I'm out of his sight I don't care what I do to keep in with the mob. So I dash off like a runaway slave, and keep out of his way as long as I can, and the next time I meet him I remember all that I had to admit the time before, and naturally I feel ashamed. There are times when I'd honestly be glad to hear that he's dead, and yet I know that if he did die I'd be more upset than ever—so I ask you, what is a man to do?

Plato, *Symposium*, 215D–16C, in Edith Hamilton and Huntington Cairns, eds., *Plato: The Collected Dialogues*, trans. Michael Joyce (New York: Pantheon, Bollingen Series 71, 1966), p. 567.

collection plate; the ethics professor who copies colleagues' new software and uses the school's equipment to play on the Internet; the psychology instructor who lectures while intoxicated and dates students (only "mature" students, of course); the activist professor whose passionate indictments of elitism or racism or sexism are simply virulent forms of the very same "isms," only in reverse.

So ingrained is contemporary suspicion of the possibility of healthy expressions of "paradigmatic integrity," that I am uncomfortable writing this passage and listing these commonplace examples of apparent gaps between teachers and what they teach. So let's be contemporary for a moment: The historical Socrates was probably not such a fine fellow, anyway. Plato probably just invented him to get back at the Sophists (Chapter 3). Once we grow up, we see through these romanticized, Sunday-school type heroes. Nobody could really live like Socrates today. But what if . . .

PHILOSOPHICAL

QUERY

• • • • • •

Can you think of other paradigmatic individuals? Remember, a paradigmatic individual is more than a merely influential teacher, adviser, social reformer, or significant religious figure. Do you think that contemporary America, with its present sense of diversity, can produce archetypal philosophers? Or must each community or ethnic group have its own human paradigms? What qualities do you think a contemporary "American sophos" must possess?

■ THE TEACHER AND HIS TEACHINGS ■

As presented by Plato, the harmony between Socrates' life and teachings transformed him from a truth-seeker into a sage, from a sage into a paradigm of the teacher-as-more-than-sage. Pierre Hadot says:

> There were several reasons for the fact that my research on the sage as a model gradually became fixed upon Socrates. In the first place, I found in him a figure who exercised a widespread influence of the greatest importance on the entire Western tradition. Secondly, and most importantly, the figure of Socrates—as sketched by Plato, at any rate—had it seemed to me one unique advantage. It is the portrait of a mediator between the transcendent ideal of wisdom and concrete human reality. It is a paradox of highly Socratic irony that Socrates was not a sage, but a "philo-sopher": that is, a lover of wisdom.[14]

For reasons that remain controversial to this day, Socrates' "electric shock" effect on Athens resulted in his indictment, conviction, and execution as a traitorous blasphemer. Speaking for the last time as a public figure, on trial for his life, the seventy-year-old philosopher repeated what he had *always* insisted: "I neither know nor think that I know."

As we learn more about Socrates' teachings and teaching method, let's see if we can gain some understanding of how it came to pass that a philosopher who insisted, under threat of death, that his wisdom consisted of knowing that he did not know still stands as *the* archetypal *wise man* in Western philosophy.

■ THE DIALECTIC ■

Socrates argued that one of the chief reasons many people cannot think clearly is that they do not even know what they are talking about. Consequently, the first order of business is to define our terms. The early dialogues of Plato reveal a Socrates constantly pushing and searching for clearer and more precise definitions of key terms. Time after time he lures a confused individual from one muddled definition to another. Then, using skillful (some would even say loaded or leading) questions, he attempts to guide his "opponent" closer to the truth by allowing the opponent to experience the logical inconsistencies in his own stated positions. Socrates was so effective with this method of philosophical teaching and inquiry that it came to be known as the **Socratic dialectic,** also known as the **Socratic method.**

The Socratic method begins with the assumption that the function of education is to draw the truth out of the pupil rather than "fill an empty vessel." In practice, it is a series of guided questions known as the *dialectical method of inquiry*. Claims are continually refined, definitions required for all key terms, logical inconsistencies brought to light and resolved. A vital aspect of Socratic teaching is the active involvement of the audience (pupils, listeners), hence the use of questions rather than straight lectures.

The dialectical process as Socrates practiced it was dynamic and hopeful. At worst, the participants learned that although they might not have found *the* answer, *the* meaning of justice, *the* good life, or courage, they were at least a bit clearer than

But I shall be asked, Why do people delight in continually conversing with you? I have told you already, Athenians, the whole truth about this matter: they like to hear the cross-examination of the pretenders to wisdom; there is amusement in it.

SOCRATES

Socratic method or Socratic dialectic
Question-and-answer technique used by Socrates to draw truth out of his pupils, often by means of achieving a clearer, more precise definition of a key term or concept.

before. At any rate, this was Socrates' experience—others were often angered and frustrated, if not humiliated, as their confusion and ignorance were exposed.

Socrates believed that the truth was somehow in each of us. The teacher's role, then, isn't to put knowledge into an empty mind, but to draw wisdom and clarity out of a disordered and confused soul. Just as a midwife does not herself give birth but, rather, aids the mother, Socrates claimed to aid others in giving birth to their own insights by *drawing out what was already there.* And just as a midwife is of no help until the mother has conceived a child, Socrates was of no help until the other person had conceived at least a sketchy idea.

For Socrates, the most important order of business was to *engage* the other person. The Socratic method in full form is more than just questions and answers. It is a highly personal activity, guided by one who knows both the general direction of the inquiry (but not "the answers") as well as the nature and needs of the individual student. It works only if the other "participant" actively listens and responds.

Socratic Irony

A key element in keeping his pupils engaged, and calling attention to the importance of meaning, was Socrates' use of **irony,** a way of communicating on more than one level. An ironic utterance has at least two levels of meaning: *the literal level,* also known as the obvious level, and *the hidden level,* also known as the real level. As a rule, the two meanings are near opposites, as in the case of the sarcastic professor who writes on a woefully inadequate term paper: "Beautiful job! You've never done better!"

By using words in unexpected ways, by meaning more than one obvious, surface-level thing, Socrates hoped to keep his listeners alert. Further, the use of irony underscored his belief that things are not always as they first appear, that there is a deeper meaning than may be apparent. Socrates used irony to keep his listeners on their toes and to avoid putting answers in their mouths. For instance, he begins his *Apology* (his defense at his trial) by referring to the "persuasive" abilities of his immediate accusers, who are Sophists. Of course, his remark is actually an ironic way of showing that these Sophists have not persuaded him of anything. His use of irony in his opening remarks gets the audience's immediate attention:

How you, O Athenians, have been affected by my accusers, I cannot tell; but I know that they almost made me forget who I was—so persuasively did they speak; and yet they have hardly uttered a word of truth. But of the many falsehoods told by them, there was one which quite amazed me;—I mean when they said that you should be upon your guard and not allow yourselves to be deceived by the force of my eloquence. To say this, when they were certain to be detected as soon as I opened my lips and proved myself to be anything but a great speaker, did indeed appear to me most shameless—unless by the force of eloquence they mean the force of truth; for if such is their meaning, I admit that I am eloquent. But in how different a way from theirs! Well, as I was saying, they have scarcely spoken the truth at all; but from me you shall hear the whole truth: not, however, delivered after their manner in a set oration duly ornamented with words and phrases . . . at my time of life I ought not be appearing before you, O men of Athens, in the character of a juvenile orator—let no one expect it of me.[15]

Ironic communication confuses those who are inattentive or not "in on" the hidden meaning. For instance, most members of Socrates' jury would have been familiar with his wranglings with Sophists and with sophistic emphasis on the arts of persuasion. A smaller group would have also responded to the irony of Socrates, whose life was devoted to following the command "Know thyself," forgetting who he was. Irony was both a crucial component of Socrates' method and a contributing factor to his ultimate trouble, because to many observers, Socrates' use of irony was just another sophistic trick.

	PHILOSOPHICAL
• • • • • •	QUERY
See how many ironic references to Sophists you can find in the preceding passage from Plato's Apology.	

■ SOCRATES AT WORK ■

Before we look further into some specific Socratic doctrines, let's enrich our sense of the dialectic as an interpersonal philosophical method. We can do that by taking an extended look at the kind of dialectical exchange with a Sophist that Socrates became famous for: precisely the sort of explosive encounter that fueled his ambiguous reputation and contributed to the animosity between Socrates and certain Sophists.

To some critics, Socrates' entire "philosophical career" was what vaudeville performers used to call a "shtick," a gimmick that gives a performer a recognizable identity to hide behind and a repertoire of predictable routines. Sophists and other critics saw him as an undemocratic elitist merely pretending to be a simple fellow, poor and modest, on a so-called quest for wisdom. According to this view, Socrates was a Sophist. From this perspective, his "Aw, shucks," seemingly meek demeanor was thought to be a ruse designed to set opponents up for the fall. That is, by lulling people into a false sense of security and trust, Socrates was able to catch them off guard and "shock" them with sneaky word tricks and leading questions. Whether there is merit to such a picture of Socrates is something you must wrestle with for yourself.

Plato provides one of the most intriguing examples of the Socratic dialectic in action early in his masterpiece, the *Republic* (Chapter 5). The passage that follows concerns a typical encounter between Socrates and a Sophist. Thrasymachus (c. 450 B.C.E.) is the kind of Sophist who is less interested in theories and philosophy than in political and social action. In Book I, section 3 of the *Republic*, Plato paints a vivid portrait of the volatile, aggressive style Thrasymachus used in confronting his opponents.

I will tell you something, Socrates [said Aristides, the son of Lysimachus and grandson of the great Aristides], something quite incredible but true. I have never learned a single thing from you, as you know yourself; but whenever I was with you I improved, even if I was only in the same house but not in the same room. . . .

The *Republic* consists of a series of dialogues between Socrates and various individuals, chiefly about the nature of justice. By skillful questioning, Socrates "reveals" that conventional notions of morality are confused and "muddle-headed." After Socrates has rejected a number of attempts to define justice, Thrasymachus literally bursts onto the scene. With energy and sarcasm, the Sophist categorically denies that any one moral standard can be equally applicable to rich and poor, strong and weak, "superior" and "inferior."

Thrasymachus goes well beyond Socrates' rejection of common conceptions of justice such as repaying debts or giving persons their "due" and substitutes unabashed self-interest for any other view of justice. He thereby transforms *moral relativism* into a hard-edged *moral realism,* contending that an unsentimental view of life shows quite clearly that *might makes right.*

Whether we like it or not, according to Thrasymachus, the values that prevail in all areas of life—economic, political, racial, educational—reflect the *interests of the strong.* Certain values dominate not because they are in some absolute sense "right," but because they are the views preferred by the most powerful individual or group. And since nature rewards power, the powerful individual is always the superior individual, the "true individual," gloriously free in his or her indifference to the puny concerns of conventional morality.

Reflecting Socrates' harsh opinion of moral realism, Plato portrays Thrasymachus as loud, offensive, and often on the verge of resorting to force. From the very start, we know we are in for an interesting experience as Thrasymachus disrupts the courteous, "philosophical" tone of the discussion.

Sophos *Versus Sophist*

Of what value is smartness of speech? Opposing a man with the mouth excites anger.

CONFUCIUS

As you read the following extended passage from the *Republic,* look for examples of irony (and sarcasm). Reflect on Thrasymachus's accusations against Socrates and his method. Study Socrates' responses. Note how Socrates manages to draw Thrasymachus into his preferred question-and-answer process—in spite of Thrasymachus's apparent awareness of the dialectic's effects and his own strong assertions that he will not participate. Be alert for the possible psychological consequences that might result from a "losing" encounter with Socrates. (And add some zest to your reading by mentally picturing the two protagonists: the volatile, younger, stronger, hotheaded Thrasymachus and the confident old master of the cross-examination.)

As our drama opens, Socrates is describing Thrasymachus's impatient interruption of a discussion Socrates was having with a man named Polemarchus:

Speak softly but carry a big stick.

THEODORE ROOSEVELT

While we had been talking Thrasymachus had often tried to interrupt, but had been prevented by those sitting near him, who wanted to hear the argument concluded; but when we paused . . . he was no longer able to contain himself and gathered himself together and sprang on us like a wild beast, as if he wanted to tear us in pieces. Polemarchus and I were scared stiff, as Thrasymachus burst out and said, "What is all this nonsense, Socrates? Why do you go on in this childish way being so polite about each other's opinions? If you really want to know what justice is, stop asking questions and then playing to the gallery by refuting anyone who answers you. You know perfectly well that it is easier to ask questions than to answer them. Give us an answer yourself, and tell us what you think justice is. And don't tell me that it's duty, or expediency, or advantage, or profit, or interest. I won't put up with nonsense of that sort; give me a clear and precise definition."

I was staggered by his attack and looked at him in dismay. If I had not seen him first I believe I should have been struck dumb; but I had noticed him when our argument first began to annoy him, and so managed to answer him, saying diffidently: "Don't be hard on us, Thrasymachus. If we have made any mistake in the course of our argument, I assure you we have not done so on purpose. For if we were looking for gold, you can't suppose that we would willingly let mutual politeness hinder our search and prevent our finding it. Justice is much more valuable than gold, and we aren't likely to cramp our efforts to find it by any idiotic deference to each other. I assure you we are doing our best. It's the ability that we lack, and clever chaps like you ought to be sorry for us and not get annoyed with us."

Thrasymachus laughed sarcastically, and replied, "There you go with your old affectation, Socrates. I knew it, and I told the others that you would never let yourself be questioned, but go on shamming ignorance and do anything rather than give a straight answer."

"That's because you're so clever, Thrasymachus," I replied, "and you know it. You ask someone for a definition of twelve and add, 'I don't want to be told that it's twice six, or three times four, or six times two, or four times three; that sort of nonsense won't do.' You know perfectly well that no one would answer you on those terms. [This person] would reply, 'What do you mean, Thrasymachus; am I to give none of the answers you mention? If one of them happens to be true, do you want me to give a false one?' And how would you answer him?"

"That's not a fair parallel," he replied.

"I don't see why not," I said: "but even if it is not, we shan't stop anyone else answering like that if he thinks it fair, whether we like it or not."

"So I suppose that is what you are going to do," he said; "you're going to give one of the answers I barred."

"I would not be surprised," said I, "if it seemed to me on reflection to be the right one."

"What if I give you a quite different and far better definition of justice? What plea will you enter then?"

"The plea of ignorance: for those who don't know must learn from those who do."

"You must have your joke," said he, "but you must pay your costs as well." [The Sophists always charged for their instruction; and Thrasymachus is having his own joke by demanding a fee for "instructing" Socrates.]

"I will when I have any cash."

"The money's all right," said Glaucon; "we'll pay up for Socrates. So let us have your definition, Thrasymachus."

Socrates is guilty of rejecting the gods acknowledged by the state and of bringing in strange deities; he is also guilty of corrupting the youth.

INDICTMENT BROUGHT AGAINST SOCRATES

"I know," he replied, "so that Socrates can play his usual tricks, never giving us his own views but always asking others to explain theirs and refuting them."

"But what am I to do?" I asked. "I neither know nor profess to know anything about the subject, and even if I did I've been forbidden to say what I think by no mean [insignificant] antagonist. It's much more reasonable for you to say something, because you say you know, and really have something to say. Do please do me a favour and give me an answer, and don't grudge your instruction to Glaucon and the others here."

Glaucon and the others backed up what I had said, and it was obvious that Thrasymachus was anxious to get the credit for the striking answer he thought he could give: but he went on pretending he wanted to win his point and make me reply. In the end, however, he gave in, remarking, "So this is the wisdom of Socrates: he won't teach anyone anything, but goes round learning from others and is not even grateful."

To which I replied, "It's quite true, Thrasymachus, to say I learn from others, but it's not true to say I'm not grateful. I am generous with my praise—the only return I can give, as I have no money. You'll see in a moment how ready I am to praise any view I think well founded, for I'm sure the answer you're going to give will be that."

"Listen then," [Thrasymachus] replied. "I define justice or right as what is in the interest of the stronger party. Now where is your praise? I can see you're going to refuse it."

"You shall have it when I [Socrates] understand what you mean, which at present I don't. You say that what is in the interest of the stronger party is right; but what do you mean by interest? For instance, Polydamas the athlete is stronger than us, and it's in his interest to eat beef to keep it; we are weaker than he, but you can't mean that the same diet is in our interest and so right for us."

"You're being tiresome, Socrates," he returned, "and taking my definition in the sense most likely to damage it."

"I assure you I'm not," [Socrates] said; "you must explain your meaning more clearly."

"Well then, you know that some states are tyrannies, some democracies, some aristocracies? And that in each city power is in the hands of the ruling class?"

"Yes."

I think that all men have a choice between various courses, and choose and follow the one which they think conduces most to their advantage.

SOCRATES

"Each ruling class makes laws that are in its own interest, a democracy democratic laws, a tyranny tyrannical ones and so on; and in making these laws they define as 'right' for their subjects what is in the interest of themselves, the rulers, and if anyone breaks their laws he is punished as a 'wrongdoer.' That is what I mean when I say that 'right' is the same thing in all states, namely the interest of the established ruling class; and this ruling class is the 'strongest' element in each state, and so if we argue correctly we see that 'right' is always the same, the interest of the stronger party.

" . . . Consider how the just man always comes off worse than the unjust. For instance, in any business relations between them, you won't find the just man better off at the end of the deal than the unjust. Again, in their relations with the state, when there are taxes to be paid the unjust man will pay less on the same income, and when there's anything to be got he'll get it all. Thus if it's a question of office, if the just man loses nothing else he will suffer from neglecting his private affairs; his honesty will prevent him appropriating public funds, and his relations and friends will detest him because his principles will not allow him to push their interests. But quite the reverse is true of the unjust man . . . the man . . . who can make profits in a big way: he's the man to study if you want to find how much more private profit there is in wrong than in right. . . . *So we see that injustice, given scope, has greater strength and freedom and power than justice; which proves what I started by saying, that justice is the interest of the stronger party, injustice the interest and profit of oneself.*" [emphasis added]

"Now," I said, "I understand your meaning, and we must try to find out whether you are right or not. Your answer defines 'right' and 'interest' . . . but adds the qualification "of the stronger party.'"

"An insignificant qualification, I suppose you will say."

"Its significance is not yet clear; what is clear is that we must consider whether your definition is true. For I quite agree that what is right is an 'interest'; but you add that it is the interest 'of the stronger party,' and that's what I don't know about and want you to consider."

"Let us hear you."

"You shall," said I. "You say that obedience to the ruling power is right and just?"

"I do."

"And are those in power in the various states infallible or not?"

"They are, of course, liable to make mistakes," he replied.

"When they proceed to make laws, then, they may do the job well or badly."

"I suppose so."

"And if they do it well the laws will be in their interest, and if they do it badly they won't, I take it."

"I agree."

"But their subjects must obey the laws they make, for to do so is right."

"Of course."

"Then according to your argument it is *right* not only to do what is in the interest of the stronger party but also the opposite."

"What do you mean?" he asked.

"My meaning is the same as yours, I think. Let us look at it more closely. Did we not agree that when the ruling powers order their subjects to do something they are sometimes mistaken about their own best interest, and yet that it is *right* for the subject to do what his ruler enjoins?"

"I suppose we did."

"Then you must admit that it is *right* to do things that are *not* in the interest of the rulers, who are the *stronger* party; that is, when the rulers mistakenly give orders that will harm them and yet (so you say) it is right for their subjects to obey those orders. For surely, my dear Thrasymachus, in those circumstances it follows that it is 'right' to do the opposite of what you say is right, in that the weaker are *ordered* to do what is against the interest of the stronger."[16]

The doer of injustice is unhappier than the sufferer.

DEMOCRITUS

And this, O men of Athens, is the truth and the whole truth; I have concealed nothing, I have dissembled nothing. And yet, I know that my plainness of speech makes them hate me, and what is their hatred but a proof that I am speaking the truth?

SOCRATES

● ● ● ● ● ●

Statistically, poorer, less-educated people make up a disproportionate segment of our prison population. Just how relevant to Thrasymachus's position is it that white-collar and celebrity criminals are often punished less severely than poor or obscure defendants are? Other studies suggest that physically attractive job candidates are most likely to be hired. Have you ever noticed how some students seem to get by mostly on cleverness and charm? Should we draw conclusions about the nature of justice from these cases or just chalk them up to the way things sometimes go? Try to separate our lip-service moral values from those we practice. Try to separate a storybook conception of life from a realistic one. Are moral realists onto something or not? Explain.

■ THE UNEXAMINED LIFE ■

Among Socratic teachings, the most persistent command was "Know thyself." The significance to Socrates of this command is underscored by the fact that he stressed its importance to his life and mission during his *Apology*. Facing the end of a long life, Socrates uttered one of the most famous statements in the history of ideas: "The unexamined life is not worth living." By this he meant, among other things, that a life devoid of philosophical speculation is hardly a *human life*. That is, it is incomplete; it is not fully functioning and so lacks virtue or excellence.

Socrates believed that the human **psyche** is the essence of humanness. The psyche was a combination of what we think of as the mind and soul: consciousness, the capacity to reason, and the ability to reflect, known as *reflective thinking*. Giovanni Reale says:

> As has recently come to light, no one prior to Socrates had understood by *soul* what Socrates understood by it, and after Socrates the whole of the West. . . . the soul for Socrates was identified *with our consciousness when it thinks and acts with our reason and with the source of our thinking activity and our ethical activity*. In short, for Socrates the soul *is the conscious self, it is intellectual and moral personhood.*[17]

An unexamined life is a life that takes the psyche for granted. An "unexamined" life is, in a sense, an unconscious life. It is lived on the minimal level: Thinking never rises above practical concerns; desires are rarely pondered; custom, habit, and unquestioned beliefs substitute for reflection and assessment. Consequently, it is possible for a very intelligent, materially successful individual to live an unexamined life. The examined life does not produce "all the answers." Instead, it results in a life devoted to knowing more, a life in which progress means shedding false beliefs, a life in which pretense is continually reduced. The examined life is lived in conscious awareness of the human condition; it is not merely spent in an uncritical attempt to satisfy various needs and desires.

psyche

Greek for "soul"; in today's terms, combination of mind and soul, including capacity for reflective thinking.

The striving to find meaning in one's life is the primary motivational force in man.

VIKTOR FRANKL

PHILOSOPHICAL

QUERY

• • • • • •

Do some informal research among your friends to get a sense of some contemporary conceptions of the soul. Compare and contrast what you discover with Socrates' conception of the psyche. How might a person's conception of the soul influence his or her response to the issue of the unexamined life?

Socratic Ignorance

When Socrates was probably in his thirties, his friend Chaerephon went to the Oracle at Delphi with a question: Is anyone wiser than Socrates? The Oracle was believed to have the gift of prophecy. Either through divine guidance or cleverness, it gave this famous, ambiguous reply: *No man is wiser than Socrates.* This can be taken to mean either (a) Socrates is the wisest man in Athens, or (b) even though Socrates is not very wise, he is as wise as anybody gets. The first interpretation makes Socrates unique. The second makes him an exemplar of the human condition.

Socrates took the Oracle's reply quite seriously, claiming that it was the turning point in his life. His first reaction to hearing the god Apollo's reply was confusion:

> I said to myself, What can the god mean? and what is the interpretation of his riddle? for I know that I have no wisdom, small or great. What then can he mean when he says that I am the wisest of men? And yet he is a god, and cannot lie; that would be against his nature. After long consideration, I thought of a method of trying the question. I reflected that if I could only find a man wiser than myself, then I might go to the god with a refutation in my hand. I should say to him, "Here is a man wiser than I am; but you said I was the wisest." Accordingly I went to one who had a reputation of wisdom, and observed him—his name I need not mention; he was a politician whom I selected for examination—and the result was as follows: When I began to talk with him, I could not help thinking that he was not really wise, although

If, as they say, I am only an ignorant man trying to be a philosopher, then that may be what a philosopher is.

DIOGENES

I am not wise.
SOCRATES

he was thought wise by many, and still wiser by himself; and thereupon I tried to explain to him that he thought himself wise, but was not really wise; and the consequence was that he hated me, and his enmity was shared by several who were present and heard me. So I left him, saying to myself, as I went away: Well, although I do not suppose that either of us knows anything really beautiful and good, I am better off than he is—for he knows nothing, and thinks that he knows; I neither know nor think that I know. In this . . . , then, I seem to have slightly the advantage of him. Then I went to another who had still higher pretensions to wisdom, and my conclusion was exactly the same. Whereupon I made another enemy of him, and of many others besides him.[18]

What point could Socrates have been making? Clearly—it seems—Socrates possessed some kind of knowledge, if not wisdom. Just as clearly—it seems—he must have believed in his own ignorance, since he alluded to it on many occasions. If we allow for an element of irony in Socrates' language, it then becomes likely that Socrates was challenging our notions of wisdom and knowledge. To certain sorts of people, Socrates' statements will remain clouded, perhaps beyond comprehension. Among them are young people whose "minds have not conceived at all" or older ones whose thoughts are already so firmly set that they can see only a phony technique used to avoid answering questions. Such people cannot conceive of their own ignorance. They are firmly convinced that they know everything important. To the Sophists, Socrates' use of "fake ignorance" was merely a clever psychological ploy to keep them off balance and on the spot. It's this sort of thing that made Thrasymachus so angry.

Shall I tell you what knowledge is? It is to know both what one knows and what one does not know.
CONFUCIUS

Since the Socratic method employs guided questions, we can conclude that Socrates *does* have some ideas about the general direction the search for answers will take and the adequacy of certain lines of analysis. But he refuses to reveal these in dogmatic form. Socrates' "ignorance" was part of his whole mission, which he saw as bringing home to others *their own* intellectual needs. Once that was accomplished, they were invited to join the search for truth using the dialectical method of question-and-answer. The essence of the Socratic method is to convince us that, although we thought we knew something, in fact we did not.

Socrates may also have been sharing his own honest doubt. Even if he knew more than he let on, which is likely, he was probably more aware of the uncertain nature and limits of knowledge (his own included) than many of us are. In this, he seems wiser than the average person in two ways. First, many of us tend to think that we know much more than we do. Second, all human knowledge is tentative and limited: We are not gods, though we sometimes act as if we were.

The oldest sage would admit at the close of a life of study his wisdom was as a raindrop to the sea. Nor is this idea new. . . . anthropologists have traced its presence in the legends and indigenous ideas of nearly every country in the world.
CHRISTMAS HUMPHREYS

The Power of Human Wisdom

Perhaps the best way to glimpse the power of Socratic ignorance is to look once more to the *Apology,* this time where Socrates makes tantalizing statements regarding his "wisdom":

I dare say, Athenians, that some of you will reply, "Yes, Socrates, but what is the origin of these accusations which are brought against you; there must have been something strange which you have been doing? All these rumours and this talk about you would never have arisen if you had been like other men: tell us, then, what is the cause of them, for we should be sorry to judge hastily of you." Now I regard this as a fair challenge, and I will endeavour to explain to you the reason why I am called wise and have such evil fame. Please to attend then. And although some of you may think that I am joking, I declare that I will tell you the entire truth. Men of Athens, this reputation of mine has come of a certain sort of wisdom which I possess. If you ask me what kind of wisdom, I reply, wisdom such as may perhaps be attained by man, for to that extent I am inclined to believe that I am wise; whereas the persons to whom I was speaking have a superhuman wisdom, which I may fail to describe, because I have it not myself; and he who says I have, speaks falsely, and is taking away my character.[19]

The Socratic distinction between "human wisdom" and "more-than-human wisdom" is a powerful one. Buddha made a similar point in his intriguing discussion of "questions not tending toward edification" (discussed in Chapter 2).

In his effort to understand why the god said no one was wiser than he, Socrates discovered how easy it is to become deluded by our own special skills. The modern tendency to compartmentalize rather than integrate our lives, combined with the respect we have for specialized skills and knowledge, might make us especially susceptible to this delusion. Television talk shows are a parade of individuals expressing their "insights" and "discoveries" in all areas of life. Psychologists discuss morals, entertainers lecture on food additives, preachers propose legislation, all sorts of people write books generalizing from their own limited experience to the human condition. They—and we—seem to assume that if you have a degree, sell lots of books, get rich, have a television or radio show, or become famous, then you *must know what you're talking about no matter what you're talking about.* Things haven't changed:

> At last I went to the artisans, for I was conscious that I knew nothing at all, as I may say, and I was sure that they knew many fine things; and here I was not mistaken, for they did know many things of which I was ignorant, and in this they certainly were wiser than I was. But I observed that even the good artisans fell into the same error as the poets—because they were good workmen they thought that they also knew all sorts of high matters, and this defect in them overshadowed their wisdom; and therefore I asked myself whether I would like to be as I was, neither having their knowledge nor their ignorance, or like them in both; and I made answer to myself and to the oracle that I was better off as I was.
>
> This inquisition has led to my having many enemies of the worst and most dangerous kind, and has given occasion to many calumnies. And I am called wise, for my hearers always imagine that I possess the wisdom which I find wanting in others; but the truth is, O men of Athens, that God only is wise; and by his answer he intends to show that the wisdom of men is worth little or nothing; he is not speaking of Socrates, he is only using my name by way of illustration, as if he said, He, O men, is wisest, who, like Socrates, knows that his wisdom is in truth worth nothing. And so I go about the world, obedient to the god, and search and make enquiry into the wisdom of anyone, whether citizen

Every man is enlightened, but wishes he wasn't.

R. H. BLYTH

If I had engaged in politics, I should have perished long ago . . . for the truth is, that no man who goes to war with you or any other multitude, honestly striving against the many lawless and unrighteous deeds which are done in a state, will save his life; he who will fight for the right, if he would live even for a brief space, must have a private station and not a public one.

SOCRATES

It is fascinating to imagine encounters between Socrates and today's confident "sages" and professional advice-givers such as television talk-show host Dr. Phil. How do you think Dr. Phil (and other celebrity gurus) would fare with Socrates as a guest?

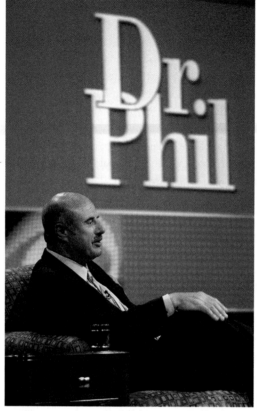

© Getty Images

or stranger, who appears to be wise; and if he is not wise, then in vindication of the oracle I show him that he is not wise; and my occupation quite absorbs me, and I have no time to give either to any public matter or interest or to any concern of my own, but I am in utter poverty by reason of my devotion to the god.[20]

PHILOSOPHICAL

QUERY

• • • • • •

Have you ever met a highly educated specialist (physician, biochemist, psychologist, philosophy teacher, preacher) who thinks nothing of pontificating on the economy, sex education, and how you should raise your child? Discuss in light of Socratic statements concerning human wisdom.

■ THE PHYSICIAN OF THE SOUL ■

Socrates' entire teaching mission centered on his conviction that *we are our souls.* That is, the "real person" is not the body, but the *psyche.* Perhaps the most important passage in the *Apology* concerns Socrates' description of himself as a kind of "physician of the soul." In Socrates' sense, "seeking my own welfare" means "seeking the welfare of my soul." Note how in the following passage

Socrates implies that he does indeed know something (that the most important thing is care of the soul) and that he views his whole public career as a teacher in light of his expanded notion of the self as the soul:

> Men of Athens, I honour and love you; but I shall obey God rather than you, and while I have strength I shall never cease from the practice and teaching of philosophy, exhorting any one whom I meet and saying to him after my manner: You, my friend,—a citizen of the great and mighty and wise city of Athens,—are you not ashamed of heaping up the greatest amount of money and honour and reputation, and caring so little about wisdom and truth and the greatest improvement of the soul, which you never regard or heed at all? And if the person with whom I am arguing, says: Yes, but I do care; then I do not leave him or let him go at once; but I proceed to interrogate and examine and cross-examine him, and if I think that he has no virtue in him, but only says that he has, I reproach him with undervaluing the greater, and overvaluing the less. And I shall repeat the same words to everyone I meet, young and old, citizen and alien, but especially to the citizens . . . For know that this is the command of the god; and I believe no greater good has happened to this state than my service to the god. For I do nothing but go about persuading you all, old and young alike, not to take thought for your persons or your properties, but first and chiefly to care about the greatest improvement of your soul. I tell you that virtue is not given by money, but that from virtue comes money and every other good of man, public as well as private. This is my teaching.[21]

To know what you do not know is best. To pretend to know what you do not know is a disease.

LAO-TZU

• • • • • •

Compare Socrates' attitude toward the soul with your own—with your religion's, if you practice one. What do you see as the main differences? What are some advantages and disadvantages of Socrates' view?

PHILOSOPHICAL

QUERY

"Oh, the Pure Innocent Child!"

Oh, tell me who was it first announced, who was it first proclaimed, that man only does nasty things because he does not know his own interests; and that if he were enlightened, if his eyes were opened to his real normal interests, man would at once cease to do nasty things, would at once become good and noble because, being enlightened and understanding his real advantage, he would see his own advantage in the good and nothing else, and we all know that not one man can, consciously, act against his own interests, consequently, so to say, through necessity, he would begin doing good? Oh, the babe! Oh, the pure innocent child!

Fyodor Dostoevsky, *Notes from the Underground,* trans. Constance Garnett, in *Existentialism from Dostoevsky to Sartre,* ed. Walter Kaufmann (New York: New American Library, 1975), p. 67.

No One Knowingly Does Evil

The fundamental Socratic imperative "Know thyself" takes on special significance in light of Socrates' view that human beings always seek what they believe to be their own welfare and cannot deliberately do otherwise. In the *Gorgias*, Socrates points out that when people do what appear to be bad or distasteful things, it is always with some ultimate good in mind:

> So it is for the sake of the good that people do all these [distasteful] actions?
> Yes, it is.
> And we have admitted that when we act for any purpose, we do not desire the action itself but the object of the action?
> Yes.
> Then we do not desire . . . these [distasteful] actions themselves; but if they are advantageous, we desire to do them; and if they are harmful, we do not. For we desire what is good . . . but things that are neither bad nor good we do not desire, nor things that are bad either.[22]

For Socrates, the good or harm in question is always determined by what benefits or harms the soul. In order to seek my soul's welfare I have to "know myself." And in order to "know myself," I have to know what kind of thing I am. Without this knowledge, I cannot know what is really good for me. In the *Protagoras,* Socrates reinforces his conviction that no one knowingly does evil:

> For no wise man, I believe, will allow that any human being errs voluntarily, or voluntarily does evil or base actions; but they are very well aware that all who do evil and base things do them against their will.[23]

• • • • • •

Do you agree that no one knowingly does evil? Explain. You might want to read the box about the Ring of Gyges in Chapter 3 (p. 71) before you answer.

Virtue Is Wisdom

virtue

From the Greek *arete,* meaning "that at which something excels," or "excellence of function."

The Sophists claimed to be "teachers of human excellence," with excellence meaning "excellence of function," or **virtue** (*arete* in Greek). Too often, however, the result, as we saw in Chapter 3, was might-makes-right moral relativism and a radical this-worldly egoism—in contrast to Socratic egoism, which centers on the soul as the true self. The Sophists looked outward for markers of well-being and success, whereas Socrates looked inward at character.

Socrates believed that human excellence (virtue for short) is a special kind of knowledge that combines technical understanding with the skill and character to apply that knowledge. One of the words Socrates used for this kind of knowledge was **techne,** the Greek term for practical knowledge of how to do things. At various times, *techne* meant "art," "skill," "craft," "technique," "trade," "system," or "method of doing something." It is the root of English words such as *technique, technical,* and *technology. Techne* is knowledge of what to do and how to do it. It is knowledge of both means and ultimate ends. Plato accused the Sophists of developing persuasive skills (rhetoric) without acquiring a corresponding knowledge of what ought to be done or avoided—that is without knowledge of ultimate ends.

For example, according to Socrates, a knowledgeable physician has both theoretical understanding and practical skill. Her *techne* is manifest by the fact that she makes her patients well. If she made them worse, we would conclude that she was not really a physician, that she lacked medical knowledge. *Techne* is not like merely cognitive knowledge of a cake recipe; it involves the skills needed to actually bake a good cake.

According to Socrates, the Sophists' lack of *techne* was evident because their teachings made people worse. Their own pupils engaged in corrupt business practices and destructive political schemes. Sometimes the Sophists' pupils even attacked their teachers and tried to cheat them out of their tuition, as we saw in the case of Protagoras's Wager (Chapter 3). Thus, the Sophists lacked knowledge of human excellence, or virtue.

Socrates believed that knowledge (wisdom) always produces behavioral results, because behavior is always guided by beliefs. For instance, if I believe that the glass of water in front of me is poisoned, I will not drink it—unless I also believe that dying will be better for me than living, given my present circumstances (say, terminal cancer of a painful sort). This rationalistic view that behavior is always controlled by beliefs about what is good and the means to that good is sometimes called **intellectualism**. Intellectualism emphasizes cognitive states (beliefs) whereas egoism emphasizes desires.

Socrates' intellectualism was part of his unusual claim that no one knowingly does wrong. According to Socrates, when we "admit" (state) that our choices are wrong, we are playing word games. To take an extreme example, a satanist who glories in "choosing" *evil* really believes in the superiority of what he is calling evil. Perhaps, according to Jews, Christians or Muslims, what he is choosing is wrong, but to the satanist, it is *really good*. If he honestly believed (knew) that X was wrong (fatal to his soul), our hypothetical satanist could not choose X, according to Socrates.

In other words, there is no such thing as true *weakness of will*. We are, implies Socrates, psychologically incapable of knowing what is good and not doing it. Conversely, we are psychologically incapable of doing what we really know (and believe wholeheartedly) will harm us. Socrates' simple psychology and intellectualism led him to the conviction that all evil is a form of ignorance, because no one knowingly wills harm to herself.[24]

For Socrates, knowledge of virtue is wisdom; it goes beyond theoretical understanding of justice or right and wrong, and includes *living* justly, living honorably and well in the highest sense. In the following passage from the *Meno,* Socrates argues that virtue is wisdom and that all things "hang upon" wisdom:

> *Socrates*: The next question is, whether virtue is knowledge or of another species?
> *Meno*: Certainly. . . .
> *Socrates*: Do we not say that virtue is good? . . .
> *Meno*: Certainly. . . .

techne

From the Greek for "art," "skill," "craft," "technique," "trade," "system," or "method of doing something"; root of English words such as *technique, technical,* and *technology*; term Socrates used when he asserted that virtue (*arete*) is knowledge or wisdom (*techne*).

intellectualism

Term used to refer to the claim that behavior is always controlled by beliefs about what is good and the means to that good.

Socrates: Then virtue is profitable?

Meno: That is the only inference. . . .

Socrates: And what is the guiding principle which makes [things] profitable or the reverse? Are they not profitable when they are rightly used, and hurtful when they are not rightfully used?

Meno: Certainly.

Socrates: Next, let us consider the goods of the soul: they are temperance, justice, courage, quickness of apprehension, memory, magnanimity, and the like?

Meno: Surely.

Socrates: And such of these as are not knowledge, but of another sort, are sometimes profitable and sometimes hurtful; as, for example, courage wanting prudence, which is only a sort of confidence? When a man has no sense he is harmed by courage, but when he has sense he is profited?

Meno: True.

Socrates: And . . . whatever things are learned or done with sense are profitable, but when done without sense they are hurtful?

Meno: Very true.

Socrates: And in general, all that the soul attempts or endures, when under the guidance of wisdom, ends in happiness; but when she is under the guidance of folly, the opposite?

Meno: That appears to be true.

Socrates: If then virtue is a quality of the soul, and is admitted to be profitable, it must be wisdom or prudence, since none of the things of the soul are either profitable or hurtful in themselves, but they are all made profitable or hurtful by the addition of wisdom or folly; and therefore if virtue is profitable, virtue must be a sort of wisdom or prudence?

Meno: I quite agree. . . .

Socrates: And is this not universally true of human nature? All other things hang upon the soul, and the things of the soul herself hang upon wisdom, if they are to be good; and so wisdom is inferred to be that which profits—and virtue, as we say, is profitable?

Meno: Certainly.

Socrates: And thus we arrive at the conclusion that virtue is either wholly or partly wisdom?

Meno: I think that what you are saying, Socrates, is very true.[25]

> *He who enjoins a knowledge of oneself bids us become acquainted with the soul.*
>
> PLATO

> *To live is not itself an evil, as has been claimed, but to lead a worthless life is.*
>
> DIOGENES

> *Either acquit me or not; but whichever you do, understand that I shall never alter my ways, not even if I have to die many times.*
>
> SOCRATES

PHILOSOPHICAL QUERY

• • • • • •

If all evil is ignorance, can we ever justly punish evildoers? Discuss.

■ THE TRIAL AND DEATH OF SOCRATES ■

For most of his long life, Socrates was able to function as a critic-at-large, questioning Athenian values and occasionally annoying important and powerful people in the process. He acquired a mixed reputation, being viewed on the one hand as a harmless eccentric and on the other as a dangerous social critic and "free-thinker"—in short, a Sophist. Socrates' philosophic method consisted of raising question after question, calling into doubt cherished, often previously unchallenged, beliefs to see if they were worthy of allegiance. Many Athenians found this skeptical attitude undemocratic, disrespectful, and threatening; they preferred unwavering loyalty to the status quo and to conventional beliefs. To these citizens, the very process of questioning fundamental values was subversive, perhaps even traitorous.

Socrates' status changed from mere annoyance to overt threat because of events associated with the bitter Peloponnesian Wars between Athens and Sparta. One of Socrates' students, Alcibiades, went to Sparta, where he advised the Spartans during the war. In some people's minds, as the teacher, Socrates was responsible for the student's act of betrayal.

Socrates further alienated himself from powerful Athenians when he resisted efforts to judge eight Athenian generals accused of poor military strategy as a group, rather than as individuals, as was their right under the Athenian constitution. Socrates was the *one member* of the Committee of the Senate of Five Hundred *to refuse*. The other 499 members initially agreed with Socrates' position, but backed down when aggressive prosecutors threatened to add to the indictment the names of Committee members who refused to ignore the constitution. The threat worked, the generals were found guilty, and the six who were already in custody were executed on the same day. This is another example of Socrates' willingness to put his principles above all other considerations (including, perhaps, his family's well-being).

Sparta defeated Athens in 404 B.C.E., and set up a Commission of Thirty to form a new Athenian government. The Thirty turned out to be a ruthless dictatorship that executed supporters of the earlier Periclean democracy and greedily confiscated their property. The Thirty lasted about eight months before being removed from power by force. Unfortunately for Socrates, among the Thirty were his close friends Critias and Charmides. Once again, in the minds of many Athenians, Socrates was guilty of treason by association.

Finally, resentment, distrust, and hostility against Socrates grew to such proportions that he was brought to trial for "not worshiping the gods of the state" and "corrupting the young." These were potentially capital offenses, and Socrates' prosecutor, Meletus, demanded death. At the time, it was customary for individuals charged with such crimes to submit to voluntary exile. Had Socrates chosen this option, there would have been no trial. Socrates, however, remained to answer his accuser before a jury of his peers.

Athenian trials consisted of two parts. First, the jury determined whether or not the accused was guilty as charged. If guilty, the second stage of the trial determined the most appropriate punishment. Socrates' jury consisted of 501 members. There was no way such a large group could reasonably debate various penalty options, so if a defendant was convicted, the prosecutor proposed a penalty and the defendant proposed a counterpenalty. Then the jury voted once more, choosing one or the other. The hope was that both sides would be moderate in their demands.

Socrates defended himself and was judged guilty by a rather close vote. The custom of the time was for those convicted to show some contrition. The greater the prosecutor's proposed penalty, the more remorse the condemned man was

No other trial, except that of Jesus, has left so vivid an impression on the imagination of Western man as that of Socrates.

I. F. STONE

expected to express. In cases where death was demanded, the proposed counterpenalty was supposed to be stiff. It might include leaving Athens forever and
giving up most or all of one's property as fines. Public humiliation was also part
of the price of escaping death. Defendants were expected to tear at their clothes,
roll on the ground, and throw dirt on themselves while crying and wailing. They
would usually have their wives and children and friends cry and plead for their
lives. An important function of the trial involved making peace with those one
had offended.

Instead of following custom, Socrates pointed out that it would be undignified
at his age to grovel for a little more life. He refused to allow his friends and family to
crawl either. To make things even worse, he reminded the jury that many of them
believed he was not guilty and had been falsely convicted. In this way, Socrates
offered to redeem the jury. At one point, he considered that since he had given up
opportunities to make money because he was trying to help others, he should perhaps be given free meals for the rest of his life. Ultimately, he made only a modest,
inadequate concession to the jury by offering to let his friends pay a fine for him.
His conviction did not upset him, for a divine sign had led him throughout:

> O my judges—for you I may truly call judges—I should like to tell you of a
> wonderful circumstance. Hitherto the divine faculty of which the internal
> oracle is the source has constantly been in the habit of opposing me even about
> trifles, if I was going to make a slip or error in any matter; and now you see
> there has come upon me that which may be thought, and is generally believed
> to be, the last and worst evil. But the oracle made no sign of opposition, either
> when I was leaving my house in the morning, or I was on my way to the court,
> or while I was speaking, at anything which I was going to say; and yet I have
> often been stopped in the middle of a speech. . . . What do I take to be the
> explanation of this silence? I will tell you. It is an intimation that what has hap-
> pened to me is good, and that those of us who think that death is an evil are in
> error. For the customary sign would surely have opposed me had I been going
> to evil and not to good.[26]

Though we cannot know the exact nature of Socrates' "divine sign," we know
that he took it seriously. One result was that Socrates himself always had a clear
sense of purpose, a vocation. At his trial he said, "My service to the god has
brought me into great poverty." For Socrates real beauty was beauty of soul, real
riches were riches of soul. Socrates was poor only by conventional standards. By
his own sense of things, his service to the god brought real riches, rather than
apparent ones.

If you think that by killing men you can prevent someone from censuring your evil lives, you are mistaken; that is not a way of escape which is either possible or honorable; the easiest and the noblest way is not to be disabling others, but to be improving yourselves. This is the prophecy which I utter before my departure to the judges who have condemned me.

SOCRATES

PHILOSOPHICAL

QUERY

• • • • • •

Some people argue that Socrates committed suicide by provoking the jury. By insisting that he was right and by refusing to show fear or at least some repentance, he drove the jury members to execute him. He knew they would get carried away, and yet he insulted them. So it is his own fault that he was executed. What do you think? Is there a defense for Socrates' actions? Who is responsible?

*D*emocracy is the best form of government. Can there be any doubt? One of the great traditions of American history has been that "any boy can grow up to be president." And certainly our history suggests a continuous (if sometimes painfully slow) movement toward extending greater and greater choices and opportunities to all our citizens. Now it's no longer "any *boy* can grow up to be president," but "any *child*." Barriers of skin color, creed, and social class are being removed. The only limits on our dreams are our own. And someday these barriers may disappear as we learn new ways to abolish disadvantages of birth or social status.

As citizens of a democracy, we are free to seek any position we wish in society. The presidency itself has only three requirements: citizenship, age, and a majority of Electoral College votes. If in practice our presidents come from the wealthier, more educated classes, they still do not need to meet any stringent requirements of self-discipline, character, or wisdom. Nor do we who elect them. This is the glory of democracy.

Picture now a November morning. A line of voters waits to elect the next president of the United States. You have spent weeks studying the televised debates (you've even read the written transcripts). You've subscribed to liberal and conservative magazines and newspapers in order to get as complete a picture of the candidates' records and the issues as you can. You've read those long political editorials in the newspaper, as well as your voter's pamphlet. Because there are a number of lesser offices, bond issues, and legislative amendments on the ballot, you've brought a written list of your carefully reasoned decisions with you to the polls.

Patiently waiting your turn, you overhear a small group of people standing in line behind you. A woman announces, "I'm voting for X. She's a woman, and that's good enough for me." Someone else says, "My dad always voted Republican, so I'm voting Democrat!" A third person chimes in, "I'm not voting for Y. He's a jerk." Someone asks about "all those propositions and stuff," and the group laughs. "Who cares?" someone else snaps. "None of that stuff makes any difference." "Yeah," another responds, "there are too many to keep straight anyway. I just vote yes, no, yes, at random." Yet another says, "As a single parent, I'm only interested in Prop. M, since I need money for child care. I'll just guess at the rest."

Disturbed by this, you suddenly notice that the man in front of you is weaving. You ask if he's sick, and he laughingly answers, with the unmistakable smell of beer on his breath: "Heck, no. I'm loaded. It's the only way to vote." You vote anyway, but can't shake your anger for a long time. It doesn't seem fair that these irresponsible votes should equal your carefully researched and reasoned decisions. They might even cancel your vote out. It's worse than unfair. It's dumb. It's not *reasonable*, you think. There should be *some* requirement for voting. Not anything unfair or discriminatory, just *reasonable*. And come to think of it, there should be some kind of test or something for politicians. They're a pretty unethical and dumb lot, too.

If you have ever had thoughts like this, your disgust and annoyance at "the way things are run around here" have probably triggered a desire for a "more

---

Poverty in a democracy is as much preferable to so-called prosperity in an autocracy as freedom is to slavery.

DEMOCRITUS

Democracy . . . is a system where anything, or almost anything, can happen. The worst, but also the best. In it one may encounter all types: the sophist and also the philosopher. That is the unique advantage of this way of life.

ANDRE KOYRÉ

How can any man be a democrat who is sincerely a democrat?

H. L. MENCKEN

ideal" society. As we all know, however, no such ideal society exists in this world, so where did you get the idea for it? It's as if you have seen beyond the way things are, seen a *higher possibility.*

Anyone who has visualized a fairer, more ideal society has already shared at least some ideas with Plato, perhaps the greatest, and certainly one of the most imposing and influential, philosophers in the Western world.

PHILOSOPHICAL

QUERY

● ● ● ● ● ●

As recent voting controversies make clear, Americans have reason to be wary of requirements for voting. In the past, voting requirements have been used to prevent women and people of certain ethnic groups from voting. On the other hand, a case might be made that by not having some minimal standard of preparedness and awareness, we make a mockery of "choosing." How can an ignorant voter "choose" anything? Does "choosing" matter? Discuss from both sides.

■ PLATO'S LIFE AND WORK ■

Our chief source of information regarding Plato's philosophy is Plato himself. We still have all the works attributed to him by ancient scholars. The most important of these are philosophical dialogues. We have already seen material from some of these in Chapters 3 and 4: the *Apology, Crito, Phaedo, Theaetetus, Timaeus, Gorgias, Protagoras, Meno,* and the *Republic.* We also have the summaries and analyses of some of Plato's doctrines left by his greatest student, Aristotle. We probably have more biographical information about Plato than about any other ancient philosopher, much of it from Diogenes Läertius's *Life of Plato.* There is also a controversial collection of thirteen letters and some dialogues whose authenticity some scholars dispute. One of these, *Letter: VII,* is of special interest because of its comments regarding the mature Plato's attitudes toward democracy in view of the way Socrates was treated by it.

Probably no single work of Western philosophy has been read by as many people as Plato's *Republic.* It is considered by most philosophers to be Plato's most impressive and important work because it presents his overall philosophy in a dramatic, organized, and brilliant form. We'll use the *Republic* as the basis for our introduction to this would-be philosopher-king, but first let us start with a brief sketch of Plato's life.

The Decline of the Aristocracy

Plato (c. 427–348 B.C.E.) is actually the nickname of Aristocles, the son of one of the oldest and most elite Athenian families. Through his mother's family he was related to a celebrated lawgiver named Solon. Plato's father's family traced its lineage to the ancient kings of Athens and even further back to Poseidon, the god of the sea. His given name, Aristocles, meant "best, most renowned." He is said to have done well at practically everything as a young man: music, logic, debate,

Plato

Perictione: Plato's Philosopher-Mother

In *On the Harmony of Women,* **Perictione** (c. 450–350 B.C.E.) calls women to philosophy in terms reminiscent of Socrates (Chapter 4), Epicurus, and Epictetus (Chapter 7). Perictione is believed to have been Plato's mother, and we hear in her work echoes of Socrates' disdain for vanity, his ideal of self-control, and his affirmation of the superiority of inner or essential beauty over mere physical attractiveness. We must wonder about the influence Perictione had on her son, as well as about the influence other forgotten and overlooked women philosophers may have had on their more famous peers. In the passage quoted here, Perictione argues that wisdom and self-control in an individual woman generate other virtues, which in turn lead to harmony and happiness for the entire community:

> One must deem the harmonious woman to be full of wisdom and self-control; a soul must be exceedingly conscious of goodness to be just and courageous and wise, embellished with self-sufficiency and hating empty opinion. Worthwhile things come to a woman from these—for herself, her husband, her children, her household, perhaps even for a city. . . .
>
> But one must also train the body to natural measures concerning nourishment and clothing, baths and anointings, the arrangement of the hair, and ornaments of gold and precious stone. Women who eat and drink every costly thing, who dress extravagantly and wear the things that women wear, are ready for the sin of every vice both with respect to the marriage bed and the rest of wrongdoing. It is necessary merely to appease hunger and thirst, even if this be done by frugal means; in the case of cold, even a goat-skin or rough garment would suffice. . . . So the harmonious woman will not wrap herself in gold or precious stone from India or anywhere else, nor will she braid her hair with artful skills or anoint herself with infusions of Arabian scent, nor will she paint her face, whitening or rouging it, darkening her eye-brows and lashes and treating her gray hair with dye; nor will she be forever bathing. The woman who seeks these things seeks an admirer for feminine weakness. It is the beauty that comes from wisdom, not from these, that gratifies women who are well-born. . . .
>
> But I think a woman is harmonious in the following way: if she becomes full of wisdom and self-control. For this benefits not only her husband, but also the children, relatives, slaves; the whole house, including possessions and friends, both fellow-citizens and foreign guest friends. Artlessly, she will keep their house, speaking and hearing fair things, and obeying her husband in the unanimity of their common life, attending upon the relatives and friends whom he extols, and thinking the same things sweet and bitter as he—lest she be out of tune in relation to the whole.

Holger Thesleff, "Pythagorean Texts of the Hellenistic Period," *Acta Academiae Aboensis, Humaniora,* trans. Vicki Lynn Harper, in *A History of Women Philosophers,* vol. 1, 600 B.C.–500 A.D., ed. Mary Ellen Waithe (Dordrecht: Martinus Nijhoff Publishers, 1987), pp. 20–21.

math, poetry. He was attractive and made his mark as a wrestler. In the military he distinguished himself in three battles and even won a prize for bravery.[1] The Greek root of Plato is *Platon,* which means "broad" or "wide"; one story is that he had wide shoulders, another that he had a wide forehead.

Plato was born two years after the death of Pericles, the great architect of Athenian democracy. Athens was fighting Sparta in the Peloponnesian Wars, which lasted more than twenty years. During that time Athens was in a state of turmoil (not unlike America now and during the Vietnam War). Great energy and expense were drained off by the war itself, as well as by disagreements over whether Athens should continue to fight and, if so, how. As we learned in Chapter 4, Athens finally surrendered to Sparta in 404 B.C.E.

Concerning the essentials I have written no book nor shall I write one.

PLATO, *LETTER: VII*

The conquering Spartans supported a group of nobles, known as the Thirty, who overthrew the democracy and ruled Athens for a short time. Plato's family were members of this group. This is the same Thirty that Socrates resisted when he was ordered to condemn and execute Leon of Salamis in violation of the Athenian constitution.

Members of the Thirty failed in their efforts to restore rule by an elite based on bloodlines, rather than on character or wisdom. Their reign lasted only about eight months before democracy was restored. It was the restored democracy, however, that tried and condemned Socrates. The impact of these events never left Plato, who was in his early twenties at the time. Looking back on this time, Plato recalled:

> Of course I saw in a short time that [the Thirty] made the former government look in comparison like an age of gold. Among other things they sent an elderly man, Socrates, a friend of mine, who I should hardly be ashamed to say was the justest man of his time . . . against one of the citizens. . . . Their purpose was to connect Socrates to their government whether he wished or not. . . . When I observed all this—and some other similar matters of importance—I withdrew in disgust from the abuses of those days.[2]

The nobles who formed the Thirty had no doubt been disturbed by changes in Athenian society brought about by the long war: the loss of elitist privileges that accompanied increased democracy, the breakdown of tradition, the Sophists' use of debaters' tricks to sway the mob. In a democracy, the cleverest, most persuasive, and most attractive speakers could control the state. Also, the emerging business class had created a power base dependent on money and aggressiveness rather than on tradition and social status.[3]

Plato's Disillusionment

Plato become increasingly discouraged by both the "mob" and the "elite." The mob, represented by the jury at Socrates' trial, was irrational and dangerous; it was swayed by sophistic appeals to emotion, not by reason. Rule by the elite, represented by the behavior of the Thirty, was cruel, self-centered, and greedy. When Plato saw that neither the aristocracy nor the common citizenry was capable of superior rule, his "disillusionment [was] fearful and wonderful to behold."[4]

Plato concluded that most people are unfit by training and ability to make the difficult and necessary decisions that would result in a just society. The "average person" lacks wisdom and self-restraint. As Plato saw things, most people make emotional responses based on desire and sentiment, rather than on rational considerations stemming from an objective view of what is genuinely good for the individual and society. What, he wondered, could be clearer proof of the mob's deficiencies than its utter failure to recognize the truth of Socrates' message? The trial and death of Socrates showed Plato what happens when justice is detached from wisdom and self-restraint and reduced to a majority vote.

> Now as I considered these matters, as well as the sort of men who were active in politics, and the laws and the customs, the more I examined them and the more I advanced in years, the harder it appeared to me to administer the government correctly. . . . The result was that I, who had at first been full of

Plato's genius is exhibited in the fact that he succeeded in eliciting from his observations of the Athenian state reflections on society and government that are true everywhere.

RAPHAEL DEMOS

Do you think I would have survived all these years if I were engaged in public affairs and, acting as good man must, came to the help of justice and considered this the most important thing? Far from it . . . nor would any other man.

SOCRATES

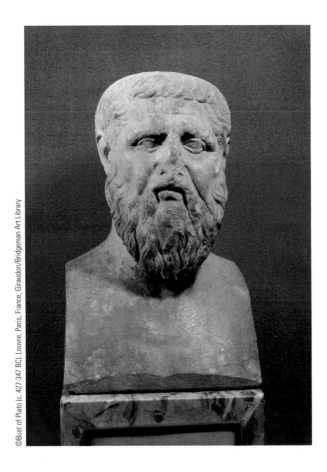

©Bust of Plato (c. 427-347 BC), Louvre, Paris, France, Giraudon/Bridgeman Art Library

This ancient bust of Plato represents one artist's conception of the philosopher.

eagerness for a public career, as I gazed upon the whirlpool of public life and saw the incessant movement of shifting currents, at last felt dizzy, and . . . *finally saw clearly in regard to all states now existing that without exception their system of government is bad.*[5] [emphasis added]

Plato would see to it that Socrates would be avenged—but by philosophy rather than by political action.

After the revolt of the Thirty and the execution of Socrates, Plato left Athens and wandered for nearly twelve years. He studied with Euclid (the great pioneer of geometry) and possibly with the hedonist Aristippus. He seems also to have gone to Egypt. During his travels he studied mathematics and mysticism, both of which influenced his later philosophy. He studied Pythagorean philosophy and was deeply influenced by its emphasis on mathematics as the basis of all things (see box "The Celestial Music of the Spheres," page 65).

The Academy

Plato was around forty years old when he founded his Academy (around 388 B.C.E.). Because, in Plato's view, "no present government [was] suitable for philosophy," the Academy was established as a philosophic retreat, isolated from the turmoil of Athenian politics, safe from the fate of Socrates. Its chief purpose was probably to educate people who would be fit to rule the just state. Plato's ideal educational program was a progressive one in which the study of mathematics, geometry, music, and so forth introduced discipline into the student's overall character and order into the student's mind. Only after the mind and soul were disciplined were a select few allowed to study ultimate philosophical principles.

Ironically, considering the importance of the Academy and the influence it was to exert, we have no solid evidence concerning when it was founded, how it was organized, what exactly was studied, or what educational techniques were used. Most of Plato's writing seems to have been finished before he founded the Academy, with the exception of a few works completed when he was an old man. His chief function at the Academy was probably as a teacher and administrator. Here Plato lived for forty years, lecturing "without notes," until he died.[6]

◼ PLATO'S EPISTEMOLOGY ◼

Socrates' death, the revolt of the Thirty, sophistic abuses, and other factors convinced Plato that a corrupt state produces corrupt citizens. He thus attempted to develop a theory of knowledge that could refute sophistic skepticism and moral relativism. Plato believed that if he could identify and articulate the difference between mere opinion and genuine knowledge, it would then be possible to identify the structure of an ideal state based on knowledge and truth—rather than the mere appearance of truth and personal whim.

Plato correctly understood that before he could provide satisfactory answers to ethical, social, political, and other philosophical questions, he must first tackle the problem of knowledge. We have seen how the conflicting opinions of the Presocratics first led to philosophical confusion and then to ethical and political abuses in the hands of the most extreme of the Sophists. Socrates' heroic effort to refute ignorance and relativism was most successful in its exposure of error and inconsistency. It was less successful in establishing any positive knowledge.

Consequently, Plato could not avoid the challenge of sophistic skepticism or ignore philosophy's reputation for generating ludicrous doctrines that contradicted each other—and themselves. Though the Presocratics, the Sophists, and Socrates had all made use of the distinction between appearance and reality, the exact nature of reality and clear rational criteria for distinguishing reality from appearance had eluded them.

Plato's Dualistic Solution

Plato concluded that the solution to the basic problem of knowledge lay in acknowledging that both Heraclitus and Parmenides were partially correct in their efforts to characterize reality (Chapter 3). Heraclitus asserted that the "one" is some kind of orderly cycle or process of change. He said that "change alone is unchanging." Parmenides, in contrast, referred to the "one" as *being*. Parmenides argued that *being* is perfect and complete or whole. It cannot move or change. Parmenidean *being* is material; "it is the *being* of the visible cosmos, immobilized, and to a great extent purified, but still clearly recognizable."

According to Plato, Heraclitus and Parmenides probably thought they were discussing things that could be sensed or perceived as part of the physical world. (We will refer to such things as "sensibles," for short.) The Sophists' skeptical arguments were also aimed at contradictions and difficulties generated by problems of sensation and perception. (See Chapter 3.)

Suppose, Plato wondered, that reality is not a single thing (a monism) but is rather a dualism. One reality might be Heraclitean and another Parmenidean; one reality in constant change and the other eternally changeless:

> After an initial critical period during which, with Socrates as spokesperson, Plato called into question his contemporaries' opinions and values, he adopted a more dogmatic approach, staking out a certain number of positions in the fields of ethics, epistemology, and ontology. In all these domains, one idea was stressed above all others: that of transcendence, implying on the one hand the division of reality into two realms—the sensible, the realm of individuals that is continually changing, and the intelligible, the realm of the absolutely immutable—and on the other hand the distinction, within each human being, between a mortal body endowed with five senses and an immortal soul that can grasp the intelligible.[7]

Of course a supposition is not evidence. Plato needed to prove the dual nature of reality. Part of the proof seemed easy enough: It is obvious that a world of "sensibles" exists. And the sensible world certainly seems to be one of change: growth cycles, soil erosion, flowing rivers, the wear and tear of the implements of daily living, and so on. Further, this change is orderly: The same seasons follow the same seasons, dogs do not give birth to stones, objects fall down not up, and so forth. So, as far as the world of sensibles is concerned, Heraclitus seems to be correct.

But a completely Heraclitean world of observable change, for all its obviousness, would be a world devoid of the possibility of knowledge and certainty, according to Plato. Such a world would be a world of appearances only, a realm of opinion, not knowledge. Plato called this condition the world of *becoming.*

■ KNOWLEDGE AND BEING ■

Attempts to explain how one kind of thing changes into another generated ambiguities and seeming contradictions: How could "one thing" somehow change into something else? In what sense can my twelve-year-old dog Daiquiri be the "same" dog she was five years ago? Does this mean that Daiquiri is both the same dog she was *and* a different dog? In what sense does the same person change from an infant into a philosophy student?

Plato recognized the full importance of the questions raised by the Presocratics concerning coherent explanations of how things change, how reality "becomes" appearance, how appearances are related to reality, and other fundamental issues. The relation between appearance and reality, the problem of "the one and the many," and the nature of change needed to be clarified before any refutation to the sophistic assault on rationality was possible.

According to Plato, the Sophists could not discover truth because they were only concerned with the Heraclitean world of sensibles, the world of ever-changing perceptions and customs. But the very essence of knowledge is unchanging. What is true is always true. Therefore, whatever is relative and *always changing* cannot be true. Truth and knowledge are found in another realm of reality: the level of *being* that Parmenides tried to characterize.

Plato . . . knew that our reason, if left to itself, tries to soar up to knowledge to which no object that experience may give can ever correspond; but which is nonetheless real, and by no means a cobweb of the brain.

IMMANUEL KANT

Plato believed that this second reality, although closely related to the world of *becoming,* exists independently of it. This other reality has many of the qualities Parmenides ascribed to the one (*being*): It is not physical, and it is not affected by space and time. According to Plato, what is eternal is *real;* what changes is only *appearance.* We can have *knowledge* of what is eternal (*being*); of appearances (*becoming*), there can be only *opinions.* Plato insisted that whatever is permanent is superior to whatever is not. Therefore, reality is superior to appearance, and knowledge (reality) is superior to opinion (appearance).

■ THE THEORY OF FORMS ■

In Plato's metaphysics, the level of *being* consists of timeless essences or entities called *Forms.* Such a metaphysics is sometimes called transcendental because it asserts that there is a plane of existence "above and beyond" our ordinary existence. To transcend anything is to go so far beyond it as to reach a qualitatively different level.

The **Platonic Forms** are independently existing, nonspatial, nontemporal "somethings" ("kinds," "types," or "sorts") that cannot be known through the senses. Known in thought, these Forms are not ideas in the usual sense. Knowledge is always about Forms.

It may be helpful to think about other meanings of the word *form.* "Form" sometimes refers to the shape, manner, style, or type of something. We make forms from which to mold dishes or statues, for example. We fill in business forms. The very notion of form implies something that provides general or essential order, structure, or shape for a particular instance. Thus, the form of something is sometimes called its structure or essence, or even its basic nature. Many of these everyday meanings involve the essence of a thing, the quality that makes it what it is. In Platonic terms, a thing's Form is what it uniquely and essentially is.

However, *exactly what Plato meant* by "Forms" has remained a subject of intense philosophical debate and disagreement from Plato's time to ours. For the last fifty years, the theory of Forms has probably been the most discussed part of Plato's philosophy among English-speaking philosophers. And, still, philosophers cannot agree on exactly what Plato meant. The complexity of the problem is further compounded by the fact that although Plato places great importance on the Forms, he does not seem to have a very well worked out theory of Forms.[8]

Nevertheless, because Plato's theory of Forms is central to the rest of his philosophy, and thus the basis for his theory of the ideal state, we need to take the time to develop a general sense of what Plato hoped to show with his theory of Forms, always keeping in mind that philosophers are still arguing over precisely what Plato meant.

What Are Forms?

The Greek root for "form" (*eidos*) is sometimes translated as "idea." Thus it is tempting to think of Forms as mental entities (ideas) that exist only in our minds. But Plato insists that the Forms are independent of any minds (real).[9] To avoid this confusion, some philosophers translate *eidos* as "archetype" or "essence."

According to Plato, each Form actually exists—pure and unchanging—regardless of continuous shifts in human opinions and alterations in the physical

Platonic Forms

Independently existing, nonspatial, nontemporal "somethings" ("kinds," "types," or "sorts") known only through thought and that cannot be known through the senses; independently existing objects of thought; that which makes a particular thing uniquely and essentially what it is.

world of sensibles. Each Form is a pure, unmixed essence that exists independently of human consciousness. It is important to be very clear about this: Although the Forms actually exist, they are not physical objects.

Forms are universal types or kinds that somehow exist outside of space and time. The physical world contains particular *instances* of the various universal Forms. Today we might call Forms abstract objects. Plato considers such abstract objects more real than concrete physical objects.

The sorts of things Plato refers to as Forms include geometrical, mathematical, and logical relations (triangularity, equivalence, identity); virtues (goodness, wisdom, courage); and sensible properties (roundness, beauty, redness). Note that the physical sensations we associate with such qualities as roundness and redness are not the same thing as *roundness* and *redness* in and of themselves.

Particular things differ in terms of what Plato variously refers to as their "participation in," "sharing in," "resembling," or "reflecting" the Form *roundness* or the Form *redness*. There is only one Form of *redness,* for instance, although there can be a virtually infinite number of particular things that "share" some element or degree of *redness,* that "resemble" or "reflect" the essence of pure *redness*. But *redness* (the Form) is always the same regardless of any changes that occur in some particular object. When, for example, a red flower fades to pale pink, its participation in the Form *redness* decreases. There is, however, no decrease in the Form *redness* itself.

What might Plato have meant by saying that particular things "resemble," "share in," "participate in," or "reflect" different Forms? Consider two apparently identical glass beads, each "reflecting" *roundness* and *identity*. Yet no sensible object is ever absolutely, truly, perfectly round, because sensible objects always contain "mixtures," "impurities," even "opposites." Under microscopic scrutiny, we would expect to find that the surface of the smoothest, purest glass bead ever discovered was minutely pitted or uneven—microscopically imperfect—yet imperfect nonetheless. At most, it might be "as round as physically possible."

According to Plato, no two beads are, or ever can be, identically round. "Aha!" you may think, "but two glass beads can be identical—especially given today's computerized technologies and sophisticated manufacturing techniques."

Stop and think a little further, though. What would it mean for two physical objects to be genuinely, absolutely, perfectly *identical?* In the strictest sense, "Two things are identical if all the characteristics of one are also possessed by the other and vice versa."[10] Is it possible for two glass beads to be *absolutely identical?* No, because in order to be identical—not just very, very similar—they would have to contain exactly the same silica molecules, atoms, quarks, neutrinos, and in exactly the same place at exactly the same time. Of course, they cannot do so, for if that were the case, there would be only one glass bead. Two very, very similar glass beads must be in two distinct places. By being in two distinct places at precisely the same moment, they are different from each other in respect to location. Thus, they are not—strictly speaking—identical.

Lastly, consider the kinds of reasons Plato might offer to support the claim that Forms exist independently of human consciousness: We have good reasons to believe that round objects existed before any perceivers (animals or people) did. Hence, roundness is not a property that depends on human minds for existence; *roundness* is more than just a human idea. *Roundness* itself—as distinct from any

I had a dream, and I heard in my dream that the primeval letters or elements out of which you and I and all other things are compounded have no reason or explanation; you can only name them, but no predicate can be either affirmed or denied of them . . . if you mean to speak of this or that thing by itself alone.

PLATO

If a man . . . does away with Forms of things and will not admit that every individual thing has its own determinate Form which is always one and the same, he will have nothing on which his mind can rest; and so he will utterly destroy the power of reasoning.

PLATO

particular round thing—is unchanging. It cannot change from being *roundness* to, say, *nearly roundness* or *oblongness* or *rectilinearity*. Following basic laws of rationality, *roundness* is either *roundness* or it is not. And so for all Forms. (For a different view of whether or not objects and properties can exist independently of perceivers, see Chapter 10.)

In general, the truths about mathematical objects exist whether we know those truths or not. Plato thinks the same is true for moral and aesthetic facts.

PHILOSOPHICAL

QUERY

• • • • • •

Reflect on the following objection to the preceding paragraphs: "The glass bead example is only playing with semantics. When we talk about two physical objects being 'identical,' we don't mean literally identical—we mean so similar that human beings are unable to distinguish one object from the other. Obviously we can distinguish different things from each other when they're right next to each other. But if we find no differences when we analyze them one at a time, we are justified in saying that they are identical, 'indistinguishable.' Identical means indistinguishable to human beings; that is, so closely resembling each other that we cannot tell them apart." How might Plato answer this objection?

Why Plato Needed the Forms

Among other things, Plato wanted the theory of Forms to provide a *rational explanation* of how knowledge is possible. The Forms are the foundation of Plato's bold answer to the Sophists' skeptical assault on knowledge and to their relativistic rejection of universal (absolute) truths. Defense of absolute, unchanging truths is difficult under the best of circumstances; it is especially difficult if we wish to move beyond merely heartfelt belief in absolutes. Plato knew that unless he could offer more than *faith* in the existence of absolutes, more than authoritarian and dogmatic pronouncements, he would fail, as a philosopher, to meet the challenge of relativism.

Plato's task here is of more than mere historical interest to us; it bears on important epistemological questions: *Is* everything a matter of opinion? If not: (1) Is there any way to *show* that knowledge is possible? and (2) Is there any way those of us who are not wise or enlightened can identify those who are? That is, if we cannot always grasp the truth, can we at least identify those who can and thereby benefit from their counsel? If the answer to 2 is "no," then we are at the mercy of unverifiable beliefs, rule by force, rhetoric, and seduction. If one opinion is ultimately as good as any other, then one form of government is no better than any other, and there is no point in seeking truth or wisdom. All that matters is surviving as comfortably as possible (in my opinion).

On the other hand, if knowledge is possible, and if some opinions really are better than others, how can we justify democracy, a form of government that treats each citizen's opinion as equal? Put more forcefully: If knowledge exists, what would justify ignoring it? Can there be any reasonable justification for ignoring the difference between knowledge and opinion?

It is hard, too, to see how a weaver or a carpenter will be benefitted in regard to his own craft by knowing this [a form], or how the man who has viewed the Idea itself will be a better doctor or general thereby. For a doctor seems not even to study health in this way, but the health of man, or perhaps rather the health of a particular man; it is individuals that he is healing.

ARISTOTLE

In struggling to develop his theory of Forms, Plato was struggling to *refute*—not just *deny*—relativism and thereby preserve the distinction between knowledge and opinion. Plato reasoned that if he could solidly establish that knowledge is possible, and that knowledge exists, then he could also justify and preserve real (objective) distinctions between right and wrong, true and false, better and worse.

• • • • • •	PHILOSOPHICAL
	QUERY

Is it possible to know that no one does know? Is it possible to know that no one does know that no one does know? Is it possible to know that no one can know that no one does know? How do you know? Or, how do you know that you don't know?

Knowledge and Opinion

For Plato, the chief distinction between knowledge and opinion is that knowledge is fixed, absolutely and eternally true (correct), whereas opinions are changeable and "unanchored." According to Plato, *scientific knowledge of particulars is impossible.* That is, fundamental knowledge of reality must always be knowledge of forms. Thus, a "science" consists of necessary and universal truths about the objects (forms) that the science studies. In all scientific subject areas, the physical objects, structural relationships, particular individuals, societies, or governments studied represent Forms. The particular things themselves are never "as real" as the Forms they participate in or resemble.

Remember, too, that for Plato, that which changes is less real than that which does not. That which changes is "lower" than that which does not. And since all particular things change, when Protagoras said that the individual is "the measure," he was, from Plato's view, talking about the level of *becoming,* about the lower level of perceptions of particular things, about the personal and individual rather than the public and universal.

In Plato's metaphysics, the level of change is the level of growth and decay, life and death—*becoming.* Only in the realm of *becoming* can opinions change from true to false. In the *Timaeus* Plato says:

> That which is apprehended by intelligence and reason is always in the same state, but that which is conceived by opinion with the help of sensation and without reason is always in a process of becoming and perishing and never really is.[11]

What Happens When We Disagree?

Granted that people and conditions change; granted that we disagree among ourselves over what is true and what is real; what happens when we disagree about knowledge?

Suppose, for example, that Michael simply cannot see or understand that 2×3 does not equal 4. In other words, for Michael, $2 \times 3 = 4$. We can say, then, that Michael has a false belief or opinion; we can also say, however, that the product of 2×3 is not a matter of opinion (Michael's or anyone's), but of fixed mathematical properties and relationships. We know this because in order to

The true lover of knowledge naturally strives for truth, and is not content with common opinion, but soars with undimmed and unwearied passion till he grasps the essential nature of things.

PLATO

To what purpose is it for philosophy to decide against common sense in this or any other matter? The material world is older, and of more authority, than any principles of philosophy. It declines the tribunal of reason, and laughs at the artillery of the logician.

THOMAS REID

understand concepts such as number, three, two, product, equivalence, and such, we have to "glimpse" their Forms. This glimpse of recognition is what understanding the concept is.

Next, consider the case of Michael's aunt, Patricia. Asked the product of 2×3, Patricia proudly says, "I know the answer. It's six!" Asked how she knows, Patricia explains, "Because mother told me so. And because my mother's mother told her." Michael's friend, Emma, also confidently agrees that $2 \times 3 = 6$. When we ask her to explain why, Emma says, "Teacher told me so."

Emma does not *know* that $2 \times 3 = 6$ any more than Michael "knows" that $2 \times 3 = 4$ or Patricia "knows" that $2 \times 3 = 6$. Unlike Michael's belief, Patricia's and Emma's beliefs are true. But they are still just *beliefs* (opinions). Patricia and Emma are lucky this time—their beliefs are "unanchored," however.

Lacking knowledge, Michael, Patricia, and Emma have no way to *determine* who is right or wrong. If they vote, they might end up with the correct answer—but only by chance. What they cannot do is willingly choose the correct answer, because they lack sufficient understanding to make an informed determination: They don't *know* what it is.

Without knowledge, we are like Michael, Patricia, and Emma: We, too, are at the mercy of luck and uninformed preference. We are "unanchored" and so can only act based on habit, tradition, personal preference, and impulse.

Throughout the *Republic* Plato repeatedly distinguishes between knowledge and opinion, warning against even true opinions that lack grounding in knowledge. Here's a typical passage:

> "But I don't think it's right, Socrates . . . for you to be able to tell us other people's opinions but not your own, when you've given so much time to the subject."
>
> "Yes, but do you think it's right for a man to talk as if he knows what he does not?"
>
> "He has no right to talk as if he knew; but he should be prepared to say what his opinion is, so far as it goes."
>
> "Well," I [Socrates] said, "haven't you noticed that opinion without knowledge is blind—isn't anyone with a true but unthinking opinion like a blind man on the right road?"
>
> "Yes."[12]

According to Plato, the Sophists failed to understand this, confusing opinion with knowledge, perception with understanding, and the realm of *becoming* with the realm of *being*. Plato's task, then, is analogous to "proving" the existence of colors to persons born blind.

When an appeal to direct experience or common understanding is not possible, an indirect approach may prove effective. If we have yet to grasp the Forms, perhaps we can get some indirect idea of them. In the *Republic,* Plato uses three different comparisons to help express various aspects of the theory of Forms: the Divided Line, the Simile of the Sun, and the Allegory of the Cave. We will study each of them. Each comparision clarifies different but interconnected aspects of the theory of Forms. Do not worry if you need to take extra time with this material. Allow each of Plato's similes to help you better grasp the whole.

▪ THE DIVIDED LINE ▪

Plato used the concept of a divided line to illustrate the relationship of knowledge to opinion, reality to appearance, metaphysics to epistemology, and the world of *being* to the world of *becoming*. The Divided Line shows that both knowledge and opinion deal with Forms, though in different ways.

The Divided Line consists of two basic sections, each unevenly divided into two segments. The four segments illustrate four ways of apprehending four components of reality; two each of being and becoming. Figure 5.1 is a representation of the Divided Line that you can refer to as you read Plato's presentation of it. Note how the four metaphysical levels of reality correspond to four epistemological ways of apprehending the Forms.

For as all nature is akin, and the soul has [already] learned all things, there is no difficulty in . . . learning . . . all the rest, if a man is strenuous and does not faint; for all enquiry is but recollection.

PLATO

METAPHYSICS	EPISTEMOLOGY		
Higher forms Example: The Good	**A** Understanding		INTELLIGIBLE WORLD
Lower forms Example: Form Human	**B** Reasoning	KNOWLEDGE	
Sensible objects Example: Mother Teresa	**C** Perception		VISIBLE WORLD
Images Example: Mother Teresa's photograph	**D** Imagination	OPINION	

Left bracket spans: BEING (Higher forms, Lower forms); BECOMING (Sensible objects, Images).

FIGURE 5.1 PLATO'S DIVIDED LINE

A + B = World of Forms (Being)

C + D = Physical World (Becoming)

Segments A, B, C, D represent decreasing degrees of truth. Each degree of truth corresponds to a different kind of thinking and different level of reality.

A: This is the level of pure intelligence or understanding. Here the soul directly apprehends truth at its highest level.

B: This is the level of reasoning; specifically, mathematical thinking and deductive reasoning.

C: This is the level of belief or common opinions about physical objects, morals, politics, practical affairs.

D: This is the level of illusion, dominated by secondhand opinions and uncritical impressions.

(This characterization of the lowest level goes beyond what Plato says in this section, but is required considering what he does say in the Allegory of the Cave, and Book X about poetry and art.)

With Figure 5.1 as a guide, let's take a look at what Plato said about the Divided Line. In this passage, Socrates is describing a conversation he had with Plato's older brother, Glaucon:

"Well, take a line divided into two unequal parts, corresponding to the visible and intelligible worlds, and then divide the two parts again in the same ratio, to represent degrees of clarity and obscurity. In the visible world, one section stands for images: by 'images' I mean first shadows, then reflections in water and other close grained, polished surfaces, and all that sort of thing if you understand me."

"I understand."

"Let the other section stand for the objects which are the originals of the images—animals, plants and manufactured objects of all kinds."

"Very good."

"Would you be prepared to admit that these sections differ in their degree of truth, and that the relation of image to the original is the same as that of opinion and knowledge?"

"I would."

"Then consider next how the intelligible part of the line is to be divided. In one section the mind uses the originals of the visible world in their turn as images, and has to base its inquiries on assumptions and proceed from them to its conclusions instead of going back to first principles: in the other it proceeds from assumption back to self-sufficient first principles, making no use of the images employed by the other section, but pursuing its inquiry solely by means of Forms. . . .

". . . it treats assumptions not as principles, but as assumptions in the true sense, that is, as starting points and steps in the ascent to the universal, self-sufficient first principle; when it has reached that principle it can again descend, by keeping to the consequences that follow from it, to a final conclusion. The whole procedure involves nothing in the sensible world, but deals throughout with Forms and finishes with Forms."[13]

Levels of Awareness

The lowest level of awareness, **D** on Figure 5.1, is the level of illusion. Virtually no one inhabits this level all the time, but we can occasionally slip into states of illusion. We slip into **D** on purpose and for fun when we go to magic shows or watch movies (which are really just light, shadows, and sound creating the illusion of depth and action). This is known as the "willing suspension of disbelief." But we can also slip into illusion without being aware of it when we hold opinions based solely on appearances, unanalyzed impressions, uncritically inherited beliefs, and unevaluated emotions. The image—opinion—I have of Mother Teresa is an example of **Level D** awareness. It is based on photographs I have seen, news clips on television, and part of a speech she gave to the United Nations that I watched on the C-SPAN cable network.

Level C on Figure 5.1 represents the second or informed level of awareness. It involves a wider range of opinions about what most of us probably think of as reality. At this level of informed awareness, we attempt to distinguish appearance from reality, but in a kind of everyday way. For example, I believe that my desk looks solid but it is actually made up of countless molecules and atoms in motion.

Human insight requires a turning around. . . . But when it is a question of thinking in earnest, when an . . . eternal truth . . . makes a claim on independent thinking, then there is something in man that rebels against the rigors of responsible self-clarification. He does not want to wake up but go on sleeping.

KARL JASPERS

I believe that the sun looks small because of its distance from earth, but in fact, it is much larger.

Strictly speaking, I do not *know* these things. I have had some science classes, and looked through microscopes and telescopes, but I do not have a scientist's sophisticated knowledge built upon rigorous deductive reasoning. At the same time, my **Level C** opinions are based on observations and perceptions of physical objects, not just on photos or representations of them. On this informed level we realize that the way things appear may not be the way they are. Most of us spend much of our lives dealing with more or less informed opinions about most things. If I had known Mother Teresa, my **Level D** image of her would have been a **Level C** informed opinion.

The next level of awareness (**B**) takes us out of the realms of becoming and opinion (**D/C**) and into the world of being and the first stage of knowledge acquired through deductive reasoning. As we've learned, Plato believed truth is changeless, eternal, and absolute and that knowledge doesn't grow or decay but just *is*. Mother Teresa the individual did grow and change, however, so **Level B** knowledge must be of a form, say the Form Human. The Form Human does not change—grow or decay—according to Plato.

At the highest level of reality (**A**), the soul has no need for perception or interpretation. Plato says that it "directly apprehends" the "absolute Form of the Good." At the highest level, reason does not—indeed it cannot—deduce the Forms. The higher Forms are directly understood, apprehended—"glimpsed"—without any mediating process or principles.

■ THE SIMILE OF THE SUN ■

Plato compared the "absolute Form of the Good" to the sun: Just as the sun (light) is necessary for vision and life, so, too, the Good makes Reality, Truth, and the existence of everything else possible. The Good exists beyond becoming at the highest reaches of being. The Good cannot be observed with the five senses and can be known only by pure thought or intelligence. The Good is the source of both the value and the existence of all other Forms. The Good is the Form of the Forms.

Comprehension of the Good is unlike other forms of knowing. It is holistic, not partial. The soul must deliberately work its way up from the lowest level of becoming to enlightenment. Experience of the Good so far transcends all other experiences that it cannot be clearly described, so Plato uses a comparison or simile to allude to the Good. We can represent Plato's comparison of the Good to the sun as shown in Figure 5.2.

VISIBLE WORLD (C + D)	INTELLIGIBLE WORLD (A + B)
The Sun	The Good
Growth	Reality
Light	Truth
Visibility	Intelligibility

FIGURE 5.2

The hierarchy of being and knowledge is reflected in Plato's simile of the sun.
A = pure understanding
B = deductive thinking
C = common opinion
D = uncritical impressions

In the following passage from the *Republic,* Plato (in the character of Socrates) compares the Good to the sun and apprehension of the Good to seeing. Note how strongly he expresses his ultimate regard for the Good:

"Well, [the sun] is the child of the Good. . . . The Good has begotten its own likeness, and it bears the same relation to sight and visibility in the visible world that the Good bears to intelligence in the intelligible world."

"Will you explain that a bit further?"

"You know that when we turn our eyes to objects whose colours are no longer illuminated by daylight, but only by moonlight or starlight, they see dimly and appear to be almost blind, as if they had no clear vision."

"Yes."

"But when we turn them on things on which the sun is shining, then they see clearly and their power of vision is restored."

"Certainly."

"Apply the analogy to the mind. When the mind's eye rests on objects illuminated by truth and reality, it understands and comprehends them, and functions intelligently; but when it turns to the twilight world of change and decay, it can only form opinions, its vision is confused and its beliefs shifting, and it seems to lack intelligence."

"That is true."

"Then what gives the objects of knowledge their truth and the mind the power of knowing is the Form of the Good. It is the cause of knowledge and truth, and you will be right to think of it as being itself known, and yet as being something other than, and even higher than, knowledge and truth. And just as it was right to think of light and sight as being like the sun, but wrong to think of them as being the sun itself, so here again it is right to think of knowledge and truth as being *like* the Good, but wrong to think of either of them as being the Good, which must be given still a higher place of honor."

"You are making it something remarkably exalted, if it is the source of knowledge and truth, and yet itself higher than they are. For I suppose you can't mean it to be pleasure?"

"A monstrous suggestion," I replied. "Let us pursue our analogy further. . . . The sun, I think you will agree, not only makes the things we see visible, but causes the process of generation, growth and nourishment, without itself being such a process. . . . The Good therefore may be said to be the source not only of the intelligibility of the objects of knowledge, but also of their existence and reality; yet it is not itself identical with reality, but is beyond reality, and is superior to it in dignity and power."[14]

Toward the end of the discussion of the Good, Glaucon remarks that the process of escaping from shadows to enlightenment "sounds like a long job." Plato-Socrates agrees, adding:

And you may assume that there are, corresponding to the four sections of the line, four states of mind: to the top section [**A**] Intelligence, to the second [**B**] Reason, to the third [**C**] Opinion, and to the fourth [**D**] Illusion. And you may arrange them in a scale, and assume that they have degrees of clarity corresponding to the degree of truth and reality possessed by their subject-matter.[15]

Just as people born blind have different meanings for color words than those who have seen colors, those on one level of reality cannot recognize what is being said by those on a higher level. They have no comparable experience. Those who reach the level of comprehending the Good are forever transformed; they are enlightened—they are wise. And the relationship between the enlightened and the unenlightened is at the heart of Plato's whole philosophy.

• • • • • •

Compare Plato's use of similes to show that there are levels of knowledge with John Stuart Mill's more "ordinary" argument regarding levels of knowledge in judgments of quality (Chapter 12). Which approach seems most compelling, if either does? Assess.

PHILOSOPHICAL

QUERY

▨ THE ALLEGORY OF THE CAVE ▨

One problem common to any hierarchical enlightenment philosophy involves the gap between what the wise master knows and the pupil's initial ignorance. Different levels of experience can create communication and comprehension gaps.

We see a similar kind of difficulty in interactions between adults and young children. Most of us—at least as we mature—have no difficulty with the concept of degrees of awareness and knowledge between adults and children. We even accept the fact that there are levels of knowledge and experience dividing adults with some form of mental impairment or limit and those of average or better mental capacities.

But what about differences between average and so-called wise or enlightened people? Do such differences really exist? If they do, are they indicators of different levels of what Plato refers to as "intelligence" or "wisdom," or are they just unprovable claims made by people who think they know more than the rest of us? What reasons do we have for believing Plato's claims about levels of being and the Good? Why should we discount the views and experiences of the vast majority of people and listen to the claims of one supposedly wiser person?

Plato responded to this important challenge by telling a story with a lesson—an allegory—in Book VII of the *Republic*. This allegory is offered not as a conclusive proof, but as a suggestive possibility. It is the summation of the exposition of Plato's theory of Forms that includes the Divided Line and the Simile of the Sun.

The Divided Line expresses Plato's hierarchical view of reality and wisdom. The Simile of the Sun characterizes the act of apprehending highest truth in the form of the Good. In the Allegory of the Cave, Plato compares the level of becoming to living in a cave and describes the ordeal necessary for the soul's ascent from shadowy illusion to enlightenment—from mere opinion to informed opinion to rationally based knowledge to wisdom. The allegory also alludes to the obligation of the enlightened wise person (say, Socrates) to return to the world of becoming in order to help others discern the Forms.

The parable [of the Cave] is unforgettable. It is a miracle of philosophical invention, providing an approach to thoughts that do not lend themselves to direct statement.

KARL JASPERS

The levels of awareness identified in the Allegory of the Cave correspond to the segments of the Divided Line referred to on page 133 in Figure 5.1: Those chained to the wall of shadows are imprisoned in the shadowy world of imagination and illusion (**D**); those loose within the cave occupy the "common sense" world of perception and informed opinion (**C**); those struggling through the passageway to the surface are acquiring knowledge through reason (**B**); the rich surface world of warmth and sunlight is the highest level of reality, directly grasped by pure intelligence (**A**).

Plato presents the allegory as part of Socrates' continuing conversation with Glaucon:

Learning without thought brings ensnarement. Thought without learning totters.

CONFUCIUS

"I want you to go on to picture the enlightenment or ignorance of our human conditions somewhat as follows. Imagine an underground chamber, like a cave with an entrance open to the daylight and running a long way underground. In this chamber are men who have been prisoners there since they were children, their legs and necks being so fastened that they can only look straight ahead of them and cannot turn their heads. Behind them and above them a fire is burning, and between the fire and the prisoners runs a road, in front of which a curtain-wall has been built, like the screen at puppet shows between the operators and their audience, above which they show their puppets."

"I see."

"Imagine further that there are men carrying all sorts of gear along behind the curtain-wall, including figures of men and animals made of wood and stone and other materials, and that some of these men, as is natural, are talking and some not."

"An odd picture and an odd sort of prisoner."

"They are drawn from life," I replied. "For, tell me, do you think our prisoners could see anything of themselves or their fellows except the shadows thrown by the fire on the wall of the cave opposite them?"

"How could they see anything else if they were prevented from moving their heads all their lives?" . . .

"Then if they were able to talk to each other, would they not assume that the shadows they saw were real things?"

"Inevitably."

"And if the wall of their prison opposite them reflected sound, don't you think that they would suppose, whenever one of the passers-by on the road spoke, that the voice belonged to the shadow passing before them?"

"They would be bound to think so."

"And so they would believe that the shadows of the objects we mentioned were in all respects real."

"Yes, inevitably."

"Then think what would naturally happen to them if they were released from their bonds and cured of their delusions. Suppose one of them were let loose, and suddenly compelled to stand up and turn his head and look and walk towards the fire; all these actions would be painful and he would be too dazzled to see properly the objects of which he used to see the shadows. So if he was told that what he used to see was merely illusion and that he was now nearer reality and seeing more correctly, because he was turned towards objects that were more real, and if on top of that he were compelled to say what each of the passing objects was when it was pointed out to him, don't you think he would be at a loss, and think that what he used to see was more real than the objects now being pointed out to him?"

"Much more real."

. . . "And if, . . . he were forcibly dragged up the steep and rocky ascent and not let go till he had been dragged out into the sunlight, the process would be a painful one, to which he would much object, and when he emerged into the light his eyes would be so overwhelmed by the brightness of it that he wouldn't be able to see a single one of the things he was now told were real. . . . he would need to grow accustomed to the light before he could see things in the world outside the cave. . . . The thing he would be able to do last would be to look directly at the sun, and observe its nature without using reflections in water or any other medium, but just as it is."

"That must come last."

"Later on he would come to the conclusion that it is the sun that produces the changing seasons and years and controls everything in the visible world, and is in a sense responsible for everything that he and his fellow-prisoners used to see."

"That is the conclusion which he would obviously reach."[16]

- - - - - -

PHILOSOPHICAL

QUERY

The Allegory of the Cave has intrigued students of Plato since it first appeared. Do you think it fairly expresses the way we experience knowledge? For instance, in childhood, everything is black and white, but with experience, we discover rich nuances and hues, as it were. What level are you on? Society in general? The world? Explain. Do you believe in levels of reality? In enlightenment? Why or why not?

■ THE RULE OF THE WISE ■

Plato's fundamental vision is deliberately hierarchical and aristocratic, rather than egalitarian and democratic. His epistemology and metaphysics reflect and encourage this kind of highly discriminating orientation.

Today, any nondemocratic philosophy is likely to be called elitist. If you believe in the fundamental equality of all people, you may be suspicious of Plato's belief in the superiority of those who have supposedly escaped the Cave and seen the Good. If you are skeptical about the possibility of any human being discovering "the truth," you may have difficulty with the idea that only exceptional, enlightened individuals are fit to govern the rest of us. But, then, aren't you dangerously close to believing that you have discovered that no one—including you—can discover the truth? Now what? This nagging suspicion will haunt philosophy for centuries, returning with a vengeance in the twentieth century. See Chapter 17.

Nonetheless, such concerns are well-founded. We are all aware of the abuses committed by Nazis, racist supremacists, and all sorts of "true believers" who are convinced that they alone know the truth and are thus superior to the rest of us.

Out of Plato come all things that are still written and debated among men of thought. Great havoc makes he among our originalities. We have reached the mountain from which all these drift boulders were detached.

RALPH WALDO EMERSON

Plato's aristocracy of wisdom, however, is not based on gender, national origin, and the like, at least in theory. It is built on Plato's conviction that enlightenment is real and that it is more than mere intellectual ability. Platonic enlightenment is the product of careful training, directed desire, hard work—and the good luck to live in an environment that does not prevent us from escaping the Cave.

> "And when he [who escaped the cave] thought of his first home and what passed for wisdom there, and of his fellow-prisoners, don't you think he would congratulate himself on his good fortune and be sorry for them?"
>
> "Very much so." . . .
>
> "And if he had to discriminate between the shadows, in competition with the other prisoners, while still blinded and before his eyes got used to the darkness—a process that might take some time—wouldn't he be likely to make a fool of himself? And they would say that his visit to the upper world had ruined his sight, and that the ascent was not worth even attempting. And if anyone tried to release them and lead them up, they would kill him if they could lay hands on him."
>
> "They certainly would."
>
> "Now, my dear Glaucon," I went on, "this [allegory] must be connected, throughout, with what preceded it [the Divided Line and Simile of the Sun]. The visible realm corresponds to the prison, and the light of the fire in the prison to the power of the sun. And you won't go wrong if you connect the ascent into the upper world and the sight of the objects there with the upward progress of the mind into the intelligible realm—that's my guess, which is what you are anxious to hear. The truth of the matter is, after all, known only to God. But in my opinion, for what it is worth, the final thing to be perceived in the intelligible realm, and perceived only with difficulty, is the absolute form of the Good; once seen, it is inferred to be responsible for everything right and good. . . . And anyone who is going to act rationally either in public or private must perceive it."[17]

Plato wrote the *Republic* to show that the levels of reality correspond to three types of people. The *Republic* is Plato's answer as to what kind of person is qualified to rule the state, based on his theory of reality.

At the beginning of the *Republic,* Socrates and his friend Glaucon have spent the day at a festival and are on their way home when another friend, Polemarchus, stops them. The dialogue begins with good-natured banter among friends.

> "Socrates," said Polemarchus, "I believe you are starting off on your way back to town."
>
> "You are right," I [Socrates] replied.
>
> "Do you see how many of us there are?" he asked.
>
> "I do."
>
> "Well, you will either have to get the better of us or stay here."
>
> "Oh, but there's another alternative," said I. "We might persuade you that you ought to let us go."
>
> "You can't persuade people who won't listen," he replied.[18]

You can't persuade people who won't listen. Plato is no doubt referring in part to the people who executed Socrates. But he may also be giving us a key to the rest of the *Republic.*

The state, if once started well, moves with accumulating force like a wheel. For good nurture and education implant good constitutions [temperaments], and the good constitutions taking root in a good education improve more and more, and this improvement affects the breed in man as in other animals.

PLATO

Socrates believed in the pursuit of wisdom through the dialectical method of question-and-answer. This required participants willing to listen actively and to respond intelligently. But what about people who cannot or will not listen? What about people who are satisfied with life in the Cave? What good is being reasonable in the face of ignorance? Will a mob listen to reason? Will the lazy?

Plato thought not. He came to believe that there were different types of human beings, with different strengths and weaknesses corresponding to each type. Not everyone is capable of participating in rational discourse. Some people lack the intellect. Some lack the will. Some even lack both. Thus it is that a wise and wonderful individual who has escaped from the Cave, like Socrates, can be brought down by his moral and intellectual inferiors who are still in it. In Plato's view, Socrates made a mistake in going to "the people" at all. Socrates himself had even said that in matters of virtue and wisdom, the majority is usually wrong, while only a few are wise.

> Wise men say . . . that heaven and earth, gods and men, are held together by the principles of sharing, by friendship and order, by self-control and justice; that, my friend, is the reason they call the universe "cosmos," and not disorder or licentiousness . . . what a mighty power is exercised, both among men and gods, by geometrical equality.
>
> PLATO

The Search for Justice

Plato argued that a reciprocal relationship exists between the individual and the kind of society he or she lives in. That means a certain kind of society produces a certain kind of individual, and certain kinds of individuals produce certain kinds of societies. In fact, Plato thought the relationship between the two was so close that a clear understanding of the just (ideal) society would yield a clear understanding of the just (healthy) individual. In the *Republic* he refers to society as "the individual writ large." The *Republic* is, consequently, a study of Plato's ideal society and, by extension, a study of types of individuals.

The first book of the *Republic* begins with a discussion of justice. But justice in this context does not mean quite what it does today. Philosophical translator H. D. P. Lee says that the Greek roots of what is usually translated as *justice* cover a cluster of meanings that no single English word does. According to Lee, *justice* in the *Republic* is a broad term covering right conduct or morality in general; the verb from the same root can mean to act "rightly" or "justly."[19] For Plato, justice involved much more than fairness under the law; it went beyond a legalistic limit. Historian of ancient Greece B. A. G. Fuller says that what Plato is interested in is nothing less than "the whole sphere of moral action, both external and internal."[20]

Various limited and specific definitions of justice are offered during the course of the *Republic*. The first one is that justice is paying our debts and telling the truth. During the course of the dialogue a variety of modifications and alternatives are discussed and rejected.

> Besides, this at any rate I know, that if there were to be a treatise or a lecture on the [ideal society], I could do it best.
>
> PLATO

Function and Happiness

The *Republic* contrasts two views of morality. One asserts that right and wrong must be determined by the consequences our acts produce, and the other holds that they can be understood only in terms of their effect on our overall functioning as human beings. The first view is sometimes called an **instrumental theory of morality**. Right and wrong are treated as *means to, or instruments*

instrumental theory of morality
Moral position that right and wrong must be determined by the consequences of acts; right and wrong viewed as means (instruments) for getting something else.

for, getting something else. Be good, get *X.* Be bad, get *Y.* Plato characterizes the instrumental view:

> For fathers tell their sons, and pastors and masters of all kinds urge their charges to be just not because they value justice for itself, but for the social prestige it brings; they want them to secure by a show of justice the power and family connexions and other things which [were] enumerated, all of which are procured by the just man of good reputation.[21]

functionalist theory of morality

Moral position that right and wrong can be understood only in terms of their effect on anything's natural function; each kind of thing has a natural purpose (function).

Plato, by contrast, argues for a **functionalist theory of morality** in which each kind of thing (including human beings) has a "natural purpose or function." Renowned Plato scholar A. E. Taylor says that in the *Republic*, "Happiness depends on conformity to our nature [function] as active beings."[22] In other words, only virtuous people can be happy.

The Greeks viewed happiness as being more than a matter of personal satisfaction. *Happiness was the result of living a fully functioning life.* It involved balance and wholeness. It required being pleased by what is good and being displeased by what is bad. For instance, under such a view, no cigarette smoker can be "happy" regardless of the pleasure derived from smoking. The reason is that no fully functioning, maximally healthy human being will enjoy polluting his or her body. (For a fuller treatment of this view of happiness, see Chapter 6.)

The Philosopher's Republic

The *Republic* reveals Plato's view that a good life can be lived only in a good society because no one can live a truly good life in an irrational, imbalanced society. Nor can one live a truly good life without having some social activities, obligations, and concerns.

Plato said that society originates because no individual is self-sufficient. The just or ideal state meets three basic categories of needs: (1) nourishing needs (food, shelter, clothing); (2) protection needs (military, police); (3) ordering needs (leadership and government). These needs are best met by members of three corresponding classes of people: (1) workers (computer programmer, banker, truck driver); (2) warriors (soldiers, police officers, firefighters); (3) guardians (philosopher-kings).

A state is "just" when it functions fully. An unjust state is dysfunctional; it fails to meet some essential need. Only when all classes of people are virtuous *according to their natures* is the state whole, healthy, balanced, and just. *The good life is nothing more—or less—than each individual functioning well according to his or her own nature, in a state that is well-ordered and wisely ruled.*

Injustice is a form of imbalance for Plato. It occurs whenever a state does not function properly. Some imbalance always results when one part of the state tries to fulfill the function of another part. Justice, happiness, and the good life are interrelated *functional results* of order. Because the essence of a thing determines its proper order, function, and proper care, only those who have seen the Forms and seen the Good know what this essence is for the state or for individuals.

The Parts of the Soul

For Plato, **virtue** is *excellence of function* (which reflects form). We must identify a thing's function before we can fully evaluate it. The healthy, good, or virtuous soul is one in which all parts function harmoniously. The human soul resembles the state in that it too is divided into three parts. The three parts of the soul are *reason, spirit,* and *appetite.*

Plato believed in weakness of will; he disagreed with Socrates' belief that "to know the good is to do the good." According to Plato, we most clearly encounter each part of our souls when we're faced with a difficult choice. Suppose, for example, that you are on a date with someone who wants to go dancing and stay out late. You, on the other hand, have an important test early the next morning. Your *reason* says: "Go home, review your notes, rest. You can go dancing another time, but you cannot make up this important test." Your *appetite* says: "I'd love a pizza. I'd love to party." Your *spirit,* which is concerned with honor, says: "This is awful! I hate it! I don't know what to do. I sort of want to study—but I'd really like to go out. Oh my, oh my!" Most of us are intimately familiar with what can be characterized as parts of ourselves. Plato called them parts of the soul.

In the *Phaedrus,* Plato compares the soul to a chariot being pulled by two horses. One horse needs no touch from the whip, responding instantly to whispers and spoken commands. The other horse is full of "insolence and pride," and "barely yields to whip and spur." The charioteer knows where he wants to go but needs the help of both horses to get there. The driver, of course, corresponds to *reason;* the horse that responds to the merest whisper corresponds to *spirit* (or will), and the bad but powerful horse represents *appetite.*

If the charioteer is unable to control both horses, he will be dragged all over the place by the stronger horse. It is the *function* and therefore the *duty* and the *right* of the charioteer to control the horses. In the *Republic,* Plato says:

> So the reason ought to rule, having the ability and foresight to act for the whole, and the spirit ought to obey and support it. And this concord between them is effected, as we said, by a combination of intellectual and physical training, which tunes up the reason by intellectual training and tones down the crudeness of natural high spirits by harmony and rhythm.[23]

The Cardinal Virtues

Plato identifies four "cardinal virtues" as necessary for a good society and for a happy individual. Cardinal virtues are essential, basic virtues that provide optimal functioning for the human soul.

Temperance is another name for self-control and moderation. It is important for the worker class, but necessary for all three classes of people. The state, too, must control itself, not yielding either to the unjust demands of other states or to a lust for expansion or power. The state must not give in to an excess of liberty or repression. The healthy state resembles the healthy person. Both are moderate, self-disciplined, and guided by reason. The healthy soul is not controlled by appetites.

Courage is the essential virtue of the warrior class. Courage is necessary to protect the community and to enforce the just laws of the guardians. In the

virtue (Platonic)
Excellence of function.

Bodily exercise, when compulsory, does no harm to the body; but knowledge which is acquired under compulsion obtains no hold on the mind.

PLATO

individual, courage is a quality of will, an essential drive that provides a person with stamina and energy.

Wisdom is the virtue associated with the guardians who are called the philosopher-kings. In the individual, wisdom is present when the rational part of the soul is healthy and in control. Wisdom is found only in a community ruled by those fit by nature and training to guide it: the philosopher-kings who have seen the Good.

Justice is the result of the other three cardinal virtues, in much the same way that bodily health is the result of the proper functioning of all organs and systems. **Justice** *is excellence of function for the whole:* Each essential element works well, and together all elements blend into a balanced system in the just state and in the just individual.

For Plato, justice extends far beyond a legal system. The just state is well, whole, vital. It nurtures each individual by providing a lifestyle appropriate to him or her.

justice (Platonic)
Excellence of function for the whole; in a just society each individual performs his or her natural function according to class; in a just individual, reason rules the spirit and the appetites.

PHILOSOPHICAL

QUERY

• • • • • •

Consider the family as a functional system: If young children are allowed to spend the money, determine bedtimes, and so on, the whole family suffers. If the parents try to live like children, the whole family suffers. If every family member is free to pick and choose what he or she feels like doing or not doing every day, there can be no family. You might try similar analyses of marriages, churches, schools, or factories. Discuss the need for hierarchy, authority, and a governing order.

■ THE ORIGIN OF DEMOCRACY ■

utopia
Term for a perfect or ideal society derived from Sir Thomas More's 1516 novel of the same name; the word was created from the Greek root meaning "nowhere."

Plato's *Republic,* and a later dialogue called *Laws,* outline **utopias**—that is, perfect, ideal societies. (Although Plato originated the idea, the word *utopia* was coined by Sir Thomas More in 1516.) A Platonic utopia would be enormously difficult, perhaps impossible, to achieve. But a consideration of Plato's program for a utopia will prove to be worthwhile on many counts.

For Plato, the ideal Form of government is rule by philosopher-kings, not democracy. Because our current culture is democratic and individualistic in so many respects, many of us view democracy as the ideal Form of government without giving any other possibilities serious consideration. For that reason alone, consideration of an elitist alternative can be illuminating. It may help us to better identify the virtues of our own society—and we may get a clearer look at its shortcomings.

In Book VIII of the *Republic,* Plato discusses different kinds of governments and the types of souls each produces. He argues that democracy grows out of a type of government called *oligarchy,* the rule of a wealthy few. Because the chief aim of the oligarchs is to get rich, they create a constitution and type of government that encourage the acquisition of property.

But just having property isn't enough. Plato asks, "Doesn't oligarchy change into democracy because of lack of restraint in the pursuit of its objective of getting as rich as possible?"[24] The seeds of democracy, according to Plato, are the love of property and riches, and a corresponding desire for a free economy: In order to preserve their wealth, oligarchs must encourage trading in real estate, heavy borrowing, and lack of self-control. In order to increase wealth, "money people" need to stimulate irrational but constant consumption by everyone else. Plato declares, "It should then be clear that love of money and adequate self-discipline in its citizens are two things that can't co-exist in any society; one or the other must be neglected."[25]

> *Oligarchy: A government resting on a valuation of property, in which the rich have power and the poor man is deprived of it.*
> PLATO

• • • • • •

Do you agree with Plato that democracy is incompatible with self-discipline? What sort of self-discipline do you think Plato was concerned about?

PHILOSOPHICAL

QUERY

In Plato's diagnosis, as the rich get richer, the poor grow angrier until they somehow overthrow the rich, either through armed revolt or by social and legal pressure. Resentful over their status, the poor initiate a program of *equality*.

> Then democracy originates when the poor win, kill or exile their opponents, and give the rest equal rights and opportunity of office. . . . There is liberty and freedom of speech in plenty, and every individual is free to do as he likes. . . . That being so, won't everyone arrange his life as pleases him best? . . . a democracy is the most attractive of all societies. The diversity of its characters, like the different colours in a patterned dress, make it look very attractive . . . perhaps most people would, for this reason, judge it to be the best form of society . . . [if they] judge by appearances.[26]

A democratic state, Plato says, will contain every type of human temperament. But the predominant characteristic of democracy is lack of guidance and self-control, lack of wisdom, and lack of temperance. Swayed by opinion, rather than grounded in knowledge, the democratic state is in a state of constant flux, always *becoming*. It is hostile to the possibility of a fixed hierarchy of being.

> In a democracy . . . there's no compulsion either to exercise authority if you are capable of it, or to submit to authority if you don't want to; you needn't fight if there's a war, or you can wage a private war in peacetime if you don't like peace. . . . It's a wonderfully pleasant way of carrying on in the short run, isn't it?[27]

Democracy is so pleasant, Plato asserts, that even those convicted of a crime in a democracy can continue "to go about among their fellows." H. D. P. Lee paraphrases Plato's description of the democratic type as "versatile but lacking principle."[28]

Most damning of all, Plato says, democracy violates the principle of functional order and rule by reason. He asserts that only very rare and exceptional individuals can grow up to be good people without strict training from infancy, in a good environment. But democracy lacks the order and balance to provide such

> *Thus the only sort of liberty that is real under democracy is the liberty of the have-nots to destroy the liberty of the haves. . . .*
> H. L. MENCKEN

> *The truth is that the common man's love of liberty, like his love of sense, justice and truth, is almost wholly imaginary.*
> H. L. MENCKEN

> *Then the master passion runs wild and takes madness into its service; any decent options or desires and any feelings of shame still left are killed or thrown out, until all discipline is swept away, and madness usurps its place.*
> PLATO

an environment. At its most extreme, the disordered, democratic soul resists all limits, both internal and social:

> All pleasures are equal and should have equal rights. [Such a character] lives for the pleasure of the moment. One day it's wine, women, and song, the next bread and water; one day it's hard physical training, the next indolence and ease, and then a period of philosophic study. . . . There's no order or restraint in [this] life and [such a person] reckons [this] way of living is pleasant, free, and happy. . . .
>
> It's a life which many men and women would envy, it has so many possibilities.[29]

The Pendulum of Imbalance

Ancient philosophers were aware that one extreme often produces another, nearly opposite, extreme in a never-ending effort to achieve balance. In Plato's view, the chief objective of democracy is "excessive liberty." In one of the more interesting and perhaps prophetic passages in the *Republic,* Plato describes the effects "too much liberty" will produce. As you read what he said so long ago, take note of parallels to our own culture.

Each individual is his own center, and the world centers in him.
SØREN KIERKEGAARD

> It becomes the thing for the father and son to change places, the father standing in awe of his son, and the son neither respecting nor fearing his parents, in order to assert his independence; and there's no distinction between citizen and alien and foreigner. And there are other more trivial things. The teacher fears and panders to his pupils, who in turn despise their teachers and attendants; and the young as a whole imitate their elders, argue with them and set themselves up against them, while their elders try to avoid the reputation of being disagreeable or strict by aping the young and mixing with them on terms of easy good fellowship. . . .
>
> You would never believe—unless you had seen it for yourself—how much more liberty the domestic animals have in a democracy. Love me love my dog, as the proverb has it, and the same is true of horses and donkeys as well. . . . Everything is full of this spirit of liberty. . . .
>
> What it comes to is this, . . . that the minds of the citizens become so sensitive that the least vestige of restraint is resented as intolerable, till finally, as you know, in their determination to have no master they disregard all laws, written or unwritten.[30]

Many admire, few know.
HIPPOCRATES

One form of *shamelessness* is an exaggerated sense of honor. In this condition, the individual is always ready to take offense. Every restriction or social limit is taken personally: "The least vestige of restraint is resented as intolerable." Consider: Some years ago, one *kindergartner* was suspended from school for patting a teacher on the bottom (sexual harassment) and another for bringing a metal nail file to school ("zero tolerance" for anything that "looks like a weapon"). A Northern California school reacted to excessive absences and poor grades by requiring students to wear uniforms—and then pressuring the entire staff to wear them, too—so as "not to make the students feel like they're different."

According to Plato, the spoiled and undisciplined person grows used to playing now and paying later. When he cannot pay his own way, Plato says, he turns to his parents to gratify his desires. He sees their estate as "his due," and "if they

Plato thought that excessive liberty always leads to its own destruction because demands for increasing individual freedom result in counterdemands for restrictions and control, as seen in the call for schoolchildren to wear uniforms instead of dress of their choice, which may be extreme or outlandish.

The greatest griefs are those we cause ourselves.

SOPHOCLES

don't give in to him, he'll try first to get his way by fraud and deceit." But "if his old mother and father put up a resistance and show fight . . . [he will not] feel any hesitation about playing the tyrant with them." What begins as unlimited freedom ends up as the tyranny over reason by the lower parts of the soul.

• • • • • •

PHILOSOPHICAL

QUERY

Can you spot any symptoms in our society of the pattern Plato attributes to injustice in individuals and the state? Can you identify individuals or groups that "fall into sickness and dissension at the slightest provocation"? What—if anything—does justice (or a lack of justice) have to do with these reactions? Explain.

The Tyranny of Excess

The ills of democracy were aggravated for Plato by a pattern of increasing self-indulgence, which he thought would pass from generation to generation, until sooner or later pleasures and excesses would actually tyrannize the soul itself.

> Isn't this the reason . . . why the passion of sex has for so long been called a tyrant? . . . And isn't there also a touch of the tyrant about a man who's drunk? . . . And the madman whose mind is unhinged imagines he can control gods and men and is quite ready to try. . . . Then a precise definition of a tyrannical man is one who, either by birth or habit or both, combines the characteristics of drunkenness, lust, and madness. . . . And how does he live? . . . When a master passion has absolute control of a man's mind, I suppose life is a round of holidays and dinners and parties and girl-friends and so on. . . . And there will be a formidable extra crop of desires growing all the time and needing satisfaction. . . . So whatever income he has will soon be expended, and he'll start borrowing and drawing on capital.
>
> . . . When these sources fail, his large brood of desires will howl aloud. . . . He *must* get something from somewhere or his life will be torment and agony.[31]

tyranny

Form of government in which all power rests in a single individual, known as the tyrant.

According to Plato, the built-in excesses of democracy already contain the seeds of tyranny. **Tyranny** is a form of government in which all power rests in a single individual, the tyrant. For Plato, the tyrant is the most imbalanced type of personality. A tyrant is always a slave to his own strong passions and desires. An individual who is controlled by drugs or lust is obviously a slave. But so is the politically powerful leader who is a slave to his own lust for power and domination.

Once again, things are not as they initially appear. What looks like freedom is in reality lack of control; what looks like power is in truth a form of enslavement.

PHILOSOPHICAL

QUERY

• • • • • •

Do you think things like the Patriot Act, V-chip, laws against hate speech, and fundamentalist reactions against "the excesses of Western democracy" support Plato's argument that the inevitable result of democracy is "too much liberty" and that widespread "abuses" of liberty lead to demands for "law and order" and, ultimately, tyranny? What other examples can you think of to buttress Plato's case? What examples to weaken it? (As you ponder this, note that calls for restrictions on personal freedom come from both liberal and conservative thinkers.)

▥ COMMENTARY ▥

The most damning charge that can be leveled at all enlightenment philosophies is that no matter how initially intriguing or appealing they seem, they remain impractical and unrealistic in the world as most of us experience and understand it. In Plato's case, we might ask ourselves whether we have any supportable firsthand evidence for believing in actual levels of reality. Does a story like the Allegory of the Cave help us determine who is enlightened and who is deluded? Do the Divided Line and Simile of the Sun do anything besides reflect certain psychological states?

On the other hand, who can doubt the need for order and balance in both the individual and society? Further, it would not be difficult to make Plato's case against the "excesses of democracy" using trends and events from our own time. We might even find some merit in his claim that letting each individual choose his or her occupation based solely (or even chiefly) on strength of desire and ambition leads to great overall unhappiness.

When we rank occupations by income and prestige, most of the tasks needed for a good society are less desirable than a few glamorous, less useful ones. Which, then, does more lasting harm: letting everyone who wishes scramble for the top of the heap or carefully matching people's basic abilities and personalities with various levels of education and occupation? We might find Plato's three categories of people—guardians, warriors, and workers—too restricting, but does that rule out a more realistic division of opportunities and social roles?

Lastly, there is much to be said for living a well-rounded life. That includes, of course, being individually balanced. A society that values specialization and material success to the extent that this society does makes personal growth (well-roundedness), as opposed to self-indulgence, difficult.

Interestingly, even though Plato's great pupil Aristotle turns away from the theory of Forms, he follows the direction in which his great teacher pointed and makes his own case for the fully functioning, whole, balanced human being. Aristotle is the subject of the next chapter.

Among the disciples of Socrates, Plato was the one who shone with a glory which far excelled that of the others and who not unjustly eclipsed them all.
ST. AUGUSTINE

Plato is dear to me, but dearer still is truth.
ARISTOTLE

▪ SUMMARY OF MAIN POINTS ▪

- Plato was a member of the Athenian aristocracy and Socrates' most famous and important pupil. Socrates' trial and death convinced Plato that Athenian democracy was irrational mob rule. He founded his famous Academy to educate wise rulers.

- In Plato's metaphysics, the highest level of reality consists of timeless "essences" called ideas or Forms. Plato divided reality into three levels. The highest level of reality is eternal and changeless *being*. The other two levels together make up *becoming*, the level of change. Knowledge is always of essence. Disagreement is only possible on the lower level of becoming.

- According to Plato, knowledge is unchanging. The Sophists could not discover truth because they were only concerned with the world of ever-changing perceptions and customs. Truth and knowledge are found at the level of being. Plato's theory of Forms was part of his refutation of sophistry.

- Plato used the concept of a Divided Line to illustrate the relationship of knowledge to opinion, reality to appearance, and the worlds of being and becoming. The Divided Line consists of two basic sections, each unevenly divided into two segments: (1) pure intelligence or understanding, (2) reasoning, (3) informed belief or ordinary opinions, and (4) illusion and imagination, dominated by secondhand opinions and uncritical impressions.

- Plato compared the "absolute Form of the Good" to the sun; the Good makes the existence of everything else possible. The Good cannot be observed with the five senses and can be known only by pure thought or intelligence. It is the source of both the value and the existence of all other Forms.

- In the Allegory of the Cave, Plato characterized three levels of awareness by referring to three distinct levels of reality: two levels of becoming and one qualitatively unique and ultimate level of being. The lowest level is inhabited by people with little or no imagination. The informed level involves a wider range of basic understanding. On the highest level, the soul has no need for perception or interpretation.

- In the *Republic,* Plato argued that there is a recipro-cal relationship between the individual and the kind of society in which he or she lives. The ideal state meets three basic categories of needs: (1) nourish-ing needs; (2) protection needs; (3) ordering needs. These needs are best met by members of three cor-responding classes of people: (1) workers; (2) war-riors; (3) guardians or philosopher-kings.

- The *Republic* contrasts two views of morality. The instrumental theory of morality asserts that right and wrong must be determined by the consequences our acts produce, and the functionalist theory of morality holds that right and wrong can only be un-derstood in terms of the way they affect our overall functioning as human beings.

- According to Plato, the just state functions fully; the unjust state is dysfunctional. Only when all classes of people are virtuous according to their natures is the state whole, healthy, balanced, and just. The good life consists of each individual functioning well according to his or her own nature, in a state that is ordered and wisely ruled.

- According to Plato, the human soul resembles the state in that it too is divided into three parts: reason, spirit, and appetite. A just (healthy, good, or virtuous) soul is one in which all parts func-tion harmoniously. The just society is one ruled by guardians in such a way that each class func-tions at its best.

- Plato identified four cardinal (essential, basic) vir-tues. The virtue of temperance is important for the worker classes but necessary for all classes of people. Courage is the essential virtue of the warrior class; in the individual, courage is a quality of will that provides a person with stamina and energy. Wisdom is the virtue associated with the guardians and the rational part of the soul. Justice, the result of the other three cardinal virtues, is excellence of function for the whole.

- Plato rejected democracy as unjust because rule by the majority usurps the rightful role of the guardian class. The result is an excess of liberty and rule by impulse, appetite, and emotion in which all classes suffer. Democracy violates the principle of functional order and rule by reason. According to Plato, the excessive liberty found in democracies contains the seeds of tyranny, a type of government in which all power rests in a single individual, the tyrant, the most imbalanced type of personality.

▥ POST-READING REFLECTIONS ▥

Now that you have had a chance to learn about Plato, use your new knowledge to answer these questions.

1. Discuss some of the personal experiences that shaped Plato's overall philosophical idealism.

2. Illustrate the Divided Line and relate each segment to Plato's epistemology as it is characterized in the Allegory of the Cave.

3. How did Plato use the sun to help explain the Good?

4. Identify and explain the three basic levels of reality.

5. Distinguish the realm of being from the realm of becoming.

6. Tell the Allegory of the Cave in your own words. Then carefully explain its purpose in Plato's philosophy.

7. Carefully explain the relationship of the individual to the state in the *Republic.* Why is the relationship significant?

8. What does Plato see as the most unjust type of person and state? Why? Do you agree? Explain.

9. Explain the origin and nature of democracy according to Plato.

PHILOSOPHY INTERNET RESOURCES

Go to the Soccio Web page at **http://philosophy.wadsworth.com/ Soccio7e** for Web links, practice quizzes and tests, a pronunciation guide, and study tips.

THE NATURALIST

Aristotle

IN ALL THINGS OF NATURE THERE IS
SOMETHING OF THE MARVELOUS.

Aristotle

For Your Reflection

Keep these questions in mind as you learn about Aristotle.

1. *What is naturalism?*
2. *How did Plato distinguish between knowledge and opinion?*
3. *What is form according to Aristotle?*
4. *What is matter according to Aristotle?*
5. *What are the Four Causes?*
6. *What is* entelechy?
7. *What is teleological thinking?*
8. *What is* eudaimonia?
9. *What is* sophrosyne?
10. *What is character?*
11. *What is the Aristotelian mean?*
12. *What is virtue according to Aristotle? Vice?*

For Deeper Consideration

A. Critics accuse Aristotle of circular reasoning when he attempts to identify goodness by first looking at the good man. Is this criticism fair? How else could one identify goodness objectively? Can goodness, or any virtue or vice, be identified objectively? How does Aristotle approach the problem of studying virtue objectively? What do you think of his strategy?

B. Increasingly, contemporary philosophers and social scientists are raising questions about the pursuit of happiness, with some suggesting that the pursuit of "happiness" leads to unhappiness and dissatisfaction. Contrast the classical notion of happiness with today's notion in terms of *eudaimonia*. Is *eudaimonia* the same thing as happiness? (Hint: Do not overlook the role of habit as it affects character.) Is today's concept of happiness healthy and reasonable? Might we benefit by modifying it along Aristotelian lines? Use your own expectations and experiences to help you dig into this interesting area of philosophy.

One of the most frustrating aspects of college can be choosing a major. Sometimes we are encouraged to decide without having had much exposure to a variety of disciplines, and some of us just may not really know who we are yet. (This condition is not confined to students or persons of any particular age.) As a result, we may change our minds as sophomores or juniors or seniors, when we realize that our initial choice was wrong for the real us. Outside the campus environment, more and more people seem to be making significant career changes at mid-life or later.[1]

What prompts a forty-five-year-old person to leave a secure job, giving up seniority and retirement benefits and medical insurance, to open a cookie shop? What makes a social worker quit work and go to law school? What drives a middle-aged man or woman to leave his or her family, lose weight, buy a sports car, and become a poet? What makes a pre-med major just nine units short of graduation drop out of school and join the Peace Corps? There are many reasons, some of which may be unwise, but some of which are good reasons.

Did you ever feel that you weren't really being yourself? What does that mean? Aren't you always yourself, even if that self is confused or inconsistent or phony? Maybe that's just who you are? On the other hand, maybe the "real you" is being denied or starved. Perhaps people who walk away from their jobs or families have been false to their "true selves" for years. Does that seem possible?

Aristotle might have thought so, even though he would not have suggested that we "find ourselves" by returning to adolescence or undertaking a self-indulgent escape from responsibility. But he did believe in a natural development of the soul/self based on an inner essence or goal. He believed that the good life involves balance and fullness. And though each of us may have individually different "selves" to develop, in Aristotle's view, all human beings share a common nature that makes it possible to identify the general outline of a good life.

> *There is perhaps nothing worse than reaching the top of the ladder and discovering that you're on the wrong wall.*
>
> JOSEPH CAMPBELL

> *You need not, and in fact cannot, teach an acorn to grow into an oak tree, but when given a chance, its intrinsic potentialities will develop. Similarly, the human individual, given a chance, tends to develop his particular human potentialities. He will develop then the unique alive forces of his real self. . . . In short, he will grow . . . toward self-realization. And that is why I speak . . . of the real self as that central force, common to all human beings and yet unique in each, which is the deep source of growth.*
>
> KAREN HORNEY

▓ WORKS ▓

Aristotle is said to have written twenty-seven dialogues on a level comparable to Plato's, and it is through these dialogues that he was best known in the ancient world.[2] Unfortunately, they were all destroyed when the Visigoths sacked Rome in 400 C.E. What we know today as the "writings of Aristotle" are really a collection of *logoi*—discourses. These apparently include notes Aristotle made for his lectures and possibly notes taken by students who attended his lectures. Of 360 works mentioned by Diogenes Läertius, forty survive today.

Aristotle's works include *Organon*, a collection of six logical treatises; *Physics; On Generation and Corruption; De Anima (On the Soul); On the Heavens; The History of Animals; On the Parts of Animals; Metaphysics; Politics; Rhetoric; Poetics;* and the *Nicomachean Ethics.*

What remains of Aristotle's work is complex, stiffly written, and often dry. But in spite of that, these notes reflect a genius whose range of interests, wonder, insight, and effort stands as a most remarkable testament to the human mind and spirit.

■ ARISTOTLE'S LIFE ■

Aristotle

The son of a court physician, **Aristotle** (384–322 B.C.E.) was born in Stagira, a Greek community in Thrace. What little we know of him comes primarily through Diogenes Läertius's compilation of the lives of ancient philosophers.

Aristotle probably learned basic anatomy and dissection from his father before he was sent to study at Plato's Academy in Athens at the age of eighteen. When he arrived practically everyone noticed him, in part because he was something of a dandy. Plato is reported to have said that Aristotle paid more attention to his clothes than was proper for a philosopher. To be fashionable, Aristotle cultivated a deliberate lisp, the speech pattern that the Greek elite used to separate themselves from the masses. (In a similar way, some people today think of an English accent as being "higher class" than a Southern drawl or Brooklyn accent.)

Despite his affectations, Aristotle almost immediately earned a reputation as one of the Academy's finest students. Diogenes Läertius says that on one occasion when Plato read aloud a difficult treatise about the soul, Aristotle "was the only person who sat it out, while all the rest rose up and went away."[3] Aristotle remained with Plato for perhaps twenty years, and Plato is supposed to have humorously remarked that his Academy consisted of two parts: the body of his students and the brain of Aristotle. Although Aristotle disagreed with Plato on important philosophical matters, he built an altar to Plato at his teacher's death.

Thirty-seven years old when Plato died, Aristotle expected to be the next master of the Academy. But the trustees of the Academy picked a native Athenian instead, because they saw Aristotle as a "foreigner." When a former classmate who had become a kind of philosopher-king over a rather large area in Asia Minor invited him to be his adviser, Aristotle accepted.

Apparently, Aristotle had little effect on his friend Hermeias's rulership, but he did manage to marry Hermeias's adopted daughter Pythias in 344 B.C.E. Pythias had a large dowry, which Aristotle happily invested. Aristotle's life was disrupted the same year, however, when his political benefactor offended the king of Persia. Shortly after Aristotle and Pythias fled to the island of Lesbos, Hermeias was crucified by the Persian king. While on Lesbos, Aristotle studied natural history, and Pythias died giving birth to their daughter. Aristotle never forgot Pythias and asked that her bones be buried with him. Aristotle later lived with a woman named Herpyllis. Their long, happy relationship produced Aristotle's son Nicomachus, to whom he dedicated the *Nicomachean Ethics*.

In 343 B.C.E. King Philip of Macedon invited Aristotle to train his thirteen-year-old son Alexander. The boy was wild and crude, but Aristotle was able to smooth his rough edges and instill in him respect for knowledge and science. As Alexander the Great, Aristotle's famous pupil ordered his soldiers to collect specimens of plant, marine, and animal life from faraway places for his old teacher.

In 340 B.C.E. Philip sent Aristotle back to Aristotle's hometown of Stagira, so that he could write a code of laws to help restore the community, which had been disrupted by a war. He did well enough that Stagira celebrated a yearly holiday in his honor. In 334 B.C.E. Aristotle at last returned to Athens, where he founded his own school, possibly with money from Alexander.

With regard to excellence, it is not enough to know, but we must try to have and use it.

ARISTOTLE

To be sure, the whirl of life and culture in contemporary America is such that we apparently feel little need of, and obviously pay no heed to, such things as the ethical and political observations of an Aristotle. For what is there to human existence, save getting ahead and having a good time?

But Aristotle did not see things this way.

HENRY VEATCH

■ THE LYCEUM ■

Aristotle named his school after the god Apollo Lyceus. The Lyceum was built near some of the most elegant buildings in Athens, surrounded by shady groves of trees and covered walkways. Socrates used to visit the same groves, remarking on what a wonderful spot they made for reflection.

Aristotle's students were known as the *peripatetic* philosophers because he often discussed philosophy while strolling with them along tree-covered walkways called the Peripatos. In addition to philosophy, Aristotle's curriculum included technical lectures for limited audiences and popular lectures of more general interest. Aristotle collected hundreds of maps, charts, and documents, forming the first important library in the West. For instance, he collected and studied 153 political constitutions.

Leadership of the Lyceum rotated among certain members of the school according to rules drawn up by Aristotle. Once a month he held a common meal and symposium at which one of the members was picked to defend a philosophical idea against criticism from everyone else. Aristotle continued to lecture and research for his entire tenure at the Lyceum.[4]

The Lyceum's students tended to be from the middle class, whereas the students at Plato's Academy were more aristocratic. For a short while the two schools were bitter rivals, but as each concentrated on its own particular interests, this rivalry died down. The Academy stressed mathematics and "pure" understanding, while Aristotle's students collected anthropological studies of barbarian cultures, chronologies of various wars and games, the organs and living habits of animals, the nature and locations of plants, and so on.[5]

The development of philosophic science as science, and, further, the progress from the Socratic point of view to the scientific, begins with Plato and ends with Aristotle. They of all others deserve to be called teachers of the human race.

G. W. F. HEGEL

The general movement, we may say, was from other-worldliness towards an intense interest in the concrete facts both of nature and history, and a conviction that the "form" and meaning of the world is to be found not apart from but embedded in its "matter."

SIR DAVID ROSS

©Alinari Archives/Corbis

Raphael's famous painting *The School of Athens* depicts Aristotle (right center, blue) conversing with Plato (left center red) and surrounded by such philosophers as Socrates, Diogenes, Heraclitus, Epicurus, Parmenides, Hypatia, Averroës, and Pythagoras.

Alexander the Great died in 323 B.C.E. Athens had smarted under a Greek unification program begun by Philip and continued under Alexander. With Alexander dead, Athens openly expressed its hostility and resentment toward all things Macedonian. Because of his long and favored place under the protection of both Philip and Alexander, Aristotle found himself in an uncomfortable position. He left Athens and the Lyceum the next year after being legally charged with not respecting the gods of the state—one of the same charges leveled at Socrates. Rather than stand trial like the crusty old *sophos*, Aristotle fled to the island of Euboea (his mother's birthplace), in his words, "lest Athens sin twice against philosophy."

In 322 B.C.E. the man who had created the first important library, tutored the greatest ruler of the ancient world, invented logic, and shaped the thinking of an entire culture died. So great was his influence on later thinkers that for hundreds of years all educated persons knew him simply as *the Philosopher*.

■ THE NATURALIST ■

Aristotelian philosophy is so complex in treatment and scope that no introductory survey can do justice to all of it. A good place to begin, however, is with a look at Aristotle's ethics and psychology, for in addition to presenting a powerful and challenging doctrine of happiness as self-realization and personal growth, they rest on Aristotle's naturalistic metaphysics.

In Plato we saw one significant expression of the search for the good life: evaluating this life by comparing it to some ideal standard and then trying to perfect this world. In a sense, Aristotle brings to full maturity a second major expression of the search for the good life: attempting to acquire facts without bias and then using that information to make this a better world.

Although Aristotle loved and respected Plato, he saw dangers in Plato's rationalistic idealism. Partly as a reaction to Plato, and partly as a consequence of his own temperament, Aristotle is sometimes said to have brought philosophy down to earth. He combined the study of humanity and nature to a degree that was not possible again, because after Aristotle no single individual could seriously hope to contribute in a major way to so many distinct fields.

Aristotle stands alone as an archetype of the philosophical naturalist. Basically, **naturalism** is the belief that reality consists of the natural world. The naturalist's universe is ordered in that everything in it follows consistent and discoverable *laws* of nature; everything can be understood in terms of those fundamental laws. Nothing exists outside of space and time. Nature always acts with a purpose, and the key to understanding anything lies in determining its essential purpose.

Philosophical naturalists deny the existence of a separate supernatural order of reality. They believe that *human beings, although special, are part of the natural order and behave according to fixed laws and principles.* Thus a clear understanding of nature is necessary to any clear conception of human behavior. Ethics and political (social) science must be based on the actual facts of life, carefully observed and collected by a scientific method—not on speculative, "otherworldly," rationalistic schemes.

All men by nature desire knowledge.

ARISTOTLE

naturalism

Belief that reality consists of the natural world; denial of the existence of a separate supernatural order of reality; belief that nature follows orderly, discoverable laws.

Aristotle based his philosophical positions on scrutiny of particular, actual things, not on the isolated contemplation of mathematical laws or "pure ideas." Let's see what Aristotle discovered when he turned his scientist's eye to the teeming natural world.

■ NATURAL CHANGES ■

Recall that the Presocratic philosophers struggled to explain how change is possible. In simplified form, the problem of explaining change was generated by a seemingly inescapable contradiction: In order for X to change into Y, then somehow X must be *both* X and Y. If X *is* Y, then X cannot be said to *become* (change into) Y. For example, water is not ice, yet we say that water "changes into" or "becomes" ice (and the opposite). But until the water becomes ice, it is not ice: It is water. When it is ice, it is no longer water.

"But," you may ask, "what about the in-between stages, the transitional period when some water molecules are freezing into ice molecules? There we have both ice and water!" Do we? That is, do we have some sort of "ice-water" molecule? If so, then it is not water or ice, but a third—different—thing. Further, we still need some clear explanation of *how* what once *was* water *is* now ice. (You may wish to review the problem of change and "Zeno's Paradoxes" in Chapter 3.)

Aristotle is sometimes called "the father of science" because he was the first Western thinker of record to provide an adequate analysis of a *process* of change based on the claim that form is inseparable from matter.

A likely impossibility is always preferable to an unconvincing possibility.
ARISTOTLE

Form

Aristotle was troubled by Platonic dualism, the division of the universe into two worlds or realms: the realm of *becoming* and the realm of *being*. (You might find it helpful to review the discussion of Plato's theory of Forms in Chapter 5.)

According to Plato, only Forms (with a capital F) are truly real; objects of sense perception are mere reflections or diluted copies of Forms. Aristotle worried that dualism leads to "otherworldliness, to a chasm between the actual and the ideal . . . [which means] that discussion of what is can never amount to more than a 'likely story,' and knowledge of what *ought to be* has little or no relevance to pressing moral, political, and social problems."[6] If Aristotle's claim that there is only one world is correct, whatever "form" is can only be an aspect of *this* world.

Aristotle argued that form can be distinguished from content only in thought and never in fact. For instance, we can make a mental distinction between shape and color, but we never encounter shapeless colors or colorless shapes. We can mentally distinguish between mortality and living things, but we will never encounter mortality-of-and-by-itself, any more than we will encounter living things without also encountering mortality. This means that mortality is a formal—or essential—aspect of living things.

Aristotle warned that we must take care not to mistake "intellectual analysis" for "ontological status." Aristotle accused Plato of doing just that by imputing actual existence to the Forms. For Aristotle, form exists *within the natural order* embedded in particular things and *cannot* exist independently.

The actuality of thought is life.
ARISTOTLE

Not everything that is faced can be changed. But nothing can be changed until it is faced.

James Baldwin

It is absurd to suppose that purpose is not present because we do not observe the agent deliberating.

Aristotle

Aristotle argued that every particular thing, considered at any given time, has two aspects. First, it shares properties with other particulars. For example, you and your philosophy professor share certain properties with each other. You also share properties with Willy the whale, with anything containing hydrogen, and so on. But there is something special, unique, or primary (basic) that you and your professor share with each other and with me. This shared quality consists of whatever answers the question "What is that?" Aristotle characterized this basic essence as the "substance" of a thing.

So, "What are you, what is your essence?" You are a mammal, an animal, a vertebrate—just like your professor, Willy, and I are. But you, your professor, and I share a common quality that Willy lacks: humanness. All human beings share qualities that Willy lacks, and Willy has qualities that we lack and that he shares with other underwater creatures. The more thorough our list of the shared, common properties that make up a thing's essential nature or form, the fuller our grasp of that form.

According to Aristotle, *form* (with a lowercase f) makes a substance what it is. This kind of substance-making form is what is meant by the essence of a thing. So we (you, your professor, and I) share a common "form," "substance," or "essence that makes us human."

After distinguishing among various ways that we talk about *being* (in reference to a thing's size, shape, and such), Aristotle says:

> Although being is used in all these ways, clearly the primary kind of being is what a thing is; for it is this alone that indicates substance. When we say what kind of thing something is, we say that it is good or bad, but not that it is three feet long or that is a man; but when we say what a thing is, we do not say that is white, hot, or three feet long, but that is a man or a god. All other things are said to be only insofar as they are quantities, qualities, affections . . . so what is primarily—not in the sense of being something, but just quite simply being—is substance.[7]

In other words, Aristotle is saying that when we characterize or define *what a thing is*, we are speaking of that thing's substance or essence. Thus, according to Aristotle, *form* is the essence of substance itself, that which makes a substance a substance.

From the Greek word for essence (*ousia*), **Aristotelian form** is that which is *in matter* and makes a thing what it is. Aristotelian form can be abstracted from matter in thought but cannot exist independently of matter. Although knowing what kind of thing a thing is can be useful, merely knowing a thing's form (essence) does not account for its particularness, its individuality. So, according to Aristotle, form is only one basic aspect of reality. The other is matter.

form (Aristotle)
From the Greek word for essence (*ousia*), that which is in matter and makes a thing what it is; can be abstracted from matter but cannot exist independently of matter.

Matter

Navigating wisely through life requires that we recognize the common features of things, their essences, natures, qualities, common characteristics, and such; it also requires dealing with specific things, with particulars. The essence that you, your philosophy professor, and I share is that we are human beings; we are also, however, particular human beings. So we also need to ask about *this* specific human being (or horse, or book, or anything).

In Aristotle's view, when we ask about *this* particular thing, we are asking about the material composition of whatever constitutes that thing, the specific stuff that makes a general form (human being) into a particular instance of that form (you, your professor, me). For Aristotle, **matter**, from the Greek *hyle*, is the common material stuff found in a variety of things; matter has no distinct characteristics until some form is imparted to it or until the form inherent in a thing becomes actualized. Thus, for Aristotle, individual things are "formed matter."

His careful studies of the natural world led Aristotle to posit a *hierarchy of forms*, moving from the simplest kinds of things to the most complex, based on each thing's function or purpose. At the highest levels, form is the "purpose," "goal," or "overall plan" of an object considered as a *whole*, as a *unity*.

Aristotle did *not* mean that the universe (nature) has been planned by something separate from it like God or Plato's Forms. Rather, he argued, order and purpose are inherent in nature. Nature is purposive. Matter provides "opportunity"; form provides "direction." Form does not—cannot—exist without matter; matter does not—cannot—exist without form. The Aristotelian universe is a continuum of *formed matter*, from the lowest, most inert things to the most complex, autonomous, and active ones. Understanding anything consists of understanding its relationships to other things on this continuum.

Change

Aristotle thought that his picture of nature as *formed matter* explained how it is that things can change. Consider once more the example of water changing into ice. When water changes into ice, some part of the water itself remains water, and some part of the water changes. The basic matter stays the same, but it changes form. As water becomes progressively colder, the behavior or properties of the molecules that constitute water change from liquid form to crystalline form.

The basic process of change—substitution of forms in stages—is the same from the simplest to the most complex things. As an acorn changes into an oak tree, a progressive succession of shapes occurs: acorn to sprout to sapling to tree. (And the tree stage itself consists of a series of shape changes as the trunk thickens and branches grow out and up.)

Guiding this series of changes, says Aristotle, is movement toward an inherent structure or form (oak tree). The acorn, for instance, contains a potential sprout—a form not yet "materialized." If conditions are right, the acorn's actual form is replaced by its potential form, and the *potential* sprout is *actualized*. The actualized sprout contains within itself the form of a potential sapling. Given the necessary material conditions, the sprout restructures its own matter into a sapling according to this "blueprint" (form of a sapling). The sapling, of course, contains the form of a potential tree, and so on.

So "change" is really a series of smaller changes in which matter loses and gains form. In complex organisms, change occurs as an orderly series of progressively complex forms. Such structured, systematic change, from simple to

matter (Aristotle)
From the Greek *hyle*, the common material stuff found in a variety of things; it has no distinct characteristics until some form is imparted to it or until the form inherent in a thing becomes actualized.

A great Hasidic rabbi by the name of Zusya once said: When I die, God will not ask me, "Why were you not Moses?" When I die, God will ask me, "Why were you not Zusya?"

complex, accounts for the qualitative distinction between change and *development* or *growth*. Development occurs when changes follow a pattern that leads toward a *goal* or *end* (purpose or function).

The goal or purpose that produces growth unites or unifies the successive changes as *stages* leading to a single goal (actualization of the ultimate form or essence). Aristotle argued that in order to understand something, it is necessary to identify its function or purpose. But there is more to a thing than its function (purpose or end). The most complete analysis or understanding of anything, Aristotle believed, could only come from asking, "What accounts for the existence of this or that thing?"

■ ARISTOTLE'S HIERARCHY ■ OF EXPLANATIONS

You may have heard the story of the three bricklayers who are asked, "What are you doing?" The first worker says, "I am laying this brick." The second answers, "I am building an arch." The third says, "I am building a cathedral." In a sense, each worker is correct. She has stated her view of her task, her sense of purpose or primary function. The story is often told to inspire us to set our sights on lofty goals. But it has another lesson, too. This story teaches us that the same thing can be characterized by distinctly different accounts or explanations, depending on the *purpose* of the account—and the purposes that together constitute the thing, process, or activity.

In the story of the bricklayers, each succeeding account includes the essence of the prior account. When the second bricklayer says, "I am building an arch," she implies, "I am laying this brick in order to make an arch." In other words, her goal is the arch. When the third bricklayer says, "I am building a cathedral," she implies, "I am laying this brick in order to make an arch in order to make a cathedral." Her goal is "higher" than that of the second worker, whose goal is, in turn, higher than that of the first bricklayer's more modest task.

In this simplistic example, we also see that a number of alternative explanations and accounts could have been given, depending on the focus (purposes) of the account giver. If the first bricklayer is a novice with no knowledge of arches or cathedrals, then she will be unable to grasp the ultimate purpose of her activity as part of a complex, goal-directed process. Her view is not incorrect; it is incomplete. She lacks adequate comprehension of the *end* of the construction process, which is only a *means* governed by a plan.

Have you noticed, however, that even the third worker's account can be broadened? We still—naturally—want to ask, "But why are you building a cathedral?" Here, too, a variety of responses will be "correct": "To make money." "To honor God." "To impress my special friend." "Because I enjoy it." The first three answers don't necessarily bring a halt to the inquiry, do they? We may still need to ask, "Why do you want money? What's the money to be used for?" "Why honor God by building a cathedral?" "What's the purpose behind trying to impress your special friend?"

One answer seems somehow different. What kind of answer might we expect to the question, "Why do what you enjoy?" We don't usually ask that question because pleasure (enjoyment) is capable of standing as an *end in itself.* That is, enjoyment is treated as an ultimate goal by many people, a goal that does not look forward toward a yet-higher goal.

Later in this chapter, we'll see what Aristotle has to say about money and other things, including pleasure, as final goals. What's important now is the concept of hierarchical ends, a hierarchy of "whys." Aristotle's hierarchical account of causation serves as a foundation for his moral psychology and greatly influenced subsequent thinkers.

■ THE FOUR CAUSES ■

Aristotle was the first philosopher to understand that not all "why" questions can be answered in the same way because there is more than one kind of *why.* In marked contrast to the single explanation view, Aristotle distinguished among four different kinds of explanations that, together, constitute a complete accounting or understanding of a thing. He referred to them as *causes.*

The Greek word for cause, *aitia,* meant "the reason for something happening." According to Aristotle, complete understanding of a thing must tell us what material the thing is made of, what form the thing takes, what triggered the events that set the thing's existence into motion, and the ultimate purpose for which the thing exists.

Aristotle's Four Causes are thus offered as accounts of (1) the material the thing is made of (*Material Cause*); (2) the form the thing takes (*Formal Cause*); (3) the triggering action or motion that begins the thing (*Efficient Cause*); and (4) the ultimate purpose or goal for which the thing exists (*Final Cause*). After describing the Four Causes, Aristotle says that "it is the business of the natural scientist to know about them all . . . [and to] give his answer to the question 'why?' in the manner of a natural scientist . . . [by referring] to them all—to the matter, the form, the mover, and the purpose."[8]

Aristotle is the first philosopher from whom we have retained a theoretical analysis of chance—which is in itself a sort of cause.
PIERRE PELLEGRIN

Material Cause

The **Material Cause** of a thing refers to the material (substance) from which the thing comes and in which change occurs. What accounts for wood becoming a bed instead of, say, a table? In his *Physics,* Aristotle points out that merely identifying the material out of which, say, a bed or statue is made does not tell us how and why that bed or that statue exists:

> Some people regard the nature and substance of things that exist by nature as being in each case the proximate element inherent in the thing, this being itself unshaped; thus, [according to such a view] the nature of a bed, for instance, would be wood, and that of a statue bronze. [Those who think this way offer] as evidence . . . the fact that if you were to bury a bed, and the moisture that got into it as it rotted gained enough force to throw up a shoot, it would be wood and not a bed that came into being. [According to this view, the bed's] arrangement according to the rules of an art . . . is an accidental attribute, whereas its substance is what remains permanently, and undergoes all these changes.[9]

Material Cause
The material (substance) from which a thing comes, and in which change occurs; first of Aristotle's Four Causes.

Nature does nothing uselessly.

ARISTOTLE

In other words, statues and beds are made of many different things, and some bronze and wood never become statues or beds. Identifying a thing's matter is a necessary part of—but not a complete—accounting for that thing. Aristotle rejects merely identifying a thing's *matter* as a complete understanding of the "how" and "why" of that thing. After all, it is not the nature of wood to become beds or the nature of bronze to become statues.

Formal Cause

Formal Cause

The shape, or form, into which matter is changed; second of Aristotle's Four Causes.

Until wood is fashioned into some particular thing, a bed or table, it is *potentially* but not *actually* a bed or table. Wood needs to be *formed* into beds and tables and other crafted objects "according to the rules of an art." It is not just wood (matter), then, that makes a bed or table, but the *form* the wood takes. Therefore, in addition to identifying the Material Cause of a thing, we need to know its **Formal Cause**, the shape, or form, into which "this matter" is changed.

It is easy enough to see how an artisan imposes form on matter; the bed-maker shapes wood into beds or tables. But what about natural things, growing things, and such? What forms natural objects? According to Aristotle, flesh and bone, for example, become flesh and bone only when their substance (matter) *forms* into "that which makes flesh, flesh" and "that which makes bone, bone." Aristotle says:

> What is potentially flesh or bone does not yet have its own nature until it acquires the form that accords with the formula, by means of which we define flesh and bone; nor can it be said at this stage to exist by nature. So in another way, nature is the shape and form of things that have a principle of movement in themselves—the form being only theoretically separable from the object in question.[10]

The basic elements that flesh or bone are made from are not—of themselves—flesh or bone. Flesh *is* (essentially and by definition) the precise "formulation" of matter-as-flesh. Bone *is* (essentially and by definition) the precise "formulation" of matter-as-bone.

Together, then, the Material and Formal Causes of a thing tell us what stuff it is composed of and how that stuff is formed. In other words, Material and Formal Causes combine to describe a particular unit of "formed matter."

Efficient Cause

But what explains *why* this bone or flesh or person or tree actually *exists*? What accounts for the potentially "formed matter" *becoming actualized?* What starts the whole process? What gets it going? What "triggers" the sequence that results in this bone or that person? Aristotle answers that a "proximate mover" "causes" a thing's "coming-to-be." Some sort of "motion" is needed to convert potentiality into actuality. Aristotle says:

> Thus the answer to the question "why?" is to be given by referring to the matter, to the essence, and to the proximate mover. In cases of coming-to-be it is mostly

in this last way that people examine the causes; they ask what comes to be after what, what was the immediate thing that acted or was acted upon, and so on in order.[11]

Aristotle named a thing's "triggering" cause the **Efficient Cause**: that which initiates activity; the substance by which a change is brought about. Although, for Aristotle, Efficient Causes, like all causes, are substances, the concept of a triggering action is probably closer to our contemporary notion of cause than the other causes Aristotle discusses.

Final Cause

Aristotle addressed one other "why" question, a question that still confounds philosophers, scientists, and theologians and that is the basis of certain "ultimate meaning" questions: What is the meaning of life? Does life have purpose? *Why* (not *how*) does this universe exist? Ultimate "why" questions are also asked and (usually) easily answered about crafted objects: "Why do these shoes exist? To keep our feet warm and protected." In the case of the shoes, note that the answer states the *reasons for which* the shoes were made, the *purpose, goal,* or *end* that the shoes exist to serve.

Aristotle called the *ultimate why* of a thing that thing's *telos*, or "final" goal, the purpose of its very existence. Thus, the very last answer in a series of "why" questions identifies the "final cause" needed to complete our understanding of the thing. A thing's **Final Cause** is that for which an activity or process takes place, a thing's very reason for being (*raison d'être*).

Another term for "final cause" is *end*, not in the sense of last event or action, but in the sense of *purpose* or *completed state*. In this sense, a thing is completed or finished in the way that a chair or painting or song is finished when the artisan has accomplished his or her goal. When living things are finished in this sense, they are said to be fully realized, mature, ripe, grown, complete, whole, or perfected. Note that, from a naturalistic perspective, referring to persons as "complete," "whole," and "perfect" does *not* carry religious or moralistic connotations. Rather, the terms connote realization, actualization, or reaching our ultimate stage of development, our end or purpose.

Aristotle claimed to have identified what he called an "inner urge" in each living thing to realize its end or purpose: a drive to develop, to become its unique self. Speaking this way, we can say that the acorn, for example, has an *inner urge* to become an oak tree, the baby has an *inner urge* to become a fully realized adult, and so forth. Aristotle characterized this inner urge to become what a thing is "meant to be" as "having its end within itself." The Greek word for this is **entelechy**, and Aristotle constructs his theory of human well-being on the concept of *entelechy*.

■ ENTELECHY ■

Aristotle thought that *entelechy* explained nature as a whole. Certainly the concept frames his entire practical philosophy. *Entelechy means that things do not just happen—they develop according to natural design.* That is, nature

---

Efficient Cause
The triggering cause that initiates activity; the substance by which a change is brought about; close to the contemporary meaning of cause; third of Aristotle's Four Causes.

Final Cause
That for which an activity or process takes place; a thing's very reason for being (*raison d'être*); fourth of Aristotle's Four Causes.

entelechy
From the Greek for "having its end within itself": according to Aristotle, an inner urge that drives all things to blossom into their own unique selves; inner order or design that governs all natural processes.

is ordered and guided internally. Sometimes Aristotle refers to *entelechy* as a "creative drive." "Such principles," he says, "do not all make for the same goal, but each inner principle always makes for the same goal *of its own [kind]*, if nothing interferes" [emphasis added].[12]

The acorn will become an oak tree if nothing stops it. But the acorn lacks the power to ensure that all its needs are met. It might fall on rocky soil, get too much or too little water, and so forth. It might become a pretty pathetic oak tree—but it will never become any kind of cedar because change occurs only within substances.

Human beings, however, are more complex than acorns. And though we must remain human beings, we may fail (for reasons to be discussed) to follow our own *entelechy*. We may never fulfill our ultimate purpose, to become our "true selves." We may remain incompletely "formed," in much the same way some plants "meant to blossom" never blossom. Malformed, they linger in hostile conditions, spindly, thin, unproductive. Materially, they remain petunias, azaleas, cherry trees; they grow but do not develop.

For Aristotle, life without full development is all too common for human beings, too. Because we are so much more complex than acorns and azaleas, the conditions necessary for fully realized human beings are correspondingly more complex. But before we look into Aristotle's formula for thriving, we need to see how and why Aristotle applied the concept of form to the human soul.

■ THE HIERARCHY OF SOULS ■

As we have seen, the Greek term for soul is *psyche*. We get the term *psychology* from it. For Aristotle, *psyche is the form of the body*. Just as we cannot even imagine a soul going to Atlanta without a body, so too, one's body is not a human being without a human soul in Aristotle's view. *Soul is entelechy.*

Aristotle believed that it is impossible to affect the body without affecting the soul or to affect the soul without affecting the body. There is no way to reach the soul except through the bodily organs (including the brain), and there is no way for the soul to act or communicate except bodily. Recently, some scientists have lent support to the view that the mind plays a role in altering the course of various autoimmune diseases, that laughter and positive attitudes have healing power. Such ideas seem to be consistent with Aristotle's insistence on the organic, holistic, inseparable union of the body and the natural soul. African, Amazonian, Native American, and other tribal cultures have long accepted this union as a fact.

Human beings are not the only *besouled* (to use one translator's beautiful word) creatures, and each kind of substance requires a different kind of study. Aristotle thought that although various kinds of souls are different enough that no single definition of *soul* can cover them all, they are similar enough that we can still recognize a common nature in all their varieties.[13]

Aristotle taught that there are three kinds of soul, which constitute a hierarchy. Each higher level on the continuum of souls contains elements of the lower levels—but the lower levels do not contain the higher. This hierarchy is based on

---

Nature, like mind, always acts for a purpose, and this purpose is its end [goal]. That it should be so is according to nature; for every part of a living body is an organ of the soul. Evidently then, all such parts are for the sake of the soul, which is their natural end.

ARISTOTLE

For Aristotle, the great philosopher of the classical period, reared to accept slavery and pursue self-centeredness, the Greek was human. The European barbarians were not human, because they were unskilled; nor were Asians human, because they lacked strength and character; women were not human either; women were halfway human and children were only potentially human. The human being par excellence is the free man of the polis of Hellas.

ENRIQUE DUSSEL

the capacities or *potentialities* possessed by each level of animal life. The more potentiality a thing has, the higher its place in the hierarchy.

The hierarchy of souls progresses from the simplest life functions to more complicated ones. The lowest type of soul is called the *vegetative,* or *nutritive,* soul. This is the minimal level of life (animate matter). *The nutritive soul absorbs matter* from other things (as food is absorbed and transformed into blood or tissue). The second level of soul is the level of sensation; here we find the *sensitive,* or *sentient,* soul. *The sensitive soul registers information* regarding the form of things, but does not absorb or become those things (as when we look at or touch something). Human souls include a third, higher level of *entelechy* called the *rational* soul, which includes the nutritive and sensitive souls, as well as capacities for analyzing things, understanding various forms of relationships, and making reasoned decisions (called *deliberation*).

The lowest level of life has the most limited potential; think, for instance, of single cells or worms. At the top of the hierarchy of souls, we observe greater capacities for discriminating among various aspects of the environment and for overriding impulse and instinct with rational deliberation based on goals and ends. We note a capacity for understanding the essence (form) of what's going on and a capacity for creative and self-conscious intelligence. These capacities are lacking in lower life-forms.

We must have richness of soul.

ANTIPHANES

Aristotle's ethics is built on this concept of a hierarchy of souls. It is sometimes classified as an ethic of *self-realization,* but a much better term would be *soul-realization.* A good way to get a basic sense of this kind of ethic is to take a look at the concept of happiness expressed in the *Nicomachean Ethics.*

▨ NATURAL HAPPINESS ▨

The classical Greeks believed, as has been noted, that virtue *arete,* was excellence of function. Happiness was also understood in terms of function: A thing was "happy" when it functioned fully and well according to its own nature. In Aristotelian terms, happiness is the state of actualizing or realizing a thing's function, its *entelechy. A good life is one that provides all the necessary conditions and opportunities for a person to become fully himself or herself—and one in which the person has the character to do so.*

I am convinced that each human being is unique and that he has a right to be his own separate self.

AARON UNGERSMA

As the French classicist Pierre Pellegrin notes, for Aristotle, virtue plays a central, but not self-sufficient, role in the pursuit of human well-being.

The translation of *arete* by virtue, while it has a long tradition of its own, still remains dangerous because of the connotations of the word. For Aristotle, *arete* is the excellence of some thing. He remarks that we can speak of the *arete* of a tool or a horse. Nonetheless, he uses the term most particularly in the ethical realm. Now "ethical" comes from *ethos* . . . which means the habitual way to be, the one that results from experience and education. If someone has acquired the habit, from childhood, of being intemperate, intemperance becomes for him a habitual, almost natural way to be. Ethical virtue then will be a state of being virtuous, rooted in the human subject by long experience. But while Aristotle acknowledges that immorality and vice can procure

"The Meaning of Our Existence Is Not Invented But Detected"

What is called self-actualization is, and must remain, the unintended effect of self-transcendence; it is ruinous and self-defeating to make it the target of intention. And what is true of self-actualization also holds for identity and happiness. It is the very "pursuit of happiness" that obviates happiness. The more we make it a target, the more widely we miss.

It may now have become clear that a concept such as self-actualization, or self-realization, is not a sufficient ground for a motivational theory. This is mainly due to the fact that self-actualization, like power and pleasure, also belongs to the class of phenomena which can only be obtained as a side effect and are thwarted precisely to the degree to which they are made a matter of direct intention. Self-actualization is a good thing; however, I maintain that man can only actualize himself to the extent to which he fulfills meaning. Then self-actualization occurs spontaneously; it is contravened when it is made an end in itself. . . .

We have to beware of the tendency to deal with values in terms of the mere self-expression of man himself. . . . If the meaning that is waiting to be fulfilled by man were nothing but a mere expression of self, or no more than a projection of his wishful thinking, it would immediately lose its demanding and challenging character; it could no longer call man forth or summon him. . . . I think the meaning of our existence is not invented by ourselves, but rather detected.

Viktor E. Frankl, *Man's Search for Meaning: An Introduction to Logotherapy* (New York: Pocket Books, 1963), pp. 8, 35–36, 156–157.

satisfactions, he posits as the basis for his ethics the principle that virtue, which implies moderation of tendencies and self-mastery, is the principal—though not the only—element in happiness (*eudaimonia*). . . . To be virtuous, then, for human beings, is to give themselves the best opportunity to realize their human nature fully.[14]

The final cause, then, produces motion through being loved.

ARISTOTLE

For Aristotle, happiness is a quality of life here and now, not something for the hereafter. It is neither entirely material nor entirely spiritual (formal). His is a philosophy of moderation in the fullest sense, based on common experience, stripped of sentimentality: Wealth is not enough to give us happiness, but poverty makes happiness impossible. Mental attitude is important, but so is physical health. No one can be happy *in the fullest sense* who is chronically ill or mentally deficient. Unattractive people are not as happy as attractive ones. No matter how great our efforts, happiness always contains an element of luck. A person raised well from infancy is a happier person than one who is not. An otherwise good life can be marred by a bad death.

PHILOSOPHICAL QUERY

• • • • •

As an example of the importance of luck in the good life, think about this Aristotelian maxim (derived from Solon): "Count no man happy until he is dead." Aristotle taught that a good life can be marred by a bad death. Discuss this general idea and then tie it to our present attitudes toward death, dying, and euthanasia.

The Good

Whereas Plato believed the Form of Good was the highest form of being, Aristotle believed the good is "that at which all things aim." In other words, the good for anything is the realization of its own nature (essence): *The good at which all things aim is their own entelechy*. When we use the expressions "for your own good," or "that's not good for you," we may have something similar in mind. "The good," then, is what's good for something's full functioning. The good encourages the development (realization) of a thing's true nature.

Because human beings are complex, consisting of all three elements of soul, it is possible to develop physically or emotionally or intellectually and still fail to realize our *entelechy*. It is also possible to lack the ability to achieve it, either because the external circumstances of our lives inhibit our full development or because some imbalance in our own characters prevents us from fully developing.

Before we go any further, it's important to be clear about the distinction between "aging" and "developing." We're probably all familiar with people who grow old without growing up. We must not confuse biological growth and maturation with personal development. Aristotle linked the two: A *fully* functioning, *completely* happy person will be mentally, physically, spiritually, financially, professionally, creatively, and socially healthy and well-rounded.

As noted in the Overview of Classical Themes (pp. 16–20), most classical philosophers included an objective component in their conceptions of happiness. This means that *entelechy* is not determined by the individual. Aristotle's view differs from those self-realization or self-fulfillment theories that claim "you can be anything you want to be." Such a claim would have struck him as

> *The intention that man should be "happy" is not contained in the plan of Creation.*
>
> SIGMUND FREUD

> *Count no man happy until he is dead.*
>
> SOLON

> *"Know thyself" has become "Do whatever you please."*
>
> BRUNO BETTELHEIM

"Can Mommy borrow your baby-blue pinafore tonight, sweetie?"

ridiculous. It is as irrational and unworthy for a human being to try to live like an animal, for example, as it is for an acorn to try to be an ear of corn—or for us to try to make a dog into a child.

| PHILOSOPHICAL | • • • • • • |
| QUERY | *Discuss some of the common obstacles to becoming a fully functioning, balanced individual.* |

Teleological Thinking

According to Aristotle, observation of the natural world (which includes human behavior) reveals that

> Every art and every scientific inquiry, and similarly every action and purpose, may be said to aim at some good. Hence the good has been well defined as that at which all things aim. . . .
>
> As there are various actions, arts, and sciences, it follows the ends are also various. Thus health is the end of medicine, a vessel of shipbuilding, victory [is the end] of strategy, and wealth [is the goal] of domestic economy. . . .
>
> . . . If it is true that in the sphere of action there is an end which we wish for its own sake, and for the sake of which we wish everything else . . . it is clear that this will be the good or the supreme good. Does it not follow that the knowledge of this supreme good is of great importance for the conduct of life, and that, *if we know it,* we shall be like archers who have a mark at which to aim, we shall have a better chance of attaining what we want?[15]

Why do people feel so crowded? Because each wants to occupy the place of the other.

RABBI ABRAHAM YAAKOV OF SADAGORA

The technical name for this kind of thinking is *teleological,* from the Greek root *telos,* meaning end, purpose, or goal. (*Entelechy* comes from the same root.) **Teleological thinking** is a way of explaining or understanding a thing in terms of its ultimate goal, or final cause. For example, in teleological terms, infancy is understood as a stage on the way to mature adulthood. Adulthood is the *telos* of infancy. Teleological thinking also refers to understanding things functionally in terms of the relationship of the parts to a whole—for example, considering a vehicle's transmission in terms of the vehicle's ultimate function: speed, traction, comfort. Both Aristotle's ethic and conception of virtue are teleological.

teleological thinking
Way of explaining things in terms of their ultimate goals; understanding things functionally in terms of the relationship of the parts to the whole.

The Science of the Good

In the first book of the *Nicomachean Ethics,* Aristotle makes a famous and insightful proclamation:

> Our statement of the case will be adequate if it be made with all such clearness as the subject-matter admits; for it would be wrong to expect the same degree of accuracy in all [subjects]. . . . [Due to the nature of our subject] we must be content to indicate the truth roughly and in outline; and as our subjects and premises are true generally *but not universally,* we must be content to arrive at conclusions which are generally true.[16]

Aristotle was aware that moral considerations involve practical judgments of particular circumstances. We might characterize his position as *formal relativism*. That means that even though there is an underlying structure, or form, of happiness for human beings, the specific way in which a particular human being realizes that form varies with his or her circumstances.

Consider an example from Aristotle: A wrestler and a young child do not eat the same kinds of foods or the same amounts; but this does not mean that the laws of nutrition are relative in the Sophists' sense of being radically determined by the individual or group. Indeed, the same natural laws apply to wrestlers and babies: Minimum protein, fat, carbohydrate, and fluid levels must be met for good health. Appropriate caloric intake should be based on actual energy output, not on a merely theoretical model, and so on. But since individual metabolisms vary, since local temperature affects metabolism, since the quality of food varies, and so forth, we must modify each person's actual diet: "We must be content to indicate the truth roughly and in outline," Aristotle reminds us.

We can identify a general outline of conduct that will lead to the best possible life, but we cannot give a precise prescription for any individual's good life. Still, Aristotle says, we can arrive at a valuable approximation of the "good life" based on human nature and the good we each seek.

According to the *Nicomachean Ethics,* the good to which all humans aspire is happiness:

> As [all] knowledge and moral purpose aspires to some good, what is in our view the good at which the political science aims, and what is the highest of all practical goods? As to its name there is, I may say, a general agreement. The masses and the cultured classes agree in calling it happiness, and conceive that "to live well" or "to do well" is the same thing as "to be happy." But as to the nature of happiness they do not agree, nor do the masses give the same account of it as the philosophers.[17]

The *Nicomachean Ethics* is a careful survey of a variety of opinions regarding what constitutes "living well" in the best, fullest sense. Although Aristotle concludes that the best life is the life of philosophical contemplation, the heart of his ethics is a philosophy of moderation, fulfillment, activity, and balance.

Eudaimonia

The word Aristotle used that is so often translated as "happiness" is **eudaimonia**. The English language does not have a good one-word equivalent for *eudaimonia*. *Happiness* is almost too bland, although it's probably the answer most of us would give if asked what we want from life (or the afterlife, in many conceptions of heaven).

Eudaimonia implies being really alive rather than just existing: fully aware, vital, alert. This is more than being free of cares or worries. Rather, *eudaimonia* implies exhilaration—great suffering and great joy, great passions. It implies a full life, not a pinched, restricted one.

A life devoted solely to pleasure, says Aristotle, is "a life fit only for cattle." Pleasure is not the *goal* of life; it's the natural companion of a full and vigorous

To attain any assured knowledge of the soul is one of the most difficult things in the world . . . if there is no . . . single and general method of solving the question of essence, our task becomes still more difficult . . . with what facts shall we begin our inquiry?

ARISTOTLE

The hell to be endured hereafter, of which theology tells us, is no worse than the hell we make for ourselves in this world by habitually fashioning our characters in the wrong way.

WILLIAM JAMES

eudaimonia
Often translated as happiness; term Aristotle used to refer to fully realized existence; state of being fully aware, vital, alert.

life. If you have ever seen an athlete or scholar or artist working very hard at what she loves, you know what Aristotle meant: Deep and satisfying pleasure *accompanies* doing what we are meant to do. But the pursuit of pleasure as an end is shallow:

> Ordinary or vulgar people conceive [the good] to be pleasure, and accordingly approve a life of enjoyment. . . . Now the mass of men present an absolutely slavish appearance, as choosing the life of brute beasts, but they meet with consideration because so many persons in authority share [such] tastes.[18]

According to Aristotle, a life devoted to acquiring wealth is also a limited one. Its focus is too narrow to nourish the natural soul's full complement of qualities and needs. Think of people who work long, stressful hours to get rich—and then think of how much life they miss in the process. They never "stop to smell the roses." The unhappy rich person is common enough to be a stereotype. Even with all the money in the world, a person still needs self-discipline and the knowledge to use his or her riches wisely. Aristotle says:

> The life of money-making is in a sense a life of constraint, and it is clear that wealth is not the good of which we are in quest; for it is useful in part as a means to something else.[19]

Aristotle also rejected fame and public success as leading to *eudaimonia* because he believed that the more self-sufficient we are, the happier we are; and

Continued observations of this basic dynamic nature of happiness, especially in clinical psychological practice, leads almost inevitably to the conclusion that deeper and more fundamental than sexuality, deeper than the craving for social power, deeper even than the desire for possessions, there is a still more generalized and more universal craving in the human makeup. It is the craving for knowledge of the right direction—or orientation.

WILLIAM H. SHELDON, M.D.

Eudaimonia results when pleasure is the natural companion of a fully functioning life, rather than the goal of life. Artisans working at their true calling—such as this eighty-year-old glassblower—combine hard work and happiness in a vital, rich way.

©Bojan Brecelj/Corbis

the famous are less self-sufficient than most: They need bodyguards, managers, financial advisers, public adulation, and so forth. There is greater peace of mind, security, and satisfaction in knowing that I can provide for my needs than there is in depending on others, as any adolescent or convalescent knows. If one's happiness depends on fame, it depends on the whims of a fickle public:

> But [the love of fame] appears too superficial for our present purpose; for honor seems to depend more upon the people who pay it than upon the person to whom it is paid, and we have an intuitive feeling that the good is something which is proper to a man himself and cannot be easily taken away from him.[20]

The Good Life Is a Process

The highest and fullest happiness, according to Aristotle, comes from a life of reason and contemplation—not a life of inactivity or imbalance, but a rationally ordered life in which intellectual, physical, and social needs are all met under the governance of reason and moderation. The "reasonable" person does not avoid life: He or she engages in it fully. A rich and full life is a social life. Aristotle says that no man would choose to live without friends, even if he could have everything he wanted on the condition that he remain solitary. According to Aristotle, human beings are political (social) creatures "designed by nature to live with others."

The rational person alone knows how to engage in life fully, since he or she alone has fully realized all three souls: the nutritive, sensitive, and rational—according to the basic form or *entelechy* of human beings.[21] *The good life must be lived fully; it is a process, an activity, a becoming, not a static condition.* Not even moral virtue is adequate for happiness by itself, because:

> [Virtue] it appears, lacks completeness; for it seems that a man may possess virtue and yet be asleep or inactive throughout life, and, not only [that], but he may experience the greatest calamities and misfortunes. But nobody would call such a life a life of happiness unless he were maintaining a paradox.[22]

Practicing a philosophy of *fully functioning* moderation is quite difficult, for it often requires that we stretch beyond those talents and areas of life we are currently satisfied with. Aristotle understood this and attempted to present practical advice that could help us come closer to living a richer, more virtuous life:

> The purpose of this present study is not . . . the attainment of theoretical knowledge; we are not conducting this inquiry in order to know what virtue is, but in order to become good, else there is no advantage in studying it.[23]

The happy man lives well and does well; for we have practically defined happiness as a sort of good life and good action.

ARISTOTLE

May God grant me power to struggle to become not another but a better man.

SAMUEL TAYLOR COLERIDGE

● ● ● ● ● ●

PHILOSOPHICAL

QUERY

Consider Aristotle's position carefully here. It might conform more closely to our true feelings about virtue than our sentimental and idealistic platitudes imply. We might be taught that "virtue is its own reward," but how many of us really think as highly of a "good" person who hides away from the world as we do of someone who has faults and makes mistakes, but gets out there and gets involved in life? Is being "good" really enough?

■ HITTING THE MARK ■

It is possible to fail in many ways . . . while to succeed is possible only in one way (for which reason also one is easy and the other difficult—to miss the mark easy, to hit it difficult).

ARISTOTLE

There are, perhaps, two ways to avoid mediocrity. The first is probably the most common today: to excel or fail at something in a big way. The other, it seems, is rarer, probably because it is so difficult for many of us: to live the fullest life possible, developing and nurturing *all* good and necessary qualities while avoiding all character defects.

Now, clearly the second way constitutes an impossible goal for a human being to meet completely. No one seems likely to avoid all defects of character. That does not, however, rule out the desirability of trying to hit this difficult mark. It's one thing to say "I can't be expected to get perfect scores on all my assignments," and quite another to jump to the conclusion "so there's no point in studying at all." Such a reaction is already extreme.

We saw that temperance was one of the cardinal virtues in Plato's *Republic* and that it was a key virtue for Socrates. Aristotle goes so far as to base his entire moral philosophy on moderation:

> First of all, it must be observed that the nature of moral qualities is such that they are destroyed by defect and by excess. We see the same thing happen in the case of strength and of health . . . excess as well as deficiency of physical exercise destroys our strength, and similarly, too much and too little food and drink destroys our health; the proportionate amount, however, produces, increases, and strengthens it. The same applies to self-control, courage, and the other virtues: the man who shuns and fears everything becomes a coward, whereas a man who knows no fear at all and goes to meet every danger becomes reckless. Similarly, a man who revels in every pleasure and abstains from none becomes self-indulgent, while he who avoids every pleasure like a

Compulsive dedication to something may result in excellence at that particular something. But Aristotle cautions that great effort in the service of anything less than the goal of well-balanced thriving results in imbalance and overall dysfunction. Does *specialized* excellence (in any field, not just bodybuilding) inhibit being truly well-rounded? Have we, as a culture, perhaps lost sight of the price we pay for narrowly *specialized* excellence?

© David Reed/Corbis

boor becomes what might be called insensitive. Thus we see that self-control and courage are destroyed by excess and deficiency and are preserved by the mean.[24]

The Principle of the Mean

The concept of moderation, what the Greeks called **sophrosyne**, seems dull and depriving to many people. It implies a life of rigid rules, no fun, playing it safe and avoiding any risks. As we have seen, however, Aristotle did not regard a narrow, boring, play-it-safe life as good. Indeed, the idea that moderation is boring is itself the product of an extreme view. The attitude that only living on the edge, going for the gusto, abandoning self-restraint, can make life interesting is one-sided.

Aristotelian moderation is based on the concept that wisdom is *hitting the mark* between too much and not enough. If you study a target, you will notice that only a small circle in the center is the bull's-eye. There is more room on the target to miss the mark than there is to hit it.

A life completely devoted to playing it safe would be off the mark—cowardly, boorish, and insensitive in Aristotle's terms. Living that way actually limits opportunities to grow and fully experience life. Living recklessly or self-indulgently, going from extreme to extreme, will not produce a good, full life either. The great artist who lives only for her work is not living a good, full life, since she indulges her work at the expense of other vital parts of herself. The scholar who hides in research does likewise. So, too, the compulsive jogger or bodybuilder. People who spend all their time doing charity work, praying, and reading holy scriptures are not balanced human beings. (Moral virtue, remember, is not enough, according to Aristotle.)

Aristotelian moderation is the crux of becoming a whole person—of actualizing our potentialities, realizing our form. Achieving it may require that we do more of the things that are difficult for us and less of those we presently enjoy. Just as a proper diet is relative (the overeater must eat less than he is used to or wants to; the anorexic must do the opposite), the goal for each is a bull's-eye.

Each person's prescription for self-realization must be determined by his or her own actual condition. Some of us must become more social, others less so. Some students need to study less to become balanced human beings; others need to study more. If we see the call to moderation in terms of *who we are right now* and what it would take to make us fuller, more balanced, more "alive" and vibrant people, it is anything but a call to boring mediocrity.

> But let us first agree that any discussion on matters of action cannot be more than an outline and is bound to lack precision. . . . And if this is true of our general discussion, our treatment of particular problems will be even less precise, since these do not come under the head of any art which can be transmitted by precept, but the agent must consider on each different occasion what the situation demands, just as in medicine and in navigation. But although this is the kind of discussion in which we are engaged, we must do our best.[25]

sophrosyne
Wisdom as moderation; hitting the mark; quality of finding the mean between excess and deficiency.

There is no greater misfortune that can befall you than to be stricken from the roster of the living while you are still living.
SENECA

Character is fate.
HERACLITUS

Character and Habit

Central to Aristotle's ethics is the notion of character. From the Greek *charakter,* a word derived from *charassein,* "to make sharp" or "to engrave," **character** refers to the sum total of a person's traits, including behavior, habits, likes and dislikes, capacities, potentials, and so on. For Aristotle, *character* referred to the overall nature or tone of a person's habits, the habitual or predictable and usual way a person behaves. A courageous person is *characteristically* brave. A slothful one is *characteristically* lazy. Moral virtues are habits, according to Aristotle, and must be ingrained in us by training. We are not born with them.

> Moral virtue comes to us as a result of habit. . . . The virtues we first get by exercising them, as also happens in the case of the arts as well. For the things we have to learn before we can do them, we learn by doing them, e.g., men become builders by building. . . . So too we become just by doing just acts, temperate by doing temperate acts, brave by doing brave acts. . . . If this were not so, there would have been no need of a teacher, but all men would be born good or bad at their craft. . . . Thus in one word, states of character arise out of like activities. That is why the activities we exhibit must be of a certain kind; it is because the states of character correspond to the difference between these. It makes no small difference, then, whether we form habits of one kind or another from our very youth; it makes a very great difference, or rather all the difference.[26]

The coward cannot wait for courage, or he will remain a coward. The coward must first act courageously if he wishes to become brave. The poor student cannot wait for motivation, but must first *act the way the disciplined student* acts in order to become a better student. Aristotle anticipated a number of contemporary psychological schools with this emphasis on habitual behavior as the prime element in shaping the human character.

Aristotle distinguishes practical wisdom from theoretical understanding and other forms of knowledge. He links practical wisdom to deliberation. Practical wisdom involves choosing the right goals *and* acting on them. Practical wisdom can help those of us lacking good habits to develop them:

> A man fulfills his proper function only by way of practical wisdom and moral excellence or virtue: virtue makes us aim at the right target, and practical wisdom makes us use the right means.[27]

But, Aristotle notes,

> our ability to perform such actions is *in no way enhanced by knowing them,* since the virtues are characteristics [that is, fixed capacities for action, acquired by habit].[28]

Merely knowing what is good and healthy does not—by itself—usually lead to doing what is good and healthy, as most of us realize. This reminds me of a saying a friend uses as a rule of thumb: "You can act yourself into right thinking, but you can't think yourself into right acting." Like all such sayings, this one needs to be taken with the proverbial grain of salt, but it does emphasize an Aristotelian point: *Happiness requires action.*

character

From the Greek *charakter,* a word derived from *charassein,* "to make sharp" or "to engrave," character refers to the sum total of a person's traits, including behavior, habits, likes and dislikes, capacities, potentials, and so on; a key element of Aristotelian ethics and psychology, meaning the overall (generally fixed) nature or tone of a person's habits.

So, as . . . Aristotle . . . insisted, wisdom is to be contrasted with cleverness because cleverness is the ability to take the right steps to any end, whereas wisdom is related only to good ends, and to human life in general rather than to the ends of particular arts.

PHILIPPA FOOT

Assume the virtue, even if you have it not,
*   For use almost can change the stamp of nature.*

SHAKESPEARE

Aristotle thought that good habits ingrained in childhood produced the happiest, best life. He said it was better to "overtighten the bow string" in youth, because aging would naturally loosen it.

Application of the Mean

A **mean** is the midpoint between two other points. On a line, it is the exact middle. *Aristotle characterized moral virtue as a mean between too little and too much*. In his terms, the mean is located between deficiency and excess. We might visualize it like this:

vice ——————— virtue ——————— vice

deficiency ——————— mean ——————— excess

One advantage of a visual aid like this is that it shows us an action can be *more or less* virtuous or vicious (meaning that it's a vice, not that it's necessarily cruel). Depending on the area encompassed by the mean, there is a certain amount of room within the general area of virtue, but there is even more room in the range of the extremes. Thus it is easier to go wrong than right.

Aristotle realized that some actions are excessive by their very nature; they can have no mean. For instance, there is no moderate, appropriate way to commit adultery. Other kinds of actions admit of degree and so can have a mean. Aristotle illustrated his point with a lengthy analysis of courage, which he placed between the deficiency of cowardice and the excess of recklessness or foolhardiness, both of which are vices. Some examples of Aristotelian vices and virtues are shown in Table 6.1.

Aristotle noted that some vices are closer to the mean than others are, because they reflect more of the virtue. In the case of courage, for instance, foolhardiness is closer to courage and so is less a vice than cowardice is. Nevertheless, foolhardiness is still a vice. This is why the coward—who is further from the mean—is more easily recognized as flawed than is the foolhardy person who takes too many or the wrong kind of risks. That's why television and movie characters are easily mistaken for being courageous when they are actually foolhardy. In real life, they are not the people to emulate.

mean
From the Latin *medius,* the midpoint between two other points; for Aristotle, moral virtue was characterized as a mean between too little (deficiency) and too much (excess).

The unforgivable sin is [to not] become all that you can as a human being, given the circumstances of life that we have to accept.

R. D. Laing

A thing moderately good is not so good as it ought to be. Moderation in temper is always a virtue; but moderation in principle is always a vice.

Thomas Paine

TABLE 6.1

∼ Aristotelian Virtues and Vices

DEFICIENCY/VICE	MEAN/VIRTUE	EXCESS/VICE
Cowardice	Courage	Foolhardiness
Anorexia	Moderation	Gluttony
Stinginess	Generosity	Profligacy
Standoffishness	Friendliness	Obsequiousness
Shyness	Pride	Vanity
Pessimism	Realism	Optimism
Celibacy	Monogamy	Promiscuity
Dullness	Well-roundedness	Wildness

His own manners will be his punishment.

CICERO

We can easily find many other examples of excess or deficiency being mistaken for valuable character traits. If we take an organic view of life, such examples show how great virtue or talent in one or two areas cannot outweigh significant deficiencies in other areas. An Aristotelian analysis of human activity as an organic complex affected by our characteristic virtues and vices can improve our moral perspective:

> It is moral virtue that is concerned with emotions and actions, and it is in emotions and actions that excess, deficiency, and the median are found. Thus we can experience fear, confidence, desire, anger, pity, and generally any kind of pleasure and pain either too much or too little, and in either case not properly. But to experience all this at the right time, toward the right objects, toward the right people, for the right reason, and in the right manner—that is the median and the best course, the course that is a mark of virtue.[29]

According to Aristotle, we become our best selves in the process of becoming fully functioning human beings.

One possible benefit of thinking of virtue as a mean between excess and deficiency is an enriched sense of virtue. Thinking only in terms of right *or* wrong can lead to a perception of virtues and vices as simple opposites, whereas Aristotle's system treats them as part of an organic whole, in which each element affects the others and the overall functioning of the organism. *Aristotelian self-realization, like happiness, is a by-product of living a well-balanced life.*

As long as you have to defend the imaginary self that you think is important, you will lose your peace of heart. As soon as you compare that shadow with the shadows of other people, you lose all joy, because you have begun to trade in unrealities, and there is no joy in things that do not exist.

THOMAS MERTON

PHILOSOPHICAL QUERY

• • • • • •

Study and discuss Table 6.1, Aristotelian Virtues and Vices, using principles from the Nicomachean Ethics *and the concept of the mean. Then add and discuss your own examples of virtues and vices.*

"They Are Obliged to Become Somebody Else"

The Trappist monk and Roman Catholic philosopher Thomas Merton (1915–1968) expressed an interesting variation of a self-realization ethic in his book *New Seeds of Contemplation*. By tying individual *entelechy* to God's will, Merton avoided the problem of relativism. His position has some of the contemporary feel of humanistic psychology, but with the added moral limits of Roman Catholic values. Merton's work is a blend of philosophy, religion, and psychology. The following passage is typical:

> Many poets are not artists for the same reason that many religious men are not saints: they never succeed in being the particular poet or the particular monk they are intended to be by God. They never

become the man or the artist who is called for by all the circumstances of their individual lives.

> They waste their years in vain efforts to be some other poet, some other saint. For many absurd reasons, they are convinced that they are obliged to become somebody else who died two hundred years ago and who lived in circumstances utterly alien to their own.

> They wear out their minds and bodies in a hopeless endeavor to have somebody else's experiences or write somebody else's poems or express somebody else's spirituality.

Thomas Merton, *New Seeds of Contemplation* (New York: New Directions, 1961), p. 98.

■ COMMENTARY ■

For Aristotle, self-realization was part of a natural process that could be understood only in terms of the whole. Self-realization was not directed by a personal God, nor was it a function of free-flowing self-expression. Aristotle saw limits as set by nature, not by the individual. He thought that he had identified a fixed, natural hierarchy within the human soul. The rational soul is "designed" to control and guide—but not crush—emotions and appetites.

Just as some actions (adultery, for instance) cannot hit a mean because their very nature is imbalanced, so, too, some personalities cannot be actualized (full-functioning) because their very essences are excessive or deficient. Some lives are such that self-actualization is impossible. An acorn that falls too close to the parent tree might lack sufficient sunlight to burgeon, or it might be carried to a hostile environment by a bird or used by an artist in a collage. Corn infected with disease will lack the material necessary to complete its development. Human beings raised in seriously defective environments or born with major genetic impairments will never fully realize their *entelechies*.

The simple call to "be yourself" may sound appealing, but it proves to be insubstantial without solid philosophical grounding. While it is possible to be too self-controlled, no substantial good can come from realizing whatever limited conception of a self we happen to feel like—and this includes a self based only on religious, moral, or personal feelings.

It is difficult to judge Aristotle's conception of the self-realized, superior person today. Clearly, his classical model of "human excellence" is alien to a culture that encourages the expression of virtually every emotion as healthy. His basic values are alien to a culture that prizes youthful spontaneity and talent over mature self-mastery and self-discipline. The modern, individualistic self is, it seems, set free without a clear direction. The Aristotelian self is crafted according to standards of excellence discovered through philosophical contemplation and careful observation.

Well begun is half done.
ARISTOTLE

The knowledge of the soul admittedly contributes greatly to the advance of truth in general, and, above all, to our understanding of Nature, for the soul is in some sense the principle of animal life. Our aim is to grasp and understand, first its essential nature, and secondly its properties.
ARISTOTLE

■ SUMMARY OF MAIN POINTS ■

- Aristotle was Plato's most illustrious pupil and tutor of Alexander the Great. In contrast to Plato's rationalistic approach, Aristotle brings to full maturity a second major approach to the study of the good life: collecting facts and using factual information to make this a better world.

- Aristotle was a philosophical naturalist. Naturalism is the belief that reality consists of the natural world and that the universe is ordered. Everything follows consistent and discoverable *laws* of nature and can be described in terms of fundamental laws.

- According to Aristotle, form can be abstracted from matter but cannot exist independently of matter; this kind of form is sometimes referred to as essence. Matter is the common material stuff found in a variety of things; it has no distinct characteristics until some form is imparted to it or until the form inherent in a thing becomes actualized. Individual things are "formed matter."

- Aristotle claimed that complete understanding of a thing required identifying its "four causes." The Four Causes are the Material Cause (the material the thing is made of); the Formal Cause (the form the thing takes); the Efficient Cause (the "triggering" motion that begins the thing); and the Final Cause (the *telos,* or ultimate purpose for which the thing exists).

● Aristotle identified what he called an "inner urge" in every living thing, a drive to become its unique self. He called this inner urge *entelechy,* meaning "having its end within itself." Things do not just happen— they develop according to natural design. Nature is ordered and guided "internally." The technical name for this kind of thinking is *teleological,* from the Greek root *telos,* meaning end, purpose, or goal.

● Aristotle taught that there are three kinds of soul and that they constitute a hierarchy. Each higher level of soul contains elements of the lower levels—but the lower levels do not contain the higher. The lowest soul is the vegetative, or nutritive, soul. The second level is the sensitive, or sentient, soul; it registers information regarding the form of things, but does not absorb or become those things. Human souls include a third, higher level of *entelechy* called the rational soul, which includes the nutritive and sensitive souls plus capacities for analysis, understanding various forms of relationships, and making reasoned decisions.

● According to Aristotle, the good is "that at which all things aim." The good at which all things aim is their own *entelechy. Eudaimonia,* which is often translated as "happiness," means being really alive rather than just existing. According to Aristotle, happiness requires activity, good habits, and practical wisdom.

● Aristotelian moderation is based on the concept of wisdom as hitting the mark (*sophrosyne*) between too much and not enough. Virtue consists of hitting the mark of moderation, and vice consists of being off by too much (excess) or too little (deficiency). Virtue is the mean between either extreme.

■ POST-READING REFLECTIONS ■

Now that you have had a chance to learn about Aristotle, use your new knowledge to answer these questions.

1. What is unusual about the nature of the writings attributed to Aristotle?

2. What do scholars mean by saying that Aristotle brought philosophy down to earth? How does this relate to Plato?

3. Why does Aristotle characterize things as "formed matter"? Explain.

4. Construct and evaluate a teleological explanation of your education.

5. In what sense can Aristotle's position be termed "formal relativism"? Is Aristotle a relativist? Explain.

6. What did Aristotle identify as the highest kind of life? Explain fully.

7. Explain the importance of *sophrosyne* and character to Aristotle's concept of happiness.

8. What is the "principle of the mean"? Give one or two examples of using it to evaluate a course of action or moral choice. Give several examples of activities for which there is no mean.

9. How do character and habit affect happiness and virtue, according to Aristotle?

10. Analyze one or two ranges of activity to show how some vices are more virtuous than others.

 PHILOSOPHY INTERNET RESOURCES

Go to the Soccio Web page at **http://philosophy.wadsworth.com/ Soccio7e** for Web links, practice quizzes and tests, a pronunciation guide, and study tips.

THE STOIC

Epictetus and Marcus Aurelius

YOU SHAME YOURSELF, MY SOUL, YOU SHAME YOURSELF,
AND YOU WILL HAVE NO FURTHER OPPORTUNITY TO RESPECT
YOURSELF; THE LIFE OF EVERY MAN IS SHORT AND YOURS IS
ALMOST FINISHED WHILE YOU DO NOT RESPECT YOURSELF BUT
ALLOW YOUR HAPPINESS TO DEPEND UPON . . . OTHERS.

Marcus Aurelius, Emperor of Rome

FOR YOUR REFLECTION

1. *What is hedonism?*

2. *What is Cyrenaic hedonism?*

3. *What is Epicurean hedonism?*

4. *What is Cynicism?*

5. *What is the relationship of Socrates to Cynicism and Stoicism?*

6. *What is the Stoic Logos?*

7. *What is under our control according to the Stoics?*

8. *What is the* cosmopolis?

9. *Who was James Stockdale?*

FOR DEEPER CONSIDERATION

A. How did the social climate of ancient Rome encourage the emergence of Stoicism? That is, in what ways can Stoicism be characterized as a response to specific living conditions? And what, if anything, explains the attraction of Stoicism to both Epictetus and Marcus Aurelius, whose lives, viewed from the outside, seem to be so radically different? What did they have in common—if indeed they had anything—that can help us understand the origins and appeal of Stoicism?

B. One popular notion of a Stoic is of an emotionally inhibited or repressed individual, someone detached and unfeeling, not engaged in life, not "living fully." Is this conception fair and accurate? Whether it is or not, what accounts for this stereotype? What would Seneca say about it? What do you think?

t's the Friday before a three-day weekend and you are looking forward to a romantic vacation on the beach with your special friend. You get off work a bit late and head for the bank to cash a check. Pulling onto the freeway, you're immediately locked into a bumper-to-bumper mass of vehicles, lurching along at fifteen miles per hour. Forty-five minutes later, still a couple of miles from the bank, you notice that you're low on fuel. You begin to steam. Someone tries to cut in front of you, and you explode in a rage, shaking your fist and shouting obscenities.

When you finally get to the bank, there's no place to park. After circling the parking lot for twenty minutes, you find a space. The line in the bank looks endless and there are only three tellers. The man in front of you has a bag of checks and cash from his business. You continue to steam. It seems like every customer chats with the tellers. And the tellers! It takes them forever to do anything. As you inch along in line you glare at various bank officers to let them know how angry you are at the inefficient way they run their bank.

By the time you get out of the bank, you're behind schedule and it's rush hour—pre-holiday, Friday-afternoon rush hour. You race out of the parking lot, squealing your tires as you cut into traffic. Rushing through an intersection at high speed, you catch the attention of a police officer. It's not enough that you get a ticket for reckless driving—the officer takes forever checking out your license and writing the ticket. When you finally get going again, you feel like a bomb about to go off.

If you have ever had an experience anything close to the one just described, you've shared the nearly universal sense of frustration, anger, and anxiety caused by "stupid people" and "events beyond our control." This kind of reaction to external events is so common that a school of philosophy sprang up to deal with just such experiences. Yet its basic tenets go against the grain for most people, at least initially. This philosophy is called **Stoicism,** and those who practice it are called **Stoics**.

Stoicism initially emerged as a reaction against the belief that pleasure is always good and pain is always bad or evil. Rather than pursuing pleasure and trying to avoid pain, the Stoic seeks serenity (peace of mind) through self-discipline. Stoicism asserts that seeking anything but self-control results in *avoidable* unhappiness. In the Stoic view, happiness comes only through detachment from all "externals." Put another way: Everything is a matter of attitude. The disciplined, reasonable person can be happy under any and all conditions.

Stoics believe that *nothing can make you happy or unhappy without your consent.* All unhappiness is the result of bad thinking, poor character, and confusing what we can control with what we cannot control. Regarding the opening story, a Stoic would diagnose your frustration and anger as self-induced. Traffic jams, lines and crowds, and cars nearly running out of gas are normal, common aspects of life. There is nothing new or surprising in anything that happens to you. In fact, nothing "happens to you." *You* are the problem.

Your medicine is in you, and you do not observe it. Your ailment is from yourself, and you do not register it.

HAZRAT ALI

Stoicism
Philosophy that counsels self-control, detachment, and acceptance of one's fate as identified by the objective use of reason.

Stoic
Individual who attempts to live according to Stoic doctrine.

In J. W. Waterhouse's romanticized painting, Diogenes ignores the blandishments of civilization from the comfort of his barrel-home. The lantern reminds us of the Cynic's quip that even with a lantern in broad daylight it is impossible to find an honest man.

Discourse on virtue and they pass by in droves; whistle and dance the shimmy, and you've got an audience.

DIOGENES

©Diogenes (d.c. 320 BC) 1882 (oil on canvas). Waterhouse, John William (1849-1917)/Art Gallery of New South Wales, Sydney, Australia/Bridgeman Art Library

PHILOSOPHICAL

QUERY

• • • • • •

Stop for a moment and reflect on this: Is it possible to be calm under all circumstances? Or do certain circumstances force us to be distressed and agitated? Why do some people seem happy in horrible circumstances, while others suffer in the midst of being loved, healthy, and financially well-off? Do you think happiness is mostly a matter of attitude or not? Discuss.

■ HEDONISM ■

To a considerable extent, Stoicism is a refutation of one of the earliest and most persistent, perhaps even the most basic, theories of happiness: Pursue pleasure (whatever suits you) and avoid pain (whatever causes you suffering and discomfort). The technical name for this kind of philosophy is hedonism. From *hedone*, the Greek root for "pleasure," **hedonism** is the general term for any philosophy that says pleasure = good and pain = evil. Some hedonists stress the pursuit of pleasure, and others emphasize avoiding pain. For a strict hedonist, nothing that provides pleasure can be bad.

hedonism

From the Greek root for "pleasure," the general term for any philosophy that says pleasure = good and pain = evil.

Simply put, a hedonist sees the happy life in terms of having the most possible pleasure and the least possible pain. The pursuit of pleasure, says the hedonist, is our birthright. The baby in the cradle coos when it is cuddled, fed, or played with. It cries when it is uncomfortable. No baby has to be taught this; it comes with the territory. We have to learn to be honest, to work hard, to delay gratification, but we do not have to learn to seek pleasure and avoid pain. On the contrary, we have to be forced to go against our basic hedonistic natures.

The difference between *philosophical* hedonism and the instinctive pursuit of immediate pleasure rests, among other things, on the possibility that although most people *think* they know what they need to be happy, a cursory look around makes it clear that many of us don't. We may be able to provide ourselves with *momentary distractions* or *isolated pleasures*, but that's not the same thing as *being happy*. The hedonistic philosopher argues that the pursuit of pleasure and flight from pain may be universal, but genuine happiness is not.

The Meaning of Life Is Pleasure

Aristippus (c. 430–350 B.C.E.) lived in the town of Cyrene on the coast of North Africa in what is now Libya. Cyrene was founded by Greek colonists on the edge of a plateau near the Mediterranean coast. The soil and climate made the area rich in flowers, fruits, and lush vegetation. By the time Aristippus was born, Cyrene was a prosperous city, noted for its marble temples, its opulent public square, and the huge, luxurious homes of its wealthiest citizens. Like ancient Athens, Cyrene's strategic location helped make it a wealthy and exciting trading center.

Aristippus was a friendly and clever young man, fond of pleasures of all sorts. He heard about Socrates while attending the Olympic Games with a friend and was so impressed that he rushed to Athens to meet Socrates. Aristippus quickly became a member of the closest, most involved groups of Socrates' followers and eventually did some teaching himself. Aristippus annoyed some of his Socratic friends, who thought he was behaving like a Sophist when he began to travel about teaching and collecting higher and higher fees. Eventually, Aristippus returned home and opened a school of philosophy in Cyrene. His doctrine of unrefined hedonism is known as **Cyrenaic hedonism,** after his hometown.

Aristippus taught that *pleasure is the principal motive for living and that pleasure is always good—regardless of its source.* He thought it was obvious, to anybody who cared to see it, that all people seek pleasure (whether they are aware of it or not). Aristippus argued that the meaning of life can only be discerned by observing our *actual behavior.* Doing so reveals that the meaning of life is pleasure. The simple, healthy, proper course of life is to follow our natural desires openly, without guilt or apology, and to learn how to most enjoy ourselves and since pleasure is the natural goal of all life, we should try to have as much intense, sensual pleasure as we can.

Aristippus asserted that because sensory pleasures are more intense than mental or emotional ones, they are the best of all. Therefore, physical pleasure is superior to all other things. Only physical pleasure makes life exciting, dynamic, worth living. Not only that, but actual pleasures of the moment are much more desirable than are potential pleasures that might (or might not) occur in the future. In the first place, we are certain only of the present; the future might not even come. And besides, things may be different for us in the future.

Being asked what was the difference between the wise man and the unwise, Aristippus said, "Strip them both and send them among strangers and you will know." To one who boasted that he could drink a great deal without getting drunk, his rejoinder was, "and so can a mule."

DIOGENES LÄERTIUS

Aristippus

Cyrenaic hedonism
Philosophy that advocates the unreflective pursuit of intense, immediate pleasure; makes no qualitative distinctions among pleasures.

It is a hard matter, my fellow citizens, to argue with the belly, since it has no ears.

CATO THE ELDER

Any distinction between good and bad pleasures was as absurd and contradictory as distinguishing between good and bad sins or good and bad virtues. The only difference among pleasures is their intensity: *Whatever pleases me most at the moment is the highest good there can be.* No pleasure can be "sick" in such a value system. No enjoyment can be wrong. No passion is evil in itself. Only loss of self-control that leads to less pleasure is wrong.

The consequence of such a view is that *whatever feels good is good.* Lacking any objective standard of comparison, the Cyrenaic hedonist concludes that the individual is the measure: of that which is pleasure, that it is pleasure; of that which is pain, that is pain. (See Protagoras, Chapter 3.) And since any pleasure is by definition good, it follows that I *ought* to be doing whatever I enjoy doing. This transforms psychological hedonism into ethical hedonism: Although we are, by nature, predisposed to seek pleasure and avoid pain, some of us become confused and our instincts and habits get corrupted. We attempt to stifle the pursuit of pleasure because we see it as somehow shameful or immoral. We may even add pain to our lives if we think that by suffering we become purified or ennobled. Our natural hedonism can be subdued by childhood training, religious indoctrination, or a puritanical culture. Thus, the Cyrenaic hedonist argues, it makes sense to advise people that they *ought* to do what they are by nature meant to do: Be happy at all costs.

> *What is the result at which all virtue aims?* Serenity.
> Epictetus

◼ EPICUREANISM ◼

Though **Epicurus** (341–270 B.C.E.) was born in the Asia Minor city of Samos, he was an Athenian citizen because his father had moved to Samos as an Athenian colonist. When he was eighteen years old, Epicurus went to Athens to complete the two years of military service required of Athenian males. The Macedonian king of Greece, Alexander the Great, had just died, and the Athenians, who had resented his rule, revolted against the regent he had imposed on them. It took less than a year for this revolt to be crushed, but Epicurus drew an important lesson from it: Political activities and ambitions are pointless.

Epicurus remained in Athens for a time and studied with followers of both Plato and Aristotle. He never accepted Plato's philosophy and came to reject Aristotle's as well. He referred to himself as self-taught and never acknowledged any philosophical teacher or master. He saw himself as a moral reformer who had discovered a brand-new message, one that could save others from unhappiness.

Epicurus

> *Guest, thou shalt be happy here, for here happiness is esteemed the highest good.*
> Motto hung over the entrance to the Garden of Epicurus

> Vain is the word of a philosopher which does not heal any suffering of man. For just as there is no profit in medicine if it does not expel the diseases of the body, so there is no profit in philosophy either if it does not expel the suffering of the mind.[1]

Epicurus called his school the Garden. A serene retreat from the social, political, and even philosophical turmoil of Athens, Epicurus's Garden became as well known for good living and pleasant socializing as it was for its philosophy. One of the unusual features of the Garden was that it welcomed everyone. It was one of the very few places in Greece where women were allowed and encouraged to interact with men as *equals.* Epicurus's Garden provided a truly unique experience for *both* men and women, since elsewhere men, as well as women, were denied the opportunity to experience equality. Epicurus also made no distinctions based on social status or race. He accepted all who came to learn: prostitutes, housewives, slaves, aristocrats. His favorite pupil was his own slave, Mysis.[2] Epicurus took as his mistress a courtesan (a kind of prostitute) named Leontium, and under his nurturing influence she wrote several books.

As you might expect, rumors were rampant about exactly what went on in the Garden. We can lose sight of the truly radical nature of Epicurus's understanding and tolerance if we judge it only in light of today's more enlightened attitudes. In his time, the mere acceptance of all races, sexes, and social classes would have been enough to brand Epicurus as a dangerous and ungrateful rebel, regardless of his philosophical ideas. Yet he went well beyond theoretical tolerance, actively welcoming and encouraging all comers. Even in our own time, such an attitude is often met with fear and criticism when it is put into practice.

Quality of Life

Neither life nor death is good or bad in itself, Epicurus said; only the quality of our pleasures or pains is important. This is a major departure from Aristippus's emphasis on intensity (quantity). Rather than seek to have the most of anything, including the longest possible life span, the wise and sophisticated Epicurean chooses to have the finest.

> Most people, however, recoil from death as though it were the greatest of evils; at other times they welcome it as the end-all of life's ills. The sophisticated person, on the other hand, neither begs off from living nor dreads not living.
>
> Life is not a stumbling block to him, nor does he regard not being alive as any sort of evil. As in the case of food he prefers the most savory dish to merely the larger portion, so in the case of time, he garners to himself the most agreeable moments rather than the longest span.[3]

Practically anything can be *desired* by someone somewhere. But that does not mean that it is *desirable.* This distinction goes beyond Aristippus's simple hedonism to a much more disciplined and subtle concept. In Epicurus's words,

> Because of the very fact that pleasure is our primary and congenital good we do not select every pleasure; *there are times when we forgo certain pleasures, particularly when they are followed by too much unpleasantness. Furthermore, we regard certain states of pain as preferable to pleasures, particularly when greater satisfaction results from our having submitted to discomforts for a long period of time. Thus every pleasure is a good by reason of its having a nature akin to our own, but not every pleasure is desirable.* In like manner every state of pain is an evil, but not all pains are uniformly to be rejected. At any rate, it is our duty to judge all such cases by measuring pleasures against pains, with a view to their respective assets and liabilities, inasmuch as we do experience the good as being bad at times and, contrariwise, the bad as being good.[4] [emphasis added]

Perhaps you associate the term *Epicurean* with expensive tastes, exotic food and drink, elegant clothing, and a life devoted to the pursuit of such pleasures. If so, you are not alone. Even in Epicurus's time, many people mistakenly thought that Epicureanism was a philosophy of expensive self-indulgence. For Epicurus,

(Epicureans) write about political order in order to prevent us from engaging in political life, about rhetoric to stop us practicing oratory, and about kingship to make us avoid the courts of Kings.

PLUTARCH

We must not make a pretense of doing philosophy, but really do it; for what we need is not the semblance of health but real health.

EPICURUS

And so we speak of pleasure as the starting point and the goal of the happy life because we realize that it is our primary native good, because every act of choice and aversion originates with it, and because we come back to it when we judge every good by using the pleasure feeling as our criterion.

EPICURUS

If only we'd stop trying to be happy we could have a pretty good time.

EDITH WHARTON

What Would Epicurus Eat?

In the *Letter to Menoeceus*, Epicurus praises self-sufficiency and easily got satisfactions, noting that "everything natural is easy to obtain and whatever is groundless is hard to obtain." Ironically, the man whose name is inaccurately linked with Epicurean delicacies believed that "simple flavors provide a pleasure equal to that of an extravagant life-style when all pain from want is removed, and barley cakes and water provide the highest pleasure when someone in want takes them."

When Indiana University professors Lisa Keele and Rondo Keele tried to find a recipe for the sort of barley cakes Epicurus might have had in mind, they found that coming up with a "derivation of a truly Epicurean [in the original sense] recipe for barley cakes was no trivial matter." Their research led them to the oldest surviving work of Latin prose, *De agricultura,* or *On Farming,* of the Roman Statesman Marcus Porcius Cato, "the elder," (234–149 B.C.E.). There, the Keeles found a recipe for a simple barley cake called *libum,* which may have been derived from a Greek sacrificial cake.

Here, then, is the Keele's "reasonably authentic" recipe for the sort of cake Epicurus might have enjoyed—with friends of course.

2 pounds (or four cups) plain cream cheese
1/2 pound (or two cups) barley flour

1 egg
a good quantity of dry bay leaves (say, 10 or more)

Place the cheese in a clean mixing bowl. Knead the cheese somewhat to soften it. Add the flour; work it in with your hands until well-mixed. Then add the egg; knead it in well too. When all is mixed, the dough should resemble the texture of wet potter's clay; mold it into a loaf shape and place it in a casserole dish, the bottom of which is lined with bay leaves. The bay leaves insure that the cake will not stick to the pan. Because the loaf will rise in the oven, make sure that the casserole dish is larger than the cake loaf. For aesthetic reasons, you may wish to smooth the top of the loaf with your hands. Place the lid on the casserole; bake in a preheated 350° oven. The cake is done when it is golden-brown and the top has cracked. This takes approximately an hour. Remove the cake from the casserole; peel the bay leaves from the bottom and discard; serve immediately or store for later use. Makes about 15 servings. Dribble with honey, if desired.

Enjoy!

See Lisa Keele and Rondo Keele, "Let Them Eat (Barley) Cake: An Epicurean Recipe to Share with Your Students," in Teaching Philosophy, *APA Newsletter*, Fall 2002, Vol. 2, no.1, pp. 208–210. Reprinted by permission.

All bodily suffering is negligible; for that which causes intense pain has a brief duration, and that which endures long in the flesh causes mild pain.

EPICURUS

however, the highest pleasures are intellectual, and the greatest good is peace of mind, not intense or exquisite physical pleasure:

> Thus when I say that pleasure is the goal of living I do not mean the pleasures of libertines or the pleasures inherent in positive enjoyment, as is supposed by certain persons who are ignorant of our doctrine or who are not in agreement with it or who interpret it perversely. I mean, on the contrary, the pleasure that consists in freedom from bodily pain and mental agitation. The pleasant life is not the product of one drinking party after another or of sexual intercourse with women and boys or of the seafood and other delicacies afforded by a luxurious table. On the contrary, it is the result of sober thinking—namely, investigation of the reasons for every act of choice and aversion and elimination of those false ideas about the gods and death which are the chief source of mental disturbances.[5]

■ THE CYNICAL ORIGINS OF STOICISM ■

As disciplined and moderate as Epicurus's refined hedonism was, it was still too soft for another important influence on Stoicism. **Cynicism** was a philosophical "school" only in the loosest sense. Founded by **Antisthenes**

(c. 455–360 B.C.E.), its most famous proponent was **Diogenes** (c. 412–323 B.C.E.). As a philosophical school, Cynicism existed from the fourth century B.C.E. until the sixth century C.E., although by the first century its reputation had seriously diminished.

Although the Cynics revolted against the rigidly ordered philosophies of Plato and Aristotle, they admired Socrates. Socrates was the model on which Antisthenes built his Cynicism, and, by extension, Socrates was a model for the Stoics. It is said that Antisthenes walked almost five miles every day to hear Socrates.

Antisthenes was apparently more impressed with Socrates' lifestyle and character than with his philosophical ideas, though Antisthenes, too, sought to base his life on the rule of reason. Socrates' disdain for fashion, his ragged, functional clothing, lack of shoes, ability to not sleep or eat for long periods, physical toughness, and forthright honesty made a tremendous impression on the young Cynic.

After Socrates' death, Antisthenes founded a school called the *Cynosarges* (the Silver Dog). The word **Cynic** comes from the Greek word for "dog," and this label was later given to Diogenes because he "lived like a dog." That is, he was unwashed and rough-looking, he scrounged for food, and he refused to follow conventional standards of dress and behavior.

Because Antisthenes attended some lectures of Gorgias the Sophist and because he stayed so close to Socrates, it is not surprising that he was especially affected by Socrates' stinging attacks on such sophistic values as power, celebrity, prestige, wealth, and clever deception. The Cynics also despised the widespread hedonism and hypocrisy that they saw throughout Athens. They believed that the very essence of civilization is corrupt: Manners are hypocritical and phony; material wealth weakens people, making them physically and morally soft; the desire for success and power produces dishonesty and dependency; flattery, fashion, and convention destroy the individual and make him or her vulnerable to the whims of fortune. And, as the tragic death of Socrates underscored, not even the wisest person can control other people or external events.

So the less an individual needs to be happy, the less vulnerable he or she is. Diogenes, for example, lived in an abandoned wine barrel on the beach and once said, "When I saw a child drinking from his hand, I threw away my cup." The Cynics lived austere, unconventional lives. They distrusted luxury as a hook that always brought complications and ultimately frustration into people's lives. What happiness was possible, according to the Cynics, came from self-discipline, rational control of all desires and appetites, and minimal contact with conventional society.

Even though Epicurus also emphasized a simple life and the avoidance of pain, the Cynics still found Epicureanism too conventional and too encouraging of dependence to suit them. The Cynics believed that the Epicureans relied too much on their friends and certain "proper" pleasures. Cynicism, on the other hand, was rough-and-tumble. Its most famous advocates were sarcastic and hostile toward conventions and institutions. Rejecting Epicurus's high esteem for friendship, Cynics relied only on themselves.

Few Cynics exhibited the moral or intellectual virtues of Antisthenes or Diogenes, however, and eventually Cynicism fell into disrepute. Later Cynics were hostile, arrogant individuals who despised everyone else and hated the society in which they lived. Indiscriminate scorn and contempt for practically everything replaced penetrating social criticism. Today the terms *cynic* and *cynical* are

Cynicism
Philosophy based on the belief that the very essence of civilization is corrupt and that civilization destroys individuals by making them soft and subject to the whims of fortune.

Cynic
Individual who lives an austere, unconventional life based on Cynic doctrine.

Lathe Biosas (Live unknown)
MOTTO OF EPICURUS

Plato winces when I track dust across his rugs: he knows that I'm walking on his vanity.
DIOGENES

A Socrates Gone Mad

Diogenes studied under Antisthenes, who, by the way, hated students. Diogenes took his master's teachings to heart and went him one better. Being called a dog was not enough for him; he actually lived with a pack of stray dogs.

Alexander the Great (356–323 B.C.E.), having heard of Diogenes, made a point of meeting him. Diogenes was sitting on the seashore when the magnificent, handsome young king of Greece and future conqueror of the known world rode up on his powerful charger. Looking down on the reclining Cynic, he said,

"I am Alexander the Great."

"I am Diogenes, the dog," replied the Cynic.

"The dog?"

"I nuzzle the kind, bark at the greedy, and bite louts."

"What can I do for you?" asked the Ruler of the World.

"Stand aside, you're blocking my light."

So impressed was Alexander with the uncompromising character of Diogenes that he later said, "If I were not Alexander, I would be Diogenes."

This sketch is based on material in Guy Davenport's *Herakleitos and Diogenes* (San Francisco: Grey Fox Press, 1979), pp. 35–37. Reprinted by permission of Guy Davenport.

commonly used to refer to a general attitude of basic contempt for people, an excessively hostile or critical stance, or a tendency to distrust other people's motives.

▦ A SCOUT FOR WISDOM ▦

I can see Antisthenes' vanity through the holes in his cloak.

PLATO

The Stoics agreed with the Cynics' admiration of Socrates' sturdy character and wholeheartedly accepted the basic Cynic premise that excessive wanting always leads to unhappiness. The Stoic Epictetus considered the Cynic as a sort of ideal, while acknowledging that most of us are not called to the Cynic's way of life, a way of life that depends on extraordinary moral, philosophical, and physical fitness according to Epictetus. Epictetus characterized the "true Cynic" as a "free open-air spirit," saying to himself:

Reason or a halter.

DIOGENES

Henceforth, my mind is the material I have to work on, as the carpenter has his timber and the shoemaker his leather: my business is to deal with my impressions aright. My wretched body is nothing to me, its parts are nothing to me. Death? Let it come when it will, whether to my whole body or part of it. Exile? Can one be sent into exile beyond the Universe? One cannot. Wherever I go, there is the sun, there is the moon, there are the stars, dreams . . . conversation with the gods. The true Cynic when he has ordered himself thus . . . must know that he is sent as a messenger from God to men concerning things good and evil, to show them that they have gone astray and are seeking the true nature of good and evil where it is not to be found.[6]

Epictetus described the Cynic as a "scout" sent "to find out what things are friendly to men and which hostile," a scout who must first do his scouting accurately, and on returning must tell the truth, not driven by fear. The Cynical roots of Stoicism are apparent in the respect and admiration that flows through Epictetus's portrait of the Cynic, who must, whenever possible, report his findings like Socrates, calling out:

"Alas! men, where are you rushing? What are you doing, O wretched people? Like blind men you go tottering all around. You have left the true path and are going off on another; you are looking for serenity and happiness in the wrong place, where it does not exist, and you do not believe when another points them out to you. Why do you look for [the true path] outside? It does not reside in the body. . . . It is not in possessions. . . . It is not in office. . . .

. . . It is where you do not expect it, and do not wish to look for it. For if you had wished, you would have found it within you, and would not now be wandering outside, nor would you be seeking what does not concern you, as though it were your own possession. Turn your thoughts upon yourselves, find out the kind of preconceived ideas you have.

. . . Look at me . . . I am without home, without a city, without property, without a slave; I sleep on the ground; I have neither wife nor children, no miserable governor's mansion, but only earth, and sky, and one rough cloak. Yet what do I lack? Am I not free from pain and fear, am I not free? When has anyone among you seen me failing to get what I desire, or falling into what I would avoid? When have I ever found fault in either God or man? When have I ever blamed anyone? Has anyone among you ever seen me with a gloomy face? And how do I face those persons before whom you stand in fear and awe? Do I face them as slaves? Who, when he lays eyes upon me, does not feel that he is seeing his king and master?"

Lo, these are words that befit a Cynic, this is his character, and his plan of life. . . . Why, then, are you even laying your hand to so great an enterprise?[7]

"The Cynic," says the Stoic, "has made all mankind his children; the men among them he has as sons, the women as daughters; in that spirit he approaches them all and cares for them all . . . as a father . . . as a brother, and as a servant of Zeus, who is father of us all."[8]

Do not craze yourself with thinking, but go about your business anywhere. Life is not intellectual or critical, but sturdy. Its chief good is for well-mixed people who can enjoy what they find, without question.

RALPH WALDO
EMERSON

Everything that happens is as normal and expected as the spring rose or the summer fruit; this is true of sickness, death, slander, intrigue, and all the other things that delight or trouble foolish men.

MARCUS AURELIUS

©Royalty-Free/Corbis

Do you think you could distinguish a contemporary Diogenes from a street person? To what extent might beliefs about the importance of money, status, material comfort, and the like blind us to accepting the possibility that at least some homeless people (and other social outcasts) are philosophical Cynics?

▪ EPICTETUS: FROM SLAVE TO SAGE ▪

Though the philosophical school known as Stoicism was founded in Greece by **Zeno** (c. 334–262 B.C.E.) around 300 B.C.E., it flourished in Rome. Because Zeno lectured at a place called the *stoa poikile,* or painted porch, his followers were known as "men of the porch"—Stoics.

Under Alexander the Great, Greece conquered the Persian empire (what is now Iran and Iraq) and established Greek rule over a large area of the Near East and Egypt. As a result, Greek culture became more sophisticated and cosmopolitan, absorbing ideas and customs from the cultures it conquered. As the Greek empire expanded, the importance of individual city-states such as Athens and Sparta diminished, and people identified themselves as part of a larger, more international community.

Alexander's empire was unstable, however, and began to fall apart almost immediately after his death. For most of the third century B.C.E. no single dominant power emerged in the Mediterranean region. By the middle of the second century B.C.E., Rome had destroyed what was left of Alexander's kingdom and annexed Greece as a Roman province called Achaia. By 100 B.C.E., Rome essentially controlled the entire Mediterranean area.

The Romans were not particularly interested in abstract, speculative thinking. Pragmatic and religiously tolerant, they borrowed heavily from Greek culture, including philosophy. Given their interest in establishing social order, the Romans were especially attracted to the Stoics' emphasis on duty and self-control.

The two most philosophically influential Stoics are a Roman slave and a Roman emperor: Epictetus and Marcus Aurelius. The Roman senator Seneca, although not a particularly original thinker, was one of the finest Stoic writers. We will be using some of his *Discourses* and *Moral Letters* to supplement our two main sources. For centuries, Stoic literature has been some of the most popular of all philosophical writings. Let's see why as we encounter the archetype of the Stoic in two radically different forms: a slave and an emperor.

Stoicism appealed to Romans living in times of great uncertainty, under emperors of widely differing abilities and virtues. It spread throughout the Roman world because it was advocated by three important public figures: Cicero (106–43 B.C.E.), Cato (95–46 B.C.E.), and Seneca (c. 4 B.C.E.–65 C.E.). Ironically, however, one of the most important Stoic philosophers was a former slave named **Epictetus** (c. 50–130 C.E.). Perhaps because a slave's life is not his own, Epictetus acquired special insight into the major issue of Stoicism: controlling what we can and accepting what is beyond our control.

We do not know much about Epictetus's early life. His mother was a slave living in Hierapolis, a city in the Asia Minor province of Phrygia. Epictetus was brought to Rome as the slave of a former slave named Epaphroditus, who seems to have been Nero's administrative secretary. Epictetus must have demonstrated unusual abilities, for Epaphroditus sent the youth Epictetus to study with Musonius Rufus, the most powerful Stoic since the days of Zeno. Even so, Epictetus never lost sight of the fact that he could be bought or sold, pampered or tortured, at his owner's whim. As a slave, he was constantly reminded that what happened to him had no bearing on his own wishes or behavior. As a slave, the only absolute

---

"What is the fruit of your Stoic doctrines?" someone once asked Epictetus. "Tranquility, fearlessness, and freedom," he answered. Controlling your emotions is difficult but can be empowering.

JAMES BOND
STOCKDALE

Misfortune is not fate but providence.

SARVEPALLI
RADHAKRISHNAN

Epictetus

Let others practice lawsuits, others study problems, others syllogisms; here you practice how to die, how to be enchained, how to be racked, how to be exiled.

EPICTETUS

control Epictetus had was over his own reactions to what happened. His motto was *Anechou kai apechou:* Bear and forbear.

Epictetus was once so badly tortured—for another slave's mistake—that his broken leg did not heal properly, and he limped for the rest of his life. The story goes that as his leg was being twisted, Epictetus reminded his master that a person's leg was likely to break under such torture. Epaphroditus ignored this, and when his leg finally broke, Epictetus said, "See, it's just as I told you." He later said, "I was never more free than when I was on the rack." He had learned that he could control his attitude, but that fate controlled his life:

> If the captain calls, let all those things go and run to the boat without turning back; and if you are old, do not even go very far from the boat, so that when the call comes you are not left behind.[9]

Freed sometime after Nero's death in the year 68 C.E., Epictetus became a well-known teacher. Sometime around the year 90, all the philosophers were ordered out of Rome by the emperor Domitian, who was angry about the encouragement certain Stoics had given to his opponents. Epictetus fled to Nicopolis in northern Greece, where he taught until he was very old. He was a popular teacher, and his schools in both Rome and Nicopolis throve during his lifetime.

A modest man, famed for his sweetness and simplicity, Epictetus lived in a sparely furnished house, content with a straw mat and pallet for a bed and a clay lamp (after his iron one was stolen). He was especially loving toward children, and he was charitable toward all those who came to him for advice and guidance. Following the example of Socrates, he published nothing. His ideas have come down to us in the form of the class notes of his student Flavius Arrianus, called the *Discourses,* and as a truly remarkable set of excerpts from them called the *Enchiridion,* also known as the *Manual* or *Handbook* (because it was made into books that were carried "at hand" into the field by Roman soldiers).[10]

> *Everything depends on the right attitude in the same way and manner as in the case of suffering. The difference lies in the fact that the right attitude is, then, a right attitude to himself.*
>
> VIKTOR E. FRANKL

■ MARCUS AURELIUS: PHILOSOPHER-KING ■

Marcus Aurelius Antoninus

Marcus Aurelius Antoninus (121–180 C.E.) was bound by duty. By temperament a scholar and a recluse, he lived surrounded with commotion, deception, and crowds. Marcus so impressed the emperor Hadrian that he advised Marcus's uncle Aurelius Antoninus (commonly known as Antoninus Pius) to adopt Marcus. When Marcus was forty, Antoninus Pius, then emperor, appointed Marcus heir over Pius's other adopted son, Lucius Verus.

When Pius died in 161, Marcus generously named his stepbrother Verus the co-emperor—against the wishes of the senate—but got little help from him. All the serious work of governing was done by Marcus. As emperor, he was obliged to contend with flatterers, liars, and enemies. He was regularly dragged away from Rome to deal with uprisings and barbarian invasions along the frontiers. He was betrayed by a trusted general and spent the last years of his life away from home on a difficult military campaign. He suffered through the deaths of four of his five sons, and he even endured unsubstantiated rumors that his wife took many lovers in his absence and that his sole surviving son was not his own. To himself, he wrote:

> Everywhere and at all times it is in thy power piously to acquiesce in thy present condition, and to behave justly to those who are about thee, and to exert thy skill upon thy present thoughts, that nothing shall steal into them without being examined.[11]

Marcus was loved by many Romans for his kindness and mercy. He refused to turn away from his incompetent stepbrother, choosing instead to carry out both their duties until Verus died in 169, after which Marcus ruled alone. He convinced the Senate to pardon the family of the traitorous general when other emperors would have destroyed it. He stood by his wife as cruel rumors about her virtue spread everywhere and his own soldiers mocked his masculinity. He went so far as to promote those accused of being her lovers when doing so was good for Rome.

> Let it make no difference to thee whether thou art cold or warm, if thou art doing thy duty; and whether thou art drowsy or satisfied with sleep; and whether ill-spoken of or praised; and whether dying or doing something else. For it is one of the acts of life, the act by which we die: it is sufficient then in this act also to do well what we have in hand.[12]

The last truly great figure of imperial Rome, Marcus combined classical philosophy with a spiritual quality that foreshadowed the Christian-influenced Scholasticism of the Middle Ages. He was also one of the kindest, wisest, and most virtuous of philosophers.

> Only attend to thyself, [Marcus,] and resolve to be a good man in every act which thou doest; and remember. . . . Look within. Within is the fountain of good, and it will ever bubble up, if thou wilt ever dig.[13]

Marcus's last years were hard and lonely, spent on a military campaign along the Danube. Yet, rather than succumb to bitterness or lash out at others, he sought solace in philosophy. Late at night, after his public duties were done, he did his duty to his soul, sitting alone in his tent writing what are popularly known as his *Meditations*, but which he addressed "To Myself." This journal is one of the finest, most widely read examples of both Stoic thought and personal reflection in Western literature.

On this last campaign, Marcus Aurelius, a man once described as "by nature a saint and sage, by profession a warrior and ruler," died at the age of fifty-nine, worn down by fatigue and toil.[14]

▪ THE FATED LIFE ▪

Though fate is an important aspect of their philosophy, the Stoics were rather imprecise about what fate meant in specific terms. In some mysterious way, the actual course of our lives is directed by the *Logos,* which the Stoics thought of as World Reason or Cosmic Mind (see Chapter 3). Sometimes the *Logos* is referred to as God, Zeus, Nature, Providence, Cosmic Meaning, or Fate. Seneca says:

> We are all chained to [fate]. . . . All of us are in custody, the binders as well as the bound . . . some are chained by office, some by wealth; some weighed

"Why Should Anywhere I Go Not Be All Right?"

One of the great joys of learning is the discovery of common themes and threads. This is especially so in matters of wisdom. The great sages are at their most powerful when they speak of acceptance in the face of great hardship. Sometimes, it seems as if one spirit speaks with many voices and accents. Compare this passage from Chuang-tzu with the passage from Marcus Aurelius on page 196.

> Tzu-lai fell ill, was gasping for breath and was about to die. His wife and children surrounded him and wept. . . . He said, "Don't disturb the transformation that is about to take place." Then, leaning against the door, he continued, "Great is the Creator! What will he make of you now? Where will he take you? Will he make you into a rat's liver? Will he make you into an insect's leg?"
>
> Tzu-lai said, "Wherever a parent tells a son to go, whether east, west, south, or north, he has to obey. The yin and yang are like a man's parents. If they pressed me to die and I disobeyed, I would be obstinate. What fault is theirs? For the universe gave me the body so I may be carried, my life so I may toil, my old age so I may repose, and my death so I may rest. Therefore, to regard life as good is the way to regard death as good.
>
> "Suppose a master foundryman is casting his metal and the metal leaps up and says, 'I must be made into the best sword. . . . ' The master foundryman would certainly consider the metal as evil. And if simply because I possess a body by chance, I were to say, 'Nothing but a man! Nothing but a man!' the Creator will certainly regard me as evil. If I regard the universe as a great furnace and creation as a foundryman, why should anywhere I go not be all right?"

Chuang-tzu, in *A Source Book in Chinese Philosophy,* trans. and comp. Wing-Tsit Chan (Princeton, N.J.: Princeton University Press, 1963), p. 197.

down by high birth, some by low; some are subject to another's tyranny, some to their own; some are confined to one spot by banishment, some by a priesthood. All life is bondage.[15]

The Stoics learned, as many of us do, that our lives are not entirely our own. This discovery did not, at least in the cases of Epictetus and Marcus Aurelius, lead to despair or escapist indulgence but, rather, to a shift in the focus of responsibility. Rather than complain about what they could not control, the Stoics chose to master what they could: their own minds. By mastering their thoughts, they believed, they could master their feelings.

Stoics believed that serenity comes to that individual whose will is in accord with the World Reason, the *Logos,* for right thinking leads to a reduction of frustration and anxiety. In the words of Epictetus,

> Remember that thou art an actor in a play, of such a kind as the author may choose: if short, a short one; if long, a long one: if he wishes you to act the part of a poor man, see that you act the part naturally: if the part of a lame man, of a magistrate, of a private person (do the same). For this is your duty, to act well the part that was given to you; but to select the part belongs to another.[16]

The Stoic Logos

Under the guidance of the **Logos,** the universe remains rational and ordered. Seneca said, "Events do not just happen, but arrive by appointment." Everything that occurs

[T]he lecture-room of the philosopher is the hospital; students ought not to walk out of it in pleasure, but in pain.

EPICTETUS

Logos (Stoic)
According to Stoic doctrine, World Reason, also referred to as Cosmic Mind, God, Zeus, Nature, Providence, Cosmic Meaning, and Fate; force that governs the universe; also see Chapter 3.

*That which happens to ...
every man is fixed in a
manner for him suitable to
his destiny. . . . For there
is altogether one fitness
and harmony. . . . And so
accept everything which
happens, even if it seems
disagreeable, because it
leads to this, to the health
of the universe and to the
prosperity . . . of the whole.*

Marcus Aurelius

is connected to everything else. Everything that exists is connected to the *Logos*. Our individual minds are "emanations" or "sparks" from the *Logos,* which is sometimes characterized as "fire." (The Stoics borrowed this idea from Heraclitus.) Our finite human reason is, thus, a small reflection of divine reason. Seneca puts it like this:

> We do not need to lift our hands to heaven . . . God is near you, with you, inside you. Yes . . . there is a holy spirit abiding within us. . . . No man is good without god.[17]

Faith in a rationally ordered universe and our intimate relation to the *Logos* are central aspects of Stoicism. If the universe is divinely ordered, then there is a plan. Things happen to us for a reason—a divinely ordained reason.

If this is true, then nothing that happens can be wrong or bad, since everything that happens is part of God's rational plan. When I truly grasp this, I will no longer fear for the future nor complain about the past or present, but can remain as calm as Zeno did when he heard that all his possessions were lost in a shipwreck and said, "Fortune bids me philosophize with a lighter pack."

©Warner Brothers/Photofest

©Wolfgang Langenstrassen/dpa/Landov

Reflect on the precarious nature of the human condition by reading the box "Why Should Anywhere I Go Not Be All Right?" on p. 193 and study these two photographs of the late actor-director Christopher Reeve. It is all too easy to think that science, good habits, and technology can give us control over our lives. Reeve's public courage and lack of self-pity remind us of Epictetus's doctrine that although the role we play in life's saga may not be up to us, how we play it is. The picture on the right shows Reeve at a dinner for the American Paralysis Association, one of a number of organizations and causes that he supported.

What can I do, then, if the course of my life's events is beyond my control? The Stoic answers that I can concentrate on developing an attitude of courageous acceptance. My efforts should be directed toward that part of my life over which I exert absolute control: my attitudes, or my will.

· · · · · ·

Do you agree that the test of faith is anxiety? Are the Stoics correct in insisting that one who truly realizes that everything is governed by a divine plan will lose all fear and anxiety? Justify your position.

PHILOSOPHICAL

QUERY

The Disinterested Rational Will

If we are "bits" of the *Logos,* it follows that our virtue and happiness will consist in being as much like the *Logos* as possible. Being perfectly rational, the *Logos* is not partisan; that is, the *Logos* is objective. It is calm and serene, viewing events with "disinterest." Seneca says:

> Just as the rays of the sun do indeed warm the earth but remain at the source of their radiation, so a great and holy soul is lowered to earth to give us a nearer knowledge of the divine; but though it is in intercourse with us, it cleaves to its source . . . it looks toward it, it seeks to rejoin it, and its concern with our affairs is superior and detached.[18]

To be *disinterested* is to have no *personal* attachments or motives. For example, a judge or a teacher should be disinterested when he passes sentence or grades papers—he should not play favorites. Marcus Aurelius was disinterested when he promoted the men accused of being his wife's lovers.

The Stoics make an intriguing case that our best chance for happiness is to adopt a disinterested attitude toward our own lives, as well as toward all life. The Stoics thought such a perspective would result not in a world of self-centered

People find no rest because of four pursuits—long life, reputation, office, possessions. Whoever has these four goals dreads spirits, fears other men, cowers before authority, and is terrified of punishment. I call him "a man in flight from things." He can be killed, he can be given life; the destiny which decides [his state of mind] is outside him.

YANG ZHU

Of the 85,000 residents of Billings, Montana, in 1993, approximately one hundred were Jews. In December 1993, someone threw a cinder block through five-year-old Isaac Schnitzer's window. The reason: a Hanukkah menorah had been sitting in it. Thousands of Billings's residents showed their solidarity with the small Jewish community by placing pictures of menorahs in their windows—and by posing for this powerful picture, a picture that reflects the *cosmopolis.*

isolationists, but in a sense of universal communion and duty. Why? Because turning to the *Logos* means looking beyond the particular laws, customs, and prejudices of one's self and society and rejecting them if they deviate from Nature/*Logos*. Unlike the hedonists, who evaluated the welfare of others only in terms of one's own happiness, the Stoics viewed all humans as citizens of a "universal city," a *cosmopolis*. Whereas the hedonist tends to be indifferent to others, the Stoic is indifferent to self (ego). When our duties are dictated by disinterested reason, rather than by custom or personal preference, we become members of a community, a human fellowship. Marcus Aurelius alludes to this in a beautiful passage:

> It is man's peculiar distinction to love even those who err and go astray. Such a love is born as soon as you realize that they are your brothers; that they are stumbling in ignorance, and not willfully; that in a short while both of you will be no more; and, above all, that you yourself have taken no hurt, for your master-reason has not been made a jot worse than it was before.
>
> Out of the universal substance, as out of wax, Nature fashions a colt, then breaks him up and uses the material to form a tree, and after that a man, and next some other thing: and not one of these endures for more than a brief span. As for the vessel itself, it is no greater hardship to be taken to pieces than to be put together. . . .
>
> Only a little while, and Nature, the universal disposer, will change everything you see, and out of their substance will make fresh things, and yet again others from theirs, to the perpetual renewing of the world's youthfulness.[19]

PHILOSOPHICAL QUERY

• • • • • •

Discuss the advantages and disadvantages of disinterestedness. When is it a virtue? When is it not? Give some examples and explain them.

Whereas other philosophies used various criteria to distinguish between good and bad emotions, the Stoics rejected emotion to the extent it was humanly possible. The best attitude, they claimed, was rational, detached acceptance.[20] Seneca says:

> Philosophers of our school reject the emotions; the [Aristotelian] Peripatetics keep them in check. I, however, do not understand how any half-way disease can be either wholesome or helpful. . . .
>
> "But," you object, "it is natural for me to suffer when I am bereaved of a friend; grant some privileges to tears which have the right to flow! It is also natural to be affected by men's opinions and to be cast down when they are unfavourable; so why should you not allow me such an honorable aversion to bad opinion?"
>
> There is no vice which lacks some plea. . . . we are in love with our vices; we uphold them and prefer to make excuses for them rather than shake them off. We mortals have been endowed with sufficient strength by nature, if only we use this strength. . . . The real reason for failure is unwillingness, the pretended reason, inability.[21]

■ STOIC WISDOM ■

By the time of Marcus Aurelius, Stoicism had a religious quality that made it especially attractive to the growing Christian community in the Roman world. As we have seen, classical philosophies were naturalistic: They placed rational humanity at the center of things. By contrast, Christian values place a personal God at the center. Though the Stoics were classical in their emphasis on the impersonal *Logos* as being material and on reason and self-control of the human will as the means to salvation, they also anticipated Christianity in their emphasis on the divine will and on our submission to it. As you will see, many of the Stoics' specific lessons also have a decidedly Judeo-Christian flavor to them. Thus, Stoicism stands as the most influential transitional philosophy between classical and Christian values. Even so, Augustine (Chapter 8) rejected Stoicism as man-centered, not God-centered.

Control Versus Influence

Given the Stoic position that our lives are fated but that our wills remain free, our first task must be to distinguish what we can control from what we cannot control. Because Stoic literature is sometimes imprecise and inconsistent, it is important to be sensitive to the distinction between *control* and *influence*.

Even though the Stoics believed in destiny, or fate, they also talked about choosing appropriate actions, in addition to just controlling our attitudes. This suggests that a given individual's fate is painted in broad strokes: *X* will not get into medical school; *Y* will marry *Z*. But *X* may have the freedom to apply to medical school, and *Y* may be free to break up with *Z* two or three times. There appear to be gaps in our fate. For instance, in the first section of the *Enchiridion,* Epictetus says:

> If then you desire . . . great things, remember that you must not (attempt to) lay hold of them with small effort; but you must leave alone some things entirely, and postpone others for the present.[22]

Later he says:

> When you are going to take in hand any act, remind yourself what kind of act it is. If you are going to bathe, [remind] yourself what happens in the [public]

If you regard yourself as a man and as a part of the whole, it is fitting for you now to be sick and now to make a voyage and run risks, and now to be in want, and an occasion to die before your time. Why, then, are you vexed? . . . For it is impossible in such a body as ours, that is, in this universe that envelops us, among these fellow-creatures of ours, that such things should not happen, some to one man, some to another.

EPICTETUS

Some things are up to us and some are not up to us. Our opinions are up to us, and our impulses, desires, aversions. . . . Our bodies are not up to us, nor are our possessions, our reputations, our public offices.

EPICTETUS

Show me a man who though sick is happy, who though in danger is happy, and I'll show you a Stoic.

EPICTETUS

"Life Passes by Like a Galloping Horse"

From the point of view of Tao, what is noble and what is humble? They all merge into one. Never stick to one's own intention and thus handicap the operation of Tao. What is much and what is little? They replace and apply to each other. . . . Time cannot be arrested. The succession of decline, growth, fullness, and emptiness go in a cycle, each end becoming a new beginning. This is the way to talk about the workings of the great principle and to discuss the principle of all things. The life of things passes by like a galloping horse. With no activity is it not changing, and at no time is it not moving. What shall we do? What shall we not do? The thing to do is to leave it to self-transformation.

Chuang-tzu, in *A Source Book in Chinese Philosophy,* trans. and comp. Wing-Tsit Chan (Princeton, N.J.: Princeton University Press, 1963), p. 206.

"None Strive to Grasp What They Already Know"

There is often chaos in the world, and the love of knowledge is ever at the bottom of it. For all men strive to grasp what they do not know, while none strive to grasp what they already know. . . . Thus, above, the splendor of the heavenly bodies is dimmed; below, the power of land and water is burned up, while in between the influence of the four seasons is upset. There is not one tiny worm that moves on earth or an insect that flies in the air but has lost its original nature. Such indeed is the world chaos caused by the desire for knowledge!

Chuang-tzu, *The Wisdom of Laotse*, trans. and ed. Lin Yutang (New York: Modern Library, 1976), p. 287.

All that happens without us knowing why is destiny. For the man who trusts destiny, there is no difference between long life and short. For one who trusts his mind, there is nothing which is agreeable or offensive.

LIE ZI

To pursue the unattainable is insanity, yet the thoughtless can never refrain from doing so.

MARCUS AURELIUS

Which of you by worrying can add a moment to his life-span?

JESUS, MATTHEW 6:27

bath; some splashing the water, others pushing against one another, others abusing one another, and some stealing.[23]

Elsewhere, Epictetus talks about choosing to be a philosopher or deciding to train for the Olympics. This implies that we have at least some degree of influence over our actions. So the Stoics must have thought that we have influence over more than just our attitudes; otherwise, such advice is illogical. Advice makes sense only where there is some choice.

Although the Stoics are theoretically inconsistent when they counsel accepting fate on the one hand and then advise us to live moderately and wisely on the other, their position contains merit because *it is consistent with common experience.* A careful survey of the human condition reveals that many of us expend a great deal of effort trying to control things that we cannot control while nearly ignoring those areas over which we do have control.

A common example will make the point. Technically speaking, you cannot *control* your grades in school, although you have considerable *influence* over them. No matter how carefully you listen to instructions, no matter how good your notes, how thorough your studying and grasp of the material, you cannot *guarantee* a passing grade in any course. Your professor might have a personal grudge against you or be depressed or ill while grading your work. A clerical error might alter your grade in a class, and the school might refuse to correct it. By the same token, you cannot even guarantee a failing grade. Another clerical error might result in an A for a class you haven't attended for weeks, or the professor might confuse your name with that of another student.

We are foolish when we exert no effort on our own behalf. We all know that. But, the Stoic reminds us, we are also foolish to believe that we *control* our GPAs. Rather than trying to control our grades, we should work wisely to *influence* them and should make sure to *control our attitudes* toward them.

This difference can be difficult to grasp in a culture that believes that "You can be anything you want to be if you work hard enough." From the Stoic point of view, it is misleading to talk about controlling our lives (or grades); we can only influence them up to a point. And we must remember this warning: *The results of our efforts are out of our hands.*

Off campus we see this as well. Jim Fixx, a well-known running enthusiast, ate sensibly and exercised regularly, yet died in his forties of an inherited heart condition. The film genius Orson Welles ate what he wished, never exercised, smoked cigars, and weighed over four hundred pounds when he died—at age seventy. Such an example is not an excuse for self-indulgence but a hard fact of life: *We do not control our destinies; we influence them just enough so that we should do our best to behave responsibly.*

This is the crux of Stoicism. The inconsistencies in Stoic writing are due, in part, to our ignorance of precisely when influence becomes control in a particular case. There are ways to learn what to try and what to avoid, but in all cases, the Stoic remains aware that the *Logos* ultimately rules the universe. The individual's task is to identify the *Logos*'s will and then put his or her will in harmony with it. While we may not have control over the events in our lives, we do have control over our happiness. The wise person is the serene individual who lives courageously and responsibly, who knowingly accepts everything that happens, be it good or bad, without becoming bitter or broken—and without resorting to distortion or denial. (See what Augustine says about this in Chapter 8.)

Some Things Are Not in Our Control

To achieve serenity and wisdom, we must remain clear about what is not in our control:

> Not in our power are the body, property, reputation, offices . . . and in a word, whatever are not our own acts . . . the things not in our power are weak, slavish, subject to restraint, in the power of others. Remember that if you think the things which are by nature slavish to be free, and the things which are in the power of others to be your own, you will be hindered, you will lament, you will be disturbed, you will blame both the gods and men.[24]

"Not in our power" means not under our control. If I realize that these things are not under my control, I can adopt a healthy attitude toward them. For instance, since my reputation is not totally up to me, I can quit trying so hard to make everyone like me. I cannot *make* anyone like me—or dislike me. My family likes me even when I'm a fool, and some people don't like me no matter how hard I try to be likable. Instead of directing my efforts where they are ineffective, I can devote them to what I have more control over: myself. In practical terms, this means that I take appropriate action and then mentally let go of the results.

Once I realize that how long I live, who likes me or doesn't, and my social status are beyond my total control, I can quit being obsessively fearful. I can manage my health with moderation, but will not be bitter if after watching my diet and exercising daily I develop cancer. Bitterness will not get me well. Bitterness, or envy, or resentment are never my fate; they are always my choice. Not getting into the university of my choice might be my fate. Resenting it for the rest of my life is not—it's my choice. I can ask you to marry me, and marry you if you say yes, but I cannot make you happy. I cannot make you stay with me. If you leave, my anger and despair are not my fate—they are my choice.

All wisdom can be stated in two lines:
What is done for you—
allow it to be done.
What you must do
yourself—make sure you
do it.
KHAWWAS

Do to me what is worthy of Thee
And not what is worthy of me.
SAADI

You cannot judge by annoyance.
IDRIES SHAH

Attachment is the great fabricator of illusions; reality can be attained only by someone who is detached.
SIMONE WEIL

PHILOSOPHICAL
QUERY

● ● ● ● ● ●

Reflect on letting go in the sense of doing what seems right and then relaxing. Provide a few of your own examples of how fear of consequences and an obsession with control can affect us. Discuss ways for identifying and striking a balance between letting go in a wise way and in an irresponsible way.

Some Things Are in Our Control

What is in our power is our free *will*. Epictetus insists, contrary to what we may believe, that we alone control our feelings. We control our feelings because we control our thinking. We can also reason out that other people's likes and dislikes are beyond our total control. This should free us from depending on other people's opinions of us for self-esteem or happiness.

> In our power are opinion, movement towards a thing, desire, aversion; and in a word, whatever are our own acts. And the things in our power are by nature free, not subject to restraint or hindrance . . . if you think that only which is your own to be your own, and if you think of what is another's, as it really is, belongs to another, no man will ever compel you, no man will hinder you, you will never blame any man, you will accuse no man, you will do nothing . . . against your will, no man will harm you, you will have no enemy, for you will not suffer any harm.[25]

I wonder how many hours of human suffering can be chalked up to trying to control how others feel about things. I also wonder if we really try to control our own thoughts. For example: Mike suffers and worries every time Helon is annoyed

Do not seek to have events happen as you want them to, but instead want them to happen as they do happen, and your life will go well.
EPICTETUS

We grow older. But it is by no means certain that we shall grow up.
WALTER LIPPMANN

By some estimates, 60 percent of Americans are overweight or obese. Some 95 percent of those who try to lose and maintain a clinically healthy weight will fail. Could being obese be part of a person's fate? Could being an alcoholic? Sexually promiscuous? Lazy? As more and more behaviors are linked to genetics, how can we distinguish between defects of character and things not in our control?

with him. He buys her flowers, is distracted at work, agonizes until she likes him again. If he had control over how she felt, he would never let her be annoyed. Since she gets annoyed and he doesn't want her to be annoyed, it follows logically (and causally) that he *cannot* control her feelings. But—irrationally—he tries to, again and again.

Suppose that Mike reads Epictetus. Now, instead of trying to make Helon feel a certain way, he tries to control his own thoughts and behavior. When he starts to worry, he consciously, and with great effort at first, forces himself not to dwell on Helon. He may not be able to stop fears about her from popping into his mind, but he can stop himself from dwelling on them. He can exert his *will* over his own thinking. He is not responsible for his first thoughts, but he is responsible for his second thoughts.

This is a difficult lesson. It may be especially difficult to accept today, when we place so much importance on relationships and when we have been told that inadequate parents and abusive spouses are often responsible for our unhappiness. Epictetus has something interesting to say about relationships.

Relationships

According to the Stoics, we suffer to the extent that we take our own lives personally. Consequently, relationships must be evaluated with the same disinterested detachment as everything else.

> Duties are universally measured by relations. Is a man a father? The [duty] is to take care of him, to yield to him in all things, to submit when he is reproachful, when he inflicts blows. But suppose he is a bad father. Were you then by nature [guaranteed] a good father? No; [just] a father. Does a brother wrong you? Maintain then your own position towards him, and do not examine what he is doing, but what you must do [in order] that your will shall be [in accord with] nature. For another will not damage you, unless you choose; but you will be damaged when you shall think that you are damaged. In this way then you will discover your duty from the relation of a neighbor, from that of a citizen, from that of a general, if you are accustomed to contemplate [your relationships].[26]

This passage is an excellent example of applying disinterested reason to daily affairs. The Stoics believed that a disinterested study of life shows that no one is *entitled* to good, healthy parents; loving, supportive brothers and sisters; obedient children; or sexy, interesting, loyal boyfriends, girlfriends, or spouses. If the *Logos* provides *everything we need* to be happy, then it is clear that no one needs good parents, and so on. The reason is obvious: Not everyone gets them. Thus, these are not things to which we are entitled or the *Logos* would have provided them.

The only way to grasp this point is to set our *feelings* aside and apply *disinterested reason* to relationships. For example, the traditional marriage vow commits each spouse to the other "for richer or poorer, in sickness and in health." This means that as a husband—not as an individual—I have obligations that stem from the nature of the marital relationship, regardless of how my wife behaves. Duties

What you're supposed to do when you don't like a thing is change it. If you can't change it, change the way you think about it.

MAYA ANGELOU

Do not be distressed, do not despond or give up in despair, if now and again practice falls short of precept. Return to the attack after each failure, and be thankful if on the whole you can acquit yourself in the majority of cases as a man should.

MARCUS AURELIUS

"These sons belong to me, and this wealth belongs to me"—with such thoughts a fool is tormented. He himself does not belong to himself; how much less sons and wealth?

BUDDHA

Do not value either your children or your life or anything else more than goodness.

SOCRATES

Olympic champion swimmer Michael Phelps and the happy graduate (facing page) have paid the price of training and self-discipline. As Epictetus said, "You will be unjust and insatiable if you do not part with price in return for which . . . things are sold." Perhaps if we remember this Stoic principle, we will not envy or resent those who have paid a price that we have not.

are not based on the personalities or preferences of the individuals involved. Similarly, as a son, I have duties toward my father whether or not I "like" him and whether or not he is a good father.

In Epictetus's time, social roles were less flexible than they are now. We have more sophisticated psychological knowledge of the damage that bad, abusive relationships can cause. So it will be necessary to modify Epictetus's strict position. But even today, I can still be a Stoic without being a martyr. I can remind myself that as long as I am in this marriage or have this job, *I* have duties that are not contingent on other people fulfilling *their* duties. What kind of teacher would I be if I did not prepare my lessons carefully just because many of my students come to class unprepared? What kind of student would you be if you whispered and passed notes to your friend just because your teacher was unprepared?

PHILOSOPHICAL
QUERY

• • • • • •

Discuss the preceding passage from Epictetus about relationships. What lessons might it have regarding our relationships and the things that make us unhappy?

Everything Has a Price

One reason we might be frustrated by events is that we tend to focus on the object of our desire while ignoring its cost. Yet everything has a clearly marked price tag. The athlete with a fine physique has paid the price of training and discipline, perhaps by giving up a broad education or full social life. The ambitious character at the office has paid the price of flattering the boss and working late while you did not have to "kiss up" and were home enjoying your family life. The A student has

©Douglas J. Soccio

I consider it a dangerous misconception of mental hygiene to assume that what man needs in the first place is equilibrium or . . . a tensionless state. What man actually needs is not a tensionless state but rather a striving and struggling for some goal worthy of him.

VIKTOR E. FRANKL

paid the price of missing many parties and other kinds of socializing. According to Epictetus, we suffer unnecessarily when we try to have things without paying the price:

> You will be unjust then and insatiable, if you do not part with the price, in return for which . . . things are sold, and if you wish to obtain them for nothing. Well, what is the price of lettuces? An obulus perhaps. If then a man gives up the obulus and receives the lettuces, and if you do not give up the obulus and do not receive the lettuces, do not suppose that you receive less than he who has got the lettuces; for as he has the lettuces, so you have the obulus which you did not give . . . you have not been invited to a man's feast, for you did not give the host the price at which the supper is sold; but he sells it for praise (flattery), he sells it for personal attention. Give him the price, if it is for your interest, for which it is sold. But if you wish both not to give the price, and to obtain the things, you are insatiable and silly. Have you nothing then in place of the supper? You have indeed, you have the [satisfaction of] not flattering . . . him . . . whom you did not choose to flatter; you have [not had to put up with him].[27]

What would you think of someone who screamed and turned red with rage when asked to pay for a basket of groceries at the market? He or she would be silly, to say the least. How is this different from the couple who once eagerly desired a baby and now resent the infant's demands? Or the married man who chafes at his

It may seem strange, but most people . . . elect not to continue with their life journeys—to stop short by some distance to avoid the pain of giving up parts of themselves. If it does not seem strange, it is because you do not understand the depth of the pain that may be involved. In its major forms, giving up is the most painful of human experiences.

M. SCOTT PECK

We can only bow our heads in the presence of those broken beneath the burden of their destiny. The capacity of the human soul for suffering and isolation is immense.

SARVEPALLI RADHAKRISHNAN

"For What Matters Above All Is the Attitude We Take Toward Suffering"

Perhaps the most philosophical and Stoic psychology today is Viktor E. Frankl's logotherapy. During World War II, Frankl (1905–1997), an Austrian Jew, was imprisoned for three years in the Nazi concentration camp at Auschwitz. Upon his release he discovered that his whole family had been destroyed. Based on his personal experience and subsequent clinical experiences with suffering, Frankl developed logotherapy, based on the definition of *Logos* as "meaning." Frankl's most famous book is *Man's Search for Meaning*. If you have not read it, I recommend it to you. Here's an extract to whet your appetite:

> Whenever one is confronted with an inescapable, unavoidable situation, whenever one has to face a fate that cannot be changed, e.g., an incurable disease, such as inoperable cancer, just then one is given a last chance to actualize the highest value, to fulfill the deepest meaning, the meaning of suffering. For what matters above all is the attitude we take toward suffering, the attitude in which we take our suffering upon ourselves. . . . Suffering ceases to be suffering in some way at the moment it finds a meaning, such as the meaning of a sacrifice. . . . It is one of the main tenets of logotherapy that man's main concern is not to gain pleasure or avoid pain, but rather to see a meaning in his life. That is why man is ready to suffer, on the condition, to be sure, that his suffering has a meaning.

From *Man's Search for Meaning: An Introduction to Logotherapy* (New York: Pocket Books, 1963), pp. 178–179. Used by permission of Beacon Press.

---

obligations? Or the woman who has a job, a social life, and three children and is surprised that she feels tired and run-down? As obvious as the notion of a price seems, many of us seem to be stunned when we are expected to pay up.

> *For humans, a life of hardship is the norm and death is the end. Abiding by the norm, awaiting my end, what is there to be concerned about?*
>
> RONG QIQI

> *Whether you like it or not, you'd better accept reality the way it occurs: as highly imperfect and filled with most fallible human beings. Your alternative? Continual anxiety and desperate disappointment.*
>
> ALBERT ELLIS AND ROBERT HARPER

Suffering and Courage

Stoicism is a "mature" philosophy in that its appeal seems to increase with experience—that is, with frustration and disappointment. Growing up emotionally and philosophically involves adopting realistic expectations and accepting one's limits. The challenge of maturity is how to do this without becoming overly negative or giving in to inertia. How can I develop an attitude of Stoic detachment and acceptance and still have hopes and take action?

The Stoics sometimes compared the *Logos* to a parent or teacher. They pointed out that hardship and suffering can be viewed as gifts, if we understand that the best teachers are strictest with those pupils in whom they see the most ability. They also noted that suffering cannot be bad by nature, or else good men like Socrates would not have suffered. In other words, who am I that I should escape the ordinary trials of life? The goal isn't to avoid them, but to use them to become a good person. Seneca said, "The greater the torment, the greater shall be the glory." He adds:

> Prosperity can come to the vulgar and to ordinary talents, but to triumph over the disasters and terrors of mortal life is the privilege of the great man.

To be lucky always and to pass through life without gnawing of the mind is to be ignorant of the half of nature. You are a great man, but how can I know, if Fortune has never given you a chance to display your prowess? You have entered the Olympic games but have no rival; you gain the crown but not the victory. . . . I can say . . . "I account you unfortunate because you have never been unfortunate. You have passed through life without an adversary; no man can know your potentiality, not even you." For self-knowledge, testing is necessary; no one can discover what he can do except by trying.[28]

Since there is really no way to avoid pain, it is especially tragic to see those who try, for not only are they doomed to failure, but they also suffer additionally because they lack character. They live at the whim of circumstances. Seneca says:

So god hardens and scrutinizes and exercises those he approves and loves; but those he appears to indulge and spare he is only keeping tender for disasters to come. If you suppose anyone is immune you are mistaken. . . . Why does god afflict every good man with sickness or grief or misfortune? Because in the army, too, the most hazardous duties are assigned to the bravest soldiers. . . . In the case of good men, accordingly, the gods follow the plan that teachers follow with their pupils; they demand more effort from those in whom they have confident expectations. . . . What wonder, then, if god tries noble spirits with sternness? The demonstration of courage can never be gentle. Fortune scourges us; we must endure it. It is not cruelty but a contest.[29]

Thus, the Stoics say, our misfortune on this earth is not a result of God's disfavor, but possibly the result of His respect or understanding of what we need to endure but would avoid if left to our own devices. Certainly faith in a divine will seems to obligate us to reach such a conclusion. Even without belief in God, we can still ask the Stoic's question: Which is more reasonable: to endure inescapable hardship and to suffer mental torment or to endure inescapable hardship but accept it with courage and magnanimity? As I have framed the question, it answers itself. Without trivializing it, we can say that Stoicism comes down to this: *While making reasonable efforts to get what we want, it is wise to learn to be happy with what we get.*

▪ THE WORLD OF EPICTETUS ▪

Perhaps the greatest testimonies to the merit of Stoicism come from those who have suffered greatly, as Frankl reminds us. One of the most interesting and compelling arguments for the practical value of a good philosophical education came from an unexpected source: a highly trained United States Navy fighter pilot.

What we know as the *Enchiridion* of Epictetus can be a powerful consolation and support to people undergoing the severest trials. In fact, **James Bond Stockdale** (1923–2005), a vice admiral (retired) in the United States Navy, credited his education in the humanities—and Epictetus in particular—with helping him survive seven and one-half years as a prisoner of war in North Vietnam, including four years in solitary confinement. Stockdale was awarded the Congressional Medal of Honor after his release.

It is the mind which moulds man's destiny, action being but precipitated thought. It follows that one's lightest thought has vast effects, not only on the thinker, but on all that lives.
CHRISTMAS HUMPHREYS

To bear pain, to endure suffering, is the quality of the strong in spirit. It adds to the spiritual resources of humanity.
SARVEPALLI RADHAKRISHNAN

Love only that which happens to thee and is spun with the thread of thy destiny. For what is more suitable?
MARCUS AURELIUS

James Bond Stockdale

©Corbis

©Courtesy of Sybil Stockdale

James Bond Stockdale credited the lessons he learned from Epictetus's *Enchiridion* with helping him to survive seven and one-half years in a North Vietnamese prison camp, confirming the Stoic belief that through great effort of will we can transform total loss into "heroic and virtuous achievement."

Lameness is an impediment to the leg, but not to the Will; and say this to yourself with regard to everything that happens. For you will find such things to be an impediment to something else, but not truly to yourself.

EPICTETUS

In April 1978 the *Atlantic Monthly* published a remarkable article by this unusual soldier-philosopher called "The World of Epictetus." Stockdale describes the brutal conditions that POWs were kept in and his own fear and despondency. As he reviewed his life from his solitary cell, Stockdale "picked the locks" to the doors of his past experiences. He recalled cocktail parties and phony social contacts with revulsion as empty and valueless. "More often than not," he said, "the locks worth picking had been old schoolroom doors."

In this passage, Stockdale testifies to the real-life value of Epictetus's *Enchiridion*:

The messages of history and philosophy I used were simple.

The first one is the business about life not being fair. That was a very important lesson and I learned it from a wonderful man named Philip Rhinelander. . . . He said, "The course I'm teaching is my personal two-term favorite—The Problem of Good and Evil—and we're starting our second term." He said the message of his course was from the Book of Job. The number one problem in this world is that people are not able to accommodate the lesson in the book.

He recounted the story of Job. It starts out by establishing that Job was the most honorable of men. Then he lost all his goods. He also lost his reputation, which is what really hurt. His wife was badgering him to admit his sins, but he knew he had made no errors. He was not a patient man and demanded to speak to the Lord. When the Lord replied in the whirlwind, he said, "Now, Job, you have to shape up! Life is not fair." That's my interpretation and that's the way the book ended for hundreds of years. I agree with those of the opinion that the happy ending was spliced on many years later. . . . People couldn't live with the original message.

Rhinelander also passed on to me another piece of classical information which I found of great value. On the day of our last session together he said, "You're a military man, let me give you a book to remember me by. It's a book of military ethics." He handed it to me, and I bade him goodbye with great emotion. I took the book home and that night started to read it. It was the *Enchiridion* of the philosopher Epictetus, his "manual" for the Roman field soldier.

As I began to read, I thought to myself in disbelief, "Does Rhinelander think I'm going to draw lessons for my life from this thing? I'm a fighter pilot. I'm a technical man. I'm a test pilot. I know how to get people to do technical work. I play golf; I drink martinis. I know how to get ahead in my profession. And what does he hand me? A book that says in part, 'It's better to die in hunger, exempt from guilt and fear, than to live in affluence and with perturbation.'" I remembered this later in prison because perturbation was what I was living with. When I ejected from the airplane on that September morn in 1965, I had left the land of technology. I had entered the world of Epictetus, and it's a world that few of us, whether we know it or not, are ever far away from.[30]

The lessons that the old Roman slave learned on the rack gave comfort and courage to a solitary prisoner of war two thousand years later in the rice paddies of Southeast Asia.

■ COMMENTARY ■

This summary glance at Stoicism shows up inconsistencies and difficulties. The nature of fate remains ambiguous: How detailed is my life script? Has the *Logos* determined that I drop a pencil or make a typing mistake as I write this? Or is my fate painted in broader strokes? If so, in what sense is it fate? Are all emotions "bad"? Is it *reasonable* to be so detached, if it's even possible? Can a disinterested person have a motive, or are motives emotional?

Such obvious problems result partly from the Stoics' near indifference to everything except the issue of how to live the least disturbed life possible. They were not concerned with providing a completely worked-out philosophical *system*. Even so, Stoicism retains an appeal that rests on genuine insights into the causes of much suffering and unhappiness. The Stoics were highly practical moral psychologists whose chief interests were ethics and psychology. As such, the most insightful of them offer sage counsel and inspiration that is as pertinent and helpful today as it was when first presented over two thousand years ago.

When I first encountered Stoicism as an undergraduate, I found it annoying. The ideal Stoic seemed to be a bland, emotionless vegetable—certainly not the kind of person I wanted to be. I needn't have worried. Stoic self-control and discipline were unable to stifle my great emotions. And so I spent too many years fuming over traffic, long lines, the way the world behaved, my teachers, my students, being alone, not being alone—life.

Today, I recognize the depth of passion behind the words of Marcus Aurelius and Epictetus. They certainly were not bland, unfeeling people. I understand how

To live under the false pretense that you will forever have control of your station in life is to ride for a fall; you're asking for disappointment. So make sure in your heart of hearts, in your inner self, that you treat your station in life with indifference, not with contempt, only with indifference.

JAMES BOND STOCKDALE

Sorrow is merely a state of mind and may not be warranted by the circumstance. Hence whether or not you feel sad over something is all in the mind.

LIE ZI

For wherever a man's place is, whether the place which he has chosen or that in which he has been placed by a commander, there he ought to remain in the hour of danger; he should not think of death or of anything but disgrace. And this, O men of Athens, is a true saying.

SOCRATES

Glory be to that God Who slays our wives and destroys our children And Whom withal we love.

PRAYER OF ATTAR

much of my own frustration has come from not looking carefully for the price tag before I rushed to the checkout.

Given the condition of our society and seemingly basic human nature, I see enough merit in Stoic wisdom to compensate for certain ambiguities and inconsistencies in its expression. If nothing else, it *sometimes* helps me sit through time-wasting and mind-numbing traffic jams and crowded waiting rooms. More important, reading Stoic works inspires me to look beyond my own immediate comfort (or discomfort), to strive for self-discipline, courage, and serenity.

Stoicism provides a counterbalance of sorts to today's love affair with instant gratification and emotional expressiveness. In its lessons on relationships and suffering, Stoicism wisely reminds us that what cannot be changed must be accepted graciously if we are ever to be happy. We live in a time when people seek external solutions to nearly every sort of predicament. Many solutions will be found. But no external solution can make us happy or unhappy, for, as a late friend used to remind me, "Happiness is an inside job."

After his 1973 release from prison, Admiral Stockdale served as president of the Naval War College in Newport, Rhode Island; president of the Citadel, the military college of South Carolina; and a senior research fellow at the Hoover Institution, located at Stanford University. In 1992, third-party presidential candidate Ross Perot asked Stockdale to be his vice presidential running mate. During an election-year debate among the three vice presidential candidates, Stockdale began, as Socrates might have, with two timeless questions: "Who am I? Why am I here?" Though the philosophical thrust of the questions was missed by most people, Stockdale's philosophical vision attracted national attention to Stoicism in general and Epictetus in particular. In 1999, Stoicism played a central role in Tom Wolfe's best-selling novel *A Man in Full*, which involved a character based loosely on Stockdale.

Stockdale remains one of our most remarkable contemporary philosophers in the original sense. The lessons of wisdom he learned are particularly compelling because they come from as broad a spectrum of experiences as is humanly possible—the extremes of defeat, degradation, torture, and isolation, on the one hand, and the heights of influence, national prominence, and academic recognition, on the other. Few of us experience such extremes in either direction; fewer yet in both. Thus, Stockdale's life and writings provide us with a rare contemporary example of the Stoic sage. Who better to have the last word in our survey of one of the most influential archetypes of wisdom?

Stoicism is certainly not for everybody, and it is not for me in every circumstance, but it is an expression in philosophical terms of how people find purpose in what they have every right to see as a purposeless world. . . . [Stoicism] speaks to people everywhere who persist in competing in what they see as a buzz-saw existence, their backs to the wall, their lives having meaning only so long as they fight for pride and comradeship and joy rather than capitulate to either tyranny or phoniness. . . .

. . . We who are in hierarchies—be they academic, business, military, or otherwise—are always in positions in which people are trying to manipulate us, to get moral leverage on us. The only defense is to keep yourself clean—never to do or say anything of which you can be made to feel ashamed. . . .

For it is better to die of hunger, exempt from fear and guilt, than to live in affluence with perturbation.

EPICTETUS

The judge will do some things to you which are thought to be terrifying; but how can he stop you from taking the punishment he threatened?

EPICTETUS

Defeat may serve as well as victory to shake the soul and let the glory out.

EDWIN MARKHAM

If you want to protect yourself from "fear and guilt," and those are the crucial pincers, the real long-term destroyers of will, you have to get rid of all your instincts to compromise, to meet people halfway.

JAMES BOND STOCKDALE

Am I personally still hooked on Epictetus's Principle of Life? Yes, but not in the sense of following a memorized doctrine. I sometimes become amused at how I have applied it and continue to apply it unconsciously. An example is the following story about myself.

As the months and years wear on in solitary confinement, it turns out each man goes crazy if he doesn't get some ritual into his life. I mean by that a self-imposed obligation to do certain things in a certain order each day. Like most prisoners, I prayed each day, month after month, continually altering and refining a long memorized monologue that probably ran to ten or fifteen minutes. At some point, my frame of mind became so pure that I started deleting any begging of God and any requests that would work specifically for my benefit. This didn't come out of any new Principle of Life that I had developed; it just suddenly started to seem unbecoming to beg. I knew the lesson of the book of Job: life is not fair. What claim had I for special consideration? And anyway, by then I had seen enough misery to know that He had enough to worry about without trying to appease a crybaby like me. And so it has been ever since.[31]

> In this day and age, the greatest devotion, greater than learning and praying, consists in accepting the world exactly as it happens to be.
>
> RABBI MOSHE OF KOBRYN

■ SUMMARY OF MAIN POINTS ■

- Hedonism is the general term for any philosophy that says that pleasure is identical with good and pain is identical with evil. Hedonists stress either the pursuit of pleasure (Cyrenaic) or the avoidance of pain (Epicurean). Cyrenaic hedonists believe that all pleasures of the same intensity are equal. They deny the possibility of qualitative differences among pleasures. Epicurean hedonism is the more refined doctrine that there are qualitative differences among pleasures.

- Antisthenes was the founder of a philosophical school known as Cynicism, and Diogenes was its most famous advocate. The Cynics believed that the very essence of civilization is corrupt, that manners are hypocritical, that material wealth weakens people, and that civilization destroys the individual and makes him or her vulnerable to the whims of fortune. According to the Cynics, the death of Socrates showed that not even the wisest person can control other people or external events. They concluded that the less an individual needs to be happy, the less vulnerable he or she will be. Cynics lived austere, unconventional lives.

- Founded in Greece by Zeno, Stoicism grew out of Cynicism and achieved widespread influence in first-century Rome, ultimately spreading throughout Christianized Europe. The Roman slave Epictetus, the Emperor Marcus Aurelius, and the senator Seneca are the most influential Stoic writers. Stoics recommended accepting whatever circumstances we are in without resentment. They believed that the cosmos is wisely governed by the *Logos* (World Reason) and that everything happens as part of a divine plan.

- According to the Stoics, human beings are bits of the *Logos* because we have rational souls. Happiness comes from the effective use of reason to alter the will. Based on their concept of a disinterested World Reason, the Stoics taught that it is wise to minimize personal attachments and motives. They rejected emotion to the extent it was humanly possible, favoring detached, rational acceptance over personal, emotional involvement.

- Though the Stoics believed that life is fated, they understood this in a loose sense. Because we cannot know precisely what our fate is, we must take reasonable action without pinning our happiness on a particular result. According to the Stoics, we can control our ideas and attitudes, but we cannot control "externals" such as reputation, social status, relationships, health, and wealth.

- Stoic virtues include strength of will, courage, dignity, and maturity. According to Stoic doctrine, everything has a price that reason can reveal. The price of happiness is personal detachment from external conditions; peace of mind comes from indifference to everything except accepting the will of the *Logos*. Stoics taught that only great struggle could produce greatness of character.

- The philosopher-warrior James Bond Stockdale refined Epictetus's Principle of Life and communicated it to a growing audience.

■ POST-READING REFLECTIONS ■

Now that you have had a chance to learn about the Stoic, use your new knowledge to answer these questions.

1. Explain the role hedonistic thinking played in the origins of Stoicism.

2. How did Cynicism influence Stoicism? Be specific.

3. What is the relationship of Socrates to Cynicism and Stoicism?

4. How are the *Logos* and fate related in Stoicism?

5. Identify and discuss possible problems with the Stoic notion of fate.

6. Stoicism was quickly absorbed into Christianity. Identify and comment on any similarities you are aware of.

7. What is the disinterested rational will, and why is it important to Stoic doctrine?

8. What do the Stoics think falls under our control? What do the Stoics think does not fall under our control? Do you agree? Why or why not?

9. Discuss the difference between avoidable and unavoidable suffering. How can we tell which is which? Why does it matter?

10. Explain the Stoic attitude toward relationships. How does it differ from today's attitudes? What do you see as important strengths and weaknesses of each perspective?

11. What does Seneca mean when he says "I account you unfortunate because you have never been unfortunate"? How do the Stoics interpret suffering? What do you think of this view?

12. What do you think of James Stockdale's claim that a good philosophical education is highly practical? Give his position and then comment on it.

 ### PHILOSOPHY INTERNET RESOURCES

Go to the Soccio Web page at **http://philosophy.wadsworth.com/ Soccio7e** for Web links, practice quizzes and tests, a pronunciation guide, and study tips.

THE SCHOLAR

Thomas Aquinas

NOW, AMONG THE INQUIRIES THAT WE MUST UNDERTAKE
CONCERNING GOD IN HIMSELF, WE MUST SET DOWN IN
THE BEGINNING THAT WHEREBY HIS EXISTENCE IS DEMONSTRATED,
AS THE NECESSARY FOUNDATION OF THE
WHOLE WORK. FOR, IF WE DO NOT DEMONSTRATE
THAT GOD EXISTS, ALL CONSIDERATION OF DIVINE THINGS
IS NECESSARILY SUPPRESSED.

Thomas Aquinas

LEARNING OBJECTIVES

- WHAT IS THEOLOGY?
- WHAT IS SCHOLASTICISM?
- WHAT IS THE ARGUMENT FROM MOTION?
- WHAT IS THE COSMOLOGICAL ARGUMENT?
- WHAT IS THE ARGUMENT FROM NECESSITY?
- WHAT IS THE PRINCIPLE OF SUFFICIENT REASON?
- WHAT IS THE PRINCIPLE OF PLENITUDE?
- WHAT IS THE ARGUMENT FROM GRADATION?
- WHAT IS THE TELEOLOGICAL ARGUMENT?

FOR YOUR REFLECTION

KEEP THESE QUESTIONS IN MIND AS YOU LEARN ABOUT THE SCHOLAR.

1. *What is theology?*
2. *What is Scholasticism?*
3. *What is the argument from motion?*
4. *What is the cosmological argument?*
5. *What is the argument from necessity?*
6. *What is the principle of sufficient reason?*
7. *What is the principle of plenitude?*
8. *What is the argument from gradation?*
9. *What is the teleological argument?*

FOR DEEPER CONSIDERATION

A. The "problem of evil" has perplexed philosophers, theologians, and others for centuries. What, exactly, is the problem and what does the traditional Judeo-Christian conception or understanding of God have to do with it? How does Thomas Aquinas approach the problem of evil? Do you think he solves it? Do you think it is solvable? Is it a real problem or not? Explain.

B. What does it mean to say that human beings are susceptible to principles of reason? What are principles of reason? What is the law of contradiction and what is its connection to the origins of Scholastic philosophy? What real-life difference does it make if we are or are not "susceptible to principles of reason"?

1 once watched a television news reporter interview a weeping woman who sat on the pile of rubble that had been her small mobile home. Everything she owned had been destroyed by a tornado. Through her tears, the victim expressed her gratitude to God for saving her life. As she explained it, she was preparing supper when she mysteriously had the urge to go to the corner market for a loaf of bread. She was gone for only a few minutes, but in those minutes the tornado struck. "If I hadn't gone for that bread," she said into the camera, "I would be dead now. God told me to go get that bread in order to save my life."

Does this mean that God *wanted* those people who were not warned to die? Suppose the woman's neighbor had been planning to go to the store but got a phone call just as he started for the door. Should we conclude that God arranged the timing of the call to make sure he didn't escape the tornado?

After all, if God is the cause of *everything* that happens, *everything* includes tornadoes and torture, as well as salvation and joy. If God knows *everything,* does He know your grade on your philosophy final right now? But if God knows things before they happen, how can *we* be held responsible for them? If God knew before you were born that you would get a C minus in philosophy, isn't *He* the "cause" of your grade, not you? But if there is even one thing that He does not know, even one thing, how can He be all-wise?

These and related questions are of more than just academic interest. They are vitally important to anyone who attempts to reconcile faith with reason. One solution to such problems has been to hold a *dual-truth point of view.* This is the position that there is one small-t truth on the finite, human level and another, superior, capital-T Truth for God. Another strategy is to declare that these problems demonstrate that the ways of God are a "mystery" to human beings. In both cases, inconsistencies and ambiguities are not so much resolved as they are evaded.

Many believers and nonbelievers alike feel cheated when asked to accept inconsistent beliefs or simply to dismiss the most vital questions of faith. If you doubt this, wander through the sections of your college library's stacks dealing with theology and religious philosophy. You will find a large number of books and articles attempting to reconcile faith with reason. If you have ever seriously wrestled with the problem of evil (How can a good, loving, wise, powerful God allow evil?) or the problem of moral responsibility (If God gave Adam and Eve a corrupt nature, how can they—and we—justly be held responsible?), you have entered a timeless struggle.

Our culture has been heavily influenced by an ongoing clash between Christian values and the values established in classical Greece. In the classical view, human beings, despite our many faults, represent the most important life-form. The classical philosopher believed that objective knowledge and logic could unlock the keys to the universe, improving our lives in the process. The good life was seen as being a product of reason. Reason was valued over faith because knowing was thought to be more useful than believing.

The Christian view presents a completely different picture. Human beings are seen as fallen and corrupt creatures, finite and ignorant. Christian theology teaches

A person who says he has faith in God's goodness is speaking as if he had known God for a long time and during that time had never seen him do any serious evil. But we know that throughout history God has allowed numerous atrocities to occur. No one can have justifiable faith in the goodness of such a God.

B. C. Johnson

God does not play dice with the universe.

Albert Einstein

For the sake of a laugh, a little sport, I was glad to do harm and anxious to damage another; and that without a thought of profit for myself or retaliation for injuries received! And all because we are ashamed to hold back when others say, "Come on! Let's do it!"

Augustine

that we are incapable of avoiding sin and the punishment of hell through our own efforts. Only the undeserved grace and sacrifice of a loving God can save us. Obedience to the revealed word of God is also necessary for salvation. Faith is valued more highly than reason because salvation is more important than worldly success in a life that is relatively brief compared with the afterlife—where we will spend eternity in heaven (if we are saved) or hell (if we are not). As a result of its emphasis on the afterlife, Christian theology is sometimes characterized as *otherworldly.*

▓ THE GOD-CENTERED UNIVERSE ▓

theology

From the Greek *theos* (God) and *logos* (study of); "talking about God" or "the study or science of God."

Whereas the classical mind was predominantly secular, the medieval mind was chiefly theological. **Theology,** from the Greek *theos* (God) and *logos* (study of), means "talking about God" or "the study or science of God." The Middle Ages saw philosophers turn from the study of man and nature to "otherworldly" inquiries and the study of God.

Rather than *discover* the truth through reason and science, the medieval scholar studied church dogma and theology in order to *explain* what God chose to reveal. Philosophers struggled with such questions as these: Are faith and reason always at odds? Can the human mind know God through reason? Does being a "good Christian" prohibit questioning and trying to understand certain things? Why did God give us the ability to reason if we are asked to ignore what reason reveals? When conflicting religious beliefs all claim to rely on divine authority and revelation, how can we choose among them?

The Seeds of Change

The Christian religion arose after the death of Jesus Christ, through the efforts of the early apostles and disciples, especially Paul. Christianity originally consisted of scattered groups of believers who anticipated the Second Coming of Christ, which would signal the end of the world. Thinking that they would soon be in heaven, early Christians saw no need to develop political interests. Similarly, they were uninterested in science and philosophy and remained indifferent to much of what went on around them. Their chief concern was salvation through faith. Expecting that the risen Christ would return at any moment, they were understandably impatient with the affairs of this world. Thus, the first Christians devoted themselves to converting non-Christians and to preparing their own souls for judgment. In a major contrast with the classical view of life, they saw no time or need to fashion philosophical, social, or moral theories.

As time passed and the world did not end, Christians found it increasingly difficult to avoid dealing with problems of the here and now. Principles and rules for interpreting the basic teachings of Christ, collected as the New Testament, became necessary when it grew clear that the Second Coming might not occur until well into the future.

Interpreting revealed sacred dogma is always dangerous, however, for once the inevitability of interpretation is accepted, the door is open to competing interpretations. If *every* claimed interpretation is reliable, God's revealed will is going to appear chaotic, inconsistent, contradictory, and capricious. There must be

The Need to Reconcile Faith and Reason

The great paradoxes of faith are sometimes superficially dismissed by people who have never really grappled with them. Their religious training may have given them simple answers to problems such as free will, evil, predestination, and God's nature. Or they may have been taught to "exalt faith" by condemning reason. It is easy to say that faith surpasses understanding until you fully grasp the complex depths and significance of these problems. Whatever our individual religious beliefs, most of us are also rational creatures for whom it is somehow unsatisfying to accept contradictions and serious inconsistencies concerning something as important as our religious faith. We are uncomfortable when we learn that we are violating rational principles.

The basic **principles of reason**—also called **rules of inference**—define the limits of rationality. That is, consistently violating them moves us to the realm of the irrational or illogical. They are true by their very structure (by definition). They cannot be rationally refuted, since we rely on them in order to reason. Contemporary logicians recognize several rules of inference. One of the most important is the law of contradiction.

The **law of contradiction** (sometimes known as the law of noncontradiction) says, No statement can be both true and false at the same time and under the same conditions. Or to use

symbols (as philosophers who study logic often do), p cannot be both p and $not\text{-}p$ at the same time. For example: Either this is a philosophy book or it is not a philosophy book. It cannot be both a philosophy book and not a philosophy book. It can, however, be a philosophy book and a doorstop at the same time. There is no contradiction involved in asserting that it is a philosophy book and more. The contradiction occurs in the mutually exclusive assertions: "This is a philosophy book" and "This is not a philosophy book."

Take a moment to reflect on the law of contradiction. See if you can get a sense of just how basic it is to rationality. Because it is a fundamental principle of reasoning, we are usually disturbed to discover that our ideas are contradictory, for such awareness commits us to resolving the contradiction or holding seemingly irrational ideas.

In matters of faith, trying to avoid the possibility of contradiction by claiming that the human mind is finite and unable to understand God and God's ways is ultimately unsatisfying, for it removes us from meaningful communication with God. If we can never fully comprehend God, if we must trust that things are not at all what they seem (for instance, that evil only appears to be evil from our level but is really good from God's), then our "solution" may not be what it appears to be, either.

criteria for distinguishing revelation from delusion and dogma from error. And there must be criteria for choosing criteria. And criteria for choosing criteria for choosing criteria . . .

Some reinterpretation of Christian teachings was clearly called for, if the Second Coming might be generations away. Giving all our goods to the poor is one thing when we expect to be in heaven in the immediate future; practical considerations complicate matters if the final judgment may be years away. As the centuries passed and the Second Coming did not occur, Christianity continued to expand: As Christian doctrine increased in complexity, theological issues added to practical complications.

▪ AUGUSTINE: BETWEEN TWO WORLDS ▪

Aurelius Augustine (354–430) has been described as "a colossus bestriding two worlds" for his efforts to synthesize early Christian theology with his own understanding of Platonic philosophy and Manichean dualism, the

principles of reason (rules of inference)
Principles (such as the law of contradiction) that define the limits of rationality by their very structure and that cannot be rationally refuted since we rely on them in order to reason.

law of contradiction
Rule of inference that says no statement can be both true and false at the same time and under the same conditions; sometimes known as the law of noncontradiction.

Aurelius Augustine

*I inquired, "Whence is evil?"
and found no result. . . .
What torments did my heart
then endure!*

AUGUSTINE

*Here proud, there
superstitious, everywhere
vain.*

AUGUSTINE

*It can hardly be right for
[an infant] . . . to cry for
everything, including things
which would harm him; to
work himself into a tantrum
against people . . . when
they do not give in to him
and refuse to pander to
whims which would only
do him harm. This shows
that, if babies are innocent,
it is not from lack of will to
do no harm, but for lack of
strength.*

AUGUSTINE

*I still thought that it was not
we who sin but some other
nature that sins within us. It
flattered my pride to think
that I incurred no guilt. . . .
My sin was all the more
incurable because I did not
think myself a sinner.*

AUGUSTINE

belief that God and Satan are nearly evenly matched in a cosmic struggle and that human beings must choose sides.

Augustine's struggle to "choose sides" began at home. He was born in the North African city of Tagaste in the province of Numidia. His mother, Monica, was a devout Christian while his father, Patricius, regularly strayed from the straight and narrow. For all of her life, Monica fought to bring Augustine into the Christian church. Meanwhile, Augustine lived it up. He had a son, Adeodatus ("gift of God"), with one mistress—he had others—and by his own account lived a wanton, worldly life until he was thirty-three years old.

> I was so blind to the truth that among my companions I was ashamed to be less dissolute than they were. For I heard them bragging of their depravity, and the greater the sin the more they gloried in it, so that I took pleasure in the same vices not only for the enjoyment of what I did, but also for the applause I won. . . . I gave in more and more to vice simply in order not to be despised. . . . I used to pretend that I had done things I had not done at all, because I was afraid that innocence would be taken for cowardice and chastity for weakness.[1]

Augustine's influence, like his life and work, emanates from the fearless way he pursues "something missing," looking for it in sex, glory (he was a fierce and effective debater), and companions, but also searching his heart and soul, his "interior teacher."

> Bodily desire, like a morass, and adolescent sex welling up within me exuded mists which clouded over and obscured my heart, so that I could not distinguish the clear light of true love from the murk of lust. Love and lust together seethed within me. In my tender youth they swept me away over the precipice of my body's appetites and plunged me into the whirlpool of sin.[2]

Eventually, under the prodding of his mother and at the bidding of Ambrose (c. 339–397), the Bishop of Milan, Augustine turned to the Bible. Sitting in a garden one day with his friend Alypius, Augustine heard the "sing-song voice of a child" saying over and over, "Take it and read, take it and read." He did, and the first passage his eyes fell upon seemed written just for him:

> Let us behave with decency as befits the day; no drunken orgies, no debauchery or vice, no quarrels or jealousies! Let Christ Jesus himself be the armour that you wear; give your unspiritual nature no opportunity to satisfy its desires.[3]

On Easter Sunday, 387, as Monica watched, Augustine, Adeodatus, and Alypius were baptized in Milan by Ambrose. Full of faith, the four left for Africa, where they planned to live ascetic lives, but Monica died before they reached Tagaste. In Tagaste, Augustine sold his inheritance, gave the money to the poor, and, with the help of friends, founded the Augustinian Order, the oldest Christian monastic order in the West. In 391, Augustine was ordained a priest by Valerius, the Bishop of Hippo, a Roman coastal city in North Africa. In 396, Augustine succeeded Valerius as Bishop of Hippo, a post he held for thirty-four years.

Augustine was a daring and active Christian bishop, just as he had been a daring and active anti-Christian Manichean. In both roles, he challenged doubters and nonbelievers to public debates, first defending Manicheanism against Christianity and then defending Christianity against Manicheanism.

After his conversion, Augustine produced more than 230 treatises, two of which, the *Confessions* (c. 400) and the *City of God* (413–426), remain important philosophical works for Christians and non-Christians alike.

In his writings, Augustine anticipates major philosophical and theological ideas concerning doubt and certainty, the divided self, consciousness, time, free will and God's foreknowledge of history. The *City of God* details the fall of Rome in terms of a full-fledged philosophy of history, the first *philosophy* of history ever. By arguing that the fall of Rome was part of the Christian—not pagan—God's plan, the *City of God* signals the end of the ancient worldview.

Augustine's *Confessions* is considered by some scholars to be the first true autobiography, a claim that is challenged by other scholars. Whether autobiography or something else, the *Confessions*, like the *Meditations* of the pagan emperor Marcus Aurelius, engages readers from divergent backgrounds. Like Marcus, Augustine takes the measure of his own soul in remarkably direct language and thereby speaks to almost anyone who has ever struggled to reconcile the longings of the heart with the demands of the mind, appetite with order, and resolve with repeated failures to live up to that resolve.

> I was held fast, not in fetters clamped upon me by another, but by my own will, which had the strength of iron chains. . . . the new will which had come to life in me . . . was not yet strong enough to overcome the old [will], hardened as it was by the passage of time. So these two wills within me, one old, one new, one servant of the flesh, the other of the spirit, were in conflict and between them they tore my soul apart.[4]

Augustine died shortly after the Vandals, who were at war with Rome, reached Hippo. He left no will, having no property. He did, however, write his own epitaph: "What maketh the heart of the Christian heavy? The fact that he is a pilgrim, and longs for his own country."

Pride and Philosophy

Combined with his Christian faith, Augustine's training in rhetoric and philosophy led him to reject Platonism, Epicureanism, and Stoicism (Chapters 5 and 7) as ways of life. Of particular concern to Augustine was the emphasis the classical Greeks, from Socrates through the Stoics, placed on human reason and the pride of place given to the human will.

Typically, the Greek philosophers held that reason is capable of distinguishing between truth and error and between reality and illusion. Even the Epicureans, with their emphasis on human happiness, stressed the importance of reason as the key to happiness in the here and now. In spite of their individual differences, the classical philosophers believed that human understanding (wisdom and knowledge) could and naturally would lead to proper emotions and proper behavior—to happiness here and now.

By Christian standards, classical humanism was too human or, rather, merely human in its indifference to the need for God's grace and guidance in

A cauldron of unholy loves bubbled up all around me. I loved not as yet, yet I loved to love.

AUGUSTINE

I searched about for something to love, in love with loving, and hating security.

AUGUSTINE

If truth were equal to our minds, it would be subject to change. Our minds sometimes see more and sometimes less, and because of this we acknowledge that they are mutable.

AUGUSTINE

If the will is wrongly directed, the emotions will be wrong; if the will is right, the emotions will be not only blameless, but praise worthy.

AUGUSTINE

the application of reason and moderation of the will. Augustine argued that, by itself, reason is powerless—even perverse—without the right will, without a will grounded in grace, love, and proper longing. Faith must precede education, for faith alone makes true understanding possible. Thus it is that faith is a necessary condition for productive philosophical inquiry.

Without faith, reason—the ground of so much classical philosophy—is, by Christian standards, unreliable, even dangerous. Left to its own devices, reason does not guide the will, but is guided—pulled hither and yon—by the will, especially if the will itself is corrupt, fallen, unsaved. The will cannot redeem itself, nor can it think itself well. To believe otherwise is to lapse into pride and ignorance.

Although Augustine may have misinterpreted some of the teachings of the Stoics and Epicureans, his uneasiness with their emphasis on the natural world and on self-willed self-control is understandable. Because Epicurus taught that the soul is physical and cannot survive in immaterial form, Augustine accuses the Epicureans of advocating the pursuit of physical pleasure to the exclusion of all else: "Eat, drink, and be merry, for tomorrow we may die."

According to Augustine, Epicureanism is fit only for swine, not for human beings. Besides debasing human beings, the Epicureans, in Augustine's view, make what God intended only as a means (appetites) into the be-all and end-all of life (satisfaction, pleasure). In so doing, Epicureans, in their retreat into the earthly Garden, satisfy themselves at the expense of the poor. In their rejection of an afterlife, they ignore their own souls.

Augustine had more respect for the Stoics. He admired their emphasis on virtues, particularly courage and integrity, but mocked the way they made serenity and detachment their chief goals, asking sarcastically, "Now is this man happy, just because he is patient in his misery? Of course not!" A steady state of serenity, regardless of what condition the world is in, strikes Augustine as an insubstantial goal. Worse yet, the Stoic's faith, like the Epicurean's, is in himself, not in God.

> By which thing it seems to me to be sufficiently proved that the errors of the Gentiles in ethics, physics, and the mode of seeking truth, errors many and manifold, but conspicuously represented in these two schools of philosophy [Epicureanism and Stoicism], continued even down to the Christian era, notwithstanding the fact that the learned assailed them most vehemently, and employed both remarkable skill and abundant labour in subverting them. Yet these errors . . . have been already so completely silenced, that now in our schools of rhetoric the question of what their opinions were is scarcely ever mentioned; and these controversies have been now so completely eradicated or suppressed . . . that whenever now any school of error lifts up its head against the truth, i.e., against the Church of Christ, it does not venture to leap into the arena except under the shield of the Christian name.[5]

Augustine took note of the description of Paul's encounter with the Stoics and Epicureans described in the Acts of the Apostles.

> While Paul was . . . at Athens . . . some of the Epicurean and Stoic philosophers joined issue with him. Some said, "What can this charlatan be trying to say?" . . . And when they had heard of the raising of the dead, some scoffed;

Now could anything but pride have been the start of the evil will?

AUGUSTINE

We see then that . . . the earthly city was created by self-love reaching the point of contempt for God . . . the earthly city glories in itself.

AUGUSTINE

When an evil choice happens in any being, then what happens is dependent on the will of that being; the failure is voluntary, not necessary, and the punishment that follows is just.

AUGUSTINE

Just as it is agreed that we all wish to be happy, so it is agreed that we all wish to be wise, since no one without wisdom is happy.

AUGUSTINE

For by the evil use of free choice man has destroyed both himself and it.

AUGUSTINE

others said, "We will hear you on this subject some other time." So Paul left the assembly.[6]

Augustine's misgivings notwithstanding, late Stoicism, especially in the *Meditations* and *Letters* of Marcus Aurelius, marks the beginning of the shift from purely pagan to Christian philosophy. Though pagan himself, Marcus in the *Meditations* expresses values and interests that become hallmarks of Christian philosophy: devaluing of this life and its temporary nature, a strong sense of duty, and the idea that human beings are related to the *Logos* (see Chapter 7).

But Marcus, like Plato and Epicurus, differed from his Christian successors, in his emphasis on human reason and his focus on this world. Augustine understood this and took up Paul's crusade against the errors of Greek philosophy. In so doing, he set in motion a major shift from the human-centric classical worldview to the God-centered medieval worldview.

> *I maintain that all attempts to employ reason in theology in any merely speculative manner are altogether fruitless.*
>
> IMMANUEL KANT

▪ THE LIFE OF THOMAS AQUINAS ▪

Thomas Aquinas (c. 1225–1274) was born near Naples.[7] His father, who was related to the count of Aquino, planned for Thomas to achieve a position of importance in the Catholic Church. To this end he enrolled Thomas in the Benedictine abbey school at Montecassino when Thomas was about five. The Benedictines are Roman Catholic monks famed for their modest lifestyle, which involves physical labor as well as spiritual discipline. As a general rule, Benedictines remain in one monastery for life. The monks of Montecassino taught close scrutiny of Scripture, careful reading and writing, and rote memory of long and complicated passages. While under their care, Thomas acquired basic religious knowledge, academic skills, and good study habits.

Thomas Aquinas

The Dominican

In 1239, Thomas was sent to study at the Imperial University of Naples, where he befriended some Dominican monks. Dominicans were dedicated to education and to preaching to common people. They took vows of poverty, chastity, and obedience. Unlike the Benedictines, who tended to establish their monasteries in the country, the Dominicans established themselves in the towns. As the spiritual authority of the Benedictine monasteries was declining, in part due to their wealth and prosperity, the Dominicans were emerging as the intellectual elite of the thirteenth century.[8]

Thomas was so attracted to the Dominican way of life that he decided to join the order. This decision disturbed his family, who had been looking forward to enjoying the advantages of being related to a powerful priest or bishop. That Thomas would become a poor monk was not in their plans.

Nonetheless, in 1243 or 1244, Thomas entered the Order of Preachers, as the Dominicans are known. His mother was so unhappy about it that she sent a distress message to his older brothers, who were soldiers. Thomas was traveling with other Dominicans when his brothers tracked him down and ordered him to

> *Of all the pursuits open to men, the search for wisdom is more perfect, more sublime, more profitable, and more full of joy.*
>
> THOMAS AQUINAS

remove his Dominican habit. When he refused, they kidnapped him. His family held Thomas captive for several months. They applied various arguments and pressures but did allow him to wear his Dominican habit and to study—though they kept him confined to his room.

One biographer reports the interesting but unlikely story that his family sent a provocatively dressed girl into his room one night while Thomas slept: "She tempted him to sin, using all the devices at her disposal, glances, caresses and gestures."[9] The saint in Thomas proved stronger than temptation, and he prayed until the girl left. In any event, Thomas managed to write a treatise *On Fallacies* while in family captivity. Finally, convinced of Thomas's sincerity and strength, his family released him. Soon after, the Dominicans sent him first to Cologne to continue his studies with the acclaimed teacher Albertus Magnus and then to the University of Paris.

The University of Paris

What we know today as universities began as medieval cathedral schools, though cathedral schools lacked central libraries and clusters of special buildings. Cathedral schools were religious in nature, originally consisting of masters and students under the authority of the supporting cathedral. These independent schools were associated with cathedrals and monasteries in such cities as Cluny, Tours, Chartres, and Paris. The cathedral of Notre Dame eventually supported more than one school. Cathedral schools spread from France to England and throughout Europe.

As the number of schools increased, they vied to possess the best libraries and faculty, and even competed over the quality and drama of great public debates called *disputations*. Associated with both the Dominicans and Franciscans, individual schools tended to specialize in copying and commenting on selected texts, in consolidating oral teachings into unified written form, or in subject areas such as rhetoric or theology. In time, individual schools merged into the University of Paris, which was closely supervised by the bishop of Paris, the chancellor of Notre Dame, and the pope.

As they developed, universities became centers of medieval learning, based in part on the quality of their faculties and in part on the availability of important new translations of philosophical texts. Most notable among these was the work of Aristotle; also significant were the great commentaries on Aristotle made by Arabian scholars from Baghdad and Spain and original Arabic and Jewish works of epistemology, metaphysics, and ethics by al-Farabi, ibn-Gabriol, Avicenna, and Averroës.

Only the clergy were permitted to study and teach at the universities, and Latin was the universal language of church and school. It is not surprising, then, that for the first time the unification, organization, and synthesis of knowledge became major philosophic tasks, strengthened by the authority and firm hierarchy of the church. The fundamental philosophical and social movement of the thirteenth century was toward the synthesis and consolidation of a single spiritual truth.[10]

Much of the teaching was conducted in the great public debates, the disputations, so the universities sought great debaters who could enhance the school's reputation by the quality of their disputations. The Dominicans were renowned

You can say that you trust God anyway—that no arguments can undermine your faith. But that is just a statement describing how stubborn you are; it has no bearing whatsoever on the question of God's goodness.

B. C. Johnson

[Religious ideas], which are given out as teachings, are not precipitates of experience or end-results of thinking; they are illusions, fulfillments of the oldest, strongest and most urgent wishes of mankind.

Sigmund Freud

If God did not exist, it would be necessary to invent him.

Voltaire

debaters, and by 1231 they held two faculty positions in theology at the University of Paris.[11]

Albertus Magnus: The Universal Teacher

While at Cologne, Thomas was encouraged in the search for philosophical unity by his teacher Albertus Magnus (Albert the Great) (c. 1200–1280), who was among the first scholars to realize the need to ground Christian faith in philosophy and science. If this were not done, the church would lose influence in the face of great advances in secular and pagan knowledge. Rather than ignore the huge quantity of learning made available by the Crusades, Albert chose to master it. He read most of the Christian, Muslim, and Jewish writers and wrote continuously about what he read. Albert was called the "Universal Teacher" because of the breadth of his knowledge and because he tried to make Aristotle accessible by paraphrasing many of his works.

Although Albert has been criticized for not being creative and consistent, his efforts at synthesis laid a foundation for Thomas Aquinas. Albert quoted extensively and without alteration, and from this Thomas learned the value of broad knowledge and extensive documentation.

If there were not a Devil, we would have to invent him.

OSCAR WILDE

©St. Thomas Aquinas (charcoal on paper), Annigoni, Pietro (1918-83)/Church of San Marco, Florence, Italy/Bridgeman Art Library

Pietro Annigoni's drawing depicts Thomas Aquinas as both scholar and man of God.

*A philosopher is a blind
man in a dark room looking
for a black cat that isn't
there. A theologian is the
man who finds it.*

H. L. MENCKEN

In his own work, however, Thomas went beyond his teacher by using his sources to construct a coherent philosophy of his own. Still, his scholarly skills owe a great deal to Albert, who recognized his ability while Thomas was still a young man, as a famous anecdote reveals: When Thomas first arrived in Paris, his rural manners, his heavyset, farm-boy physique, and slow, quiet ways earned him the nickname "the Dumb Ox," and his handwriting was so bad that others could barely read it. Yet he studied hard and remained good-natured as the other students laughed at him— until the day he answered one of Albert the Great's questions with such stunning brilliance that the master said to the others: "We call this man the Dumb Ox, but someday his bellow will be heard throughout the whole world."

The Task of the Scholar

*My father taught me that
the question "Who made
me?" cannot be answered,
since it immediately suggests
the further question "Who
made God?"*

JOHN STUART MILL

Shortly before Thomas was born, the church had forbidden the teaching of Aristotle's natural science and *Metaphysics*. His Unmoved Mover was an impersonal, natural force—not a loving, personal God. *Entelechy* (soul) was part of nature, inseparable from the body that housed it, and so it seemed that Aristotle's naturalism denied the possibility of personal immortality. (See Chapter 6.)

Yet the thorough, systematic quality of Aristotle's work on scientific thinking, logic, and nature gradually won more and more medieval converts. As Aristotle's influence spread throughout the University of Paris, questions arose regarding both the relationship of Aristotle's classical naturalism to orthodox Christianity and the accuracy of newly arrived Arabian commentaries on Aristotle. The faculty realized that Aristotle would have to be integrated into Christian theology. This task became the great, courageous accomplishment of Tommaso d'Aquino, "the Dumb Ox of Sicily."

In 1252 Thomas received his master's degree from the University of Paris, where he was also lecturing. He taught theology at the papal court in Rome in 1259, and from 1268 to 1272 lectured in Paris once more. During the twenty years that he was an active teacher, Thomas wrote disputations on various theological questions, commentaries on books of the Bible, commentaries on twelve works of Aristotle and others, and nearly forty other miscellaneous notes, sermons, lectures, poems, and treatises. His crowning achievements are the multivolume summaries of arguments and theology known as the *Summa Theologica* and *Summa contra Gentiles*.

Thomas was sent to Naples to establish a Dominican school in 1272, and in 1274 he was commanded by Pope Gregory X to attend the Council of Lyons. He died on the trip to Lyons on March 7, 1274. As reported by Brother Peter of Montesangiovanni, his last hours reflected his submission to the authority of the church.

■ THE WISDOM OF THE SCHOLAR ■

Scholasticism
Christian philosophy
dominating medieval
Europe from about 1000 to
1300 that stressed logical
and linguistic analysis
of texts and arguments
in order to produce a
systematic statement
and defense of Christian
beliefs.

The term **Scholasticism** refers to mainstream Christian philosophy in medieval Europe from about 1000 to about 1300, just after the death of Aquinas. It comes from the Greek *scholastikos,* meaning "to enjoy leisure" or "to devote one's free time to learning."

Scholastic philosophy rested on a strong interest in logical and linguistic analysis of texts and on arguments producing a systematic statement and defense of Christian beliefs. As the revealed word of God, the Bible was central to this project, but always was interpreted in accord with the authority of the church and the wisdom of selected earlier Christian writers.

A central effort of Scholastic philosophers was the attempt to reconstruct Greek philosophy in a form that not only was consistent with but also supported and strengthened Christian doctrine. An important aspect of this effort was the imposition of a hierarchy of knowledge, in which the highest place was held by revelation, as interpreted by the church; next were faith and theology; philosophy came last, subordinated to both faith and revelation.[12]

Medieval scholars were the first *professors of philosophy;* their task was to teach, to expound on texts, to write about them, to debate in class and in public, and to publish great educational summations of official doctrine.[13] Generally viewed as the most complete realization of medieval Scholasticism, Thomas Aquinas is the archetype of the scholar. Unlike modern professional philosophers, Thomas was not free to *pursue* the truth wherever it led; he *started from the truth*—always ultimately supporting Christian doctrine.

In Scholastic philosophy, the *way* a case was made and analyzed became an integral part of what was being claimed, and method remains an important concern to today's scholars. Logic and linguistic analysis were vital elements in proving a case—as they are today. Scholarly, intellectual standards were developed for documenting an argument with citations from approved sources—standards that any student who has ever written a research paper will recognize. In fact, in the first twelve questions of the *Summa Theologica,* Thomas refers to other authors 160 times.

Scholastic philosophers had to present their arguments publicly and defend them against all comers—a precursor to the modern professor's obligation to publish, present, and defend papers. Subject matter became specialized, and a universal impersonal, technical, scholarly style of writing was developed to communicate with a select audience of students and teachers devoted to mastering an elaborate professional technique.[14]

The emergence of the Scholastic *professor of philosophy* reflects a move away from the importance of a particular philosopher, away from the *sophos* whose work closely reflected his life, to a less personal view of the individual thinker as a part of a scholarly community. Thus, although Thomas's work reflected his life, the product of his work is scholarly and technical in ways unlike anything produced before. He says:

> That which a single man can bring, through his work and his genius, to the promotion of truth is little in comparison with the total of knowledge. However, from all these elements, *selected and coordinated and brought together,* there arises a marvelous thing, as is shown by the various departments of learning, which by the work and sagacity of many have come to a wonderful augmentation.[15] [emphasis added]

> *Science has not killed God—quite the contrary. It is clearer now than ever that what we can learn from science is limited to what is abstract and quantifiable. Because of what science has achieved, the unresolved (and undoubtedly unresolvable) dilemmas of what Unamuno called the "man of flesh and bone; the man who is born, suffers, and dies—above all, who dies"—are more poignant, the mysteries deeper. God is needed now more than ever.*
>
> RENÉ J. MULLER

> *Take from your scientific work a serious and incorruptible method of thought, help to spread it, because no understanding is possible without it. Revere those things which go beyond science, which really matter, and about which it is so difficult to speak.*
>
> WERNER HEISENBERG

▪ WHY DO PEOPLE ARGUE ABOUT ▪ SPIRITUAL MATTERS?

Absent some sort of objective proof or rational argumentation, all we have to offer those who disagree with us about spiritual and religious matters are appeals to bald assertions of our sincerity, insistent claims that we are

The creationist, whether naive Bible-thumper or an educated bishop, simply postulates an already existing being of prodigious complexity. If we are going to allow ourselves the luxury of postulating organized complexity without offering an explanation, we might as well make a job of it and simply postulate the existence of life as we know it!

RICHARD DAWKINS

"saved" or happier than they are, and other "bits of autobiography." Although we may believe that we are discussing the content of our beliefs, we are actually reporting information about ourselves (hence, "autobiography"). As a result, those who already believe what we do continue to believe what we do. And while those who do not believe what we do may have learned something about *us,* we have provided them with no evidence demonstrating the actual merits of the beliefs themselves.

But, clearly, our great and persistent disagreements over matters of faith are not meant to be reduced to assertions of personal feelings (subjective states) but, rather, are intended to be about claimed realities, about *what is true,* about whether or not God actually exists—objectively, really. Otherwise, there is nothing to dispute.

Consider the hypothetical case of Ross, who believes that only God X exists; Dean, who believes that only God Y exists; and Joe, who believes that no god whatsoever exists. If Ross, Dean, and Joe were simply reporting subjective states, they would not need argumentation, because they would each be right. "Right" would be equivalent to "reporting present beliefs accurately." But Ross, Dean, and Joe think that they are doing more than reporting products of thinking. And, hence, as reasoning creatures, as rational agents, they are compelled to apply "laws of reason" to their beliefs. If the phrase "laws of reason" seems too authoritarian or dated to you, try the more expansive and less imposing term "standards of evidence." The main point here is to note that, for the most part, we agree with Ross, Dean, and Joe: Our religious questions are about what is real, what exists, what is true. They are not just about what people feel or think is true.

In Thomas's time, as in our own, there were conflicting claims about what constituted proper standards of evidence for evaluating matters of theology, church authority, and religious faith in general. One view held that all truth claims must be tested against *revealed* truths. From this perspective, *revelation* was the chief and only reliable source of knowledge of God and God's ways. At the opposite extreme were those philosophers and scientists who argued that truth could only be *discovered through concrete experience and deductive reasoning.*

God and Natural Reason

It is clear from what has been said that there is a substance which is eternal and unmovable and separate from sensible things.

ARISTOTLE

Thomas approached this problem from an Aristotelian, "naturalistic" position. This is sometimes referred to as *natural theology* because it appeals to what Thomas calls *natural reason* or *natural intelligence.* By "natural" here, Thomas means "of this world"—not sloppy or undisciplined. Natural reason is, thus, reason unaided by divine revelation, and natural theology is theology based on appeals to natural reason. Although Thomas had great respect for, and submitted to, church authority, his efforts to prove God's existence begin with appeals to concrete experience and empirical evidence, rather than with revelations or dogma—an argument style favored by Aristotle. (You may wish to review the material concerning Aristotle's ideas regarding form, matter, change, and cause in Chapter 6.)

As we review selected passages from Thomas, keep in mind that no introductory survey can do justice to the complexity of Thomas's thought. So although what follows is a plausible interpretation of some of the most studied and disputed arguments in the history of philosophy, it cannot serve as a definitive account.

Thomas's Five Ways are so influential and persuasive that I am sure you've already thought about some of them, at least in simplified form. You may even think of them as your own since popularized versions of them have become staples of Christian "apologetics," the offering of reasons to justify the divine origin of faith. To get the most out of your efforts, I recommend approaching the Five Ways as a whole, focusing on what Thomas is arguing and why it matters, before accepting or rejecting the individual arguments. That being accomplished, you'll be in a good position to assess not only this particular version of Thomas's arguments, but also more general issues of faith and evidence.

■ PROVING THE EXISTENCE OF GOD ■

Although Thomas believed in God, he also thought God's existence could be demonstrated by natural reason. To this end, he offered his famous five proofs for the existence of God. Each proof follows a basic pattern, beginning with some natural effect with which we are all familiar, such as movement or growth. Thomas then tries to show that the only possible explanation for this effect is God. *The Five Ways are cause–effect arguments, beginning with our experience of effects and moving toward their cause, God.*

The Five Ways are most effective if viewed as parts of a single argument. The first three ways deal with avoiding an infinite chain of causes in nature. Their conclusion is that an Unmoved Mover/Uncaused Cause must exist—that is, a being whose existence depends only on its own essence and not on anything external to itself. But Aristotle said much the same thing without concluding that a personal god exists; such an impersonal cause could just as easily be basic matter and energy. The fourth and fifth ways are thus crucial. They are needed to introduce some hierarchical quality into the overall description of causes and effects that can transform them into a personal god.

Theology is an effort to explain the unknowable in terms of the not worth knowing. . . . [It] is not only opposed to the scientific spirit; it is opposed to every other form of rational thinking.

H. L. MENCKEN

The First Way: Motion

The Five Ways begin with the argument Thomas thought was the easiest to understand, the **argument from motion**. Starting with the indisputable observation that things are moving, the argument points out that motion must be given to each object by some other object that is already moving. (By "motion," Thomas means both linear motion and more complex "life-motion," animating motion.) For instance, a rack of balls at rest on a billiard table is set in motion only after being struck by the *already moving* cue ball. In turn, the cue ball is set in motion after being struck by the tip of the *already moving* cue stick. But the cue stick cannot move unless something *already moving* moves it: a gust of wind, an earthquake, a cat, or the billiards champion Minnesota Fats. Similarly, I am given life (ani-motion) by my *already moving* (alive) parents, who had to be given life by their already moving parents, who . . .

It *might* be possible to keep imagining an infinite chain of things already in motion moving other things. But no such infinite regress can account for the fact

argument from motion
Attempt to prove the existence of God based on the reasoning that to avoid an infinite regress, there must be an Unmoved Mover capable of imparting motion to all other things; Aristotelian argument that forms the basis for the first of Thomas Aquinas's Five Ways.

that things are *actually in motion*. Given that things are moving, we know that some *first already moving thing* had to move other not-yet-moving things. Thomas reasoned that some "first mover" had to exist outside the series of *becoming*—some force or being with the ability to move other things without itself needing to be moved by any outside force. God is just such an Unmoved Mover. Here is Thomas's argument:

> Therefore, whatever is moved must be moved by another. If that by which it is moved be itself moved, then this also must needs be moved by another, and that by another again. But this cannot go on to infinity, because then there would be no first mover, and, consequently, no other mover, seeing that subsequent movers move only inasmuch as they are moved by the first mover; as the staff moves only because it is moved by the hand. Therefore it is necessary to arrive at a first mover, moved by no other; and this everyone understands to be God.[16]

PHILOSOPHICAL

QUERY

• • • • • •

Is there any other explanation for motion besides an "unmoved mover"? If so, what is it? If not, is Thomas's conclusion sound? Convincing?

The Second Way: Cause

The explanation just given for the movement of billiard balls and children is incomplete. We can still ask what accounts for the very existence of billiard balls, cue sticks, Minnesota Fats, and parents. Thomas answered with a second argument, similar in pattern to his first, but based on the Aristotelian concept of cause. Because the second argument concerns the initiating cause of the existence of the universe, it is called the **cosmological argument**, from the Greek word *kosmos,* meaning "world," "universe," or "orderly structure."

In a nutshell, the cosmological argument asserts that it is impossible for any natural thing to be the complete and sufficient source of its own existence. In order to cause itself, a thing would have to precede itself. Put another way, in order for me to be the source of my own existence, I would have to exist before I existed. This is as absurd as it is impossible.

In broad strokes, my existence is explained by my parents' existence, and theirs by my grandparents' existence, and so on. But if *every* set of parents had to have parents, there could never be any parents at all. At least one set of parents must not have had parents. In the Bible, this is Adam and Eve. But even Adam and Eve did not cause their own existence. They were created by God, who creates but is uncreated. This is why it is said that "God always was, is, and will be."

In Thomas's understanding of things, any series or system of causes and effects requires an originating cause. In order to avoid an infinite regress of causes, which he thought was impossible, there had to be an Uncaused Cause.

cosmological argument

From the Greek word *kosmos,* meaning "world," "universe," or "orderly structure"; argument for the existence of God that because it is impossible for any natural thing to be the complete and sufficient source of its own existence, there must be an Uncaused Cause capable of imparting existence to all other things; Aristotelian argument that forms the basis for the second of Aquinas's Five Ways.

The cosmological argument is based on Aristotle's concept of *efficient cause*. (See Chapter 6.) Efficient cause is the force that initiates change or brings about some activity. The efficient cause in the development of a human fetus, for example, is the entire biochemical process of changes in the mother's womb that nurtures the growing fetus. In the case of an acorn, the efficient cause that produces an oak tree consists of rain, sun, soil, and temperature interacting to initiate growth and development. Thomas argues:

> In the world of sensible things we find there is an order of efficient causes. . . . Now in efficient causes it is not possible to go on to infinity, because in all efficient causes following in order, the first is the cause of the intermediate cause, and the intermediate is the cause of the ultimate cause, whether the intermediate cause be several, or one only. Now to take away the cause is to take away the effect. Therefore, if there be no first cause among efficient causes, there will be no ultimate, nor any intermediate, cause. . . . Therefore it is necessary to admit a first efficient cause, to which everyone gives the name God.[17]

• • • • • •

Discuss the cosmological argument. Is Thomas's reasoning sound or not? Are you comfortable with the possibility that there is no "first cause"? If there isn't, can we explain the existence of the universe at all? Discuss.

PHILOSOPHICAL

QUERY

The Third Way: Necessity

Thomas's third proof, the **argument from necessity**, may seem odd to you. It is based on the difference between two classes of things: those whose existence is only contingent or *possible* and those whose existence is *necessary*. Contingent things might or might not exist, but they do not have to exist, and they all eventually cease to exist. You and I do not exist of necessity: We just happen to exist given the particular history of the world. Our existence is contingent, dependent on something else. This is true, in fact, of every created thing in the universe. It is even possible and imaginable that the universe itself never existed or that someday it will cease to exist. In other words, the universe is also contingent.

But, Thomas pointed out, it is not possible to conceive of a time in which nothing whatsoever existed. There would be no space; time itself would not exist. There would be no place for something to come into existence from or move to. There would be nowhere for anything to move, if there were anything to move, which there would not be. Without movement, there would be no passage of time. If no time passes, nothing happens. *Thus, if nothing had ever existed, nothing would always exist.* But all around us we see things in existence. Therefore, there was never no-thing. Getting rid of the double negatives, this becomes: There was always something—or there is something that always existed and always will. (See Democritus, Chapter 3.)

argument from necessity
Argument for the existence of God based on the idea that if nothing had ever existed, nothing would always exist; therefore, there is something whose existence is necessary (an eternal something); Aristotelian argument that forms the basis for the third of Aquinas's Five Ways.

The logic of Thomas's Third Way relies on the principle of sufficient reason and the principle of plenitude. According to the **principle of sufficient reason**, nothing happens without a reason. Consequently, no *adequate* theory or explanation can contain any brute, crude, unexplained facts. The **principle of plenitude** is the metaphysical principle that given infinity and the richness of the universe, any real possibility must occur—at least once. Based on these two principles, Thomas concluded that there must be something whose existence is necessary and not just possible. There needs to be some reason that what is possible actually happens. In short, God's existence is necessary. As Thomas puts it,

> We find in nature things that are possible to be and not to be, since they are found to be generated, and to be corrupted, and consequently, it is possible for them to be and not to be. But it is impossible for them always to exist, for that which can not-be at some time is not. Therefore, if everything can not-be, then at one time there was nothing in existence. Now if this were true, even now there would be nothing in existence, because that which does not exist begins to exist only through something already existing. . . . Therefore, we cannot but admit the existence of some being having of itself its own necessity, and not receiving it from another, but rather causing in others their necessity. This all men speak of as God.[18]

principle of sufficient reason

The principle that nothing happens without a reason; consequently, no adequate theory or explanation can contain any brute, crude, unexplained facts. First specifically encountered in the work of the medieval philosopher Peter Abelard (1079–1142), it is usually associated with the rationalist philosopher Gottfried Wilhelm Leibniz (1646–1716), who used it in his famous "best of all possible worlds" argument.

PHILOSOPHICAL QUERY

principle of plenitude

The name given by American historian of ideas Arthur O. Lovejoy (1873–1962) to the metaphysical principle that, given infinity, any real possibility must occur (at least once).

argument from gradation

Argument for the existence of God based on the idea that being progresses from inanimate objects to increasingly complex animated creatures, culminating in a qualitatively unique God; Aristotelian argument that forms the basis for the fourth of Aquinas's Five Ways.

• • • • • •

Scholastic arguments often hinged on whether or not something was conceivable (clearly imaginable). One cardinal principle held that no one could even conceive of absolute nothingness. Do you agree? Explain. Whether or not you agree, do you find the argument from necessity convincing? Discuss.

The Fourth Way: Degree

The first three arguments for the existence of God fail to establish the existence of a good and loving being. They only deny the possibility of an infinite series of causes and effects, an infinity of *becomings*. Even if some element or entity functions as an ever-existing Prime Mover or Uncaused Cause, these characteristics alone do not describe God. In the fourth and fifth arguments, Thomas makes a qualitative shift in his proofs.

The Fourth Way rests on the idea of qualitative differences among kinds of beings. Known as the **argument from gradation**, it is based on a metaphysical concept of a hierarchy of souls. (See Chapter 6.) In ascending order, being progresses from inanimate objects to increasingly complex animated creatures. (For instance, a dog has more being than a worm, and a person more than a dog.) Thomas believed that what contemporary philosopher Arthur O. Lovejoy called "the great chain of being" continued upward through angels to God.

This chain of being, Thomas thought, is reflected in the properties of individual things, as well as in the kinds of things that exist. For example, there are grades of goodness, going from the complete lack of goodness (evil) to pure goodness (God), from the complete lack of honesty to complete honesty, from utter ugliness to sublime beauty, and so forth. In very general terms, existence flows downward from perfection and completeness to varying lower stages, each descending level possessing less being.

Of the Five Ways, the significance of this argument can be especially difficult for contemporary thinkers to grasp because it rests on a metaphysical world-view that is alien to many of us today. Yet we cannot just dismiss it as a quirk of the medieval mind-set. The Five Ways form a cumulative argument. The first three arguments cannot establish the existence of a *qualitatively different kind of being*. The fifth argument, as we shall see, only establishes that the universe is ordered. Without the argument from gradation, Thomas can make a case only for an eternal something that follows orderly patterns. But this "something" is almost a contemporary scientist's description of the universe; it is certainly not a description of God. Without the introduction of qualitatively different kinds of entities, Thomas cannot establish the existence of God by rational argument. Here is Thomas's argument from gradation:

> Among beings there are some more and some less good, true, noble, and the like. But *more* and *less* are predicated of different things according as they resemble in their different ways something which is the maximum, as a thing is said to be hotter according as it more nearly resembles that which is hottest; so that there is something which is truest, something best, something noblest, and, consequently, something which is most being, for those things that are greatest in truth are greatest in being. . . . Therefore there must also be something which is to all beings the cause of their being, goodness, and every other perfection; and this we call God.[19]

Creation produces myriad forms. Whatever one's form, one should cherish and take care of it and use it to live well.

LIE ZI

© Douglas J. Soccio

According to the principle of gradation, the little girl and her grandfather in this photo have more "being" than the dogs, which have more than the trees. Does such a view reflect reality or does it foster a kind of arrogance in which we see ourselves as superior to—rather than a part of—the natural world? Does the way the dogs and humans are engaged with one another tell us anything significant about the principle of gradation?

• • • • • •

Do you have any sense of grades of being? Is there anything in your own experience that supports Thomas's argument? Discuss the argument from gradation.

The Fifth Way: Design

teleological argument

Also called the argument from design, this widely known argument for the existence of God claims that the universe manifests order and purpose that can only be the result of a conscious intelligence (God); Aristotelian argument that forms the basis for the fifth of Aquinas's Five Ways and the basis of William Paley's watchmaker argument.

Thomas's **teleological argument**, also called the argument from design, is one of the most widely known and used arguments for the existence of God. Teleological thinking, as we learned in Chapter 6, is a way of understanding things in terms of their *telos,* or end. For example, infancy is understood in relationship to adulthood: The adult is the *telos* of the infant; the oak tree is the *telos* of the acorn. When archaeologists uncover some ancient artifact unlike anything ever seen before, they often recognize that it was made for a purpose, a *telos,* even if they do not know what specific purpose. In other words, they infer the existence of a designer who shaped the mysterious object.

Thomas asserts that the entire natural world exhibits order and design. Water behaves in orderly ways, as do rocks, crabs, clouds, reindeer, and people. Today, we are even more aware of the complex interrelatedness of the natural world than Thomas was: Rain forests in the Amazon basin scrub the atmosphere in ways that affect the whole earth; this is their *telos.* Cells and chromosomes, molecules, atoms, and subatomic particles exhibit order, with each performing a specific function, a *telos.* On inspection, the universe reveals order; otherwise, we could not quantify scientific laws.

Order, Thomas argued, implies intelligence, purpose, a plan. Here again he follows the pattern of starting with common observations and searching for principles to explain them. In this case, Thomas held that the order we observe in inanimate nature cannot come from matter itself, since matter lacks consciousness and intelligence. Design, by its nature, implies conscious intent. Thus, if the world exhibits evidence of design, it follows logically that there must be a Designer:

> We see that things which lack knowledge, such as natural bodies [matter and inanimate objects], act for an end, and this is evident from their acting always, or nearly always, in the same way, so as to obtain the best result. Hence it is plain that they achieve their end, not fortuitously, but designedly. Now whatever lacks knowledge cannot move towards an end, unless it is directed by some being endowed with knowledge and intelligence; as the arrow is directed by the archer. Therefore some intelligent being exists by whom all natural things are directed to their end; and this being we call God.[20]

• • • • • •

Is order the same thing as design? Does the universe seem to be ordered and "intelligently" designed? Discuss. (For more on this intriguing topic, see Chapter 10.)

create us so that we do not suffer or do wrong? These are always unanswerable questions, for they amount to asking why did God create *this* universe?

As a Christian philosopher, Thomas pursued his natural theology as far as he could, but he refused to speculate on God's ultimate motives. In the end, he accepted the limits of the human mind when it confronts the infinite. There's even a tradition that Thomas turned toward mysticism late in his life. He is supposed to have said that everything he had written was "as straw"—but he wouldn't say what he "saw" that taught him that.

Thomas's philosophy is alive today as a vital component of Roman Catholicism, but the impact of his great efforts extends beyond the church. He is the first philosopher to have actually produced a comprehensive, logically ordered synoptic (holistic) science, when science is understood as *organized knowledge*. That is, he fulfilled the promise of Aristotle and actually produced a cohesive *system* that included all the known sciences of his time.

Of course, the fragmentation and specialization of knowledge today make such an achievement virtually impossible. That does not reduce the desirability, and perhaps the need, for a cohesive, consistent, all-encompassing philosophy, even if it must be less grand. From Thomas we can learn more than the Scholastic method. In his great effort we see that faith need not be a substitute for philosophical rigor. We see that in spite of the confusions and problems in his arguments, it is still preferable to balance faith with reason rather than to believe, not in humility, but in ignorance.

The logical and theoretical questions Thomas faced still confront basic Christian doctrine. Questions about ultimate causes remain beyond the scope of science, but they do not disappear just because scientists cannot answer them. In Thomas Aquinas we encounter a rare, magnificent attempt to blend faith, reason, and experience into wisdom. If so comprehensive a system is no longer possible, it does not follow that no comprehensive vision is possible. The very effort to construct a consistent, coherent philosophy may be worth more than any risk to our faith in science or religion.

Thomas squarely faced the tension between reason and faith and, without abandoning either, gave faith his ultimate allegiance. The next major figure in the history of philosophy, René Descartes, faced the same tension, but gave himself to reason. In so doing, he ushered in the modern era.

> *Do not be concerned about what speaker you are listening to; instead, when something good is said, commit it to memory. Be sure that you understand whatever you read. Make sure you know the difficulties and store up whatever you can in the treasure-house of the mind; keep as busy as a person who seeks to fill a vessel.*
> THOMAS AQUINAS

> *Religions are the great fairy-tales of the conscience.*
> GEORGE SANTAYANA

> *My life is still governed by a faith I no longer have.*
> ERNEST RENAN

■ SUMMARY OF MAIN POINTS ■

● Augustine's efforts to synthesize early Christian theology with his own understanding of Greek philosophy and Manichean dualism anticipate major philosophical and theological ideas concerning doubt and certainty, the divided self, consciousness, time, free will and God's foreknowledge of history, and the philosophy of history.

● Augustine rejected Epicureanism and Stoicism for placing too much value on human reason and will. According to Augustine, reason is powerless and perverse without a will grounded in grace, love, and proper longing. For Augustine, faith alone makes understanding possible; faith is a necessary condition for productive philosophical inquiry.

- Scholastic philosophy was a product of a hierarchical society based on a God-centered view of the universe. Scholastic philosophy developed out of efforts to reconcile Aristotle's naturalism with the increasingly complex theological problems that developed when it became clear the Second Coming of Christ might not occur for generations.

- Scholastic philosophy rested on logical and linguistic analysis of texts and arguments for the ultimate purpose of producing a systematic statement and defense of Christian beliefs. The reconciliation of faith and reason was based, in part, on the law of contradiction: No statement can be both true and false at the same time and under the same conditions.

- Thomas Aquinas introduced new levels of thoroughness, scholarship, and methodical rigor to philosophy in the form of his massive summaries known as *summae*. Thomas's efforts to prove the existence of God using the Five Ways are among the most widely studied examples of Scholastic thinking. The Five Ways are the argument from motion; the cosmological argument; the argument from necessity; the argument from gradation; and the argument from design.

- Thomas's logic relies on two principles: The principle of sufficient reason is the idea that nothing happens without a reason, that no *adequate* theory or explanation can contain any brute, crude, unexplained facts. The principle of plenitude is the metaphysical principle that given infinity and the richness of the universe, any real possibility must occur—at least once.

- The problem of evil derives from the apparently inescapable conclusion either that God cannot prevent evil, and is therefore not all-powerful, or that God will not prevent evil, and is therefore not all-good. Thomas answers the problem of evil from two directions: First, he argues that evil is not a positive thing, but a lack of goodness. Hence, it cannot come from God. Second, Thomas returns to the importance of love, asserting that God created the universe in order to multiply His love. Because love cannot be forced, it always requires freedom of choice. Genuine freedom of choice includes the real possibility of evil. God does not will evil; He wills freedom and love.

▣ POST-READING REFLECTIONS ▣

Now that you have had a chance to learn about the Scholar, use your new knowledge to answer these questions.

1. Compare and contrast the classical worldview with the medieval.

2. What basic conditions led to the development of Christian philosophy? Where did the need for interpretation come from?

3. In your own words, describe the chief characteristics of Scholastic scholarship.

4. In what ways is the medieval scholar the forerunner of the modern professor?

5. Which of the Five Ways do you think is the weakest? Explain why.

6. Which of the Five Ways do you think is the most convincing? Explain why.

7. In general terms, compare and contrast scientific attempts to explain the origin of the universe with theological or philosophical ones.

8. What is evil, according to Thomas?

9. According to Thomas, what is the relationship of free will to love?

PHILOSOPHY INTERNET RESOURCES

Go to the Soccio Web page at **http://philosophy.wadsworth.com/ Soccio7e** for Web links, practice quizzes and tests, a pronunciation guide, and study tips.

Overview of Modern Themes

Good sense is of all things in the world the most equally distributed . . .
is by nature equal in all men.

RENÉ DESCARTES

'Tis not contrary to reason to prefer the destruction of the whole world to the
scratching of my finger.

DAVID HUME

Sapere aude!—Dare to reason! Have the courage to use your own minds!—is
the motto of the enlightenment. . . . If I have a book which understands for
me, a pastor who has a conscience for me, a doctor who decides my diet, I
need not trouble myself. If I am willing to pay, I need not think. Others will
do it for me.

IMMANUEL KANT

It is generally agreed that the modern era, also known as the *Enlightenment* or the Age of Reason, began in the first half of the seventeenth century with the publication of two seminal texts: Sir Francis Bacon's *Novum Organon* (1620) and René Descartes's *Discourse on Method* (1637). This does not mean that Bacon and Descartes—by themselves—created a new philosophical era. Their ideas were, of course, reactions and responses to the ideas of both earlier and contemporary writers and thinkers.

In the realm of philosophy, Descartes challenged and ultimately rejected the cumbersome and complex disputations and speculations of Scholastic philosophy in favor of his own simpler, more "natural" appeals to "common reason"—written in ordinary French rather than in scholarly and obscure Latin. Along with Descartes (Chapter 9), our look at the origins of modern philosophy includes David Hume (Chapter 10) and Immanuel Kant (Chapter 11).

▪ REASON, REFORMATION, ▪ AND REVOLUTION

Together, what we now refer to as the *Reformation* and the *Copernican Revolution* signaled a major shift away from the medieval worldview, with its organic emphasis on a God-centered, earth-centered universe in which everything had an allotted place in a fixed hierarchy. The modern worldview, in stark contrast, moved the earth from the center of the universe and put the reasoning *individual* at the forefront of philosophy. Objective and methodical reason replaced faith as the path to truth.

In the medieval worldview, everything was understood in terms of its place in the whole scheme of things. God ruled the universe, the pope ruled the church, the king ruled the state, and so on down through lords, merchants, craftsmen, and serfs. In such a worldview, social order was transformed into a divine purpose that was reflected in a hierarchy of authority that permeated the entire universe. Throughout the Middle Ages, most Europeans accepted that this hierarchy came from God—and therefore accepted the authority of God's church and pope as legitimate.

The Reformation

By the fourteenth century, the authority of the Roman Catholic Church and of the pope had eroded. The credibility of the papacy was severely damaged by a series of disputes and scandals as popes began to keep church offerings for their own use and to sell offices and ecclesiastical titles. These abuses led to cries for reform.

What is known today as the Protestant Reformation began in Germany on October 31, 1517, when **Martin Luther** (1483–1546), a Roman Catholic Augustinian monk and professor at the University of Wittenberg, nailed ninety-five theses (criticisms of church teachings and practices) to the church door. The papacy viewed this as a gesture of rebellion rather than a call for debate and labeled Luther a heretic. Luther persisted, and in 1520 he published three significant treatises: *An Open Letter to the Christian Nobility of the German Nation Concerning the Reform*

This illustration from Martin Luther's Bible shows God as the orderer of the Ptolemaic universe. So convinced was Luther of the accuracy of this picture of the heavens, that he called Copernicus "that fool [who would] reverse the entire art of astronomy. . . . Joshua bade the sun and not the earth to stand still."

of the Christian Estate, The Babylonian Captivity of the Church, and *A Treatise on Christian Liberty.*

On April 18, 1521, Luther stood before the Holy Roman Emperor Charles V and an assembly of German nobility at the Diet at Worms. Luther refused to recant unless he could be proven wrong by the Bible *or by clear reason.* Luther's bold words of refusal to bow to institutional or civic authority in matters of truth still ring: "Here I stand; I can do no other." Although Luther and his ideas generated popular support, he was formally excommunicated in 1521.

Church authorities realized Luther's ideas and actions constituted a public challenge to the entire medieval and Scholastic worldview. By asserting that the individual's channel to God was "justification by faith" rather than by "works" (that is, living a good life in accord with the teachings of the church), Luther made the individual believer his or her own authority.

In addition to rejecting "works," Luther rejected the sacraments and confession—two important Catholic practices that made the institutionalized church an essential part of salvation. Moreover, if, as Luther claimed, the institution and *authority* of a church are unnecessary, then "every believer is a priest." Despite having been labeled a heretic, Luther had enough political support in Germany that the church was reluctant to use force against him. He went on to establish his own church—which, ironically, very quickly institutionalized its own rigid requirements and began ejecting heretics.

The philosophical significance of Luther's move lay in its implication that individual experience and interpretation are more truly Christian than unquestioning acceptance of an official, authoritative position. Luther's revolt against institutionalized authority is one of the major markers of the decline of the medieval worldview.

As doubts grew about the legitimacy or necessity of an authoritarian, institutionalized church hierarchy, reliance on individual reasoning and experience increased. And since the reach of the medieval church extended into the teachings and practices of science, challenges to authoritarian and archaic science paralleled challenges to theology.

The Copernican Revolution

In the Middle Ages, it was commonly believed that the universe was carefully created by a God of harmony and design and that human beings were the very purpose of creation. The heavens themselves, so it was believed, reflected this: God made the sun and moon to shine upon *us* and placed the earth so that the rest of the universe revolved around *us*. As part of this divine harmony, the natural (physical) world was also thought to reflect spiritual order.

This *geocentric* worldview, with the earth at the center of the universe, can be both comforting and reassuring: If the universe physically manifests a sense of divine order and purpose, then each of us is assured that we "belong" where we are, socially and geographically. The universe is our neighborhood and earth is "home"—the universe is not a cosmic accident of such immensity that it lacks a fixed center and reduces the entire earth to less than a speck.

But as it became clearer and more widely known that the earth is a sphere, with no fixed up or down, the old worldview began to totter. Once Luther's contemporary Nicolaus Copernicus mapped the heavens, it toppled.

Some ancient Greek astronomers—in particular, the philosopher Aristarchus of Samos (third century B.C.E.)—had concluded that the earth revolves around the sun. Most of Aristarchus's writings were lost, however, and later astronomers rejected his ideas, partly because they seemed contrary to common experience and partly because they conflicted with Aristotle's teachings. Aristotle believed the earth was the unmoving center of the universe and that the sun, moon, and planets moved in semiregular "epicycles" around it. Ptolemy, an astronomer of the second century C.E., gave Aristotle's ideas even more weight by designing a mathematical model that seemed to predict planetary motions quite well.

By the fifteenth century, however, calculations using the Ptolemaic model no longer matched the observed positions of the planets. This inspired **Nicolaus Copernicus** (1473–1543) to look for a more accurate model. His proposal that the sun is the center of the solar system set in motion a revolution in thinking. He made his case in such a way that knowledgeable astronomers realized the entire Ptolemaic model had to be revised.

Copernican astronomy directly refuted Aristotle, who believed that the earth was the center of the universe. Because Thomas Aquinas and the church were so closely tied to Aristotelian philosophy and science, any major threat to Aristotle threatened church authority. If the church—guided by God—was in error here, where else might it be in error? Copernicus was sensitive enough to the church's attitude toward criticism and unofficial doctrines that he withheld publication of his discoveries until shortly before he died.

Once Copernicus's work was known, the earth was "cut loose" from its central place of honor, both physically and psychologically, and became just one more planet revolving around the sun. If the earth was reduced in significance, what about us? This major change in perspective did not *feel right* to either Catholic or Protestant theologians. Thus, Martin Luther called Copernicus "that fool [who would] reverse the entire art of astronomy. . . . Joshua bade *the sun* and not the earth to stand still."[1]

Luther's opinion notwithstanding, Copernicus was no fool. Although the details of his model were inaccurate (for instance, he thought the earth's path around the sun was a circle, but it really is an ellipse), his hypothesis that the earth is part of a sun-centered system was correct. Copernicus developed this hypothesis by applying careful calculations to careful observations. The danger in his position can be clearly observed if we speak bluntly: Copernicus rendered both church authority and the consensus of unqualified nonastronomers irrelevant. His careful application of reason and observation began revolutions in both astronomy and philosophical thought.

Where Are We, Then?

The struggle for authority, for the right to determine truth, between the church and science, that began in the early Enlightenment continued until God was reduced to the role of spectator. Faith in God was replaced by faith in the orderly discovery of laws of nature and in the power of human reason to ensure continuous progress and improvement of the human condition.

It was taken for granted that the scientific method could and would unlock all the mysteries of the universe. Given the wealth of scientific discoveries in physics, optics, astronomy, biology, and so on, it was but a simple step to conclude that God (if there is a God) has created a universe of such regularity and order that He no longer need bother running it. Further, having imbued us with reason, God has no need to govern or rescue us.

For almost three centuries, many "enlightened" thinkers remained convinced that, with the exception of "idiots," people possessed an innate, virtually equal capacity for rational thinking that could be nurtured, developed, and tapped to produce progressively better lives for each generation. Out of this optimism emerged modern anti-authoritarian democratic principles, founded on unalienable "natural rights" and rational self-interest.

You might recognize this optimistic faith in science and rational self-interest as a fundamental element of American thinking. Indeed, the framers of our Constitution were children of the Enlightenment who believed that science and universal reason would combine to produce a rational, free, ever-progressing society.

A major task of the Enlightenment was to start anew—just like America, just like each new wave of immigrants—and to use reason to accomplish a kind of individual and cultural *rebirth,* uncluttered by past superstitions and unprovable beliefs, to create a "new world" based on objective, universal knowledge.

THE RATIONALIST

René Descartes

BUT WHAT THEN AM I?
A THING WHICH THINKS.

René Descartes

For Your Reflection

KEEP THESE QUESTIONS IN MIND AS YOU LEARN ABOUT
THE RATIONALIST.

1. *What is rationalism?*
2. *What is the coherence theory of truth?*
3. *What is the "methodic doubt"?*
4. *What are innate ideas?*
5. *What are* a priori *ideas?*
6. *What is* a posteriori *knowledge?*
7. *What is skepticism?*
8. *What is the* cogito?
9. *What is the "evil genius"?*
10. *What is materialism?*
11. *What is Cartesian dualism?*
12. *What is the ontological argument?*
13. *What is the mind–body problem?*

For Deeper Consideration

A. Descartes asserts that whatever we recognize "clearly and distinctly" is true. What does he mean? Assess the criticism that this formulation fails to meet its own standard. Is the criticism sound? Do you agree that Descartes's rationalism is based on subjective states rather than on reasons understood "clearly and distinctly"? In other words, is Descartes's standard of truth chiefly rational or psychological?

B. Descartes says that "it were far better never to think of investigating the truth at all, than to do so without a method." Why was he so troubled by disorganized thinking and blind curiosity? What do you think he might say to us about basing our opinions regarding global warming, creation versus evolution, and other controversial matters on what we "learn" from movies, TV, the Internet, politicians, and professors? What methods do you use to choose among competing "experts" and positions? Is Descartes suggesting that we should become experts in choosing experts? Or is he arguing for something else entirely, and if so, what and why?

By the seventeenth century, developments in modern science, combined with a decline in the authority of a single (Roman Catholic) church, signaled the end of the medieval era and the beginning of what we now refer to as the modern worldview. In philosophy, the result of these changes was a shift away from metaphysics toward epistemology.

As remarkable as it may seem, René Descartes was the first philosopher to study the *process of thinking* itself. In so doing, he began what philosophers refer to as the *epistemological turn*, a major transformation in the character of philosophy that would ultimately require a century and a half to complete, culminating with Immanuel Kant's *Critique of Pure Reason* (Chapter 11).

Whereas earlier philosophers sought knowledge about the good life, nature, the soul, God, the ideal society, and so forth, from Descartes forward, modern philosophers increasingly devoted themselves to acquiring knowledge about knowledge. The power of Descartes's original insight becomes clear once it is articulated: *Before we can reasonably evaluate any beliefs about reality, we must inquire into the nature of the "instrument" we use to observe it.*

■ THE PROBLEM OF AUTHORITY ■

Modern philosophy emphasizes methodology, technique, and personal, social, and historical *detachment*. Its origins lie in the decline of a stable social order, the loss of central authority by the Roman Catholic Church, and the proliferation of scientific advances. More sophisticated mathematics and improved scientific instruments had resulted in discoveries that challenged and contradicted Aristotelian naturalism. Scientists were able to move beyond metaphysical speculations to careful observations. No authority—religious or political—could refute what the individual observer *saw* or the individual mind *calculated* for itself.

Descartes was a Catholic, but his argument that each individual possesses the "natural light of reason" and needs no intervening authority to interpret "the great book of the world" may remind you of Luther's claim that each person can go directly to God without the church as an intermediary. In other words, Descartes, like Luther, set aside the so-called accumulated wisdom of the past, insisting that each person must examine what is true and false afresh.

Descartes's scientific interests led him to observe and experiment for himself, and he soon discovered that Aristotle's authoritative writings on nature contained many errors.

> But so soon as I had achieved the entire course of study at the close of which one is usually received into the ranks of the learned, . . . I found myself embarrassed with so many doubts and errors that it seemed to me that the effort to instruct myself had no effect other than the increasing discovery of my own ignorance. And yet I was studying at one of the most celebrated schools in Europe.[1]

In Descartes's time, the distinction between science and philosophy was not clear. His interests and abilities in philosophy, mathematics, and science made this

All that is comes from the mind.

THE *DHAMMAPADA*

As soon as age permitted me to emerge from the control of my tutors, I quitted the study of letters . . . resolving to seek no other science than that which could be found in myself, or at least in the great book of the world.

RENÉ DESCARTES

Method consists entirely in the order and disposition of the objects toward which our mental vision must be directed if we would find out any truth. We shall comply with it exactly if we reduce involved and obscure propositions step by step to those that are simpler, and then starting with the intuitive apprehension of all those that are absolutely simple, attempt to ascend to the knowledge of all others by precisely similar steps.

RENÉ DESCARTES

confusion especially intolerable to him. He expected scientific claims to be provable by appeals to observation and clear thinking. So he made a radical proposal: Let's start fresh, throwing out everything we think we know, and build a system of knowledge based entirely on ideas whose truth can be clearly and distinctly known—to us, firsthand.

RENÉ DESCARTES: THE SOLITARY INTELLECT

René Descartes (1596–1650) was born into an old and respected family in the French province of Touraine. His mother died of tuberculosis a year after his birth, and Descartes believed he inherited a frail constitution from her. His father was a famous lawyer, whose career kept him away from home for months at a time.

When he was approximately nine years old, Descartes was sent to the Jesuit college at La Flèche, where his physical weakness and mental strength were both acknowledged—he was allowed to sleep later than the other students (a lifelong habit). At La Flèche Descartes studied Greek, Latin, history, liberal arts, science, mathematics, and philosophy, in addition to music, dancing, and fencing.

After completing his studies at La Flèche, Descartes spent the next few years living the life of the young gentleman he was. He practiced his fencing, rode horses, and—already in love with mathematics—briefly took up gambling to see if he could devise a system to break the bank. At the University of Poitiers, he earned degrees in civil and canon law.

In 1618, when Descartes was twenty-two years old, the Thirty Years' War broke out. To the surprise of his friends, a strong, healthy Descartes enlisted in the army of the Prince of Nassau and later joined the army of the Duke of Bavaria. It is not clear whether he ever saw combat.

On November 10, 1619, Descartes had a revelation that transformed him and ultimately changed the direction of Western philosophy. As he later wrote, "I remained the whole day shut up alone in a stove-heated room, where I had complete leisure to occupy my thoughts."[2] There, Descartes says, he "discovered the foundations of a wonderful new science." The next night, full of excitement and anticipation over his discovery, he had three dreams, in one of which he heard a clap of thunder. He took it to be "the Spirit of Truth descending to take possession" of him. Descartes believed he had been divinely encouraged to establish a universal method of reasoning, based on mathematical principles, which, if followed carefully enough, would guarantee the absolutely certain truth of its results.

After this remarkable experience, Descartes's outward life seemed little changed. His inheritance, first from his mother and then from his father, had freed him from the need to make a living, so he traveled, studied, conversed, and wrote. He lived alone most of his life, except for his servants, and during a twenty-year period lived in twenty different houses.

Solitary and secretive, Descartes preferred to avoid the distractions and commotion of city life and social involvements. Most of his philosophical discourse took the form of letters. There were times when he didn't want his friends to know where he was; he even asked them not to write to him for a

---

René Descartes

I shall not say anything about Philosophy, but that, seeing that it has been cultivated for many centuries by the best minds that have ever lived, and that nevertheless no single thing is to be found in it which is not the subject of dispute, and in consequence which is not dubious, I had not enough presumption to hope to fare better there than other men had done. And also, considering how many conflicting opinions there may be regarding the self-same matter, all supported by learned people, while there can never be more than one which is true, I esteemed as well-nigh false all that only went as far as being probable.

RENÉ DESCARTES

while. Descartes thought he worked better this way, completely free to devote all his energy, at his own pace, to his studies. In a letter to a friend, Descartes wrote from Amsterdam: "And thus in this large city where I now am, since I seem to be practically the only one here who is not a merchant or in trade; all are so bound up in their profitable business transactions that I could remain here my entire life without being noticed by anyone."[3] Living this way, Descartes was able to study philosophy, geometry, physics, optics, circulation, and other subjects. Conducting experiments and dissections, as well as making important discoveries in mathematics, he rejected the Scholastic model of science and philosophy, turning instead to firsthand observations and deductions.

In 1635 Descartes had an illegitimate daughter (who died at the age of five) with a servant girl. Later, he referred to the episode as "a dangerous commitment" from which he had "extricated" himself. He was not entirely immune to the charms of women, however. He had a close six-year correspondence with Princess Elizabeth, daughter of the dethroned queen of Bohemia. When she was nineteen, the princess read his *Discourse on Method* and was surprised and delighted to discover philosophy written in clear, everyday language.

Through a friend who had become the French ambassador to the court of Queen Christina of Sweden, Descartes was ultimately convinced in September 1649—against his better judgment—to join her court in Stockholm. He was not happy there. He had little time for his experiments, and the queen forced him to break his lifelong habits of sleeping late and working at leisure—she wanted to be tutored in philosophy at five in the morning! This forceful woman even managed to get Descartes to write a ballet. The cold weather and austere conditions weakened his already frail health. By the end of January 1650, he was ill with pneumonia. He died February 11, two months before his fifty-fourth birthday.

René Descartes stands not only as the father of modern philosophy, but also as the original archetype of the modern rationalist: He boldly relied on the disciplined use of his own reason; he refused to accept as true anything that did not square with what he had personally verified as true; he exalted the thinking, conscious self as the foundation of all certainty.

▪ RATIONALISM ▪

Rationalism is an epistemological position in which reason is said to be the primary source of all knowledge, superior to sense evidence. Rationalists argue that only reason can distinguish reality from illusion and give meaning to experience.

In general, rationalists believe that abstract reasoning can produce undeniable, absolutely certain truths about nature, existence, and the whole of reality. Many of these ultimate truths can be discovered without observation, experiment, or even experience. These are called *a priori* or, sometimes, **innate ideas**. Thus, to the rationalists, reason—not empirical observation—is the ultimate test of truth.

According to the **coherence theory of truth**, new or unclear ideas are evaluated in terms of rational or logical consistency and in relation to already established truths. The ultimate criteria for basic, originating truths are clarity and distinctness. Once fundamental truths are established, the rationalist uses a

---

Descartes' metaphysics, as he so clearly sees himself, is the natural product of a precious ingredient of the past which today is in danger of rapid extinction—privacy—that marvelous compound of withdrawal, self-reliance, quiet, solitude, contemplation, and concentration which seems the exclusive possession of a bygone age.

A. W. LEVI

rationalism
An epistemological position in which reason is said to be the primary source of all knowledge, superior to sense evidence. Rationalists argue that only reason can distinguish reality from illusion and give meaning to experience.

***a priori* ideas (innate ideas)**
Truths that are not derived from observation or experiment, characterized as being certain, deductive, universally true, and independent of all experience.

coherence theory of truth
Truth test in which new or unclear ideas are evaluated in terms of rational or logical consistency and in relation to already established truths.

deductive, mathematical/logical method to test and establish other, more complex ideas. True ideas are coherent (rationally consistent) with each other, and the rationalist's aim is to achieve absolute certainty of the sort possible in mathematics. "My method," said Descartes, "contains everything which gives certainty to the rules of arithmetic."

The coherence theory of truth is in direct opposition to the correspondence theory of truth (Chapter 10) and differs from the other major theory of truth, the pragmatic theory (Chapter 15).

Against Disorganized Thinking

Descartes's first philosophical work was *Rules for the Direction of the Mind*. The twenty-one principles contained in *Rules* reappear in Descartes's major philosophical works, *Discourse on Method* and *Meditations on First Philosophy*.

Rule 3 advises: *Once we have chosen a subject to study, we should confine ourselves to what we can clearly intuit and deduce with certainty for ourselves.* We must not rely on what others have thought or on our own as-yet-untested beliefs. We must look for ourselves, with new eyes and new understanding. Referring to the Scholastics, among others, Descartes cautions that "in a too absorbed study" of the works of earlier thinkers, we become "infected with their errors, guard against them as we may."

This is a general caution against authoritarian thinking, in which we give more weight to the opinions of others than to our own experience and clear thinking. When we accept views *solely* on the weight of the authority or prestige of those who hold them, or because of loyalty to a cause or belief structure, we become nonrational at best. We become memorizers, not thinkers.

Descartes points out that it is common to overlook clear, simple truths (intuitions) when we do encounter them. We quickly complicate them with cloudy but elaborate "explanations." He speculates that we surround the truth with ambiguities because we are afraid that the simplicity of our discoveries will make them seem unimportant. He adds:

> For we shall not, e.g., turn out to be mathematicians though we know by heart all the proofs others have elaborated, unless we have an intellectual talent that fits us to resolve difficulties of any kind. Neither, though we may have mastered all the arguments of Plato and Aristotle, if yet we have not the capacity for passing solid judgment on these matters, shall we become Philosophers; we should have acquired the knowledge not of a science, but of history.[4]

PHILOSOPHICAL

QUERY

• • • • • •

Use Descartes's distinction between memorizing ideas and understanding them to examine your own education. Describe the distinction between learning to love psychology or literature and becoming a historian of psychology or literature in Descartes's terms. Speculate on ways this distinction might be used to reform education.

"Beyond Intellect There Is Yet Another Stage"

In 1091, the Persian philosopher **Abu Hamid Muhammad al-Ghazali** (1058–1111) was appointed professor of Islamic theology at the Nizamiyah College in Baghdad. In 1095, al-Ghazali, by then a man of great influence, suffered a spiritual crisis and nervous breakdown that resulted in a speech impediment that prevented him from lecturing. He left the college and ultimately embraced a mystical form of Islam known as *sufism*. Al-Ghazali briefly returned to teaching, but eventually quit for good and founded a monastic community in Tus, the city of his birth.

The passage that follows is from his work *The Deliverance from Error*. Note how al-Ghazali's work anticipates Descartes's first meditation by five hundred years. Whereas Descartes exalted reason over faith, al-Ghazali "transcended" reason with the mystic's direct and immediate experience of God (Allah).

> To thirst after a comprehension of things as they really are was my habit and custom from a very early age. . . . as I drew near the age of adolescence the bonds of mere authority . . . ceased to hold me and inherited beliefs lost their grip upon me, for I saw that Christian youths always grew up to be Christians, Jewish youths to be Jews and Muslim youths to be Muslim. . . .
>
> I therefore said within myself: "To begin with, what I am looking for is knowledge of what things really are, so I must undoubtedly try to find what knowledge really is." It was plain to me that sure and certain knowledge is that knowledge in which the object is disclosed in such a fashion that no doubt remains along with it, that no possibility of error or illusion accompanies it, and that the mind cannot even entertain such a supposition. Certain knowledge must also be infallible. . . . Thus, I know that ten is more than three. Let us suppose that someone says to me: "No, three is more than ten, and in proof of that I shall change this rod into a serpent": and let us suppose that he actually changes the rod into a serpent and that I witness him doing so. No doubts about what I know are raised in me because of this. The only result is that I wonder how he is able to produce this change. Of doubt about my knowledge there is no trace.
>
> After these reflections I knew that whatever I did not know in this fashion and with this mode of certainty is not reliable and infallible knowledge; and knowledge that is not infallible is not certain knowledge. . . .
>
> Thereupon I investigated the various kinds of knowledge I had, and found myself destitute of all knowledge with this characteristic of infallibility except in the case of sense-perception and necessary truths. . . .
>
> I proceeded therefore with extreme earnestness to reflect on sense-perception and on necessary truths, to see whether I could make myself doubt them. The outcome of this protracted effort was that I could no longer trust sense-perception either. . . .
>
> . . . "Do you not see," [my ego] said, "how, when you are asleep, you believe things and imagine circumstances, holding them to be stable and enduring, and, so long as you are in that dream-condition, have no doubts about them? . . . Why then are you confident that all your waking beliefs, whether from sense or intellect, are genuine? They are true in respect of your present state; but it is possible that a state will come upon you whose relation to your waking consciousness is analogous to the relation of the latter to dreaming. In comparison with this state your waking consciousness would be like dreaming! When you are in this state, you will be certain that all the suppositions of your intellect are empty imaginings. . . . "
>
> It became clear to me . . . that what is most distinctive about mysticism is something which cannot be apprehended by study, but only by immediate experience . . . by ecstasy and by a moral change. What difference between *knowing* the definition of health and satiety . . . and *being* healthy and satisfied! . . .
>
> Beyond intellect there is yet another stage. In this another *eye* is opened, by which he beholds the unseen, what is to be the future, and other things which are beyond the ken of intellect.

Abu Hamid Muhammad al-Ghazali, *The Deliverance from Error*, in *The Faith and Practice of Al-Ghazali*, trans. W. Montgomery Watt (London: George Allen and Unwin, 1953), pp. 21–68.

Addressing the fact that we are bombarded with conflicting knowledge claims, Rule 4 succinctly states: *There is need of a method for finding the truth.*

> So blind is the curiosity by which mortals are possessed, that they often conduct their minds along unexplored routes, having no reason to hope for success. . . . it were far better never to think of investigating truth at all, than to do so without a method. For it is very certain that unregulated inquiries and confused reflections of this kind only confound the natural light and blind our mental powers. . . . In [method] alone lies the sum of all human endeavour, and he who would approach the investigation of truth must hold to this rule.[5]

PHILOSOPHICAL
QUERY

* * * * * *

People who have little or no scientific education sometimes engage in fierce debates about cloning, brain death, and evolution. Individuals who don't keep up with world events nonetheless express opinions about foreign affairs, balancing the federal budget, or the meaning of the First Amendment. Have you ever been guilty of investigating "the most difficult questions with so little regard for order"? Discuss the general advantages of "method," and identify one or two current areas of controversy that might benefit from "method."

■ THE METHOD OF DOUBT ■

Descartes believed that a mathematically precise method was the only reliable way to discover the truth about the universe. He proposed to use the new spirit of scientific inquiry and mathematical rigor to reexamine—everything! His effort not only marks the beginning of an entirely new philosophical orientation, but it also remains fascinating and relevant.

Descartes attacked earlier philosophy on the grounds that it did not demand rational comprehension from the individual intellect. It did not rest *solely* on ideas known through "the clear light of natural reason."

> I thought that the sciences found in books—and those at least whose reasonings are only probable and which have no demonstrations, composed as they are of the gradually accumulated opinions of many different individuals—do not approach so near to the truth as the simple reasoning which a man of common sense can quite naturally carry out respecting the things which come immediately before him.[6]

So long as we have the body . . . we shall never attain completely what we desire.

PLATO

"Common sense," which Descartes also referred to as *natural reason,* is the ability to think that is found in all normal humans. It does not depend on divine revelation or special education—at least according to Descartes. Though not everyone has the talent for or interest in refined thinking, Descartes believed all reasoning individuals could apply his method to basic questions concerning human nature, truth, and the existence of God.

Good sense is of all things in the world the most equally distributed, for everybody thinks himself so abundantly provided with it, that even those most difficult to please in all other matters do not commonly desire more of it than they already possess. It is unlikely that this is an error on their part; it seems rather to be evidence in support of the view that the power of forming a good judgment and of distinguishing the true from the false, which is properly speaking what is called Good Sense or Reason, is by nature equal in all men. Hence too it will show that the diversity of our opinions does not proceed from some men being more rational than others, but solely from the fact that our thoughts pass through diverse channels and the same objects are not considered by all. For to be possessed of good mental powers is not sufficient; the principal matter is to apply them well. The greatest minds are capable of the greatest vices as well as of the greatest virtues, and those who proceed very slowly may, provided they always follow the straight road, really advance much faster than those who, though they run, forsake it.[7]

> *Descartes has transformed wisdom into a work, a project, a making, a determinate problem, for he denies that he can work with anything else.*
>
> ROBERT E. MEAGHER

* * * * * *

PHILOSOPHICAL QUERY

Comment on the preceding passage. Do you agree with Descartes? Why? Is common sense the same thing as good sense? Analyze the notion of common sense. Do you really think there is such a thing? What is your evidence either way?

The Cartesian "I" and Methodic Doubt

Descartes did not write in Latin, the "universal language of scholars," but in everyday French. His aim was to reach beyond the confines of the university and church to a wider audience of European intellectuals. Consequently, Descartes cast all his works in the first person to describe both his *conclusions* and his *thinking process.* He wanted to call our attention to the actively reasoning mind itself. Until Descartes, philosophers tended to focus on the content of ideas and on their logical relations to each other, not on the mind. Although "reason" was discussed and referred to, and often cited as the guide by which we should live, the "reasoning thing" itself was not directly studied.

> *For those who like a dramatic and specific date, the simple but far-reaching phrase of Descartes, "I think, therefore I am," will do very well for the beginning [of the Age of Reason]: 1657.*
>
> CRANE BRINTON

As you study Descartes's ideas, don't always interpret the "I" as referring to Descartes—allow it also to refer to you while you are reading (and, I hope, thinking along with) the words Descartes wrote. By occasionally becoming the "I" yourself, you can participate in the *conscious flow* of Descartes's reasoning in a way that will help you evaluate his arguments as if they were your own. You will be reflecting and meditating on your own conscious mind.

Descartes was convinced that he could apply a mathematically oriented method to the most fundamental problem of all: How can I know that I know anything? In geometry, he pointed out, we begin with self-evident truths such as "A straight line is the shortest distance between two points." More complex theorems based on these truths are then called upon to prove less-evident truths. Descartes proposed applying this basic method to philosophy. In his *Rules,* he stated that *we must not accept anything we can doubt at all.*

In his effort to base his philosophy on an absolutely certain foundation, Descartes had a culture-altering insight. He discovered **methodic doubt.** Simply put, *methodic doubt involves deliberately doubting everything it is possible to doubt in the least degree. Whatever remains will be known with absolute certainty.* In order to apply methodic doubt, Descartes had to rely on a standard of truth that could tell him whether or not it was reasonable to doubt something.

methodic doubt
Cartesian strategy of deliberately doubting everything it is possible to doubt in the least degree so that what remains will be known with absolute certainty.

Standard of Truth

No matter what method we employ in a search for truth, we must have some criterion for distinguishing truth from falsity. Descartes proposed that we "might assume as a general rule that the things which we conceive very clearly and distinctly are all true." He defined *clear* as "that which is present and apparent to an attentive mind," and *distinct* as "that which is so precise and different from all other objects that it contains within itself nothing but what is clear." We might say that for Descartes, knowledge requires precision and detail.

Throughout his philosophical writings Descartes appeals to clear and distinct knowing as the ultimate standard to be used in accepting or rejecting ideas. To produce the most certain conclusions possible, he rejected *anything* he did not know "clearly and distinctly." He also believed that certain very basic propositions *need only to be understood* to be recognized as true. To understand something clearly and distinctly, according to Descartes, is a matter of perceiving that there are no reasonable grounds on which it can be doubted. In other words, *to recognize something clearly and distinctly is to know that it is true.*

Some philosophers are troubled by Descartes's standard of truth. They claim that *the standard itself* is ambiguous and subjective and thus cannot be known with clarity and distinctness. They accuse Descartes of basing his rationalism on the subjective states of the perceiver; they interpret this to mean that, in spite of his talk about reason, Descartes actually bases much of his philosophy on his feelings and moods. Their point is that "clear and distinct" vary from individual to individual; I might be convinced I know something clearly and distinctly and still be wrong about it.

Perceiving something clearly and distinctly is essentially a matter of perceiving certain logical relationships.

HARRY G. FRANKFURT

PHILOSOPHICAL

QUERY

• • • • • •

A common criticism of Descartes's standard of truth is that he failed to apply it to itself: Do we know with clarity and distinctness that only what we know with clarity and distinctness is true? *Can we know it? Not if, as critics claim, Descartes's standard is itself unclear and ambiguous. Do you have a clear and distinct idea of Descartes's criterion? How can we tell when an inability to perceive something clearly and distinctly is the fault of the individual or of the quality of the idea? Discuss carefully.*

Innate Ideas

As you wrestle with these issues, keep in mind that getting started is the most difficult part of establishing a new or original philosophical orientation. We must begin with initially unquestioned assumptions and basic principles. To a certain extent, some ideas must be known before we can know anything else. These ideas must be first or *prior* to knowing everything else. *A priori* ideas are characterized as being certain, deductive, universally true, innate, or independent of all experience. **A priori** knowledge is derived from reason without reference to sense experience. Truths of reason and laws of logic are usually thought to be *a priori*. Examples include "All triangles contain 180°" and "Every event has a cause."

In contrast to *a priori* knowledge, **a posteriori** knowledge is empirical knowledge derived from sense experience. This kind of knowing comes from the accumulation of experience. It is not regarded as certain or necessary, because the conditions under which it is acquired change, perceivers vary, and factual relationships change. For example, the statement "My shirt is white" can be true for a particular set of circumstances today and false tomorrow. "My shirt is white" is not universally or eternally true in the way that "Every event has a cause" is. *A posteriori* truths are also called factual truths or truths of fact, as opposed to rational truths. (Not all philosophers agree that *a priori* truths exist. For example, the empiricists, whom we will meet in Chapter 10, insist that all knowledge comes from sense experience.)

As a brilliant geometer, Descartes was familiar with the axioms for geometric proofs, which he characterized as *a priori* ideas. He believed we are born with certain ideas "implanted" in us by God. For example, we are born with the idea of a triangle in our minds. When we see triangles or triangular-shaped objects, we are reminded of this innate idea. Descartes often appeals to the standard of clarity and distinctness as if its truth should be obvious to us with a bit of reflection. All we need is to be "reminded" of it to recognize its truth.

> **a priori knowledge**
> Derived from reason without reference to sense experience. Examples include "All triangles contain 180°" and "Every event has a cause."

> **a posteriori knowledge**
> Empirical knowledge derived from sense experience and not regarded as universal because the conditions under which it is acquired change, perceivers vary, and factual relationships change.

● ● ● ● ● ●

PHILOSOPHICAL

QUERY

Is Descartes correct? What about seemingly sincere, rational, and intelligent people who say they do not, perhaps cannot, see the truth of this idea about innate ideas? Compare Descartes's problem here with Plato's problem of accounting for ignorance of the Forms. Do you think Forms are innate ideas? Are innate ideas Forms? (See Chapter 5.)

■ THE CARTESIAN GENESIS ■

To summarize: Descartes wanted to find an absolutely certain, indubitable starting point for his philosophy. He chose a form of deliberate, methodological skepticism that we have labeled *methodic doubt*. As we will see from the work of David Hume (Chapter 10), there are degrees of skepticism,

> *Descartes' success is indicated by the extent to which the central notions of his philosophy became the common conception of man and the universe for nearly three centuries.*
>
> ALEXANDER SESONSKE
> AND NOEL FLEMING

© Chronicle Features, 1989

Even if life and all of you and everything is like just a dream I'm having, I still figure I'm going to need all the money I can lay my hands on.

progressing from total doubt about everything to temporary or particular doubt invoked just for the process of analysis. Descartes's skepticism is part of his method, and is, consequently, of the temporary—but still serious—sort. He does not really doubt everything he challenges in his *Meditations;* rather, systematically doubting is the *process* of Cartesian inquiry, not the end result. Descartes hoped to use skepticism to establish complete certainty.

In the *Meditations,* Descartes begins by asking if it is rationally possible to doubt everything. He reasons that by doing this, he will quickly discover if there is any certain, undoubtable truth. In the course of this inquiry, Descartes tears down the old world of Scholastic philosophy, unquestioned beliefs, and ambiguous ideas and attempts to replace it with a brand-new, certain, clearly proved, rational order. He suggests that his readers reflect on one meditation a day, reading carefully and leisurely. After six days, Descartes, like God in the biblical book of Genesis, will have finished with his own creation. The attentive, rational reader, by becoming the Cartesian "I" in the manner noted earlier, will also have torn down and rebuilt his or her previously unquestioned house of beliefs on a solid, rational foundation.

Descartes begins the *Meditations* by giving his methodic doubt the widest possible scope. He calls Meditation I *Of the things which may be brought within the sphere of the doubtful.* In the first two paragraphs, Descartes invokes the skeptical method and introduces the standard of clarity and distinctness and immediately points out that it would be impossible to examine every belief he currently holds. Instead, he will examine the origins and foundations of basic kinds of beliefs. If

Consciousness is a disease.
Miguel de Unamuno

there is *any* possibility, however remote, that they could be mistaken, Descartes will reject them and every idea that depends on them:

> It is now many years since I detected how many were the false beliefs that I had from my earliest youth admitted as true, and how doubtful was everything I had since constructed on this basis; and from that time I was convinced that I must once and for all seriously undertake to rid myself of all the opinions which I had formerly accepted, and commence to build anew from the foundation if I wanted to establish any firm and permanent structure in the sciences. . . .
>
> Now for this object it is not necessary that I should show that all of these are false—I shall perhaps never arrive at this end. But inasmuch as reason already persuades me that I ought no less carefully to withhold my assent from matters which are not entirely certain and indubitable than from those which appear to be manifestly false, if I am able to find in each some reason to doubt, this will suffice to justify my rejecting the whole. And . . . owing to the fact that the destruction of the foundations of necessity brings with it the downfall of the rest of the edifice, I shall only in the first place attack those principles upon which all my former opinions rested.[8]

Above all, Descartes admired almost nothing and no one.

C. Adam

PHILOSOPHICAL QUERY

• • • • • •

How carefully have you examined your own fundamental beliefs? What—if anything—is wrong with trusting beliefs handed down by others? Why not rely on the testing of others, trusting their conclusions? Discuss. Also comment on the tendency to believe something if it could possibly be correct. What is the relationship between possible and plausible, and what might it have to do with this entire issue? Explain.

Maybe It's All a Dream?

Like most of us, prior to his investigations, Descartes had uncritically assumed that the most true and certain things known come from the senses. For example, it seems "obviously true" that my computer exists as I type this sentence, and it seems "obviously true" that the book you are reading exists. What could be more certain than simple, direct sensations and perceptions of our immediate environment?

Ah, but our senses sometimes deceive us. For example, we may think we are looking at an airplane and later discover that it is a bird. Witnesses to crimes disagree over descriptions of perpetrators, and we sometimes think we recognize the figure coming down the sidewalk, only to be wrong. Even so, aren't we always sure of immediate sensations? Though our senses may deceive us about distant events, there are many other things we know through our senses "as to which we cannot reasonably have any doubt." Descartes reflects:

In the interplay of reality and illusion, how can you be sure that you are now not dreaming and that events seen during a state of dream may be closer to the truth?

Lie Zi

> At the same time I must remember that I am a man, and that consequently I am in the habit of sleeping, and in my dreams representing to myself the same things or sometimes even less probable things, than those who are insane do

in their waking moments. How often has it happened to me that in the night I dreamt that I found myself in this particular place, that I was dressed and seated near the fire, whilst in reality I was lying undressed in bed! At this moment it does indeed seem to me that it is with eyes awake that I am looking at this paper; that this head which I move is not asleep, that it is deliberately and of set purpose that I extend my hand and perceive it; what happens in sleep does not appear so clear and distinct as does all this. But in thinking over this I remind myself that on many occasions I have in sleep been deceived by similar illusions, and in dwelling carefully on this reflection I see so manifestly that there are no certain indications by which we may clearly distinguish wakefulness from sleep that I am lost in astonishment. And my astonishment is such that it is almost capable of persuading me that I now dream.[9]

> It seems to me that the greatest lesson of adult life is that one's own consciousness is not enough.
>
> SIR FRED HOYLE

With this example, Descartes rejects sense knowledge as a sufficient foundation for certainty. In so doing, he also rejects the primacy of the external, physical world because it is *possible* that the whole so-called real world is nothing but an elaborate mental construct, a hallucination. Remember, in the interest of constructing a flawless philosophy, Descartes is being ultracautious. He will not settle for degrees of probability, no matter how "virtually certain" they may be. Whether or not you consider it *probable* that your world is a dream, Descartes points out that it is at least *possible*.

But even if the world is a dream, it still has regularity and predictability, doesn't it? Maybe the world is just a dream implanted in the mind by God.

PHILOSOPHICAL QUERY

• • • • • •

How do we know the difference between a dream or hallucination and reality? Seriously consider how a confused person might verify that he or she is or is not dreaming.

> After the guarantee of the criterion of clear and distinct ideas has been elaborated, however, it turns out that the relations apprehended by reason are but misleading representatives of the true relations whose basic nature must remain a mystery to us. There is a powerful and basic undercurrent of irrationalism in Descartes, the first of the modern rationalists.
>
> LEONARD G. MILLER

The Evil Genius

Perhaps, like Descartes, you are having some trouble seriously doubting your experiences of the real world. Descartes says, "These ancient and commonly held opinions [that I am not dreaming] still revert frequently to my mind." To better test his most persistent beliefs, Descartes decides to allow himself deliberately "to be deceived, and for a certain time pretend that all these opinions are entirely false and imaginary." Descartes is in no danger of losing his bearings; this is still methodic doubt, not real confusion or delusion. He even says not to worry about giving in to too much doubt and distrust, since he is "not considering the question of action, but only of knowledge."

At this point, Descartes introduces one of the most intriguing figures in the history of philosophy, the *evil genius*:

> I shall then suppose, not that God who is supremely good and the fountain of truth, but some evil genius not less powerful than deceitful, has employed his

whole energies in deceiving me; I shall consider that the heavens, the earth, colours, figures, sound, and all other external things are nought but the illusions and dreams of which this genius has availed himself in order to lay traps for my credulity; I shall consider myself as having no hands, no eyes, no flesh, no blood, nor any senses, yet falsely believing myself to possess all these things; I shall remain obstinately attached to this idea, and if by this means it is not in my power to arrive at the knowledge of any truth, I may at least do what is in my power [i.e., suspend my judgment], and with firm purpose avoid giving credence to any false thing, or being imposed upon by this arch deceiver, however powerful and deceptive he may be.[10]

This cold possibility of ultimate delusion concludes the first Meditation. Descartes has reduced his world to himself and one all-powerful, all-evil source of deception. He reasons that if he can find one anchor point of undoubtable certainty in the midst of the possibility of error in *all* quarters of his life, he will have found his unshakable foundation.

● ● ● ● ● ●

PHILOSOPHICAL

QUERY

Before reading any further, stop for a moment and play with Descartes's idea of an evil genius. Try to get into the spirit of doubting as much as you can. Do not be limited by what you actually doubt; this is an intellectual exercise, not a personal confession. See if you can extend the range of what might on the remotest possibility be false or other than you think it is. Can you be absolutely sure that there is no evil genius?

Cogito, Ergo Sum

Could the evil genius so arrange things that nothing is as I think it is? In the physical realm he could. He could trick me into thinking that I have a body when I don't, that things have shapes, colors, and so on, that they really don't. Descartes says that—as difficult as it is to imagine—he might even be able to deceive me regarding certain innate, *a priori* ideas, so that maybe 7 + 5 does not really equal 12 or triangles don't have three sides. If I can be tricked into thinking things exist that do not exist, and if I can be fooled into thinking things do not exist when they really do, then maybe I am being deceived about my own existence. Is there anything the evil genius cannot trick me about? Maybe I don't really exist?

What is important is not liberation from the body but liberation from the mind. We are not entangled in our own body, but entangled in our own mind.

THOMAS MERTON

> Not at all; of a surety I myself [must] exist since I persuaded myself of something [or merely because I thought of something]. But [what if] there is some deceiver or other, very powerful and very cunning, who ever employs his ingenuity in deceiving me. Then without doubt I exist also if he deceives me, and let him deceive me as much as he will, he can never cause me to be nothing so long as I think that I am something. So that after having reflected well and carefully examined all things, we must come to the definite conclusion that this proposition: I am, I exist, is necessarily true each time that I pronounce it, or that I mentally conceive it.[11]

Frank and Ernest reprinted by permission of Bob Thaves.

Cogito, ergo sum
Latin for "I think,
therefore I am."

This is the famous "cogito," from the Latin sentence ***Cogito, ergo sum,*** meaning *I think, therefore I am.* In some ways, this Cartesian insight, more than anything else, marks the beginning of the modern worldview.

Note the difference between "Descartes thinks, therefore Descartes exists" and "I think, therefore I exist," where the "I" refers to whoever speaks or thinks the sentence. The cogito must be understood in the first person. In that form, it meets Descartes's conditions for being utterly unshakable. No rational person can doubt his or her own existence as a conscious thinking entity—while being aware of thinking about anything.

Cogito ergo non dormio.
(I think, therefore I am not asleep.)

Descartes interprets this to mean that while bodily existence may seem more solid and certain than ideas, mental existence is in actuality more certain. He goes on:

> I find here that thought is an attribute that belongs to me; it cannot be separated from me. I am, I exist, that is certain. But how often? . . . to speak accurately [at this stage of the Meditations] I am not more than a thing which thinks, that is to say a mind or soul, or an understanding, or a reason, which are terms whose significance was formerly unknown to me. I am . . . a real thing and really exist; but what thing? I have answered: a thing which thinks.
>
> . . . What is a thing which thinks? It is a thing which doubts, understands, [conceives], affirms, denies, wills, refuses, which also imagines and feels.[12]

Hamlet did think a great many things; does it follow that he existed?

JAAKO HINTIKKA

Descartes argues that we identify and know everything—including bodily and material things—through the mind. He grounds all knowledge in mental states, in awareness. Thus the foundation of Descartes's philosophy and, to a considerable extent, of the modern worldview is the thinking self. Although Descartes was a rationalist, the thrust of the cogito is not *reasoning* but *self-awareness.* Augustine had a similar formula: "I doubt, therefore I am," and in *Nausea* Jean-Paul Sartre wrote, in effect, "I am nauseated, therefore I exist."

So far, Descartes has established that the thinking thing possesses absolute certainty of its own existence as a consciously thinking thing. Thus there is one rather limited fact I know with certainty. Do any other insights follow from this bedrock experience of self-consciousness? Can Descartes move from it to re-create the external world?

"Quod Si Fallor, Sum: If I Am Mistaken, I Exist"

More than twelve centuries before Descartes's attempt to refute skepticism with the certain knowledge of his own existence (the cogito), Augustine (Chapter 8) used a remarkably similar argument for the same purpose in *The City of God*.

> The certainty that I exist, that I know it, and that I am glad of it, is independent of any imaginary and deceptive fantasies.
>
> In respect of these truths I have no fear of the arguments of the [Skeptics]. They say, "Suppose your arguments are mistaken?" I reply, "If I am mistaken, I exist." A non-existent being cannot be mistaken; therefore I must exist, if I am mistaken.

> . . . Since therefore I must exist in order to be mistaken, then even if I am mistaken, there can be no doubt that I am not mistaken in my knowledge that I exist. It follows that I am not mistaken in knowing that I know. And when I am glad of those two facts, I can add the fact that of that gladness to the things I know, as a fact of equal worth. For I am not mistaken about the fact of my gladness, since I am not mistaken about the things which I love. Even if they were illusory, it would still be a fact that I love the illusions.

Augustine, *The City of God*, trans. Henry Bettenson (Harmondsworth, England: Penguin, 1972), 11.26.

• • • • • •

PHILOSOPHICAL

QUERY

When I was a student I felt compelled to challenge anything presented to me as being irrefutable. As soon as I heard about the cogito I assumed I would be able to refute it, to show that it was not necessarily true. That proved easier said than done. Try for yourself; it is interesting, and it is the only way to grasp Descartes's point. Discuss your efforts.

■ THE INNATE IDEA OF GOD ■

Descartes begins the third Meditation still treating everything he thinks of as part of himself, as merely "perceptions and imaginations" from his own mind. That being so, his next step is to survey his own thoughts, to see whether there might be something he has overlooked or been unaware of so far. He reasons that the most important issue is the existence of God:

> I must inquire whether there is a God as soon as the occasion presents itself; and if I find that there is a God, I must also inquire whether He may be a deceiver; for without a knowledge of these two truths I do not see that I can ever be certain of anything.[13]

In other words, if Descartes can establish the existence of God rationally, he will have a foundation for truth concerning other ideas. If God is not an evil deceiver, Descartes argues, He will have created the reasoning mind to seek and know the truth. Rationally verifying the existence of God will not only guarantee the possibility of knowledge with certainty, but will also bridge the gaps between religion and science and between the imagination and reality. If God is the source of reason, then it follows that He wills the use of reason in pursuit of truth. If so, then God is the impetus behind science. If God is not a deceiver, then He will have given Descartes the ability to distinguish the real from the merely imagined. Thus the issue of God's existence and nature is crucial to Descartes's entire rationalistic enterprise.

The Perfect Idea of Perfection

As a rationalist, Descartes cannot appeal to Aquinas's arguments for the existence of God (Chapter 8) because they are based on claims about the external world, the existence of which Descartes has yet to establish. Indeed, Descartes needs to establish the existence of God in order to establish the existence of the external world. Descartes can—at this point—only examine the nature and quality of his own ideas.

> I shall now close my eyes, I shall stop my ears, I shall call away all my senses, I shall efface even from my thoughts all the images of corporeal things, or at least (for that is hardly possible) I shall esteem them as vain and false; and thus holding converse only with myself and considering my own nature, I shall try little by little to reach a better knowledge of and a more familiar acquaintanceship with myself.[14]

Clearly, Descartes says, the *idea* of God exists. He notes the obvious: Such an idea does exist—he has it. But does it follow that an *object* corresponding to this idea exists?

> Hence there remains only the idea of God, concerning which we must consider whether it is something which cannot have proceeded from me myself. By the name of God I understand a substance that is infinite [eternal, unchangeable], independent, all-knowing, all-powerful, and by which I myself and everything else, if anything else does exist, has been created. Now all these characteristics are such that the more diligently I attend to them, the less do they appear capable of proceeding from me alone; hence, from what has been already said, we must conclude that God necessarily exists.[15]

Descartes's position amounts to this: I have in me the clear and distinct idea of a perfect, infinite being. Where could I, an imperfect, finite creature, ever get the idea of infinite perfection? A perfect being is not just a bigger, stronger, quantitatively improved Descartes. If my idea of God were merely of a kind of superhuman being, then I might have created it out of wishful thinking. But how could I even have a notion of infinite perfection, or want to be more perfect myself, "unless I had within me some idea of a Being more perfect than myself, in comparison with which I should recognize the deficiencies of my nature?"[16] In other words, because of its very uniqueness, the idea of an infinite, perfect being must come from just such a being: God.

Note that Descartes has ruled out the idea of an infinite regress of causes. He is also appealing to a version of the principle of sufficient reason (Chapter 8). No matter how far the chain of causes extends, nothing is sufficient to explain (cause) the idea of a perfect, infinite being but a perfect, infinite being.

> And although it may be the case that one idea gives birth to another idea, that cannot continue to be so indefinitely; for in the end we must reach an idea

whose cause shall be so to speak an archetype, in which the whole reality [or perfection] which is so to speak objectively [or by representation] in these ideas is contained formally [and really]. Thus the light of nature causes me to know clearly that the ideas in me are like [pictures or] images which can, in truth, easily fall short of the perfection of the objects from which they have been derived, but which can never contain anything greater or more perfect.[17]

In other words, Descartes's mind cannot be the cause of this one special idea. If Descartes were the cause of Descartes, then he would have given himself all the perfections associated with God. So ultimately something other than Descartes must be its cause. The same is true of any so-called evil geniuses or angels or other not-perfect, finite beings.

Descartes, for all his dislike of Scholastic philosophy, follows a Scholastic line in his analysis of these matters. He seems to be saying that not only is God a perfect being, but the idea of God is also a "perfect idea." If it is, he reasons, where could it come from? Imperfect creatures such as ourselves can imagine only imperfect ideas; we could not come up with the idea of a *perfect* anything without help. Where could the idea of perfection come from? Only from a mind more perfect than ours.

> It is perfectly evident that there must be at least as much reality in the cause as in the effect; and thus since I am a thinking thing, and possess an idea of God within me, whatever in the end be the cause assigned to my existence, it must be allowed that it is likewise a thinking thing and that it possesses in itself the idea of all the perfections I attribute to God. . . . But if it derives its existence from some other cause than itself, we shall again ask, for the same reason, whether this second cause exists by itself or through another, until from one step to another, we finally arrive at an ultimate cause, which will be God.[18]

Descartes determines that he cannot have "received" the idea of God through the senses, nor has it suddenly burst upon his consciousness. He cannot have imagined it, for he lacks the ability to improve upon or to detract from it. Consequently, he says, "the only alternative is that it is innate in me, just as the idea of myself is innate in me."[19]

Descartes's conception of God as a perfect being includes the qualities of all-knowing, all-powerful, all-loving, all-good. Descartes posits that such a God would not let him be constantly deceived by either himself or some evil genius. If, the argument goes, God gave us reason and faculties of perception, they must be basically accurate and reliable. God's existence is crucial to the Cartesian Genesis.

> And the whole strength of the argument which I have here made use of to prove the existence of God consists in this, that I recognize that it is not possible that my nature should be what it is, and indeed that I should have in myself the idea of a God, if God did not veritably exist—a God, I say, whose idea is in me, i.e., who possesses all those supreme perfections of which our mind may indeed have some idea but without understanding them all, who is liable to no errors or defect [and who has none of all those marks which denote imperfection]. From this it is manifest that He cannot be a deceiver, since the light of nature teaches us that fraud and deception necessarily proceed from some defect.[20]

When a person is in any state of consciousness it logically follows that he is not sound asleep.

NORMAN MALCOLM

It must always be recollected, however, that possibly I deceive myself, and that what I take to be gold and diamonds is perhaps no more than copper or glass.

RENÉ DESCARTES

Descartes's Ontological Argument

In the fifth Meditation, Descartes presents an argument for the existence of God based on the claim that it is impossible to conceive of or even imagine God without also thinking of existence. The very essence of the idea of God includes "all perfections," and certainly existence is a perfection. This line of reasoning is known as an ontological argument. The term *ontology* derives from the Greek roots *onta,* "truly real," and *logos,* "study of." An **ontological argument** is an attempt to prove the existence of God by referring either to the meaning of the word *God* when it is understood a certain way, or by referring to the purportedly unique quality of the concept of God.

The purest form of the ontological argument first occurs in the *Proslogion* of St. Anselm (1033–1109). A Benedictine monk who eventually became the archbishop of Canterbury, Anselm attempted to provide a rational basis for Christian doctrine. He asserted that the very idea of God "contains existence" because *by definition* God is "that than which nothing greater can be conceived." And of any two things, a real one is "greater" than an imaginary one. Hence, an existing God is greater than a merely imaginary God. Therefore, by definition, the term *God* refers to a real, existing being. When we use *God* to refer to a fantasy being, we have changed its meaning.

For Descartes, the idea of God (infinite perfection) is unique. It is an idea that can only be caused by something external to Descartes. More than that, it is an idea that must resemble the being that it is an idea of. That is not to say that our limited grasp of this privileged idea is adequate. Of course we cannot comprehend God. But we can, Descartes believes, clearly and distinctly grasp the uniqueness of the idea of God, and in so doing, we understand that existence is part of God's essence. He writes:

> This indeed is not at first manifest, since it would seem to present some appearance of being a sophism. For being accustomed in all other things to make a distinction between existence and essence, I easily persuade myself that the existence can be separated from the essence of God, and that we can thus conceive God as not actually existing. But, nevertheless, when I think of it with more attention, I clearly see that existence can no more be separated from the essence of God than can its having its three angles equal to two right angles be separated from the essence of a [rectilinear] triangle, or the idea of a mountain from the idea of a valley; and so there is not any less repugnance to our conceiving a God (that is, a Being supremely perfect) to whom existence is lacking (that is to say, to whom a certain perfection is lacking), than to conceive of a mountain which has no valley.
>
> But although I cannot really conceive of a God without existence any more than a mountain without a valley, still from the fact that I conceive of a mountain with a valley, it does not follow that there is such a mountain in the world; similarly although I conceive of God as possessing existence, it would seem that it does not follow that there is a God which exists; for my thought does not impose any necessity upon things, and just as I may imagine a winged horse, although no horse with wings exists, so I could perhaps attribute existence to God, although no God existed.

---

ontological argument

An attempt to prove the existence of God either by referring to the meaning of the word *God* when it is understood a certain way or by referring to the purportedly unique quality of the concept of God.

From the "I conquer" applied to the Aztec and Inca world and all America, from the "I enslave" applied to Africans sold for gold and silver acquired at the cost of the death of the Amerindians working in the depths of the earth, from the "I vanquish" of the wars of India and China to the shameful "opium war"— from this "I" appears the Cartesian ego cogito. . . .

ENRIQUE DUSSEL

But a sophism is concealed in this objection; for from the fact that I cannot conceive a mountain without a valley, it does not follow that there is any mountain or any valley in existence, but only that the mountain and the valley, whether they exist or do not exist, cannot in any way be separated one from the other. While from the fact that I cannot conceive God without existence, it follows that existence is inseparable from Him, and hence that He really exists; not that my thought can bring this to pass, or impose any necessity on things, but, on the contrary, because the necessity which lies in the thing itself, i.e. the necessity of the existence of God determines me to think in this way. For it is not within my power to think of God without existence (that is of a supremely perfect Being devoid of a supreme perfection) though it is in my power to imagine a horse either with wings or without wings.[21]

PHILOSOPHICAL QUERY

● ● ● ● ● ●

Some philosophers doubt that we really do have a clear and distinct (precise) idea of God. Reflect on the idea of God. Is it clear and distinct? Do you have a clear and distinct idea of perfection—in beings or automobiles or marriages or anything? Does Descartes's argument?

Reconstructing the World

Having shown that at least one mind (his own) and God exist, Descartes concludes his project by reestablishing knowledge of the objective existence of the external world:

> Nothing further now remains but to inquire whether material things exist. . . . And certainly I at least know that these may exist. . . . For there is no doubt that God possesses the power to produce everything that I am capable of perceiving with distinctness.[22]

Descartes reasons that since he has a clear and distinct idea of himself *both as a mind and as having a body,* he must of necessity be both a mind and a body. But the idea of being both mind and body is neither innate nor known to be true with deductive certainty. Thus, the idea of the body must originate outside Descartes's mind.

> And . . . because I know that all things which I apprehend clearly and distinctly can be created by God as I apprehend them, it suffices that I am able to apprehend one thing apart from another clearly and distinctly in order to be certain that one is different from the other, since they may be made to exist in separation at least by the omnipotence of God. . . . On the one side, I have a clear and distinct idea of myself inasmuch as I am only a thinking and unextended thing, and as, on the other, I possess a distinct idea of body, inasmuch as it is only an extended and unthinking thing, it is certain that this I [that is to say, my soul by which I am what I am], is entirely and absolutely distinct from my body and can exist without it.

Descartes' Meditations probably rivals Plato's Republic as the work most frequently read or recommended as an introduction to philosophy.

ALEXANDER SESONSKE
AND NOEL FLEMING

... But, since God is no deceiver, it is very manifest that He does not communicate to me these ideas immediately and by Himself. ... I do not see how He could be defended from the accusation of deceit if these ideas were produced by causes other than corporeal objects. Hence we must allow that corporeal things exist.[23]

Descartes reasoned that his own ideas of body and mind must be basically sound, since God allowed him to know clearly and distinctly that he is both. At this point, the Cartesian Genesis is essentially complete. All that remains are the details of reconstructing knowledge of the world on a solid base by carefully following the rules of method.

▪ THE CARTESIAN BRIDGE ▪

materialism (behaviorism, mechanism, reductionism)
Belief that everything is composed of matter (and energy) and can be explained by physical laws, that all human activity can be understood as the natural behavior of matter according to mechanical laws, and that thinking is merely a complex form of behaving: The body is a fleshy machine.

Descartes was a devout Catholic who took his religion seriously. He was aware of the challenge to religion posed by advances in physics and astronomy and the reemergence of **materialism** (also known as **behaviorism, mechanism,** or **reductionism**). Other philosophers, most notably Thomas Hobbes (1588–1679), were arguing that everything is composed of matter (and energy) and can be explained by physical laws. This means all human activity can be understood as the natural behavior of matter according to mechanical laws. Thus, thinking is merely a complex form of behaving, and the body is a fleshy machine. The so-called mind can be reduced to the brain, and thinking and acting can be reduced to biochemical brain states and stimulus-response reactions. Since the laws of physics are universal, there can be no such thing as a free will. If everything is material, there can be no such thing as an immaterial soul. (This point of view, which is held by many scientists and philosophers today, will be discussed more fully in Chapter 10.)

dualism
Any philosophical position that divides existence into two completely distinct, independent, unique substances.

Like the theologians, Descartes was alarmed by the amoral, secular nature of this particular view of the universe. Yet, as we have noted, he was a scientist himself, and his philosophy was designed to bridge the growing gap between the "new science" and religion. By showing that the mind is different in kind from the body, Descartes hoped to prove that the discoveries of the physicists posed no threat to free will or the existence of an incorporeal soul. The laws of physics apply only to matter, but the mind (soul) is an incorporeal thinking substance. Mind and body are two completely different kinds of substances. Thus, science turns out to be the language of bodies; it cannot address minds or souls, so it is no threat to the church or basic Christian theology.

monism
General name for the belief that everything consists of only one, ultimate, unique substance such as matter or spirit.

Cartesian Dualism

Any philosophical position that divides existence into two completely distinct, independent, unique substances or kinds of things is a form of **dualism**. The distinction can be between mind and body, natural and supernatural, spirit and matter, soul and body, good and evil, and so on. (**Monism** is the general name for the belief that everything consists of only one, ultimate, unique substance, such as matter; **pluralism** is the name for the belief in more than one substance.)

pluralism
The belief that more than one reality or substance exists.

Cartesian dualism refers to Descartes's conviction that human beings are a mysterious union of mind (soul) and body, of incorporeal substance and corporeal substance, with each realm operating according to separate sets of laws. The mind follows the laws of reason but otherwise is free. The body is governed by the laws of physics and falls under the rule of cause and effect: The human body is no freer than any other material thing. The soul is somehow dispersed to all parts of the body, but thinking enters the brain through the pineal gland.

> And as a clock composed of wheels and counter-weights no less exactly observes the laws of nature . . . if I consider the body of a man as being a sort of machine so built up and composed of nerves, muscles, veins, blood, and skin, that though there were no mind in it at all, it would not cease to have made the same motions as at present, exception being made of those movements which are due to the direction of the will, and in consequence depend upon the mind.[24]

If we can understand thinking without ever referring to the body, and if we can understand the body without ever referring to the mind/soul, then minds and bodies are essentially independent of each other. Science can study bodies and the natural world without ever treading in theology. Initially, this rationale seems satisfactory. Indeed, it fits the commonsense view of Christian theology and ordinary experience. Thus, Cartesian dualism allows for the doctrine of the soul's continued existence after the body's death. Further, by defining himself as *thinking substance* rather than corporeal, Descartes reaffirms the primacy of the soul over the body. Human beings are essentially spiritual beings who happen to inhabit bodies. As a devout believer, Descartes appears to have found a way to salvage his faith from the threats of purely materialistic science. As a scientist, he has freed science to progress without church interference, since scientific discoveries are about the body and have no real bearing on the nature of the soul.

There is no simple entity that you can point to and say: this entity is physical and not mental.

BERTRAND RUSSELL

The Mind–Body Problem

Dualism generates one of the most tenacious of philosophical questions: What is the relationship of the mind to the body? Yet so appealing is dualism to philosophers, preachers, psychologists, and most of the rest of us that in his influential and controversial book, *The Concept of Mind,* contemporary philosopher Gilbert Ryle refers to it simply as "the official doctrine." Ryle says:

> The official doctrine, which hails chiefly from Descartes, is something like this. With the doubtful exceptions of idiots and infants in arms every human being has both a body and a mind. Some would prefer to say that every human being is both a body and a mind. His body and his mind are ordinarily harnessed together, but after the death of the body his mind may continue to exist and function.[25]

Corollaries of the official doctrine are found in beliefs about the immortality of the soul and reincarnation. Corollaries are implicit in psychological theories that view the mind as something other than the brain and that differentiate mental states from bodily conditions and behavior. The official doctrine is reflected in ordinary language when we talk about *having* a body and in common experience when we feel as if "we" are somehow *in* our bodies.

Such a dualistic mode of perception not only impedes a holistic theory of liberation, but it is also substantially responsible for constructing the very world of alienation from which we seek liberation . . . operating on three levels: (1) alienation from oneself; one's own body; (2) alienation from one's fellow person in the "alien" community; (3) alienation from the "world": from the visible earth and sky.

ROSEMARY RADFORD RUETHER

Darrow's Trip to Goofville

If I am told that next week I shall start on a trip to Goofville; that I shall not take my body with me; that I shall stay for all eternity: can I find a single fact connected with my journey—the way I shall go, the part of me that is to go, the time of the journey, the country I shall reach, its location in space, the way I shall live there—or anything that would lead to a rational belief that I shall really take the trip? Have I ever known anyone who has made the journey and returned? If I am really to believe, I must try to get some information about all these important facts.

Clarence Darrow, "The Myth of the Soul," *The Forum* 80 (October 1928).

Religious and metaphysical versions of the official doctrine sometimes compare the soul to a driver and the body to a car. At death, we get out of the car or—if you believe in reincarnation—trade the old body in for a new one. Descartes rejects the car–driver type of analogy and unites mind and body into "one whole."

> Nature also teaches me by these sensations of pain, hunger, thirst, etc., that I am not only lodged in my body as a pilot in a vessel, but that I am very closely united to it, and so to speak so intermingled with it that I seem to compose with it one whole. For if that were not the case, when my body is hurt, I who am merely a thinking thing, should not feel pain, for I should perceive this wound by the understanding only, just as a sailor perceives by sight when something is damaged in his vessel; and when my body has need of drink or food, I should clearly understand the fact without being warned of it by confused feelings of hunger and thirst. For all these sensations of hunger, thirst, pain, etc., are in truth none other than certain confused modes of thought which are produced by the union and intermingling of mind and body.[26]

There does seem to be, so far as science is concerned, nothing in the world but complex arrangements of physical constituents. All except for one place: consciousness.

J. J. C. SMART

(The "union" or "intermingling" occurs, as noted earlier, in the pineal gland. Descartes apparently devoted some time to dissecting animal carcasses in order to study this mysterious gland.)

Dualism *feels consistent* with certain common experiences, but inconsistent with others: If I hit my thumb with a hammer, I experience no mind–body split. Yet there are serious consequences if we reject dualism in favor of a materialistic, behavioristic monism: When we reduce mental states to physical states, do we lose the possibility of free will, moral responsibility, and the possibility of survival after death? Such beliefs are important to the very meaning of life for many people, real enough and important enough so that any difficulties of *explaining* mind–body interaction pale beside the consequences of rejecting dualism.

The relation between the body and the mind is so intimate that, if either of them got out of order, the whole system would suffer.

MOHANDAS GANDHI

But the fact that millions of people believe something does not make it true. Cartesian dualism—indeed, metaphysical speculation itself—stands in direct opposition to another major modern philosophical archetype: the skeptical questioner who turns to experience rather than to the mind for knowledge. The skeptic is the subject of Chapter 10. Chapters 14–17 deal with existential and postmodern rejection of abstract metaphysics.

PHILOSOPHICAL

QUERY

● ● ● ● ● ●

How plausible is this "official doctrine"? On Descartes's own terms, how "clearly and distinctly" do we understand the relationship of the mind to the body? How can a completely nonphysical thing interact with a completely physical thing? To ask Mark Twain's insightful question, How come the mind gets drunk when the body does the drinking? Why does my mind react to what happens to my body with such intensity if it's not part of my body?

■ FROM COSMOS TO MACHINE ■

As noted in Chapter 3, ancient Greek philosophy developed in a series of increasingly abstract steps, until growing concern with logical consistency and rules of thinking led to theories that, though logically consistent, did not match observed facts.[27] One result of this split between common experience and the claims of early philosophers was the alienation of philosophy from the life concerns of most people. Historian of philosophy Amaury de Riencourt says, "The absolute predominance of the dissociating, analytical masculine principle in Greek thought is obvious—hence its strength and its weakness."[28]

As the early Greeks developed and refined rational skills, they increasingly valued personal detachment and the suppression of traits that today we associate with maternal and caring qualities. Objectivity and emotional detachment—qualities traditionally associated with masculinity—were considered essential aspects of knowledge, and subjectivity and emotional involvement were considered hindrances.

According to feminist philosopher of culture **Susan Bordo** (b. 1947), this "masculinizing" of philosophical thought reached a watershed at the beginning of the modern period. In *The Flight to Objectivity: Essays on Cartesianism and Culture*, Bordo argues that "Cartesian modernity is inherently linked to the repression of nature and women."[29] This repression, she suggests, is motivated by revulsion and uneasiness that modernity has traditionally associated with the daily lives of women.[30] Women's lives are circumscribed by menstruation, childbirth, nursing, caring for others. In short, women's experiences are *embodied* experiences that cannot be abstracted into distinct mental and physical substances. Bordo's point is that the daily lives of women do not reflect Cartesian dualism.

Bordo's critique of modern philosophy adds a feminist perspective to the radical sorts of criticism brought to bear on objectivity and rationality by Marx, Kierkegaard, James, and Nietzsche. (See Chapters 13–16.)

We are all familiar with the dominant Cartesian themes of starting anew, alone, without influence from the past or other people, with the guidance of reason alone.

SUSAN BORDO

Susan Bordo

PHILOSOPHICAL

QUERY

● ● ● ● ● ●

Do you think that Cartesian dualism reflects men's lives more than women's? Do you think Cartesian dualism reflects anyone's life?

According to Bordo, modernity rests on Descartes's attempt to *reconstruct the world* based solely on his own clear and distinct ideas. She says, "We are all familiar

"None Strive to Grasp What They Already Know"

In a remarkably insightful and timeless passage, the Taoist sage Chuang-tzu speaks across generations and cultures:

> There is often chaos in the world, and the love of knowledge is ever at the bottom of it. For all men strive to grasp what they do not know, while none strive to grasp what they already know. . . . Thus, above, the splendor of the heavenly bodies is dimmed; below, the power of land and water is burned up, while in between the influence of the four seasons is upset. There is not one tiny worm that moves on earth or an insect that flies in the air but has lost its original nature. Such indeed is the world chaos caused by the desire for knowledge!

Chuang-tzu, *The Wisdom of Laotse,* trans. and ed. Lin Yutang (New York: Modern Library, 1976), p. 287.

A sword that repelled a huge army in days past is no longer useful. Similarly, some of the dictums of the people of old may no longer be applicable in today's world.

LIE ZI

with the dominant Cartesian themes of starting anew, alone, without influence from the past or other people, with the guidance of reason alone."[31] The result, Bordo argues, is that *objectivity,* rather than *meaning,* became the chief philosophical issue. But as long as human beings are "embedded in nature," embodied and subject to its rhythms, such detachment is impossible.

In Bordo's view, Descartes's particular genius was the way in which he laid a philosophical foundation for transforming the initial experience of alienation and loss that accompanied the Copernican Revolution into an optimistic, objective method for understanding, dominating, and managing nature. (See the Overview of Modern Themes.) According to Bordo, Cartesian rationalism required sundering the organic ties between the person (subject) and the world (object). As Bordo sees it, starting with Descartes, modern philosophy reacted to the new cosmic order with an exaggerated emphasis on objectivism and mechanism. As a result, the modern vision of the universe is one of a complex machine, not an organic whole (cosmos):

> This re-visioning of the universe as a *machine*—most often, a clockwork— was not the work of philosophers alone. Astronomy and anatomy had already changed the dominant picture of the movements of the heavens and the processes of the body by the time the *Meditations* were written. But it was philosophy . . . that provided the cosmology that integrated these discoveries into a consistent and unified view of nature. . . . Nature became *defined* by its lack of affiliation with divinity, with spirit. All that which is god-like or spiritual—freedom, will, and sentience—belong entirely and exclusively to *res cogitans* [the thing that thinks]. All else—the earth, the heavens, animals, the human body—is merely mechanically interacting matter.[32]

If a kind of Cartesian ideal were ever completely fulfilled, i.e., if the whole of nature were only what can be explained in terms of mathematical relationships—then we would look at the world with that fearful sense of alienation, with that utter loss of reality with which a future schizophrenic child looks at his mother. A machine cannot give birth.

KARL STERN

Bordo goes on to suggest that the masculinization of science involves more than just the historical fact of male dominance of the sciences, noting that "the most interesting contemporary discussions of the 'masculinist' nature of modern science describe a . . . characteristic cognitive style, an epistemological stance which is required of men *and* women working in the sciences today."[33] Bordo does not, however, see modernity as entirely negative:

Inspired by the work of [Carol] Gilligan, [Nancy] Chodorow, [Susan] Harding, and [Evelyn Fox] Keller, feminist theory has been systematically questioning the historical identification of rationality, intelligence, "good thinking," and so forth, with the masculine modes of detachment and clarity, offering alternative models of fresher, more humane, and more hopeful approaches to science and ethics.[34]

If Bordo and other critics of depersonalization are generally correct (see Chapters 13–17), the scientific, technological, and cultural advances generated by modern science and philosophy carry a high price. This price includes widespread alienation from the natural world; fear and revulsion in the face of "messy" aspects of life such as birthing, caring, and dying; and the trivialization of the family in the name of "justice" and "objectivity."

▪ COMMENTARY ▪

Descartes's rationalism was inspired by a vision and three dreams, which he interpreted as a divine calling to establish his method of rational inquiry. Through the innovative use of methodic doubt, he established one irrefutable certainty, the cogito. Descartes claimed that God's existence was the foundation for all knowledge and for the general reliability of the "natural light" of reason, yet, for the contemporary observer, the cogito is more solidly grounded than the proof for God.

To a considerable extent, the modern era is grounded in Cartesian self-consciousness, self-reflection, and self-analysis. In its emphasis on an individual's inquiry after truth rather than official answers, Cartesian rationalism seems to pave the way for social and political democracy. The irony in this is that we note a kind of cool, analytic detachment as Descartes makes himself the subject of study in a new way. As the modern era develops, purity of method ultimately takes precedence over the search for wisdom. This trend might be a consequence of the detached, depersonalized quality of rationalistic analysis that emerged in the work of Descartes.

The benefits of the Cartesian revolution include the use of clearer, simpler, ordinary language (an idea that significantly influenced subsequent philosophers). Descartes paved the way for psychological studies by showing that the "thinking thing" is not a neutral "window," but a dynamic entity whose very nature affects its observations and conclusions. He initiated the study of knowledge and the sources of knowledge that continues to this day. Even the rationalists' great epistemological opponents, the empiricists, found themselves responding partly to issues raised by rationalism.

Unlike others of his time (and ours), Descartes refused to bow before authority, choosing to accept only what he knew for himself. He stands out as an archetype of the rationalist for his unwillingness to settle for inconsistencies and contradictions between his faith and his intellect. If his notion of "clear and distinct" is itself cloudy, if his introduction of God is suspicious, and if his attempt to account for mind–body interaction is unsatisfying, he is nonetheless remarkable for squarely facing up to the need to reassess his belief system for himself. Descartes tried not to believe what he could not clearly understand. That in itself is a remarkable achievement.

If I write in French, which is the language of my country, rather than in Latin, which is that of my teachers, that is because I hope that those who avail themselves only of their natural reason in its purity may be better judges of my opinions than those who believe only in the writings of the ancients . . . those who unite good sense with study . . . alone I crave for my judges.

RENÉ DESCARTES

■ SUMMARY OF MAIN POINTS ■

● Descartes's scientific and mathematical interests demanded clear, provable evidence of a sort lacking in Scholasticism's cumbersome reliance on authority and resulted in a radical proposal: Start fresh; throw out everything we think we know and build a system based entirely on ideas whose truth can be clearly and distinctly known to us firsthand. Rationalists rely on the coherence theory of truth: New or unclear ideas are evaluated in terms of rational or logical consistency and in relation to already established truths.

● Reliance on reason as the ultimate source of knowledge is a form of rationalism, the notion that abstract reasoning can produce absolutely certain truths about reality and that some important ultimate truths can be discovered without observation, experiment, or experience. Such truths are known as innate ideas or *a priori* ideas. Ideas derived from experience are known as *a posteriori* ideas.

● Descartes's interest in the "thinking thing itself" was the first major step in a shift in emphasis in modern philosophy from metaphysics to epistemology. He recognized the need for orderly thinking, which he called *method*. This paved the way for the modern emphasis on technique (method) and marks a major change from metaphysical, authoritarian medieval thinking to epistemological, technical modern thinking.

● Descartes employed *methodic doubt* in his effort to find one absolutely certain and undoubtable idea. Methodic doubt is a form of skepticism that rejects any idea that could possibly be false, no matter how remote that possibility. Methodic doubt coupled with the concept of the evil genius led Descartes to raise questions about whether or not he was dreaming and about the existence of his own body and of the entire external world.

● Even an evil genius could not shake one fundamental idea: "I think, therefore I am." This is known as the cogito. Having found an undoubtable truth, Descartes tried to build a reliable foundation for knowledge on the innate idea of God. He did this by appealing to an argument that attempts to prove the existence of God by showing that the idea "God" cannot be derived from human experience; it can only come from the actual existence of God.

● Having established the existence of God to his satisfaction, Descartes believed he had clearly and distinctly demonstrated the reliability of reason and the possibility of certain knowledge, since if God is all-knowing, all-good, and all-powerful, He would not let us live in constant ignorance.

● Descartes rejected the materialists' challenge to the notion of free will with Cartesian dualism, the belief that two completely different kinds of things exist, bodies and minds, and that human beings are a mysterious union of both. Dualism, however, generates the mind–body problem: What is the relationship of the mind to the body? How can a nonmaterial thing (mind) affect a material thing (body)?

● According to Susan Bordo, a "masculinizing" of modern philosophical thought reached a watershed at the beginning of the modern period. Bordo asserts that Cartesian modernity is inherently linked to the repression of both nature and women. Bordo argues that the daily lives of women do not reflect Cartesian dualism because women's experiences are embodied experiences that cannot be abstracted into distinct mental and physical substances.

■ POST-READING REFLECTIONS ■

Now that you have had a chance to learn about the Rationalist, use your new knowledge to answer these questions.

1. What was Descartes's proposal, and how did his Scholastic education influence it?

2. Give a brief summary of the role methodic doubt plays in Descartes's overall effort to discover certain knowledge.

3. How is skepticism important to Cartesian philosophy?

4. What is the evil genius, and what is its significance to the Cartesian Genesis?

5. Can the Evil Genius refute the cogito? Is there any way to "refute" the cogito?

6. Give Descartes's argument for the existence of God in your own words, then analyze it. Is it convincing? Why or why not?

7. How did Descartes answer the materialists' rejection of free will?

8. What is the mind–body problem? How does Descartes deal with it? Is he successful? Why or why not?

PHILOSOPHY INTERNET RESOURCES

Go to the Soccio Web page at **http://philosophy.wadsworth.com/ Soccio7e** for Web links, practice quizzes and tests, a pronunciation guide, and study tips.

THE SKEPTIC

David Hume

I AM UNEASY TO THINK I APPROVE OF ONE OBJECT,
AND DISAPPROVE OF ANOTHER; CALL ONE THING BEAUTIFUL,
AND ANOTHER DEFORM'D; DECIDE CONCERNING TRUTH
AND FALSEHOOD, REASON AND FOLLY, WITHOUT KNOWING
UPON WHAT PRINCIPLES I PROCEED.

David Hume

FOR YOUR REFLECTION

KEEP THESE QUESTIONS IN MIND AS YOU LEARN ABOUT THE SKEPTIC.

1. *What is a skeptic?*
2. *What is empiricism?*
3. *What is the "epistemological turn"?*
4. *What is the correspondence theory of truth?*
5. *How do primary qualities differ from secondary qualities?*
6. *What is idealism (immaterialism)?*
7. *What is "epistemological dualism"?*
8. *What is the difference between impressions and ideas?*
9. *What is the "empirical criterion of meaning"?*
10. *What is the bundle theory of the self?*
11. *What is inductive reasoning?*

FOR DEEPER CONSIDERATION

A. How did distinguishing between the knower and the known generate Locke's egocentric predicament? Is the predicament an inescapable feature of strict empiricism? Is there any way to get beyond my own sensations and establish solid (nonsubjective) knowledge of things-in-themselves, knowledge of an "objective" reality? How?

B. When he died, there was a commonly held belief that David Hume was an atheist. Why did so many people think that he was an atheist (a notion that is still widely held by those who only know a smattering of his philosophy)? That is, what ideas did he espouse that might lead to such a conclusion? And if he wasn't an atheist, what position did he hold in regard to God's existence and nature—and why is that position possibly more troubling than atheism?

A friend of mine once told me that her third cousin could move objects by psychokinesis—that is, by mind power. She insisted that she had seen him send ashtrays and glasses across a room, without touching them or leaving his chair, merely by concentrating very deeply. I was intrigued, because I had known this woman for years, and she seemed intelligent and sane to me—yet I had never seen such a phenomenon for myself. I asked to be allowed to witness this amazing feat, but was told that, sadly, this remarkable individual had died some years before. This did not surprise me, and I may have been too blunt in saying so. "You don't believe me, do you?" my friend said, obviously annoyed with me. "You never believe anything! You're too skeptical."

A **skeptic** is a person who demands clear, observable, *undoubtable* evidence—based on experience—before accepting any knowledge claim as true. The word *skepticism* (from the Greek *skeptesthai,* "to consider or examine") refers to both a school of philosophy and a general attitude. Originally, a skeptic was a special kind of doubter, one who withheld judgment while waiting for better evidence. Sextus Empiricus (c. 200) even devised a *skeptical grammar,* which ends every proposition with "so it seems to me at the moment." There are variations of skepticism, progressing from total doubt about everything to temporary or particular doubt invoked just for the process of analysis—what Descartes called "methodic doubt" (Chapter 9).

My friend's reaction was common: She took my demand for firsthand evidence personally. That is, she interpreted it as an attack on her integrity. She would have preferred that I accept her claim as true simply because we were friends. I have reacted to requests for evidence the same way myself. Yet if we are seriously interested in the pursuit of truth in general, or in the truth of a specific claim, we must demand more than the personal testimony of others, no matter how sincerely they may give it or how much we may care for them.

skeptic

From the Greek *skeptesthai,* "to consider or examine"; a person who demands clear, observable, undoubtable evidence before accepting any knowledge claim as true.

● ● ● ● ● ●

Have you ever been angry or insulted when someone pressed you for evidence? Or has anyone ever gotten angry with you for asking for evidence? Why do you suppose that is? Is it rude to ask "How do you know that?" or "Can you prove that?" when people make claims about important, or even not so important, things? Analyze this question and see if you can justify not asking for evidence.

PHILOSOPHICAL

QUERY

Scepticism is . . . a form of belief. Dogma cannot be abandoned; it can only be revised in view of some more elementary dogma which it has not yet occurred to the sceptic to doubt; and he may be right in every point of his criticism, except in fancying that his criticism is radical and that he is altogether a sceptic.

GEORGE SANTAYANA

Standards of evidence vary with conditions. The more important the issue is, the stricter our standards must be. And the more important the issue is, the greater is our obligation to demand evidence. Expertise and training—as well as time, interest, and ability—also matter when we are justifying our beliefs. Ideally, we should accept as true only what we can verify for ourselves. Often, however, we must rely on the testimony of qualified experts, but this differs considerably from relying on unverified testimony. My friend was not qualified to determine the genuineness of psychic experience. Accepting her claim at face value would have been unreasonable; it would require discounting my own experience without ever having seen the phenomenon for myself or having read about incontrovertible, repeatable, carefully controlled cases of similar powers.

Yet consider how rarely we demand good evidence for beliefs and knowledge claims. We buy so-called health foods on the recommendation of neighbors and fellow students. Political candidates make claims about education, the environment, even moral values. Automobile manufacturers make claims for the reliability and safety of their vehicles. Political action groups make claims concerning abortions, racial prejudice, toxic effects, crime rates, drugs, and so forth. How often have you asked for verification of such claims? When a salesperson makes claims about this refrigerator or that DVD player, do you ask for supporting data?

All of these issues involve knowledge claims. In technical language, they are *epistemological issues*. The study of the theory of knowledge, **epistemology,** is the branch of philosophy concerned with the origins, quality, nature, and reliability of knowledge. Beginning with Descartes, Western philosophy has been dominated by epistemological issues.

epistemology

Branch of philosophy that studies the nature and possibility of knowledge.

PHILOSOPHICAL

QUERY

• • • • • •

Who is a qualified expert in areas such as psychic phenomena, miracles, nutrition, or philosophy? What is the relationship between the reports of experts and your own experience? When the two conflict, which should you trust? Why? How do you know?

■ JOHN LOCKE ■

Attempts to answer fundamental epistemological questions gave rise to the two major orientations of modern philosophy. The first, as we learned in Chapter 9, is rationalism. The other is known as **empiricism,** from the Greek root *empeiria*, meaning "experience."

Empiricists believe that all ideas can be traced back to *sense data*. Abstractions and complex beliefs are said to be combinations and mental alterations of original impressions and perceptions, as when, for example, we imagine a man with a horse's head. Empiricists believe that reason is unable to provide knowledge of reality; such knowledge can only be derived from experience. The strictest empiricists believe that even mathematical and logical principles are derived from experience. A potent form of empiricism emerged with the advent of modern philosophy. Because its three founding philosophers were all British, it has come to be called *British empiricism*.

The earliest of the three British empiricists, **John Locke** (1632–1704), was disturbed by the confusion and uncertainty surrounding seventeenth-century philosophy and theology. Like Descartes, he was troubled by Scholastic philosophy (Chapter 8), which he had encountered as a student at Oxford. He was especially critical of its emphasis on formal disputations and debates, which he said were "invented for wrangling and ostentation, rather than to discover

empiricism

Belief that all knowledge is ultimately derived from the senses (experience) and that all ideas can be traced to sense data.

John Locke

the truth." Locke's *An Essay Concerning Human Understanding,* published in 1690, established the groundwork for empiricism as it is generally understood today.

Educated as a physician, Locke was aware of the great changes and progress being generated by science. Trained to rely on his own powers of perception, he pointed out that as a physician you cannot "wait until you have reached mathematical certainty about the correct treatment" before helping a patient. You have to observe and act based on what you perceive. You must turn to the facts.[1]

In the winter of 1670, Locke had a series of philosophical discussions concerning morality and religion with some friends. It wasn't long before the friends found themselves confused and puzzled. Their inability to reach clearly right or wrong answers—in the way a chemist or baker often can—had a profound effect on Locke. He realized he had to take a step back and examine the nature and limits of knowledge before trying to sort out the truth or falsity of specific ideas:

> After we had awhile puzzled ourselves, without coming any nearer a resolution of those doubts which perplexed us, it came into my thoughts that we took a wrong course; and that before we set ourselves upon inquiries of that nature, it was necessary to examine my own abilities, and see what *objects* our understanding were, or were not, fitted to deal with.[2]

Without some clear idea of the ultimate source of knowledge in a given area, we have little hope for resolving philosophical agreements. If you have ever been involved in a nearly endless and unsettled disagreement over social, moral, political, or religious issues at some casual gathering, you know what Locke experienced. Each person seems to have an unstated set of rules and assumptions regarding what is obviously true and what is ridiculous, which sources of information are reliable and which are not. Without a clearly stated and agreed-upon set of basic principles, such discussions often amount to nothing more than each person repeatedly affirming a set of favored beliefs and denouncing all others.

Locke's solution was to study the origins of our ideas to better understand the nature and process of acquiring knowledge. He hoped he could thereby find a way to settle difficult issues. Although his philosophy contains its own inconsistencies, Locke initiated an emphasis on logical rigor and analytic precision that would shake the foundations of many of our most cherished beliefs. He began by calling for philosophers to refocus their attention "outward," on experience.

Experience Is the Origin of All Ideas

According to Locke, all *ideas* originate in *sensation* and *reflection*. Specifically, he says we can think about things only *after we have experienced them*. In other words, all ideas originate from sense data. For example, no one born blind can ever have an idea of color, according to this theory. Those of us who are sighted "abstract" the *idea of color* from specific sense data by reflecting on, say, red, green, yellow, and blue circles. In doing so, we note that they have two common qualities,

Let us then suppose the Mind to be, as we say, a White Paper, void of all Characters, without any Ideas; How comes it to be furnished? . . . To this I answer in one word, From Experience

JOHN LOCKE

Scepticism, while logically impeccable, is psychologically impossible, and there is an element of frivolous insincerity in any philosophy which pretends to accept it.

BERTRAND RUSSELL

Reason is, and ought only to be the slave of passions, and can never pretend to any other office than to serve and obey them.

DAVID HUME

circularity and color. Our blind friend can trace their shape and thus acquire sensations of circularity, but color, which is only perceived through sight, will remain unknown.

As part of his empirical inquiry into the nature of human understanding, Locke attempted to explain and classify different kinds of ideas and the ways we arrange sense data from simple into increasingly complex and abstract ideas. He insisted that all ideas are *copies* of the things that caused the basic sensations on which they rest. Ideas are less intense copies, or images, of sensations. Your idea of a baseball, for example, is a copy of the set of sensations and impressions you have received from seeing and handling actual baseballs. If your idea of a baseball includes the shape of a cube, it is a poor copy. It does not *correspond* to reality.

This position is known as the *copy theory* or *representation theory* or, most recently, **correspondence theory of truth,** a term attributed to contemporary philosopher Bertrand Russell. The correspondence theory of truth is a truth test that holds that an idea (or belief or thought) is true if whatever it refers to actually exists. In other words, an idea is defined as true if it corresponds to a fact. The procedure for checking the truth of an idea is called *confirmation* or *verification* (see Chapter 17).

Favored by empiricists, the correspondence theory of truth is in direct contrast with the *coherence theory of truth* favored by rationalists (see Chapter 9) and differs from the other major truth theory, the *pragmatic theory of truth* (see Chapter 15).

correspondence (copy or representation) theory of truth
Truth test that holds that an idea (or belief or thought) is true if whatever it refers to actually exists (corresponds to a fact).

Locke's Rejection of Innate Ideas

In Chapter 9, we learned that Descartes, as a rationalist, believed in a special class of ideas known as **a priori** or **innate ideas.** So-called innate ideas are truths that are not derived from observation or experience; they are characterized as being certain, deductive, universally true, and independent of all experience. Examples of innate ideas include mathematical equivalences, such as "2 + 3 = 5," and deductive principles of reason, such as "Every event has a cause" and "All triangles contain 180°."

In the *Meditations*, Descartes based a major part of his case for the certainty of reason—as well as for general reliability of the senses and knowledge of the existence of an external world—on the clarity and distinctness of "the innate idea of God." (See pages 261–265.) But if Locke's view proves to be the correct one, Descartes's entire project collapses. Whereas Descartes's prototype of reason was modeled after mathematical (deductive) reasoning, Locke's model was fashioned from his experiences as a physician.

In Locke's estimation, Cartesian-style speculation (abstract thinking modeled after geometric method) can at best "amuse our understanding with fine and useless speculations." It cannot, however, adequately deal with concrete problems. When used for more than amusement, Cartesian-type reasoning is dangerous because it distracts "our inquiries from the true and advantageous knowledge of things." All that can result from such "idle speculation," suggests Locke, is "to enlarge the art of talking and perhaps [lay] a foundation for endless disputes."

innate ideas (*a priori* ideas)
Truths that are not derived from observation or experiment; characterized as being certain, deductive, universally true, and independent of all experience.

It cannot provide useful knowledge, the way, say, Isaac Newton's new scientific reasoning could.[3]

Locke accused the rationalists of labeling their pet ideas "innate" in order to convince others to accept them secondhand, without question:

> We may as rationally hope to see with other men's eyes, as to know by other men's understandings. So much as we ourselves consider and comprehend of truth and reason, so much we possess of real and true knowledge. The floating of other men's opinions in our brains, makes us not one jot the more knowing, though they happen to be true.
>
> When men have found some general propositions that could not be doubted of as soon as understood, it was, I know, a short and easy way to conclude them innate. This being once received, it eased the lazy from the pains of search, and stopped the inquiry of the doubtful concerning all that was once styled innate. And it was of no small advantage to those who affected to be masters and teachers, to make this the principle of principles,—*that principles must not be questioned.* . . . [This] put their followers upon . . . [a] posture of blind credulity.[4]

From Locke's point of view, Descartes's attempt to introduce a method of inquiry that would free us from the dogmatic shackles of Scholasticism merely results in another dogmatism, a rationalistic one.

Locke argued that without appealing to the ultimate test of experience, reason has no "ground," or standard, for distinguishing truth from fantasy. Modifying a characterization used by some rationalistic philosophers, who compared the mind to a pantry well stocked with "innate ideas," Locke suggested that the mind is better compared to an empty pantry, waiting to be stocked by experience.[5] But Locke's most famous comparison was to describe the mind at birth as a completely blank tablet, or clean slate, a **tabula rasa,** to use the Latin equivalent:

> *All ideas come from sensations or reflection*—Let us then suppose the mind to be, as we say, white paper, void of all characters, without any ideas:—How comes it to be furnished? . . . Whence has it all the *materials* of reason and knowledge? To this I answer, in one word, from EXPERIENCE. In that all our knowledge is founded; and from that it ultimately derives itself.[6]

Locke's Dualism

Although Locke rejected Descartes's theory of innate ideas, he did agree with Descartes that "something substantial" underlies and holds together the sensible qualities of experience (color, taste, size, shape, location, sound, motion, and such). This substantial something is *substance,* a complex idea according to Locke.

> The mind being, as I have declared, furnished with a great number of simple ideas, conveyed in by the senses as they are found in exterior things, or by reflection on its own operations, takes notice also that a certain number of

Unless some things are certain, it is held, nothing can be even probable.

A. J. AYER

tabula rasa
Latin expression for a "clean slate," used by John Locke to challenge the possibility of innate ideas by characterizing the mind at birth as a blank tablet or clean slate.

Strictly speaking, nothing exists except sensations (and the minds which perceive them).

W. T. STACE

these simple ideas go constantly together; which being presumed to belong to one thing, and words being suited to common apprehensions . . . are called, so united in one subject, by one name; which, by inadvertency, we are apt afterward to talk of and consider as one simple idea, which indeed is a complication of many ideas together: because . . . not imagining how these simple ideas *can* subsist by themselves, we accustom ourselves to suppose some *substratum* wherein they do subsist, and from which they do result, which therefore we call *substance*.[7]

Locke proceeds to argue that we have only an obscure idea of substance "in general." He claims that upon analysis, we have no clear, distinct idea of substance itself, but only a notion of "such qualities which are capable of producing simple ideas in us." Locke says that if pressed to explain "what is the subject wherein colour or weight inheres," all we can offer is "the supposed, but unknown, support of those qualities we find existing, which we imagine cannot subsist . . . without something to support them."[8]

Having affirmed the general idea of substance, Locke next inquires into *kinds of substances.* He reports that observation and experience reveal that certain sorts of simple ideas seem to cluster together. From these clusters of simple ideas, we form ideas of "a man, horse, gold, water," and so on. According to Locke, although philosophers might have trouble describing it, our everyday experiences confirm the existence of substance:

> I appeal to every one's own experience. It is the ordinary qualities observable in iron, or a diamond, put together, that make the true complex idea of those substances, which a smith or a jeweler commonly knows better than a philosopher; who, whatever *substantial forms* he may talk of, has no other idea of those substances, than what is framed by a collection of those ideas which are found in them.[9]

It is genius, and the want of it, that adulterates philosophy, and fills it with error and false theory.

THOMAS REID

According to Locke, the substance that holds "extended things" together, things known through sensible qualities, is *matter.* Locke claims that upon reflection, the "same thing happens concerning the operations of the mind, viz. thinking, reasoning, fearing, &c." That is, we identify a "thinking substance":

> . . . some other *substance,* which we call *spirit;* whereby . . . supposing a substance wherein thinking, knowing, doubting, and a power of moving, &c., do subsist, we have as clear a notion of the substance of spirit, as we have of body; the one being supposed to be (without knowing what it is) the *substratum* to those simple ideas we have from without; and the other supposed (with a like ignorance of what it is) to be the *substratum* to those operations we experiment in ourselves within.[10]

Thus, Locke affirms the existence of two substances: *matter* and *mind.* So, although Locke rejected Descartes's rationalism and theory of innate ideas, he accepted a Cartesian-type of *dualism,* in which mind and matter are viewed as different kinds of substance.

Primary and Secondary Qualities

In addition to distinguishing between two kinds of substance, Locke distinguished between two kinds of qualities. **Primary qualities** are sensible qualities that exist independently of any perceiver. Shape, size, location, and motion are examples of primary qualities. **Secondary qualities** are qualities whose existence depends on a perceiver. Examples of secondary qualities include color, sound, taste, and texture. Thus, we can say that primary qualities are *objective* properties of things; they exist in the *object*. Secondary qualities depend on—"exist in"—a knowing or perceiving *subject;* thus, they are said to be *subjective* properties.

We have seen the importance of this basic objective–subjective distinction many times. It is at the heart of the quarrels between the Sophists and Plato, as well as the earliest efforts of philosophers to identify reality and to distinguish it from appearance. Locke's distinction between primary qualities (located in independently existing material objects) and secondary qualities (located in subjective mental acts and perceptions) is important because so much is riding on it.

If primary qualities do not exist, then what of the possibility of objective knowledge? What can we know of the existence of an independent reality? In other words, some real distinction between primary and secondary qualities *seems* necessary for confirmation of the "world of common sense." The "world of common sense" is simply a term for the widely held view that an objective world exists independently of our perceptions and that it exists "out there" and not simply as a figment of our imaginations or mental construct.

primary qualities
According to Locke, objective sensible qualities that exist independently of any perceiver; shape, size, location, and motion are examples of primary qualities.

secondary qualities
According to Locke, subjective qualities whose existence depends on a perceiver; color, sound, taste, and texture are examples of secondary qualities.

Locke's Egocentric Predicament

Locke holds a position known as **epistemological dualism,** the view that knowing contains two distinct aspects: the knower and the known. Given the basic empiricist premise that all knowledge comes from our own ideas, which in turn are based on our own sensations and perceptions, epistemological dualism presents us with a fundamental problem: If all knowledge comes in the form of my own ideas based on sense data, how can I verify the existence of anything external to the sensations that constitute sense data? That is, won't the very process of verification take place within the realm of my own ideas?

This problem has been termed Locke's **egocentric predicament** because Locke's copy theory seems to put us in the egocentric position of being able to know only a world of our own mental construction, a self-limited world. Indeed: If there is no "external world," can there be any mind other than my own? How could I know? How could I distinguish another mind from my own—if all I ever know are my own subjective perceptions?

And if, as Locke suggests, all true ideas are based on sense data that correspond to something else, how can we ever verify the objective, independent existence of an external reality? How can we ever apply Locke's own standards of verification to his notion of primary qualities?

At this point, it seems as if all I can know are my own perceptions (secondary qualities). As soon as I am *aware* of them, I have labeled and organized

epistemological dualism
The view that knowing consists of two distinct aspects: the knower and the known.

egocentric predicament
Problem generated by epistemological dualism: If all knowledge comes in the form of my own ideas, how can I verify the existence of anything external to them?

"If Physics Is to Be Believed"

We think that the grass is green, the stones are hard, and the snow is cold. But physics assures us that the greenness of the grass, the hardness of the stones, and the coldness of snow are not the greenness, hardness, and coldness that we know in our own experience, but something very different. The observer, when he seems to himself to be observing a stone, is really, if physics is to be believed, observing the effects of the stone upon himself.

Bertrand Russell, *Our Knowledge of the External World as a Field for the Scientific Method in Philosophy* (Chicago: Open Court, 1915).

them. That is, even if external objects exist, the process of perceiving sense data is a process of becoming aware of *my ideas*. I don't ever seem to be able to actually experience *things-in-themselves*. If, as Locke claims, my ideas are "messages" from my senses, how can I—or anyone—verify that the messages come from *independently existing things*? Locke himself asks, "How shall the mind, when it perceives nothing but its own ideas, know that they agree with things themselves?"

Locke tries to avoid the egocentric predicament by asserting that we "somehow know" that mental and physical substances—and an objective external reality—exist. We just don't have a clear idea of the *difference* between minds and bodies or other aspects of ultimate reality:

> Sensation convinces us that there are solid extended substances [matter and bodies]; and reflection that there are thinking ones [minds, souls]; experience assures us of the existence of such beings; and that one has the power to move body by impulse, the other by thought; this we cannot have any doubt of. Experience, I say, every moment furnishes us with clear ideas both of one and of the other. But beyond these ideas, as received from their proper sources, our faculties will not reach.[11]

Suppose that a [plain] man meets a modern philosopher, and wants to be informed what smell in plants is. The philosopher tells him that there is no smell in plants, nor in anything but the mind; that it is impossible there can be smell but in a mind; and that all this hath been demonstrated by modern philosophy. The plain man will, no doubt, be apt to think him merry.

THOMAS REID

In other words, Locke holds on to both a commonsense view of reality *and* his copy theory of truth, even though he cannot verify either by appealing to the copy theory. In spite of his major differences with Descartes, Locke draws surprisingly similar conclusions for similar reasons.

Both Locke and Descartes shied away from pursuing the logical consequences of their basic premises. Descartes was able to establish the momentary certainty of the cogito but had difficulty moving beyond his own mind when he attempted to provide a certain foundation for the external world and God's existence. Locke was able to demonstrate the importance of experience as an element of knowledge and show that many of our ideas are based on sensation and experience. He was also able to show the inadequacy of pure reason as a foundation for all knowledge. But, like Descartes, Locke was unable to move from direct knowledge of his own ideas to direct knowledge of external reality.

Pursued to its logical conclusion, Locke's empiricism does seem to end in the egocentric predicament. If it does, not only are we denied knowledge of an external, independent reality, but we are also denied the possibility of knowing God, for what simple sensations and experiences can there be on which the idea of God rests? Locke chose, in the end, to affirm certain beliefs at the expense of philosophical consistency. The second of the British empiricists tried to be more consistent.

• • • • • •

PHILOSOPHICAL

QUERY

Reflect on the claim that ideas are copies of sensations by considering these ideas: love, God, perfection, wisdom. Can you identify the precise *sensations to which they correspond?*

■ GEORGE BERKELEY ■

George Berkeley

idealism (immaterialism)
Belief that only ideas (mental states) exist; the material world is a fiction—it does not exist.

George Berkeley (1685–1753) was an Anglican bishop who posed one of the most quoted and least understood questions in the history of ideas: Does a tree falling in the forest make a sound if no one is there to hear it? Berkeley's answer is no, and it is based on a clear sense of the predicament Locke's empiricism generated.

From a commonsense point of view it may seem absurd to deny the existence of a material world, but Berkeley pointed out that on closer examination it makes more sense to deny the existence of matter than it does to affirm it. Don't pass over this point too quickly. Taking empiricism a logical step further than Locke, Berkeley argues that the material world does not exist. Only ideas exist, and ideas are mental states, not material objects. This makes Berkeley an **idealist** or **immaterialist:** The idea of matter existing without mental properties is self-contradictory, for there is no way to conceive of what an unperceived, unexperienced existence would consist of. We can conceive of things only in terms of the perceptions (ideas) we have of them.

Berkeley challenged Locke's copy theory of truth by pointing out that the so-called objects Locke thought our ideas correspond to lack any fixed nature. They are constantly changing. There is no "thing" to copy, Berkeley said, only a cluster of constantly changing perceptions:

> [Some hold that] real things, it is plain, have a fixed and real nature, which remains the same notwithstanding any change in our senses or in the posture and motion of our bodies; which indeed may affect the ideas in our minds, but it were absurd to think they had the same effect on things existing without the mind.
>
> . . . How then is it possible that things perpetually fleeting and variable as our ideas should be copies or images of anything fixed and constant? Or, in other words, since all sensible qualities, as figure, size, color, etc., that is, our ideas, are continually changing upon every alteration in the distance, medium, or instruments of sensation—how can any determinate, material objects be properly represented or painted forth by several distinct things each of which is so different from and unlike the rest? Or, if you say it resembles some one only

of our ideas, how shall we be able to distinguish the true copy from all the false ones?[12]

According to Berkeley, all the qualities we assign to material objects are relative to the perceiver, what Locke called "secondary" qualities. For example, the coffee I am drinking is hot or cold depending on my perception of it. It is absurd to ask if it is *really* hot or cold. But, you might point out, it has an objective temperature, say 120° Fahrenheit—only, however, when someone measures it, that is, only when someone perceives a thermometer registering 120° Fahrenheit. Even so, you're probably tempted to respond, it *does have* a certain temperature regardless of whether or not someone is aware of it.

Does it? What kind of temperature is it if no one anywhere is aware of it? And how can we ever—*in fact* or *in theory*—verify the existence of a thing's temperature *when no one is aware of it?* If there is an "objective, real" temperature, we will never know it.

We can know things only in terms of some perception of them through the senses, or as ideas perceived by the mind. And this being so, Berkeley argued, we know only perceptions—not *things-in-themselves,* only *things as perceived.* What difference does it make to insist that things exist independently of perceptions? If they do, we have no awareness of them, and they have no effect on us, so they are of no importance to us. When they do affect us, we perceive them. Thus, if no one or no thing were around to perceive the famous tree falling all alone in the forest, it would be absurd to say that it made a sound.

In *Three Dialogues Between Hylas and Philonous,* written in 1713, Berkeley points out that there is no difference between sound as perceived by us and sound as it is in itself. We may define sound in terms of what is perceived: sensations, atmospheric disturbances, decibels, waves, marks on a graph, or whatever, but in all cases sound remains *something that is perceived.*

> *Philonous:* It should follow then, that, according to you, real sounds may . . . never [be] heard.
> *Hylas:* Look you, Philonous, you may, if you please, make a jest of my opinion, but that will not alter the truth of things . . . sounds too have no real being without the mind.[13]

Berkeley takes the radical—but logically correct—step of concluding that this is true of everything. We know things only as different kinds of ideas about them. Berkeleian ideas imply consciousness, perception. It is self-contradictory to discuss ideas we do not know we have.

PHILOSOPHICAL
QUERY

• • • • • •

Think about the notion of mind *as contrasted to the* brain *and* brain *states. It seems clear that our behavior, moods, and even thoughts can be influenced by factors we are unaware of. These might include fatigue, hunger, the effects of medication, allergies, neurological disorders, and so on. Could we also have ideas, motives, and emotions we are unaware of? That is, could we have an "unconscious mind"?*

"This Moping Method of Study"

Learning has been [a] great . . . loser by being shut up in colleges and cells, and secluded from the world and good company. By that means every part of what we call *belles lettres* became totally barbarous, being cultivated by men without any taste for life or manners, and without that liberty and facility of thought and expression which can only be acquired by conversation. Even philosophy went to wreck by this moping recluse method of study, and became chimerical in her conclusions, as she was unintelligible in her style and manner of delivery; and, indeed, what could be expected from men who never consulted experience in any of their reasonings, or who never searched for that experience, where alone it is to be found, in common life and conversation?

David Hume, "Of Essay Writing," in *Of the Standard Taste and Other Essays,* ed. John W. Lenz (Indianapolis: Bobbs-Merrill, 1965), p. 39.

It is equally absurd to posit an independent, external reality, for if it exists, we cannot have anything to do with it. If we accept Locke's starting point that all knowledge derives from experience, Berkeley reasons, we must conclude that all knowledge is limited to ideas, because *we experience things only as ideas.* So-called material or physical *states* are perceptions, mental acts. Pain is a perception; sweet and sour are perceptions; the moon is a perception; my own body is known to me only as a series of perceptions. **Esse est percipi**: To be is to be perceived.

As Descartes pointed out, there can be no doubt about my existence while I am aware of it: To think is to exist. Berkeley adds that to exist is to be thought about: Nothing, not even an unthinking thing, can exist unless something perceives it.

> The table I write on I say exists; that is, I see and feel it: and if I were out of my study should say it existed; meaning thereby that if I was in my study I might perceive it, or that some other spirit actually does perceive it. . . . This is all that I can understand by these and the like expressions. For as to what is said of the *absolute* existence of unthinking things [matter], without any relation to their being perceived, that to me is perfectly unintelligible. Their *esse is percipi;* nor is it possible they should have any existence out of the minds or thinking things which perceive them.[14]

Had Berkeley continued working out the logical consequences of his position, he would have had to accept a disturbing picture of reality: Only particular, immediate perceptions can be known to exist.

Berkeley stopped short of the skeptical conclusions implied by his premises. He introduced God as a guarantee that he had a continuing self, that he existed during deepest sleep, and that there was indeed an external world, safely encapsulated in the never-resting, all-perceiving mind of God. His successor, David Hume, did not stop, but pursued skeptical logic to unsettling consequences.

Esse est percipi
Latin for Berkeley's belief that "to be is to be perceived."

David Hume

■ DAVID HUME: THE SCOTTISH SKEPTIC ■

David Hume (1711–1776) stands out in the history of ideas for the fearless consistency of his reasoning. I am aware of few other philosophers who so relentlessly and thoroughly follow the premises and principles on which his or her philosophy rests to such chilling and disturbing conclusions. Many great thinkers ultimately shied away from the logical conclusions of their ideas for personal, social, or religious reasons. Hume refused to do so. So powerful is his analysis that it effectively destroyed many important philosophies that went before it and much of the philosophy, science, and commonsense beliefs that follow it. Ironically, the wielder of perhaps the sharpest philosophical ax was one of the sweetest, most accessible figures in Western philosophy.

Hume was born in Edinburgh, Scotland, and raised by his mother under a strict Presbyterian regimen. He attended three-hour morning services, went back for an hour in the afternoon, and joined in family prayers every evening. His father died the year after he was born, leaving his son a small income. Hume enrolled in the University of Edinburgh when he was twelve years old, but after three years dropped out without a degree, planning to devote himself to philosophy and literature. A short time later, Hume admitted he had lost the faith of his childhood, writing that once he read Locke and other philosophers, he never again "entertained any belief in religion."[15]

The small income his father left allowed him only the barest existence, and Hume's family tried to persuade him to do something more practical and profitable than just study literature and philosophy. He studied law from 1726 to 1729, but the experience was so unpleasant that he had a breakdown and for a time lost interest in everything. In his own words, "The law appeared nauseous to me."[16]

Hume moved to London "to make a very feeble trial for entering into a more active scene of life," though he must have had a somewhat active social life in Scotland, for on March 5 and again on June 25 of 1734 he was accused of being the father of Agnes Galbraith's child. Hume escaped censure by the church because he was out of Scotland, but poor Agnes was required to wear sackcloth in front of the congregation and be put on public display in the pillory for three consecutive Sundays.

Meanwhile, Hume was working for a merchant in Bristol, but "in a few months I found that scene totally unsuitable to me." He moved to France, where living expenses were lower, finally settling near Descartes's old college at La Flèche. There the Jesuits allowed him full access to their first-rate library. Already his skeptical, questioning mind and discomfort in the face of any authority not supported by clear evidence stood out. One of the Jesuits described Hume as "too full of himself . . . his spirit more lively than solid, his imagination more luminous than profound, his heart too dissipated with material objects and spiritual self-idolatry to pierce into the sacred recesses of divine truths."[17]

The Skeptical Masterpiece

The Jesuits were correct in one aspect of their assessment of Hume, for they recognized a mind given to no allegiance but its own experiences interpreted in an unforgiving rational light. While in France, Hume had what contemporary philosopher Richard Watson calls a "skeptical crisis." In six weeks he gained sixty pounds, and remained a "fat, jolly fellow for the rest of his life."[18] He also completed the first two books of his powerful and disturbing *Treatise of Human Nature.*

In 1737 Hume returned to England hoping to publish the *Treatise* and immediately ran into objections from publishers. In December 1737 he wrote, "I am at present castrating my work, that is, cutting out its noble parts, . . . endeavoring it shall give as little offense as possible."[19] Hume found most resistance to his analysis of miracles. He agreed to remove the most offensive passages, but did not destroy them. In this censored form, the two-volume *Treatise* was published anonymously in January 1739. Hume received fifty pounds and twelve copies as his total payment. At the age of twenty-seven, he had written one of the major works of modern philosophy.

In the *Treatise* Hume makes compelling arguments *against* materialism, the possibility of a spiritual, supernatural reality, and personal immortality—this in the watered-down version! Pushing beyond Locke and Berkeley, Hume argued that neither matter nor mind exists. (A standing joke at the time referred to Berkeley and Hume with the slogan "No matter; never mind.")

The uncensored version of the *Treatise* does not stop there. Hume ultimately reduces reason to the "slave of the passions" and alters the conventional picture of the nature of science by denying cause and effect as they are generally understood. Thus Hume challenged established religious beliefs, moral judgments, reason and rationalism, earlier forms of empiricism, and the certainty of science. He denied the existence of a "fixed self," the possibility of personal immortality, and the possibility of miracles. It would not be surprising if such a book provoked a great storm of controversy. Ultimately, Hume's book did just that, but not among the general public and not right away. The second, uncensored, edition of the *Treatise* was not published until after Hume's death.

> *There is indeed nothing more ridiculous than to imagine that any motion or modification of matter should produce thought.*
>
> Thomas Reid

An Honest Man

Unable to earn his living as a writer, Hume applied for a professorship at the University of Edinburgh, but was rejected. He took a somewhat humiliating job as the tutor of a young nobleman, who shortly went insane. Hume was ultimately dismissed and had to sue for his salary. He eventually secured a position as secretary to a general who was on a mission to Turin, Italy. Hume, having apparently gained more weight, began wearing a scarlet uniform. His appearance unsettled the young Earl of Charlemont, who wrote as follows: "His face was broad and fat, his mouth wide, and without any other expression than that of imbecility. . . . The corpulence of his whole person was far better fitted to communicate the idea of a turtle-eating alderman than that of a refined philosopher."[20]

Hume returned to London in 1748 and published *An Enquiry Concerning Human Understanding.* In 1749 he went back to Edinburgh and in 1751 published *An Enquiry Concerning the Principles of Morals.* These works reach the same conclusions as the *Treatise,* but in a softer tone.

> *Shall we esteem it worthy the labour of a philosopher to give us a true system of the planets, and adjust the position and order of those remote bodies; while we affect to overlook those, who, with so much success, delineate the parts of the mind, in which we are so intimately concerned?*
>
> David Hume

The softer tone was not to last, for in about 1751 Hume wrote the most devastating, direct, and irreverent of his works, the *Dialogues Concerning Natural Religion*. In it Hume mounts an unrelenting attack on the argument from design (see Chapter 8) and other attempts to demonstrate the existence of or understand the nature of God. At the urging of friends, Hume withheld the *Dialogues* from publication. They were finally published in 1779, three years after his death.

Hume wearied of the heated discussion his philosophical reasonings provoked and turned to politics and history. He finally achieved some success as an author with *Political Discourses* (1751) and *Essays on Various Subjects* (1753). The theory of economics discussed in the *Essays* was substantial enough to influence the great economist Adam Smith.

In 1752 Hume was elected keeper of the library for the Faculty of Advocates in Edinburgh. The pay was low, but Hume was delighted with the job because it gave him control of thirty thousand volumes. Taking advantage of this opportunity, he researched and wrote *History of England*. He was a competent enough historian that Edward Gibbon, the author of *The Decline and Fall of the Roman Empire* (1776), cited him as an influence.

Hume published his *History* in six volumes, in reverse order, beginning with the years 1603–1649 and ending with the period from Julius Caesar to Henry VII in 1485. His attitudes toward Parliament and Bonnie Prince Charlie were unorthodox, and the controversy aroused by the first volume was so intense that Hume grew depressed and planned to move back to France. But France and England were at war, and the second volume was nearly done. So Hume revised the first volume and continued with the others. By the publication of the sixth volume, Hume's popularity as a writer had soared. James Boswell referred to him as "the greatest writer in Britain," and Voltaire said Hume's work was "perhaps the best history ever written in any language."[21] (Today, hardly anyone reads Hume's *History of England,* but no truly educated person fails to read something of Hume's philosophy.)

In spite of his success, Hume remained troubled by the unrelenting attacks from ecclesiastical and other sources. Relief arrived in the form of an appointment as deputy secretary to the Earl of Hertford, ambassador to France. Hertford also arranged that Hume should receive a pension of two hundred pounds for life.

Hume's writing was more popular in France than in England, and by the time he returned to France he was almost a cult figure. The aristocracy loved him (the ladies most of all), and he loved them (the ladies most of all). The Earl of Hertford found that Hume was more popular and respected than the earl was. Once at a party an envious French intellectual made fun of Hume's weight, quoting the Gospel verse "And the word was made flesh." One of Hume's many lady admirers quickly countered, "And the word was made lovable."

After Britain appointed a new ambassador to France in 1765, Hume worked for a time as undersecretary at the Foreign Office in London. He retired to Edinburgh in 1769, being, in his own words, "very opulent (for I possessed a revenue of £1,000 a year), healthy, and though somewhat stricken in years, with the prospect of enjoying long my ease, and of seeing the increase of my reputation."[22]

'Tis impossible upon any system to defend either our understanding or senses; and we but expose them farther when we endeavour to justify them. . . . Carelessness and inattention alone afford us any remedy. For this reason I rely entirely upon them; and take it for granted, whatever may be the reader's opinion at this present moment, that an hour hence he will be persuaded there is both an external and internal world.

DAVID HUME

As a philosophical critic Hume has few peers. No one has challenged more sharply rationalism's central thesis that matters of fact can be known without recourse to experience; nor has anyone revealed more clearly the severe problems raised by insisting that all factual claims be empirically verified.

JOHN W. LENZ

Hume's home (on, fittingly, St. David Street) became an intellectual salon for Scottish celebrities, including Adam Smith. Hume was a friendly, supportive, encouraging mentor, despite the rigor and iconoclasm of his intellect. He remained a popular guest, even if he occasionally broke a host's chair.[23] He once proposed a tax on obesity but thought its passage unlikely because it might put the church in danger, and he blessed Julius Caesar for preferring fat men.

Part of Hume's charm came from his personal modesty. These days celebrities and television "personalities" in their teens think nothing of writing a two- or three-hundred-page autobiography, yet one of the finest minds ever to have written considered it sufficient to pen an eight-page one—and then only shortly before he died. In it he wrote:

> In the spring of 1775 I was struck with a disorder in my bowels, which at first gave me no alarm, but has since, as I apprehend it, become mortal and incurable. I now reckon upon a speedy dissolution.
>
> I have suffered very little pain from my disorder; and what is more strange, have, notwithstanding the great decline of my person, never suffered a moment's abatement of my spirits; insomuch that were I to name the period of my life which I should most choose to pass over again, I might be tempted to point to this later period. I possess the same ardor as ever in my study, and the same gaiety in company. I consider, besides, that a man of sixty-five, by dying, cuts off only a few years of infirmities.[24]

In 1775 Hume lost seventy pounds due to his illness. In 1776, he was prepared to die "as fast as my enemies, if I have any, could wish, and as easily and cheerfully as my best friends could desire."[25]

Even in his last hours, Hume was not spared the attentions of the devout. James Boswell was troubled that the agnostic Hume, whom many erroneously believed to be an atheist, could be so cheerful in the face of death. But Hume did not deny the existence of God, a position known as *atheism;* rather, he adopted the agnostic view that we do not know enough to assert or deny the existence of God.

Happiness in the face of death was thought to be a virtue of the devout believer, not the skeptical agnostic. Unrelenting even at the end, Boswell asked the dying Hume if he did *now* finally believe in an afterlife. Hume answered, "It is a most unreasonable fancy that we should exist forever." Asked if he didn't at least think the possibility of another plane of existence was desirable, the dying skeptic answered, "Not at all; it is a very gloomy thought." A small parade of women visited Hume, begging him to believe, but he distracted them with humor.[26]

David Hume died free of much pain on August 25, 1776. The story goes that a large crowd attended his burial, despite heavy rain. Someone was heard to say, "He was an atheist." "No matter," a voice answered from the crowd. "He was an honest man."

▪ HUME'S SKEPTICAL EMPIRICISM ▪

Hume's philosophy rests on the rejection of overly abstract, obscure, bloated speculations. Hume found most metaphysical speculation irrelevant to the lives of ordinary people. It was poorly worded, unclear, and based on

Hume was a wonderful man. He and Benjamin Franklin used to have grand times together in Paris, eating and drinking and playing whist, and pulling bluestocking ladies down to sit on their fat laps.

RICHARD WATSON

As sure, therefore, as the sensible world really exists, so sure is there an infinite omnipresent Spirit, who contains and supports it.

GEORGE BERKELEY

unverified assumptions; it was also, he observed, never-ending. No metaphysical issue was ever clearly and thoroughly settled. For each theory about the soul or nature or reality, there were opposing theories and modifications, apparently infinite in number.

Hume thought such "abstruse speculation" was useful only to individuals with some theological motive, who, "being unable to defend [their views] on fair grounds, raise these entangling brambles to cover and protect their weaknesses." The only way to rid ourselves of these pointless excursions, he claimed, is to inquire seriously and thoroughly into the nature of human understanding, "and show, from an exact analysis of its powers and capacity, that it is by no means fitted for such remote and abstruse subjects."

In other words, Hume continued the "epistemological turn," moving further away from metaphysics than Locke and Berkeley had. Although he said we must "cultivate true metaphysics with some care in order to destroy the false," Hume moved modern philosophy firmly into the realm of epistemology.

> Accurate and just reasoning is the only catholic remedy, fitted for all persons and all dispositions; and is alone able to subvert that abstruse philosophy and metaphysical jargon, which, being mixed up with popular superstition, renders it in a manner impenetrable to careless reasoners, and gives it the air of science and wisdom.[27]

Impressions and Ideas

In *An Enquiry Concerning Human Understanding,* Hume set out to modify Locke's theory of ideas in a way that removed any metaphysical residue. He began by pointing out the very obvious difference between, say, the painful perception of excessive heat or the pleasure of comforting warmth and the memory of such perceptions. There is also, he noted, a difference between anticipating a perception in the imagination and actually perceiving it. He says, "The most lively thought is still inferior to the dullest sensation." This kind of distinction also applies to "mental perceptions," such as anger and hate.

Hume thought Locke was correct in claiming that thought is a "faithful mirror, and copies objects truly." But he reminds us not to overlook a vital fact: The copies are always duller and fainter than the original perceptions on which they are based. Hume proposes that we distinguish "ideas" from "impressions":

> Here therefore we may divide all perceptions of the mind into two classes or species, which are distinguished by their different degrees of force and vivacity. The less forcible and lively are commonly denominated *Thoughts* or *Ideas.* The other species wants a name in our language, and most others. . . . Let us, therefore, use a little freedom, and call them *Impressions;* employing that word in a sense somewhat different from the usual. By the term *impression,* then, I mean all our more lively perceptions, when we hear, or see, or feel, or love, or hate, or desire, or will. And impressions are distinguished from ideas, which are the less lively perceptions, of which we are conscious, when we reflect on any of those sensations or movements above mentioned.[28]

One has no knowledge of the sun but only of an eye that sees a sun, and no knowledge of the earth but only of a hand that feels an earth.

ARTHUR
SCHOPENHAUER

We declare at the outset that we do not make any positive assertion that anything we shall say is wholly as we affirm it to be. We merely report accurately on each thing as our impressions of it are at the moment.

SEXTUS EMPIRICUS

More careful analysis of ideas, no matter how fanciful, creative, or original, reveals that "all this creative power of the mind amounts to no more than the faculty of compounding, transposing, augmenting, or diminishing the materials afforded us by the senses and experience." In other words, all ideas can be traced to impressions and, thus, are derived from experience, even if they become so abstracted and diluted that they no longer resemble any identifiable impressions. If you doubt this, Hume says the only way to refute him is to produce an idea not derived from impressions or from combining and altering the ideas that impressions generate. Modifying Locke's copy theory of ideas, Hume developed an empirical test of meaning:

> When we entertain, therefore, any suspicion that a philosophical term is employed without any meaning or idea (as is a bit too frequent), we need to enquire, *from what impression is that supposed idea derived?* And if it be impossible to assign any, this will serve to confirm our suspicion. By bringing ideas into so clear a light we may reasonably hope to remove all dispute, which may arise, concerning their nature and reality.[29]

The **empirical criterion of meaning** holds that all *meaningful* ideas can be traced to sense experience (impressions). Beliefs that cannot be reduced to sense experience are technically not "ideas" at all: They are *meaningless utterances*.

empirical criterion of meaning
Meaningful ideas are those that can be traced back to sense experience (impressions); beliefs that cannot be reduced to sense experience are not "ideas" at all, but meaningless utterances.

• • • • • •

PHILOSOPHICAL QUERY

Apply the empirical criterion of meaning to such concepts as God, love, creativity, and intelligence. What, in general, do you see as the strengths and weaknesses of this criterion?

The Self

As we have seen, Descartes based modern philosophy on the thinking thing, the self. What could be more certain than the existence of my self? But what exactly does the word *self* refer to? Applying his empirical criterion of meaning, Hume argues that we do not have any idea of self as it is commonly understood:

The solution to the problem of identity is, get lost.
NORMAN O. BROWN

> For from what impression cou'd this idea be deriv'd? This question 'tis impossible to answer without a manifest contradiction and absurdity; and 'tis a question, which necessarily must be answer'd, if we wou'd have the idea of self pass for clear and intelligible. But self or person is not any one impression, but that to which our several impressions and ideas are suppos'd to have a reference. If any impression gives rise to the idea of self, that impression must continue invariably the same, thro' the whole course of our lives; since self is suppos'd to exist after that manner. But there is no impression constant and invariable. Pain and pleasure, grief and joy, passions and sensations succeed each other, and never all exist at the same time. It cannot, therefore, be from any of these impressions, or from any other, that the idea of self is deriv'd; and consequently there is no such idea.[30]

If we have no specifc *impression* of self, then what are we? Hume gives one of the most intriguing, yet elusive, answers in modern philosophy:

> For my part, when I enter most intimately into what I call *myself,* I always stumble on some particular perception or other, of heat or cold, light or shade, love or hatred, pain or pleasure. I never can catch *myself* at any time without a perception, and never can observe any thing but the perception. When my perceptions are remov'd for any time, as by sound sleep; so long am I insensible of *myself,* and may truly be said not to exist. And were all my perceptions remov'd by death, and cou'd I neither think, nor feel, nor see, nor love, nor hate after the dissolution of my body, I shou'd be entirely annihilated, nor do I conceive what is farther requisite to make me a perfect non-entity. If any one upon serious and unprejudic'd reflexion, thinks he has a different notion of *himself,* I must confess I can reason no longer with him. All I can allow him is, that he may be in the right as well as I, and that we are essentially different in this particular. He may, perhaps, perceive something simple and continu'd, which he calls *himself;* tho' I am certain there is no such principle in me.
>
> But setting aside some metaphysicians of this kind, I may venture to affirm of the rest of mankind, that they are nothing but a bundle or collection of different perceptions, which succeed each other with an inconceivable rapidity, and are in a perpetual flux and movement.[31]

bundle theory of the self
Humean theory that there is no fixed self, but that the self is merely a "bundle of perceptions"; a self is merely a habitual way of discussing certain perceptions.

In such passages, Hume sounds very much like a Buddhist or Hindu. He has dissolved the self into a flickering series of perceptions with no underlying, constant *thing* to unite them. What has come to be known as Hume's **bundle theory of the self** is difficult for most of us to accept. Yet Hume's position is more consistent than are some that are more comforting and popular.

PHILOSOPHICAL QUERY

• • • • • •

Where and what are "you" in the midst of some exciting experience that totally absorbs your consciousness? That is, what happens to your self when you are not aware of it? What exactly are you aware of when you are self-conscious? A "self" or sweaty palms, uncomfortable desks, boring lectures? Discuss.

Personal Immortality

If we cannot speak clearly about the self, what happens to the common belief that the self (or the soul) survives after bodily death?

Hume says, in his straightforward fashion, that there can be no persistent identity for us. We speak of "the oak tree" in the backyard, but, in fact, each time we see it, "the oak tree" is different. It may have a different number of leaves, and certainly it has changed in some ways, even when we cannot discern these changes. Any change in a thing changes its identity. In what sense can a two-hundred-pound man who has been married twice and fathered children be the same person who

The sceptic wishes, from considerations of humanity, to do all he can with the arguments at his disposal to cure the self-conceit and rashness of the dogmatists.
Sextus Empiricus

was once a fifty-pound third-grader? In what sense are you the same person who began reading this book? Your mind—or brain—has different ideas. Your body has different cells. As Heraclitus noted, "We cannot step twice into the same river, for the water into which we first stepped has flowed on."

In other words, identity is not a property of things, but a mental act. Our minds *confer* identity on things; we do not perceive it. A self is merely a habitual way of discussing certain perceptions.

> The whole of this doctrine leads us to a conclusion, which is of great importance in the present affair, *viz.* that all the nice and subtle questions concerning personal identity can never possibly be decided, and are to be regarded rather as grammatical than as philosophical difficulties. . . . We have no just standard, by which we can decide any dispute concerning the time, when [things] acquire or lose a title to the name of identity. All the disputes concerning the identity of connected objects are merely verbal, except so far as the relation of parts gives rise to some fiction or imaginary principle of union, as we have already observ'd.[32]

Strictly speaking, Hume is correct. We do not *perceive* identity. Yet something gives order and continuity to our experiences, and Hume does not deny that. Rather, he insists on clearer, more precise talking, reasoning, and thinking about this and other important matters. In the process, Hume challenges the limits of reason and, perhaps, of knowledge.

▦ THE LIMITS OF REASON ▦

In a sense, Hume stops at the first part of Berkeley's position:

> The mind has never anything present to it but the perceptions, and cannot possibly reach any experience of their connexion with objects. The supposition of such a connexion . . . is, therefore, without any foundation in reasoning.[33]

We have no way of empirically establishing the independent existence of an external world, or of what many of us mean by "reality." We can only know our own perceptions, ideas, and experiences.

> As several impressions appear exterior to the body, we suppose them also exterior to ourselves. The paper, on which I write at present, is beyond my hand. The table is beyond the paper. The walls of the chamber beyond the table. And in casting my eye towards the window, I perceive a great extent of fields and buildings beyond my chamber. From all this it may be infer'd, that no other faculty is requir'd, besides the senses, to convince us of the external existence of body. But to prevent this inference, we need only weigh the three following considerations. *First,* That, properly speaking, 'tis not our body we perceive, when we regard our limbs and members, but certain impressions, which enter by the sense; so that in ascribing a real and corporeal existence to these impressions, or to their objects, is an act of the mind as difficult to explain, as that which we examine at present. *Secondly,* Sounds

Nihil in intellectu quod prius non fuerit in sensu. *(Nothing is in the intellect which was not in the senses first.)*

THOMAS AQUINAS

and tastes, and smells, tho' commonly regarded by the mind as continu'd independent qualities, appear not to have any existence in extension, and consequently cannot appear to the senses as situated externally to the body. . . . *Thirdly,* Even our sight informs us not of distance or outness (so to speak) immediately and without certain reasoning and experience, as is acknowledg'd by the most rational philosophers.[34]

If, as Hume thought, there is no rational evidence whatsoever for belief in an external reality, then why is the notion so popular? Hume suggests that the imagination accounts for the universal notion of the independent existence of an external world. It is the nature of the imagination to complete and fill in gaps between perceptions. If we regularly experience very much the same perceptions—say, of the oak tree in the yard or our own face—we overlook the gaps between different perceptions. Hume says we "feign" or fabricate continuity. I assume that because my face looks "the same" this morning as yesterday morning, it has existed continuously all night (and at other times) when I had no perception of it.

Further, our experiences tend to occur with a kind of pattern or regularity, which Hume refers to as *coherence.* That is, when I turn my head to the left, my view in the mirror is a particular perception. When I tilt forward, I have a completely different perception, and so on. When I turn around and use a hand mirror to examine the thinning hair on the back of my head, I have yet another perception. What I never have is an impression of my whole head—and neither do you have an impression of my whole head. No one does. But because my various views always follow a pattern, my imagination feigns or fabricates an idea of my whole head.

According to Hume, this process explains our belief in an external world. This "natural quality" of the mind is much more powerful than logical reasoning; it always reasserts itself after being challenged on logical grounds.

There is a great difference betwixt such opinions as we form after a calm and profound reflection, and such as we embrace by a kind of instinct or natural impulse, on account of their suitableness and conformity to the mind. If these opinions become contrary, 'tis not difficult to foresee which of them will have the advantage. As long as our attention is bent upon the subject, the philosophical and study'd principle may prevail; but the moment we relax our thoughts, nature will display herself, and draw us back to our former opinion. . . . [35]

If Hume is correct, nature and reason are adversaries: "Nature is obstinate, and will not quit the field, however strongly attack'd by reason; and at the same time reason is so clear in the point, that there is no possibility of disguising her."

A completely nonrational life would be barely human, however. Even the most primitive, nontechnical, "natural" cultures depend on reason. What Hume suggests is a kind of fluctuating balance between reason and nature, or between logic and emotion. His skepticism indicates that a completely rational view of reality is not possible, or at least not for more than brief, concentrated periods. It suggests that reason, the great ideal of so many philosophers, is, in fact, the slave of emotions, shaped by psychology and biology.

I said that I could not imagine being an atheist any time before 1859, when Darwin's Origin of Species *was published. "What about Hume?" replied the philosopher. "How did Hume explain the organized complexity of the living world?" I asked. "He didn't," said the philosopher. "Why does it need any special explanation?"*

RICHARD DAWKINS

PHILOSOPHICAL

QUERY

• • • • • •

Have you been able to take Hume's strictest claims seriously? That is, have you seriously considered the possibility that we lack knowledge of the external world? Discuss some factors that make taking this idea seriously so difficult. Can you spot any errors in Hume's reasoning?

▨ THE LIMITS OF SCIENCE ▨

Scientific reasoning rests on a pattern of **inductive reasoning,** which results in generalized rules or principles. Simplistically, induction reasons from the particular to the general or from "some" to "all." Scientific principles are never based on experience with *all* things of a certain kind. Newton did not have to observe the behavior of all bodies to conclude they are subject to gravity. He based his conclusion on the behavior of just some bodies.

Scientists assume that such inferences are reliable because they identify *causal patterns.* In Hume's time, cause and effect were defined in terms of a *necessary connection.* That is, *A* was said to cause *B* if the occurrence of *A always and without exception* was followed by the occurrence of *B*. But if Hume's epistemology is correct, how can we perceive the actual connection, the causal relationship? Strictly speaking, all we actually observe is *A* followed by *B*. We observe constant conjunction. That is, a perception of *A* is always (or so far) followed by a perception of *B*. But that is a temporal sequence, not a necessary connection. If Hume is correct there is no empirical evidence for the existence of cause and effect:

> We have sought in vain for an idea of power or necessary connexion in all the sources from which we could suppose it to be derived. It appears that, in single instances of the operation of bodies, we never can, by our utmost scrutiny, discover anything but one event following another, without being able to comprehend any force or power by which the cause operates, or any connexion between it and its supposed effect. The same difficulty occurs in contemplating the operations of mind on body—where we observe the motion of the latter to follow upon the volition of the former, but are not able to observe or conceive the tie which binds together the motion and volition, or the energy by which the mind produces this effect. The authority of the will over its own faculties and ideas is not a whit more comprehensible: So that, upon the whole, there appears not, throughout all nature, any one instance of connexion which is conceivable by us. All events seem entirely loose and separate. One event follows another; but we can never observe any tie between them. They seem *conjoined,* but never *connected.* And as we can have no idea of any thing which [is not based on an impression], the necessary conclusion *seems* to be that we have no idea of connexion or power at all, and that these words are absolutely without any meaning, when employed either in philosophical reasonings or common life.[36]

What *do we observe* that we call cause and effect? Hume answers that we observe a series of recognizable impressions and that we come to expect the first

inductive reasoning
Reasoning pattern that proceeds from the particular to the general or from "some" to "all" and results in generalized rules or principles established with degrees of probability.

It follows from this definition of cause, that night is the cause of day, and day the cause of night. For no two things have more constantly followed each other since the beginning of the world.

THOMAS REID

part of the series to be followed by the second part. When we are correct, we assume the connection is causal. But we cannot observe that one event *must* follow the other. All we *know* is that one event *happens* to follow another. We may have observed this pattern countless times, but that does not logically justify inferring any sort of necessity.

In other words, the mind creates the ideas of causality and necessity; we do not observe them. The best we can do is take for granted that the future will resemble the past: There is no way to prove that it must. We are psychologically constructed so that we have no choice but to *believe in* cause and effect. And for the most part, our inferences regarding the predictability and uniformity of experience have been borne out. But, Hume cautions, we should not forget that the real origin of science lies in the operation of the human mind. We believe in an independent, external reality because we cannot help it.

■ THE LIMITS OF THEOLOGY ■

Given his radical view of cause and effect, it is not surprising that Hume rejected all efforts to use causality to prove the existence of God. The cosmological argument and the argument from motion (Chapter 8) were meaningless for him. The ontological argument (Chapter 9) was meaningless as well, because the very qualities ascribed to God—perfection, omniscience, omnipotence, and so forth—do not correspond to specific impressions. They are empty noises.

Besides rejecting these arguments, Hume wrote perhaps the most devastating and complete critique of the argument from design, also known as the teleological argument (see Thomas Aquinas's fifth way in Chapter 8). After taking the briefest look at this compelling bit of logical analysis, we can understand why Hume withheld publication of his *Dialogues Concerning Natural Religion* during his lifetime.

Recall that the core of the argument from design is the belief that all about us we see evidence of God's handiwork. We perceive order and harmony and beauty throughout the universe. We sense divine purpose in a beautiful sunset or an ocean breeze; we feel God's presence in the miracle of childbirth or the renewing of the seasons. But as Hume points out, that's not the whole picture.

> But were this world ever so perfect a production, it must still remain uncertain, whether all the excellences of the work can justly be ascribed to the workman. If we survey a ship, what an exalted idea must we form of the ingenuity of the carpenter, who framed so complicated, useful, and beautiful a machine? And what surprise must we feel, when we find him a stupid mechanic, who imitated others, and copied an art, which, through a long succession of ages, after multiplied trials, mistakes, corrections, deliberations, and controversies, had gradually been improving? Many worlds might have been botched and bungled, throughout an eternity, ere this system was struck out: Much labor lost: Many fruitless trials made: And a slow, but continued improvement carried on during infinite ages in the art of world-making. . . .

Did I show you a house or palace, where there was not one apartment convenient or agreeable; where the windows, doors, fires, passages, stairs, and the whole economy of the building were the source of noise, confusion, fatigue, darkness, and extremes of heat and cold; you would certainly blame the contrivance, without any farther examination. . . . If you find many inconveniences and deformities in the building, you will always, without entering into any detail, condemn the architect.[37]

There is even less reason to infer the existence of a good god once one takes a thorough, objective look at life:

But allowing you, what never will be believed; at least, what you never possibly can prove, that animal, or at least human happiness, in this life, exceeds its misery; you have yet done nothing: For this is not, by any means, what we expect from infinite power, infinite wisdom, infinite goodness. Why is there any misery at all in this world? Not by chance surely. From some cause then. Is it from the intention of the Deity? But he is perfectly benevolent. Is it contrary to his intention? But he is almighty. Nothing can shake the solidity of this reasoning, so short, so clear, so decisive. . . .

Look round this universe. What an immense profusion of beings, animated and organized, sensible and active! You admire the prodigious variety and fecundity. But inspect a little more narrowly these living existences, the only beings worth regarding. How hostile and destructive to each other! How insufficient all of them for their own happiness! How contemptible or odious to the spectator! The whole presents nothing but the idea of a blind nature, impregnated by a great vivifying principle, and pouring forth from her lap, without discernment or parental care, her maimed and abortive children.[38]

Based solely on our observations of human experience, we find insufficient evidence to assume the existence of a good, all-wise, all-powerful god. Imagine what kind of argument Hume could have made had he known of the Holocaust or Darfur.

At this point in the dialogue, Hume has the person representing orthodox belief object, asking, "What *data* have you for such extraordinary conclusions?" Hume makes his most important and devastating point:

This is the topic on which I have all along insisted. I have still asserted that we have no *data* to establish any system of cosmogony [theory of the origins of the universe]. Our experience, so imperfect in itself, and so limited both in extent and duration, can afford us no probable conjecture concerning the whole of things.[39]

Strictly speaking, our own little corner of the universe is too small to permit useful generalizations about the whole. To conclude yea or nay about God's existence and nature is beyond the limits of both reason and experience.

In a note added to the *Dialogues* just before his death, Hume stated that *"the cause or causes of order in the universe probably bear some remote analogy to human intelligence."* But he insisted that this analogy does not suggest that God exists, at least not the God of Judeo-Christian-Islamic religions.

> *Christianity does not—and cannot—explain how a God who is infinitely powerful and infinitely loving came to create a universe which turned out to be not very good.*
>
> ARNOLD TOYNBEE

PHILOSOPHICAL

QUERY

• • • • • •

Take a moment to reconsider the argument from design (Chapter 8) in light of modern-day horrors such as chemical warfare, environmental disasters, AIDS, crack babies, crime rates, world hunger, and homelessness amid plenty. Do such examples refute the notion of design or not? Of intelligent design?

Doubt is the nerve of all fresh and durable thinking. If Aristotle was right in the first book of his Metaphysics *when he said that philosophy began in wonder, philosophy could not have got very far if she had not doubted searchingly.*

PHILIP P. HALLIE

I found a certain boldness of temper growing on me, which was not inclined to submit to any authority in these subjects [philosophy and literature]. . . . When I was about eighteen years of age there seemed to be opened up a new scheme of thought, which transported me beyond measure, and made me, with an ardor natural to young men, throw up every other pleasure or business to apply myself entirely to it.

DAVID HUME

▪ THE LIMITS OF ETHICS ▪

As we have seen, reason has played a dominant role in Western philosophy. Plato argued that reason's function is to rule the appetites and emotions. The Stoics attempted to control their passions through reason. Descartes attempted to replace the authority of the church with the authority of reason. Descartes was not alone in his vision of reason as the ground of all knowledge, including moral knowledge. The seventeenth and eighteenth centuries are sometimes characterized as the Age of Reason. Attempts to ground morals in reason continue in the present. Hume, in contrast, challenged the role of reason in morality in an unprecedented way and achieved results similar to his critiques of theology and metaphysics.

Hume insisted that morality is grounded in sentiment, not reason. His devastating attack on any "metaphysic of morals" has had an enormous influence on modern and postmodern conceptions of morality, value judgments, and the possibility of moral knowledge. Immanuel Kant (Chapter 11) would ultimately refer to Hume's work as a "scandal in philosophy."

In his *Treatise of Human Nature,* Hume asserts that "reason alone" can never provide a motive for any action:

Nothing is more usual in philosophy, and even in common life, than to talk of the combat of passion and reason, to give the preference to reason, and to assert that men are only so far virtuous as they conform themselves to its dictates. Every rational creature, 'tis said, is oblig'd to regulate his actions by reason; and if any other motive or principle challenge the direction of his conduct, he ought to oppose it, 'till it be entirely subdu'd, or at least brought to a conformity with this common principle. On this method of thinking the greatest part of moral philosophy, ancient and modern, seems to be founded; nor is there an ampler field, as well for metaphysical arguments, as popular declamations, than this suppos'd pre-eminence of reason above passion. . . .

In order to shew the fallacy of all this philosophy, I shall endeavour to prove *first,* that reason alone can never be a motive to any action of the will; and *secondly,* that it can never oppose passion in the direction of the will.[40]

Hume did not deny that reason plays a role in making moral judgments. Rather, he argued that reason's role is secondary to the role of moral feelings or *sentiments,* because reason can never provide ultimate ends:

It appears evident that the ultimate ends of human actions can never . . . be accounted for by *reason,* but recommend themselves entirely to the sentiments and affections of mankind, without any dependence on the intellectual faculties. Ask a man *why he uses exercise;* he will answer, *because he desires to*

©Douglas J. Soccio

Consider the ongoing controversy surrounding gay marriage. To what extent do you think the persistence and intensity of this matter involves moral "sentiment"? Take a close, thoughtful look at the happy couple in this photograph and reflect on the extent to which *feelings* influence our moral values. According to Hume, what we call "virtues" are traits of character that we find agreeable, and what we call "moral judgments" are matters of taste, feeling, or "sentiment." If there is more to morality than sentiment and taste, what is it? If Hume is right, what is the best way to approach moral disagreements?

keep his health. If you then enquire, *why he desires health,* he will readily reply, *because sickness is painful.* If you push your enquiries farther, and desire a reason *why he hates pain,* it is impossible that he can ever give any. This is an ultimate end, and is never referred to any other object.[41]

According to Hume, although reason has a useful role to play in moral discernment, moral judgments themselves ultimately rest on "some internal sense or feeling which nature has made universal in the whole species."[42] Reason helps us clarify experience. It helps us identify facts. It does not, however, evaluate them: "Reason is, and ought only to be the slave of the passions, and can never pretend to any other office than to serve and obey them."[43]

The Facts, Just the Facts

Hume's analysis of moral judgments resembles his analysis of causality. Recall that, according to Hume, we do not actually perceive "necessary connection," but, rather, associate the feeling of necessity with certain related events (events constantly conjoined). Moral judgments are like causal judgments: They are mental associations or projections, not *perceptions* of facts. When we like a certain quality, we call it a virtue or label it "good" or "right." When we dislike something, we call it a vice or label it "wrong" or "bad." These evaluations are not derived from reason, but from experience. It is "just a fact" that a certain combination of conditions produces cold or heat; likewise, it is "just a fact" that we associate some experiences with good feelings (these are desired) and some with bad feelings (these are disliked). In other words, through experience, we learn to associate certain facts with positive sentiments (being good or desired) and other facts with negative sentiments (being bad or disliked). The facts themselves are value neutral.

Americans especially might take their cue today from their forebears in the eighteenth century in making an approach to Hume's philosophy. For in 1787, when the statesmen of the new American republic were discussing for many arduous months their design of a new constitution for the United States, they alluded almost daily to various writings of Hume.

CHARLES W. HENDEL

In the important and influential Part I of Book III of his *Treatise,* Hume makes a crucial distinction between *facts* and *values* (evaluations of facts). According to Hume, *facts themselves are valueless.* Moral judgments (like all evaluations) are not judgments of facts but reports of moral sentiments or feelings. Hume's fact-value distinction has exerted tremendous influence on all moral philosophy since. In the *Treatise* he says:

> But can there be any difficulty in proving, that vice and virtue are not matters of fact, whose existence we can infer by reason? Take any action allow'd to be vicious: Willful murder, for instance. Examine it in all lights, and see if you can find the matter of fact, or real existence, which you call *vice.* In whichever way you take it, you find only certain passions, motives, volitions and thoughts. There is no matter of fact in the case. The vice entirely escapes you, as long as you consider the object. You can never find it, till you turn your reflexion into your own breast, and find a sentiment of disapprobation, which arise in you towards this action. Here is a matter of fact; but 'tis the object of feeling, not of reason. It lies in yourself, not in the object. So that when you pronounce any action or character to be vicious, you mean nothing, but that from the constitution of your nature you have a feeling or sentiment of blame from the contemplation of it. Vice and virtue, therefore, may be compar'd to sounds, colours, heat and cold, which according to modern philosophy, are not qualities in objects, but perceptions in the mind.[44]

To fully grasp what Hume is saying, it helps to distinguish between *descriptive language* and *normative language.* Descriptive language—as the name suggests—is devoid of all subjective, evaluative characterizations. Using Hume's example of "willful murder," we might expect to find descriptive language in a police report: "Dean Fetters shot J. Scott Vargas in the chest six times. Vargas fell to the floor. He lost three quarts of blood and died at 6:15 P.M." and so on. No matter how precise and elaborate a purely factual description of the circumstance is, it will contain no moral judgments. Indeed, the moral judgment of murder is like the legal judgment of murder. Although we base both judgments on our beliefs about the facts, murder (in either the moral or legal sense) is an interpretation of the facts—not a description or observation. No one sees murder. We see Fetters shoot Vargas. We do not see murder. In a court of law, we *decide* murder (or not). In the moral case, we react subjectively to the facts and feel murder (or not). Moral judgments, according to Hume, are like judgments about art or food—matters of moral taste or sentiment.

The intercourse of sentiments, therefore, in society and conversation, makes us form some general inalterable standard, by which we may approve or disapprove of characters and manners. And tho' the heart does not take part with those general notions, or regulate its love and hatred by them, yet are they sufficient for discourse, and serve all our purposes in company, in the pulpit, in the theatre, and in the schools.

DAVID HUME

PHILOSOPHICAL QUERY

• • • • • •

Hume's point here is very important. Don't rush by it. Take a moment and try to write a purely factual description of something you believe is immoral. Do you agree with Hume that the facts are value neutral and that all moral judgments are reports of feelings associated with certain facts? Explain why or why not.

Moral Sentiments

Hume believed that the task before him was a "question of fact, not of abstract science" and that success was possible only by "following the experimental method, and deducing general maxims from a comparison of particular instances." Using the fact–value distinction, he attempted a reformation of moral philosophy, announcing that it was time to "reject every system of ethics, however subtle or ingenious, which is not founded on fact and observation."

Hume's efforts did, indeed, launch a revolution in moral philosophy. He helped establish a method of "ordinary language analysis" that became especially influential in the early part of the twentieth century and whose influence is still significant. (See Chapter 17.) Notice how the empirical criterion of meaning affects Hume's language analysis in the following passage. Also note the role he gives reason.

> The very nature of language guides us almost infallibly in forming a judgment of [matters of Personal Merit]; and as every tongue possesses one set of words which are taken in a good sense, and another in the opposite, the least acquaintance with the idiom suffices, without any reasoning, to direct us in collecting and arranging the estimable or blamable qualities of [people]. The only object of reasoning is to discover the circumstances on both sides, which are common to these qualities; to observe that particular in which the estimable qualities agree on one hand, and the blamable on the other; and thence to reach the foundation of ethics, and find those universal principles, from which all censure or approbation is ultimately derived.[45]

In all cases of moral judgment, what we call virtues are the traits that we, in fact, find agreeable. The feeling of agreeableness is what makes them virtues to us. We do not find them agreeable because they are virtues. We call them virtues because we find them agreeable. That's an important distinction.

We sometimes lose sight of the fundamental nature of all value judgments because we use different terms to distinguish among variations of experience. Put another way, different pleasures are like different flavors; all the good flavors are pleasing, yet we call some sweet, some sour, some chocolate, some lime, some fruity, some salty, and so forth. Similarly, all unpleasant sentiments are alike, yet we call some disgusting, some ugly, some evil, some bad, some cowardly, and so forth.[46]

What, then, is unique to that "peculiar kind" of sentiment that Hume calls moral? Hume says that *moral sentiment is a disinterested reaction to character (motive).* Moral virtue is *disinterested approbation* (liking or approval) of character or motive. Moral vice is *disinterested disapprobation* (disliking or disapproval) of character or motive. According to Hume, careful language analysis reveals that, *as a matter of fact,* moral judgments are disinterested judgments of character.

Accurate and just reasoning is the only catholic remedy, fitted for all persons and all dispositions; and is alone able to subvert that abstruse philosophy and metaphysical jargon, which, being mixed up with popular superstition, renders it in a manner impenetrable to careless reasoners, and gives it the air of science and wisdom.

DAVID HUME

Rejection of Egoism

By asserting that moral judgments are disinterested, Hume rejected egoism. (See Chapters 3, 4, 11, 12, 16, and 17 for more about the relationship of self-interest to morality.) In his forceful attack, he refers to egoism as "a principle . . . supposed to prevail among many." Hume characterizes egoism as the belief that

> . . . all *benevolence* is mere hypocrisy, friendship a cheat, public spirit a farce, fidelity a snare to procure trust and confidence, and that while all of us, at bottom, pursue only our private interest, we wear these fair disguises, in order to put others off their guard, and expose them the more to our wiles and machinations.[47]

Hume argues that egoism is utterly inadequate as an account of real life. A clear look at the facts makes it plain that we have other motives than these. He rejects egoism as factually inaccurate and overly simplistic, warning that the love of such contrived simplicity "has been the source of much false reasoning in philosophy." He says:

> The most obvious objection to the selfish hypothesis is that, as it is contrary to common feeling and our most unprejudiced notions, there is required the highest stretch of philosophy to establish so extraordinary a paradox. To the most careless observer there appear to be such dispositions as benevolence and generosity; such affections as love, friendship, compassion, gratitude.[48]

Hume's attack on egoism is withering in its clarity and appeal to everyday experience. He rejects and ridicules the complications implicit in the belief that our real motives are always some form of narrow self-interest. Consider, Hume suggests, feelings of grief. Which is more absurd: to assume that all feelings of grief over the deaths of our loved ones are really disguised self-interest or to accept them as we experience them? Are we, Hume asks, ready to believe that our loving pets are really motivated solely by self-interest? Obviously not. The most cursory glance at our actual experiences with animals shows that conditioning (or even instinct) does not adequately describe all acts of animal loyalty and affection. Does this mean that animals can express disinterested benevolence but human beings cannot? Hume thought such an idea was preposterous.

According to Hume, pure self-love is another of the fictions that results from rationalistic thinking that loses touch with actual experience because it is not based on empirical facts. When we take our actual experience into account, self-love is not an adequate explanation of human motivation.

> Where is the difficulty in conceiving, that . . . from the original frame of our temper, we may feel a desire of another's happiness or good, which by means of that affection, becomes our own good, and is afterwards pursued, from the combined motives of benevolence and self-enjoyments? Who sees not that vengeance, from the force alone of passion, may be so eagerly pursued, as to make us knowingly neglect every consideration of ease, interest, or safety; and, like some vindictive animals, infuse our very souls into the wounds we give an enemy; and what a malignant philosophy it must be, that will not allow to humanity and friendship the same privileges which are indisputably granted to the darker passions of enmity and resentment.[49]

Even an act performed out of love is supposed to be "unegoistic"? But you blockheads!

FRIEDRICH NIETZSCHE

Soon or late, it is ideas, not vested interests which are dangerous for good or evil.

JOHN MAYNARD KEYNES

"Emotions May Be Helpful and Even Necessary"

Alison Jaggar is one of a number of contemporary philosophers who are raising questions about the heavy emphasis placed on reason by Western philosophers. Jaggar argues that emotions are also vital aspects of anyone's picture of reality because they help determine what we notice or ignore, and impart degrees of interest and importance to experience. According to Jaggar, emotions select, direct, and help define observations and experiences. Yet, Jaggar notes, traditional Western philosophy has viewed emotion as inferior to reason and even viewed emotions as subversive hindrances to knowledge. Jaggar denies that a gap exists between emotion and knowledge: Far from being hindrances to the construction of knowledge, she says, "emotions may be helpful and even necessary." In *Love and Knowledge: Emotion in Feminist Epistemology*, she writes:

From Plato until the present, with a few notable exceptions, reason rather than emotion has been regarded as the indispensable faculty for acquiring knowledge. . . . [Objective] testability became accepted as the hallmark of natural science; this, in turn, was viewed as the paradigm of genuine knowledge. . . . Because values and emotions had been identified as variable and idiosyncratic, [the objective standard] stipulated that trustworthy knowledge could be established only by methods that neutralized the values and emotions of individual [thinkers].

Alison M. Jaggar, "Love and Knowledge: Emotion in Feminist Epistemology," in *Women, Knowledge, and Reality: Explorations in Feminist Philosophy*, eds. Ann Garry and Marilyn Pearsall (Boston: Unwin Hyman, 1988), pp. 123ff.

■ COMMENTARY ■

In the end, Hume compared full-blown skepticism to doubting the existence of an external reality, pointing out that the issue cannot be settled logically and rationally. No one can actually live as a skeptic:

> To whatever length anyone may push his speculative principles of scepticism, he must act . . . and live, and converse like other men. . . . It is impossible for him to persevere in total scepticism, or make it appear in his conduct for a few hours.[50]

Having reasoned carefully and thoroughly, without shying away from what he discovered, no matter how alien to common sense or established knowledge and custom, no matter how foreign to his heart's desire, the great archetype of the skeptic expresses a timeless lament in his own fashion:

> Where am I, or what? From what causes do I derive my existence, and to what condition shall I return? Whose favour shall I court, and whose anger must I dread? What beings surround me? and on whom have I influence, or who have influence on me? I am confounded with all these questions, and begin to fancy myself in the most deplorable condition imaginable, environ'd with the deepest darkness, and utterly depriv'd of the use of every member and faculty.

Never [a] literary attempt was more unfortunate than my Treatise of Human Nature. *It fell dead-born from the press, without reaching such distinction as even to excite a murmur among the zealots.*

DAVID HUME

Most fortunately it happens, that since reason is incapable of dispelling these clouds, nature herself suffices to that purpose, and cures me of this philosophical melancholy and delirium. . . . I dine, I play a game of backgammon, I converse, and am merry with my friends; and when after three or four hours' amusement, I wou'd return to these speculations, they appear so cold, and strain'd and ridiculous, that I cannot find in my heart to enter them any farther.[51]

What, then, is the point of these difficult and frustrating skeptical inquiries if, in the end, not even Hume takes them seriously? Ah, but he does take them seriously. Using careful observation and analysis, Hume raises important points about both the limits of reason and the needs of the human heart.

Hume exposes cloudy and meaningless language and bogus theorizing. He shows clearly the ultimate inadequacy of rational and empirical efforts to prove God's existence or infer His nature. In Hume's own time, a great scientific revolution had already established the force and usefulness of the scientific method. His analysis of cause and effect, as he acknowledges, does not destroy science but, rather, modifies a bit of what some see as its arrogance. Neither science nor theology can explain the ultimate origins of life or the ultimate nature of reality.

Hume has shown us how little we actually *know* of the most important and most common aspects of existence: self, personal identity, cause and effect, reality, the external world, the universe, and God. Read correctly, I think, Hume reveals that the power of logic and reason are, nevertheless, not all-powerful. He also shows that many of the great theological and metaphysical beliefs to which so many are devoted are barely intelligible. In other words, Hume teaches us that neither the scientist nor the philosopher nor the priest has *the* method and *the* answer to timeless questions.

When you reach the fork in the road, take it.

Yogi Berra

Hume reminds us that there is no absolute certainty in life, only enough uniformity to live reasonably well, if we are lucky. He also shows that belief without reason is often meaningless, but that a life based solely on reason is not possible. We live and act on what George Santayana calls *animal faith:* a force within us that *trusts something* in spite of the limits of our experience and reason.

Hume, the archetypal skeptic, suggests that a person will always be more than philosophy, religion, or science can hope to know:

It seems, then, that nature has pointed out a mixed kind of life as the most suitable to the human race, and secretly admonished them to allow none of these biases to *draw* too much, so as to incapacitate them for any other occupations and entertainments. Indulge your passion for science, says she, but let your science be human, and such as may have a direct reference to action and society. Abstruse thought and profound researches I prohibit, and will severely punish, by the pensive melancholy which they introduce, by the endless uncertainty in which they involve you, and by the cold reception which your pretended discoveries shall meet with, when communicated. Be a philosopher; but amidst all your philosophy, be still a [human being].[52]

■ SUMMARY OF MAIN POINTS ■

- A skeptic is a person who demands clear, observable, undoubtable evidence based on experience before accepting any claim as true. Empiricism is the belief that all knowledge is ultimately derived from the senses (experience). Empiricists believe that all ideas can be traced to sense data. There are no innate ideas. At birth the mind is a clean slate, or *tabula rasa*.

- John Locke claimed that all ideas are copies of the things that caused the basic sensations on which they rest. Today Locke's copy theory is known as the correspondence theory of truth: an idea (or belief or thought) is true if whatever it refers to actually exists. The copy theory generates what is called the egocentric predicament: If all knowledge comes in the form of my own ideas, how can I verify the existence of anything external to them? Locke distinguished between *primary qualities* and *secondary qualities*. Primary qualities are sensible qualities that exist independently of any perceiver. Secondary qualities are qualities whose existence depends on a perceiver. Although he rejected Descartes's rationalism and theory of innate ideas, Locke accepted a Cartesian type of *dualism,* in which mind and matter are viewed as different kinds of substance.

- Locke's successor, George Berkeley, rejected the correspondence theory, pointing out that there is no fixed "thing" to copy; we know only perceptions. Berkeley's formula is *esse est percipi:* To be is to be perceived. This view is known as idealism or immaterialism. Berkeley shied away from the logical consequences of immaterialism and posited the existence of a universal perceiver (God) to account for the existence of the external world and regularity of nature.

- David Hume rejected metaphysical speculation as meaningless and irrelevant to the lives of ordinary people. He asserted that no metaphysical issue was ever clearly and thoroughly settled. Hume modified Locke's theory of ideas by distinguishing between two kinds of perceptions: ideas and impressions. All ideas can be traced to the impressions on which they are based. All ideas are derived from experience.

- Hume established an empirical criterion of meaning: All meaningful ideas can be traced to sense experience (impressions). Beliefs that cannot be traced to sense experience are technically not ideas at all; they are meaningless utterances. Strict application of the empirical criterion of meaning led Hume to skeptical conclusions regarding some of our most fundamental beliefs. Hume thought that imagination, rather than reason or experience, accounts for the persistence of our belief in the independent existence of an external world and that imagination ultimately overrides reason.

- Hume argued that the self is only a bundle of impressions and that identity is a mental act, not a property of things. Therefore, personal immortality is a meaningless concept. He also argued that cause and effect are products of imagination and that the argument from motion and the ontological argument are meaningless. According to Hume, the argument from design fails because human experience cannot provide sufficient evidence of order on earth, much less order in the universe. Hume denied the possibility of rationalistic ethics and claims that all moral judgments are based on sentiments.

■ POST-READING REFLECTIONS ■

Now that you have had a chance to learn about the Skeptic, use your new knowledge to answer these questions.

1. Outline the development of the "epistemological turn" from Descartes through Locke and Berkeley to Hume.

2. In your own words, reconstruct the basic empirical critique of rationalism.

3. What is the *tabula rasa*? What is its significance to Locke's empiricism?

4. Explain the philosophical significance of the question "Does a tree falling in the forest make a sound if no one is there to hear it?" Then answer it as Berkeley would.

5. Why is the distinction between impressions and ideas important to Hume's philosophy?

6. Apply the empirical criterion of meaning to an example of your own choosing.

7. How does Hume's bundle theory of the self affect his reasoning regarding personal identity and immortality.

8. How does Hume account for the external world?

9. Sketch Hume's analysis of cause and effect.

10. Summarize and analyze Hume's critique of the argument from design.

11. Construct a Humean analysis of some contemporary moral issue. What are the advantages of Hume's approach? The disadvantages?

12. Why does Hume say "I am ready to throw all my books and papers into the fire, and resolve never more to renounce the pleasures of life for the sake of reasoning and philosophy"?

PHILOSOPHY INTERNET RESOURCES

Go to the Soccio Web page at **http://philosophy.wadsworth.com/ Soccio7e** for Web links, practice quizzes and tests, a pronunciation guide, and study tips.

THE UNIVERSALIST

Immanuel Kant

TWO THINGS FILL THE MIND WITH EVER NEW
AND INCREASING ADMIRATION AND AWE . . .
THE STARRY HEAVENS ABOVE
AND THE MORAL LAW WITHIN.

Immanuel Kant

LEARNING OBJECTIVES

- WHAT IS THE DIFFERENCE BETWEEN "NONMORAL" AND "IMMORAL"?
- WHAT IS KANTIAN FORMALISM?
- WHAT IS CRITICAL PHILOSOPHY?
- WHAT ARE PHENOMENAL AND NOUMENAL REALITY?
- WHAT ARE PRACTICAL REASON AND THEORETICAL REASON?
- WHAT IS A MAXIM? WHAT MAKES A MAXIM MORAL?
- WHAT IS A HYPOTHETICAL IMPERATIVE?
- WHAT IS THE "PRACTICAL IMPERATIVE"?
- WHAT IS A THOUGHT EXPERIMENT?
- WHAT IS THE ORIGINAL POSITION, AND HOW IS IT RELATED TO THE "VEIL OF IGNORANCE"?

FOR YOUR REFLECTION

KEEP THESE QUESTIONS IN MIND AS YOU LEARN ABOUT THE UNIVERSALIST.

1. *What is the difference between "nonmoral" and "immoral"?*
2. *What is Kantian formalism?*
3. *What is critical philosophy?*
4. *What are phenomenal and noumenal reality?*
5. *What are practical reason and theoretical reason?*
6. *What is a maxim? What makes a maxim moral?*
7. *What is a hypothetical imperative?*
8. *What is the "practical imperative"?*
9. *What is a thought experiment?*
10. *What is the original position, and how is it related to the "veil of ignorance"?*

FOR DEEPER CONSIDERATION

A. What did Kant mean by "a scandal in philosophy"? How did this scandal prompt Kant to complete the epistemological turn and generate what has been called Kant's "Copernican revolution in philosophy"?

B. What is the "categorical imperative," and how is the notion of moral duty crucial to Kant's attempt to establish a universal moral principle? What does Kant mean by duty? How does the categorical imperative help us identify our duty in particular cases and connect us to the Kantian kingdom of ends?

Moral issues confront us daily. We live in a time troubled by intense moral controversies concerning abortion, euthanasia, affirmative action, terrorism, capital punishment, substance abuse, monetary fraud, governmental deception, the environment, aid to the homeless, welfare, the rights of disabled persons, parental influence in the schools, pornography, AIDS, smoking in public, and sexual conduct. Such issues have political, financial, legal, religious, and psychological aspects. But in their *moral dimensions,* they touch upon our most fundamental values concerning good and bad, personal worth and character, respect for ourselves and others—in sum, what it means to be a human being.

The word **moral** comes from the Latin *moralis,* meaning "custom," "manner," or "conduct." Moral refers to what people consider good or bad, right or wrong. There are two contrasting words: **nonmoral (amoral)** and **immoral**. The *moral–nonmoral* distinction is *descriptive*. It makes no value judgment and only distinguishes moral concerns from nonmoral ones, such as economic, mechanical, nutritional issues. The *moral–immoral* distinction is *prescriptive;* it makes a value judgment about what we ought to do. The distinction between moral and immoral is equivalent to that between right and wrong or good and bad.

The moral dimension confronts us in courtrooms, classrooms, at work, and at home, as we try to determine who is or is not *responsible* for this or that act. Moral responsibility is different from the factual issue of determining who did what. It has to do with punishment or forgiveness; it affects whether we see a sexual offender as bad or sick, whether we scold a child or hug her, whether a criminal defendant is imprisoned, hospitalized, or released. Morality seems to be inseparable from responsibility.

Responsibility, in turn, implies freedom of choice, the ability to decide on one course of action over another, to think and behave one way instead of another way. For example, a person unwillingly drugged is not held morally accountable for actions performed under the influence of the drug, but a person who willingly gets drunk and then drives probably is.

Lawyers, theologians, psychologists, and parents continually wrestle with issues of free, responsible choice. Yet scientific evidence of causal patterns suggests that more and more conduct once labeled immoral may be beyond our control. Biopsychologists and geneticists continue to discover physical and biochemical "causes" of behavior.

But if all nature is *governed* by laws of chemistry and physics, laws that admit of no exceptions, then I can no more be held responsible for helping you across the street than you can be held responsible for striking me with an ax because you're bored. If our behavior is determined by genetic influences, how can we ever hold anyone responsible for anything? And if we cannot, how do we justify moral sanctions? Stripped of the possibility of moral choice, how different am I from any other animal?

Troubled by scientific and philosophic arguments against the possibility of human freedom and responsibility, Immanuel Kant completed the epistemological turn begun by René Descartes (Chapter 9) by challenging Hume's skepticism (Chapter 10).

moral
From the Latin *moralis,* meaning "custom," "manner," or "conduct"; refers to what people consider good or bad, right or wrong; used descriptively as a contrast to *amoral* or *nonmoral* and prescriptively as a contrast to *immoral.*

nonmoral (amoral)
Not pertaining to moral; a value-neutral descriptive claim or classification.

immoral
Morally wrong, bad, or not right; a moral value judgment or prescriptive claim.

It is precisely in knowing its limits that philosophy consists.

IMMANUEL KANT

PHILOSOPHICAL
QUERY

• • • • • •

Think for a moment about a nonmoral world, a world in which no one is held morally accountable. In such a world, every action would be viewed as the inevitable result of genetic, social, and historical causes. What are the advantages of such a view? The disadvantages? Think about some time when you made an excuse for yourself, claiming that you "couldn't help" doing or not doing something. What is gained and lost by making such excuses?

■ THE PROFESSOR ■

Immanuel Kant (1724–1804) was born in Königsberg in what was then known as East Prussia (now Kaliningrad in the former Soviet Union). His parents were poor but devout members of a fundamentalist Protestant sect known as Pietism. Pietists rejected the idea of imposing a church and priests between the individual and God, preferring to rely on immediate personal appeal to God. They emphasized faith and repentance and lived severe, puritanical lives.

When he was eight years old Kant was sent to a school founded by a local Pietist preacher. The regimen was exceptionally strict, beginning daily at five-thirty in the morning. Students received an hour's instruction in Pietism, and each class period concluded with a prayer. Sundays were devoted almost completely to religious activity. Later in life, Kant said that he resented the school's heavy emphasis on a theology of terror and piety—fear of hell and trembling before a vision of a wrathful God. Yet he never lost his regard for righteousness and moral severity. As an old man, Kant spoke respectfully of his parents' faith, saying, "People may say what they will of Pietism. Those in whom it was sincere were worthy of honor. They possessed the highest thing that man can have—the quiet, the content, the inner peace, which no suffering can disturb."[1]

At the age of sixteen, Kant entered the University of Königsberg, where he studied for six years. Upon leaving the university, he refused a lucrative offer to become a Lutheran minister, choosing instead to continue his studies. For the next nine years he supported himself with meager earnings as a private tutor. In 1755, Kant received the equivalent of today's doctoral degree. This earned him the privilege of lecturing at the university as a *Privatdozent,* a private teacher whose salary was paid directly by his students. The more students he attracted and retained, the more money he earned. Kant became a popular lecturer, and in 1770, when he was forty-six, the university hired Kant as a professor of logic and metaphysics. Though the salary was small, Kant was pleased with his improved status.

Immanuel Kant

It is indeed true that I think many things with the cleverest conviction, and to my great satisfaction, which I never have the courage to say, but I never say anything that I do not think.

IMMANUEL KANT

The life of Immanuel Kant is hard to describe; he had neither life nor history in the proper sense of the words.

HEINRICH HEINE

The Solitary Writer

For the most part, Kant's life is noteworthy for not being noteworthy. He probably never traveled more than sixty miles from his birthplace during his entire life. One

A Beloved Teacher

I have had the good fortune to know a philosopher who was my teacher. In the prime of his life he possessed the joyous courage of youth, and this also, as I believe, attended him to extreme old age. His open, thoughtful brow was the seat of untroubled cheerfulness and joy, his conversation was full of ideas most suggestive. He had at his service jest, witticism, and humorous fancy, and his lectures were at once instructive and most entertaining. . . . No cabal or sect, no prejudice or reverence for a name, had the slightest influence with him in opposition to the extension and promotion of truth. He encouraged and gently compelled his hearers to think for themselves. . . . This man, whom I name with the greatest gratitude and reverence, is Immanuel Kant; his image stands before me, and is dear to me.

Johann Gottfried Herder (1744–1803), quoted by Will and Ariel Durant in *Rousseau and Revolution*, vol. 10 of *The Story of Civilization* (New York: Simon & Schuster, 1967), p. 532.

biographer said, "Kant's life was like the most regular of regular verbs," to which another added, "But it was not a *conjugated* verb. For Kant never married."[2]

Kant lived most of his life on a rigid schedule. The poet Heinrich Heine described Kant's penchant for routine:

> I do not believe that the great cathedral clock of this city accomplished its day's work in a less passionate and more regular way than its countryman, Immanuel Kant. Rising from bed, coffee-drinking, writing, lecturing, eating, walking, everything had its fixed time: and the neighbors knew that it must be exactly half past four when they saw Professor Kant, in his gray coat, with his cane in his hand, step out of his housedoor, and move toward the little lime tree avenue, which is named after him, the Philosopher's Walk. Eight times he walked up and down that walk at every season of the year, and when the weather was bad, or the gray clouds threatened rain, his servant, old Lampe, was seen anxiously following him with a large umbrella under his arm like an image of providence.[3]

Kant is reported to have missed his walk only once, when he became so absorbed in reading Rousseau's *Émile* that he forgot to take it.

Kant was a prolific writer. His works include the difficult but revolutionary *Critique of Pure Reason* (1781 and a second edition in 1787), *Prolegomena to Any Future Metaphysics* (1783), *Foundations of the Metaphysics of Morals* (1785), *Critique of Practical Reason* (1788), *Critique of Judgment* (1790), and *Religion Within the Limits of Reason Alone* (1793).

The *Critique of Pure Reason* is one of the most difficult books ever written. Philosophy majors approach it with dread and then forever after boast proudly if they manage to read the entire thing. Kant once said that he did not fear being refuted; he feared not being understood. He had good reason to fear.

When I could have used a wife, I could not support one; and when I could support one, I no longer needed any.

IMMANUEL KANT

On August 16, 1783, he wrote that his work was "the result of reflection which occupied me for at least twelve years":

> I brought it to completion in the greatest haste within four or five months, giving the closest attention to its contents, but with little thought of the exposition, or of rendering it easy of comprehension by the reader—a decision which I have never regretted, since otherwise, had I longer delayed and sought to give a more popular form, the work would probably never have been completed at all.[4]

Kant admitted that he deliberately left out illustrative examples because they would just add length to an already massive work. Besides, he added, examples are only necessary for popular appeal "and this work can never be made suitable for popular consumption."[5] When he sent the metaphysician Marcus Herz the manuscript of the *Critique of Pure Reason,* Herz sent it back only half read, saying, "If I finish it I am afraid I shall go mad."[6]

Kant's work was made difficult by another factor: Because he was trying to express new concepts, he felt that he had to invent new meanings for Latin terms or coin new phrases in German; he also gave his own unusual meanings to common terms and sometimes used the same term to mean different things. All of that notwithstanding, the little professor's big, difficult books forever altered Western thinking.

Kant retired from public lecturing in 1797, and although he physically declined, he remained a prolific writer. Immanuel Kant died a lonely old man who had never seen a mountain or the sea. Yet he shook the foundations of Western philosophy to such an extent that it has been said that whether or not philosophers agree or disagree with Kant, they must face him. Above his grave in the Königsberg Cathedral, his own words are inscribed, "The starry heavens above me; the moral law within me."

The philosopher-poet Friedrich Schiller, referring to the richness, complexity, and importance of Kant's philosophy, as well as its impact on the many philosophers whose work is in one way or another a response to Kant's, said, "See how a single rich man has given a living to a number of beggars."[7]

Kant's work was important and troubling, for it included devastating critiques of rationalism and empiricism (the dominant philosophical schools of the day), as well as popular theology. It is said that some clergymen called Immanuel Kant a dog, and others called their dogs Immanuel Kant.

■ A SCANDAL IN PHILOSOPHY ■

In Chapter 10, we saw how radical Hume's skepticism was. Hume was one of the most troublesome philosophers of his or any time. His critique of empiricism led him to such disturbing conclusions as we can never know cause and effect, the self, or the external world. He also argued that moral judgments are somehow like matters of taste. Hume's withering *Dialogues Concerning Natural Religion* applied a strictly rational analysis to cherished arguments for the existence of God and showed them to be illogical and unpersuasive. With his strict understanding of knowledge and reason, Hume concluded that reason is

The goodly burghers of Königsberg had an infallible way of setting their clocks. Every afternoon, precisely at three-thirty, Immanuel Kant left his house for his daily stroll.

HENRY THOMAS AND
DANA LEE THOMAS

[Kant] is often pictured as an old bachelor whose every activity was scheduled with such precision that neighbors could set their watches when he stepped out of his house each day at half past four to walk up and down his small avenue eight times.

SAMUEL ENOCH STUMPF

[Kant] arose at five every morning, was in bed by ten every night, and the townspeople used to set their watches by his three o'clock walk.

BURTON F. PORTER

and ought to be "the slave of the passions." Hume's philosophy made the external world unknowable and rendered reason impotent to unlock the secrets of nature. His critique of rationalistic ethics seemed to show that reason was utterly incapable of motivating people. In other words, Hume undercut the very essence of optimistic Enlightenment thinking.

Kant was one of the first thinkers to realize the consequences of Hume's relentless attack on the scope of reason. In the preface of his *Prolegomena to Any Future Metaphysics,* Kant wrote:

> Since the origin of metaphysics so far as we know its history, nothing has ever happened which could have been more decisive to its fate than the attack made upon it by David Hume. He threw no light on this species of knowledge, but he certainly struck a spark by which light might have been kindled had it caught some inflammable substance and had its smouldering fire been carefully nursed and developed.
>
> . . . However hasty and mistaken Hume's inference may appear, it was at least founded upon investigation, and this investigation deserved the concentration of the brighter spirits of his day as well as determined efforts on their part to discover, if possible, a happier solution of the problem in the sense proposed by him.
>
> But Hume suffered the usual misfortune of metaphysicians, of not being understood. It is positively painful to see how utterly his opponents . . . missed the point of the problem; for while they were ever taking for granted that which he doubted, and demonstrating with zeal and often with impudence that which he never thought of doubting, they so misconstrued his valuable suggestion that everything remained in its old condition, as if nothing happened.[8]

The seeds of what Kant referred to as a "scandal" in philosophy were planted when Descartes doubted his own existence and divided everything into two completely distinct substances: minds and bodies. Descartes was never able to account satisfactorily for mind–body interaction or to establish with certainty the existence of an external, material world. Although Descartes refused to follow his rationalistic premises to their logical conclusions, the Continental rationalists who came after him did. Because their model of certainty was mathematical and geometric, they moved further and further away from experience. As a result, they established grand systems of logical relationships ungrounded in observation or perception.

The British empiricists chose another tack, viewing the human mind as the passive receiver of impressions and experiences. But this view leads to the unfortunate conclusion that all certain knowledge is confined to ideas. Ironically, though they began with experience, the empiricists were unable to get back to it. The result was Hume's admission that we must believe in an external world, in selves, and in causes and effects, without ever knowing them.

As it has so often in history, scientific progress challenged the dominant philosophies of the day. As Kant noted, something was drastically wrong with philosophy if between them the two major philosophical schools at the time denied the importance of perception, denied the possibility of knowledge of cause and effect, denied the verifiable existence of the external world, and rendered reason

But Hume suffered the usual misfortune of metaphysicians, of not being understood. It is positively painful to see how utterly his opponents . . . missed the point of the problem; for while they were ever taking for granted that which he doubted, and demonstrating with zeal and often with impudence that which he never thought of doubting, they so misconstrued his valuable suggestion that everything remained in its old condition, as if nothing happened.

Immanuel Kant

[T]he Enlightenment has not remained incomplete, but unenlightened.

H. Böhme and
G. Böhme

impotent as a motivator in human affairs, while science—not to mention common sense and everyday experience—clearly showed otherwise.

You might ask why Kant did not abandon philosophy if it was so out of touch, so bizarre? Why not just accept the supremacy of science and let philosophy die of irrelevance? Kant found this course unsatisfying, for science was unveiling a mechanistic universe in which everything (at least once fully understood) would ultimately be shown to follow universal, unchanging laws of nature. If such a picture is complete and accurate, then God is unnecessary, free will is an illusion, and morality is impossible. If we have no choice but to follow "laws of nature," then values as they are usually understood disappear. Our behavior is only more complex than that of rocks or worms—it is not different in kind. The murderer and the saint are both following inescapable patterns of cause and effect.

How, Kant asked, could science, which was clearly making progress, be headed for conclusions that reduced human life to blind mechanism? How could two radically different philosophies each reach such odd, unacceptable results? Was it possible to synthesize science with the good parts of rationalism and empiricism in a way that would give a rational account of the world without stripping us of moral worth and dignity? Surely there had to be better alternatives than the cold, unfree world of science or the unverifiable, impractical worlds of rationalistic and skeptical philosophy.

I have therefore found it necessary to deny knowledge in order to make room for faith.

IMMANUEL KANT

PHILOSOPHICAL
QUERY

• • • • • •

Do you think morality must disappear if everything we do can be explained according to scientific laws and patterns? Could there be another kind of morality based on laws of behavior and biopsychology? Why or why not? What is lost in the purely "scientific" view? Anything important? Explain.

■ KANT'S COPERNICAN REVOLUTION ■

In response to the "scandal in philosophy," Kant turned to an analysis (which he called a critique) of *how* knowledge is possible. In the process, he posited an underlying *structure* imposed by the mind on the sensations and perceptions it encounters. We can think of this structure as the *formal* component of knowing. For this reason, Kant is known as a formalist. Kant theorized that neither reason by itself nor sensation by itself can give us knowledge of the external world. Knowledge is the result of the interaction between the mind and sensation. Knowledge and experience are shaped, structured, or formed by special regulative ideas called *categories*. This theory is known as **Kantian formalism,** *Kantian idealism,* or *transcendental idealism.*

Kant noted that Descartes's principal error began with a failure to understand scientific method. Galileo had changed science by establishing a "common plan of procedure," a method for studying phenomena. Though Descartes had understood the importance of method, he had not fully understood that the *scientific* method is *both* empirical *and* rational. Kant realized that the empiricists were

Kantian formalism
Theory that knowledge is the result of the interaction between the mind and sensation and is structured by regulative ideas called categories; also known as *Kantian idealism* and *transcendental idealism.*

A Diderot Pictorial Encyclopedia of Trades & Industry, Dover Publications

This illustration of a print shop from Denis Diederot's *Encyclopédie* illustrates the Enlightenment's optimistic faith in the spread of knowledge through free exchange of ideas. Does today's interest in the Internet reflect similar faith in the spread of knowledge through free exchange of ideas?

guilty of a similar error of incompleteness by discounting the importance of reason. Knowledge, as the scientific method shows, consists of both a rational and a perceptual (empirical) component. It requires both a subject (a knowing mind) and an object (that which is known).

The common belief during Kant's time, however, was that truth occurs when ideas in the mind agree with external conditions or objects, the "copy theory" (see Chapter 10). For example, if I think this book has a red cover, my idea is true if the cover actually is red. But as Kant realized, if all knowledge fits that model, we could never discover general laws of nature. We could discover only that *this* apple falls, not that all bodies are subject to gravity—because we never experience all bodies. Hume understood this but was willing to limit the domain of knowledge to particulars, in the end asserting that we could *only believe* in the most important aspects of our existence: the regularity of experience, the existence of an external world, the existence of a unified self, cause and effect, and a moral order.

If we accept Hume's initial premises, his conclusions follow. However, close inspection of the way science is actually done shows that scientists make precisely the kinds of generalizations Hume's *theory* says we cannot make. Kant said that *when a theory results in conclusions that are clearly inconsistent with experience, real-world evidence must outweigh theoretical consistency.* And everyday experience shows that knowledge of causes and effects, the external world, and the self exists.

According to Kant, the scientific method is obviously more reliable and complete than Hume's philosophy. How do they differ? Kant pointed out that scientific thinking involves the *activity* of asking questions and framing hypotheses. Scientific thinking is not merely the passive recording of whatever happens; it

[T]he demand for intellectual honesty is itself dishonest. . . . Rather, knowledge comes to us through a network of prejudices, opinions, innervations, self-corrections, presuppositions and exaggerations.

THEODOR ADORNO

requires the *active* setting up of controlled experimental conditions.[9] And this suggests that knowledge is a kind of *interaction*, a two-way street between the knower (the subject) and the known (the object).

Kant realized that he was proposing to change fundamental assumptions about the structure of knowledge, much as Copernicus had changed our assumptions about the structure of the universe. After astronomers had failed for centuries to make consistent sense of an earth-centered universe, Copernicus proposed a revolutionary hypothesis: that the sun is at the center, that the earth is part of a solar system. This assumption dissolved the great difficulties of the past and produced new, predictable knowledge. Kant was advocating a Copernican revolution in philosophy: He would reverse the course of his philosophical predecessors and assume that *instead of the mind having to conform to what can be known, what can be known must conform to the mind.*

Critical Philosophy

Descartes began the epistemological turn by focusing on the mind as a rational substance. But by concentrating on the mind's rational function, he ignored its *organizing function* and so was unable to avoid generating conclusions that do not square with experience. The British empiricists, culminating with Hume, took the second step and demonstrated both the importance of experience and the limits of *a priori* reason. So strict was Hume's emphasis on experience as the sole source of knowledge that, coupled with the empiricists' view of the mind as a passive, neutral blank tablet, he was forced to conclude we cannot "know" that anything happens of necessity or even that we have a self.

Kant proposed a radical alternative, which we can think of as the third and final step of the epistemological turn: a critical analysis of what kind of knowledge we actually have based on a new view of the mind as actively interacting with impressions and perceptions.

Hume had insisted that all knowledge begins in experience with sense impressions. But Hume confused knowledge that is *triggered* by experience with knowledge that is *based* on experience. Kant raised the possibility that our "faculty of knowledge" (mind, for short) might add something to the raw data of experience. Because experience *triggers* and hence *accompanies* all knowledge, we may fail to notice the effects the mind has on experience:

> But though all our knowledge begins with experience, it does not follow that it all arises out of experience. For it may well be that even our empirical knowledge is made up of what we receive through impressions and of what our own faculty of knowledge (sensible knowledge serving merely as the occasion) supplies from itself. If our faculty of knowledge makes any such addition, it may be that we are not in a position to distinguish it from the raw material, until with long practice of attention we have become skilled in separating it.
>
> This, then, is a question which at least calls for closer examination, and does not allow of any offhand answer:—whether there is any knowledge that is thus independent of experience and even of all impressions of the senses. Such

knowledge is entitled *a priori,* and distinguished from the *empirical,* which has its sources *a posteriori,* that is, in experience.[10]

Kant asked a basic question: *Is metaphysics possible?* Can we know things beyond immediate experience? That is, does the human mind have the capacity for *a priori* knowledge, knowledge derived from reason without reference to sense experience? (See Chapters 9 and 10.) In answer, Kant proposed a critical reexamination of metaphysics. Metaphysics, as distinct from science, is an attempt to acquire and systematize knowledge derived by reason, not experience. Kant referred to earlier metaphysical philosophies as *dogmatic,* by which he meant, among other things, that they were *uncritical efforts* to understand the nature of whatever lies beyond immediate experience.

Critical philosophy is the name given to Kant's effort to assess the nature and limits of "pure reason" (reason unadulterated by experience) in an effort to identify the actual relationship of the mind to knowledge. "Pure knowledge" is not morally pure, but refers, rather, to *independent reasoning* (*a priori* reasoning)— that is, to knowledge *not derived from* the senses.

Phenomena and Noumena

According to Kant, our knowledge is *formed* by two things: our actual experiences *and* the mind's faculties of judgment. If Kant is correct, then we cannot know reality as it is. We can know reality only as it is organized by human understanding. **Phenomenal reality** is Kant's term for the world as we experience it. **Noumenal reality** is his term for reality as it is independent of our perceptions, what we commonly call "objective reality." All we can *know* is perceived reality. This is not the same thing as saying that we each have our own private, subjective reality. All other things being equal, Kant says, the human mind imposes uniform categories on reality. Because the faculty of understanding is uniform, all functioning minds impose the same basic order on experience. We might think of Kant's distinction as between *human reality* and *pure reality.*

Although we never experience pure reality, we can nonetheless know (understand) that our minds do not just invent the world. In Kant's language, the mind imposes order on a world of things-in-themselves. Things-in-themselves are *noumena,* things as they exist independently of us. We know *that they exist,* but we can never know them, because in the act of imposing order, the mind changes things-in-themselves to a comprehensible form.

For example, the human ear cannot hear the noumena—the full spectrum of air vibrations known as sound. We cannot hear the highest-pitched sounds a dog hears or the lowest pitches an elephant hears. Human beings would not know that these other wavelengths of sound exist without the help of dog and elephant ears or sensitive instruments. We can experience only what our human faculty of understanding is capable of processing.

Why make such a distinction, since we will never experience noumena? Kant's response is twofold. First, the distinction shows us the limits of human understanding. Second, such a distinction is necessary in order to establish a foundation for a moral philosophy capable of preserving our moral autonomy

critical philosophy
Kant's term for his effort to assess the nature and limits of "pure reason," unadulterated by experience, in order to identify the actual relationship of the mind to knowledge.

phenomenal reality
Kant's term for the world as we experience it.

noumenal reality
Kant's term for reality as it is, independent of our perceptions; what is commonly called "objective reality."

There will always be metaphysics in the world, and what is more, in everyone, especially in every thinking man.

IMMANUEL KANT

and sentiments in light of the onslaught from science and Humean philosophy. But to accomplish this second goal, Kant must first somehow connect human reality to pure reality.

Transcendental Ideas

Hitherto it has been assumed that all our knowledge must conform to objects. But all attempts to extend our knowledge of objects by establishing something in regard to them by means of concepts have, on this assumption, ended in failure. We must, therefore, make trial whether we may not have more success if we suppose that objects must conform to our knowledge.

IMMANUEL KANT

Kant argues that although we cannot directly experience noumena, a special class of *transcendental ideas* bridges the gap between the phenomenal and noumenal worlds. Empirical ideas are validated by sense data (experience). Transcendental ideas are "triggered" by experience when we rely on them to impose unity on the totality of our experiences. They "unify" or "make possible" having experience in the first place. Without some sort of unifying structure, Kant argues, the mind could not "experience" raw sense data. It would be meaningless, undifferentiated—unexperienced. Transcendental ideas do not correspond to any specific experience, but they "make experience possible."

Kant identified three transcendental ideas: *self, cosmos* (totality), and *God*. Kant also called them *regulative ideas* because they "regulate" and synthesize experience on a grand scale.

> Everything that has its basis in the nature of our powers must be appropriate to, and consistent with, their right employment—if we can only guard against a certain misunderstanding and so discover the proper direction of these powers. We are entitled, therefore, to suppose that transcendental ideas . . . have an excellent, and indeed indispensably necessary, regulative employment, namely, that of directing the understanding towards a certain goal upon which the routes marked out by all its rules converge.[11]

According to Kant, pure reason synthesizes all our psychological activities into a unity by positing the idea of *self*:

> The first [regulative] idea is the "I" itself, viewed simply as thinking nature or soul . . . ; in a word, the idea of a simple self-sustaining intelligence. [Reason operates] to represent all determinations as existing in a single subject, all powers, so far as possible, as derived from a single fundamental power, all change as belonging to the states of one and the same permanent being.[12]

PHILOSOPHICAL

QUERY

• • • • • •

Have you ever met or heard of someone with no idea of self? What would such a person be like? What about people with multiple personality disorder? One woman claims to have ninety-four "personalities." Would such a person have ninety-four "selves" too?

Pure reason also attempts to lend unity to experience by synthesizing all events into a single totality or *cosmos*. Although the idea of cosmos helps organize and frame our experience, we cannot establish (prove) its actual existence. The idea of cosmos remains, for Kant, a deep instinctive need that reason satisfies. But it remains a "mere idea"—though a most important one.

> The second regulative idea of merely speculative reason is the concept of the world in general. . . . The absolute totality of the series of . . . conditions . . . is an idea which can never be completely realised in the empirical employment of reason, but which yet serves as a rule that prescribes how we ought to proceed in dealing with such series. . . . Cosmological ideas are nothing but simply regulative principles, and are very far from positing . . . an actual totality.[13]

PHILOSOPHICAL

QUERY

• • • • • •

Think carefully about your own sense of the universe. How real is the universe to you? Do you know or think of it as an actual, existing thing? Or does it, upon reflection, serve a function along the lines that Kant suggests? Does it help organize and support your understanding in a "regulative" way? What are the implications of Kant's position in regard to scientific attempts to discover the origin of the universe and in regard to religious beliefs in creation?

God, or "the highest intelligence," is Kant's third regulative idea.

> The third idea of pure reason, which contains a merely relative supposition of a being that is the sole and sufficient cause of all cosmological series, is the idea of *God.* We have not the slightest ground to assume in an absolute manner [the existence of] the object of this idea.[14]

By "mere" or "pure" idea, Kant means that God is not the kind of thing that can be verified by an appeal to experience. We know that some people don't believe in God and that others dismiss the idea of God as being unimportant. Kant, however, claims that it is not possible to dismiss the *idea of God,* since it forms one of the organizing structures or categories of reason.

PHILOSOPHICAL

QUERY

• • • • • •

Do you think it's possible for a human to never, ever consider the idea of God? Do you know anyone who never has? Is Kant perhaps onto something, at least regarding the importance of the idea of God? How important and necessary (unavoidable) do you think the idea of God is to the human mind? Explain.

Kant goes on to say that we must act as if self, cosmos, and God refer to existing things but that, as in the case of all noumena, there is no way empirically to verify that they do. God, self, and cosmos are nonetheless real. They refer to universal ideas that regulate human understanding. But if the rest of

Kant's epistemology is correct, God, self, and cosmos remain, like other things-in-themselves, known only through the operations of reason, rather than through experience.

The Objectivity of Experience

In very simple terms, Kant's complex project attempts to show that experience is possible only under a certain general condition: objectivity. Kant argues, that there must be a real—objective—distinction between how the world seems to me and how the world is *in order for me to have any experience at all.*[15]

Crudely put, if there were no difference between the world and me, I could not even have an idea of "having an experience." But I do have experience. Indeed, the skeptical arguments of Hume only make sense if Hume (or any skeptic) understands that he has experience. But experience itself presupposes precisely what the skeptic doubts: his own independent existence as a unified, continuing self that is part of an objective order, subject to causal laws.[16]

Although commentators on Kant understandably disagree over the precise nature of his *argument* here, the disagreement seems to center on the concept of the unity of self that allows me to say (and experience) that this thought or this sensation belongs to *me,* belongs to *one thing,* belongs to a unity that exists prior to *any* empirical verification. For Kant, such a transcendental sense of unity is necessary in order for *me* to have any experience—and, of course, without "me" the whole world ceases to exist.

This awareness of transcendental unity is possible because I *am aware of my own existence and identity through time.* And I can only be aware of my identity through time because I situate or locate myself in a world of actually existing things, things that endure through time. These things have the capacity to be other than I perceive them. They are not merely my perceptions. Thus, they must exist objectively.

You may need to study the preceding passages more than once and may wish to do additional reading to get a better grasp of Kant's complicated, but influential, critical philosophy. And your philosophy instructor might have other interpretations of Kant. That's not surprising given both the complexity of Kant's subject matter and his complex treatment of it.

Kant himself is inconsistent in his treatment of the noumenal world and regulative transcendental ideas, sometimes talking about them as mental constructs and other times suggesting they are existing entities. That's not surprising either, since, if he is correct, the human need for unity and transcendence is very strong. One defense of Kant's inconsistencies might be the force and power of regulative ideas. They may not give us new empirical knowledge, but they allow us to meet our persistent metaphysical longings for an ordered, objective world.

For many people, one of the great weaknesses of the strictest empirical theories of knowledge is that by ruling out knowledge of the existence of God, mind (soul), and other transcendental metaphysical beliefs, these theories fail to satisfy deep, nearly universal needs. Kant deserves credit for recognizing and respecting these needs and for offering a rigorous and sustained explanation and defense of the kind of thinking that springs from them. (Of course, longing for something

In this enquiry I have made completeness my chief aim, and I venture to assert that there is not one single metaphysical problem which has not been solved, or the solution of which the key at least has not been supplied.

IMMANUEL KANT

And thus I conclude the analytical solution of the main question which I had proposed: "How is metaphysics in general possible?" by ascending from the data of its actual use, as shown in its consequences, to the grounds of its possibility.

IMMANUEL KANT

to be true does not mean that it is true. And as philosophers, we do not want to accept as true whatever we deeply long for just because we long for it.)

Having at least a rudimentary sense of Kant's critical project and methods, we are ready to turn to a more accessible, and equally influential, aspect of Kantian philosophy—his categorical imperative and the universalist moral philosophy on which it rests.

▪ THE METAPHYSICS OF MORALS ▪

You may have identified a basic strategy throughout Kant's philosophy so far. Kant shows great respect for powerful and persistent ways of thinking, even if they seem difficult to justify philosophically. I have in mind, for example, the persistence of belief in cause and effect, self-identity, the external world, and God. To establish his "metaphysics of morals," Kant starts with the hypothesis that somehow such ideas can be justified *because we keep relying on them.* Given how they work in our lives and their apparent universality, such ideas must have more than just the psychological value Hume assigned them.

Using the distinction between the phenomenal world and the noumenal world, Kant asserts that it is possible to be both determined, or unfree (in the phenomenal world), and free (in the noumenal world). We have a phenomenal self that falls under the laws of nature and behavior and a noumenal self that is free. Thus, free will exists in the noumenal world. This means we are free and morally responsible even though from the empirical, scientific view of life, we cannot *experience* our freedom but only *think* of it. It is a mistake to attempt an empirical proof of human freedom. Science describes the phenomenal world, but it cannot deal with the noumenal world.

Although there is only one reason, one faculty of understanding, Kant distinguishes two functions of reason, which he called theoretical reason and practical reason. **Theoretical reason,** including scientific reasoning, is confined to the empirical, phenomenal world. Interaction with the world of experience produces laws of behavior that force reason to view everything mechanically. Theoretical reason thus concludes that human beings, like all phenomena, are governed by cause and effect in the form of inescapable laws of nature. Limited by the way the mind can understand the phenomenal world, we must accept that there is no freedom on that level. If freedom is necessary for morality, we must find our freedom elsewhere.

According to Kant, we use **practical reason** to move beyond the phenomenal world to the moral dimension. Practical reason begins with knowledge about moral conduct and produces religious feelings and intuitions. Practical reason helps us deal with the moral freedom provided by free will. In his *Critique of Practical Reason,* Kant says that no matter how many natural causes and sensations might "drive" a person, "they cannot produce [a state of] *being under obligation,* they cannot account for moral duty."[17] The feeling of duty comes from within; it comes from being rational.

Kant uses the term *practical* reason to indicate that we do not act on impulses and desires alone. We also act from *conscious choice* based on our general

If I am asked "What is good?" my answer is that good is good, and that is the end of the matter. Or if I am asked "How is good to be defined?" my answer is that it cannot be defined, and that is all I have to say about it.

G. E. MOORE

theoretical reason
According to Kant, a function of reason confined to the empirical, phenomenal world.

practical reason
According to Kant, moral function of reason that produces religious feelings and intuitions based on knowledge of moral conduct.

"Metaphysical Moments"

The name metaphysics is apt to suggest something difficult, unusual, and remote. Yet it has its familiar side. Most of us have times at which, in reflection, we seem to be confronted not with any particular isolated problem or any particular aspect of our experience, but with experience, or life, or existence, *as a whole*. These might be called our metaphysical moments. It is not easy to give a detailed description of them and for our purpose it is not necessary. Indirectly and roughly, however, it is possible to identify them by saying that if they did not occur there would be no point in religion and little in many works of art and philosophy.

S. Körner, *Kant* (Baltimore: Penguin, 1955), p. 13.

principles. In direct opposition to Hume's claim that reason cannot be a motivator, Kant argues that we can consciously act when no desire is involved at all.[18] Consider, for example, the kind of inner conflict you might experience between a strong desire to buy a new CD and your awareness of your duty to repay a friend from whom you borrowed money. You can *choose* to repay your friend because you ought to, even though you do not want to. (This is not the same thing as doing something to avoid feeling guilty: That does involve desire.)

PHILOSOPHICAL

QUERY

• • • • • •

What would a person be like who could choose only what he or she desired? Do you think it is possible to choose to do something if no desire whatsoever is involved? Explain.

The Moral Law Within

It is clear, then, that the idea of a fixed method, or of a fixed theory of rationality, rests on too naive a view of man and his social surroundings. To those who look at the rich material provided by history . . . it will become clear that there is only one principle that can be defended under all stages of human development. It is the principle: anything goes.

PAUL FEYERABEND

For Kant, morality is a function of reason. Specifically, morality is based on our consciousness of necessary and universal moral laws (or rules, as Kant calls them). Moral rules of behavior differ from other, pragmatic rules because moral rules alone have the quality of being thought of as universal and necessary. And since only *a priori* judgments are universal and necessary, moral judgments must be *a priori*. This is why the empiricists could not discover them.

Thus the moral law cannot be discovered in actual behavior. It is a function of reason, a component of how we think. From this it follows that only rational creatures can be moral and held morally accountable. It also follows that any and all rational creatures are moral beings. The capacity for reason is the source of morality. Reason imposes moral obligation.

Imagine a world in which *no one* had any moral obligations. Would any rational creature desire to live in it? Kant answers with a resounding no! Therefore, he reasoned, morality is absolutely necessary for human relationships. Empirical studies can identify only what people *actually do*; they cannot identify what we *ought to do*. Whereas Hume (Chapter 10) dealt with the is/ought (fact/value) issue by denying that "ought" refers to any fact, it seemed obvious to Kant that the very essence of moral judgments involves *duty*, what we ought to do. Again, Kant begins his inquiry with awareness of and respect for the way we actually think. He notes that very few people consistently think of their own moral judgments as mere matters of custom or taste. Whether we actually live up to our moral principles or not, we think of moral judgments as concerned with how people ought to behave.

Thus, if we begin with the *actual form* of moral judgments as they occur in our lives, we see that they are judgments of duty. As an example, Kant offered the moral judgment "We ought to tell the truth," which he said has the same status as "Every change must have a cause." (Hume rejected the idea of cause.) Just as we cannot begin to think of or even experience anything without already assuming the principle of cause and effect, Kant thought that we cannot function without a sense of duty. Practical reason *imposes* the notion of *ought* on us.

Morality and practical reason rely on concepts that transcend particular facts and immediate experience. Practical reason deals with human behavior and relationships by continually monitoring how we ought to behave. Further, practical reason goes beyond merely addressing how we ought to behave in particular circumstances and generates universal principles that apply to everyone's behavior in similar circumstances at all times.

> *Nowadays everyone in the world is deluded about right and wrong, and confused about benefit and harm. Because so many people share this sickness, no one perceives that it is a sickness.*
>
> Lao Zi

PHILOSOPHICAL QUERY

• • • • • •

Psychologists have identified a character disorder that is labeled as either "sociopathic" or "antisocial personality disorder." One component of this diagnosis is that such people are amoral, lacking any conscience. Do you know people without any sense of moral duty? What are they like? Does the existence of such people mean there is no such thing as a necessary, universal moral law? Discuss.

The Good Will

For Kant, goodness depends not on our behavior but on our will, on what we intend to do if circumstances do not prevent it. Kant insisted that morality was entirely a matter of reason and good will, not, as some believe, a matter of consequences or action.

It's important to note that Kant conceives of the good will as a component of rationality. He argues that "ought implies can," by which he means it must be possible for human beings to live up to their moral obligations. Yet circumstances sometimes prevent us from doing the good we want to do. I may sincerely wish to minister to the sick, but be physically or financially unable. I may diligently try to love my neighbor, only to be rebuffed by him. Thus, Kant reasons, I must not be judged on the consequences of what I actually do but on my reasons. Put another way, morality is a matter of motives.

> *Morality is not properly the doctrine of how we should make ourselves happy, but how we should become worthy of happiness.*
>
> Immanuel Kant

> A good will is good not because of what it performs or effects, not by its aptness for the attainment of some proposed end, but simply by virtue of the volition, that is, it is good in itself, and considered by itself is to be esteemed much higher than all that can be brought about by it in favour of any inclination, nay, even of

the sum-total of all inclinations. Even if it should happen that, owing to special disfavour of fortune, or the niggardly provision of a step-motherly nature, this will should wholly lack power to accomplish its purpose, if with its greatest efforts it should yet achieve nothing, and there should remain only the good will (not, to be sure, a mere wish, but the summoning of all means in our power), then, like a jewel, it would still shine by its own light, as a thing which has its whole value in itself. Its usefulness or fruitlessness can neither add to nor take away anything from this value.[19]

We must not, of course, confuse a good will with rather halfhearted good wishes. After all, "The road to hell is paved with good intentions." I have the will to do something, in Kant's words, only when I "summon all the means within my power." This is much more than merely wishing to be good. It is certainly more than a cheerful expression of moral platitudes.

PHILOSOPHICAL

QUERY

• • • • • •

Does the idea of a good will help our analysis of the sociopath in the preceding Philosophical Query? Explain.

Inclinations, Wishes, Acts of Will

The majesty of duty has nothing to do with the enjoyment of life.

Immanuel Kant

In Kantian terminology, decisions and actions based on impulse or desire are known as *inclinations,* and Kant was convinced that morality could not be "reduced to" inclinations because inclinations are notoriously unreliable and inconstant. Inclinations are not products of practical reason; indeed, they are not products of reason at all. We can see this clearly when we consider the behavior and motivations of dogs, cats, and infants. Dogs, cats, and infants have very strong inclinations: to eat this but not that, now but not later, and so on. But in Kant's sense of the term, they do not have "a will"; they cannot *act from a will.*

Now it is important to be clear here. "Having a will" and "acting from a will" have a precise meaning for Kant, a meaning connected to acting from "internal commands" or maxims that are the result of rational deliberation. So, although we sometimes call infants or pets "willful," from a Kantian point of view, they are merely manifesting powerful inclinations, not a will. *Willing X* requires consciously and deliberately committing ourselves to bringing about *X.* There is something "wholehearted" and conscious about willing.

Look at the means a man employs; consider his motives. A man simply cannot conceal himself!

Confucius

We can see that Kant's strong sense of willing is not so far from everyday language as it might first appear if we consider what we mean by "willpower." We often lament lacking the willpower to stop smoking, start exercising, stop overeating, study for philosophy class, and so on. We say, "She meant well" and "If wishes were horses, then beggars would ride." In other words, we distinguish between merely wanting, wishing, or being inclined, and actually *willing* something, seriously committing ourselves wholeheartedly, consciously, and consistently—regardless of our inclinations and desires. We do not ordinarily talk about "wish power" or "want power."

In contrast to inclinations, acts of will reflect autonomy, the capacity to choose clearly and freely for ourselves, without "outside" coercion or interference. With inclinations, it is as if "one part of me wants to be healthy but another part of me wants to enjoy a smoke now." Rather than making a focused, unified, whole-hearted commitment not to smoke, I make a "halfhearted gesture."

When we *will* something, we issue ourselves a kind of internal command, or order, of the type: "I refuse to eat meat" or "I will not lie." These *subjective intentions* can be framed as *maxims*, the reason or rule according to which an act is done (or not done). In these two examples, maxims might be framed as "Do not eat meat" and "Do not lie." In a sense, when I will something, I pass a law, framed as my maxim—and I obey my own law. I am both a lawgiver and a servant of the law.

Kant's moral philosophy is his attempt to distinguish morally proper maxims and motives from morally unacceptable ones. Ultimately, Kant thought that he was able to identify the "supreme moral principle," the moral motive that distinguishes the good will from all other motives.

■ MORAL DUTY ■

Kant thought it was crucially important to distinguish moral motives from other kinds of motives. I might tell the truth to impress you or to avoid going to jail for perjury. Obviously, such considerations (motives) are not moral. I may give money to charity in order to cut my tax bill. I might do what I think God commands in order to go to heaven or to escape hell, but then my motive is self-interest. Only when I do a thing solely because it is my duty do I have a good will.

What, then, is duty? Kant says, "*Duty is the necessity of acting from respect for the [moral] law.*"[20] He goes on to explain that duty does not serve our desires and preferences (he calls these "inclinations"), but, rather, *overpowers* them. Put another way, duty excludes considerations of personal preference or profit and loss from moral calculation. For example, suppose I have criticized my boss to others. When she asks me whether I've done this, I decide to tell her the truth because I am not sure what my co-workers have already told her. Even though I do my duty, I cannot get moral credit for it, according to Kant, because my decision is based on something other than moral duty—it's based on not getting fired.

> Thus the moral worth of an action does not lie in the effect expected from it, nor in any principle of action which requires to borrow its motive from its expected effect. For all these effects—agreeableness of one's condition, and even the promotion of the happiness of others—could have been also brought about by other causes so that for this there would have been no need of the will of a rational being; whereas it is in this alone that the supreme and un-conditioned good can be found. The preeminent good which we call moral can therefore consist in nothing else than *the conception of law* in itself, which certainly is only possible in a rational being, in so far as this conception, and not the expected effect, determines the will.[21]

Moral judgement belongs, as does religious judgement, to a level of ignorance at which even the concept of the real, the distinction between the real and the imaginary, is lacking.

FRIEDRICH NIETZSCHE

One of the mistakes oftenest committed, and which are the sources of the greatest practical errors in human affairs, is that of supposing that the same name always stands for the same aggregation of ideas.

JOHN STUART MILL

If this seems unduly strict (and it has to many philosophers), keep in mind that decisions based on "inclinations" are often inconsistent and always relative. My inclination might be to renege on a loan or to be rude to a dirty, smelly customer. How can anyone rely on me if I only follow my inclinations? My inclination on the day I asked you to dinner might have been to keep our date, but by Friday my inclination might be to stay home alone. And I might not be inclined to call and inform you of this, either. Imagine the chaos of a world in which our obligations were tied to our moods.

According to Kant, moral obligations cannot be grounded in whims and personal taste. Moral duty must be confined to considerations of the form: *What are the universal obligations of all persons in similar circumstances?* My duty cannot be based on what I want to do, what I like or don't like, whether or not I care about the people involved. Kant's next step was to devise a way to determine exactly what our duty is in this or that case, to ask, *What is the moral law?* Kant's answer is one of the most intriguing and widely debated principles in all moral philosophy.

Words are used of God and creatures in an analogical way.
THOMAS AQUINAS

PHILOSOPHICAL

QUERY

• • • • • •

Do you think it is possible to have only one motive for an action? Is it common to have only one motive? Is it important to distinguish moral motives from pragmatic ones? Why? Compare Kant with Hume on the issue of moral sentiments.

Hypothetical Imperatives

Kant argues that the moral quality of an act is determined by the *principle* to which the will consciously assents. If, for instance, I resolve to feed the hungry and mistakenly serve tainted meat at a charity dinner, my intention is praiseworthy even though my action results in sickness or death. If, on the other hand, I intend to poison my sick wife in order to inherit her fortune and mistakenly give her a chemical that cures her, I am morally guilty of murder, for that was what I consciously willed.

Since they affect behavior, moral principles are always framed as commands, according to Kant. He refers to commands by their grammatical designation as *imperatives.* Examples of imperatives are "Shut the door," "Always brush your teeth after eating," "Love your neighbor as yourself," and "Double-space your term paper."

Imperatives that tell us what to do under specific, variable conditions are called **hypothetical imperatives.** In logic, a hypothetical proposition takes the form "*If* this, *then* that." These are also called conditional propositions because they set up a *conditional* relationship: *If* it rains, *then* postpone the picnic. The imperative "Postpone the picnic" is binding only in the condition of rain. According to Kant, all empirical or factual imperatives are hypothetical because they are binding only so long as certain conditions apply.

There are a variety of *kinds* of hypothetical imperatives. Some are technical, applying to chemists or surgeons or bakers. Others are social, telling us how to

hypothetical imperatives
Propositions that tell us what to do under specific, variable conditions.

CALVIN AND HOBBES © Watterson. Reprinted with permission of UNIVERSAL PRESS SYNDICATE. All rights reserved.

be popular or get dates. Some are legal, and so on. No hypothetical imperative is binding on everyone or even on one person all the time. When factual conditions change, so do hypothetical imperatives. No hypothetical imperative is *a priori*. All are relative.

In fact, Kant says, "the imperatives of prudence do not, strictly speaking, command at all."[22] No one has a necessary obligation to be practical, to make money, to eat wisely. Thus, though hypothetical imperatives can help us deal with life, they cannot be a basis for determining moral duty.

The Categorical Imperative

According to Kant, what is needed is a **categorical imperative,** a command that is universally binding on all rational creatures. This alone can guide the good will. Indeed, the good will is precisely that which summons all its powers in order to obey just such an imperative.

Moral duty must be universally—not conditionally—binding. What principle can we follow that is not conditional? After considering the difference between telling the truth because it is a duty and telling it because it might yield some payoff, Kant concludes that acting from duty is always based on the principle of a "conception of the law in general."

categorical imperative
According to Kant, a command that is universally binding on all rational creatures; the ultimate foundation of all moral law: "Act as if the maxim of thy action were to become a universal law of nature."

Men are good in one way
but bad in many.

ARISTOTLE

The way to appraise a
"way of life" may well be by
considering what's in it for
you; the way to appraise
the moral value of a course
of action is by considering
what's in it for everyone.

JAN NARVESON

Even apart from the value
of such claims as "there is
a categorical imperative
in us," one can still always
ask: what does such a claim
tell us about the man who
makes it?

FRIEDRICH NIETZSCHE

What Kant means can be characterized as *acting on the principle of acting on principle.* In the case of telling the truth, I tell the truth because I have a basic, general obligation to tell the truth—period. This obligation is general in the sense that I must not base it on particular considerations at all. I must not be partial to myself and my fears or my wants. Kant thus strips the good will of every Humean sentiment, every impulse, appetite, fear, preference, or other practical or person-specific consideration. What's left?

> There remains nothing but the universal conformity of [the will's] actions to law in general, which alone is to serve as its principle, *i.e.,* I am never to act otherwise than *so that I could also will that my maxim should become a universal law.* Here, now, it is the simple conformity to law in general, without assuming any particular applicability to certain actions, that serves the will as its principle, and must so serve it, if duty is not to be a vain delusion and a chimerical notion.[23]

Kant formulated the categorical imperative as "*Act as if the maxim of thy action were to become a universal law of nature.*" In other words, we must act only according to principles we think should apply to everyone. Because a free will is a necessary condition of morality, Kant reminds us that the "universal law" in question comes from our own rational, willing assent—it is not imposed on us from the outside. Obeying God or nature or any other *overpowering force* out of fear or necessity is not moral. If we obey out of fear, our motive is partial and pragmatic; if we have no choice but to obey, we are not free. Moral law is obligatory because it springs from our own rational nature and becomes law only when we willingly assent to it.

PHILOSOPHICAL
QUERY

• • • • • •

To get a clearer sense of the power of the categorical imperative to clarify the nature of various forms of behavior, formulate and then analyze the maxims that are required to justify the following: charging things on credit without being sure you can pay them off on time; enrolling in two different high-demand courses so that you can check them both out and drop the one you don't like; having unprotected sex without knowing if you are HIV positive; talking in the theater; forcing schools to teach the values of your religion.

The Kingdom of Ends

Judaism would reject the
Kantian axiom, "I ought,
therefore I can": it would
claim, instead, "Thou art
commanded, therefore thou
canst."

ABRAHAM JOSHUA
HESCHEL

Kant believed that as conscious, rational creatures, we each possess intrinsic worth, a special moral dignity that always deserves respect. Kant uses a beautiful expression to describe the moral universe, the universe of all moral beings, of all creatures possessing intrinsic worth. He refers to it as the *kingdom of ends,* a kingdom in which everyone is an end in himself or herself, and no one is just a means to be used and tossed aside. In other words, we are more than mere objects to be used to further this or that end. We are *persons,* reasoning creatures capable of monitoring and guiding our own behavior according to principles. Thus, the ability to reason carries with it an obligation to respect the rights of others to reason for themselves.

©Michael Dwyer/Stock, Boston

Kant held that, as conscious, rational creatures we each possess dignity that deserves universal respect and that is not contingent on how likable we are, how attractive, successful, and so forth. In this photo, the caregiver's sense of dignity is apparent in the way he is helping another man find clothes that fit. His posture reflects patience and concern—as well as his own dignity.

Moral dignity is not contingent on anything. It is not a function of how likable we are, how attractive, talented, clean, or even good we are. It is not contingent on how well we use our reason or on whether we use it at all. We possess intrinsic worth (moral dignity) just because we *can* reason.

We have seen that, according to Kant, our basic obligations to one another cannot rest on inclinations or sentiments (desires), for that amounts to saying we have no moral obligations. Imagine a wedding in which the bride or groom promised to love, cherish, and respect the other "as long as I feel inclined to." The very concept of duty implies acting in an appropriate way regardless of our sentiments, convenience, comfort, or other personal factors. In Kant's terms, this is an objective duty toward other rational beings—exactly what Hume denied:

> Man and generally any rational being *exists* as an end in himself, *not merely as a means* to be arbitrarily used . . . but in all his actions, whether they concern himself or other rational beings, must be always regarded at the same time as an end. All objects of inclination have only a conditional worth; for if the inclinations and the wants founded on them did not exist, then their object would be without value. . . . Rational beings . . . are called *persons,* because their very nature points them out as ends in themselves. . . . These, therefore, are not merely subjective ends whose existence has a worth *for us* as an effect of our action, but *objective ends,* that is, things whose existence is an end in itself: an end moreover

We do not need science and philosophy to know what we should do to be honest and good, yea, even wise and virtuous.

IMMANUEL KANT

So sharply and clearly marked are the boundaries of morality and self-love that even the commonest eye cannot fail to distinguish whether a thing belongs to one or the other.

IMMANUEL KANT

for which no other can be substituted . . . for otherwise nothing whatever would possess *absolute worth;* but if all worth were conditional and therefore contingent, then there would be no supreme practical principle of reason whatever.

If then there is a supreme practical principle or, in respect of the human will, a categorical imperative, it must be one which, being drawn from the conception of that which is necessarily an end for everyone because it is *an end in itself,* constitutes an *objective* principle of will, and can therefore serve as a universal practical law. The foundation of this principle is: *rational nature exists as an end in itself.*[24]

Kant formulates the categorical imperative around the concept of dignity in a way that is sometimes referred to as the **practical imperative** or **principle of dignity**: "*Act in such a way that you always treat humanity, whether in your own person or in the person of another, never simply as a means but always at the same time as an end.*"[25] I confess I'm partial to this particular principle. It has, I believe, much to teach us.

If, for example, I view my students only as a way to make a living, or only as a captive audience to indoctrinate with my views, I treat them as means to an end without honoring their basic dignity as persons. We violate this principle of dignity when we hurl ethnic or gender insults at one another, for then we are treating other persons as means of venting rage or expressing feelings. No abusive parent or spouse treats the objects of his or her abuse as *persons.* In the kingdom of ends, there are no slaves, no sweatshops, no terrorists, no bullies, no rude clerks or surly customers, no unprepared teachers or students—only respectful and respected *persons.*

Yet in fact, my students *are a means* to an income for me. I *am a means* to a degree or meeting a requirement for them. A boss and an employee are each a *means* and an *end.* Note that Kant's principle does not preclude this. Rather, it adds a dimension of universal respect to all human relationships: We are means *and* ends.

practical imperative (principle of dignity) Kant's formulation of the categorical imperative based on the concept of dignity: "Act in such a way that you always treat humanity, whether in your own person or in the person of another, never simply as a means but always at the same time as an end."

PHILOSOPHICAL

QUERY

• • • • • •

Consider the actual case of the parents who conceived a child for the express purpose of producing a bone marrow donor for their nineteen-year-old daughter who has leukemia. Doctors advised the parents that a bone marrow transplant was the only hope of saving their daughter's life. Unable to find a compatible donor match, the parents took the desperate step of having another child, and in 1991 bone marrow from the specially conceived child, then just over one year old, was transplanted to her nineteen-year-old sister. Can the parents' action be morally justified? Explain.

John Rawls

■ A KANTIAN THEORY OF JUSTICE ■

In 1971, Harvard professor **John Rawls** (1921–2002) published *A Theory of Justice,* which became one of the most significant philosophical books of our time. Rawls's attempt to refine Kant's moral philosophy greatly influenced political scientists, economists, and moral philosophers.

According to Rawls, the fundamental principles of justice are those principles to which "free and rational" persons would agree if they were in an "original position" of equality. Of course, Rawls continued, we are not in and cannot create a position of perfect equality. How, then, he asked, can we ever determine what justice is, since any inquiry into justice will be influenced by our actual—and unequal—circumstances?

One way to deal with the limits imposed by our actual circumstances is known as a thought experiment. A **thought experiment** is a way of using our imaginations to test a hypothesis that cannot be tested in fact. During a thought experiment, we think rather than field-test a hypothesis, using reasoned imagination to provide the necessary conditions for the experiment and then reasoning out the most likely consequences according to our hypothesis.

Kant had already tried to overcome the limits of personal circumstances and bias with the categorical imperative, which is supposed to overlook all merely personal considerations and inclinations. Rawls used a thought experiment as part of an attempt to improve upon Kant's efforts to overcome the limits of personal concerns in ethical deliberations.

The **original position** of equality is Rawls's term for an imaginary setting in which we can identify the fundamental principles of justice from an *objective, impartial* perspective—as "rational agents," rather than as "interested parties." And this is where the thought experiment comes in. We "enter into the original position" by imaginatively placing ourselves behind what Rawls terms a "veil of ignorance." The **veil of ignorance** is a problem-solving device that prevents us from knowing our social status, what property we own, what we like and don't like, how intelligent we are, what our talents and strengths are, "and the like." In other words, the veil of ignorance is a way of adopting an objective (or at least disinterested) perspective. In the following passage, Rawls introduces the veil of ignorance and the original position:

> The original position is not, of course, thought of as an actual historical state of affairs, much less as a primitive condition of culture. It is understood as a purely hypothetical situation characterized so as to lead to a certain conception of justice. . . . Among the essential features of this situation is that no one knows his place in society, his class position or social status, nor does any one know his fortune in the distribution of natural assets and abilities, his intelligence, strength, and the like. I shall even assume that the parties do not know their conceptions of the good or their special psychological propensities. The principles of justice are chosen behind a veil of ignorance. This assures that no one is advantaged or disadvantaged in the choices of principles by the outcome of natural chance or the contingency of social circumstances.[26]

Rawls goes on to argue that persons in the original position "would all agree"—being rational and mutually disinterested—to principles of equal political liberty and opportunity. That is, any *rational agent* looking out for his own self-interest would agree to two basic principles: (1) everyone has an equal right to "the most extensive basic liberty compatible with a similar liberty for others," and (2) any social and economic inequalities must be such that "they are both (a) reasonably expected to be to everyone's advantage and (b) attached

thought experiment
A way of using our imaginations to test a hypothesis; we think rather than field-test a hypothesis, using reasoned imagination to provide the necessary conditions for the experiment, and carefully reasoning out the most likely consequences according to our hypothesis.

original position
John Rawls's imaginary setting in which we can identify the fundamental principles of justice from an objective, impartial perspective, as rational agents, rather than as "interested parties": similar to the "state of nature" in the social contract theories of Thomas Hobbes, Jean-Jacques Rousseau, and John Locke.

veil of ignorance
John Rawls's mechanism for imaginatively entering into the original position by avoiding all personal considerations in the process of determining principles of justice; the veil of ignorance is a problem-solving device that prevents us from knowing our social status, what property we own, what we like and don't like, how intelligent we are, what our talents and strengths are, and so on.

to positions and offices open to all."[27] When the two principles conflict, *reason directs us* to defer to the first.

According to Rawls, "whenever social institutions satisfy these principles those engaged in them can say to one another that they are cooperating on terms to which they would agree if they were free and equal persons whose relations with respect to one another were fair."[28]

PHILOSOPHICAL

QUERY

• • • • • •

Conduct your own thought experiment by using the concept of a veil of ignorance to write a code of conduct for college courses. Imagine that you do not know if you are a pupil or professor, or any other personal factors. Does the veil of ignorance aid in such tasks, or is something overlooked? Explain.

What About Family Justice?

Susan Moller Okin

Family justice must be of central importance for social justice.

SUSAN MOLLER OKIN

The traditional canon is elitist . . . concerned with the writing primarily of privileged white men. Women's writing, writing of people of color, people of the working class—these voices need to be brought into . . . study.

SUE HOWARD

In *Justice, Gender, and the Family,* **Susan Moller Okin** (1946–2004) analyzes Rawls's theory of justice, with special attention to issues of gender and the family. Okin points out that no adequate theory of justice can fail to include an analysis of justice within the family, since the family—in whatever form—is still the primary shaper of personality, as well as of basic attitudes of self-respect (self-esteem), gender, and ethnicity. In sum, justice cannot be separated from considerations of justice for each specific member of the family. Clearly, in our present society, wealth, equality, and liberty are not evenly or justly apportioned. Okin continues:

> Yet, remarkably, major contemporary theorists of justice have almost without exception ignored the situation I have just described [the status of all family members]. They have displayed little interest in or knowledge of the findings of feminism. They have largely bypassed the fact that the society to which their theories are supposed to pertain is heavily and deeply affected by gender, and faces difficult issues of justice stemming from its gendered past and present assumptions. Since theories of justice are centrally concerned with whether, how, or why persons should be treated differently from one another, this neglect seems inexplicable.[29]

Okin argues that Rawls's analysis of justice is "ambiguous" regarding gender because she says, he rarely indicates "how deeply and pervasively gender-structured" this society is. Further, Okin points out, Rawls fails to mention that *Kant did not intend for his moral theory to apply to women.* Okin asserts that in his discussion of Sigmund Freud's theory of the formulation of the male superego, Rawls simple ignores the fact that Freud thought that women's moral development was *psychologically deficient.* Okin concludes that

> Thus there is a blindness to the sexism of the tradition in which Rawls is a participant, which tends to render his terms of reference more ambiguous than they might otherwise be. A feminist reader finds it difficult not to keep asking, Does this theory apply to women?[30]

According to Okin, Rawls's work is "ambiguous" rather than flatly sexist because he does acknowledge that sex is one of the morally relevant contingencies that are to be hidden behind the veil of ignorance. But reconsider Rawls's language regarding these contingencies in light of Okin's observations:

> Among the essential features of this situation is that no one knows *his* place in society, *his* class position or social status, nor does any one know *his* fortune in the distribution of natural assets and abilities, *his* intelligence, strength, and the like.[31] [emphasis added]

Rawls had hoped that the veil of ignorance could be used to "correct for" the "arbitrariness of the world" by putting people in a position to reason independently of "morally relevant contingencies" such as actual social status, talent, ethnicity, *and the like.* As "pure rational agents," they would think from an identical standpoint. Each one's perspective would be the perspective of all. Okin notes that "one might think that whether or not they knew their sex might matter enough to be mentioned." "Perhaps," she suggests, "Rawls meant to cover it by his phrase 'and the like,' but it is also possible that he did not consider it significant."[32]

■ COMMENTARY ■

Kant remains *the* major figure in modern philosophy. His effort to understand how the mind *knows* has shaped a significant portion of the field. Kant is also a major influence in modern psychology. In fact, many of the epistemological issues he raised are now being addressed by the cognitive sciences, which are devoted to unraveling the mysteries of perceiving, learning, knowing, and thinking.

In the field of ethics, three imposing visions dominate modern philosophy. One is Kantian formalism, the second is Humean subjectivism (Chapter 10), and the third is utilitarianism (the subject of Chapter 12). We will address some criticisms of Kantian ethics in the process of understanding the major alternative to it in the next chapter. Even so, some general remarks are in order here.

In spite of the difficulty of his arguments and writing style, Kant's moral philosophy has proved to be influential beyond philosophical circles. Part of its power lies in a deep sense that it is wrong to make ourselves the exception in moral matters. If something is right (or wrong) for one person, it seems only fair that it be right (or wrong) for other persons in similar circumstances. We are offended when others make themselves or their loved ones exceptions to their own purported moral rules. This sense of offense may stem from a glimmer of a "moral law within."

Kant's categorical imperative is a more refined and sophisticated version of the Golden Rule: "Do unto others as you would have them do unto you." Kant understood that a sloppy formulation of the Rule can be interpreted as saying "Treat others as you would *like* to be treated." Such a formulation generates what I call the Sadomasochistic Paradox, from an old joke in which a masochist says to a sadist, "Hurt me!" and the sadist replies, "No." The point, of course, is that how we *want* to be treated varies and is often determined by our individual tastes, background, personal beliefs, and temperament. This is certainly not a

Today women are talking to each other, recovering an oral culture, telling our life-stories, reading aloud to one another the books that have moved and healed us, analyzing the language that has lied about us, reading our own words aloud to each other . . . to name and found a culture of our own.

ADRIENNE RICH

One race there is of men, one of gods, but from one mother we both draw our breath.

PINDAR

The notion of happiness is so indefinite that although every man wishes to attain it yet he never can say definitely and consistently what it is that he really wishes and wills.

IMMANUEL KANT

very reliable standard for treating others. If we lack self-respect or have some psychological quirk, we might want to be treated very poorly indeed. Kant's insistence that duty rise above inclination is meant to prohibit such individualistic interpretations of the Rule.

A common criticism of Kant's moral philosophy is that it promotes rash and irresponsible behavior by exempting us from responsibility for the consequences of our actions. After all, if the only truly good thing is a good will or motive, then all that matters morally is my intention—not the results of my behavior. Sophisticated Kantians point out, however, that any universalizable maxim must include concern for and consideration of the likely consequences of action. No defensible moral duty can condone indifference to what happens to others.

Another intriguing problem has to do with the conscience of a fanatic. By stressing the rational aspects of morality, Kant might have given too little weight to important psychological factors. A famous example involves a Nazi who is willing to universalize this maxim: "Always annihilate those whom you judge to be inferior and impediments to human progress." When it is pointed out that the Nazi could become the target of annihilation if he turns out to be an impediment to human progress, he is expected to see the "unreasonableness" of his maxim. If he still holds to it, knowing that it could result in his own destruction, he is said to be a fanatic. But isn't this judgment based on our own inclinations (sentiments) and beliefs about what is reasonable? Yet how else can we determine what's rational? Did Kant merely use his own Western European Christian background to define "reasonable"? Is he, perhaps, guided by moral sentiment after all—as Hume thought? This is a complex and important problem, one even the finest moral philosophers still struggle with.

Being "rational" is clearly not all that matters, as the harm caused by "rational" criminals, frauds, toxic polluters, and others clearly demonstrates. Experience offers countless examples of dangerous, immoral schemes hatched by rational individuals lacking good will. Equally dangerous is the well-intentioned but shortsighted or incompetent individual whose motives are unassailable, yet whose actions generate harm. The best will must be combined with a certain minimum of intelligence, insight, and ability. Just as being rational is not a sufficient condition for being moral, neither is having a good will.

Because we lack the ability to frame moral rules so clearly that they do not generate problems, attempting to apply the categorical imperative to specific cases is often quite difficult. Suppose, for instance, that you promise a friend to repay borrowed money whenever he requests it. One evening your friend and a drug dealer show up. Your friend demands the money to buy an ounce of heroin. Should you repay it? Which is more important, keeping a promise or looking out for a friend's welfare when he or she is unable to? Can a drug user be rational when compelled by a powerful addiction? Does treating my friends as ends entail protecting them from themselves or letting them make their own choices no matter how harmful the consequences?

Can I frame a moral maxim to guide me in choosing between conflicting moral rules in such a case? I could add qualifications to my rules, but what is the purpose or benefit of having rules if they require so many qualifications that they cease to function as moral maxims? It is not clear there is *any* maxim that can be

The altruism which in my view underlies ethics is not to be confused with generalized affection for the human race. It is not a feeling.

THOMAS NAGEL

Man can never escape the ideal or absolute . . . man cannot be an animal; he can only be a philosopher or anthropologist who asserts that men are animals and ought to live like them.

EMIL L. FACKENHEIM

Kant can justly be called the father of modern philosophy, for out of him stem nearly all the still current and contending schools of philosophy. . . .

WILLIAM BARRETT

universalizable without qualification and still function as more than a very loose guideline.

In spite of such difficulties, I remain especially impressed by Kant's pattern of starting with commonly accepted ideas like causality, the unitary self, and free will and then trying to determine how the mind can know them. The result is certainly not a simplistic epistemology or moral philosophy. Kant presented a radically new picture of the mind as an active organizer and questioner of sensation. He identified important limits of empiricism and rationalism and identified vital questions that wait to be answered. His insistence that "reason demands" a noumenal world beyond immediate experience and the reach of science remains a profound expression of a moral sense shared by many people.

How often we seem to forget that others are *persons* when we use them as status symbols or see only their outward appearance or religious or political beliefs. Imagine a world in which clerks and medical doctors and parents and children and spouses and students and teachers and politicians and police officers and everyone else followed this principle. If I can remember that I live in a kingdom of ends, I can transform my relationships from a sort of bartering for favors or competing for power and success. I can elevate my life to something beyond a contest in which I and mine must struggle against a "different" and "inferior" them. In the kingdom of ends, it is always *us*.

Deficiency in judgment is just what is ordinarily called stupidity, and for that there is no remedy.

IMMANUEL KANT

■ SUMMARY OF MAIN POINTS ■

- Kant fully understood the serious implications of the "scandal in philosophy" that resulted from Hume's devastating use of the empirical criterion of meaning and the failure of rationalism and empiricism to adequately account for knowledge of the external world, cause and effect, and knowledge in general while science clearly showed otherwise.

- Kant developed a special kind of analysis called a critique, which combined reason and experience in order to avoid the errors of rationalism and empiricism. Critical philosophy attempts to discover whether a *priori* knowledge and metaphysics are possible. Kant claimed that knowledge is formed by actual experience and faculties of judgment called categories of understanding. We know reality only as it is organized by human understanding (phenomenal reality), not reality as it is (noumenal reality).

- Kant distinguished between theoretical reason and practical reason. Theoretical reason is confined to the phenomenal world; practical reason moves beyond the phenomenal world to the moral dimension. Practical reason reveals a moral dimension

based on our consciousness of necessary and universal moral laws, which Kant calls rules or maxims.

- Moral rules cannot be discovered empirically; reason imposes moral obligation. Reason reveals that morality is a matter of moral duty (good will) rather than consequences. Moral duty must be confined to considerations of the form: What are the universal obligations of all persons in similar circumstances? The moral quality of an act is determined by the principle to which the will consciously assents. Moral obligations are not hypothetical and dependent on individual circumstances but, rather, categorical, universally binding on all rational beings.

- Kant called the universal command that infuses all moral obligations the categorical imperative: Act as if the maxim of thy action were to become a universal law of nature. A special formulation of the categorical imperative acknowledges this worth: Act in such a way that you always treat humanity, whether in your own person or in the person of another, never simply as a means but always at the same time as an end.

- John Rawls, an influential modern philosopher, constructed a theory of justice designed to overcome the limits of personal bias that prevent us from basing our moral and social values on objective and impartial rational principles.

- Susan Moller Okin argues that overlooked gender bias remains present in both the language and choice of examples Rawls employed in his influential attempt to refine Kant's modern moral philosophy. Okin analyzes Rawls's theory of justice with special attention to issues of gender and the family, arguing that Rawls's position is "ambiguous" regarding gender because he rarely indicates how deeply and pervasively gender-structured this society is.

■ POST-READING REFLECTIONS ■

Now that you have had a chance to learn about the Universalist, use your new knowledge to answer these questions.

1. Why did Kant think it necessary to posit the existence of the noumenal world?

2. How does Kant answer Hume's bundle theory of the self? Do you think he is successful?

3. Describe the moral dimension as Kant understood it.

4. Explain the reasoning behind Kant's efforts to make morality a matter of motives, not consequences.

5. What is a good will, according to Kant, and why does he claim that the only thing good in itself is a good will?

6. For Kant, how does *willing X* differ from *wanting X,* and why is this distinction important?

7. What is a maxim? What makes a maxim *moral* in Kantian terms?

8. What is the basis of our intrinsic worth, according to Kant? How does this Enlightenment conception of moral (human) dignity differ from today's broader understanding of human worth?

9. What Kantian problem was Rawls addressing with his theory of justice? What did Rawls offer as an alternative?

10. What oversight did Susan Moller Okin identify in modern theories of justice, including Rawls's? Why does she say that Rawls's theory of justice is ambiguous?

 PHILOSOPHY INTERNET RESOURCES

Go to the Soccio Web page at **http://philosophy.wadsworth.com/ Soccio7e** for Web links, practice quizzes and tests, a pronunciation guide, and study tips.

THE UTILITARIAN

John Stuart Mill

THE UTILITARIAN STANDARD . . . IS NOT THE AGENT'S OWN GREATEST HAPPINESS, BUT THE GREATEST AMOUNT OF HAPPINESS ALTOGETHER, AND IF IT MAY POSSIBLY BE DOUBTED WHETHER A NOBLE CHARACTER IS ALWAYS THE HAPPIER FOR ITS NOBLENESS, THERE CAN BE NO DOUBT THAT IT MAKES OTHER PEOPLE HAPPIER, AND THAT THE WORLD IN GENERAL IS IMMENSELY A GAINER BY IT. UTILITARIANISM, THEREFORE, COULD ONLY ATTAIN ITS END BY THE GENERAL CULTIVATION OF NOBLENESS OF CHARACTER.

John Stuart Mill

FOR YOUR REFLECTION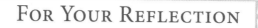

KEEP THESE QUESTIONS IN MIND AS YOU LEARN ABOUT THE
UTILITARIAN.

1. *What is psychological hedonism?*
2. *What is ethical hedonism?*
3. *What is the principle of utility?*
4. *What is simple utilitarianism?*
5. *What is the "hedonic calculus"?*
6. *What is the greatest happiness principle?*
7. *What is the "egoistic hook"?*
8. *What is refined utilitarianism?*
9. *What is altruism?*

FOR DEEPER CONSIDERATION

A. Analyze Bentham's claim that all pleasures are equal. What was Mill's basic argument against this claim? Did he make a convincing case? Explain why or why not.

B. How does Mill distinguish between happiness and contentment? Why is this distinction vital to his utilitarian philosophy? What role does education play here? Has your education lived up to Mill's hopes? If yes, in what ways? If no, why not?

*T*wo *competing impulses* struggle to control the general direction of any society: a desire for change and progress and a desire for security and order. To do justice to both tendencies, free societies struggle to balance individual rights and freedoms with the general social welfare, what's best for everyone. The problem is, not everyone agrees about what's best for everyone.

As contemporary life grows more complex and the world more populous, competing interests, limited resources, and conflicting beliefs make dealing with all sorts of issues increasingly touchy. What seems obvious, fair, and just to one group often seems unfair and unjust to other groups. The wants of the privileged appear to conflict with the wants—and needs—of the many.

If you traveled to work or school today on a major roadway, you may have benefited from someone else's loss. Suppose that when the community decided to build the highway that now benefits you and thousands of others, engineers determined that the best route for most people cut straight through a family farm. Based on that information, the local government, on behalf of the majority of citizens, would try to buy the land. Such an offer is technically only a courtesy, for virtually every community in this country can appropriate private land—at a "fair market price"—under what is called the right of eminent domain. If the owners don't want to sell, they can be forced to on the grounds that the general welfare takes precedence over individual preferences.

The use of eminent domain to promote the "greater good" is an application of a philosophical principle that's become so entrenched in our culture that many of us take it for granted. It is the principle that, although individual rights and desires must be respected, the good of the majority ultimately takes precedence over the happiness of any one individual or small group of individuals. Greatest-happiness reasoning limits when we can run our loud leaf blowers; it also prevents us from refusing to rent apartments to people of ethnicities, gender orientations, or ages we may not like.

Immediately after the events of September 11, 2001, the federal government initiated time-consuming and annoying security checks at airports. A year later, security procedures were modified in an effort to balance security and convenience for the largest number of travelers while jeopardizing the smallest number. From matters of the gravest concern to mundane decisions about what to have for dinner, groups almost instinctively try to make as many people as possible as happy as possible.

In this chapter, we'll look at utilitarianism, a modern application of hedonism that was first formulated by the British philosopher Jeremy Bentham. Bentham's simple utilitarianism was refined by his friend and student John Stuart Mill into one of today's most influential moral and social philosophies. (Hedonism is discussed in Chapter 7.)

> *It is vain to talk of the interest of the community, without understanding what is in the interest of the individual. A thing is said to promote the interest, or to be for the interest, of an individual when it tends to add to the sum total of his pleasures; or, what comes to the same thing, to diminish the sum total of his pains.*
>
> JEREMY BENTHAM

▨ SOCIAL HEDONISM ▨

Modern utilitarianism developed as a response to social conditions created by the Industrial Revolution—which in Britain ran roughly from 1780 to 1835. As the term implies, this era was characterized by massive social

Now, pleasure is in itself a good; nay, even setting aside immunity from pain, the only good; pain is itself an evil; and, indeed, without exception, the only evil; or else the words good and evil have no meaning. And this is alike true of every sort of pain, and every sort of pleasure. It follows, therefore, immediately and incontestably, that there is no such thing as any sort of motive that is in itself a bad one.

JEREMY BENTHAM

change and upheaval generated by new scientific manufacturing techniques that, in turn, produced geographic, familial, spiritual, and economic disruption as a newly created class of "workers" competed for jobs that were often repetitious, dangerous, poorly paid—degrading and dehumanizing.

The advent of efficient steam and water power made large factories practical. Cloth weaving, for example, had once been a cottage industry, but the textile mills could make cloth much more cheaply. Hordes of workers sought jobs in the mill towns and cities, creating large slums. Between 1800 and 1831, the English cities of Leeds, Sheffield, Manchester, and Liverpool nearly doubled in population. Shabbily constructed buildings rented at such high prices that they paid for themselves in five years. Of course, such high rents resulted in overcrowding, as poorly paid workers lived two and three families to an apartment. In Manchester in 1845, for example, twenty-seven cases were documented of up to seven people trying to sleep in one bed.[1]

In 1798, **Thomas Malthus** (1766–1834), an Anglican minister, published a work titled *An Essay on the Principle of Population as It Affects the Future Improvement of Society*. In it, Malthus expressed grave doubts about the feasibility of social reform:

> I have read some . . . speculations, on the perfectibility of men and society, with great pleasure. I have been warmed and delighted with the enchanting picture which they hold forth. I ardently wish for such happy improvements. But I see great and, to my understanding, unconquerable difficulties in the way to them.[2]

The "great difficulties" Malthus feared were overpopulation and underproduction of food. He argued that although food production increases arithmetically (1 to 2 to 3 to 4 to 5 to 6, and so on), unchecked population growth progresses geometrically (1 to 2 to 4 to 8 to 16 to 32, and so forth). Thus, according to Malthus, unchecked population inevitably outgrows the food supply.

Troubled by both the growing slums in the cities and efforts to improve living conditions for the poor, Malthus concluded that there could be no justification for helping the disadvantaged. Raising wages would only enable the poor to marry younger and have even more children; the population would outgrow the food supply, and poverty would return anyway. Welfare programs would only result in increased "idleness" and encourage large families—with the same result.

It is clear that any society where the means of subsistence increase less rapidly than the numbers of the population is a society on the brink of an abyss. . . . Destitution is fearfully prolific.

M. LOUIS BLANC

Malthus argued that the only way to avoid such harsh "natural cures" as epidemics and the "historical cure" of war or rebellion was to stop helping the poor and remove all restraints on the free enterprise system. Buyers, sellers, bosses, workers, and owners must be left to their own struggle. The law of supply and demand would make it more difficult for the poor to afford to marry early or support very many children, thereby checking the geometrical rise of population.

The conservative British ruling class eagerly embraced Malthusian principles. Factory owners and businessmen were able to justify low wages as their "duty." The evils of the Industrial Revolution could be rationalized away by blaming the miserable living and working conditions of the poor on the poor themselves. And certainly these conditions were discouraging.

In such a context, Jeremy Bentham's insistence that legislators consider the greatest happiness of the greatest number of people can be seen as the radical philosophy that it was.

• • • • • •

PHILOSOPHICAL

QUERY

Think carefully about Malthus's arguments. Can you think of any current evidence to support Malthus's view? Can you think of any evidence against it?

▓ PHILOSOPHY AND SOCIAL REFORM ▓

Jeremy Bentham (1748–1832) directly challenged the owners, bosses, and ruling classes when he insisted that "each counts as one and none more." Bentham blasted those in power for pursuing their own narrow, socially destructive goals instead of pursuing happiness for everyone.

Bentham's solution was to establish democratic rule by the whole people, rather than by a select class. If "the rulers are the people," as Bentham believed, then "all government is in itself evil," and the only justification for government is to prevent worse evils. For Bentham, the legitimate functions of government are social reform and the establishment of the conditions most conducive to promoting the greatest happiness for the greatest number of people. This proved to be a nearly irresistible philosophy for many.

Although much nineteenth-century philosophy had been a response to Kant's work, with the notable exceptions of G. W. F. Hegel and Arthur Schopenhauer, many philosophers rejected Kant's elaborate systems and transcendental metaphysics. They viewed metaphysics as cumbersome, irrelevant, and meaningless— unverifiable by science and unclear according to the empirical criterion of meaning (see Chapter 10). Philosophers' interest shifted from the search for transcendental truth or systemic coherence to practical remedies for the pressing problems of society. They explored social and political philosophy, empirically based ethics, and the application of scientific knowledge to immediate problems of human happiness.

Predictably, this secular, fact-oriented approach revived belief in the cultural relativity of values and beliefs. Philosophers no longer felt obliged to produce elaborate theories or systems, since they thought even their own theories had to be culturally limited. By contrast, particular strategies and factual information were thought to be reliable, provided they were "scientific" and "objective."

Moreover, the new scientific view of an evolving universe made elaborate metaphysical theories seem irrelevant. If the universe and everything in it is slowly changing, then any fixed "grand theory" would apply for a brief time at best. Growing belief in evolution resulted in efforts to identify an evolutionary view of ideas, rather than a search for *the* static truth.

Lastly, the social change and turmoil generated by the Industrial Revolution, the French Revolution, and the Napoleonic Wars cast serious doubts on the adequacy of Kant's ethic of *good will*. Looking about them, philosophers noted that

Jeremy Bentham

I would have the dearest friend I have to know that his interests, if they come in competition with those of the public, are as nothing to me. Thus I would serve my friends—thus I would be served by them.

JEREMY BENTHAM

As for me, when you want a laugh, you will find me in fine fettle, fat and sleek, a hog from Epicurus's herd.

HORACE

what actually happens to people is of supreme importance. A clear need for fact-based, humanistic reform emerged.

Science became the new hope for this reform, replacing Enlightenment conceptions of reason. Scientists and reformers believed that the application of scientific methods of inquiry could identify and eliminate poverty, crime, ignorance, and other sources of widespread misery. Social and political issues eventually dominated metaphysical concerns. Epistemology was important only to the extent that it related to verifiable, immediate improvements in society. If the Enlightenment was the Age of Reason, the nineteenth century began as the Age of Reform. (How it ended is another story.)

■ THE PRINCIPLE OF UTILITY ■

In contrast to Kant, who would have dismissed Bentham's work as "anthropology," Bentham attempted to base his philosophy on careful consideration and observation of social conditions and actual human behavior. Like Aristippus before him (Chapter 7), Bentham declared that careful observation of actual behavior makes it crystal clear that pain and pleasure shape all human activity. As he says in the famous opening passage of *An Introduction to Principles of Morals and Legislation*:

> I. Nature has placed mankind under the governance of two sovereign masters, *pain* and *pleasure*. It is for them alone to point out what we ought to do, as well as determine what we shall do. On the one hand the standard of right and wrong, on the other the chain of causes and effects, are fastened to their throne. They govern us in all we do, in all we say, in all we think: every effort we can make to throw off our subjection will serve but to demonstrate and confirm it. In words man pretends to abjure their empire; but in reality he will remain subject to it all the while. The *principle of utility* recognizes this subjection and assumes it for the foundation of that system, the object of which is to rear the fabric of felicity by the hands of reason and of law. Systems which attempt to question it deal in sounds instead of sense, in caprice instead of reason, in darkness instead of light.[3]

psychological hedonism

The belief that all decisions are based on considerations of pleasure and pain because it is psychologically impossible for human beings to do otherwise.

ethical hedonism

The belief that although it is possible to deliberately avoid pleasure or choose pain, it is morally wrong to do so.

In other words, Bentham espouses both **psychological hedonism** (pain and pleasure "determine what we shall do") and **ethical hedonism** (pain and pleasure "alone . . . point out what we ought to do"). Thus, the principle of utility is sometimes referred to as the *pleasure principle*.

The term *utility* has two related meanings. Utility can refer to a thing's usefulness, to how well it performs a specific function. In this sense, a strictly utilitarian automobile might have standard wheels and only the most practical accessories, such as rear-window defrosters or antilock brakes. Although this no-frills notion of utility enters into Bentham's meaning, he generally uses the term to mean *pleasure-producing* or *pain-avoiding*. We might simplify that to *pleasure-maximizing*, if we remember that sometimes the best we can do to maximize pleasure is minimize pain.

Having asserted both ethical and psychological hedonism, and having described what he meant by utility, Bentham made a move that revolutionized the concept of hedonism: He enlarged the ethical interests of the hedonist. And since he thought we are all hedonists whether we know it or not, this amounted to enlarging everyone's general ethical obligation. Bentham transformed personal hedonism into a potent social and ethical philosophy, using the **principle of utility:** *Act always to promote the greatest happiness for the greatest number.*

Although Bentham's successor John Stuart Mill coined the term *utilitarianism,* philosophers sometimes also refer to Bentham's philosophy as utilitarianism. To avoid confusion, we'll refer to Bentham's philosophy as *simple utilitarianism* to distinguish it from Mill's more refined and elaborate version, which we'll refer to as *utilitarianism.*

> **principle of utility**
> Always act to promote the greatest happiness for the greatest number.

The Hedonic Calculus

Bentham wanted to make ethics a science. To that end, he tried to base his philosophy on observations of actual conditions and to derive principles of behavior from facts. Bentham thought he had found a scientific way to calculate the proper course of action for any circumstance. He called his technique the *hedonic calculus.* John Stuart Mill sometimes referred to the calculus as Bentham's "method of detail," because it considered various factors.

To introduce mathematical precision to the difficult task of weighing alternative courses of action, Bentham proposed the notion of "units" of pleasure or pain, which he called *hedons* or *lots.* (Some contemporary philosophers use the term *utiles.*) Thus, when contemplating an action, we add units of pleasure or subtract units of pain. Bentham identified four elements that affect pleasure or pain themselves, two that affect action related to pleasure or pain, and one based on the number of people affected. The seven elements are:

> *Morality, the science of human happiness, [is] the principle which binds the individual to the species, and the inducements which are calculated to persuade us to model our conduct on the way most conducive to the advantage of all.*
>
> WILLIAM GODWIN

1. *Intensity.* How strong is the pleasure?
2. *Duration.* How long will the pleasure last?
3. *Propinquity.* How soon will the pleasure occur?
4. *Certainty.* How likely or unlikely is it that the pleasure will occur?
5. *Fecundity.* How likely is it that the proposed action will produce more pleasure?
6. *Purity.* Will there be any pain accompanying the action?
7. *Extent.* How many other people will be affected?

Positive units of pleasure or negative units of pain can be attached to each of these seven elements. The resulting unit totals can then be compared, and if the balance is on the positive (pleasure) side, the proposed choice is good; if the balance is on the negative (pain) side, the choice is bad. If a hedonic calculation results in more units of pleasure, we should perform the contemplated action; if more units of pain, we should not. Bentham believed that each of us already uses hedonic calculation on a commonsense, intuitive level; in his view, he was simply adding scientific rigor to our informal methods of choosing pleasure and avoiding pain.

The Egoistic Foundation of Social Concern

Like Aristippus, Bentham claimed that psychological egoism is natural and universal. Psychological egoism asserts that we are always interested chiefly in our own welfare, whether or not we admit it. That's not to say we don't care about anyone or anything else, but this caring is based on how things affect our own happiness. People we love give us pleasure, and pleasure is in our self-interest. People we hate cause us pain, which is not in our self-interest. To those who cause us neither pain nor pleasure, we remain indifferent.

If the psychological egoist is correct, all ethical systems, regardless of their terminology, attempt to maximize pleasure and minimize pain. They may speak of right and wrong, good and bad, and so forth, but these terms all reduce to pleasure and pain. Reason is simply a tool that helps us determine whether our actions will result in more pain or more pleasure. Bentham's calculating concept of reason contrasts significantly with Kant's concept of the good will (Chapter 11).

Building on this egoistic foundation, Bentham thought that if people could be shown how a better society for others would result in less pain and more pleasure for *them,* genuine social reform would occur. That is, natural self-interest provides an *egoistic hook* that shows how our individual welfare is inseparable from social welfare. Thus, the proper role of government must be to ensure that the *enlightened self-interest* of each individual is allowed to develop. Further, to promote the greatest possible happiness for the greatest number, laws and regulations must be not only fair and effective but also designed to motivate people to consider others' welfare as well as their own.

Bentham, along with other liberal laissez-faire reformers, made a revolutionary connection between the welfare of the individual and the welfare of the community by trying to *show* how clear-thinking "selfishness" could produce a better world. Rather than chastise us for being self-interested, Bentham sought to take advantage of it.

Let's examine Bentham's egoistic hook by considering an actual issue. During a heated debate over a severe cut in tax money available for schools, a number of letters to the editor of a local newspaper made this basic point: "I have paid my dues. My children are grown and I've paid taxes for years. Why should I pay to send someone else's children to school? Let their families pay." These letters reflected a disappointing lack of enlightened self-interest. It is in every individual's self-interest—even individuals who don't have children themselves—to see that all children get a good education. Poorly educated people are much more likely to be unemployed or dependent on government assistance than are adequately educated ones. Moreover, if poorly educated people turn to crime for survival, the rest of us will have to live in fear and to pay for more judges, district attorneys, police officers, and jails; we'll see a general decline in our own social services. Thus, it is clearly in every individual's interest for as many children as possible to grow up to be well-educated, productive (happy) members of society.

Bentham's move was motivationally brilliant. In one fell swoop he found a way to link individual self-interest and the good of the community. Egoistic utilitarian logic is concrete and practical, based on everyday concerns and foreseeable consequences. We need not be able to reason abstractly to understand the basic appeal

The problem about appealing ultimately to human desires is that this appears to exclude rational criticism of ethical motivations at the most fundamental level.

THOMAS NAGEL

Have I a genius for anything? What can I produce? . . . What, of all earthly pursuits, is the most important? Legislation. Have I a genius for legislation? I gave myself the answer, fearfully and tremblingly: "Yes."

JEREMY BENTHAM

of the greatest happiness principle. Such reasoning, though effective, remains egoistic and potentially destructive, for whatever sense of community it creates is based chiefly on selfish concerns, not compassion or empathy.

The Question Is, Can They Suffer?

By appealing to the egoistic hook, Bentham extended the ethical reach of the pleasure principle beyond the merely human community to include any creature with the capacity to suffer.

Although the *Introduction to Principles of Morals and Legislation* begins with the ringing announcement that nature has placed *mankind* under the governance of pain and pleasure, Bentham used the fact of suffering to push the moral domain well beyond Kant's kingdom of ends and beyond other Enlightenment philosophies that treat rationality as the source of morality. As far as Bentham was concerned, suffering makes moral claims on us whether or not the sufferer can reason.

In this, Bentham disagreed with René Descartes (Chapter 9), whose dualism led him to conclude that bodies are soulless, unself-conscious objects and that, consequently, animals are meaty machines, bodies without souls. Shortly after reading Descartes's ideas about animals in the posthumously published *Treatise on Man,* the French philosopher Nicolas Malebranche (1638–1715) put Descartes's dualistic thinking into practice as he was walking along with some friends. When a friendly dog came up to them, eagerly looking for attention, Malebranche knelt down and patted it. Then, when he was sure that his friends were watching, he stood up and kicked the poor creature in the stomach as hard as he could. As the dog yelped off, the philosopher noted that it was just a machine.[4]

The Dutch rationalist Baruch de Spinoza (1632–1677) admitted that animals suffer, but argued that we are within our moral rights to "use them as we please, treating them in the way which best suits us; for their nature is not like ours, and their emotions are naturally different from human emotions."[5]

Immanuel Kant, recall, argued that moral dignity is a function of rationality. Kant, like Spinoza, understood that animals suffer, but insisted that they lack any moral worth or dignity. Animals are excluded from the kingdom of ends because they cannot reason from moral maxims. According to Kant, even though we have *no duties toward the animals themselves,* we should treat them humanely, because treating animals humanely is good practice for treating people humanely:

> So far as animals are concerned, we have no direct duties. Animals are not self-conscious and are there merely as means to an end. That end is man. . . . Our duties towards animals are merely indirect duties toward humanity. . . . Thus, if a dog has served his master long and faithfully, his service, on the analogy of human service, deserves reward, and when the dog has grown too old to serve, his master ought to keep him until he dies. Such action helps to support us in our duties towards human beings. . . . Tender feelings towards dumb animals develop humane feelings towards mankind.[6]

Bentham rejected any notion that animals lack moral worth simply because they cannot reason, comparing such thinking to racist thinking. Note how far

This, then, is our Bentham. He was a man both of remarkable endowments for philosophy, and of remarkable deficiencies for it: fitted, beyond almost any man, for drawing from his premises conclusions not only correct, but sufficiently precise and specific to be practical: but whose general conception of human nature and life furnished him with an unusually slender stock of premises.

JOHN STUART MILL

Bentham seems to have moved beyond simple, egoistic hedonism in the following passage:

> The day may come when the rest of animal creation may acquire those rights which never could have been witholden from them but by the hand of tyranny. The French have already discovered that the blackness of the skin is no reason why a human being should be abandoned without redress to the caprice of a tormentor. It may one day come to be recognized that the number of the legs, the villosity of the skin, or the termination of the os sacrum [tailbone], are reasons equally insufficient for abandoning a sensitive being to the same fate. What else is it that should trace the insuperable line? Is it the faculty of reason, or perhaps the faculty of discourse? But a full-grown horse or dog is beyond comparison a more rational, as well as more conversable animal, than an infant of a day, or even, a month old. But suppose they were otherwise, what would it avail? The question is not, Can they reason? nor Can they talk? but, Can they *suffer?*[7]

For all Bentham's personal empathy and kindness, his *philosophy* remained egoistic at base. Its full moral force did not emerge until John Stuart Mill's suffering produced a more refined, clearly altruistic application of it.

■ JOHN STUART MILL ■

John Stuart Mill (1806–1873), one of the most interesting figures in philosophy, began life with nearly equal doses of favor and misfortune. A lucid defender of individual liberty, his childhood was severely restricted, his emotional needs virtually ignored.

Mill's parents were estranged—in his words, living "far apart, under the same roof, as the north pole from the south." Mill's contemporary biographer, A. Bain, described John Stuart Mill's father, James Mill, as unfeeling. James Mill believed that the best way to love his children was by identifying and prohibiting their "vices."[8]

John Stuart Mill's destiny was sealed when Jeremy Bentham befriended his father, who became one of Bentham's younger disciples. From Bentham, James Mill came to believe that all minds are the same at birth and that proper education—begun early enough—would produce a healthy, rational child. Bentham and James Mill decided to use little John Stuart to show just how effective Bentham's ideas were. They gave him a rigorous education, carefully planned to produce a champion of utilitarianism.

Basing their program in part on Bentham's own experiences as a child prodigy, the experimenters saw to it that John Stuart learned Greek and arithmetic at three; Latin, geometry, and algebra at eleven; and logic and philosophy at twelve. Though not everything went smoothly (young John Stuart had some trouble with Plato's *Theaetetus*), he was such a whiz at math that he had to teach himself once he had surpassed his father's abilities.[9] In an effort to refine John Stuart's thinking and to prevent "the mere cramming of the memory," James Mill forced John Stuart to try to learn everything for himself before James would even consider explaining it. In his touching *Autobiography,* John Stuart Mill characterized his education:

> Most boys or youths who have had much knowledge drilled into them have their mental capacities not strengthened, but overlaid by it. They are crammed

If all mankind minus one were of one opinion, and only one person were of the contrary opinion, mankind would be no more justified in silencing that one person than he, if he had the power, would be justified in silencing mankind.

JOHN STUART MILL

John Stuart Mill

Judgment is given to men that they may use it. Because it may be used erroneously, are men to be told that they ought not to use it at all?

JOHN STUART MILL

with mere facts, with the opinions and phrases of other people, and these are accepted as a substitute for the power to form opinions of their own; and thus the sons of eminent fathers, who have spared no pains in their education, so often grow up mere parroters of what they have learnt, incapable of using their minds except in the furrows traced for them. Mine . . . was not an education of cram. My father never permitted anything that I had learnt to degenerate into a mere exercise of memory. He strove to make the understanding not only go along with every step of teaching, but, if possible, precede it. Anything which could be found out by thinking, I never was told, until I had exhausted my efforts to find it out for myself.[10]

Because John Stuart Mill ultimately proved to be brilliant, Bentham and James Mill "produced" not just a champion of utilitarianism, but a true genius. John Stuart Mill said his education gave him a quarter of a century advantage over others his age—but added that any average, healthy boy or girl could achieve the same results with the same training.[11] The personal cost, however, was high: Mill's education robbed him of his childhood. His father's strict control, though typical of the time, stifled any expression of emotion or spontaneity.

> I was so much accustomed to expect to be told what to do, either in the form of direct command or of rebuke for not doing it, that I acquired a habit of leaving my responsibility as a moral agent to rest on my father, my conscience never speaking to me except by his voice.[12]

Later, a friend would say of Mill, "He had never played with boys; in his life he never knew any."[13] In an early version of his *Autobiography,* Mill said: "Mine was not an education of love but of fear. . . . My father's children neither loved him, nor, with any warmth of affection, anyone else."[14] This is not true of Mill himself, for as we'll see, Mill dearly loved one woman his entire adult life.

Mill's Crisis

When he was twenty, Mill began to pay the high price of his hothouse education in earnest with a depression or breakdown he described as a "dry heavy dejection."

> I seemed to have nothing left to live for. At first I hoped that the cloud would pass away of itself; but it did not. A night's sleep, the sovereign remedy for the smaller vexations of life, had no effect upon it. In vain I sought relief from my favourite books, those memorials of past nobleness and greatness from which I had always hitherto drawn strength and animation. I read them now without feeling, or with the accustomed feeling *minus* all its charm; and I became persuaded that my love of mankind, and of excellence for its own sake, had worn itself out.[15]

Mill blamed the strict, critical, analytic environment he was raised in for robbing him of his feelings by insisting that only facts and reasons, only the objective, mattered. But a finely honed analytic mind, unaided by emotion, cannot provide life with meaning:

> I was . . . left stranded at the commencement of my voyage, with a well equipped ship and rudder, but no sail; without any real desire for the ends

When someone brought his son as a pupil, [Aristippus] asked a fee of 500 drachmae. The father objected, "For that sum I can buy a slave." "Then do so," was [Aristippus's] reply, "and you will have two."

Diogenes Laërtius

se mind
ould bear
rse of
... the plan of paying
no regard to others except
so far as their own private
interest compels.

JOHN STUART MILL

which I had been so carefully fitted out to work for; no delight in virtue or the general good, but also just as little in anything else.[16]

Mill was eventually able to pull himself out of his depression and begin the process of becoming a more integrated person by studying music and Romantic poetry. After reading a passage about the way a father's death affected his son in the memoirs of a French writer, Mill had an emotional catharsis that opened him to a wider range of experience. Aided by his superior intellect, Mill developed a fuller and deeper insight into the human condition than his two teachers knew. Although he had bouts of depression for the rest of his life, and although he is reported to have remained rather serious, John Stuart Mill became a compassionate champion of the oppressed and a brilliant defender of classical liberal principles.

Redemption and Balance

Mill's rigid training was also balanced and softened by his remarkable relationship with Harriet Taylor. The couple fell in love when Mill was twenty-four and Harriet was married to a merchant quite a bit older than she was. The relationship began with discussions of Mill's writings and Harriet's plans (she wanted to be a writer also). As Mill began to spend all his free time at the Taylors' house, it eventually became obvious to Harriet's husband that the relationship was more than simple friendship.

Ultimately, an arrangement was worked out so that Mill could stay with Mrs. Taylor when her husband was away, and she could stay with Mill during the summer and on weekends. This arrangement lasted more than fifteen years. Two years after Harriet's husband died, she and Mill were finally married. After seven years of marriage, Harriet Taylor Mill died suddenly, while the couple was in Avignon. A grieving Mill said, "The spring of my life is broken." Mill credited his wife with influencing his work for the better, saying:

The joy of understanding
is a sad joy, yet those who
have once tasted it would
not exchange it for all the
frivolous gaieties and empty
hopes of the vulgar herd.

ANATOLE FRANCE

> What was abstract and purely scientific was generally mine; the properly human element came from her: in all that concerned the application of philosophy to the exigencies of human society and progress, I was her pupil. . . . Her mind invested all ideas in a concrete shape, and formed to itself a conception of how they would actually work: and her knowledge of the existing feelings and conduct of mankind was so seldom at fault that the weak point of any unworkable suggestion seldom escaped her.[17]

Those who knew them both suggested that Mill's vision of Harriet was more loving than it was objective. There may be some truth to that, but there can be no doubt that her relationship with Mill was beneficial and encouraging. Mill insisted that Harriet gave him a better sense of what truly mattered—and what did not—than he had on his own.

Mill's writings show the breadth and balance he worked so hard to develop: *System of Logic* (1843), *Principles of Political Economy* (1848), *On Liberty* (1859), *Representative Government* (1861), *Utilitarianism* (1863), the posthumous *Autobiography* (1873), and *Three Essays on Religion* (1874). His "On the Logic of the

Mill on Women's Rights

As I have already said more than once, I consider it presumption in anyone to pretend to decide [what] women are or are not, can or cannot be, by natural constitution. They have always hitherto been kept, as far as regards spontaneous development, in so unnatural a state that their nature cannot but have been greatly distorted and disguised; and no one can safely pronounce that if women's nature were left to choose its direction as freely as men's, and if no artificial bent were attempted to be given to it except that required by the conditions of human society, and given to both sexes alike, there would be any material difference, or perhaps any difference at all, in the character and capacities which would unfold themselves.

John Stuart Mill, "On the Subjection of Women," in *Human Worth*, eds. Richard Paul Janaro and Darwin E. Gearhart (New York: Holt, Rinehart & Winston, 1972), p. 53.

Moral Sciences" has been described as "the most enduring essay on the method of the social sciences which has ever been written."[18]

In 1873, a fatigued Mill went to Avignon, where Harriet had died so suddenly in 1858. After an especially strenuous day, he developed a high fever and died at sixty-seven on May 7, 1873. John Stuart Mill was buried in Avignon beside his beloved Harriet. So ended the remarkable life of this archetypal utilitarian, a lover of liberty and equality, reason and feeling, who worked tirelessly to improve the lot of all people.

■ REFINED UTILITARIANISM ■

Mill could not accept Bentham's simple version of hedonism, for Bentham, like Aristippus, leveled all pleasures. He did not assign higher importance to moral, intellectual, or emotional pleasures. His only criteria are those included in the hedonic calculus. All other factors being equal, for Bentham, the crucial difference between two pleasures is merely intensity. "Prejudice apart, the [child's] game of push-pin is of equal value with the arts and sciences of music and poetry. If the game of push-pin furnish more pleasure, it is more valuable than either."[19]

Bentham even referred to a "moral thermometer," implying that the only difference among various kinds of behavior was the "degree" of pleasure they produced. Mill, who had been salvaged and made whole by love, music, and poetry, knew better. He knew from personal experience that pleasures differ in *kind* as well as in *degree* and identified with the Epicurean hedonists: "There is no known Epicurean theory of life which does not assign the pleasures of the intellect, of the feelings and imagination, and of the moral sentiments, a much higher value as pleasure than those of mere sensation."[20]

By introducing the notion of *quality* into utilitarianism, Mill refuted the orthodoxy he had been raised to defend. In his analysis of this crucial issue, Mill offers a most persuasive solution to a question we have encountered before: *Is there any way to prove that supposedly "enlightened" opinions and judgments are more than mere opinions?* Mill doesn't address the issue directly in terms of wisdom and

The bad part of [Bentham's] writings is his resolute denial of all that he does not see, of all truths but those which he recognizes.

JOHN STUART MILL

Among the great social thinkers of the nineteenth century. . . . Mill alone tried to do justice to all the competing drives and motives of human nature; he would never banish from his consciousness the many-sidedness and many-leveledness of social reality.

LEWIS S. FEUER

enlightenment, but he does address the heart of the matter: *Is there an objective way to settle disagreements involving "levels" of knowledge and value disputes?*

Having inherited a dislike of abstract theories and systems and having been trained as a social empiricist, Mill approached this ancient problem in a straightforward way. He included an objective component in the assessment of pleasure. In *Utilitarianism,* Mill writes:

> If I am asked what I mean by difference of quality in pleasures, or what makes one pleasure more valuable than another merely as a pleasure, except its being greater in amount, there is but one possible answer. Of two pleasures, if there be one which all or almost all who have experience of both give a decided preference, irrespective of any feeling of moral obligation to prefer it, even though knowing it to be attended with a greater amount of discontent, and would not resign it for any quantity of the other pleasures which their nature is capable of, we are justified in ascribing to the preferred enjoyment a superiority in quality, so far outweighing quantity as to render it, in comparison, of small account.[21]

In other words, only those fully acquainted with two pleasures can decide which, if either, is better. If there is no consensus among them, then there is no objective difference in quality, only difference in taste or preference. For example, only people well enough versed in two (or more) kinds of music actually know whether one is qualitatively better than another. This is a necessary, *empirical criterion.* Many of us can only (honestly) say, "I don't like such and such, but then I've never really tried to understand it." If we really want to compare various kinds of music, we must either listen widely and carefully or ask those who know a great deal about music. If a consensus exists among those familiar with the types being compared, then on Mill's criterion, we have discovered a qualitative difference. Of course, the same pattern applies to comparing the competing pleasures/values of reading Shakespeare or romance novels, playing basketball or playing checkers.

Man does not strive for pleasure, only the Englishman does.

FRIEDRICH NIETZSCHE

PHILOSOPHICAL QUERY

• • • • • •

Can you identify any pleasures "which all or almost all who have experience of both give a decided preference, irrespective of any feeling of moral obligation to prefer it, even though knowing it to be attended with a greater amount of discontent, and would not resign it for any quantity of the other pleasures which their nature is capable of"?

It is not what earnest people renounce that makes me pity them, it is what they work for. . . . So much tension is hysterical and degrading; nothing is ever gained by it worth half what it spoils. Wealth is dismal and poverty cruel unless both are festive. There is no cure for birth and death save to enjoy the interval.

GEORGE SANTAYANA

Higher Pleasures

Mill argued that there are *empirical grounds* for asserting that what we might call "refined pleasures" are preferable to and hence better than the "cruder pleasures."

> Now it is an unquestionable fact that those who are equally acquainted with, and equally capable of appreciating and enjoying, both, do give a most marked preference to the manner of existence which employs their higher faculties. Few human creatures would consent to be changed into any of the lower animals, for a promise of the fullest allowance of a beast's pleasures; no intelligent

Mill claimed that some pleasures are qualitatively better than others. How did Mill make his case? What method did he provide for ranking pleasures? Compare playing classical music to playing video games using Mill's method for assessing the relative qualities of various pleasures.

© Douglas J. Soccio

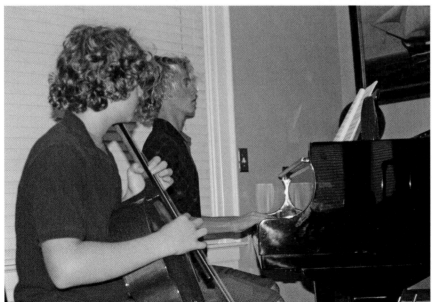

© Douglas J. Soccio

human being would consent to be a fool, no instructed person would be an ig-noramus, no person of feeling and conscience would be selfish and base, even though they should be persuaded that the fool, the dunce, or the rascal is bet-ter satisfied with his lot than they are with theirs. They would not resign what they possess more than he for the most complete satisfaction of all the desires which they have in common with him. If they ever fancy they would, it is only in cases of unhappiness so extreme that to escape from it they would exchange their lot for almost any other, however undesirable in their own eyes. A being of higher faculties requires more to make him happy, is capable probably of more acute suffering, and certainly accessible to it at more points, than one of an inferior type; but in spite of these liabilities, he can never really wish to sink into what he feels to be a lower grade of existence.[22]

This is an interesting argument. Consider typical reactions to individuals with diminished mental or emotional capacities. We love and, perhaps, pity the men-tally retarded, but we do not wish to join them. Techniques to control emotional disturbances by removing the possibility for emotion are properly seen as a last resort. Though we may jokingly claim that ignorance is bliss, few of us would consciously choose bliss if the price is ignorance.

Would you count as a human being (I will not say a true man) one whose supreme good consists of flavors and colors and sounds? He should be crossed off the roster of the noblest of all living species.
SENECA

PHILOSOPHICAL QUERY

• • • • • •

What would we make of someone who did choose ignorance? Could such a person be sane and rational? Reflect on the following: To be considered sane and rational, a person must recognize the value of both sanity and reason. If so, then by definition no sane or rational person can choose a radical diminishment of an essential capac-ity such as knowledge. What do you think of this argument?

Not everyone agrees with Mill that the "higher" faculties and their pleasures are superior, however. Many people live as if their values regarding pleasures are just the opposite from Mill's. Not only are their lives not devoted to the use and development of their higher faculties, but these people also seem actively to dis-courage their higher faculties. Why are the "higher" pleasures unpopular if they are objectively superior?

Lower Pleasures

Mill argues that there is no inconsistency between an appreciation of the supe-riority of the higher pleasures and succumbing to the temptation of more easily secured lesser pleasures. He recognizes that character and habit are major compo-nents of our judgment and behavior:

To the person with a toothache, even if the world is tottering, there is nothing more important than a visit to the dentist.
GEORGE BERNARD SHAW

Men often, from infirmity of character, make their election for the nearer good, though they know it to be the less valuable; and this no less when the choice is between two bodily pleasures than when it is between bodily and mental. They pursue sensual indulgences to the injury of health, though perfectly aware that health is the greater good. It may be further objected that many who begin with youthful enthusiasm for everything noble, as they advance in years sink into indolence and selfishness. But I do not believe that those who undergo this very common change voluntarily choose the lower description of pleasures in preference to the higher. I believe that before they devote themselves exclusively to the one, they have already become incapable of the other. Capacity for the nobler feelings is in most natures a very tender plant, easily killed, not only by hostile influences, but by mere want of sustenance; and in the majority of young persons it speedily dies away if the occupations to which their position in life has devoted them, and the society into which it has thrown them, are not favorable to keeping that higher capacity in exercise. Men lose their high aspirations as they lose their intellectual tastes, because they have not time or opportunity for indulging them; and they addict themselves to inferior pleasures not because they deliberately prefer them, but because they are either the only ones to which they have access or the only ones which they are any longer capable of enjoying. It may be questioned whether anyone who has remained equally susceptible to both classes of pleasures ever knowingly and calmly preferred the lower; though many, in all ages, have broken down in an ineffectual attempt to combine both.[23]

When Mill speaks of character, he refers to socially conditioned habits. Though there are always exceptions, consider the enormous social pressures that can interfere with nurturing "higher" sentiments: Can we reasonably expect children raised in extreme poverty, violence, turmoil, and instability to develop their higher faculties in school, if every afternoon they return to an empty apartment or social jungle? Can we reasonably expect working parents to find time to work extra hours, raise healthy children, maintain their homes, and *then* develop and nurture their own higher faculties? Compare the numbers of people flocking to inane but easily understood movies with those trickling into museums or art houses. Bombarded on all sides by seductive chemicals and toys, fatigued from self-imposed and inescapable pressures, we find that the lure of philosophy or literature or poetry can pale beside the temptations of a new mountain bike, escapist movie, relationship, or basketball game.

The only part of the conduct of anyone for which he is amenable to society is that which concerns others. Over himself, over his own body and mind, the individual is sovereign.

JOHN STUART MILL

■ ALTRUISM AND HAPPINESS ■

Having added the notion of quality to utilitarianism, Mill expands Bentham's appeal to enlightened self-interest into a full-fledged altruistic social philosophy. We have seen the general utilitarian connection between our own happiness and the happiness of others expressed in Bentham's conception of enlightened self-interest. Mill's argument in this regard is less problematic than Bentham's because it is based on a more solid relationship between the individual and the group. Mill asserts that, ultimately, utilitarianism rests on "the social feelings of mankind; the desire to be in unity with our fellow creatures." **Altruism,** from the Latin *alter,* "other," is the capacity to promote the welfare of others; altruism stands in clear contrast to egoism. According to Mill's altruistic utilitarianism, no individual's self-interest is *more* or *less* important than any other's self-interest.

altruism
From Latin for "other"; the capacity to promote the welfare of others; opposed to egoism.

"What a Terrible Punishment It Would Be to Lack a Body!"

The most obvious fact which philosophers refuse to see is that we have got a body. Tired of seeing our moral imperfections and our savage instincts and impulses, sometimes our preachers wish that we were made like angels, and yet we are at a total loss to imagine what the angel's life would be like. We either give the angels a body and a shape like our own—except for a pair of wings—or we don't. . . . I sometimes think that it is an advantage even for angels to have a body with the five senses. If I were to be an angel, I should like to have a school-girl complexion, but how am I going to have a school-girl complexion without a skin? I still should like to drink a glass of tomato juice or iced orange juice, but how am I going to appreciate iced orange juice without having thirst? How would an angel paint without pigment, sing without the hearing of sounds, smell the fine morning air without a nose? How would he enjoy the immense satisfaction of scratching an itch, if his skin doesn't itch? And what a terrible loss in the capacity for happiness that would be! Either we have to have bodies and have all our bodily wants satisfied, or else we are pure spirits and have no satisfactions at all. All satisfactions imply want.

I sometimes think what a terrible punishment it would be for a ghost or an angel to have no body, to look at a stream of cool water and have no feet to plunge into it and get a delightful cooling sensation from it, to see a dish of Peking or Long Island duck and have no tongue to taste it, to see crumpets and have no teeth to chew them, to see the beloved faces of our dear ones and have no emotions to feel toward them. Terribly sad it would be if we should one day return to this earth as ghosts and move silently into our children's bedroom, to see a child lying there in bed and have no hands to fondle him and no arms to clasp him, no chest for his warmth to penetrate to, no round hollow between cheek and shoulder for him to nestle against, and no ears to hear his voice.

Lin Yutang, *The Importance of Living* (New York: Capricorn Books, 1974), pp. 25ff.

I must again repeat, what the assailants of utilitarianism seldom have the justice to acknowledge, that the happiness which forms the utilitarian standard of what is right in conduct is not the agent's own happiness, but that of all concerned. As between his own happiness and that of others, utilitarianism requires him to be as strictly impartial as a disinterested and benevolent spectator.[24]

Mill wanted to show that as civilization advances, the social spirit grows. In the effort, he made an eloquent defense of the importance of universal education to general happiness.

For Mill, the function of education is twofold: to instill the skills and knowledge necessary for an individual to live well and productively and to create healthy, altruistic citizens. But to fulfill the second mandate, education must become a lifelong activity. People must be given opportunities to grow as part of their daily lives. They must be given fulfilling work and sufficient leisure to nurture more than their belly or bank account. The heart of such reform efforts must be widespread, ongoing, high-quality education.

Next to selfishness, Mill says that the principal cause of an inability to be happy for an extended period is a lack of mental cultivation.

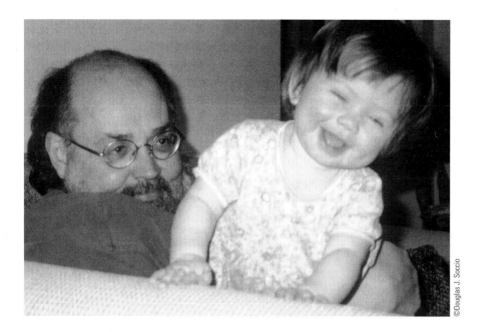

©Douglas J. Soccio

"I sometimes think what a terrible punishment it would be for a ghost or an angel to have no body. . . . Terribly sad it would be if we should one day return to this earth as ghosts and move silently into our children's bedroom, to see a child lying there in bed and have no hands to fondle him and no arms to clasp him, no chest for his warmth to penetrate to, no round hollow between cheek and shoulder for him to nestle against, and no ears to hear his voice."

LIN YUTANG

A cultivated mind (and I do not mean that of a philosopher, but any mind to which fountains of knowledge have been opened, and which has been taught, in any tolerable degree, to exercise its faculties) finds sources of inexhaustible interest in all that surrounds it; in the objects of nature, the achievements of art, the imaginations of poetry, the incidents of history, the ways of mankind, past and present, and their prospects in the future. It is possible, indeed, to become indifferent to all this, and that too without having exhausted a thousandth part of it; but only when one has had from the beginning no moral or human interests in these things, and has sought in them only the gratification of curiosity.[25]

Mill was convinced that science and clear utilitarian thinking could produce a better environment, one conducive to altruism as well as the mental, emotional, and physical development and well-being of individuals.

Utilitarian Social Logic

An excellent example of enlightened utilitarian reasoning can be found in a brief examination of the rationale behind school desegregation and busing, which caused so much controversy beginning with the civil rights movement of the 1950s and lasting into the 1970s. At the time, some people argued for "separate but equal" schooling for black and white children. Close analysis of actual conditions showed that "separate but equal" was not possible, because most entirely black schools were in communities with inadequate tax bases to support good schools. Wealthier communities attracted the best teachers because they could offer better salaries, facilities, equipment, and teaching conditions.

How could utilitarian social reformers use empirical information to improve education for all children? One utilitarian solution to school integration was to

One of the great drawbacks to the self-centered passions is that they afford so little variety. The man who loves only himself cannot, it is true, be accused of promiscuity in his affections, but he is bound in the end to suffer intolerable boredom from the invariable sameness of the object of his devotion.

BERTRAND RUSSELL

What Mill obviously thought needed advocating is that people have regard for other people's happiness, i.e., the general happiness.

JAN NARVESON

take advantage of the self-interest of those parents with the most social and political influence. How could this be done? By sending *their children* to schools in other neighborhoods. The corollary to this, of course, involved busing black children to white schools. Even if many families resented school busing and integration, in the long run their unhappiness would be balanced against a greater good for society as a whole.

What is utilitarian about this? Recall that Mill argued that we must be dispassionate, impartial spectators to everyone's interest, our own included. When I am not thinking exclusively of my own child, for example, it's clear that everyone is better off if all children go to good schools. But if I cannot—or will not—think dispassionately and objectively, I must be given a *personally effective motive,* an egoistic hook. One way to hook me is to send my child to an inferior school, so that my self-centered interest *in my own child* can be tapped to improve that school's quality, which will benefit other people's children as well as my own.

Until we all possess the "nobler sentiments" Mill praised, we may need to be moved to act for the general good by considerations of narrow self-interest. Believing that *consequences* matter at least as much as motives, a utilitarian might be satisfied (at least initially) with getting me to help improve the school system even if I am coerced to do so by law. This kind of forced stretching of my concerns also falls under the heading of ongoing social education.

> *Overcome, you higher men, the petty virtues, the petty prudences, the sand-grain discretion, the ant-swarm inanity, the miserable ease, the "happiness of the greatest number!"*
>
> FRIEDRICH NIETZSCHE

PHILOSOPHICAL QUERY

• • • • • •

Identify and discuss one or two current issues in which this kind of utilitarian appeal to altruism through self-interest might be effective. Explain your reasoning, and discuss some of the details involved in implementing your suggestions.

Happiness and Mere Contentment

> *Each person possesses an inviolability founded on justice that even the welfare of the society as a whole cannot override.*
>
> JOHN RAWLS

Mill, however, was not satisfied with merely modifying behavior. He wanted to reform character, too. In this regard, he distinguished between what he called happiness and "mere contentment." Mere contentment, as Mill understood it, is a condition of animals and those unfortunate people limited to enjoying lower pleasures. A major goal of Mill's utilitarianism is to make as many people as possible as *happy* as possible, not as *content* as possible.

> The ultimate end, with reference to and for the sake of which all other things are desirable (whether we are considering our own good or that of other people), is an existence exempt as far as possible from pain, and as rich as possible in enjoyments, both in point of quantity and quality . . . secured to all mankind; and not to them only, but so far as the nature of things admits, to the whole sentient creation.[26]

Mill argued that the principal cause of unhappiness is selfishness. He believed that happiness requires a balance between tranquillity and excitement, and selfishness robs us of both. It robs us of tranquillity because it is never satisfied, and it diminishes our possibilities for excitement (or stimulation) by narrowing our range of interests. Could that be why so many people seem to need artificial or extravagantly orchestrated excitement?

> When people who are tolerably fortunate in their outward lot do not find in life sufficient enjoyment to make it valuable to them, the cause generally is, caring for nobody but themselves. To those who have neither public nor private affections, the excitements of life are much curtailed, and in any case dwindle in value as the time approaches when all selfish interests must be terminated by death; while those who leave after them objects of personal affection, and especially those who have also cultivated a fellow-feeling with the collective interests of mankind, retain as lively an interest in life on the eve of death as in the vigor of youth and health.[27]

Men who are devoid of integrity and who live for food and nothing else . . . surely they are no better than beasts? If you are no better than a dog or chicken, others will not rely on you. Danger and disgrace will then befall you.

LIE ZI

• • • • • •

PHILOSOPHICAL

QUERY

Examine the preceding quoted passages in light of your own experience. Can you make any connection between periods of boredom and extreme self-interest? If Mill is correct, how could a bored individual become an interested one?

▓ MILL'S PERSISTENT OPTIMISM ▓

Mill thought that no insurmountable reasons or conditions existed to prevent the emergence of a truly healthy society.

Genuine private affections, and a sincere interest in the public good, are possible, though in unequal degrees, to every rightly brought up human being. In a world in which there is so much to interest, so much to enjoy, and so much also to correct and improve, everyone who has this moderate amount of moral and intellectual requisites is capable of an existence which may be called enviable; and unless such a person, through bad laws, or subjection to the will of others, is denied the liberty to use the sources of happiness within his reach, he will not fail to find this enviable existence, if he escape the positive evils of life, the great sources of physical and mental suffering—such as indigence, disease, and the unkindness, worthlessness, or premature loss of objects of affection.[28]

Altruism itself depends on a recognition of the reality of other persons, and on the equivalent capacity to regard oneself as merely one individual among many.

THOMAS NAGEL

According to Mill, the chief task of all right-thinking, well-intentioned people is to address those causes of social misfortune that can be avoided or altered. Mill argued that liberty of thought and speech are absolutely necessary for the general happiness, since we can determine the truth only by an ongoing clash of opinions. He worried about what has been called "the tyranny of the majority" and warned against the very great, and often ignored, dangers of assigning too much weight to majority beliefs. (When we succumb to rule by majority rule, we elevate considerations of quantity over more substantial qualitative matter.)

In the end, Mill remained an optimist who believed that by applying reason and good will, the vast majority of human beings could live with dignity, political and moral freedom, and harmonious happiness. He believed that "the wisdom of society, combined with the good sense and providence of individuals," could

John Stuart Mill argued that, for our own peace of mind, we need to provide social support for those in need—because we never know when we will need help. The quality of life without general assistance would diminish for all of us, Mill insisted.

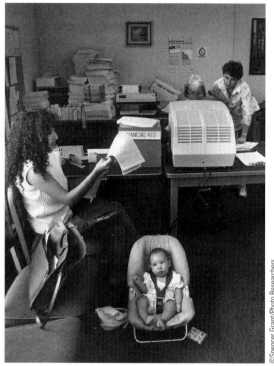

©Spencer Grant/Photo Researchers

extinguish poverty completely and that scientific progress, along with "good physical and moral education," could alleviate the scourge of disease.

We should seek the general happiness because it will make us happier. No doubt Mill, like many others, thought that this was true as it may well be. But this is not relevant. For utilitarianism is out to show that we ought to have regard for the interests of other people on moral grounds.

JAN NARVESON

As for the vicissitudes of fortune, and other disappointments connected with worldly circumstances, these are principally the effect of either gross imprudence, of ill-regulated desires, or of bad or imperfect social institutions. All these grand sources, in short, of human suffering are in a great degree, many of them almost entirely, conquerable by human care and effort; and though their removal is grievously slow—though a long succession of generations will perish in the breach before the conquest is completed, and this world becomes all that, if will and knowledge were not wanting, it might easily be made—yet every mind sufficiently intelligent and generous to bear a part, however small and inconspicuous, in the endeavor will draw a noble enjoyment from the contest itself, which he would not for any bribe in the form of selfish indulgence consent to be without.[29]

Mill's optimism is based on his view of a social human nature and a deep, nearly universal, sense of connectedness. It is a vision that sees no *inevitable* competition between my needs and yours, between ours and everyone else's:

Dissent and dissenters have no monopoly on freedom. They must tolerate opposition. They must accept dissent from their dissent.

ABE FORTAS

The deeply rooted conception which every individual even now has of himself as a social being tends to make him feel it is one of his natural wants that there should be harmony between his feeling and aims and those of his fellow creatures. If differences of opinion and mental culture make it impossible for him to share many of their actual feelings—perhaps make him denounce and defy those feelings—he still needs to be conscious that his real aim and theirs do not conflict; that he is not opposing himself to what they really wish for, namely, their own good, but is contrary, promoting it. . . . This conviction is the ultimate sanction of the greatest happiness morality.[30]

In so many ways, our lives, and those of people in many other countries, have directly benefited from the seed Jeremy Bentham and James Mill planted in John Stuart Mill—in my opinion the finest archetype of a utilitarian social reformer so far.

■ COMMENTARY ■

Although the basic appeal of Bentham's utilitarianism is obvious, Bentham's failure to consider the quality of pleasures is, I think, a fatal flaw. Moreover, the hedonic calculus is arbitrary and subjective, not scientific, as Bentham claimed. It is also probably unworkable. Yet Bentham's attempt to construct a fact-based social ethic is important and generally helpful. It saves both Bentham and Mill from what some philosophers see as Kant's overemphasis on the good will at the expense of actual consequences. It also may provide a more feasible moral code for the average person than does Kant's, since it relies less on abstract reasoning and more on such common practices as calculation of self-interest and desire for basic, identifiable happiness.

The difficulties with Mill's philosophy, as might be expected, are more subtle. He fails to completely resolve the tension between hedonism and altruism, though his "altruistic hedonism" is truly different from Bentham's more egoistic hedonism—if indeed Mill's position is hedonistic. Mill's consideration of quality is important and necessary if utilitarianism is to be anything more than another appeal to pleasure. His attempts to rate the quality of pleasures according to the judgment of those who have experienced them is intriguing, but probably cannot be empirically supported. After all, couldn't there be some people well versed in, say, both art movies and slasher movies who prefer the latter?

And let's not overlook the possible influence of social class and training involved in ranking pleasures. It may be tempting to say that the general public has low taste, but is this anything but the opinion of an educated, culturally conditioned elite? Mill was an aristocrat—by influence, intellect, and training. Today, postmodern philosophers claim that distinguishing between higher and lower pleasures reflects an inbred, elitist cultural bias.

Other contemporary moral philosophers have uncovered interesting and troubling problems with utilitarianism in general. Some of these stem from the possibility that an emphasis on the greatest happiness of the greatest number can result in immoral actions. Suppose, for instance, that the vast majority (the greatest number) of a community derives great pleasure (the greatest happiness) from harassing a small minority? There seem to be no clearly utilitarian grounds on which to condemn them. If enough Nazis derive enough pleasure from exterminating a Jewish minority, aren't they thereby generating the greatest happiness for the greatest number? Mill could argue (as he did, in effect, in his essay "On Liberty") that the rights of minorities must be protected from what Alexis de Toqueville called "the tyranny of the majority," since everyone is likely to be in a minority on some issue. But that's a factual prediction. What if the present majority doesn't believe Mill, or care?

It is better to be a human being dissatisfied than a pig satisfied; better to be Socrates dissatisfied than a fool satisfied. And if the fool, or the pig, is of a different opinion, it is because they only know their own side of the question. The other party to the comparison knows both sides.

JOHN STUART MILL

Problems also arise when we treat the principle of utility as a way of averaging out "units" of happiness. Is there no difference between a community of fifty persons in which one hundred units of pleasure are distributed among twenty people and another fifty-person community in which everybody has two units? In both cases the "totality of pleasure" remains the same.

Even if we know an action will result in the greatest possible happiness for the greatest number, we can—and should—still ask, "But is it right?" The fact that such a question is meaningful suggests that morality is based on more than just considerations of happiness, even the happiness of everybody. Indifference to our own or others' happiness violates the Kantian principle of dignity, but so does a strictly utilitarian exclusion of everything but considerations of happiness.

All that being so, Bentham and Mill have given us one of the most important ethical philosophies of the modern era. If we look beyond their philosophies, we see two diligent social reformers whose lives certainly transcended hedonism. Both lived altruistically. In their efforts to make philosophy matter, both reaffirm the pursuit of wisdom. And time after time, Mill's strongest arguments move well beyond strictly defined utilitarian principles. Without directly referring to wisdom, Mill's educational philosophy is nonetheless a call to wisdom.

Consider, in closing, the following passage from Mill's *Autobiography*. Referring to the time of his crisis, it reveals that early on, Mill's wisdom was deeper than his utilitarianism could accommodate.

> I never, indeed, wavered in the conviction that happiness is the test of all rules of conduct, and the end of life. But now I thought that this end was only to be attained by not making it the direct end. *Those only are happy (I thought) who have their minds fixed on some object other than their own happiness;* on the *happiness of others,* on the *improvement of mankind,* even on some art or pursuit, followed not as a means, but as itself an ideal end. *Aiming thus at something else, they find happiness by the way.* The enjoyments of life (such was now my theory) are sufficient to make it a pleasant thing, when they are taken *en passant,* without being made a principal object. Once make them so, and they are immediately felt to be insufficient. They will not bear a scrutinizing examination. Ask yourself whether you are happy, and you cease to be so. The only chance is to treat, not happiness, but some end external to it, as the purpose of life.[31]

Make haste and enjoy life while you have it. Why care what happens when you are dead?

LIE ZI

In the golden rule of Jesus of Nazareth, we read the complete spirit of the ethics of utility.

JOHN STUART MILL

■ SUMMARY OF MAIN POINTS ■

● Jeremy Bentham resurrected hedonism, adding a social component. He reasoned that if pleasure is good, more pleasure is better. This led him to introduce the greatest happiness principle (also known as the principle of utility): That action is best which produces the greatest happiness for the greatest number. The greatest happiness principle was a direct challenge to the conservative ruling class in Britain, since, according to Bentham, "each counts as one and none more," worker and owner alike.

● Known today as simple utilitarianism, Bentham's philosophy was an attempt to avoid the errors of irrelevant metaphysical theories by basing moral and social policies on experience and scientific principles. Bentham's hedonic calculus was a crude method of reducing issues to simple calculation of units of pleasure versus units of pain. Bentham attempted to take advantage of our "natural" egoism by using reason to show that each individual's welfare ultimately depends on the welfare of the community. The appeal to self-interest as a way of improving overall social conditions is known as the egoistic hook.

- Bentham extended the ethical reach of the pleasure principle beyond the human community to any creature with the capacity to suffer, arguing that the notion that animals lack moral worth simply because they cannot reason is akin to racist thinking. According to Bentham, suffering makes moral claims on us whether or not the sufferer can reason.

- John Stuart Mill coined the term *utilitarianism* and refined Bentham's principle of utility by distinguishing between pleasures on the basis of quality as well as quantity. Mill's concept of happiness is more complex than Bentham's and extends beyond simple concern with pleasure. Mill believed that there is an empirical basis supporting his claim that refined pleasures are objectively better than crude ones: Those familiar with both consistently prefer refined pleasures (philosophical speculation, classical music, poetry) to crude pleasures (eat, drink, and be merry).

- Mill disagreed with Bentham's insistence that all motives are egoistic and based his more refined philosophy on "the social feelings" of all people for unity with each other. Mill believed in the possibility of altruism, the capacity to promote the welfare of others. He argued that lack of altruistic feelings and ignorance of the higher pleasures were products of poor education and harsh conditions, not qualities of human nature. According to Mill, selfishness and lack of mental cultivation are the chief causes of unhappiness, and both can be cured with a proper education and legislation.

■ POST-READING REFLECTIONS ■

Now that you have had a chance to learn about the Utilitarian, use your new knowledge to answer these questions.

1. Identify and discuss some of the social and economic factors that influenced Bentham's development of simple utilitarianism.

2. What is "the Malthusian universe"?

3. Apply Bentham's hedonic calculus to a problem in your own life. Does doing so help you deal with it in a "scientific" way—or does it complicate the problem? If it complicates things, is this due to some flaw in the calculus or to its novelty?

4. What role does psychological egoism play in Bentham's simple utilitarianism?

5. Did Bentham include animals in the moral domain? Why or why not?

6. What was Mill's crisis? How did it affect his subsequent philosophizing?

7. How does Mill account for the predominance of lower pleasures? Do you agree? Why?

8. How does Mill account for the rarity of higher pleasures in so many lives? Do you agree? Why?

9. Express Mill's vision in your own words.

10. Is Mill a utilitarian? Why is the question raised at all? Answer it based on what you have just learned about this issue.

PHILOSOPHY INTERNET RESOURCES

Go to the Soccio Web page at **http://philosophy.wadsworth.com/ Soccio7e** for Web links, practice quizzes and tests, a pronunciation guide, and study tips.

THE MATERIALIST

Karl Marx

THE PHILOSOPHERS HAVE ONLY INTERPRETED THE WORLD
IN VARIOUS WAYS: THE POINT IS TO CHANGE IT.

Karl Marx

KEEP THESE QUESTIONS IN MIND AS YOU LEARN ABOUT
THE MATERIALIST.

1. *What is bourgeoisie?*

2. *What is the proletariat?*

3. *What is the "dialectical process of history"?*

4. *What does Marx mean by* mystification?

5. *What is Marxian materialism?*

6. *What are the three components of the material base of society?*

7. *What is the difference between the superstructure and substructure of society?*

8. *What is capitalism?*

9. *What is "surplus value"?*

10. *What does it mean to be co-opted?*

FOR DEEPER CONSIDERATION

A. The concept of alienation is a central component of Marx's critique of capitalism. How does Marx link alienation to capitalism? How does alienated life differ from species-life? If you are not convinced by his arguments, does that mean that you are living in a state of alienation? That is, is there a way to reject Marx's argument that does not open you up to a charge of failing to grasp what Marx is saying because you have been co-opted by a capitalistic culture and education?

B. What did Marx see as the inherent contradiction in capitalism? How is the contradiction related to his prophecy of violent revolution? What conditions might explain the so-far failure of the predicted Marxian revolution and current spread of global capitalism? Can you find evidence to support Marx's prophecy as correct in general but, perhaps, inaccurate in its estimation of when and how capitalism will be overthrown?

*H*ave *you* *ever* really resented your job, or where you live, yet felt trapped by economic circumstances, unable to improve the basic conditions of your life? Or perhaps your education is uninspiring, something you feel pressured to do in order to get a good—or just an adequate—job? Most of us probably have felt such frustration occasionally. Sometimes, our lives seem to be controlled by our jobs and the need to earn a decent living. It seems as if money determines everything.

In Chapter 12, we learned how Jeremy Bentham and John Stuart Mill hoped to reform society by applying the greatest happiness principle and an empirically based social hedonism to social problems. Mill and Bentham were not the only social reformers inspired by the great inequities of the nineteenth century's fast-moving industrialization, however. Reform movements under the general banners of socialism and communism spread throughout France and Germany. What all these reformers had in common was a clear sense of injustice and increasing inequality. Where they differed, and often significantly, was on the exact causes (and cures) of the dismal living conditions of the working class.

Besides utilitarianism, another, influential theory emerged at roughly the same time. We know it today as Marxism, after its founder Karl Marx. The sheer social and political impact of Marxism warrants a careful look. But, as you will discover, *philosophical Marxism* is not at all what most people think of as Marxism (communism)—and it is not what today's Marxists or communists practice either. Let's see, then, what philosophical Marxism is and what has made it so attractive to so many people.

> *All official and liberal science defends wage-slavery in one way or another, whereas Marxism has declared relentless war on that slavery. To expect science to be impartial in a society of wage-slavery is as silly and naive as to expect impartiality from employers on the question as to whether the workers' wages should be increased by decreasing the profits of capital.*
>
> V. I. LENIN

▦ THE PROPHET ▦

Karl Marx (1818–1883) was born in Trier, Germany. His father was a respected lawyer, and both parents were Jewish. Marx's father eventually distanced himself from the local Jewish community, however, and changed the family name from Levi to Marx, most likely for social and business reasons.

Early on, Karl Marx proved to be highly intelligent and obsessively interested in nearly everything. He was also very independent and hard to control. At seventeen, Marx entered the University of Bonn to study law. He enjoyed himself, writing romantic poems, socializing, spending more money than he had, even fighting in a duel—not to mention getting arrested once for disorderly conduct. His conventional father was not at all happy with his son's behavior and insisted that Marx transfer to the more serious and prestigious University of Berlin.

Marx's stay at Berlin proved to be crucial to his later philosophical growth. Big, busy, and ugly, Berlin epitomized the nineteenth-century idea of a modern city. It was a magnet for social agitators, radicals, and other intellectuals. Imagine the impact such an environment would have on a bright, curious, somewhat rebellious young man from a conservative small-town background.

Karl Marx

> *All I know is that I am not a Marxist.*
>
> KARL MARX

Marx's Hegelian Roots

Georg Wilhelm Friedrich Hegel (1770–1831) was clearly the dominant thinker being read in every major German university when Marx was a student. Though Hegel was primarily a philosopher, his influence spread across intellectual and artistic disciplines. In those days, one was either a Hegelian or an anti-Hegelian, but no serious German intellectual could ignore Hegel's philosophy. Hegel's works include *The Phenomenology of Mind (or Spirit)* (1807), *Science of Logic* (1812, 1816), *Encyclopedia of the Philosophical Sciences in Outline* (1817), and *Philosophy of Right* (1821).

Hegel was influenced by Kant's attempt to answer Hume's assault on reason. Hegel pushed Kant's claim that the mind imposes categories (concepts) on experience to a different conclusion. Rather than appeal to unknowable *noumena* to avoid slipping into Humean skepticism, Hegel argued that Kant's *categories of thought* are actually *categories of being*. (See Chapter 11.) According to Hegel, it is contradictory to assert that noumena are unknowable because to do so we must somehow know that noumena exist—and whatever exists is knowable.

For Hegel, Kant's categories exist independently of any specific individual's mind. They are mental processes *and* objective realities. In Hegelian philosophy, Reality is referred to as Absolute Thought, Mind, Spirit, or Idea. Hegel believed that it is the unique task of philosophy to discover the relationships of particular aspects of Reality to the Whole, which is a single, evolving substance known as Absolute Spirit or Absolute Mind. "History" is the all-encompassing Absolute Spirit self-actualizing into perfection.

Known as **absolute idealism**, Hegel's philosophy holds that the only way Mind can be recognized is as "continuously developing consciousness." The pattern that all consciousness follows constitutes a "dialectical process." As Hegel uses the term, **dialectic** refers to a three-step pattern in which an original idea (thought or condition) known as a *thesis* is opposed by a contrary idea (thought or condition) known as an *antithesis*. The interaction or struggle between the thesis and antithesis produces a new idea (thought or condition) that combines elements from the others, known as the *synthesis*.

Once established, the synthesis becomes the thesis for a new cycle until everything is realized in the infinite synthesis of Absolute Spirit. Each resulting level of consciousness includes its predecessors. According to Hegel, the ongoing dialectic represents the actual structure of reality: the unfolding thought of the cosmic *Geist* (Mind, or Spirit).

Hegel believed that it was possible to construct a complete picture of reality, a grand system that would incorporate all of philosophy, science, theology, art, history, and such. In fact, he insisted that it is impossible to understand anything except as it relates to the Whole. Thus, for Hegel, everything is always developing according to the dialectical process.

According to Hegel, previous philosophers were unaware that they were working with a particular stage of the development of Reason as it unfolds in history or that they themselves were products of the *zeitgeist*, the "spirit of the age." Failing to recognize the *dialectical process* of which they were a part, earlier philosophers mistook something "abstracted" from the Whole for a fixed, independent entity.

---

absolute idealism (Hegelian)

Term used to identify Hegel's particular form of German idealism; a monistic philosophy that is based on an all-encompassing Absolute Spirit that is self-actualizing into perfection; Reality (Absolute Mind or Absolute Spirit) is independent of any individual's mind; not to be confused with Berkeleian idealism (immaterialism), in which objective reality is said to exist in the individual's mind.

dialectic (Hegelian)

According to Hegel, a three-step pattern in which an original idea, known as a thesis, struggles with a contrary idea, known as an antithesis, to produce a new synthesis that combines elements of both.

It's possible that I shall make an ass of myself. But in that case one can always get out of it with a little dialectic. I have, of course, so worded my proposition as to be right either way.

MARX TO ENGELS, 1857

But things can only be understood when they are experienced in relationship to the Ultimate Synthesis toward which all history is unfolding. History does not "just happen." It is the rational development of progressively inclusive stages toward realization in Absolute Spirit.

Hegel was a grand systematizer—some would say *the* grand systematizer. He thought of history as the unfolding of the Absolute Idea of God (Absolute Spirit). He saw philosophy as the attempt to construct a comprehensive picture of *everything as it relates to everything.*

The young Marx was deeply influenced by Hegel, from whom he derived the crucial concept of alienation and the notion of historical evolution as an ongoing struggle.

Other Influences

During this time, Marx became acquainted with a number of radical "freethinkers." These excited young people spent hours arguing the finer points of Hegelian philosophy. Marx thrived on the heady combination of intellectual stimulation and radicalism. Despite all the time spent in coffeehouses and beer halls, Marx completed his doctoral work in philosophy with a dissertation on the materialistic philosophy of Democritus and Epicurus. He planned to be a professor of philosophy.

Life had other plans, however. Marx had been living on money from his father. When his father died about the time of Marx's graduation, he left only enough to support Marx's mother and younger siblings. This would have been no real problem if Marx had been able to secure an appointment as a professor. But by now the Prussian government had grown wary of the young, radical Hegelians and issued a decree prohibiting them from university employment.

Fortunately, Marx was offered a job by a liberal publisher named Moses Hess. Hess, himself a Hegelian, wanted Marx to help him edit a new, vocal "democratic journal" called *Rheinische Zeitung.* Even at this early age, Marx was an impressive figure. Writing about Marx to a friend, Hess said:

> He is the greatest, perhaps the one genuine philosopher now alive and will soon draw the eyes of all Germany. Dr. Marx is still very young (about twenty-five at most) and will give medieval religion and politics their *coup de grace.* He combines the deepest philosophical seriousness with the most biting wit. Imagine Rousseau, Voltaire, Holbach, Lessing, Heine, and Hegel fused into one person—I say fused, not thrown in a heap—you have Dr. Marx.[1]

Marx's admiration for Hegel was altered by an article called *Theses on the Hegelian Philosophy* by Ludwig Feuerbach (1804–1872). Feuerbach was a materialist who challenged Hegel's notion that the driving force behind historical eras was their *zeitgeist.* Feuerbach argued that any given era was the accumulation of the actual, concrete material conditions of the time—not some abstract "spirit of the age." So important were material conditions, according to Feuerbach, that they controlled not just the way people behave, but also *how they think* and *what they believe.* Different material conditions result in what we think of as different cultural eras. After reading Feuerbach, Marx retained Hegel's belief in the dialectics of history and a single reality, but concluded that reality was material, not spiritual.

To be sure, labor produces marvels for the wealthy, but it produces deprivation for the worker. It produces palaces, but hovels for the worker. It displaces labor through machines, but it throws some workers back into barbarous labor and turns others into machines. It produces intelligence, but for the worker it produces imbecility and cretinism.

KARL MARX

The less you are and the less you express of your life— the more you have and the greater is your alienated life.

KARL MARX

A chance combination of events in a thinker's life sometimes has a lasting and profound effect on his or her later theories. In Marx's case, a series of articles he had been doing for Hess on the exploitation of peasants in the wine-growing Moselle Valley crystallized his understanding of Feuerbach's thesis. Observing the way the landowners repressed the workers, actively inhibiting and even punishing their efforts at self-improvement, Marx concluded that material conditions did indeed dominate all others.

The Wanderer

Like many social reformers and agitators, Marx paid a price for his outspoken concern for the downtrodden and his vehement attacks on those he saw as their oppressors. After Marx wrote a series of bitter editorials criticizing the Russian government, the rulers of Prussia—afraid of offending their powerful neighbor— shut down Hess's journal. This was April 1843, the same year Marx married Jenny von Westphalen.

Having a wife, no job, and no longer a Hegelian, Marx sought what he hoped would be a freer intellectual climate: He and Jenny moved to Paris. One of the social and political hubs of Europe at the time, Paris attracted thinkers and doers from around the world with its unique atmosphere of openness and encouragement. Naturally, such a climate attracted the most intense and talented freethinkers and radicals. It was not long before Marx felt right at home.

In Paris, Marx discovered another congenial group of radical thinkers, this time centered on the economic ideas of the Comte de Saint-Simon (1760–1825). Saint-Simon was especially interested in the emergence of a powerful new middle class, known as the bourgeoisie. He concluded that *economic conditions determine history.* More specifically, Saint-Simon argued that historical change is the result of *class conflict:* Those who control the material necessary for production are in a perpetual struggle with those who do not. This idea, as we shall see, had a major impact on Marx's thinking.

Marx also befriended various revolutionary groups of exiled German workers. These workers were influenced by an organized group of French laborers who agitated for radical changes in the conditions of workers and in the relationship between workers and owners. Because they demanded that property be held in common and shared by all, they were known as *communists.* Members of this group helped Marx develop a keen sense of the proletariat, or working class. He now possessed the seeds of his own philosophy.

Within a year of moving to Paris, Marx was expelled from the city, and from 1845 to 1848, he and his family lived in Brussels. While there, he helped organize the German Workers' Union, which became part of an international Communist League in 1847. Its first secretary was Marx's friend and collaborator Friedrich Engels. Marx and Engels wrote the official statement of beliefs and doctrines of the Communist League, which was published in 1848 as *The Manifesto of the Communist Party* (now known simply as *The Communist Manifesto*). It may be the most important and influential revolutionary tract ever written.

Marx next went to Cologne to help agitate for a revolt in Germany. His timing was poor, however, as a more conservative tide was sweeping across France

> The very idea of distributive justice, or of any proportionality between success and merit, or between success and exertion, is in the present state of society so manifestly chimerical as to be relegated to the regions of romance.
>
> JOHN STUART MILL

and Germany. Marx was formally expelled from Germany by the government, and he returned to Paris. Not yet thirty-two years old, he was already perceived as a dangerous revolutionary. He had barely returned to Paris when the French government again made him leave.

In August 1849, Marx's friends gave him enough money to move to London. England, in spite of the flaws Marx and Engels would find in its class structure and capitalist economy, proved a haven of freedom of thought and expression. Thus, in one of the ironies of history, the great critic of capitalism found the freedom to criticize capitalism only in a capitalistic environment.

Marx never left London. For almost a decade, he spent long days in the reading rooms of the British Museum, researching some, but mostly writing. After returning home, he often continued working late into the night. He and his family lived a hand-to-mouth existence, moving from one shabby apartment to another, unable to pay rent. One time they were evicted without anything when the landlord confiscated their few possessions in lieu of rent. Food and medicine were always scarce. Their poverty was so dire that two sons and a daughter died in childhood.

> *The Communists disdain to conceal their views and aims. They openly declare that their ends can be attained by the forcible overthrow of all existing social conditions. Let the ruling classes tremble at a Communist revolution. The proletarians have nothing to lose but their chains. They have a world to win. Working men of all countries unite!*
>
> THE COMMUNIST MANIFESTO

Friedrich Engels

Friedrich Engels (1820–1895), the son of a wealthy German textile manufacturer, went to Paris to meet Marx, after sending him some articles Engels had written criticizing English economists. The meeting changed forever the lives of both men and the shape of the world. They remained friends and collaborators until Marx's death.

In 1844, Engels published *The Condition of the Working Class in England.* His writing was strong, practical, and effective. He went on to write a series of attacks on the most important English economists of the day, accusing them of rationalizing and justifying the abuses the middle and upper classes heaped upon the poor. He saw their economic theories as capitalistic propaganda, rather than honest economic or historical research. As he and Marx discussed these essays, each realized that he had finally found someone who understood the power of economic and material conditions. It has been said that Marx was the deeper thinker, but Engels added breadth and fire to Marx's ideas.

Engels had a gift for acquiring the hard facts Marx needed to support his philosophical arguments and for making Marx's often difficult and obscure thinking easier to follow. Thus Engels played a crucial role in the spread and acceptance of Marxist thinking. Engels and Marx worked together for over forty years, and Engels supported Marx and his family through the long years of poverty in London. When Marx died, Engels protected, advocated, and interpreted Marx's philosophy for the rest of the world.

Friedrich Engels

Vindication

At forty-two, Marx was considered an old man. Poverty and exile had worn him down, and his influence over revolutionary thinkers had begun when he was so

> *It is not the consciousness of men that determines their existence, but on the contrary, their social existence determines their consciousness.*
>
> KARL MARX

young that he was seen as a member of the old guard. His influence grew, however, with the emergence of the militant German Social Democracy party. After Marx became their authority on socialist theory, his financial condition improved. Then, in 1864, the International Workingmen's Association was established by revolutionaries in France and England. They, too, turned to Marx, and he came to dominate their general council. He tolerated no deviance from his views and used any means necessary to defeat those who dared challenge him.

During this time Marx began *Das Kapital*. The first of its three volumes appeared in 1867. This massive work established Marx's reputation as a philosopher. It eventually became what is sometimes referred to as "the Communist Bible," probably because of its nearly mythical status, and possibly because more people claim to give their allegiance to it than have actually read it.

As his health declined, Marx was unable to devote the same care and attention to the two remaining volumes of *Das Kapital* that he had to the first. In fact, he never finished them. What we know as the second and third volumes were extensively edited by Engels in 1885 and 1894, after Marx's death. In many ways, they are inferior to the first volume. (What is called the fourth volume was ultimately compiled later.)

In 1881, Marx's wife Jenny died after a long and painful bout with cancer. The death of the woman who had stood by the exiled, reviled philosopher through poverty and the loss of three children broke his spirit. He lived for fifteen more months in a state of grief and despair. Karl Marx died sleeping in a favorite armchair on March 14, 1883, two months after the death of his oldest daughter. His funeral was attended by his family and a few friends. At the funeral of his old friend, Engels said:

> Just as Darwin discovered the law of development of organic nature, so Marx discovered the law of the development of human history: the simple fact that man must first of all eat, drink, have shelter and clothing, before he can pursue politics, science, art, religion, etc.; that therefore the production of the immediate means of subsistence, and consequently the degree of economic development of a given epoch, form the foundation on which state institutions, legal conceptions, art and even religious ideas have evolved and in the light of which they must, therefore, be explained.
>
> Marx was before all else a revolutionist. His real mission in life was to contribute, in one way or another, to the overthrow of capitalistic society, and to the liberation of the proletariat, which he was the first to make conscious of its own position and needs. Fighting was his element. And he fought with a passion, a tenacity, and a success few could rival.
>
> His name will live through the ages, and so also will his work.[2]

■ DIALECTICAL MATERIALISM ■

From Hegel, Marx took the ideas that there is only one uniform reality and that history is an evolutionary cycle governed by an internal **dialectical process**, in which progress occurs as the result of a struggle between two opposing conditions. From Feuerbach, Marx concluded that reality is material and that

The society of money and exploitation has never been charged, so far as I know, with assuring the triumph of freedom and justice.

ALBERT CAMUS

The state is not abolished, it withers away.

FRIEDRICH ENGELS

dialectical process (Hegelian)

Internally governed evolutionary cycle in which progress occurs as the result of a struggle between two opposing conditions.

AKG London

The German workers depicted grinding silverware in this 1887 engraving were typical of the alienated proletarians championed by Marx and Engels. Could they even afford to own the very utensils they worked so hard to produce?

consequently the material conditions of life control reality. And from Saint-Simon, Marx learned to observe the relationship between the owning/governing class and the producing/exploited class. Combining these elements with a deep concern for the conditions of workers and a keen awareness of the importance of economic conditions to other aspects of life, Marx constructed a social-political-economic philosophy known variously as Marxism, communism, historical materialism, Marxian dialectics, historical dialectics, or dialectical materialism.

According to Marx's dialectical materialism, history is the ongoing result of a constant tension between two classes, an upper class of rulers/owners and a ruled and exploited underclass. From the struggle between different economic interests emerges a brand-new economic structure. Marx saw conflicting economic interests in terms of two classes, the **bourgeoisie**, or middle class, and the **proletariat**, or working class. The bourgeoisie consists of those who do not produce anything yet who own and control the means of production. The proletariat consists of all those whose labor produces goods and provides essential services, yet who do not own the means of production.

Marx took Hegel's concept of the dialectical process and applied it to historical stages, which he called "the five epochs of history." Named after their dominant economic system, these epochs are (1) primitive/communal, (2) slave, (3) feudal, (4) capitalist, (5) socialist/communist. Marx argued that as each epoch develops, its basic economic structure matures. Changes in the economic structure change the material conditions of people's lives. These altered material conditions eventually amount to new social structure.

Then begins an epoch of social revolution. With the change of the economic foundations, the entire immense superstructure is more or less rapidly

bourgeoisie
All those who do not produce anything, yet who own and control the means of production.

proletariat
All those whose labor produces goods and provides essential services, yet who do not own the means of production.

What is competition from the point of view of the work man? It is work put up to auction.

M. Louis Blanc

transformed. In considering such transformation a distinction should always be made between the material transformation of the economic conditions of production, which can be determined with the precision of natural science, and the legal, political, religious, esthetic, or philosophic—in short, the ideological forms, in which men become conscious of the social conflict and fight it out.

No social order ever perishes before all the productive forces for which there is room in it have developed; and new higher relations of production never appear before the material conditions of their existence have nurtured in the womb of the old society itself. Therefore mankind always sets itself only such tasks as it can solve; since, looking at the matter more closely, it will always be found that the task itself arises only when the material conditions for its solution already exist, or are at least in the process of formation.[3]

According to Marx, since the great injustices of capitalism (thesis) result from the private ownership of property, a new socialistic economy (antithesis) will eventually emerge in which private property is abolished. Society will at last be able to provide decent, meaningful lives to virtually everyone (synthesis). As a result, no one will need private property or wealth. Instead of having to compete for a good life, we will live harmoniously, doing creative, satisfying work that benefits us individually at the same time it benefits society collectively. There will be only one class, hence no class conflict. The economy will reach a state of balance, and history as such (not the world, just history as class struggle) will end.

Socialism will never destroy poverty and the injustice and inequality of capacities.
LEO TOLSTOY

PHILOSOPHICAL QUERY

· · · · · ·

Contemporary economists note that although the American economy is remarkably strong and that many people are wealthier than ever, even more working Americans are losing economic ground. Do you think the gap between owners/investors and workers is closing or widening? Cite some contemporary examples to support your view.

Economic Determinism

mystification

Use of cloudy abstractions to create elaborate metaphysical systems that distract us from concrete material reality.

Marx radically transformed Hegel's dialectic by confining it to the material world. He objected to excessively abstract philosophy, referring to it as **mystification**: the use of cloudy abstractions to create elaborate metaphysical systems that distract us from concrete material reality. Marx thought that instead of clarifying ideas, Hegel and other "abstractionists" and idealists make them "mysterious" and vague.

Mystifying logic, like money, does not *produce* anything, it merely alters relationships. Hegel's great error, and that of philosophers in general, according to Marx, is *abstraction*. That is why, according to Marx, most philosophy lacks

"This Society Is Irrational as a Whole"

Herbert Marcuse (1898–1979) argued that no one, Marx included, could have predicted the rapid, qualitative changes in technology that have altered the very nature of work for most people. Physical conditions of employment continue to improve for virtually all workers. Then, too, many of us have been co-opted by a taste of the pie in the form of high-definition television sets, stereos, nice cars, and so on. In other words, we are distracted from our true condition by being in a position to buy (or charge) technologically sophisticated, comforting goods. Yet we remain slave laborers, paying inflated prices for what we get and still doing meaningless work.

> This society is irrational as a whole. Its productivity is destructive of the free development of human needs and faculties, its peace maintained by the constant threat of war, its growth dependent on the repression of the real possibilities for pacifying the struggle for existence—individual, national, international. This repression, so different from that which characterized the preceding, less developed stages of our society, operates today not from a position of natural and technical immaturity but rather from a position of strength. The capabilities (intellectual and material) of contemporary society are immeasurably greater than ever before—which means that the scope of society's domination over the individual is immeasurably greater than ever before. Our society distinguishes itself by conquering the centrifugal social forces with Technology rather than Terror, on the dual basis of an overwhelming efficiency and an increasing standard of living. . . .
>
> The fact that the vast majority of the population accepts, and is made to accept, this society does not render it less irrational and less reprehensible. The distinction between true and false consciousness, real and immediate interest still is meaningful. But this distinction itself must be validated. Men must come to see it and to find their way from false to true consciousness, from their immediate to their real interest. They can do so only if they live in need of changing their way of life, of denying the positive, of refusing. It is precisely this need which the established society manages to repress to the degree to which it is capable of "delivering the goods" on an increasingly large scale, and using the scientific conquest of nature for the scientific conquest of man.

Herbert Marcuse, *One-Dimensional Man: Studies in the Ideology of Advanced Industrial Society* (Boston: Beacon Press, 1964), pp. x, xiv.

substance. Like Bentham and Mill, Marx believed sweeping metaphysical systems and grand-sounding statements about human dignity and virtue pale beside the actual, concrete, *existing conditions* under which the poor barely survive.

In the *Manifesto,* Marx asserts that "man's ideas, views and conceptions, in one word, man's *consciousness,* changes with every change in the conditions of his material existence, his social relations, and his social life." When Marx talks about "material conditions," he means more than just natural physical and biological conditions. He includes economic and social relationships.

Thus Marxian materialism should not be confused with scientific materialism (Chapters 9 and 10), which leads to the conclusion that all behavior is governed by strict laws of cause and effect. Marx is a *social determinist,* not a *hard determinist.* Hard determinists deny the possibility of free will or free action. **Marxian materialism**, by contrast, sees a reciprocal relationship between individuals and their environment.

Marxian materialism
Form of social determinism based on a reciprocal relationship between individuals and their environment; distinguished from strict materialism and hard determinism.

economic
In philosophical Marxism, the complete array of social relationships and arrangements that constitutes a particular social order.

substructure of society
In philosophical Marxism, the material substructure or base of society determines the nature of all social relationships, as well as religions, art, philosophies, literature, science, and government.

means of production
In philosophical Marxism, the means of production include natural resources such as water, coal, land, and so forth; a part of the substructure of society.

forces of production
In philosophical Marxism, the forces of production are factories, equipment, technology, knowledge, and skill; a part of the substructure of society.

relationships of production
In philosophical Marxism, relationships of production consist of who does what, who owns what, and how this affects members of both groups; a part of the substructure of society.

Marx criticized other forms of materialism for failing to understand just how important the role of human consciousness is in shaping society:

> The distinctive character of social development as opposed to the natural process of development lies in the fact that human consciousness is involved. . . . *Intelligent social action is creative action.* . . . By acting on the external world and changing it, man changes his own nature. . . . The material doctrine that men are products of circumstances and a changed upbringing forgets that it is men that change circumstance, and that the educator himself needs educating.[4]

This reciprocity between individuals and their circumstances is, of course, a dialectical relationship. Marx believed that his brand of economic materialism avoids the futility and degradation he saw in scientific materialism, while still acknowledging the importance of the material conditions of our lives.

Engels referred to Marx's philosophy as *dialectical materialism,* but Marx himself referred to it as *naturalism.* Both characterizations express its overall thrust. Marx's emphasis, like that of his great utilitarian contemporary John Stuart Mill, is on the here and now. Like Mill, Marx refers to what he is doing as "social science." He believed his unique mixture of idealistic (Hegelian) and materialistic principles was the *only way* to understand and predict the course of history:

> We see here how consistent naturalism or humanism is distinguished from both idealism and materialism, and at the same time constitutes their unifying truth. We see also that only *naturalism* is able to comprehend the process of world history.[5]

According to Marx, the process of human history is shaped by inseparable social and economic conditions, much more so than by ideas. Unlike philosophers and other intellectuals who attribute great power to ideas such as democracy or truth, Marx proposed a radical view of ideas, namely, that *the economic structure of a culture creates and forms its ideas.* For Marx, the term **economic** refers to the complete array of social relationships and arrangements that constitutes a particular social order. He assigns a crucial role to the material base of society.

Collectively, this material base is known as the **substructure of society**. Specifically, the substructure of society consists of three components: (1) **means of production** (natural resources such as water, coal, land, and so forth); (2) **forces of production** (factories, equipment, technology, knowledge, and skill); and (3) **relationships of production** (who does what, who owns what, and the effects of this division on each group).

The material substructure determines the nature of all social relationships (parent–child, boss–employee, ruler–citizen, and so on), as well as religions, art, philosophies, literature, science, and government. According to Marx, the material substructure of any society produces ideas and institutions that are compatible with it. Because ideas and institutions emerge from and depend on the economic structure of society, Marx refers to them as the **superstructure of society**. In other words, economics (the substructure) drives ideas, art, religion, and philosophy (the superstructure).

> In the social production which men carry on they enter into definite relations that are indispensable and independent of their will; these relations of production correspond to a definite stage of development of their material powers of production. The sum total of these relations of production constitutes the economic structure of society—the real foundation on which rise legal and political superstructures and to which correspond definite forms of social consciousness. The mode of production in material life determines the general character of the social, political, and spiritual processes of life.[6]

The relationship between the economic structure of a society and the kinds of people, ideas, and institutions it produces will become clearer as we take an extended look at Marx's critique of capitalism.

superstructure of society
According to philosophical Marxism, the super-structure of a culture consists of the ideas and institutions (religious beliefs, educational systems, philosophies, the arts, and such) compatible with and produced by the material substructure of the society.

• • • • • •

Analyze your education from the standpoint of relationships of production. What—and whose—values does public education really serve?

PHILOSOPHICAL

QUERY

■ CRITIQUE OF CAPITALISM ■

Given the importance Marx placed on the economic structure of society, it is not surprising that he developed a detailed critique of the prevailing nineteenth-century relationship of production, **capitalism**. Although many of Marx's ideas are clearly revolutionary, and although he did predict a violent overthrow of capitalism, Marx never actually made a moral judgment of capitalism. He thought of his analysis as "pure social science." His aim was to describe current social and economic conditions objectively, identifying their causes and predicting the next historical change.

In Marx's opinion, tension under capitalism increases as *inequities of distribution* destroy any correlation between how much an individual contributes or produces and how much he or she receives. There is a fundamental contradiction at the heart of capitalism: The law of supply and demand determines prices, yet the large pool of workers keeps wages low. Manufacturers keep prices higher than the actual cost of production; thus, over time, workers get less and less for their effort. The result is **surplus value**, which the owners accumulate in the form of capital. Those who contribute the least profit the most.

The bitter irony, Marx says, is that most of the people who suffer under capitalism have been conditioned by it to value it. They support a tax system that favors the rich, dreaming of the day when they, too, will be rich enough to benefit from it. Yet, the laws determining who is allowed to own what, and who gets to keep what, are written by those who already own. Education is controlled by that same class, so even the most deprived children grow up believing in free enterprise and "fair competition," only to be condemned to lives of poverty, or at least constant financial anxiety.

capitalism
Economic system in which the means of production and distribution are all (or mostly) privately owned and operated for profit under fully competitive conditions; tends to be accompanied by concentration of wealth and growth of great corporations.

surplus value
Term Marx used to refer to the capital accumulated by owners; the result of keeping prices higher than the costs of production at the expense of workers.

According to Marx, one of the bitterest ironies of capitalism is that those who suffer the most under capitalism have been conditioned to value it. The old woman in this picture may have worked very hard her entire life, yet remained unable to purchase expensive clothes like those in the store window. Would Marx find that appalling? What do you think?

© Thomas Craig/Index Stock Imagery/PhotoLibrary

PHILOSOPHICAL

QUERY

• • • • • •

Compare kinds of contribution: Who contributes more—the builders who construct houses or the developers who finance them? Who contributes more—the president of a corporation or the secretaries? Are such comparisons fair? Are ideas contributions? Analyze the concept of "contribution."

The Bourgeoisie and the Proletariat

What else does the history of ideas prove than that intellectual production changes character in proportion as material production is changed? The ruling ideas of each age have ever been the ideas of its ruling class.

The Communist Manifesto

Marx's critique of capitalism rests on an analysis of the two classes that have emerged under capitalism. In *The Communist Manifesto,* he characterizes the bourgeoisie as disdainful of everything but capital. The government is nothing but "a committee for managing the common affairs of the whole bourgeoisie." In other words, the government is not "of, by, and for the people," but "of, by, and for the important people." The bourgeoisie reduces everything to crude calculations of self-interest and personal wealth:

[The bourgeoisie] has left no other nexus between man and man than naked self-interest, than callous "cash payment." It has drowned the most heavenly ecstasies of religious fervour, of chivalrous enthusiasm, of Philistine sentimentalism, in the icy water of egotistical calculation. It has resolved personal worth into exchange value, and in place of the numberless indefea-sible chartered freedoms, has set up that single, unconscionable freedom—Free Trade. In one word, for exploitation, veiled by religious and political illusions, it has substituted naked, shameless, direct, brutal exploitation.

The bourgeoisie has stripped of its halo every occupation hitherto honoured and looked up to with reverent awe. It has converted the physician, the lawyer, the priest, the poet, the man of science, into its paid wage earners.

The bourgeoisie has torn away from the family its sentimental veil, and has reduced the family relation into a mere money relation.[7]

Some of the complaints people express about today's health care crisis seem to support Marx's concerns. We lament the demise of the family doctor who made house calls. We resent arriving on time for appointments only to be kept waiting and then having to pay high fees for a cursory examination or a battery of tests whose chief purpose is to protect the doctor from a malpractice suit. Could these be examples of what Marx said happens when a profession is reduced to a "mere money relation"?

Marx and Engels claim that the bourgeoisie, with its hunger for more, cannot rest, cannot leave any corner of the world unexploited and unspoiled.

Constant revolutionising of production, uninterrupted disturbance of all social conditions, everlasting uncertainty and agitation distinguish the bourgeois epoch from all earlier ones. All fixed, fast-frozen relations . . . are swept away, all new-formed ones become antiquated before they can ossify. . . .

The bourgeoisie has through its exploitation of the world market given a cos-mopolitan character to production and consumption in every country. . . . It com-pels all nations, on pain of extinction, to adopt the bourgeois mode of production; it compels them to introduce what it calls civilisation into their midst, i.e., to be-come bourgeois themselves. In one word, it creates a world after its own image.[8]

What the bourgeoisie therefore produces, above all, are its own gravediggers. Its fall and the victory of the proletariat are equally inevitable.

THE COMMUNIST MANIFESTO

But whatever form they may have taken, one fact is common to all past ages, viz., the exploitation of one part of society by the other. No wonder, then, that the social consciousness of past ages, despite all the multiplicity and variety it displays, moves within certain common forms, or general ideas, which cannot completely vanish except with the total disappearance of class antagonisms.

THE COMMUNIST MANIFESTO

● ● ● ● ● ●

PHILOSOPHICAL

QUERY

Do you think that the growth of complex, international corporations, mul-tinational trade alliances, and Internet commerce that are fueling what some observers refer to as the "global economy" or "world village" are signs of a spread-ing bourgeoisie? Is the "capitalist class" creating "a world after its own image"?

The bourgeoisie cannot actually produce all that it needs and wants, Marx pointed out. Its enormous wealth and comfort have resulted from the exploitation of a great underclass, the proletariat. These are the people who actually provide the goods and services society requires to function. Controlled by the bourgeoisie, they are even compelled to produce frivolous luxuries whose real purpose is to generate ever-escalating production. Not only are the workers paid as little as the bourgeoisie can get away with in order to maximize profit, but they are also seduced by bourgeoisie-controlled education and media to consume these over-priced, useless products. Thus, the proletarians are trapped in a never-ending cycle of debt, denied significant influence over their own work, and tricked and

Not only has the bourgeoisie forged the weapons that bring death to itself; it has called into existence the men who are to wield those weapons—the modern working class—the proletarians.

THE COMMUNIST MANIFESTO

coerced into furthering the power and advantage of their own exploiters. As *The Communist Manifesto* explains it:

> In proportion as the bourgeoisie, i.e., capital, is developed, in the same proportion is the proletariat, the modern working class, developed—a class of labourers, who live only so long as they find work, and who find work only so long as their labour increases capital. These labourers, who must sell themselves piecemeal, are a commodity, like every other article of commerce, and are consequently exposed to all the vicissitudes of competition, to all the fluctuations of the market.
>
> . . . But the price of a commodity, and therefore, also of labour, is equal to the cost of production. In proportion, therefore, as the repulsiveness of the work increases, the wage decreases. . . . The more openly this despotism proclaims gain to be its end and aim, the more petty, the more hateful and the more embittering it is.[9]

If you have ever worked on an assembly line, or at picking fruits and vegetables, or in meat- or fish-packing plants, you will instantly understand the relationships of production that Marx and Engels are describing. Some of the most difficult and "repulsive" jobs are the most necessary to society—yet those who perform them are paid little and often respected less. Those who produce the least in Marxian terms work in air-conditioned offices, are supported by hard-working staffs, and may receive salaries, bonuses, and stock options worth hundreds of thousands—if not millions—of dollars.

Communism is a society where each one works according to his ability and gets according to his needs.

PIERRE-JOSEPH PROUDHON

PHILOSOPHICAL

QUERY

• • • • • •

Analyze some corporate scandals of the last few years from a Marxist perspective. Pay particular attention to the enormous compensation packages paid to CEOs in contrast to the devastating pension plan and stock market losses incurred by average workers.

The rushed existence into which industrialized, commercialized man has precipitated himself is actually a good example of an inexpedient development caused entirely by competition between members of the same species. Human beings of today are attacked by so-called manager diseases, high blood pressure, renal atrophy, gastric ulcers, and torturing neuroses: they succumb to barbarism because they have no more time for cultural interests.

KONRAD LORENZ

Co-Option and Class Struggle

Marx and Engels were among the first modern philosophers to recognize the plight of women in modern society. When physical strength became less important, employment opportunities expanded for women and for men unable to do strenuous manual labor. But the work available and the pay offered were often substandard. Garment factories, for example, paid (and still pay) low piecework wages.

> The less skill and exertion of strength implied in manual labour, in other words, the more modern industry becomes developed, the more is the labour of men superseded by that of women. Differences of age and sex no longer have any distinctive social validity for the working class. All are instruments of labour, more or less expensive to use, according to their age and sex.[10]

According to philosophical Marxism, workers are exploited, even if *they* do not realize it. The fact that a powerless group submits to economic exploitation "willingly" does not alter the nature of the exploitative relationship. Just as abused spouses or children may lose the ability to perceive reality and hence mistakenly see themselves as somehow causing or deserving abuse, so too exploited workers, after generations of capitalistic conditioning through schools and the media, may fail to recognize their actual social condition.

We have already seen how working-class and middle-class people can come to identify with the *possibility* of acquiring wealth rather than with their *actual chances* of doing so. In other words, we may identify with the *system* rather than with our true role in it. Marxists refer to this as being **co-opted**. You are co-opted when you are tricked, seduced, or somehow convinced to further interests that are to your ultimate disadvantage—and think that you do so willingly.

All history, according to Marx and Engels, is the history of a class struggle in which the bourgeoisie forges the instrument of its own destruction as it grows smaller but richer and more powerful. In our own time, social scientists are discussing the "shrinking middle class," the growing disparity between the haves and the have-nots. Escalating housing prices keep more and more working-class families from owning property. Two-income families alter childrearing practices and family interactions. As the divorce rate remains high, people suffer the economic (not to mention psychic) cost of supporting two separate households. Unmarried mothers of young children face the dilemma of working and paying high child-care costs, or not working and living at or below the poverty level on state assistance or often inadequate child-support payments. Medical insurance is now priced beyond the reach of so many working- and middle-class people that many observers despair of ever finding a way to provide adequate care to all Americans.

Marx and Engels predicted that such conditions will not change until the proletariat becomes *fully aware* of itself, until people whose class interests are identical see that they are identical. Presently, however,

> . . . the labourers still form an incoherent mass scattered over the whole country, and broken up by their mutual competition. If anywhere they unite to form more compact bodies, this is not yet the consequence of their own active union, but of the union with the bourgeoisie, which class, in order to attain its own political ends, is compelled to set the whole proletariat in motion, and is moreover yet, for a time, able to do so. At this stage, therefore, the proletarians do not fight their enemies, but the enemies of their enemies . . . every victory so obtained is a victory for the bourgeoisie.[11]

Under capitalism, it is in the bourgeoisie's short-term interest for different ethnic, gender, age, and religious groups to distrust and despise one another, Marx and Engels point out. So, for instance, a Marxist might argue that the bitter debate over affirmative action serves the bourgeoisie by obscuring the fact that *most people of all backgrounds are being kept out of the wealthy classes*. Indeed, for the bourgeoisie as a class, nothing could be better than for "token" members of all disadvantaged groups to become publicly successful through education and hard work. This will co-opt others in those groups to "behave" and work hard while dreaming of "making it." Real change will come only when the exploited identify with one another and not with their ethnicity, religion, gender, or age, say Marx and Engels in *The Communist Manifesto*.

co-opt

In Marxian social analysis, co-option occurs when workers identify with the economic system that oppresses them by confusing the remote possibility of accumulating wealth with their actual living and working conditions; being co-opted also refers to anyone who is somehow convinced to further interests that are to her or his ultimate disadvantage.

The oppressed are allowed once every few years to decide which particular representatives of the oppressing class are to represent and repress them.

KARL MARX

Differences of age and sex have no longer any distinctive social validity for the working class. All are instruments of labour, more or less expensive to use, according to their age and sex.

THE COMMUNIST MANIFESTO

This organisation of the proletarians into a class, and consequently into a political party, is continually being upset again by the competition between the workers themselves. But it ever rises up again, stronger, firmer, mightier. It compels legislative recognition of particular interests of the workers, by taking advantage of the divisions among the bourgeoisie itself. . . . The bourgeoisie itself, therefore, supplies the proletariat with its own elements of political and general education, in other words, it furnishes the proletariat with weapons for fighting the bourgeoisie.[12]

PHILOSOPHICAL

QUERY

● ● ● ● ● ●

Discuss the possibility that affirmative action and similar social reform efforts actually serve the interests of an exploitative class by creating increased consciousness of difference and division. Are efforts to "honor diversity" aiding or hindering class consciousness? Is there a better solution to social inequality? If so, what?

All previous historical movements were movements of minorities, or in the interest of minorities. The proletarian movement is the self-conscious, independent movement of the immense majority, in the interest of the immense majority.

THE COMMUNIST
MANIFESTO

The business of America is business.

CALVIN COOLIDGE

The inherent vice of capitalism is the unequal sharing of blessings; the inherent virtue of socialism is the equal sharing of miseries.

WINSTON CHURCHILL

alienation
According to Marx, condition of workers separated from the products of their labor; primarily an objective state, but can also refer to not feeling "at one" with the product of labor.

As capitalism becomes increasingly efficient, it produces more than it can consume, and its technological progress renders large numbers of workers obsolete. Marxists say the result is an overburdened welfare state that provides barely enough sustenance—and no dignity—to its displaced workers.

The modern labourer, on the contrary, instead of rising with the progress of industry, sinks deeper and deeper below the conditions of existence of his own class. He becomes a pauper, and pauperism develops more rapidly than population or wealth. And here it becomes evident that the bourgeoisie . . . is unfit to rule because it is incompetent to assure an existence to its slave within his slavery, because it cannot help letting him sink into such a state, that it has to feed him, instead of being fed by him. Society can no longer live under the bourgeoisie; in other words, its existence is no longer compatible with society. . . . The development of modern industry, therefore, cuts from under its feet the very foundation on which the bourgeoisie produces and appropriates products.[13]

Marx and Engels predicted that more and more workers would suffer as the bourgeoisie acquired capital at their expense and that the workers' unhappiness, frustration, and indignation would erupt in violent revolution. After the revolution a new social order would emerge, from which all class distinctions, private ownership of the means of production, and exploitation would disappear forever.

What happened? Is the revolution behind schedule or is it not going to come at all? To address this issue, we need to look at one of the most important aspects of Marxist theory, one that is often overlooked by capitalistic critics of Marxism.

■ ALIENATION ■

One of Marx's most interesting and compelling notions centers on the concept of **alienation**, a term he derived from Hegel. Marx thought of alienation as the most destructive feature of capitalism. Indeed, he thought it revealed an inherent irrationality, an inherent evil in the very basis of capitalism. Alienation occurs when the worker no longer feels at one with the product of his or her labor. An alienated individual rarely feels at home with himself or herself, or with others. Alienation is a state of powerlessness, frustration, repressed resentment, and despair. It results from the transformation of a human being into a commodity.

Marx was convinced that we are happiest not when we are idle but when we are engaged in meaningful work. Meaningful work can be work of virtually any kind so long as the worker has control over its products. This is necessary psychologically, not just morally. Imagine the suffering of a designer whose boss controls what brushes, pens, and colors the designer can use; how much time can be devoted to each project; what is good enough (or not); what happens to the designs. No matter how much such a designer produces, he or she will suffer. Being detached from the work, prevented from exercising personal judgment and applying personal standards, the artist is alienated from his or her own work.

Anyone who takes a job *solely* on the basis of what it pays becomes alienated, in Marx's sense, by reducing himself or herself to a money-making machine. Possessions and money to buy them become more important than time to do things right, than the experience itself, and than the people involved. Soon, the alienated worker sees those he or she works for or provides services to as the means to a paycheck, not as full human beings. This is what Marx meant when he said, "The *increase in value* of the world of things is directly proportional to the *decrease in value* of the human world." And, of course, full functioning and **eudaimonia** are impossible in such conditions; this is a "kingdom of means," not a "kingdom of ends."

According to Marx, alienation even extends to our relationship with nature (as environmentalists remind us today). Nature provides the material basis for all work. Yet unchecked capitalism uses up nature, because the capitalist does not feel part of nature. The alienated worker sees money, rather than the natural world that provides bread and milk and fruit and wood, as the means of life. Alienated from nature, we cannot see what we really depend on.

> The more the worker *appropriates* the external world and sensuous nature through his labor, the more he deprives himself of the *means of life* in two respects; first, that the sensuous world gradually ceases to be an object belonging to his labor, a *means of life* of his work; secondly, that it gradually ceases to be a *means of life* in the immediate sense, a means of physical subsistence of the worker.[14]

eudaimonia
Often translated as "happiness"; term Aristotle used to refer to fully realized existence; state of being fully aware, vital, alert.

* * * * * *

PHILOSOPHICAL QUERY

Discuss some examples of ways alienation spreads from the workplace into society at large and the home in particular. Has it spread to your life? To school?

Because so many of us must work to live, most of us spend a high percentage of our lives at our jobs. If we are alienated there, we are likely to be alienated elsewhere, for we cannot avoid being shaped by all those hours at work. Marx describes alienation as *externalization:* Work is seen as something I *do,* not as an expression of who I *am*. When I am in a state of alienation, I develop a habit of separating myself from nature and other people. I lose touch with myself, becoming alienated from who I really am, or at least from who I *ought to be.*

What constitutes the externalization of labor?

First is the fact that labor is *external* to the laborer—that is, it is not part of his nature—and that the worker does not affirm himself in his work but denies himself, feels miserable and unhappy, develops no free physical and mental energy but mortifies his flesh and ruins his mind. The worker, therefore, feels at ease only outside work, and during work he is outside himself. He is at home when he is not working and when he is working he is not at home. . . . External labor, labor in which man is externalized, is labor of self-sacrifice, of penance. Finally, the external nature of work for the worker appears in the fact that it is not his own but another person's, that in work he does not belong to himself but to someone else . . . the activity of the worker is not his own spontaneous activity. It belongs to another. It is the loss of his own self.

The result, therefore, is that . . . the worker . . . feels that he is acting freely only in his animal functions—eating, drinking, and procreating, or at most in his shelter and finery—while in his human functions he feels only like an animal. The animalistic becomes human and the human becomes animalistic.[15]

To the extent that Marx is correct, it is no wonder we are so interested in our weekends and vacations, in our leisure: Only there do we feel fully free to be ourselves. Most of the week we sell our bodies and souls out of necessity: The capitalist machine demands that we work. Marx did not believe humans are by nature lazy. Quite the contrary; he believed we *want* and *need* meaningful work. Our obsessions with leisure, our absenteeism, our efforts to strike it rich or retire as early as possible only testify to the deep degree of alienation we must be experiencing in our work.

Species-Life

Marx distinguishes alienated life from species-life. **Species-life** is fully human life, life lived productively and consciously. **Alienated life**, in contrast, creates a sense of distance from nature and renders people unconscious of precisely how unhappy, unspontaneous, and unfulfilled they really are. In other words, alienation prevents us from being fully human. Thus alienation is anti-species or anti-human.

Marx, we see at last, is propounding not just an economic theory, but a sophisticated philosophy of *self-actualization.* He thinks that in the next historical stage, people will work to fulfill themselves, for the creative, self-actualizing joy of it. If that is difficult to believe, Marx says, it is because we are so alienated from human nature (our species) that we can conceive of work only in distorted, alienated terms.

To be alienated is to feel separated from the world as we experience it daily, from the "center" of ourselves, and from others who are having the same problem. Alienation is what a man feels when he has lost his sense of belonging to the world.

RENÉ J. MULLER

The philosopher, who is himself an abstract form of alienated man, takes himself as the yardstick of the alienated world. The whole history of alienation . . . is . . . nothing but the history of the production of abstract thought.

KARL MARX

species-life
Fully human life lived productively and consciously; not alienated.

alienated life
Unconscious, unspontaneous, and unfulfilled life; deprived of fundamental conditions necessary for self-actualization.

"Automatons Cannot Love"

Psychologist and "socialist humanist" philosopher Erich Fromm (1900–1980) wrote in a Marxian vein about self-actualization and love in his influential book *The Art of Loving*. Specifically, Fromm attempted to show how the structure of capitalistic society shapes our personal relationships. Fromm argued that alienated people cannot really love—themselves, one another, or God. Along the way he raised some disturbing questions about our society.

> Modern capitalism needs men who co-operate smoothly and in large numbers; who want to consume more and more; and whose tastes are standardized and can be easily influenced and anticipated. . . . who can be guided without force, led without leaders, prompted without aim—except the one to make good, to be on the move, to go ahead.
>
> What is the outcome? Modern man is alienated from himself, from his fellow man, from nature. He has been transformed into a commodity, experiences his life forces as an investment which must bring him the maximum profit obtainable under existing market conditions. Human relations are essentially those of alienated automatons. . . . man overcomes his unconscious despair by the routine of amusement, the passive consumption of sounds and sights offered by the amusement industry; furthermore by the satisfaction of buying ever more things, and soon exchanging them for others. . . .

> The situation as far as love is concerned corresponds, as it has to by necessity, to this social character of modern man. Automatons cannot love; they can exchange their "personality packages" and hope for a fair bargain. . . .
>
> Just as automatons cannot love each other, they cannot love God. The *disintegration of the love of God* has reached the same proportions as the disintegration of the love of man. This fact is in blatant contradiction to the idea that we are witnessing a religious renaissance in this epoch. Nothing could be further from the truth. What we witness (even though there are exceptions) is a regression to an idolatric concept of God, and a transformation of the love of God into a relationship fitting an alienated character structure. The regression to an idolatric concept of God is easy to see. People are anxious, without principles or faith, they find themselves without an aim except the one to move ahead; hence they continue to remain children, to hope for father or mother to come to their help when help is needed. . . . belief in God and prayer is recommended as a means to increase one's ability to be successful. Just as modern psychiatrists recommend happiness of the employee in order to be more appealing to the customers, some ministers recommend love of God in order to be more successful.

Erich Fromm, *The Art of Loving* (1956; reprint, New York: Perennial Library, 1974), pp. 70–71, 72–73, 89.

What makes something "work" is not whether it is difficult or easy, but *how we relate to it*. If we are involved in and care about it, if, in Marx's expression, we are "at home," we do not look upon a task as work. If we have significant say over how we do something, and do it for reasons we understand and for values we hold, we may not like what we do, but we are not alienated from it. If we act from love when we cut the grass for our parents or help a friend move furniture, we are not alienated.

The animal is immediately one with *its life activity*, not distinct from it. The animal is its life activity. Man makes his life activity itself into an object of will and consciousness. He has conscious life activity. It is not a determination with which he immediately identifies. Conscious life activity distinguishes

All of Marx's major predictions have turned out to be wrong.

ROGER KIMBALL

The teaching of Marx is all-powerful because it is true. It is complete and harmonious, providing men with a consistent view of the universe, which cannot be reconciled with any superstition, any reaction, any defence of bourgeois oppression. It is the lawful successor of the best that has been created by humanity in the nineteenth century—German philosophy, English political economy, and French socialism.

V. I. LENIN

man immediately from the life activity of the animal. Only thereby is he a species-being. Or rather, he is only a conscious being—that is, his own life is an object for him—since he is a species-being. Only on that account is his activity free activity. Alienated labor reverses the relationship in that man, since he is a conscious being, makes his life activity, his *essence*, only a means for his *existence*.[16]

If capitalism were destroyed, Marx thought, we would revert to species-life. Once freed from the irrational, destructive pressure to survive only at the expense of others, we would be free to develop as human beings, to actualize ourselves as productive workers who find joy and fulfillment in personally meaningful work. If we are unable to accept that vision of ourselves right now, Marx would say it is because we are living alienated lives to one degree or another. Our distrust of Marx's utopia becomes a symptom of our distorted view of human nature. What we think of as human nature—people hustling for a buck, scheming to strike it rich, and looking forward to the day they can quit working—is not *human* nature at all. It is alienation.

PHILOSOPHICAL QUERY

• • • • • •

Identify and discuss activities in which you participate in species-life. Contrast such experiences with alienated activity. What can you do to decrease periods of alienation and increase your own species-life?

Almost all the prophecies of Marx and his followers have already proved to be false, but this does not disturb the spiritual certainty of the faithful . . . . In this sense Marxism performs the function of a religion, and its efficacy is of a religious character. But it is a caricature and a bogus form of religion.

LESZEK KOWLAKOWSKI

■ COMMENTARY ■

Although Marx seems to have confused the evils of industrialization with capitalism, his critique of the excesses of capitalism has much to teach us about the relationship of the material conditions of people's lives to the ideas and beliefs they hold. His assessment of the evils of "the bourgeoisie" reminds us of the dangers of class disparity and the harm that can come from separating reward from performance and from determining human worth in monetary terms. Overall, his cultural critique raises important questions about the meaning of work and human dignity that are, if anything, as pressing in this era of downsizing and global conglomerates as they were in Marx and Engels's time.

I confess that I am conflicted about the strong strain of resentment and bitterness that runs through contemporary political Marxism. On the one hand, a certain amount of resentment is understandable given the disparities between the laboring classes of the world and the nonlaboring classes who control enormous pockets of wealth. But anger alone—even righteous, justified anger—cannot construct a healthy or just society.

On the other hand, I am dismayed at the lack of sustained "middle-class" anger about inequitable social conditions and the egregious disparities between the treatment of corporate CEOs and their workers. One only needs to think of the scandals of recent years involving financial institutions and various high-tech companies. Losses were anything but evenly distributed across the workforce.

Marx did not allow for the possibility of societal self-correction, serial social revolutions, and consciously guided change, nor could he fully anticipate the shape of the modern economy or the positive features of postindustrial capitalism. Nor did he, nor could anyone, imagine the effects of the great technological revolution we are living through. Indeed, its full effects are probably beyond our comprehension, too.

Lastly, in spite of his genuine concern for the alienated, degraded worker, Marx himself seems to rob individuals of any significant capacity for self-determination. Marx's emphasis on classes and class struggle does not pay enough respect to the individual. One of the major problems with political Marxism is its tendency to sacrifice the individual for the good of the collective. In his zeal to stress the causal properties of the material substructure of society, Marx grants too little importance to the role of ideas and individuals as agents of social progress. It seems to me that in the final analysis, Marx romanticized the proletariat and vilified the bourgeoisie, thereby oversimplifying relations between those two classes.

Still, Marx's vision of a fuller, better life places him among the champions of the oppressed and exploited. Like a prophet, Marx calls us to account for our sins; like a prophet, he indicates a general direction for our future. Perhaps that is enough. The rest, in any event, is up to us.

> *Marxism is a doctrine of blind confidence that a paradise of universal satisfaction is awaiting us just around the corner.*
> LESZEK KOWLAKOWSKI

> *Communism, like any other revealed religion, is largely made up of prophecies.*
> H. L. MENCKEN

▦ SUMMARY OF MAIN POINTS ▦

- Marx combined Hegel's dialectical view of history with Feuerbach's concept of a materialist *zeitgeist* (spirit of the age) to produce historical materialism, the view that history is the ongoing result of a dialectical process that consists of an interaction between an original condition (thesis) and a contrary condition (antithesis) to produce a new condition containing elements of the thesis and antithesis (synthesis). Each synthesis becomes the thesis for a new dialectical cycle driven by constant tension between two classes: the exploiters and the exploited.

- Marx identified five epochs of history that constitute the dialectical development of history: (1) primitive/communal, (2) slave, (3) feudal, (4) capitalist, (5) socialist/communist. As each epoch develops, its basic economic structure matures and the material conditions under which people live change. According to Marx, ideas, values, and thinking itself are shaped by material conditions and social relations.

- Marx argued that the economic structure of a culture creates and forms its own ideas. Most important is the material substructure, which consists of three components: (1) the means of production (natural resources); (2) the forces of production (factories, equipment, technology, and knowledge); (3) the relationships of production, which constitute a complex system that shapes everything else. The material substructure produces ideas and institutions compatible with it. These comprise the culture's superstructure and include art, science, philosophy, religion, and government.

- Marx was sharply critical of capitalism, which he saw as a stage on the way to a classless socialistic economy. In his view, the capitalist substructure contains a fundamental contradiction in the tension between the owners' desire to keep wages low while prices fluctuate according to the law of supply and demand.

- Under capitalism, the two struggling classes are the bourgeoisie and the proletariat. The bourgeoisie consists of those who own the means of production but do not produce anything; it views everything in terms of money and self-interest. The proletariat consists of those who produce things but do not own the means of production (including their own time and labor).

- Marx predicted that the demands of the bourgeoisie would result in an ever-growing proletariat whose living conditions would continue to decline until the proletariat would rise up in violent revolt and destroy the bourgeoisie and capitalism, leading to the next historical epoch, socialism.

- The most destructive feature of capitalism, according to Marx, is alienation, which occurs when the worker no longer feels at one with the product of his or her labor; it is a state of powerlessness, frustration, and despair. Capitalism alienates people from one another, from nature, and from work. Marx distinguished alienated life from species-life, which is lived productively and consciously. Species-life is fully human life, a product of self-actualization (which capitalism inhibits).

■ POST-READING REFLECTIONS ■

Now that you have had a chance to learn about the Materialist, use your new knowledge to answer these questions.

1. Describe the social conditions that led Marx and Engels to write *The Communist Manifesto*.

2. What was Feuerbach's influence on Marx?

3. What was Hegel's influence on Marx?

4. Explain why Marx's philosophy is sometimes called "historical materialism."

5. Give one or two examples of Marxian mystification.

6. Describe capitalism in terms of the relationships of production.

7. What is the significance of the bourgeoisie to philosophical Marxism?

8. What is the significance of the proletariat to philosophical Marxism?

9. Explain the importance of class consciousness and class struggle to Marxism. What role does consciousness play in species-life, according to Marx?

10. Are Marx's two categories of social class (the bourgeoisie and the proletariat) adequate to describe today's economic conflicts? Are there additional social classes that Marx does not address, and if so, what are they?

11. Is class conflict an outmoded way of understanding current economic conditions, given what we now know about ethnic and gender disparities?

 PHILOSOPHY INTERNET RESOURCES

Go to the Soccio Web page at **http://philosophy.wadsworth.com/ Soccio7e** for Web links, practice quizzes and tests, a pronunciation guide, and study tips.

THE EXISTENTIALIST

Søren Kierkegaard

THE QUESTION IS NOT WHAT AM I TO *BELIEVE*,
BUT WHAT AM I TO *DO*?

Søren Kierkegaard

FOR YOUR REFLECTION

KEEP THESE QUESTIONS IN MIND AS YOU LEARN ABOUT THE
EXISTENTIALIST.

1. *What is existentialism?*

2. *What was the Kierkegaard family curse?*

3. *Who was Regina Olsen, and what role did she play in Kierkegaard's philosophy?*

4. *What is inauthenticity?*

5. *What is authenticity?*

6. *What does Kierkegaard mean by "passion"?*

7. *What does Kierkegaard mean by "becoming a subject"?*

8. *What are the "stages on life's way"?*

9. *What is the Kierkegaardian leap of faith?*

10. *What does Kierkegaard mean by "edification"?*

FOR DEEPER CONSIDERATION

A. Why does Kierkegaard insist that the "present age" lacked authentic passion? Does the widespread use of the word *passion* these days—such as, "Music is my passion," "My kids are my passion"—suggest that he was onto something or just the opposite—that today's world is more authentic than Kierkegaard's and, thus, his critique of inauthenticity is dated?

B. Sketch and analyze Kierkegaard's critique of "false Christianity" by contrasting Kierkegaard's existentialist idea of faith with more common conceptions of faith as belief. What, for Kierkegaard, constitutes "being a Christian"? Why did—and do—so many people who see themselves as Christians find Kierkegaard's point of view offensive and wrongheaded? What do you think? Or is this a matter of thinking?

Has it perhaps occurred to you that something fundamentally important seems to be missing from most (or all) of the philosophies we have studied so far? Has the ancient challenge to philosophy been answered for *you*: "Philosophy, what practical difference do you make to *me?*" Perhaps you've wondered what, if any, bearing the categorical imperative has on your actual, day-to-day moral *living*. Do "proofs" for the existence of God, such as those offered by Thomas Aquinas, provide you with a living faith? Do they enhance your relationship with a living God? What do the rigorous inquiries of Hume or Descartes have to do with the concrete and immediate choices facing you as an "existing individual"? As a seeker of wisdom, do you wonder whether a utilitarian calculus or Marxian assessment of history makes any real difference to the daily sufferings of real people?

If it sometimes seems to you that philosophy has passed over the genuine (real-life) concerns of individuals, you are not alone. One of the most influential, intriguing, and arresting responses to the massing of society and the resultant loss of genuine respect for the individual goes under the name **existentialism**. Existentialism refers to any philosophy that asserts that the most important philosophical matters involve fundamental questions of meaning and choice as they affect actual—existing—individuals. Existential themes include choice, freedom, identity, alienation, inauthenticity, despair, and awareness of our own mortality. Existentialists point out that objective science and rationalistic philosophy cannot come to grips with the real problems of human existence: "What am *I* to do?" "To what can *I* commit myself?" "What does *my* life mean?" Existentialists believe that general answers, grand metaphysical systems, and supposedly objective and rational theories cannot address the existential (living, concrete) concerns of individuals.

The early existentialists were among the first to identify major issues unique to postindustrial, highly specialized, technical, sophisticated societies: increased loss of individuality, increased pressure to conform, the threat to human freedom and dignity from science and bureaucracy. Philosopher of history Samuel Enoch Stumpf says:

> Existentialism was bound to happen. The individual had over the centuries been pushed into the background by systems of thought, historical events, and technological forces. The major systems of philosophy had rarely paid attention to the uniquely personal concerns of individuals. Although Aristotle, for example, wrote a major treatise on ethics, Montaigne could say that "I can't recognize most of my daily doings when they appear in Aristotle." Nietzsche also wrote that "to our scholars, strangely enough, the most pressing question does not occur: to what end is their work . . . useful?". . . [Traditional] philosophy for the most part dealt with technical problems of metaphysics, ethics, and the theory of knowledge in a general and objective manner, which bypassed the intimate concerns of [people] about their personal destiny. Historical events, particularly wars, showed a similar disregard for the feelings and aspirations of individuals. And technology . . . soon gathered a momentum of its own, forcing [people] to fit their lives into the rhythm of machines.

existentialism
Term used to refer to any philosophy that emphasizes fundamental questions of meaning and choice as they affect existing individuals; existential themes include choice, freedom, identity, alienation, inauthenticity, despair, and awareness of our own mortality.

Technological progress creates more problems than it solves. Efficiency experts or social engineering will not redeem humanity. Important as their contributions may be, they do not reach the heart of the problem.

ABRAHAM JOSHUA HESCHEL

Everywhere [people] were losing their peculiarly human qualities. They were being converted from "persons" into "pronouns," from "subjects" into "objects," from an "I" into an "it."[1]

Ironically, today too many people talk about existentialism as if it were a clearly defined school of philosophy. It is not. Let's resist reducing the existentialists to an abstraction, to a category, by acknowledging that there is no such thing as an existentialist school of philosophy.

In this chapter, we take a look at one of the most important, intriguing, and controversial thinkers first associated with that label, Søren Kierkegaard, a fierce champion of the real, the concrete, the existing individual.

PHILOSOPHICAL
QUERY

• • • • • •

Reflect back over your philosophical studies so far. Can you recognize yourself in the philosophies you've studied? In which ones?

■ SØREN KIERKEGAARD ■

The most important work of **Søren Kierkegaard** (1813–1855) was virtually ignored during his lifetime, partly because he wrote in Danish, partly because of what he wrote, partly because of his brilliant use of sarcasm and irony. For this reason, and because of the issues he dealt with, Kierkegaard is an "untimely" philosopher who seems more contemporary than his chronological place in history. Some 150 years later, Kierkegaard's journals and essays have a living quality that still engages and disturbs many a reader. His work is not easy to fathom, but it is well worth the struggle.

Because he rebelled against "the system" and against objectivity, Kierkegaard's work confounds easy classification (which would delight him). His "unscientific" and "unsystematic" attacks on conventional Christian theology and dogma, on science, and on professional philosophy took the form of satirical essays, parables, anecdotes, and real and fictional journals. What are scholars and philosophers to make of a writer who asserted that "truth is subjectivity" and "the System is a lie"? How can we assess the inconsistencies and lack of a coherent philosophy in a writer who boldly denounced both systematic consistency and coherence?

As we shall see, Kierkegaard's work represented a radical shift in philosophers' orientation from objectivity to subjectivity, from efforts to impose rational consistency to a search for authentic existence. Kierkegaard said, "The question is not what am I to *believe* [think, understand], but what am I to *do?*"

Søren Kierkegaard

Had I to carve an inscription on my grave I would ask for none other than "the individual."

SØREN KIERKEGAARD

The Family Curse

Kierkegaard saw himself as a disciple of Socrates. And like Socrates, Kierkegaard's life and work make a seamless whole. We cannot know Kierkegaard the existentialist without meeting Kierkegaard the individual. Born in Copenhagen,

© Reuters/Mario Anzuoni/Landov

Compare your first impression of these Ms. America contestants with your impression of the Grammy Award winners. Is your initial reaction the common one among college students—dismissive of the Ms. America contestants as robotic clones who have "sold out" while seeing Taboo, Fergie, will.i.am, and apl.de.ap as somehow more authentic and individualistic?

© Mike Blake/Reuters/Landov

Are Taboo, Fergie, will.i.am, and apl.de.ap more authentic than the Ms. America contestants because they appeal to a more authentic crowd? Can there be such a thing as a crowd of true individuals? Is authenticity an authentic goal?

Denmark, this youngest of seven children was deeply and permanently influenced by his father Michael, a strict and devout Lutheran. One day, while herding sheep, young Michael cursed God over the conditions of his life. Until his death, he never forgot what he had done and never forgave himself for his youthful outburst. Though he grew up to become a successful merchant, Michael Kierkegaard remained consumed by what he saw as his unforgivable blasphemy. Years later, weakened by grief and loneliness, he had sexual relations with a housemaid immediately after his first wife died. Overwhelmed with guilt and sadness, consumed by these two "great sins," Michael lived without peace of mind or genuine hope, seeing himself only as a sinner.

As the youngest son of an elderly father, Søren was his father's favorite, and to him went Michael's legacy: a sense of despair and melancholy, an obsession with the nature and possibility of a finite individual's relationship with an infinite God. Unusually intelligent and sensitive, Søren had few close friends as a child and spent most of his formative years in the company of his father.

In 1830, Kierkegaard enrolled in the University of Copenhagen to study theology. The "unforgiven" father wanted his son to become a minister. Kierkegaard soon discovered, however, that theology did not interest him as much as philosophy and literature. He spent the next ten years living a collegiate life devoted primarily to drinking and attending the theater. He became known for his good taste in food, clothes, and other aesthetic delights. During this time, he lost interest in religion and became estranged from his father.

Father and son made peace before Michael died in 1838, and Michael confessed the two sins of his past to his son. Kierkegaard referred to the confession as "a great earthquake" and became consumed by its implications. He returned to the study of theology, passing his exams with honors in 1840. The next year he preached his first sermon and submitted a master's thesis on Socratic irony.

The Universal Formula

At about the same time, at age twenty-seven, Kierkegaard fell in love with Regina Olsen, the attractive fourteen-year-old daughter of an important government official. When Regina turned seventeen, the couple became formally engaged, but almost immediately Kierkegaard broke the engagement. For the rest of his life, he struggled to understand, explain, and justify this action. In his *Journals* he wrote, "It was a time of terrible suffering to have to be so cruel and at the same time to love her as I did. She fought like a tigress. If I had not believed that God had lodged a veto, she would have been victorious."[2]

Kierkegaard might have had more than one motive for breaking up with Regina. He might have been afraid of committed marriage. He might have found her cheery temperament incompatible with his somber melancholy. He might have feared that his depressions would harm her. He might have been a cad, as the popular opinion in Copenhagen had it. Perhaps all these motives played a part.

But of special interest to us is Kierkegaard's later interpretation of his "sacrifice" of Regina. Two weeks after he broke the engagement, Kierkegaard fled to Berlin, where he wrote *Either/Or: A Fragment of Life* (1843), his first important work, and *Repetition: An Essay in Experimental Psychology* (1843), through which he hoped to reestablish his relationship with Regina. But before he could publish *Repetition,* Kierkegaard learned of Regina's engagement to a former boyfriend. Stunned, hurt, and despairing, Kierkegaard destroyed the last ten

I owe everything I am to the wisdom of an old man and the simplicity of a young girl.

SØREN KIERKEGAARD

More profound and subtle— and far more dangerous— is the peril of men in such numbers that each is induced to become a number himself and is steadily losing the vital differences on which his integrity as an individual depends, and substituting a kind of common denomination of the spirit in areas which were once his own and highly differentiated, enabling him to exorcise conformity and make a contribution uniquely his own to the life of his time.

LAURENS VAN DER POST

pages of his original manuscript, which addressed his hope of a reconciliation with Regina.

For the rest of his short life, Kierkegaard claimed he had "offered up" his love for Regina Olsen as a sacrifice to God, just as Abraham offered Isaac in the Old Testament story (Genesis 22). Kierkegaard had thought he had to choose *either* God *or* "the world," and that choosing one excluded the other entirely. Torn between a career as a minister and a comfortable, middle-class life with Regina, he thought he had discovered a way to have both. Kierkegaard's solution was his discovery of what he saw as the "universal formula" revealed in the story of Abraham and Isaac: Having finally blessed Abraham and Sarah with a son in their old age, God then tested Abraham's faith by sending an angel to him, demanding the blood sacrifice of Isaac. Abraham submitted to God's will in a supreme act of faith, resisting the pull of his love for Isaac and resisting the moral code of his time that forbade such human sacrifice. At the last moment God stopped Abraham and returned Isaac to him. Kierkegaard interpreted this story to mean: If you give something up for God, you get it back *plus* the love and salvation of God. In other words, by giving something up, you get to keep it! Applying this "formula" to his predicament of "*Either* devote my life to God *or* live in comfort with Regina," Kierkegaard "reasoned" a way to have both. He was consequently stunned when he lost her. What went wrong? Didn't Kierkegaard do just what Abraham had done? Was his reasoning somehow flawed?

In his later works, Kierkegaard wrestled with the basic existential problems exemplified in this episode from one individual's life: What am I to *do* when confronted with the awesome finality of any choice? Can I objectively and scientifically model my relationship with God after Abraham's? Or Paul's? Or Christ's? How can I know what God wants *me* to do? Can I *reason* it out? What do *universal principles* have to do with *this choice?* Kierkegaard concluded that universal principles must give way to individual predicaments.

> All logical thinking employs the language of abstraction. . . . It is easier to indulge in abstract thought than it is to exist.
>
> SØREN KIERKEGAARD

Kierkegaard's? Works

Interestingly, ironically, and characteristically, Kierkegaard tweaked the noses of his fellows by writing about authenticity and identity under various pseudonyms. Unlike more conventional pseudonymous writers, he was not trying to hide. There was no point to that in a provincial little city like Copenhagen, where he was widely known. The various and odd characters he presents as the "authors" of his writings are existential personas for modes of existence, ways of living, that many of us experience. They are part of a Socratic program designed to prevent Kierkegaard's readers from keeping a safe distance, designed to prevent objective responses. It would not do for Kierkegaard to challenge abstract, detached philosophizing and thinking with his own abstract, detached arguments and analyses. Better to assume the stance and, most importantly, the voice of one who actually lives this way or that way.

Kierkegaard's "authors" and their works can be confusing to sort out, much as our real selves can be difficult to sort out. The authors sometimes appear

> Perhaps I am a man of exceptional moods. . . . At times I suffer from the strangest sense of detachment from myself and the world about me; I seem to watch it all from the outside, from somewhere inconceivably remote, out of time, out of space, out of the stress and tragedy of it all.
>
> H. G. WELLS

in more than one essay, intermingling like parts of a single self-in-progress. Kierkegaard sometimes lists himself as editor or "responsible for publication" of the pseudonymous works. He also credits some work to himself.

Kierkegaard's pseudonyms are particularly clever considering his interest in identity, meaningfulness, and authenticity and his efforts to engage his readers in a dialectical "conversation": Nicolaus Notabene (N.N. was a Danish abbreviation indicating anonymity, and *nota bene* is Latin for "note well"; in other words, pay attention); Virgilius Haufniensis (Watchman of Copenhagen); A. B. C. D. E. F. Godthaab, also known as A. B. C. D. E. F. Resenblad; Inter et Inter (Latin for "between and between"); Procul (Latin for "from a distance").

Johannes de Silentio (John the Silent) is the "silent" author who has so much to say in *Fear and Trembling: A Dialectical Lyric* (1843). Frater Taciturnus (Brother Who Keeps Silent) is the author of the third (religious) section of *Stages on Life's Way*. Victor Eremita, the Victorious Hermit, is the "publisher" of volumes 1 and 2 of *Either/Or: A Fragment of Life* (1843). The Either part of *Either/Or* is "authored" and also "edited" by an aesthete known only as A, who claims to have been given the famous *Diary of a Seducer* by someone named Johannes, "nicknamed the Seducer." The *Diary* is part of *Either/Or.*

The Or part of *Either/Or* is, naturally, by B, also known as Judge William. Judge William is also the author of part two (the ethical part) of *Stages on Life's Way* (1845), which was "collected, forwarded to the press and published by" one Hilarius Bookbinder, *Hilarius* being Latin for "merry" or "joyful." The first (aesthetic) section of *Stages on Life's Way* is credited to William Afham. Afham means "by him," and William Afham says his work is "by himself."

Johannes Climacus, a philosophical character named after a Greek monk, is listed as the author of *Philosophical Fragments, Or a Fragment of Philosophy* (1844). The *Concluding Unscientific Postscript to the "Philosophical Fragments"* (1846) is characterized as "An Existential Contribution" by him as well, with Søren Kierkegaard said to be "responsible for publication." *Sickness Unto Death* (1849) and *Training in Christianity* (1850) are by Anti-Climacus. Unlike Johannes Climacus, who cannot ascend higher than reason and logic can take him, Anti-Climacus can and does. In his journals Kierkegaard writes that "Climacus is lower, denies he is a Christian. Anti-Climacus is higher, a Christian on an extraordinarily high level. . . . I would place myself higher than Johannes Climacus, lower than Anti-Climacus."

By "hiding in plain sight," by playing games about serious matters and devoting minute scrutiny to mundane ones, Kierkegaard dares us to look for the "reasons" behind the poses. If we do, he hopes to engage us in a Socratic exchange that results in deep reflection and change on our part.

The Christian

inauthenticity
Condition that results when the nature and needs of the individual are ignored, denied, and obscured or sacrificed for institutions, abstractions, or groups.

Struggling with the existential predicament of choice and commitment, Kierkegaard grew increasingly interested in what it means to be a Christian. He became convinced that institutionalized Christianity suffers from the same inauthenticity as other institutions. **Inauthenticity** results when the nature and needs of the individual are ignored, denied, obscured, or made less important than institutions, abstractions, or groups. **Authenticity** is the subjective condition of an individual living honestly and courageously in the moment without refuge in excuses and without reliance on groups or institutions for meaning and purpose. Given the stakes—salvation or damnation—Kierkegaard turned his penetrating wit and scathing criticism to the task of distinguishing inauthentic "institutionalized Christianity" from authentic Christianity.

Kierkegaard published three important attacks on the Danish Church: *The Sickness Unto Death* (1849), *Training in Christianity* (1850), and *For Self-Examination* (1851). When his "attacks on Christendom" were largely ignored, Kierkegaard decided to make a clear, dramatic existential step: He had to break officially with the church. At the time of this decision, the head of the Danish Church was Bishop J. P. Mynster, who had been a close friend of Michael Kierkegaard. Because Søren himself respected and cared for the old man, he delayed his break until Mynster died, whereupon he published a vehement attack on "false Christianity" in an article called "Was Bishop Mynster a Witness for the Truth?" Kierkegaard's answer was an unequivocal "No!" He argued that the bishop was a witness to an error, a witness to false Christianity.

Both the clergy and the general public rose to the defense of the beloved bishop. Kierkegaard continued to hammer away at what he saw as false Christianity, hypocrisy, inauthenticity, and "mere living." As a contrast to inauthentic Christianity, Kierkegaard countered with his famous "leap of faith," a *blind* commitment to God made each instant, made without guarantees, made alone, made in fear and trembling. The leap of faith is completely "existential," made with absolutely no assurance of any kind, no support, no "reason." Consequently, Kierkegaard strenuously rejected any institutionalized religion of formulas, guarantees, security, and "group salvation."

On October 2, 1855, Kierkegaard was nearly broke. He visited his banker brother-in-law to withdraw the last of his money. On his way home, he fell to the street, paralyzed from the waist down. Destitute, helpless, and weak, Kierkegaard died quietly November 11, 1855. He was only forty-two years old.

authenticity
Subjective condition of an individual living honestly and courageously in the moment, refusing to make excuses, and not relying on groups or institutions for meaning and purpose.

That Individual

Søren Kierkegaard was buried in the huge Cathedral Church of Copenhagen. His eulogy was delivered to a crowd of both friends and enemies by his brother Peter, a respected member of the Danish Church. Upset with the way the institution had violated the spirit of its great critic, his nephew caused a scene at the graveside. The irony of such a funeral would not have been lost on Kierkegaard.

The most interesting epitaph for Kierkegaard, however, is found in his own bitterly ironic words:

> The Martyrdom this author suffered may be briefly described thus: He suffered from being a genius in a provincial town. The standard he applied . . . was on the average far too great for his contemporaries; it raised the price on them too terribly; it almost made it seem as if the provincial town and the

What I really lack is to be clear in my own mind what I am to do. The thing is to understand myself, to see what God really wants me to do; the thing is to find a truth that is true for me, to find the idea for which I can live and die.

SØREN KIERKEGAARD

Rembrandt's powerful depiction of the angel staying Abraham's hand just before the sacrifice of Isaac captures the moment of "infinite resignation" that Kierkegaard imagined he could duplicate in his own relationship with his beloved Regina Olsen. Where did Kierkegaard go wrong—if he did go wrong?

© *The Sacrifice of Abraham*/1625 (oil on canvas), Rembrandt, Harmensz van Rijn, (1606-69) (studio of)/Hermitage, St. Petersburg, Russia/Bridgeman Art Library

majority in it did not possess [absolute authority], but that there was a God in existence.

Yet it is true that he found also here on earth what he sought. He himself was *that individual* if no one else was, and he became that more and more. It was the cause of Christianity he served, his life from childhood on being marvelously fitted for such a service. Thus he carried to completion the task of translating completely into terms of reflection what Christianity is, what it means to be a Christian. . . .

. . . he could not ascribe [the grand enterprise he undertook] to any man, least of all would he ascribe it to himself; if he were to ascribe it to anyone, it would be to Providence, to whom it was in fact ascribed, day after day and year after year, by the author, who historically died of a mortal disease but poetically died of longing for eternity, where uninterruptedly he would have nothing else to do but to thank God.[3]

For all their power, allure, and effectiveness, it is not clear that must-have technological marvels, such as ubiquitous Internet access and trend-setting iPhones, help us live more meaningful lives, lives grounded in what Kierkegaard described as an "idea for which I can live and die." Do these devices, perhaps, have an opposite effect and sink us deeper into "the crowd," thereby distracting us from ourselves?

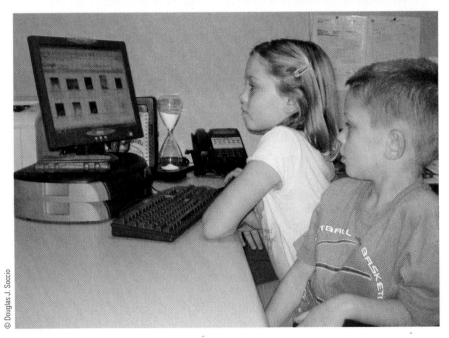

▦ TRUTH AS SUBJECTIVITY ▦

Perhaps the major existential issue is "What am *I* to *do?*" Not "How is an individual to live?" but "How am *I* to *exist?*" As Kierkegaard pointed out, any choice, once made, rules out *all* other possibilities. To be fully conscious of this is to experience what Nietzsche (Chapter 16) called *fatefulness,* the fact that our actions and choices create our individual destiny. Deciding to take a philosophy class—or deciding not to take one; deciding to marry that person—or not to

"We Are Being Destroyed by Our Knowledge"

Our culture is superficial today, and our knowledge dangerous, because we are rich in mechanisms and poor in purposes. The balance of mind which once came of a warm religious faith is gone; science has taken from us the supernatural bases of our morality, and all the world seems consumed in a disorderly individualism that reflects the chaotic fragmentation of our character. . . . We move about the earth with unprecedented speed, but we do not know, and have not thought, where we are going, or whether we shall find any happiness there for our harassed souls. We are being destroyed by our knowledge, which has made us drunk with our power. And we shall not be saved without wisdom.

Will Durant, *The Mansions of Philosophy: A Survey of Human Life and Destiny* (New York: Simon & Schuster, 1929), pp. vii, viii, xff.

marry that person; checking the air in a car's tires—or not checking it: On such inescapable daily choices hang the quality and shape of individual lives. The basic fact of Kierkegaard's *project,* as he referred to his existentialism, is the dilemma of lived choices:

> *It is not so much a question of choosing the right as the energy, the earnestness, the pathos with which one chooses. Thereby the personality announces its inner infinity, and thereby, in turn, the personality is consolidated.*
>
> SØREN KIERKEGAARD

What I really lack is to be clear in my mind *what I am to do,* not what I am to know, except in so far as a certain understanding must precede every action. The thing is to understand myself, to see what God really wishes *me* to do; the thing is to find a truth which is true *for me,* to find *the idea for which I can live and die.* What would be the use of discovering so-called objective truth, of working through all the systems of philosophy and of being able, if required, to review them all and show up the inconsistencies within each system;—what good would it do me to be able to explain the meaning of Christianity if it had *no* deeper significance *for me and for my life;*—what good would it do me if the truth stood before me, cold and naked, not caring whether I recognised her or not, producing in me a shudder of fear rather than a trusting devotion? I certainly do not deny that I still recognise an *imperative of understanding* and that through it one can work upon men, *but it must be taken up into my life,* and *that is* what I now recognise as the most important thing. That is what my soul longs after, as the African desert thirsts for water. That is what I lack, and that is why I am left standing like a man who has rented a house and gathered all the furniture and household things together, but has not yet found the beloved with whom to share the joys and sorrows of his life.[4]

PHILOSOPHICAL

QUERY

• • • • • •

How do you make life choices? Do you make them clearly and consciously, or do things just somehow happen? Is it possible to choose without being fully engaged? Does your religion or philosophy help you make concrete choices? Does a psychological theory?

Kierkegaard insisted that no amount of objective, systematic, abstract knowledge could ever provide a meaning for life. He did not deny the value of objective knowledge, which he refers to as an *imperative of understanding,* but he pointed out that the "objective facts" of a life cannot account for its existential quality. In *Either/Or,* he tells the story of a man who decides to scientifically and objectively study a Christian, in order to understand what it is to "be a Christian." Following his subject about, the observer notes what he eats, where he goes, when he reads the paper, what paper he reads, what brand of tobacco he smokes, and so on. After amassing quite a quantity of factual, objective data, the observer laments, "But he does just what I do!"

Kierkegaard's point, made ironically, is that objective information reveals facts or truths, not truth. What makes one individual a Christian and another a non-Christian, Kierkegaard claims, cannot be reduced to the objective conditions of their lives but is a quality of their *inner condition: Truth is a subjective condition, not an objective one.*

The implications of this claim—that scientific, or objective, impersonal, understanding can never pass beyond factual description—are radical. According to Kierkegaard, objective understanding cannot reveal truth; it cannot give Kierkegaard—or any existing individual—reasons to live; it cannot answer the most important question: What am I to do? Objective, scientific, philosophical, and theological systems and arguments cannot provide "*the idea for which I can live and die.*" In an era seduced by faith that science (or "technology") inevitably leads to "progress," Kierkegaard's existential critique challenges "science" ("the system" or "the establishment") to answer: Give *me* a reason for which *I* can live and die.

Kierkegaard wanted to pass from fragmentation to integration. In his terms, he wanted to alter his life from a "chance assemblage of mere details" into an existence with a "focus and center." But the modern age, with its drive toward massive institutions, infatuation with objectivity, and reliance on the scientific understanding of human behavior, inhibits personal integration. Neither scientific, objective understanding nor elaborate, abstract Hegelian philosophical systems can deal with "*that individual.*" Systems and theories only identify patterns and abstractions. They never even see "the existing individual."

> Just as desert travellers combine into great caravans from fear of robbers and wild beasts, so the individuals of the contemporary generation are fearful of existence, because it is God-forsaken; only in great masses do they dare to live, and they cluster together en masse in order to feel that they amount to something.
>
> SØREN KIERKEGAARD

Objectivity as Untruth

As we have seen again and again, for the most part, philosophers have traditionally agreed that arguments and evidence should be evaluated rationally and objectively. Until relatively recently, evidence of partiality or bias has been seen as a serious weakness in a philosopher's or scientist's arguments.

Kierkegaard vehemently disagreed. He considered objectivity, impersonality, and impartiality as dangerous, insulting, and ugly delusions. Not only is impartiality impossible, but claims of objectivity and disinterest are always lies. In the first place, preferring objectivity and impartiality to subjective involvement is itself a bias: *Favoring objectivity is a form of partiality.* Worse, our desire for objectivity deceives us by obscuring our individual (subjective) responsibility for our evaluations. The philosopher who says, "Reason demands that we must reject X because it is inconsistent" has herself *subjectively chosen* certain values: objectivity and consistency. Moreover, "reason" is a mere abstraction, a noble-sounding term that conceals an

> Mass society, with its demand for work without responsibility, creates a gigantic army of rival siblings.
>
> ALEXANDER MISTERLICH

individual, subjective choice. But anything that obscures the existing individual interferes with authenticity, honesty, and passionate commitment—existence.

To complicate matters, the impersonal quality of objective language reduces the uniqueness of individual existence to generalizations, abstractions, and features in common. But the vital issues of existence confront the complex, individually existing self, not the general self of psychologists and philosophers; not Descartes's "thing which thinks"; not Kant's "rational being"; not Hume's "bundle of perceptions." (See Chapters 9–11.) Objectivity, by its very nature, is cool, detached, impersonal. Existence, however, is not:

> The difficulty that inheres in existence, with which the existing individual is confronted, is one that never really comes to expression in the language of abstract thought, much less receives an explanation. . . . Abstract thought . . . ignores the concrete and the temporal, the existential process, the predicament of the existing individual arising from his being a synthesis of the temporal and the eternal situated in existence. . . .
>
> . . . Existing is ordinarily regarded as no very complex matter, much less an art, since we all exist; but abstract thinking takes rank as an accomplishment. But to really exist . . . that is truly difficult.[5]

Descartes, and all those who followed his lead, reduced existence to believing: "I *think,* therefore I am." Abstract, rationalistic philosophies ignore the real predicament of actual existence: deciding what to do. Actual decisions are not the neat, reasonable calculations of philosophers, nor are they the products of systematic scientific thinking. Enlightenment philosophies and all metaphysical systems merely observe life from a distance; they do not take part in it.

The Present Age

Kierkegaard viewed the mid-nineteenth century as an era of passionless mediocrity and conformity. He lamented the *massing of society,* by which he meant the diminution of the individual's role in the face of mass production, the pernicious influence of the press (mass media), and the loss of truth in the face of objectivity and abstraction. Kierkegaard included what he saw as the inflated reputation of science and technological solutions to human problems as factors contributing to the massing of society. In *Either/Or,* Kierkegaard began a profound and eloquent analysis of conformism and mediocrity:

> Let others complain that the age is wicked; my complaint is that it is wretched, for it lacks passion. Men's thoughts are thin and flimsy like lace, they are themselves pitiable like lacemakers. The thoughts of their hearts are too paltry to be sinful. For a worm it might be regarded as a sin to harbor such thoughts, but not for a being made in the image of God. Their lusts are dull and sluggish, their passions sleepy. They do their duty, these shopkeeping souls, but they clip the coin a trifle . . . ; they think that even if the Lord keeps ever so careful a set of books, they may still cheat Him a little. Out upon them! This is the reason my soul always turns back to the Old Testament and to Shakespeare. I feel that those who speak there are at least human beings: they hate, they love, they murder their enemies, and curse their descendants throughout all generations, they sin.[6]

Let us labor under no illusions. There are no easy solutions for problems that are at the same time intensely personal and universal, urgent and eternal.

ABRAHAM JOSHUA HESCHEL

Because the contemporary individual has no comprehensive picture of the social universe within which he lives and of the structure of modern society, he pays the price of meaninglessness and insignificance in his daily work and even a spiritual isolation from his fellows.

A. W. LEVI

In an essay called *The Present Age* (1846), which, according to philosopher William Barrett, "has become the source of nearly all the Existentialist criticisms of modern society," Kierkegaard continued his attack on conformity.[7] "The crowd," he points out, overwhelms the individual, yet the individual feels frightened and lost without "the crowd." The mediocre, alienated individual needs a group to identify with, to provide "peer approval." Yet, Kierkegaard insists, a collective identity is always somehow false; in order to belong, to fit in, we must betray some part of ourselves, must cease living our own lives and begin living "a kind of life."

PHILOSOPHICAL QUERY

• • • • • •

In the 1993 trial of four men for allegedly attacking truck driver Reginald Denney during the Los Angeles riots triggered by the verdict in the first Rodney King beating trial, a sociologist testifying for the defense argued that the accused were not responsible for their actions because they were caught up in the "crowd contagion" of the moment. What do you think of such a defense? Analyze your own behavior as part of a group or crowd. Do you find that it is always "somehow false"? Is it possible to be more yourself in a crowd than when alone? If so, why?

The intelligence of any group of people who are thinking as a "herd" rather than individually is no higher than the intelligence of the stupidest members.

MARY DAY WINN

An Age of Virtual Equality

According to Kierkegaard's view of "the crowd," modern people are anonymous creatures who depend on experts to point the way to salvation or personal growth. As you read the following passage, think about the many coalitions, committees, and other groups that continue to spring up in our own times:

> The present age tends toward a mathematical equality in which it takes so and so many to make one individual. Formerly the outstanding individual could allow himself everything and the individual in the masses nothing at all. Now everyone knows that so and so many make an individual, and quite

consistently people add themselves together (it is called joining together, but that is only a polite euphemism) for the most trivial purposes. Simply in order to put a passing whim into practice a few people add themselves together, and the thing is done—they dare to do it. . . .

The individual no longer belongs to God, to himself, to his beloved, to his art or to his science; he is conscious of belonging in all things to an abstraction to which he is subjected by reflection.[8]

[I]n a universe suddenly divested of illusions and lights, man feels an alien, a stranger. His exile is without remedy since he is deprived of the memory of a lost home or the hope of a promised land. This divorce between man and his life, the actor and his setting, is properly the feeling of absurdity.
ALBERT CAMUS

If Kierkegaard is correct, rather than being ourselves, we tend to conform to an image or idea associated with being a certain *type* of person. That's what Kierkegaard means by belonging to an "abstraction" (an image or idea) created by "reflection" (self-conscious thinking). Thus, for example, a woman consciously tries to be "a Christian" or "a lawyer" based on some collective abstraction, some image or idea. She attempts to conform to a pattern. Sometimes, it does seem as if many of us do indeed govern our lives by abstractions based on age, ethnicity, and gender.

To the extent that we do see ourselves and others as *abstract types,* we deal with generalizations rather than with concrete specifics; we overlook individual qualities. Certainly no one disputes the usefulness of generalizations. They provide us with the ability to identify patterns, to recognize principles of behavior, and so forth. What they do not—and cannot—do is recognize *existing individuals.* From an existentialist perspective, all acts of generalizing and abstracting require *leveling.* And for Kierkegaard, leveling, as the word itself suggests, is not a process of exaltation but of reduction to mediocrity—reduction to numerical equality at the expense of authenticity:

The abstract principle of leveling . . . like the biting east wind, has no personal relation to any individual, but has only an abstract relationship which is the same for everyone. There no hero suffers for others, or helps them; the taskmaster of all alike is the leveling process, which itself takes on their education. And the man who learns most from the leveling and himself becomes greatest does not become an outstanding man or hero—that would only impede the leveling process, which is rigidly consistent to the end; he himself prevents that from happening because he has understood the meaning of leveling: he becomes a man and nothing else, in the complete equalitarian sense.[9]

All our norms are nothing but desires in disguise.
ABRAHAM JOSHUA HESCHEL

We do not err because truth is difficult to see. It is visible at a glance. We err because this is more comfortable.
ALEXANDER SOLZHENITSYN

In courtrooms and classrooms, we use abstractions and utilitarian calculations to level ourselves so that "everyone is treated the same." The press levels presidents and celebrities through exposés of their personal lives. The underlying message is "They're no different from us." Indeed, they are not, but the leveling nature of these exposés, coupled with the sameness and mediocrity of so many of the people we elect to office and turn into celebrities, lends support to a Kierkegaardian conclusion that the modern age remains an era of increasing dullness, conformity, and lack of genuine individuals.

PHILOSOPHICAL

QUERY

• • • • • •

Identify some current examples of leveling, and discuss the general notion of leveling. Must efforts at furthering equality result in leveling? Is leveling possibly desirable?

This picture of Muslim school girls attending the funeral of a friend is a hauntingly beautiful reminder that underneath the particularities of culture and ritual lurk profound human longings for meaning, belonging, and significance, longings Kierkegaard expressed in a cry de profundis, from the depths: "It must be terrible on the day of judgment, when all souls come back to life—to stand there alone, *alone* and *unknown* to all."

Philosophers and critics offer a variety of interpretations of Kierkegaard's writings. This is not surprising given Kierkegaard's penchant for irony, "indirection," and Socratic engagement. I suspect that he would be delighted with the *fact* of these myriad interpretations, even if he should object to their content. One point seems clear, however: Kierkegaard identified and addressed one of the crucial issues of our time: How can we be our "true selves" in an age dominated by ever more sophisticated ways of influencing our thoughts, feelings, and actions? How can we find sufficient passion and clarity of focus to become ourselves in a world seduced by objectivity and conformity and run by ever more massive institutions?

▦ BECOMING A SUBJECT ▦

According to Kierkegaard, my life is the proof that I believe: If I am to be anything, really be something—that is, if I am to *exist*—my life must be a different kind of life than it would be if I believed otherwise. If, for instance, I truly believe that something is sinful or that some practice is morally obligatory, my life must reflect that belief. It won't do to say and think and feel one way but live another.

> Everyone with some capacity for observation who seriously considers what is called Christendom, or the conditions in a so-called Christian country, must surely be assailed by profound misgivings. What does it mean that all these thousands and thousands call themselves Christians as a matter of course? These many, many, many men, of whom the greater part, so far as one can judge, live in categories quite foreign to Christianity! . . .
>
> If, then, according to our assumption, the greater number of people in Christendom only imagine themselves to be Christians, in what categories do they live? They live in aesthetic, or at the most aesthetic-ethical categories.[10]

Philosophy teaches that the way is to become objective, while Christianity teaches that the way is to become subjective, i.e., to become a subject in truth.

SØREN KIERKEGAARD

How can we deny that life is absurd when we look into the face of this little girl and at the solitary figure of the little boy, bonded slaves forced to extract slate from mines and toil in unsafe workshops to produce boxes of fifty pencils for meager pay, so meager that many of them will die of malnutrition or injury without ever earning release from their parents' debts? Alas, relentless poverty, hardship, and suffering are the daily lot of millions of children—and adults. For what purpose?

©Sophie Elbaz/Sygma/Corbis

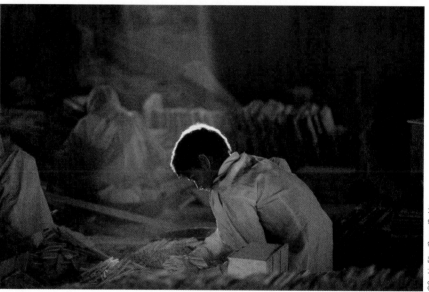

©Sophie Elbaz/Sygma/Corbis

In Kierkegaard's language, I *exist*—as a Christian, specifically, but, to an extent, as anything—only when I *appropriate* my belief by taking it up subjectively, inwardly. I must believe *in it*, not merely believe it. I must be faithful to my faith by living it. "Only when reflection comes to a halt can a beginning be made, and reflection can only be halted by something else," Kierkegaard says, "and this something else is something quite different from the logical, being a resolution of the will."[11]

Mere cognitive assent, objective understanding, will not do because objectivity demands so little of me. Objectively, I can know things without caring about them. Indeed, the essential feature of objectivity is lack of passion. Objective truths are not about *us*. Using Kierkegaard's term, they are not *present*. They are detached, "out there." Detachment blinds us to existence, makes us into "persons of a sort," living, as it were, "lives of a sort":

> It is impossible to exist without passion, unless we understand the word "exist" in the loose sense of a so-called existence. Every Greek thinker was therefore essentially a passionate thinker. I have often reflected how one might bring a man into a state of passion. I have thought in this connection that if I could get him seated on a horse and the horse made to take fright and gallop wildly, or better still, for the sake of bringing passion out, if I could take a man who wanted to arrive at a certain place as quickly as possible, and hence already had some passion, and could set him astride a horse that can scarcely walk—and yet this is what existence is like if one has become consciously aware of it. Or if a driver were otherwise not especially inclined toward passion, if someone hitched a team of horses to a wagon for him, one of them a Pegasus and the other a worn-out jade, and told him to drive—I think one might succeed. And it is just this that it means to exist, if one is to become conscious of it. Eternity is the winged horse, infinitely fast, and time is a worn-out jade; the existing individual is the driver. That is to say, he is such a driver when his mode of existence is not an existence loosely so called; for then he is no driver but a drunken peasant who lies asleep in the wagon and lets the horses take care of themselves. To be sure, he also drives and is a driver; and so there are perhaps many who—also exist.[12]

The difficulty that inheres in existence, with which the existing individual is confronted, is one that never really comes to expression in the language of abstract thought, much less receives an explanation.

SØREN KIERKEGAARD

● ● ● ● ● ●

Why do you think Kierkegaard makes one of the horses "a Pegasus" and the other "a worn-out jade"? Who was Pegasus? What is a worn-out jade? (Hint: This has something to do with Kierkegaard's profound interest in his and our relationship to God.)

PHILOSOPHICAL

QUERY

There is a qualitative difference between what we often call existence and what Kierkegaard means by truly existing. So-called existence is the half-conscious routine of going about our daily affairs, conforming to the conventions of the day, or robotically rebelling against them, rejecting one crowd in favor of another, merely "switching places," living what we sometimes characterize as horizontal, flat lives.

Objective approaches to philosophy fail us when it comes to learning how to exist because they try to instruct us, to inform us. Kierkegaard's philosophy, in contrast, aims to edify us, to change us. It is not, nor does it aim to be, neutral, systematic, and speculative; it is deliberately and necessarily passionate, practical, and subjective—existential, in the full sense of the word. Kierkegaard is not trying to prove something in the ordinary sense of proving via appeals to logic and reason. He is trying to edify us, to engage and encourage us to become more conscious of the extent to which we exist—as opposed to merely live. He cannot do that by way of generalizations and "proofs." No one can.

Abstract thought . . . ignores the concrete and the temporal, the existential process, the predicament of the existing individual arising from his being a synthesis of the temporal and the eternal situated in existence.

SØREN KIERKEGAARD

The most crucial task for Kierkegaard, and, he believes, for anyone, is living "in the truth" by *becoming a subject,* a proper, authentic self or person.[13] If we do not, then we remain, in Kierkegaard's caustic phrase, "a subject of sorts."

This is a long way from Descartes's "I think, therefore I am," grounded as it is in rational reflection. Not for Kierkegaard Descartes's genteel meditations in a cozy study. Kierkegaard's "I am" suffers and struggles, faces the "predicament" of decision at every moment. Eternity is always at stake, not rational certainty, not the conclusion of some tidy syllogism. The Kierkegaardian self wants desperately to do what is right, yet lacks—and will always lack—sufficient information, sufficient objective knowledge upon which to act. To act is not merely to behave but rather to assent with my whole being. This is the difference between being an observer or a participant.

To Kierkegaard, objectivity is "easy" because it is superficial, blind and unresponsive to inner reality, to human be-ing, to our existential predicament. Kierkegaard was, of course, affected by his own interior struggles to make sense of his father, the family curse, guilt, and his conflicted feelings regarding Regina Olsen as an impediment to living a religious life. Objectively, these may not seem like "real" problems, and, perhaps, objectively, they were not. But subjectively, personally, "in truth," they were genuine predicaments, the sorts of predicaments any of us face when we dig deep and reflect on what really faces us.

From a child I was under the sway of a prodigious melancholy, the depth of which finds its only adequate measure in the equally prodigious dexterity I possessed of hiding it under an apparent gaiety and joie de vivre.

SØREN KIERKEGAARD

PHILOSOPHICAL

QUERY

• • • • • •

Compare Kierkegaard's claims about the limits of objectivity and reason with Hume's assertion that "reason is and ought to be the slave of the passions" (Chapter 10).

In his writings, Kierkegaard left a record of his own "becoming a subject" through conflict, self-recrimination, accusation, guilt—all the messy stuff that constitutes the foundation of any self's existence:

> Then it was that the great earthquake occurred, the terrible revolution. . . . Then I suspected that my father's great age was not a divine blessing but rather a curse; that the outstanding intellectual gifts of our family were given in order that we should rend each other to pieces: then I felt the stillness of death ground around me when I saw in my father an unhappy man who was to outlive us all, a cross on the tomb of his hopes. There must be guilt upon the whole family, the punishment of God must be upon it.[14]
>
> I have just returned from a party of which I was the life and soul; wit poured from my lips, everyone laughed and admired me—but I went away— and the dash should be as long as the earth's orbit _____
> _____
> _____ and wanted to shoot myself.[15]

I was so completely shaken that I understood perfectly well that I could not possibly succeed in striking the comforting and secure *via media* in which most people pass their lives: I had either to cast myself into perdition and sensuality [by choosing Regina Olsen], or to choose the religious absolutely as

I still remember the impression it made upon me when some years ago . . . father said very solemnly: "there are offenses which one can only fight against with God's continual help." I hurried down to my room and looked at myself in the glass.

SØREN KIERKEGAARD

the only thing—either the world in a measure that would be dreadful, or the cloister. . . . I had become thoroughly aware how impossible it would be for me to be religious only up to a certain point.[16]

It must be terrible on the day of judgment, when all souls come back to life—to stand there alone, *alone* and *unknown* to all.

I am a *Janus bifrons;* I laugh with one face, I weep with the other.17

When we approach Kierkegaard objectively, he appears almost pitiful. His obsession with the family curse and decision to abandon Regina Olsen have been a rich vein for armchair psychologists to mine, easy to trivialize as self-delusions, rationalizations, symptoms of neurosis. But when we think back to our own existential struggles about romantic relationships, career choices, getting a divorce, abandoning or joining a church, having a baby or an abortion, we realize that objective advice, information, facts, and statistics are beside the point. We cannot move, cannot choose by being objective and rational; living is not a simple, zero-sum, clear, obvious best-choice game.

To objective observers, our waffling, tortured yes–no–maybe–I–don't–know–okay–wait–not–yet–maybe struggles can seem trivial, not worth the agony; so they present their objective solutions to our subjective predicaments as if they were obvious. We know better. Kierkegaard insists that all such cases are similar, at least in the sense of the anxiety and agony that they bring with them—or ought to bring if we are paying attention. Every decision we make rules out all other possibilities. Either Regina Olsen or not; either God or not. Either *we exist* or not.

> *I am left standing like a man who has rented a house and gathered all the furniture and household things together but has not yet found the beloved with whom to share the joys and sorrows of his life.*
>
> Søren Kierkegaard

• • • • • •

Think back to the example of a cart being hauled by a Pegasus and a worn-out jade. Is Kierkegaard's reason for choosing those two horses getting perhaps a bit clearer?

PHILOSOPHICAL

QUERY

▪ Stages on Life's Way ▪

According to Kierkegaard, existing, becoming a subject, is possible only when we have the—not a—God-relation: "Without God [a man] is never essentially himself (which one is only by being before God) and therefore never satisfied with being himself."[18]

In a secular age, this seems unnecessarily provincial. Isn't it possible to become one's authentic self without relating to the God of the Bible, without becoming a Christian (in Kierkegaard's sense), say by way of a passionate commitment to an ethical or social ideal or even by living passionately and authentically as an atheist? Not for Kierkegaard, who insists that anyone who truly knows himself thereby knows that the need for God is real. Living as if the God-relation is one optional choice among many *equally plausible* and possible choices is delusional, a kind of living (nonexistence) disguised as a life.

Can Kierkegaard "prove" this, prove that God exists, that the Christian way is authentic? No, and recall that he is not interested in proving anything in the

> *Never try to make anyone like yourself—you know, and God knows, that one of you is enough.*
>
> Ralph Waldo Emerson

The Socratic ignorance, which Socrates held fast with the entire passion of his inwardness, was thus an expression for the principle that the eternal truth is related to an existing individual, and that this truth must therefore be a paradox for him as long as he exists.

SØREN KIERKEGAARD

ordinary sense of proving. "One is deluded," he says, in "thinking that [one] could demonstrate that God exists."[19]

(A)ssume that the critics have succeeded in proving about the Bible everything that any learned theologian in his happiest moment has wished to prove about the Bible. These books and no others belong to the canon; they are authentic . . . —one may well say, that it is as if every letter were inspired. . . .

Well, then, everything being assumed in order with respect to the Scriptures—what follows? Has anyone who previously did not have faith been brought a single step nearer to its acquisition? No, not a single step. Faith does not result simply from scientific inquiry; it does not come directly at all. On the contrary, in this objectivity one tends to lose that infinite personal interestedness in passion which is the condition of faith.[20]

PHILOSOPHICAL

QUERY

• • • • • •

Contrast Kierkegaard's approach to theological arguments to Aquinas's Five Ways and Descartes's ontological argument. (See Chapters 8 and 9.)

In lieu of arguments, Kierkegaard offers a series of sketches and descriptions of a dialectical process that involve what David E. Cooper calls "*intimations* of a self-reflective kind that indicate, however inchoately, something about themselves."[21] If we have somehow escaped from or not yet given ourselves over entirely to "the crowd," we may be receptive to these intimations of despair, "the sickness unto death" that afflicts so many of us.

According to Kierkegaard, we are in despair whether we know it or not because we have a "double nature" composed of the infinite and finite, the temporal and the eternal. This is not some sort of Cartesian dualism. Our dual nature does not consist of two substances, but of one "self" struggling to exist between the pull of the world and eternity:

Man is a synthesis of the infinite and the finite, of the temporal and the eternal, of freedom and necessity, in short a synthesis. A synthesis is a relation between two factors. So regarded, man is not yet a self.[22]

The difficulty persists, in that existence itself combines thinking with existing, in so far as the thinker exists. . . .

SØREN KIERKEGAARD

Ironically, the despair that I try so hard to deny becomes my gateway to salvation. It is the spring that sets in motion three explicit ways of choosing to live that Kierkegaard refers to as *stages on life's way*. In ascending order, they are aesthetic, ethical, religious ways of living.[23]

The Aesthetic Stage

We have already seen what life is like at the crowd stage of living, the stage of crude, utilitarian "mathematical equality" and personal inauthenticity. When we are sunk far into the crowd, absorbed by it, we are too unaware of ourselves as selves to exist. We are too unreflective to *be* an individual person in any meaningful sense at all. Most of us, however, are not sunk so far into the crowd that we are utterly without some intimation that our lives remain "far . . . from what a man's life ought to be."[24] This nagging intimation is a sign that we are not totally in thrall to the crowd but, perhaps, at what Kierkegaard calls the aesthetic stage of life.

The aesthetic stage is characterized by the pursuit of pleasure, not just in art and music, but especially in the pursuit of sensuous pleasure. The aesthete is crafty, seductive, and energetic in his or her efforts to find meaning in aesthetic experience. This is a way of life that cultivates easy, uncommitted enjoyment, a life of whim and caprice, focused on the here and now. Its enemies are boredom, frustration, dissatisfaction.

Although the aesthete chooses, choosing is taken lightly because, well, what difference does any particular choice make? I mean, nothing fateful hangs in the balance, does it? The important point is to avoid getting entangled in tedious, boring decisions. As Kierkegaard characterizes him, the aesthete tends to be either superficially easygoing or superficially cynical.

The aesthetic stage on life's way is amoral, and the legendary seducer Don Juan is an exemplar. Don Juan lives for the sensuous romantic moment and uses whatever crafty strategies he thinks will get him what he wants. His lovers are never real to him, not existing individuals, but tokens. As a result, there is a drab sameness to Don Juan's life in spite of its apparent colorful variety. The seducer is doomed to ceaselessness, because, ultimately, he is bored or cynical no matter how many conquests he has. On the surface, the sophisticated aesthete is the life of the party—but—and here, as Kierkegaard wrote, the dash ought to be as long as the orbit of the earth. An aesthete whom Kierkegaard refers to only as A presents his worldview in stark, cynical terms:

> (T)he world goes from bad to worse, and . . . its evils increase more and more, as boredom increases, and boredom is the root of all evil.
>
> The history of this can be traced back to the very beginning of the world. The gods were bored, and so they created man. Adam was bored because he was alone, and so Eve was created. Thus boredom entered the world, and increased in proportion to the increase of population. Adam was bored alone; then Adam and Eve were bored together; then Adam and Eve and Cain and Abel were bored *en famille;* then the population of the world increased, and the peoples were bored *en masse.* To divert themselves, they conceived the idea of constructing a tower high enough to reach the heavens. This idea itself is as boring as the tower was high, and constitutes a terrible proof of how boredom gained the upper hand. . . .
>
> All men are bores. . . . Those who bore others are the mob, the crowd, the infinite multitude of men in general. Those who bore themselves are the elect, the aristocracy; and it is a curious fact that those who do not bore themselves usually bore others, while those who do not bore themselves entertain others.[25]

The aesthetic stage is, Kierkegaard implies, where most of us live most of our lives. At this stage, we flit from this to that without ever wholeheartedly and consciously committing to anything, not really committing. We toss aside marriages, families, careers because we are bored. We set off on quests to "find ourselves"

The real subject is not the cognitive subject, since in knowing he moves in the sphere of the possible; the real subject is the ethically existing subject.

SØREN KIERKEGAARD

I feel so dull and so completely without joy, my soul is so empty and void that I cannot even conceive what would satisfy it—oh, not even the blessedness of heaven.

SØREN KIERKEGAARD

in ways that are "congenial," but not authentic. We resist submitting to something higher than ourselves and struggle, futilely, to stay in control. Kierkegaard's aesthete wants an interesting life above all, and on his terms:

> If I had a humble spirit in my service, who, when I asked for a glass of water, brought me the world's costliest wines blended, in a chalice, I should dismiss him, in order to teach him that pleasure consists not in what I enjoy but in getting my own way.[26]

The aesthetic way of living is, ironically, boring—and worse: "every aesthetic life view is despair."[27] It has about it a fundamental sameness and sadness. Aesthetic satisfactions are subject to whims of circumstance. Thus, the aesthete is never *a* self but only a *multiplicity* without the "unifying power of personality."[28] The synthesis of spirit and the world fails. What can a poor, bored, fatigued aesthete do to find relief? Kierkegaard says that the aesthete must consciously choose despair and face up to his predicaments as predicaments. He must stop distracting himself and stop living only for himself.

The Ethical Stage

The next stage on life's way is the ethical stage, a way of life that involves making a commitment to the norms, principles, and customs of society. The ethical life is devoted to general principles. It moves beyond the narcissistic motives of the aesthete. Here, one plants oneself via principled commitment. In this way, Kierkegaard says, I "infinitize" myself; that is, I move upward to the level of universalized ethical behavior that, ironically, serves my "finite" aesthetic nature better than the uncommitted aesthetic life does. A faithful, happy marriage, for instance, is more satisfying than the pursuit of ceaseless, increasingly meaningless seduction after seduction.

The ethical man or woman is earnest. He or she seriously chooses an ethical code by which to live. In so doing, the ethical person achieves a degree of unity that the aesthete does not. The ethical person accomplishes this by forcing an either/or option: either a moral life or an amoral life. Kierkegaard's ethical man, the Judge, says:

> It is not so much a question of choosing the right as of the energy, the earnestness, the pathos with which one chooses. Thereby the personality announces its inner infinity, and thereby, in turn, the personality is consolidated. . . .
>
> My either/or does not in the first instance denote the choice between good and evil; it denotes the choice whereby one chooses good *and* evil/ or excludes them. Here the question is under what determinants one would contemplate the whole of existence and would himself live. That the man who chooses good and evil chooses good is indeed true, but this becomes evident only afterwards; for the aesthetical is not the evil but the neutrality. . . . It is, therefore, not so much a question of choosing between willing the good *or* the evil, as of choosing to will. . . . Here you see again how important it is that a choice be made, and that the crucial thing is not deliberation but the baptism of the will which lifts up the choice into the ethical.[29]

Dread is a desire for what one fears, a sympathetic antipathy.

SØREN KIERKEGAARD

The only reality that exists for an existing individual is his own ethical reality. To every other reality he stands in a cognitive relation; but true knowledge consists in translating the real into the possible.

SØREN KIERKEGAARD

In other words—at this stage—what matters is an ethical will. Do not be surprised if the Judge reminds you of Kant (Chapter 11). Kant's moral philosophy centers on the will, on having a moral motive and making a deliberate, rational commitment to universal moral laws and treating all persons as ends-in-themselves. Kantian morality exemplifies the ethical stage. And that, for Kierkegaard, is why Kant's philosophy and essentially any modern (Enlightenment), purely humanistic philosophy fails. It exalts human reason and makes man his own lawgiver, which he never can be:

> Kant held that man was his own law (autonomy), *i.e.,* bound himself under the law which he gave himself. In a deeper sense that means to say: lawlessness or experimentation. It is no harder than the thwacks which Sancho Panza applied to his own bottom. . . . There [must be] some third and compelling factor, which is not the individual himself. . . .
>
> Not only is the law which I give myself . . . not a law; but there is a law which is given to me by one higher than I. And not only that; but that lawgiver takes the liberty of joining in at the same time in the character of education and applies the compulsion.
>
> Now if during the whole of his life a man never acts in so decisive a way that the educator [God] can get a hold on him: well, then the man is certainly allowed to live complacently in a state of illusion, imagination, experimentation—but that also connotes: the greatest lack of grace.[30]

Modern faith in mankind, Kierkegaard insists, turns everything upside down, giving man—not God—the final say, making man—not God—the arbiter of good and evil. Yet we cannot reason out how we ought to act any more than a man can determine for himself by himself if he is being reasonable. To what part of himself can he turn to decide which of two contradictory options is true? Will he not then have to assess *that part of himself* with yet another himself *ad infinitum*?

Ultimately, nothing can be resolved on the ethical level. To get beyond it, to get *somewhere,* we must make a leap of faith. We must move beyond the merely ethical stage to the religious stage.

The Religious Stage

Kierkegaard believed that Kantian (and Enlightenment) notions of human autonomy result in despair because, in the end, everything hinges on our human judgment and human judgment is always subject to doubt. No matter how carefully we think and analyze, we can never be sure that we are right. Our ethics are constantly being challenged and revised—by us. We give ourselves ethical "laws" but ignore and repeal them as our moods and circumstances change. Consequently, we live without authenticity, security, and stability. Although we may put on a good front, we are shadowed by a sense of unease, even, perhaps, dread and despair. We have intimations of arbitrariness, partiality, and falsity.

This is not to say that we do not make intense, passionate commitments to ethical (and spiritual) principles. We do. But in the end our commitments are really to ourselves. The more serious we are about doing what is right, the less

The real action is not the external act, but an internal decision in which the individual puts an end to the mere possibility and identifies himself with the content of his thought in order to exist in it.

SØREN KIERKEGAARD

When I think of something good that I intend to do, is this identical with having done it? By no means. But neither is it the external that constitutes the criterion of action; for the human being who does not own a penny can be as charitable as one who gives away a kingdom.

SØREN KIERKEGAARD

sure we are about what we are doing. If we are sure, we cannot, in Kierkegaard's sense, be right, for such certainty is inhuman—or more than human (as Socrates understood).

Nor will it do to say that we have done the best we can. The best we can do is never enough to alleviate our anxiety about our existence—if we take it seriously, that is.

> No earnest doubt, no really deep concern, is put to rest by the saying that one does what one can. If a man is sometimes in the right, sometimes in the wrong, to a certain degree in the right, to a certain degree in the wrong, who, then, is to decide this except man; but in deciding it may he not be to a certain degree in the right, to a certain degree in the wrong? . . . We have, then, only the choice of being nothing before God, or the eternal torture of beginning over again every instant, but without being able to begin.[31]

It is necessary to "leap" toward the religious, and specifically toward God, if one is ever to escape the despair that Kierkegaard thought was ever present in other ways of living: the crowd life, the aesthetic life, and the ethical life.

The Kierkegaardian leap of faith is controversial theologically and philosophically, involving, as it does, a tricky double-movement, a paradox, and what Kierkegaard calls the *teleological suspension of the ethical*. Consider the case of Abraham once more, this time from what it must be like to be in Abraham's shoes.

Had Abraham been an ethical man he would not have considered sacrificing his son Isaac for the *possibility* that God had ordered him to do so. As an ethical man, a thinker, Abraham would have concluded that God does not command us to murder and not to murder. What categorical imperative could a Kantian Abraham will: If you believe that God wants you to kill your son, you must kill him? That will not do—"believe" is too vague, too psychological to be the basis of such an imperative.

Okay, then how about: If you are certain that God wants you to kill your son, you must do it? But what kind of human being can ever be certain of such a thing? Don't we, as reasonable observers of the human scene, see all sorts of evil things done by individuals who are certain that God has commanded them to do them? Yet we do not grant their subjective certainty the status of moral duty. Truth may be subjectivity, but beliefs are not true just because they are subjective.

To see what Kierkegaard is trying to express, imagine, as best you can, that you are in Abraham's shoes, that you believe that you have received a message from God to violate what you believe is a fundamental, universal moral principle. Recall that "in his heart" Abraham does the deed: He was in motion when the angel stopped his arm. Kierkegaard writes (thinking, no doubt, also of himself and Regina Olsen):

> With Abraham the situation was different. By his act he overstepped the ethical entirely and possessed a higher *telos* outside of it, in relation to which he suspended the former [the ethical]. For I should very much like to know how one would bring Abraham's act into relation with the universal, and whether it is possible to discover any connection whatever between what Abraham did and the

How terrible about the man who once as a little boy, while herding sheep on the heaths of Jutland, suffering greatly, in hunger and want, stood upon a hill and cursed God—and the man was unable to forget it even when he was eighty-two years old.

SØREN KIERKEGAARD

universal . . . except the fact that he transgressed it. It was not for the sake of saving a people, not to maintain the idea of the state, that Abraham did this. . . . Abraham's whole action stands in no relation to the universal, is a purely private understanding. Therefore, whereas the tragic hero is great by reason of his moral virtue, Abraham is great by reason of his personal virtue. In Abraham's life there was no higher expression of the ethical than this, that the father shall love his son. Of the ethical in the sense of morality there can be no question in this instance. Insofar as the universal was present, it was indeed cryptically present in Isaac, hidden, as it were, in Isaac's loins, and must therefore cry out with Isaac's mouth, "Do it not! Thou art bringing everything to naught."

Why then did Abraham do it? For God's sake, and (in complete identity with this) for his own sake. He did it for God's sake because God required this proof of his faith; for his own sake he did it that he might furnish the proof. The unity of these two points of view is perfectly expressed in the word which has always been used to characterize the situation: it is a trial, a temptation. . . . in this case the temptation is itself the ethical—which would keep him from doing God's will. . . .

Therefore, though Abraham arouses my admiration, he at the same time appalls me. . . . he who gives up the universal in order to grasp something still higher which is not the universal—what is he doing? . . . And if . . . the individual was mistaken—what can save him? . . . Him the beholder cannot understand nor let his eye rest confidently upon him. . . .

. . . As the individual he became higher than the universal; that is the paradox which does not permit of mediation. . . . To him who follows the narrow way of faith no one can give counsel.[32]

From any perspective but that of faith, what Abraham did was *absurd*. He made a choice in a paradoxical state of tension. Objectively, there were no grounds to justify his choice and—this is important—Abraham knew it. He could not consult with his fellow tribesmen nor with his wife Sarah. He knew in advance what they would say. No universal moral code could help him. He faced an individual predicament.

> When the question is treated in an objective manner it becomes impossible for the subject to face the decision with passion, least of all in an infinitely interested passion. It is a self-contradiction and therefore comical, to be infinitely interested in that which in its maximum still always remains an approximation. If, in spite of this, passion is nevertheless imported, we get fanaticism.[33]

For Kierkegaard, the ethical is the universal and is its own end and fulfillment (*telos*). "Its task," Kierkegaard says, "is to . . . abolish its particularity in order to become universal."[34] This Abraham refused to do. He transcended the ethical plane by teleological suspension of the ethical.

> (F)aith is this paradox, that the particular is higher than the universal—yet in such a way, be it observed, that . . . the individual, after having been in the universal, now as the particular isolates himself as higher than the universal. If this be not faith, then Abraham is lost, then faith has never existed in the world . . . .[35]

Dread is an alien power which takes hold of the individual, and yet one cannot extricate oneself from it, does not wish to, because one is afraid, but what one fears attracts one.

SØREN KIERKEGAARD

Kant is wrong. The Enlightenment is wrong. Universal, generalized humanistic ethics are inadequate. They cannot deal with the existing individual. Only faith (the religious stage) allows us to be our authentic, existing selves. If we are to *exist*, we must be willing (in the strong sense of willing) to suspend the ethical. Individually, objectively, and ethically, this is dangerous, unacceptable, absurd. From a rational, human, and humane perspective, it is absurd that God would ask me (were I Abraham) to kill my son. The whole history of man's relation to God is ethically absurd.

■ DANGEROUS STUFF ■

One problem with the Abraham example is its "bigness." If we are not careful, we might conclude that for Kierkegaard religion involves that kind of big, socially dangerous decision. Not so. Kierkegaard takes pains to remind us in different ways that the small particularities of everyday life also involve the God-relation and that any decision we are trying to make—to go to the park, say, or buy a cup of coffee—can generate an irresolvable series of questions if we try to choose objectively. There will be no stopping point.

If I buy this coffee, am I selfish for not giving the money to the poor? Which poor? Is it universally good to give money to "the poor"? How much? How do I know? If I don't buy this coffee might the barista lose his job, the coffee shop owner her shop? Silly questions? Maybe, from the outside. But not if I am earnest about doing the right thing—not merely doing my best.

I cannot think my way out of these predicaments—and once I am conscious of my dual nature, time-bound and facing eternity, they seem to be everywhere. If I am to exist, to "become a subject," I must somehow unite these two natures by obeying God while admitting that I will never know for sure that I am obeying God. I must, paradoxically, know that I do not know—yet believe anyway. Does this "make sense"? Not really. But Kierkegaard is not trying "to make sense." He is trying to edify us.

> I am not a Christian, and unfortunately, I cannot make it apparent that the others are not either—indeed, that they are even less so than I. This is because they imagine themselves to be, or they lie their way into being [Christian]. . . . My task is a Socratic task, to revise the definition of being a Christian. I myself do not call myself a Christian (keeping the ideal free), but I can make it apparent that the others are even less so.[36]

This is precisely the sort of claim that makes many philosophers and theologians uneasy. Once we throw out, or set aside, appeals to ethics, objectivity and reason, are we not so far into the realm of the subjective that we are back to the Sophists? Isn't Kierkegaard's view of "existing" and authentic Christianity just one more opinion among others, no "truer" than any other? Why should we accept it?

No *reason*—but perhaps there is something—an intimation, perhaps—that Kierkegaard has a valuable lesson to teach us, even if we cannot, or will not, go all the way with him. Perhaps the lesson is that present-day America resembles Kierkegaard's Copenhagen in that a vast majority of Americans claim to "believe

If I had not been a penitent, . . . had not been melancholy, my union with [Regina Olsen] would have made me happier than I had ever dreamed of being. But in so far as I was what, alas, I was, I had to say that I could be happier in my unhappiness without her than with her.

SØREN KIERKEGAARD

Existence . . . is a difficult category to deal with; for if I think it, I abrogate it, and then I do not think it. It might therefore seem to be the proper thing to say that there is something that cannot be thought, namely existence.

SØREN KIERKEGAARD

in God" and most of those identify themselves as Christians. But what does that mean existentially, in the living? Whatever it means, for Kierkegaard, being a Christian does not—cannot—mean living comfortably.

> All "humanity's" shrewdness is directed toward one thing, toward being able to live without responsibility. The significance of the priest for our society ought to be to do everything to make every person eternally responsible for every hour that he lives, even in the least things he does, because this is Christianity. But, his significance for society is to guarantee hypocrisy, while society pushes off the responsibility from itself onto "the priest."[37]

Are we not, then, priest and nonpriest, our own religious authority, our own self-created church? And if we are, are we not but one very small step away from being our own god? Kierkegaard would not disagree.

> Whoever you are, whatever your life might be, my friend, by ceasing to participate, (if you do) in public worship as it presently is (with its claim to being the Christianity of the New Testament) you will continually have one sin fewer, and a great sin: You are not taking part in making a fool of God.[38]

I have an existential map; it has "you are" here written all over it.

STEVEN WRIGHT

◾ COMMENTARY ◾

Kierkegaard is one of the philosophers sure to be found in virtually any popular bookstore. Other philosophers write as well or better. Other philosophers address important issues more consistently and less personally. But few speak to certain important problems of our time as pointedly as Kierkegaard does. He understands the dangers of deferring choices to outsiders, to experts, to "the crowd," and the pressures caused by the massing of society.

Despite our many freedoms, increased leisure, and psychological sophistication, authenticity seems rare in all walks of life, not the least of which is religion. Kierkegaard's great virtue is his reclamation of the existing individual from philosophical, theological, political, and scientific abstraction as he or she struggles to make life meaningful amidst a bombardment of answers and options. Kierkegaard's critique of abstract philosophy and Enlightenment reasoning reminds us that individuals construct philosophies, individuals interpret revelations, individuals draw scientific conclusions, individuals decide what is objective and reasonable.

Yet Kierkegaard seems to swing too much in the direction of subjectivity and individuality. For all his insight and prophetic power, he was unable to overcome his own alienation from science and objectivity. Surely, not even the leap of faith can completely ignore ethical considerations and objective reality. Even though a lack of passion is deadly, the presence of passion is no guarantee of authenticity. Blind, uncontrollable passion can destroy individuality as surely as excessive abstraction. Anyone who has been "consumed" or "swept away" by passion knows that it is possible to lose ourselves in passion as well as in crowds.

Yet perhaps our biggest danger today is not too much passion, but too much resentment, envy, narcissism, and sentimentality masquerading as passion; not the risky leap of faith, but the false-faith of mass-movement, fanatical religion or

Wherever and whenever men evaluate their age and their culture . . . Kierkegaard will be read—despite his exaggeration, his one-sidedness, and his radical subjectivity. Indeed, he will be read because of these qualities.

W. T. JONES

salad-bar spirituality; not too much subjectivity, but too much self-centeredness and too little honest reflection. One might even say that in spite (or because?) of our knowledge of the biology of the human psyche, we still encounter few authentic individuals.

Modern science continues to discover knowledge of many things; nonexistentialist philosophy continues to refine and clarify our capacities for understanding. But should they achieve every one of their goals this minute, we would still have no answer to the profoundest existential questions for ourselves: What is it to be a human being? Is our suffering and struggling worth living for? Has it a meaning? Has *my life* a meaning?

With or without God; with or without loving families; with or without wise advisers; with or without children; with or without jobs; with or without formal education; of whatever age, race, gender—Kierkegaard's question haunts all of us, tracks us like a Socratic hound: What are we—you and I and they—to *do*? Sometimes, when I am in a certain frame of mind, I think I can hear the tortured Dane who tried so hard to mend the rend between the self and the world: "(E)verything goes on as usual, and yet there is no one who believes in it."[39]

▓ SUMMARY OF MAIN POINTS ▓

● Søren Kierkegaard claimed that truth is subjectivity and the crowd is untruth. He rejected the view that science and objective truth could provide meaning for the individual. He criticized conformity and the degradation that he claimed results when theories and systems are used to explain and define individuals.

● For Kierkegaard, the most important issue facing any individual is how to relate to God. He criticized efforts to reduce that relationship to a performance contract and rejected as "false Christianity" all efforts to objectify faith or base belief on facts (science).

● Kierkegaard criticized what he saw as the inflated reputation of science and the massing of society, which he thought combined to alienate individuals from themselves by leveling everyone "toward a mathematical equality." People are pressured to conform to types, becoming abstractions rather than authentic individuals. Both mass movements and objective knowledge fail to address the individual.

● According to Kierkegaard, we exist only when we appropriate our beliefs by taking them up subjectively and passionately by "becoming a subject."

Rationality and objectivity are hindrances to authenticity because they distance us from our existential predicaments. Existing, becoming a subject, is possible only when we have the God-relation. For Kierkegaard, nothing else suffices.

● Rather than proofs for his views, Kierkegaard presents a series of edifying sketches and discourses describing three stages on life's way. In ascending order they are the aesthetic, ethical, and religious stages. The aesthetic stage is a futile fight against boredom characterized by the pursuit of pleasure, especially sensuous pleasure. It is the most common stage. Next is the ethical stage, a way of life that involves making commitments to the norms of society; it is devoted to general (universal) principles that are continually revised according to changing humanistic values.

● For Kierkegaard, the religious stage of life is the highest. It is the only authentic way of living. Only the religious life acknowledges our dual nature and provides a way for the individual to transform the particular into the universal. This is accomplished by a teleological suspension of the ethical, a leap of faith.

■ POST-READING REFLECTIONS ■

Now that you have had a chance to learn about the Existentialist, use your new knowledge to answer these questions.

1. Explain what Kierkegaard meant when he said that "truth is subjectivity." Is this the same as "truth is relative"?

2. How did Kierkegaard's application of the universal formula to his particular predicament influence his subsequent thinking? That is, what did he learn about love, faith, and the "God-relation" from his own experience?

3. Why is "becoming a subject" so important to Kierkegaard's philosophical enterprise?

4. Characterize the aesthete and the aesthetic stage on life's way.

5. Characterize the ethical individual and the ethical stage on life's way.

6. Characterize the religious individual and the religious stage on life's way.

7. How are the stages on life's way related?

8. What is the paradox at the heart of the leap of faith?

9. Why does Kierkegaard think that subjectivity is truth but objectivity is untruth? And what does this imply regarding efforts to scientifically and factually ground faith?

10. What role does edification play in Kierkegaard's writing? How does his extensive use of pseudonyms further this project?

11. Was Kierkegaard a Christian? Is this a trick question? Is asking if it is a trick question a trick question? Explain.

PHILOSOPHY INTERNET RESOURCES

Go to the Soccio Web page at **http://philosophy.wadsworth.com/ Soccio7e** for Web links, practice quizzes and tests, a pronunciation guide, and study tips.

THE PRAGMATIST

William James

AS A RULE WE DISBELIEVE ALL FACTS AND THEORIES
FOR WHICH WE HAVE NO USE.

William James

LEARNING OBJECTIVES

- WHAT IS *PRAGMATISM*?
- WHAT IS *PRAGMATICISM*?
- WHAT IS THE "PRAGMATIC THEORY OF MEANING"?
- WHAT IS THE "PRAGMATIC METHOD"?
- WHAT IS MEANT BY THE "CASH VALUE" OF AN IDEA?
- WHAT IS DETERMINISM?
- WHAT DOES IT MEAN TO BE "HEALTHY-MINDED"?
- WHAT DOES IT MEAN TO BE "MORBID-MINDED"?
- WHAT IS A SELF-FULFILLING PROPHECY?
- WHAT IS THE "PRAGMATIC PARADOX"?

FOR YOUR REFLECTION

KEEP THESE QUESTIONS IN MIND AS YOU LEARN ABOUT THE
PRAGMATIST.

1. *What is* pragmatism?
2. *What is* pragmaticism?
3. *What is the "pragmatic theory of meaning"?*
4. *What is the "pragmatic method"?*
5. *What is meant by the "cash value" of an idea?*
6. *What is determinism?*
7. *What does it mean to be "healthy-minded"?*
8. *What does it mean to be "morbid-minded"?*
9. *What is a self-fulfilling prophecy?*
10. *What is the "pragmatic paradox"?*

FOR DEEPER CONSIDERATION

A. Rationalists insist that truth is universal, that is, *contextless*. James rejects this notion and argues that "truth happens to an idea." What does he mean? What evidence does he offer to support his position? Provide one or two current examples of what seems to be "truth happening" to an idea. Is that what really goes on, or does truth only appear to happen? That is, does our opinion of truth change even though "the truth" does not? What's the difference, if any, between "the truth" and our sincere opinion of what's true? What would James say?

B. James says that living "at home in the universe" depends on believing things that suit us temperamentally, and he divides the human temperament into two types: the tender-minded and the tough-minded. Contrast these two types by categorizing political parties, churches, academic subjects, and tastes in art or music as tender-minded or tough-minded. Is it easy, or possible, to find pure examples of each type? Do nations and historical eras fall into these categories? What did James think happens to us if we can't find beliefs that resonate with our temperamental type? Do you agree, or do you think that we can and should mold our temperaments to fit the facts—"the truth"?

In Chapter 1 we saw that philosophy has a reputation for being dangerous and subversive, for destroying people's beliefs without replacing them. We also noted that it has the almost contradictory reputation of being irrelevant, of making no real difference in our lives. "Philosophy bakes no bread," it is said. We have seen very powerful minds disagree about the most fundamental things: Does the "mind" exist? Do we have free will? Do the consequences of our actions matter if the motives are good? What is knowledge? Is reason more reliable than experience, or is it the other way around? Is there only one reality? Is there a God? What is virtue? Can we know anything? Is objectivity possible?

What can a reasonable person, a person of so-called common sense, make of all this? It seems as if each of the great philosophers builds a whole system around one or two insights. These systems can appear farfetched and bizarre compared with life as most of us experience it; though intellectually stimulating and interesting, they hardly seem *useful*. Isn't life too short to waste on philosophical arguments full of abstract terms that have no practical use except perhaps to provide philosophers with jobs?

The first truly great American philosopher demanded that philosophy answer these kinds of questions. **William James** (1842–1910) was the most original and influential advocate of **pragmatism**, an empirically based philosophy that defines knowledge and truth in terms of practical consequences. Like Mill, Marx, and Kierkegaard, James believed that philosophy must be more than a mere intellectual enterprise. For James, philosophy's true purpose is to help us live by showing us how to discover and adopt beliefs that fit our individual needs—and temperaments. James thus shifted the focus of inquiry from the search for objectively true universal beliefs to the search for *beliefs that work for us*. His philosophy is provocative, enthusiastic, optimistic, and vigorous; it speaks to the nearly universal need for ideas and truths that matter to individuals. Voicing the lament of the common person—"What difference does this or that philosophy make to my life?"—James offers an uncommonly rich answer.

pragmatism
From the Greek for "deed"; belief that ideas have meaning or truth value to the extent that they produce practical results and effectively further our aims; empirically based philosophy that defines knowledge and truth in terms of practical consequences.

■ An American Original ■

William James was both a product and shaper of his time. The last half of the nineteenth century was a period of great confidence in science. People believed in continuous progress, influenced in part by a social interpretation of Darwin's theory of evolution that promised never-ending growth and improvement. This was also an age of bold action, as the Rockefellers and Carnegies and Vanderbilts carved up the land and established great industrial empires. People were impatient, wanting to move on, to get things done. In America, especially, this was an era of expansion, of strength. James captured this spirit so well and expressed himself in such a clear, powerful, "anti-intellectual" way that he became one of the best-known, most popular, and most influential American philosophers so far.

William James

The Education of a Philosopher

William James's father was a restless man, so William spent a considerable part of his childhood moving about. In 1855, James's father lost faith in American education and moved the entire family to Europe. They left America in June; in August, James's father sent William and his younger brother Henry (who became the famous novelist) to school in Geneva; by October the entire family had moved to England. Later they moved to France. In Boulogne, sixteen-year-old William started college and for the first time managed to attend the same school for an entire year.

That spring, however, the Jameses moved to Rhode Island. William wanted to continue his college studies, but his father was unimpressed with American colleges and prevented him from attending. A year and a half later, the family moved back to Switzerland. By this time, William's early interest in science had been replaced by a desire to be an artist, but after a year of art study, he turned back to science.

In 1861, William James entered Harvard as a chemistry major. His interests shifted to biology, anatomy, and ultimately physiology. James was so impressed by Jean Louis Agassiz (1807–1873), one of Harvard's most influential faculty members, that he accompanied him on an expedition to the Amazon. After eight months, James had had enough. He said, "When I get home I'm going to study philosophy all my days," but what he actually did was return to Harvard Medical School, where he had already taken some classes.

During his years as a student, James suffered mentally and physically. He described himself as being "on the continual verge of suicide." Unable to continue his medical studies because his hospital work put too much strain on his back, he went to Germany for the mineral baths. His letters home were funny and lighthearted, but elsewhere he noted that "thoughts of the pistol, the dagger and the bowl" were never far from him.[1] When he felt up to it, he returned to medical school and ultimately passed his licensing exam at age twenty-six. Later in the same year, though, he went into a severe depression, writing in his diary, "Nature & life have unfitted me for any affectionate relations with other individuals."[2] He was in a constant state of anxiety and dreaded being alone.

James was saved by an idea from the French philosopher Charles Renouvier (1815–1903), who had characterized free will as the ability to hold on to one idea among a number of possibilities. Willing himself to hold on to the idea of health and well-being, James effectively *decided* to get well: He *willed* himself well, by concentrating all his mental energy to produce "the self-governing resistance of the ego to the world."[3] James announced, "My first act of freedom will be to believe in free will." His depression lifted like a veil, and he was at last free to follow the restless intellect he had inherited from his father. As a result of his lingering sickness and unhappiness, he developed an interest in the relationship between mind and body. Speaking of James, a friend said:

> "Active tension," uncertainty, unpredictability, extemporized adaptation, risk, change, anarchy, unpretentiousness, naturalness—these are the

Pragmatic Study Habits

It is your relaxed and easy worker, who is in no hurry, and quite thoughtless most of the while of consequences, who is your efficient worker; and tension and anxiety, and present and future, all mixed up together in our mind at once, are the surest drags upon steady progress and hindrances to our success....

My advice to students . . . would be somewhat similar. Just as a bicycle chain may be too tight, so may one's carefulness and conscientiousness be so tense as to hinder the running of one's mind. Take, for example, periods when there are many successive days of examination impending. One ounce of good nervous tone in an examination is worth many pounds of anxious study for it in advance. If you really want to do your best in an examination, fling away the book the day before, say to yourself, "I won't waste another minute on this miserable thing, and I don't care one iota whether I succeed or not." Say this sincerely, and feel it; and go out and play, or go to bed and sleep, and I am sure the results next day will encourage you to use the method permanently.

William James, "The Gospel of Relaxation," in *Talks to Teachers of Psychology*, quoted in Lin Yutang, *The Wisdom of America* (New York: John Day, 1950), p. 243.

qualities of life which James finds most palatable, and which give him the deepest sense of well-being. They are at the same time the qualities which he deems most authentic, the accents in which the existent world speaks to him most directly.[4]

In 1872, James completed his education and took a job teaching physiology at Harvard. Within three years he was made assistant professor and remained affiliated with Harvard for nearly thirty-six years—the rest of his professional life.

In 1876, James's father announced to William, "I have met your future wife." And indeed he had. Alice Gibbens was a bright, vibrant, strikingly honest young woman. Though they fell in love, William declared himself unfit to marry her and sent her a series of self-critical, suffering letters designed to discourage any thoughts of marriage. Alice understood William well and so went to Quebec, saying she did so "to remove temptation from his path." The distance apparently diminished James's fears, however, and made Alice even more appealing. His letters became ardent efforts at courtship. Two years after his father's announcement, William and Alice were married.[5]

Though William James had found the support and care he needed to help steady his restless temperament and tendency to depression, for the rest of his life he struggled to remain healthy, using his particular good humor, aggressive intellect, and psychological insights—but he gave credit for what success he achieved to his wife for saving him.

The problem of human freedom is confused somewhat by the distinction between the self and the will. The will is only the self in its active side and freedom of the will really means freedom of the self. It is determination by the self.

SARVEPALLI
RADHAKRISHNAN

The Philosopher as Hero

James's interest in medicine and physiology developed into curiosity about psychology, and in 1878 the Henry Holt Company signed him to write a

The late nineteenth century teetered between pessimistic despair and optimistic faith in scientific progress. Thomas Eakins's painting *The Agnew Clinic* depicts the kind of medical theater William James might have attended as a medical student.

The Agnew Clinic by Thomas Eakins. ©Geoffry Clements/Corbis

psychology textbook. It took him twelve years to finish *Principles of Psychology* (1890), but the wait was worth it, and the book's wide appeal established James as an important figure in the early history of modern psychology.

About this time, his focus began to shift once more. He became increasingly interested in philosophy, but because of his broad interests, his bouts with depression, and his experience in science, medicine, and psychology, he saw philosophy in a different light than did most professional philosophers of his time. James regarded philosophy as a matter of personal involvement, as a function of the will, and as a means to overcome despair and futility. He developed the kind of philosophy *he needed to cope* with his life and presented it in an appealing and powerful series of lectures that made it accessible to others.

Much of James's work is couched in heroic, often masculine terms, which were more fashionable and common then than they are now. But we would be doing ourselves and James a serious disservice if we rejected his philosophy for that reason. Pragmatism is not a *male* philosophy but, rather, a philosophy that includes an element of heroic struggle, a philosophy of courage and action, a philosophy of vitality. A product of his times, James expressed these values in typically masculine terms. He was trying to resist inertia, to resist giving in to self-pity and self-defeat—and he used a vocabulary of heroic action to do so. James called on us to become consciously responsible for our lives by strenuous exertion of will. In our contemporary era, which seems so often to reduce us to the helpless products of environment and heredity, a philosophy like James's is a refreshing vote of confidence in the individual human spirit.

If . . . man's nature . . . makes him do what he does, how does his action differ from that of a stone or a tree? Have we not parted with any ground for responsibility? . . . Holding men to responsibility may make a decided difference in their future behavior; holding a stone or tree to responsibility is a meaningless performance.

JOHN DEWEY

James himself did not actually live the kind of life he described as ideal. But he wanted to. He recognized the dangers and limits of too much sentimentality, too much "tender-mindedness," and offered what he saw as a healthier, more useful alternative. He understood—from his own weaknesses—the frustration of being unable to stick to anything, the frustration of not knowing what we want, the frustration of trying to make up our minds and choose one important thing. James's own experiences convinced him that life was too important, too complex, too rich to reduce to any of the philosophical systems that had gone before. And so he refused to offer a system; instead, he offered a *method* for marshaling the will. But his method was grounded in philosophy, because only philosophy "has the patience and courage to work continually at a problem when common sense and even science have long since set it aside or given it up."[6]

The Philosopher as Advocate

William James published his first philosophy book, *The Will to Believe and Other Essays in Popular Philosophy,* in 1896. In 1898, he was invited to give the Gifford Lectures in Edinburgh, Scotland, a rare honor for an American. These lectures were published in 1902 as *The Varieties of Religious Experience.* A classic of contemporary philosophy, this superb book still sells widely, its popularity extending far beyond academic circles.

After returning to Harvard, James delivered a series of lectures on pragmatism and repeated these lectures at Columbia University to an audience of more than one thousand people. They were published as *Pragmatism* in 1907. *Pragmatism* also sold well and attracted the interest of both scholars and the general public. James was cheered up by its reception, to the point of announcing to his brother:

> I shouldn't be surprised if ten years hence it should be rated as "epoch-making," for of the definitive triumph of that general way of thinking I can entertain no doubt whatever—I believe it to be something quite like the protestant reformation.[7]

James's work became so influential that he effectively altered the shape of what came to be known as American philosophy. He taught, among others, Supreme Court Justice Oliver Wendell Holmes, Teddy Roosevelt, writer Gentrude Stein, and philosopher George Santayana. (Of all his students, he particularly disliked Roosevelt and Santayana.)

In 1907, the same year *Pragmatism* appeared, James retired from Harvard at the age of sixty-five. Responding at last to the criticism that he had failed to present a sustained, systematic explanation of his ideas, James resolved to craft a fuller expression of pragmatism in his remaining years. To his brother he wrote, "I live in apprehension lest the Avenger should cut me off before I get my message out. I hesitate to leave the volumes I have already published without their logical complement."[8]

James compiled a volume of essays, *The Meaning of Truth,* and one of lectures, *A Pluralistic Universe.* He hoped these books would be considered more scholarly and systematic than his others, but they were not the "logical complement" he

There are some people, and I am one of them, who think that the most important and most practical thing about a man is still his view of the universe. We think that for a landlady considering a lodger it is important to know his income, but still more important to know his philosophy.

G. K. Chesterton

If we take the whole history of philosophy, the systems reduce themselves to a few main types which, under all the technical verbiage in which the ingenious intellect of man envelops them, are just so many visions, modes of feeling the whole push, and seeing the whole drift of life, forced on one by one's total character and experience, and on the whole preferred—there is no other truthful word—as one's best working attitude.

William James

sought. Alas, the Avenger did cut off the old rebel, the anti-intellectual champion of living philosophy, and these final books were published one year after his death, in 1911. Ironically, perhaps, William James remained truer to his philosophy than if he had written a more scholarly, systematic version of it, for then he would have been required to present an appeal to the abstract and logical niceties he had spent his whole life denouncing.

The very last words of James's very last essay reflect the spirit of pragmatism better than any scholarly system: "There is no conclusion. What has concluded that we might conclude regarding it? There are no fortunes to be told and there is no advice to be given. Farewell."[9]

▩ CHARLES SANDERS PEIRCE ▩

The first expression of pragmatism actually appears in the work of **Charles Sanders Peirce** (1839–1914). The son of a Harvard mathematics professor, Peirce studied philosophy, science, and mathematics, receiving a master's degree in mathematics and chemistry from Harvard. After working at the Harvard astronomical observatory for three years, he went to work for the United States Coastal and Geodetic Survey, where he remained for thirty years. He also lectured briefly at Johns Hopkins University. A brilliant but eccentric man, Peirce was never able to secure a full-time university position. As a result, he had a difficult time publishing his work. The last years of his life were clouded by physical infirmity, poverty, and social isolation and rejection. Through it all, William James remained his friend, supporting him and presenting his ideas to a wide audience. After Peirce's death, his writings were collected and published. Although massive and difficult, his work has achieved a measure of success and is experiencing renewed interest among philosophers.

Peirce's "Pragmaticism"

Peirce first presented what he referred to as "pragmatism" in an 1878 article titled "How to Make Our Ideas Clear," written for a popular magazine. This essay was ignored by philosophers until James devoted a series of lectures to it. James had intended only to present Peirce's ideas to a wider audience, but Peirce so strenuously objected to James's version of pragmatism that he "gave" him the term and coined yet another one for himself, *pragmaticism:*

> [The] word "pragmatism" has gained general recognition in a generalized sense that seems to argue power of growth and vitality. The famed psychologist, James, first took it up. . . . So then, the writer, finding his bantling "pragmatism" so promoted, feels that it is time to kiss his child good-by and relinquish it to a higher destiny; while to serve the precise purpose of expressing the original definition, he begs to announce the birth of the word "pragmaticism," which is ugly enough to be safe from kidnappers.[10]

Peirce was not just being cranky in insisting on clear and precise use of his term. His philosophy rested on a new theory of meaning. He coined the term *pragmaticism* from the Greek word *pragma,* which means "an act" or "a consequence."

Charles Sanders Peirce

I regard Logic as the Ethics of the Intellect—that is, in the sense in which Ethics is the science of the methods of bringing Self-Control to bear to gain our Satisfactions.

CHARLES SANDERS PEIRCE

He wanted to show that the meanings of words depend on some kind of action. Peirce argued that ideas are meaningful only when they translate into actions and predict experiences associated with actions.

Pragmatic Theory of Meaning

Peirce argued that the *only differences between the meanings of words are how they test out in experience.* He thus equated meaning with the effects related to words, saying, "Our idea of anything *is* our idea of its sensible effects." Meaningful statements refer to predictable, observable, practical effects (consequences). "Consequently, the sum of experimental phenomena that a proposition implies makes up its entire bearing upon human conduct."[11] If a word cannot be tied to any observable practical results, it is thereby meaningless, for its meaning is the sum total of its practical consequences.

Peirce's scientific background and interests influenced his strong dislike for the kind of vague, abstract rationalism found in Descartes and other "impractical" system spinners. Descartes had separated the mind and thinking from any necessary connection with experience. Peirce pointed out, however, that all thinking and all meaning are *context dependent.* Context includes material, social, and emotional components, as well as an intellectual one.

Agreeing with the empiricists, Peirce argued that meaning is based on experience and determined by experiment. He did not mean just formal, scientific experiment, but also the kind of informal testing we do every day, as when, say, we test a recently varnished tabletop to see whether it is hard yet. We "test" to see whether it is appropriate to apply the word *hard* to this surface; we "experiment" by looking to see whether it looks damp, by touching it lightly, and so on. Things are not hard in some abstract, ideal, constant sense but in the real world of causal and material relationships.

> Let us illustrate this rule by examples; and, to begin with the simplest one possible, let us ask what we mean by calling a thing *hard.* Evidently that it will not be scratched by many other substances. The whole conception of this quality, as of every other, lies in its conceived effects. There is absolutely no difference between a hard thing and a soft thing so long as they are not brought to the test.[12]

If there is no way of testing the effects of words (and ideas), no way of verifying their public consequences, they are meaningless. *Meaningful ideas always make a practical difference.*

> *The rational purport of a word or other expression lies exclusively in its conceivable bearing upon conduct; if one can define accurately all the conceivable experimental phenomena which the affirmation or denial of a concept implies, one will have therein a complete definition of the concept, and there is absolutely nothing more in it. . . .*
>
> CHARLES SANDERS PEIRCE

▓ PRAGMATISM ▓

Like Peirce, James yearned for a philosophy free of "meaningless abstractions," a philosophy that stretched far beyond the merely technical and rationally coherent to embrace the whole of life. Building on Peirce's foundation, James advocated a new vision of a philosophical approach that he claimed others had recognized before, but only in parts. In the process, James went beyond Peirce's intentions and used pragmatism to present a moral

Materialism fails on the side of incompleteness. Idealism always presents a systematic totality, but it must always have some vagueness and this leads to error. . . . But if materialism without idealism is blind, idealism without materialism is void.

CHARLES SANDERS
PEIRCE

The philosophy which is so important in each of us is not a technical matter, it is our more or less dumb sense of what life honestly and deeply means.

WILLIAM JAMES

We all, scientists and non-scientists, live on some inclined plane of credulity. The plane tips one way in one man, another way in another; and may he whose plane tips in no way be the first to cast a stone.

WILLIAM JAMES

theory and to make a case for religious belief. We might even say he made pragmatism into a kind of philosophical religion. That is, James attempted to present a philosophy that could provide values and ideals worth striving for and that could satisfy our need to believe without appealing to metaphysical abstractions.

Pragmatic Method and Philosophy

James reflected a growing trend among philosophers to resist the abstract, to demand relevance and immediacy, and to deal with the "living issues" that face us. As he put it, "The whole function of philosophy ought to be to find out what definite difference it will make to you and me, at definite instants of our life, if this world-formula or that world-formula be the true one." There is a strong moral tone implicit in this position: It is not enough for philosophers to tackle questions of consistency or spin out grand theories. People are struggling through their lives, suffering, rejoicing, searching, and dying. We have a right—indeed, an obligation—to ask, "What difference does the theory of forms make to me, *now*? How is my life *different* if a tree falling in the forest does or does not make a sound? What *practical difference* does it make to me if the mind and body are two different substances?"

James often talked about feeling "at home" in the universe. Pragmatism was meant to be a *method* for solving those problems that interfere with feeling at home. James looked for what he called the *cash value* of statements, the practical payoff, and he rejected any philosophy that lacked it. This includes virtually all metaphysics.

> The pragmatic method is primarily a method of settling metaphysical disputes that otherwise might be interminable. Is the world one or many?—fated or free?—material or spiritual?—here are notions either of which may or may not hold good of the world; and disputes over such notions are unending. The pragmatic method in such cases is to try to interpret each notion by tracing its respective practical consequences. What difference would it practically make to anyone if this notion rather than that notion were true? If no practical difference whatever can be traced, then the alternatives mean practically the same thing, and all dispute is idle. Whenever a dispute is serious, we ought to be able to show some practical difference that must follow from one side or the other's being right. . . .
>
> A pragmatist turns his back resolutely and once and for all upon a lot of inveterate habits dear to professional philosophers. He turns away from abstraction and insufficiency, from verbal solutions, from bad *a priori* reasons, from fixed principles, closed systems, and pretended absolutes and origins. He turns toward concreteness and adequacy, toward facts, toward action and toward power.[13]

James referred to theories as "only man-made language, a conceptual shorthand . . . in which we write our reports of nature" and he added that "languages, as is well known, tolerate much choice of expression and many dialects."[14]

If any theory with a practical payoff is true, does it not follow that one theory is as good as another to those who believe it? It would if James were advocating sophistic relativism, but for the most part, he did not see pragmatism that way. He saw it as a *method,* rather than a collection of beliefs. Thus, he saw a use

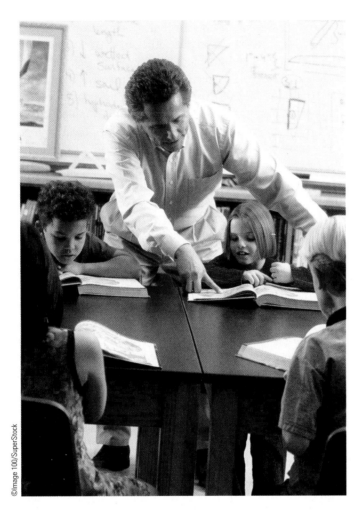

©Image 100/SuperStock

Peirce and James thought that the process of testing and reevaluating ideas is vital to human happiness. As our beliefs change, our notions of what is desirable change. But these changes can be slow. For example, some people are still uncomfortable with the idea of a male teaching preschool. As more men do, however, our ideas on this matter will be reevaluated.

for various theories of verification and meaning as long as they are ultimately used to determine the "cash value" of beliefs. We might benefit from using both empirical and rational criteria, for instance.

> Pragmatism . . . asks its usual question, "Grant an idea or belief to be true," it says, "what concrete difference will its being true make in any one's actual life? How will the truth be realized? What experiences will be different from those which would obtain if the belief were false? What, in short, is the truth's cash-value in experiential terms?"
>
> The moment pragmatism asks this question, it sees the answer: *True ideas are those that we can assimilate, validate, corroborate and verify. False ideas are those that we cannot.* That is the practical difference it makes to us to have true ideas; that, therefore, is the meaning of truth, for it is all that truth is known as. . . .
>
> Our account of truth is an account of truths in the plural, of processes. . . . Truth for us is simply a collective name for verification-processes.[15]

From a strictly logical perspective, James's position seems to contradict itself, much as strict relativism contradicts itself: He asserts the truth of his theory, which in turn seems to deny the possibility of "a truth." If a theory is merely a "man-made language," then why should we speak James's language?

Many of you are students of philosophy, and have already felt in your own persons the scepticism and unreality that too much grubbing in the abstract roots of things will breed. This is, indeed, one of the regular fruits of the overstudious career. Too much questioning and too little active responsibility lead, almost as often as too much sensualism does, to the edge of the slope, at the bottom of which lie pessimism and the nightmare or suicidal view of life. But to the diseases which reflection breeds, still further reflection can oppose effective remedies.

WILLIAM JAMES

A possible answer is to view James as an *advocate,* whose chief purpose isn't to present a strict *argument* but, rather, to make a broad enough case to convert and convince a wide audience. If we accept at face value James's insistence that he was offering us a *method* to live by, then we have to approach him differently than if he were offering a philosophy as such. Indeed, James himself sometimes refers to pragmatism as a *creed.* A philosophical creed is a body of beliefs we can devote our lives to, whereas a philosophical *argument* is an attempt to make a rational case; the former appeals primarily to our hearts, the latter to our minds.

Pragmatism has been called "philosophically crude" because of its apparent indifference to theoretical precision and consistency. Yet it can be argued that precision and consistency *pay* in some areas—science and medicine, for instance—but *cost* in others—for example, when we demand rigor and precision that are inappropriate for the issue before us.

James believed our lives are shaped by our beliefs. And we *need to believe more than we can ever "prove" by overly strict, objective, neutral standards,* which he calls "agnostic rules for truth-seeking." He says, "If one should assume that pure reason is what settles our opinions, he would fly in the teeth of the facts." What does settle our opinions, then? James answers, the *will to believe.* And what we believe is a function of whether we are tough- or tender-minded.

> *All our scientific and philosophic ideals are altars to unknown gods.*
> WILLIAM JAMES

The Temper of Belief

In addition to being a philosopher, James was an innovative, groundbreaking psychologist; as such, he refused to confine philosophy to the intellectual realm. For him, the function of philosophy shifted from revealing "the truth" to learning how to live in the world. In psychological terms, pragmatic philosophy is meant to provide a way of becoming better adjusted to the world. This helps account for the inconsistency that troubles more traditional philosophers: Living "at home in the universe" does *not,* at least according to James, depend on knowing and believing what is true, but on believing things that suit *us.*

We can classify people, James thought, into two temperamental types:

> Now the particular difference of temperament that I have in mind in making these remarks is one that has counted in literature, art, government, and manners as well as in philosophy. In manners we find formalists and free-and-easy persons. In government, authoritarians and anarchists. In literature, purists or academicals, and realists. In art, classics and romantics. You recognize these contrasts as familiar; well, in philosophy we have a very similar contrast expressed in the pair of terms "rationalist" and "empiricist," "empiricist" meaning your lover of facts in all their crude variety, "rationalist" meaning your devotee to abstract and eternal principles. . . .
>
> I will write these traits down in two columns. I think you will practically recognize the two types of mental make-up that I mean if I head the columns by the titles "tender-minded" and "tough-minded" respectively.

THE TENDER-MINDED	THE TOUGH-MINDED
Rationalistic (going by "Principles"),	Empiricist (going by "facts"),
Intellectualistic,	Sensationalistic,
Idealistic,	Materialistic,
Optimistic,	Pessimistic,
Religious,	Irreligious,
Free-willist,	Fatalistic,
Monistic,	Pluralistic,
Dogmatical.	Sceptical.

Each of you probably knows some well-marked example of each type, and you know what each example thinks of the example on the other side of the line. They have a low opinion of each other. Their antagonism, whenever as individuals their temperaments have been intense, has formed in all ages a part of the philosophic atmosphere of the time. It forms a part of the philosophic atmosphere today. The tough think of the tender as sentimentalists and soft-heads. The tender feel the tough to be unrefined, callous, or brutal. Their mutual reaction is very much like that that takes place when Bostonian tourists mingle with a population like that of Cripple Creek. . . . [But] few of us are tender-footed Bostonians pure and simple, and few are typical Rocky Mountain toughs, in philosophy. Most of us have a hankering for the good things on both sides of the line.[16]

James thought philosophy had been dominated historically by extremists, so that most philosophies are unbalanced in either the tough or tender direction. The same might be said of contemporary philosophy. Today's tough-minded philosophies view scientific knowledge as the only secure kind; they include the strictest forms of behavioristic psychology and analytically oriented philosophies, and they apply such rigid standards of meaning that most basic, meaning-of-life questions are dismissed as meaningless. The extremes of tender-minded philosophy include anti-intellectual theology, pop psychologies, and "metaphysics." Such extremism has rendered philosophy inappropriate for the vast majority of us, who are a mixture of tough and tender. But because we are easily persuaded, we end up trying to follow fashion or what James called the "most impressive philosopher in the neighborhood"—or the most impressive theologian, politician, or psychologist.

James believed that when we succumb to the "most impressive philosopher in the neighborhood," we do psychic violence to our unexpressed, preconscious sense of the world. We deny important parts of ourselves and exaggerate others. When we try to live according to beliefs that do not suit us, we become dissatisfied and unhappy. The issue, then, for James is how to find a *cause,* how to find beliefs worth living for, worth fighting and dying for—how to find a philosophical religion.

This life is worth living, we can say, since it is what we make it, from the moral point of view; and we are determined to make it from that point of view so far as we have anything to do with it, a success.

WILLIAM JAMES

My strongest moral and intellectual craving is for some stable reality to lean upon, and as a professed philosopher pledges himself publicly never to have done with doubt on these subjects, but every day to be ready to criticize afresh and call in question the grounds of his faith the day before, I fear the constant sense of instability generated by this attitude would be more than the voluntary faith I can keep going is sufficient to neutralize.

WILLIAM JAMES

PHILOSOPHICAL

QUERY

• • • • • •

If James is correct, those who criticize his free-floating style and apparently inconsistent views might be expressing their tough-minded temperaments. Do you agree with his distinction between tough- and tender-mindedness? Does it account for philosophical differences? Is it possible to evaluate this distinction without falling into one camp or the other? Which side are you on? Discuss the distinction.

The Will to Believe

According to James, we live according to beliefs that are products of our own temperaments and experience; our beliefs are not the products of abstract reasoning. Rather, we manage to find reasons to believe what we want and need to believe. And we have the right to do that, according to James, who once said he would have been better off titling his famous lecture *The Right to Believe* rather than *The Will to Believe*.

Because life *demands* a response, *demands* action, we have no choice but to believe *something*. Life presents us with what James calls *forced options*. We must make decisions whether we want to or not (even "not deciding" is a decision). We *cannot* remain detached and disinterested; life simply does not allow it. We are compelled to decide and to act, and reason is not a sufficient force for action. We do not act on what we understand, but on what we believe. The rationalist's and skeptic's demands for certainty cannot be met, yet we continue to live and act—without intellectual certainty.

> I, therefore, for one cannot see my way to accept the agnostic rules for truth-seeking, or willfully agree to keep my willing nature out of the game. I cannot do so for the plain reason that *a rule of thinking which would absolutely prevent me from acknowledging certain kinds of truth if those kinds of truth were really there, would be an irrational rule.* . . . If we had an infallible intellect with its objective certitudes, we might feel ourselves disloyal to such a perfect organ of knowledge in not trusting to it exclusively. But if we are empiricists, if we believe that no bell in us tolls to let us know for certain when truth is in our grasp, then it seems a piece of idle fantasticality to preach so solemnly our duty of waiting for the bell. Indeed we *may* wait if we will—I hope you do not think I am denying that—(we ought, on the contrary, delicately and profoundly to respect one another's mental freedom) but if we do wait, we do so at our own peril as much as if we believed.[17]

The intellect does not discover the truths in which we believe; the will creates truth.

Individual action is a means and not our end. Individual pleasure is not our end; we are all putting our shoulders to the wheel for an end that none of us can catch more than a glimpse at—that which the generations are working out.

CHARLES SANDERS
PEIRCE

Truth Happens to an Idea

The rationalists' model of truth was taken from logic and mathematics. Rationalists said truth is universal, which amounts to saying it is *contextless*. The sum "2 + 2 = 4" is true at all times, in all languages, for all creeds, for all ages, ethnicities, and genders of people, in all conditions of health or sickness. Indeed, because it is true for all "rational entities," it is true throughout the universe. (See Chapters 5 and 9.)

James rejected this simplistic, universalist notion of truth. He said experience makes it clear that ideas *become* true. Elsewhere, he said "truth *happens* to an idea." We *decide* whether or not an idea is true by "testing" it, as Peirce pointed out. James extended Peirce's pragmaticist theory of truth:

> Any idea upon which we can ride, so to speak; any idea that will carry us prosperously from any one part of our experience to any other part, linking things satisfactorily, working securely, simplifying, saving labor, is true for just so much, true in so far forth, true instrumentally.[18]

If James is correct, we accept ideas as true only after we test them against our past experiences. Even if we have a tendency to reject new ideas, the public, communitywide aspect of truth-seeking (which Peirce emphasized) forces us—or most of us—to test and reevaluate ideas, keeping some and discarding others as we and the world change.

We have all witnessed this process. It is especially clear in the areas of moral and religious belief (areas James thought vital to human happiness). For example, looking back over history, we see that ideas about vice have changed. Few contemporary Americans believe that it is wrong for women to appear in public with bare ankles, but many people used to believe that it was. Churches regularly convene councils to modify basic articles of faith, and entirely new religions emerge when old ones no longer *pay.*

Individuals and groups may simply refuse to accept changes, but on the whole, our beliefs do change, and thus our notion of what is true about the world changes—though, as James observed, we try to hang on to as many of our old ideas as possible until

> The individual . . . meets a new experience that puts them to a strain. Somebody contradicts them; or in a reflective moment he discovers that they contradict each other; or he hears of facts with which they are incompatible; or desires arise in him which they cease to satisfy. The result is an inward trouble to which his mind till then had been a stranger, and from which he seeks to escape by modifying his previous mass of opinions . . . until at last some new idea comes up which he can graft upon the ancient stock. . . .
>
> This new idea is then adopted as the true one. It preserves the older stock of truths with a minimum of modification, stretching them enough to make them admit the novelty, but conceiving them in ways as familiar as the case leaves possible. [A radical] explanation, violating all our preconceptions, would never pass as a true account. . . . We would scratch around industriously till we found something less eccentric. The most violent revolutions in an individual's beliefs leave most of his old order standing.[19]

Ideas are tested and accepted or rejected based on how well they work for us. Sometimes we see the virtue in a new idea; other times, we can no longer live with the stress and energy it takes to hold on to an old one. So there is no such thing as disinterested truth. *Pragmatic truth is human truth.* "Purely objective truth," James asserts, "plays no role whatsoever, is nowhere to be found." He adds that the

Truth is made, just as health, wealth, and strength are made, in the course of experience.

WILLIAM JAMES

Man is not to blame for what he is. He didn't make himself. He has no control over himself. All the control is vested in his temperament—which he did not create—and in the circumstances which hedge him round from the cradle to the grave and which he did not devise. . . . He is as purely a piece of automatic mechanism as is a watch. . . . He is a subject for pity, and not blame.

MARK TWAIN

William James believed that as conditions change "truth happens to an idea." Changes in health care and medical technology have led to longer lives for more people, yet not everyone wants to stay alive at any cost. So we find ourselves wrestling with ancient philosophical questions about the meaning of life, the virtues of suffering, and the right to die. Truth is happening here.

©Peter Menzel/Stock, Boston

most absolute-seeming truths "also once were plastic": "They were called true for human reasons. They also mediate between still earlier truths and what in those days were novel observations."[20]

Useful, human truth is alive; rationalistic, abstract, dogmatic truth is "the dead heart of the living tree." Truth grows.

PHILOSOPHICAL

QUERY

• • • • • •

Can you think of recent examples supporting the claim that "truth happens to an idea"? Some Protestant churches, for example, have begun revising their policies regarding birth control, abortion, and gay marriages because older beliefs lack "cash value" for many of today's churchgoers. These churches usually experience a period of soul-searching turmoil, wrestling with the dilemma of holding on to old beliefs or losing touch with their congregations. Can you cite one or two recent examples of truth happening to an idea from current events or from your own situation?

The Dilemma of Determinism

James agreed with most moral philosophers that free will is a necessary condition for moral responsibility. He offered a unique and intriguing argument for believing in free will in a famous essay titled "The Dilemma of Determinism." James begins with a novel admission: "I disclaim openly on the threshold all pretension to prove to you that freedom of the will is true. The most I hope is to induce some of you to follow my own example in assuming it true, and acting as if it were true." Having warned us not to expect an airtight argument, James goes on to present a compelling case nonetheless.

Determinism is the belief that everything that happens must happen exactly the way it does. Some materialistic philosophers and scientists say determinism is inevitable since all matter is governed by cause and effect and follows laws of nature. Possibilities are identical to actualities; the future is already contained in the present. We cannot influence the future; it lacks ambiguity, having been sealed in the distant past. James asks:

> What does determinism profess? It professes that those parts of the universe already laid down absolutely appoint and decree what the other parts shall be. . . . Indeterminism, on the contrary, says that the parts have a certain amount of loose play on one another, so that the laying down of one of them does not necessarily determine what the others shall be. It admits that possibilities may be in excess of actualities, and that things not yet revealed to our knowledge may really in themselves be ambiguous.[21]

Does determinism square with our actual feelings? James suggests that we answer this question by considering a newspaper article about the brutal murder of a woman by her husband. Ignoring his wife's screams for mercy, the husband chopped her to pieces. James asks whether any sane person can read such an account and not feel deep regret. But if the determinists are right, what is the point of regret? Determinists have no reasonable grounds for regretting anything.

> The judgment of regret calls the murder bad. Calling a thing bad means, if it means anything at all, that the thing ought not to be, that something else ought to be in its stead. Determinism, in denying that anything else can be in its stead, virtually defines the universe as a place in which what ought to be is impossible—in other words, as an organism whose constitution is afflicted with an incurable taint, an irremediable flaw. . . .
>
> It is absurd to regret the murder alone. It could not be different. . . . But how then about the judgments of regret themselves? If they are wrong, other judgments, judgments of approval, ought to be in their place. But as they are necessitated, nothing else could be in their place; and [for the determinist] the universe is just what it was before—namely, a place in which what ought to be appears impossible.[22]

Isn't it virtually impossible to think that such a murder "ought" to have occurred, given past conditions? Isn't it virtually impossible to be indifferent that it occurred? If James is correct, no sane person can help feeling some degree of sadness and regret when confronted by such horrors. Yet, if the determinists are correct, such feelings are utterly pointless. *There is no rational ground for moral feelings, because "ought" can have no meaning.* If the determinists are correct, we are caused to have senseless, absurd, utterly false feelings and ideas.

James acknowledged that there is no scientific and objective way to refute such a possibility. But he insisted that our deep, unshakable moral sense of right and wrong, combined with our feelings of regret, make a *compelling* case for our *need* and *right* to believe in free will. We have to believe at least in the possibility, however remote, that some children will not be abused because some adults

determinism
Belief that everything that happens must happen exactly the way it does because all matter is governed by cause and effect and follows laws of nature.

I suppose life has made him like that, and he can't help it. None of us can help the things life has done to us. They're done before you realize it, and once they're done they make you do other things until at last everything comes between you and what you'd like to be.

EUGENE O'NEILL

"The Problem Is Not a Real One"

It must be observed that those learned professors of philosophy or psychology who deny the existence of free will do so only in their professional moments and in their studies and lecture rooms. For when it comes to doing anything practical, even of the most trivial kind, they invariably behave as if they and others were free. They inquire from you at dinner whether you will choose this or that dish. They will ask a child why he told a lie, and will punish him for not having chosen the way of truthfulness. All of which is consistent with a belief in free will. This should cause us to suspect that the problem is not a real one; and this I believe is the case. The dispute is merely verbal, and is due to nothing but a confusion about the meanings of words.

W. T. Stace, *Religion and the Modern Mind* (New York: Lippincott, 1952), p. 279.

choose to help them; we have to believe that some bad will be avoided and some good done by our actions.

The Inner Sense of Freedom

The concept of responsibility offers little help. The issue is controllability. . . . What must be changed is not the responsibility of autonomous man but the conditions, environmental or genetic, of which a person's behavior is a function.

B. F. Skinner

James believed that change, surprise, and chance are regular parts of our experience. "There are novelties, struggles, losses, gains . . . some things at least are decided here and now . . . the passing moment may contain some novelty, be an original starting-point of events, and not merely a push from elsewhere."[23]

James appealed directly to our *inner sense of freedom* to verify his claim, a sense shared by most people. (The possible exceptions are philosophical and psychological extremists). He was convinced that most of us have a deep "spiritual need" to believe that we are active agents who exert control over significant aspects of our lives, that we affect events, that we make a difference. We *need* this belief for our spiritual and mental well-being—and we have a *right* to believe what we need to believe.

James thought the prestige and influence of science make people try to believe in determinism, but he did not believe that the evidence supporting determinism is conclusive. Echoing Hume, he claimed that we need to believe in a "more rational shape" for nature than our individual experience reveals. Consequently, we *believe* in the uniformity of laws of nature. But this uniformity of nature cannot be conclusively proved true, as Hume showed (Chapter 10). Belief in free will cannot be conclusively proved to be correct either, James noted, but this does not make it inferior to belief in determinism. The basic unprovable status of both beliefs is similar.

All the magnificent achievements of mathematical and physical science— our doctrines of evolution, of uniformity to law, and the rest—proceed from our indomitable desire to cast the world into a more rational shape in our minds than the shape into which it is thrown there by the crude order of our experience. . . . I, for one, feel as free to try conceptions of moral as of mechanical or logical rationality. If a certain formula for expressing the nature of the world violates my moral demand, I shall feel as free to throw it overboard, or at least doubt it, as if it disappointed my demand for uniformity of sequence, for example; the one demand being, so far as I can see, quite as subjective and emotional as the other is. The principle of causality, for example—what is it but a postulate, an empty name covering simply a demand that the sequence of events shall one day manifest a deeper kind of belonging of one thing with another than the mere arbitrary juxtaposition which now phenomenally appears? It is as much an altar to an unknown god as the one Saint Paul found at Athens. All our scientific and philosophic ideals are altars to unknown gods. Uniformity is as much so as is free will.[24]

In the absence of conclusive proof, we are free to *decide* which belief better suits our needs. Believing as he did in the primacy of morality, James asserted that belief in free will better serves our need for "moral rationality." And since neither belief can be conclusively rejected, he argued that we have the right to test belief in free will against our regular experiences. If it "pays" more than believing that we have no control over our lives, then clearly it is the superior belief.

Perhaps the strongest argument against determinism is the fact that almost no one really believes that absolutely everything he or she thinks, hopes, and does was determined from the first moments of the existence of the universe. Life presents us with inescapable moments of choice. How we respond is what matters most.

> Each man must act as he thinks best; and, if he is wrong, so much the worse for him. We stand on a mountain pass in the midst of whirling snow and blinding mist, through which we get glimpses now and then of paths which may be deceptive. If we stand still we shall be frozen to death. If we take the wrong road we shall be dashed to pieces. We do not certainly know whether there is any right one. What must we do? "Be strong and of a good courage." Act for the best, hope for the best, and take what comes.[25]

How can we know what is best? James says that we must discover the essence of the good.

	PHILOSOPHICAL
• • • • • •	QUERY

Do you find it impossible to doubt that you possess free will—at least sometimes? Is belief in the possibility of free will necessary for your happiness?

Morality and the Good

James rejected metaphysical attempts to define the good. He argued that the only way to understand the good life was to study what people actually want and strive for. He surveyed and rejected strictly Aristotelian, hedonistic, Christian, Kantian, and utilitarian ethics (Chapters 6, 7, 8, 11, and 12), though he borrowed from each.

Various essences of good have thus been . . . proposed as bases of the ethical system. . . .

No one of the measures that have actually been proposed has, however, given general satisfaction. . . . The best, on the whole, of these marks and measures of goodness seems to be the capacity to bring happiness. But in order not to break down fatally, this test must be taken to cover innumerable acts and impulses that never *aim* at happiness; so that, after all, in seeking for a universal principle we inevitably are carried onward to the *most* universal principle— that *the essence of good is simply to satisfy demand.* The demand may be for anything under the sun. There is really no more ground for supposing that all our demands can be accounted for by one universal underlying kind of motive than there is ground for supposing that all physical phenomena are cases of a single law.[26]

We have a basic obligation to "maximize satisfactions" and minimize frustrations, not just for ourselves but for others as well, according to James. Such a course is most likely to lead to happiness and increase the world's stock of goodness. Yet maximizing satisfaction must remain a fundamental, general obligation. The sheer number of people, coupled with the sheer number of demands we each have, makes being more specific impossible. All we can do is try our best to increase the general level of satisfaction and goodness, while remaining aware of our fallibility.

James did not offer an ethical *theory* as such, though he suggested moral guidelines. He proposed a form of altruistic utilitarianism based on an optimistic vision of social progress. He believed modern civilization is better than past eras were—he cited examples of slavery and torture—because the constant give-and-take, the "push and pull," of history results in continual refinement of satisfactions. The radical's forward drive is compensated for by the conservative's inertia; the dreamer's whimsy balances and is balanced by the scientist's objective eye, and so on.

It is important not to lose sight of the fact that James was also a psychologist and scientist. He gave more credence to observation and experience than to systematic argument. Further, he did not believe in universal moral principles or in the possibility of any finite, closed expression of morality. Thus, from his perspective, the kind of argument and system that would satisfy most philosophers would also falsify the reality of moral experience.

The Heroic Life

William James believed that life without heroic struggle is dull, mediocre, and empty. He was thinking of two approaches to life. In one, we choose (will) safety, security, and compliance. We try to avoid risks, try to avoid stress, try to avoid hassles. The other kind of life deliberately includes danger, courage, risk; it is based on a will to excitement and passion.

James was not advising us to take up hang gliding and shooting the rapids. He was talking about a "real fight" for something important, about the struggle between good and evil. He said evil is "out there," to be resisted and fought. We might find it in the form of discrimination or toxic dumping. When we do, we can ignore it, make a token effort at resisting it by voicing our objections, or actually do something. If we confront it, we could lose our jobs, money, time, or solid A grade-point average. We might fail. We might even be wrong: What we perceived as evil might not be evil. But at least we fought for or against something.

> For my own part, I do not know what the sweat and blood of this life mean, if they mean anything short of this. If this life be not a real fight, in which something is eternally gained for the universe by success, it is no better than a game of private theatricals from which we may withdraw at will. But it *feels* like a real fight—as if there were something really wild in the universe which we, with all our idealities and faithfulnesses, are needed to redeem: and first of all to redeem our own hearts from atheisms and fears. For such is a half-wild, half-saved universe adapted. The deepest thing in our nature is . . . this dumb region of the heart in which we dwell alone with our willingness and unwillingness, our faiths and fears.[27]

According to James, struggle and effort are vital elements of the good life. He believed that the "strenuous mood" is superior to sitting back and drifting along. Thus, he did not think much of the Epicurean ideal of the retreat to the Garden or of Stoic detachment when either meant reduced involvement in life and diminished passions, though he did admire the Stoic emphasis on strength of will (Chapter 7).

James thought he had identified a natural fact of life: An active, strenuous approach is healthier and more satisfying than a passive, easygoing one.

> The deepest difference, practically, in the moral life of man is the difference between the easy-going and the strenuous mood. When in the easy-going mood, the shrinking from present ill is our ruling consideration. The strenuous mood, on the contrary, makes us quite indifferent to present ill, if only the great ideal is to be attained. The capacity for the strenuous mood probably lies slumbering in every man, but it has more difficulty in some than in others in waking up. It needs wilder passions to arouse it, the big fears, loves, and indignations; or else the deeply penetrating appeal of some of the higher fidelities, like justice, truth, or freedom. Strong belief is a necessity of its vision; and a world where all the mountains are brought down and all the valleys are exalted is no congenial place for its habitation.[28]

What sort of thing would life really be, with your qualities ready for a tussle with it, if it only brought fair weather and gave those higher faculties of yours no scope?

WILLIAM JAMES

We are all ready to be savage in some cause. The difference between a good man and a bad one is the choice of the cause.

WILLIAM JAMES

• • • • • •

PHILOSOPHICAL

QUERY

Discuss your formal and informal education in terms of the preceding passage. Have you been encouraged to adopt a strenuous mood or an easygoing one? Give some specific examples. Do you think James is on the right track? Why or why not?

Choosing a Philosophy Is a Test of Character

It is simply our total character and personal genius that are on trial; and if we invoke any so-called philosophy, our choice and use of that also are but revelations of our personal aptitude or incapacity for moral life. From this unsparing practical ordeal no professor's lectures and no array of books can save us. The solving word, for the learned and the un-learned man alike, lies in the last resort in the dumb willingnesses and unwillingnesses of their interior characters, and nowhere else. It is not in heaven, neither is it beyond the sea; but the word is very nigh unto thee, in thy mouth and in thy heart, that thou mayst do it.

William James, "The Moral Philosopher and Moral Life," in *The Will to Believe and Other Essays in Popular Philosophy* (1897; reprinted in *Human Immortality,* New York: Dover, 1956), pp. 214–215.

■ PRAGMATIC RELIGION ■

James had deep respect for a religion that enriches our lives, that has "cash value." He noted that people in all cultures turn to a god (or gods) who *gets things done,* an active god, a god of the "strenuous mood," not a passive, ineffective god. This led James to offer an intriguing suggestion: If people do not believe in God, it might be because God is not *doing anything* in their lives. In *The Varieties of Religious Experience,* James attempted to discover how God *works* in people's lives. Combining an empirical, psychological study of a number of cases with a keen philosophical analysis, *Varieties* is one of James's most influential, popular, and still widely read works.

James asserted that we judge the truth of religious ideas by what he calls their "immediate luminousness," adding, "in short, *philosophical reasonableness and moral helpfulness* are the only available criteria." He concluded that religious faith is important and meaningful on pragmatic grounds: Its presence or absence makes a clearly observable, practical, and concrete difference in our lives.

Certain of our positivists keep chiming to us that, amid the wreck of every other god and idol, one divinity still stands upright,—that his name is Scientific Truth, and that he has but one commandment, but that one supreme, saying, Thou shalt not be a theist.

WILLIAM JAMES

The practical needs and experiences of religion seem to me sufficiently met by the belief that beyond man and in a fashion continuous with him there exists a larger power which is friendly to him and his ideals. All that the facts require is that the power shall be other and larger than our conscious selves.

God is the natural appellation, for us Christians at least, for the supreme reality, so I will call this higher part of the universe by the name of God. We and God have business with each other; and in opening ourselves to his influence our deepest destiny is fulfilled.[29]

James thought that a religious orientation is more effective than a nonreligious one because it encompasses more. It derives from and addresses a wider range of experiences, including a wider, more expansive consciousness than a purely secular point of view. Besides the obvious psychological benefits of having God as a support and comfort, religious conversion can open us up and make us more responsive to all of life, according to James.

A Religious Dilemma

In his study of religious experience, James distinguished between two basic personalities, the "healthy-minded" and the "morbid-minded." Healthy-minded people "look on all things and see that they are good." Such people are vital, enthusiastic, and exuberant. In contrast, the attitude of the morbid-minded person is "based on the persuasion that the evil aspects of our life are its very essence, and that the world's meaning most comes home to us when we lay them most to heart."[30] In other words, morbid souls are negativistic and pessimistic.

Interestingly, James the optimist says morbid-minded persons have a clearer, more realistic perspective than healthy-minded ones because they recognize a wider range of experience.

> The method of averting one's attention from evil, and living simply in the light of good is splendid as long as it will work. It will work with many persons; it will work far more generally than most of us are ready to suppose; and within the sphere of its successful operation there is nothing to be said against it as a religious solution. But it breaks down impotently as soon as melancholy comes. . . .
>
> The normal process of life contains moments as bad as any of those which insane melancholy is filled with, moments in which radical evil gets its innings and takes its solid turn. The lunatic's visions of horror are all drawn from the material of daily fact. Our civilization is founded on the shambles, and every individual existence goes out in a lonely spasm of helpless agony. If you protest, my friend, wait till you arrive there yourself! . . . The completest religions would therefore seem to be those in which the pessimistic elements are best developed.[31]

To better grasp this point, think of what it means to be *always* joyful and enthusiastic in a world such as ours. This lopsided kind of "healthy-mindedness" might result from a lack of true empathy with the condition of other people. A shallow enough view of things can result in a childish (not childlike) view of life in which nothing is really bad. Or, if it is bad, it is not *that* bad. Or, if it is *that* bad, then it is somehow deserved.

In his analysis of healthy- and morbid-mindedness, James is interested in identifying the most practical spiritual balance. A soul that is blocked off from a major portion of experience (which, for want of a better word, we may refer to as evil) will be less effective, less "alive," than a soul that is not blocked off.

One cannot criticize the vision of a mystic—one can but pass it by, or else accept it as having some amount of evidential weight.

WILLIAM JAMES

God is real since he produces real effects.

WILLIAM JAMES

The healthy-minded . . . need to be born only once . . . sick souls . . . must be born twice—born in order to be happy. The result is two different conceptions of the universe of our experience.

WILLIAM JAMES

• • • • • •

PHILOSOPHICAL QUERY

What do you think of James's claim that morbid-minded people have a fuller, more realistic view of things than healthy-minded ones? How would you classify yourself? Discuss some of the strengths and weaknesses of both orientations.

■ TRUTH IS ALWAYS PERSONAL ■

By the end of his life, James increasingly equated "true" with "useful." In "Is Life Worth Living?" he uses an analogy of a trapped mountain climber to illustrate his claim that sometimes psychological survival rests on the *will to believe whatever is necessary:*

> Suppose, for instance, that you are climbing a mountain, and have worked yourself into a position from which the only escape is by a terrible leap. Have faith that you can successfully make it, and your feet are nerved to its accomplishment. But mistrust yourself, and think of all the sweet things you have heard the scientists say of *maybes,* and you will hesitate so long that, at last, all unstrung and trembling, and launching yourself in a moment of despair, you roll into the abyss.
>
> In such a case (and it belongs to an enormous class), the part of wisdom as well as of courage is to *believe in the line of your needs,* for only by such belief is the need fulfilled.[32]

Thus, we see in James, as in Kierkegaard (Chapter 14), a turning of the tables as it were, so that subjectivity takes precedence over objectivity. Truth is always personal. In the end then, is James merely another Sophist advocating radical relativism born of his inability or unwillingness to understand and accept objective reality and the universal truths that flow from it? Is James manifesting "weakness" in his unwillingness to accept the world as it really is, in his refusal to face the hard fact that the world does not conform to our wishes?

James's ultimate position is that beliefs are "adaptations." As such, they can only be justified if they help us navigate our way through life. He did not think that encouraging wholehearted faith in *necessary* beliefs is the same thing as asserting that any belief that one holds is necessary *simply because one holds it.*

James's basic goal was to free us from enslavement to the notion that we *must believe* whatever science asserts—regardless of the consequences to our spiritual health and general well-being. Specifically, James argued that science should be evaluated in terms of the extent to which scientific beliefs are conducive to human happiness. Accordingly, if belief in scientific determinism and materialistic reductionism are inimical to human happiness, then disbelief is necessary for psychic survival and vitality.

For example, in testimony before the Massachusetts legislature, James spoke against a bill that would have prohibited Christian Scientists from practicing what were called "mind cures." "You are not to ask yourselves," James told the legislators, "whether these mind-curers really achieve the successes that are claimed. It is enough for you as legislators to ascertain that a large number of your citizens . . . are persuaded that a valuable new department of medical experience is by them opening up."[33]

As we have learned, for James, "the truth" is not the chief value. Usefulness is, but usefulness in the moral sense of producing healthy results. We can turn to James's personal life for an example of the kind of "necessary belief" that James considered preferable to the truth. James considered Charles Sanders Peirce his friend and mentor, despite Peirce's rejection of James's pragmatism. Unlike James,

Please remember that optimism and pessimism are definitions of the world, and that your own reactions to the world, small as they are in bulk, are integral parts of the whole thing, and necessarily help to determine the definition.

WILLIAM JAMES

Our own universe, of which we see only a small part today, may not be unique. Its beginning is not the beginning of everything. Other universes may exist at an earlier stage.

VICTOR WEISSKOPF

Peirce was unable to support himself as a philosopher, and James wanted to help his friend. Knowing that Peirce would not welcome charity, James supported and protected Peirce with money that James told him came from Peirce's many anonymous admirers. In fact, the money came from James. In this kind of case, James practiced his own principle: Better a *necessary lie* than a destructive—and unnecessary—truth.

Danger Signs

Viewed from a modern or Enlightenment perspective, William James, like Kierkegaard and Nietzsche (Chapters 14 and 16), is seen as an advocate of a potentially explosive, "anti-intellectual," "unscientific," subjectivistic philosophical doctrine. James believed that there are no neutral observers of the human condition. Everything is a "point of view." According to James, moral absolutes are impossible, and attempts to impose them are especially bad. At best, we can have moral rules of thumb, flexible guidelines. James says:

> There is hardly a good which we can imagine except as competing for the possession of the same bit of space and time with some other imagined good. . . . Shall a man drink and smoke, or keep his nerves in condition?—he cannot do both. Shall he follow his fancy for Amelia or for Henrietta?—both cannot be the choice of his heart. Shall he have the dear old Republican party, or a spirit of unsophistication in public affairs?—he cannot have both, etc. So that the ethical [or materialistic] philosopher's demand for the right scale of subordination in ideals is the fruit of an altogether practical need. Some part of the ideal must be butchered, and he needs to know which part. It is a tragic situation, and no mere speculative conundrum, with which he has to deal.[34]

What the hell, reality is a nice place to visit but you wouldn't want to live there.

JOHN BARTH

Ultimately, James came to the "inconclusive conclusion that since nothing can be proved one way or the other, each of us is entitled to believe whatever he wants to believe."[35] "We all," he said, "scientists, and non-scientists, live on some inclined plane of credulity. The plane tips one way in one [person], another way in another; and may [the person] whose plane tips in no way be the first to cast a stone."[36] And since belief in scientific method is merely *one belief* competing among many possible beliefs, belief in scientific method is no more sacrosanct than any other belief. Science, like various philosophies and religions, must compete for our allegiance against other visions and belief systems.

According to James, faith in science can be as powerful and effective as faith in religion or philosophy. He is not advocating that we commit ourselves to whatever whim or fancy strikes us. The vision that best suits our individual natures will win out. James's position is that we are entitled to commit ourselves to whatever beliefs best express our deepest selves, the fundamental quality of our "passional life." He was less worried about being "duped" by a false belief than he was about being unhappy:

> He who says, "Better go without belief forever than believe a lie!" merely shows his own preponderant private horror of becoming a dupe. He may be critical

of many of his desires and fears, but this fear he slavishly obeys. He cannot imagine any one questioning its binding force. For my own part, I have also a horror of being duped; but I can believe that worse things than being duped may happen to a [person] of this world.[37]

We might say that for James, it is better to truly believe a personally useful lie than to pretend to believe a personally incompatible truth. James's plane tips away from theoretical completeness and purity toward the concrete, existing individual.

Probably a crab would be filled with a sense of personal outrage if it could hear us classify it without ado or apology as a crustacean, and thus dispose of it. "I am no such thing," it would say: "I am MYSELF, MYSELF alone."[38]

■ COMMENTARY ■

William James's vigorous pragmatism straddled two philosophical worlds, the modern and the postmodern. He is said to have anticipated many contemporary philosophical questions. Whatever we make of his philosophy, James reminds us, will *not* be based on "pure," objective criteria. It will—and can only—be based on what we passionately and deeply need to believe.

Like Kierkegaard before him (Chapter 14) and Nietzsche, his great German contemporary (Chapter 16), James was a foe of the passionless life, the "uncommitted" life. Like Kierkegaard and Nietzsche, James challenged science's claim to ultimate, objective, universal, and absolute authority. For James, it is far better to believe passionately in a "lie" than it is to halfheartedly accept a "truth." He did not see the neatly ordered universe of the optimistic Enlightenment philosophers. The Jamesian universe is pluralistic, expansive, incomplete, and unpredictable. It is *wide open*. To survive and thrive in such a universe, James thought, we need resourcefulness, good humor, stamina, and the willingness to risk living according to convictions that cannot be objectively, universally, and scientifically established beyond doubt.

The most significant weakness in James's pragmatism is so much a part of what he saw as his mission that we must consider it from two perspectives. By tying truth to "what works" *for us,* James cuts himself off from any possibility of objective verification. Yet many philosophers still hold that the truth must refer to something beyond and not entirely determined by the individual. James seems to blur the distinction between truth and how we discover it. Although we do test ideas by acting on them and by comparing them with our more established beliefs, their *truth* is independent of this process. Penicillin remains an effective antibiotic whether or not I believe that it is, for example.

There are two different issues here. If we are looking at factual matters, this criticism of pragmatism is persuasive. But if we consider beliefs about moral and spiritual concerns, as well as some social and psychological beliefs, pragmatism has something important to say. We distort James's position if we lump both general categories of belief statements together.

Yet it is essential to realize that our way of perceiving the world in everyday life is not radically affected by scientific conceptions. For all of us—even for the astronomer, when he goes home at night—the sun rises and sets, and the earth is immobile.

PIERRE HADOT

Consider, on James's behalf, the pattern that social scientists refer to as a **self-fulfilling prophecy.** This is a belief that affects events in such a way that it causes itself to come true. For example, a man who believes his date will not like him might project a mood of surly defensiveness and hostility or passive, defeatist self-pity. Either mood could alienate his companion, who otherwise would have found him quite pleasant. If so, his prophecy of "She won't like me" has fulfilled itself. Similarly, students who expect to do poorly in a given course might not learn because they are frightened or depressed by their expectations of failure; they might unconsciously devote less energy to their studies than they would have if they had believed more in themselves. Conversely, students who expect to do well might be more open and pleasant in class, which can inspire the professor to be a better teacher; they might ask more questions, pay more attention, and so on, thereby fulfilling their own beliefs.

Ironically, in recent years, certain work emerging from the *scientific* study of belief has been interpreted as supporting James's sense that the "best" beliefs are not always the "truest" ones.[39] Lyn Abramson, of the University of Wisconsin, and Lauren Alloy, of Temple University, report that "normal, healthy" people are subject to a variety of "cognitive illusions." Among these are mild, factually unwarranted optimism and insensitivity to failure. Combined, these two "illusions" result in tendencies to make "straightforwardly false" judgments. Ironically, because they often do not suffer from such illusions, clinically depressed individuals are "Sadder But Wiser," to use the subtitle from one of Abramson and Alloy's better-known papers. In other research, social psychologist Shelley Taylor has found that victims of trauma and illness who are "unjustifiably optimistic" tend to be better adjusted and happier than more "realistic" victims of similar circumstances. Lastly, Daniel Goleman is one of a number of neo-Freudians who argue that forgetting unpleasant events (repression) is an important component of mental health.[40]

This raises the basic **pragmatic paradox:** *Pragmatism works only if we believe our ideas are true according to nonpragmatic criteria.* For instance, can I really just say to myself, "Well, belief in God makes people feel secure and gives their lives meaning. I would like to feel secure and find a purpose for my life. Therefore, I shall believe in God"? Does not such belief work only when I sincerely believe it to be true—objectively and factually true, not just true because I believe it is true? Paradoxically, it seems as if only by believing in a nonpragmatic view of truth can pragmatism work.

William James spoke eloquently for the person of "moderate" convictions and temperament and for the virtues of the active, vigorous struggle for good. He offered a persuasive and unique defense of our right to believe. He showed that faith in a higher power cannot be dismissed as a form of psychological infantilism and that its grounding in personal conviction is as solid as faith in science. Further, he showed that religious faith has restorative and unifying powers often missing from faith in science. James defended the common sense of the average person without pandering to it and called on us to test the higher life of the "strenuous mood." All in all, these are impressive accomplishments.

self-fulfilling prophecy
A belief that affects events in such a way that it causes itself to come true; an example is the student who does poorly on an exam because she expects to fail it.

pragmatic paradox
Pragmatism works only if we believe that our ideas are true according to nonpragmatic criteria.

■ SUMMARY OF MAIN POINTS ■

● William James's pragmatism is based on Charles Sanders Peirce's pragmatic theory of meaning: Ideas are meaningful only when they translate into actions and predict experiences associated with actions. James argued that philosophy should make a "definite difference" in people's lives, and he attempted to construct a philosophical religion that could provide beliefs worth living and dying for. Pragmatism was meant to be a method for helping us feel "at home" in the universe.

● Pragmatism rejects any philosophy that lacks "cash value." James believed that virtually no metaphysical theory has any practical payoff (cash value). "True ideas," he said, "are those that we can assimilate, validate, corroborate and verify. False ideas are those we cannot." Pragmatic truth is human truth. James expanded the realm of philosophy beyond "revealing the truth" to providing a way to become better adjusted to the world.

● James divided people into tough-minded or tender-minded types, claiming that historically philosophy has been dominated by extremists of one type or the other and thus has remained unbalanced. He advocated what he saw as a more useful combination of these two extremes. Because life demands an active response, we have no choice but to believe something. We face "forced options." The intellect does not discover the truths in which we believe; the will to believe creates truths.

● The pragmatic life rejects determinism as incompatible with our immediate sense of freedom.

According to James, determinism—the idea that everything must happen exactly the way it does—is incompatible with our spiritual need for freedom. Determinism has less cash value than belief in freedom, and since neither belief can be proved conclusively, the pragmatic thing to do is believe in what we need to be happy—freedom. Feelings of regret reflect our deep belief in free will.

● Since we cannot escape choice, James advocated what he called the "heroic life," rejecting life without struggle as dull, mediocre, and empty. The heroic life is characterized by a "real fight" for something important; it is about the struggle between good and evil. James distinguished between two basic personalities: The healthy-minded personality looks at all things as good; healthy-minded people are exuberant, vital, and enthusiastic. The morbid-minded personality sees the very essence of life as evil, untrustworthy, and troublesome; morbid-minded people are negativistic and pessimistic.

● Religious faith is important on pragmatic grounds: Its presence or absence makes an observable, practical difference in people's lives. James believed a religious orientation is more effective than a non-religious one because it encompasses more. Profound religious (rebirth) experience makes it possible to be both morally decent (without descending into the pessimism of morbid-mindedness) and happy (without resorting to the limited perspective of healthy-mindedness).

■ POST-READING REFLECTIONS ■

Now that you have had a chance to learn about the Pragmatist, use your new knowledge to answer these questions.

1. How did James's personal life influence some of his major pragmatic beliefs?

2. What prompted Charles Sanders Peirce to change the name of his philosophy to "pragmaticism"?

3. Illustrate the pragmatic theory of meaning with your own example.

4. What is the core question at the heart of the pragmatic method? Why did James believe that

asking that question is so important? What does the answer to the question reveal to us?

5. Discuss James's notion of the "will to believe." In what sense do "reasons serve the will," according to James? Do you agree with him? Why or why not?

6. How does James deal with the dilemma of determinism? What do you think of his strategy? Does it square with your sense of the world and

of yourself? Is his "answer" to the dilemma really an answer? If not, is there a better answer, or any answer?

7. Why was James dissatisfied with metaphysical efforts to define the good? What did he propose in their place?

8. Explain what James meant by the "heroic life." In his opinion, what aspects of life call for a heroic response? Why? What factors make it difficult for some people to live such a life?

9. What was James driving at when he claimed that a religious orientation is more effective than a nonreligious one? What reasons did he have for this belief? Do you share his opinion? Why or why not?

10. Why was James critical of optimism? What does he offer as a better—healthier—alternative?

PHILOSOPHY INTERNET RESOURCES

Go to the Soccio Web page at **http://philosophy.wadsworth.com/ Soccio7e** for Web links, practice quizzes and tests, a pronunciation guide, and study tips.

THE ANTI-PHILOSOPHER

Friedrich Nietzsche

WHO IS MOST INFLUENTIAL.—WHEN A HUMAN BEING
RESISTS HIS WHOLE AGE AND STOPS IT AT THE GATE TO
DEMAND AN ACCOUNTING, THIS MUST HAVE INFLUENCE.
WHETHER THAT IS WHAT HE DESIRES IS IMMATERIAL;
THAT HE CAN DO IT IS WHAT MATTERS.

Friedrich Nietzsche

LEARNING OBJECTIVES

- WHAT IS "MODERNITY"?
- WHAT IS "PESSIMISM"?
- WHAT IS "TRAGIC OPTIMISM"?
- WHAT IS "NIETZSCHEAN PERSPECTIVISM"?
- WHAT IS "NIHILISM"?
- WHAT IS THE "OVERMAN"?
- WHAT IS THE "UNDERMAN"?
- WHAT IS SLAVE MORALITY?
- WHAT IS MASTER MORALITY?
- WHAT IS *RESSENTIMENT*?

For Your Reflection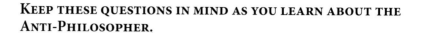

Keep these questions in mind as you learn about the Anti-Philosopher.

1. *What is "modernity"?*
2. *What is "pessimism"?*
3. *What is "tragic optimism"?*
4. *What is "Nietzschean perspectivism"?*
5. *What is "nihilism"?*
6. *What is the "overman"?*
7. *What is the "underman"?*
8. *What is slave morality?*
9. *What is master morality?*
10. *What is* ressentiment?

For Deeper Consideration

A. Nietzsche's critique of modernity accuses modern Western culture of being moralistic, mendacious, and *antinature*. What is it about modernity—and about being moralistic in particular—that troubles Nietzsche so? What does he offer as a healthier alternative? (Does he offer an alternative or a prophecy? What's the difference between the two?)

B. What did Zarathustra mean when he said that God is dead and we have killed him? Who was Zarathustra? What is his relationship to the overman? How is nihilism related to the death of God? If, as Nietzsche/Zarathustra insists, God is dead, why does belief in God thrive in today's world? Indeed, poll after poll reports that America is among the most "religious" countries, with upwards of 80 percent of Americans attesting to belief in God. And the current attacks on Western culture by fundamentalist Muslims testify to deep-seated belief in God. How would Nietzsche assess these conditions? Does widespread belief in God invalidate Nietzsche's pronouncement?

*P*erhaps no philosopher of modern times has provoked as much controversy as **Friedrich Nietzsche** (1844–1900). Of small physical stature, so nearsighted he was nearly blind, plagued by headaches, nausea, loneliness, and depression, Nietzsche voiced an explosive philosophy that attracts and offends people more than a century after his death. One of a handful of philosophers who can be called "best-selling" authors, Nietzsche's work has a poetic, confrontational style that is both exhilarating and disturbing.

Although he died in 1900, Nietzsche thought of himself as a cultural prophet of the next two centuries. In *The Will to Power* he says:

> What I relate is the history of the next two centuries. I describe what is coming, what can no longer come differently. . . . This future speaks even now in a hundred signs, this destiny announces itself everywhere; for this music of the future all ears are cocked even now. For some time now, our whole European culture has been moving as toward a catastrophe, with a tortured tension that is growing from decade to decade: restlessly, violently, headlong, like a river that wants to reach the end, that no longer reflects, that is afraid to reflect.[1]

Nietzsche saw himself as the first to recognize the symptoms of a profound sickness at the core of *modernity*. **Modernity** refers to the historical period of nineteenth- and twentieth-century nation-states and to a corresponding set of cultural conditions and beliefs dominated by Enlightenment ideals. Modernity includes faith in science, objective truth, and rationality; expectations of inevitable progress; capitalism, urbanization, and large-scale industrial enterprise; mass literacy, media, and culture; political democracy; anti-traditionalism; individualism; and secularization.

Nietzsche's most famous (or infamous) pronouncement that "God is dead" is part of a generalized assessment of modernity that consists of integrated negative and positive stages. The negative stage may be the most recognized because of Nietzsche's uniquely engaging and confrontational style of writing. Perhaps less well known—at least by the general public—is Nietzsche's life-affirming call to those who recognize the *great opportunity* for self-creation present in the death of God and all that flows from it.

Although Nietzsche is popularly credited with being the first truly postmodern philosopher, with Nietzsche nothing is that simple; or perhaps, as many philosophers insist, with Nietzsche nothing is clear. Depending on one's perspective, Nietzsche's work is either enriched or weakened by the use of cryptic utterances, biting irony, hyperbole, deliberate contradiction, and phrases and assertions that are carefully crafted to provoke the reader. Contemporary philosophers and critics disagree about whether Nietzsche was a philosopher of sustained brilliance, sporadic insight, raving irrationality—or even a philosopher at all. What is beyond dispute, however, is his enormous influence on and significance for twentieth-century and contemporary thought. Love him or hate him, Nietzsche remains an aesthetic, literary, psychological, and philosophical force to be reckoned with. He is, at the very least, a worthy adversary.

I have chosen for myself the word immoralist *as a mark of distinction and badge of honour.*

FRIEDRICH NIETZSCHE

modernity

The historical period of nineteenth- and twentieth-century nation-states and a corresponding set of cultural conditions and beliefs dominated by Enlightenment ideals, including faith in science, objective truth, and rationality; expectations of inevitable progress; political democracy; capitalism; urbanization; mass literacy; mass media; mass culture; anti-traditionalism; large-scale industrial enterprise; individualism; and secularization.

By the second half of the nineteenth century, art and literature, as well as philosophy, began to reflect a romanticized vision of Schopenhauer's pessimism. Caspar David Friedrich's painting *The Polar Sea* depicts glaciers destroying a ship: a symbol of overcivilized, industrialized man's inevitable defeat by the primal forces of irrational nature.

© Ship in the Polar Sea, 1824 (oil on canvas). Friedrich, Casper David (1774-1840)/Hamburger Kunsthalle, Hamburg, Germany/Bridgeman Art Library

Friedrich Nietzsche, the iconoclastic son of a preacher, was a deeply spiritual atheist who lived and died in lonely obscurity. He stands outside of the common categories of philosophy. He is *sui generis*—of his own kind. I have tried to express something of this uniqueness by treating him as an *anti-philosopher*. He became that over the course of his life, but he was always an outsider.

■ THE OUTSIDER ■

Nietzsche was born in the Prussian village of Röcken. When he was four years old, his father, a Lutheran minister, died, leaving the pious little boy to the care of his mother, grandmother, two aunts, and sister. As the only male in the household, young "Fritz" became the center of attention, coddled and protected. Nietzsche's studious demeanor and religious piety earned him the nickname "the little pastor."

Nietzsche originally planned to follow in his father's footsteps and become a Lutheran minister, but in his late teens, something changed. The "good boy" lost interest in his studies. He questioned the existence of God and even sneaked away and got drunk—on a Sunday.

Friedrich Nietzsche

At twenty, Nietzsche enrolled in the University of Bonn. Freed from the pampering and domination of five women, faced with uncertainties about his faith and childhood plans for the future, Nietzsche, like Kierkegaard, went through a period of rebellious high living.

Nietzsche tried his best to fit into the raucous life of late-nineteenth-century German students: drinking, boisterous singing, romantic pursuits, duels. Nietzsche joined a student club, caroused, and even fought a halfhearted duel. Yet, for all his efforts, Nietzsche was not "one of the guys." He was personally disgusted with drunken excess, smoky beer halls, and the "coarse, Philistine spirit" of his fellows. The little pastor found that kind of student life intolerable and ultimately suffered a nervous collapse.

Nietzsche left Bonn and enrolled in the University of Leipzig. There he had the good fortune to meet Professor Friedrich Ritschl, who kindled in him a passion for philology, the study of classical philosophy and literature. Ritschl recognized that Nietzsche was a brilliant scholar and encouraged and stimulated his genius.

Despite his academic brilliance, however, Nietzsche was already a lonely man, truly an outsider. When he first moved to Leipzig, he was still shaken by his disillusionment with Bonn and by the emptiness he felt at having lost his religious faith. He went through the motions of being actively interested in his life, but found himself torn by doubts. Hedonistic pursuits left him disgusted and depressed, yet the way of the church remained closed off to him.

While in this state, Nietzsche came across the work of **Arthur Schopenhauer** (1788–1860). Schopenhauer's philosophy is known as **pessimism**, the belief that life is disappointing and that for every satisfied desire, ten new unsatisfied ones emerge; our only hope is detachment and withdrawal. In his book *The World as Will and Idea,* Schopenhauer argued that life is nothing more than a constant will to survive. We are pawns of a life force, and our best hope is to detach our individual will from the cycle of wanting-getting-wanting more. Life, in Schopenhauer's vision, is an irrational, purposeless striving for a pointless existence. According to Schopenhauer, what little salvation there is comes only from resisting the blind will to *live at all costs* and curtailing our desires.

Given his mental turmoil and deep dissatisfaction, Nietzsche responded enthusiastically to Schopenhauer. He craved some kind of meaning but was unable to find it in either pleasure or religion. At a precarious time in his life, Schopenhauer gave him something to hold on to.

> It seemed as if Schopenhauer were addressing me personally. I felt his enthusiasm, and seemed to see him before me. Every line cried aloud for renunciation, denial, resignation. Here I saw a mirror in which the world, life, my own mind were reflected in fearful grandeur. Here the wholly disinterested and heavenly eye of art looked at me; here I saw illness and salvation, banishment and refuge, hell and heaven.[2]

From Schopenhauer, Nietzsche concluded that life makes no objective, absolute sense. Life is not the result of a divine plan, nor is nature orderly in any way that we can discern. Rather, life is the expression of *will*. Schopenhauer characterized the ultimate will as the will to live; Nietzsche disagreed. He insisted that

I think of myself as the scrawl which an unknown power scribbles across a sheet of paper, to try out a new pen.

FRIEDRICH NIETZSCHE

pessimism
Schopenhauer's theory that life is disappointing and that for every satisfied desire, new desires emerge; our only hope is detachment and withdrawal.

Did you ever say Yes to joy? O my friends, then you said Yes to all woe as well. All things are chained and entwined together, all things are in love. . . .

FRIEDRICH NIETZSCHE

will to power

Nietzsche's term for what he thought is a universal desire to control others and impose our values on them.

life is governed by the **will to power**, a universal desire to control others and impose our values on them.

Beyond the Academy

Schopenhauer's pessimism, paradoxically, invigorated Nietzsche, and in 1868 Ritschl recommended him for a chair in classical philology. Ritschl was especially conservative, not given to excessive praise or hasty conclusions regarding the area of study to which he had devoted his life, so the recommendation he wrote for Nietzsche is all the more significant:

> However many young talents I have seen develop under my eyes for thirty-nine years . . . Nietzsche . . . is the first from whom I have ever accepted any contribution [to the philological journal *Museum*] at all while he was still a student. . . . He is the idol, and without wishing it, the leader of the whole younger generation of philologists here in Leipzig who—and they are rather numerous—cannot wait to hear him as a lecturer. You will say, I describe a phenomenon. Well, that is just what he is—and at the same time pleasant and modest. . . .
>
> . . . He will simply be able to do anything he wants to do.[3]

Though Nietzsche lacked his doctorate, his brilliance and Ritschl's strong advocacy combined to secure the position for him. "In *Germany,*" Ritschl wrote, "that sort of thing happens absolutely never."

Nietzsche was only twenty-four when he was appointed professor. The university hurriedly conferred the doctorate on him—without requiring an examination—and Nietzsche plunged into a heavy academic routine. But his heart and mind could not be confined to the limits of philology or philosophy—or any other academic area as then defined.

In spite of noble intentions, Nietzsche was not a particularly effective professor. His lectures were often complex and difficult to follow, and fewer and fewer students attended them. He did not socialize well and found his colleagues difficult. Academic routine drained him. His sole comforts came from his own writing and a few close friends.

Tragic Optimism

In 1870, the Franco-Prussian War broke out. Nietzsche volunteered as a medic and served for a short time before returning to Leipzig in poor health. Germany humbled both Austria and France in the war. Under the powerful vision of Otto von Bismarck (1815–1898), small German principalities were unified into a single, powerful state dominated by Prussia. Nietzsche saw Bismarck as an example of a "higher morality" based on strength, power, and the will to dominate. He was impressed that Bismarck ruled by "blood and iron."

About this time, Nietzsche became intrigued with Darwinism. Combining Bismarck's will to power and domination with Darwin's idea of evolution, Nietzsche transformed Schopenhauer's pessimism into his own utterly unique doctrine of *overcoming*. Schopenhauer was right, Nietzsche thought, in recognizing that life consists of continual struggle and hardship.

> *That everyone can learn to read will ruin in the long run not only writing, but thinking too.*
>
> FRIEDRICH NIETZSCHE

> *Another century of readers— and the mind itself will stink.*
>
> FRIEDRICH NIETZSCHE

> *Life is no argument. The conditions of life might include error.*
>
> FRIEDRICH NIETZSCHE

But Schopenhauer's reaction—retreat and renunciation—struck Nietzsche as weak-willed and decadent. He concluded that Schopenhauer's pessimism was unhealthy and life-denying.

Nietzsche's solution was **tragic optimism**, the sense of joy and vitality that accompanies the superior individual's clear-sighted imposition of his own freely chosen values on a meaningless world. The superior person is the person who neither shrinks from struggle nor struggles blindly, controlled by a pessimistic instinct to survive at any cost. The superior person *wills* to live deliberately and consciously. The superior person *overcomes* pessimism without retreating into lies about ultimate meaning or purpose. In Nietzsche's view, Schopenhauer failed to recognize that the struggle to survive aims at the dominance of the strongest and the fittest. The tragic optimist imposes meaning on a meaningless universe and overcomes his or her own innate fears and weaknesses.

tragic optimism
According to Nietzsche, the sense of joy and vitality that accompanies the superior individual's clear-sighted imposition of his own freely chosen values on a meaningless world.

Zarathustra Speaks

Citing ill health, Nietzsche resigned from the university in 1879, when he was thirty-four. He was granted a pension. Nietzsche knew he needed to break free from the confines of academic scholarship and carve out his own path. He came to see himself as the prophet of a higher, healthier morality, a morality so far beyond conventional values that it required the revaluation of all values. He took to referring to himself as an *immoralist* and an *iconoclast*. He spoke of "doing philosophy with a hammer"—tapping on the statues of great idols to see which are hollow and then smashing them to bits.

One does not kill by anger but by laughter. Come, let us kill the Spirit of Gravity!
FRIEDRICH NIETZSCHE

Freed from the demands of the university, Nietzsche polished and refined both his thinking and his writing. His greatest work was accomplished in the ten-year period following his retirement from teaching. For a time, he lost some of his ferocity—mellowed, perhaps, by the physical and cultural climates of Switzerland and Italy, where he spent most of his time.

His most "cheerful" books, *The Dawn of Day* (1881) and *The Gay Science* (1882), were written while he was friends with Lou Salome, a witty, appealing young Jewish intellectual. Nietzsche was quite taken with her. In their walks and talks together he found a special kind of companionship. He seems to have found in her both a disciple and a lover. We do not know whether he ever proposed to her, as she later claimed. In any case, Lou Salome ultimately left Nietzsche for another man. (Years later, when Nietzsche was famous, Lou Salome capitalized on her relationship with him.)

Devastated by her abandonment, Nietzsche retreated to the Swiss Alps. In this agonizingly lonely, hurt, and bitter mood, he produced his most famous work, *Thus Spake Zarathustra* (1885). The title comes from the Sanskrit phrase *Iti vuttakam,* meaning "Thus spoke the Holy One."[4] Nietzsche used the name of the ancient Persian prophet Zoroaster, but created his own Zarathustra. *Zarathustra* was a call to rise above decadence and mediocrity. Nietzsche later described *Zarathustra* as a revelation:

> One hears—one does not seek; one takes—one does not ask who gives; a thought suddenly flashes up like lightning, it comes with necessity, unhesitatingly—I have never had any choice in the matter.[5]

Will the true Nietzsche please stand up? In an ironic fashion sure to delight the iconoclast, some philosophers have great difficulties taking Nietzsche seriously in light of his many personae, his romantic and ambiguous language, in short, his slipperiness. So what, if anything, are we to make of this May 13, 1882, photograph of the young prophet of the overman, with his best friend Paul Reé and the woman he once professed to love, Lou Salome?

It is better to be envied than pitied.

HERODOTUS

Nietzsche's Zarathustra is at once a great destroyer of false values and in the same instant a creator of new, higher, healthier values. Nietzsche said that Zarathustra "as a type . . . *overtook* me."[6] Zarathustra the destroyer-creator announces the arrival of the next evolutionary type, the *Übermensch,* or the overman.

Nietzsche followed *Zarathustra* with what many consider the two most coherent statements of his philosophy, *Beyond Good and Evil* (1886) and *Toward a Genealogy of Morals* (1887). Consisting mostly of aphorisms and short essays, both books are essentially commentaries on the gospel of the overman espoused in *Zarathustra.* Nietzsche's purpose is clear: to destroy conventional morality and replace it with a higher "immoral" ideal.

A Special Kind of Courage

Writer Stefan Zweig's touching description of Nietzsche reminds us that there are many kinds of courage, many ways to be strong:

> Carefully the myopic man sits down to a table; carefully, the man with the sensitive stomach considers every item on the menu: whether the tea is not too strong, the food not spiced too much, for every mistake in his diet upsets his sensitive digestion, and every transgression in his nourishment wreaks havoc with his quivering nerves for days. No glass of wine, no beer, no alcohol, no coffee at his place, no cigar and no cigarette after his meal, nothing that stimulates, refreshes, or rests him; only the short, meager meal and a little urbane, unprofound conversation in a soft voice with an occasional neighbor (as a man speaks who for years has been unused to talking and is afraid of being asked too much).
>
> And upon entering again into the small, narrow, modest, coldly furnished *chambre garnie,* where innumerable notes, pages, writings, and proofs are piled up on the table, but no flower, no decoration, scarcely a book and rarely a letter. Back in a corner, a heavy and graceless wooden trunk, his only possession, with the two shirts and the other worn suit. Otherwise only . . . manuscripts, and on a tray innumerable bottles and jars and potions; against the migraines, which often render him all but senseless for hours, against his stomach cramps, against spasmodic vomiting, against the slothful intestines, and above all the dreadful sedatives against his insomnia, chloral hydrate and Veronal. A frightful arsenal of poisons and drugs, yet the only helpers in the empty silence of this strange room in which he never rests except in brief artificially conquered sleep. Wrapped in his overcoat and a woolen scarf (for the wretched stove smokes and does not give warmth), his fingers freezing, his double glasses pressed close to the paper, his hurried hand writes for hours—words the dim eyes can hardly decipher. For hours he sits like this and writes until his eyes burn.

Stefan Zweig, quoted in *The Portable Nietzsche,* trans. Walter Kaufmann (New York: Penguin, 1968), p. 104. Reprinted by permission.

To a friend Nietzsche wrote, "If I could give you an idea of my feeling of loneliness! I have nobody among the living or among the dead, to whom I feel related. This is indescribably horrible!" (This photograph was taken at Villa Silberblick in Weimar, shortly before Nietzsche's death).

The Last Philosopher

I shall be asked why I have really narrated all these little things which according to the traditional judgement are matters of indifference . . . Answer: . . . It is precisely here that one has to begin to learn anew.

FRIEDRICH NIETZSCHE

During this period of his life, Nietzsche lived modestly in rooming houses, refusing to succumb to pessimism. Overwhelmed by disappointment and loneliness, disturbed by what he saw as rampant mediocrity and hypocrisy, Nietzsche struggled on with his writing. Less than three years before his final collapse, he wrote:

> What found expression [in even my earliest work] was . . . a *strange* voice . . . one who concealed himself for the time being under the scholar's hood. . . . Here was a spirit with strange, nameless needs. . . . What spoke here was a mystical, almost maenadic [frenzied] soul that stammered with difficulty, a feat of the will, as in a strange tongue, almost undecided whether it should communicate or conceal itself. It should have *sung,* this "new soul"—and not spoken![7]

The last years of Nietzsche's life were tragic. His health deteriorated even further, and he became increasingly, bitterly isolated and lonely.

> I call myself the last philosopher because I am the last man. Nobody talks to me but myself, and my voice comes to me like that of a dying person. . . . Though I try to conceal my loneliness from myself—the terrible loneliness of the last philosopher!—and make my way into the multitude and into love by lies, for my heart cannot bear the terror of the loneliest loneliness and compels me to talk as if I were two.[8]

[Nietzsche] had more penetrating knowledge of himself than any other man who ever lived or ever was likely to live.

SIGMUND FREUD

As his disappointments mounted, Nietzsche quarreled with practically everyone, his human contact reduced to innkeepers, shop clerks, and others with whom he had only superficial interactions. To a friend he wrote, "For the lonely one, even noise is a consolation. If I could give you an idea of my feeling of loneliness! I have nobody among the living or among the dead, to whom I feel related. This is indescribably horrible!"[9] For a soul with so much to *sing,* this must have been among the worst rebuffs of all.

In January 1889 in Turin, Italy, Nietzsche had another breakdown. His mother brought him home to Germany, and his life ended much as it had begun, in the care of his mother and sister. After their mother's death, Nietzsche's sister moved him to Weimar, where the prophet of struggle and overcoming spent the rest of his life half-paralyzed, slipping in and out of sanity. The "loneliest philosopher" died about midday, August 25, 1900.

PHILOSOPHICAL

QUERY

• • • • • •

Some postmodern philosophers claim that all philosophy is a form of autobiography. By that they mean that all philosophy—and indeed all thinking and perceiving—expresses and reflects uniquely personal qualities of the philosopher. In your opinion, do the life circumstances *of philosophers help us evaluate their philosophical writings? Do you think* autobiographical *considerations are significant? Insignificant? Discuss and explain.*

■ TRUTH IS A MATTER OF PERSPECTIVE ■

When Nietzsche says, "I call myself the last philosopher because I am the last man," he may be referring to his doctrine of the more-than-human overman. (See the preceding section.) If so, then by referring to himself as the last philosopher, Nietzsche is signaling that he is the last "merely human" philosopher. This may have been what he had in mind, since he thought that the next stage of cultural and human evolution would necessitate the destruction of all present value systems, including modern philosophical ones based on the possibility of objectivity.

According to Nietzsche, aesthetic vision (art or taste) is the basis of meaning, not science, not religion, not morality, not rationality. And for Nietzsche, like his Irish contemporary Oscar Wilde (1854–1900), art is a matter of *semblance*, a *pose*, "technically" a matter of *masks* and *lies*. Nietzsche wrote:

> I never failed to sense a *hostility to life*—a furious, vengeful antipathy to life itself [behind faith in absolutes]: for all of life is based on semblance, art, deception, points of view, and the necessity of perspectives and error.[10]

Nietzsche's controversial status as a philosopher is due, at least in part, to assertions of a form of relativism known as *perspectivism*. **Nietzschean perspectivism** is the contention that every view is only one among many possible interpretations, including, especially, Nietzschean perspectivism, which itself is just one interpretation among many interpretations. But, as the critic Alexander Nehamas reminds us:

> If every view is only an interpretation, and if, as perspectivism holds, there are no independent facts against which various interpretations can be compared, what is the object at which the many interpretations that we consider interpretations *of* Nietzsche are directed? . . . If perspectivism is correct, and, as it seems to claim, every interpretation creates its own facts, then it may seem impossible to decide whether any interpretation is or is not correct. And if there is nothing of which all these are interpretations, then the very idea of interpretation, which seems to require at least that there be something there to be interpreted, begins to appear suspect itself.[11]

We have already encountered this issue of the apparent self-contradiction at the heart of radically relativistic doctrines. (See Chapters 1, 3, and 4, for example.) There is, however, a characteristically postmodern quality to Nietzsche's perspectivist assertions: By repeatedly calling attention to his own aesthetic perspectivism, Nietzsche models what he asserts in a flagrantly self-referential way. He exuberantly adopts *points of view*, which he also refers to as *experiments*, thereby preventing his readers from forgetting that they, too, have points of view—from forgetting that they, too, conduct moral, philosophical, and spiritual *experiments*.

Nietzsche has seldom been treated as a philosopher at all. . . . His language would have been less colorful had he known what he was trying to say, but then he would not have been the original thinker he was, working through a set of problems which had hardly ever been charted before. Small wonder his maps are illustrated, so to speak, with all sorts of monsters and fearful indications and boastful cartographic embellishment.

ARTHUR C. DANTO

Nietzschean perspectivism
The contention that every view is only one among many possible interpretations, including, especially, Nietzschean perspectivism, which itself is just one interpretation among many interpretations.

anti-philosopher

A radical critic of the techniques and doctrines of modern science and philosophy. The anti-philosopher disputes the possibility of objectivity and universality and rejects the absolute authority of reason; anti-philosophers also reject the possibility of a *neutral stance* or *perspectiveless perspective*.

Thus, whatever positive position Nietzsche takes is also a negative position—experimentally, from one point of view. In "Attempt at a Self-Criticism," Nietzsche refers to what he labels a deep *antimoral propensity* in his writing. As we will see later, this does not mean that Nietzsche himself has no moral code whatsoever; it means that Nietzsche's value system is anti-moral *from the perspective* of conventional (Christian) morality. Similarly, from the standpoint of most modern philosophy, Nietzsche can be considered an *anti-philosopher*.

An **anti-philosopher** is a radical critic of certain techniques and foundational doctrines of modern science and philosophy who disputes the possibility of objectivity and universality and who rejects the absolute authority of reason. In other words, the anti-philosopher rejects the possibility of a *neutral stance* or *perspectiveless perspective*.

PHILOSOPHICAL

QUERY

• • • • • •

Do you think that the presence of a perspective makes a neutral stance impossible? What do you think neutral *means in this kind of case? Does it mean* perspective-less*? If it means something else, what else? Are perspectives the same things as biases? Discuss and explain.*

■ ATTACK ON OBJECTIVITY ■

Schopenhauer, though a pessimist . . . played the flute. Every day, after dinner: one should read his biography on that. And incidentally: a pessimist, one who denies God and the world but comes to a stop before morality—who affirms morality and plays the flute—what? is that really—a pessimist?

FRIEDRICH NIETZSCHE

What criteria for truth can Nietzsche, as an anti-philosopher, offer in place of objectivity and universality, and what standard of interpretation can he offer *in lieu* of rationality? Instead of recognizable philosophical *arguments*, Nietzsche offers a twofold *appeal*. The first component of this appeal, directed at our aesthetic sensibilities (taste), calls on us to "justify life as an aesthetic phenomenon." The second component of Nietzsche's anti-philosophical appeal rests on what he calls the *will to power*. Neither component *depends* on reason or scientific inquiry for justification.

In "On Truth and Lie in an Extra-Moral Sense," Nietzsche says that knowledge itself is an invention, and he goes so far as to doubt even our capacity for self-knowledge:

What, indeed, does man know of himself! Can he even perceive himself completely . . . ? Does not nature keep much the most from him, even about his body, to spellbind and confine him in a proud, deceptive consciousness, far from the coils of his intestines, the quick current of his bloodstream? . . .

In view of this, whence the urge for truth?[12]

The clear implication is that if nature keeps "much the most" from us concerning our very own selves, we have no chance of *discovering* the objective truth about anything. We can only *invent truths* according to our individual needs. Truths are aesthetic creations that serve the will to power. Truth is

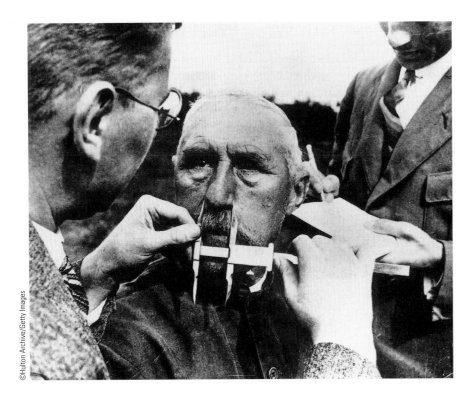

This picture depicts a Nazi-supported "scientific" system of race determination applied to a German man. Considering some of the horrific uses of "rationality" and "technology" during the past century, is optimism justified? Is the notion of "progress" intelligible on any broad scale? Yet, what better alternative is there to scientific rationality? (Is this issue framed fairly?)

The twentieth century is the age of Nietzsche, as he predicted it would be: the age of dictators unmoved by any moral tradition, of wars made more deadly and devastating by the progress of science; the age of the "death of God" for those who lead the parade in thought and power.

WILL AND ARIEL DURANT

seen as a function of the *physiology* and *pathology* of the individual, not some absolute, unchanging—objective—fact of nature or proposition derived from reason.

In Chapter 14, we saw how Enlightenment faith in reason and science produced Kierkegaard's sharp existential counterreaction. Among the nineteenth-century criticisms raised against faith in "scientific" rationality and objectivity (*scientism*), Nietzsche's cultural critique stands out for its intensity and scope. (See Chapter 15 for the pragmatic reaction to modern philosophy.)

Nietzsche's assault on objectivity includes rejecting the Cartesian notion of a unitary, fixed, rational self. Adopting a view similar to Hume's, Nietzsche insisted that the idea of a self that persists throughout a person's lifetime is a *fiction* or *metaphor*, not a fact. Metaphysicians, Christians, and scientists, Nietzsche said, are all prone to the same error: They believe that terms such as "substance," "God," and "gravity" refer to things as they objectively exist; consequently, they fail to grasp their metaphorical or fictive nature.

Moreover, according to Nietzsche, a *single hidden agenda* lurks behind science, philosophy, and religion: Scientists, philosophers, and "true believers" of all types seek power over the world, over other people, even over themselves. This natural impulse to dominate and control is often disguised as *influencing, controlling, managing, understanding,* or *improving* life, nature, the environment, society, and human behavior. Whatever we call them, Nietzsche insists, these desires are manifestations of the *will to power*.

Both Nietzsche and Socrates are intensely personal thinkers, actively engaged in changing, in one way or another, the moral quality of the life of the people around them, though they pursue their goals in radically different ways. . . . Both desperately need their audience's attention.

ALEXANDER NEHAMAS

©Hulton Archive/Getty Images

▦ THE WILL TO POWER ▦

Call it what we wish—objectivity, truth, or wisdom—Nietzsche says the single goal of science, religion, and philosophy is the exertion of power. Thus, it is "*mendacious*" for scientists (or priests or philosophers) to think of themselves as disinterested, detached, rational spectators capable of neutral, objective judgment. Nietzsche equates the will to *truth* with the will to *power* and asserts that power is the basis of the distinction between good and evil:

> What urges you on and arouses your ardour, you wisest of men, do you call it "will to truth"? . . .
>
> [I]t is a will to power; and that is so even when you talk of good and evil and of the assessment of values. . . .
>
> Where I found a living creature, there I found will to power; and even in the will of the servant I found the will to be master. . . .
>
> And life itself told me this secret: "Behold," it said, "I am that *which must overcome itself again and again.*"[13]

The positive force of Nietzsche's concept is captured in contemporary philosopher Philip Novack's characterization of the will to power:

> What, then, is the will to power? It is life's intrinsic and inexorable ache for *more.* Living processes incessantly seek the enjoyment of their own sensorium, the unblocked expression of their vitality, the radiance of their health, the overcoming of resistances, and the amplification of their self-feeling. Life in each and every one of its infinite manifestations carries within it a will to fulfillment, a will to expansion, a will to deeper, fuller being. . . . The will to power, Nietzsche tells us, includes but exceeds the will to self-preservation. For it seeks not only the continuance of life, but *more* life, an *intensification* of life.[14]

From a Nietzschean point of view, modernity—with its mass movements, reliance on technology, science, educated *reasonableness,* and Christianized emphasis on altruism—devolves away from the *intensification* of life toward the mere extension and preservation of it.

▦ THE DISEASES OF MODERNITY ▦

In contrast to the seemingly intelligible, manageable, tamable world of the scientist and modern philosopher, and in contrast to the God-centered, created world of the theistic believer, Nietzsche offers another perspective:

> And do you know what "the world" is to me? Shall I show it to you in my mirror? This world: a monster of energy, without beginning, without end; a firm, iron magnitude of force that does not grow bigger or smaller, that does not expend itself but only transforms itself; as a whole, of unalterable size, a household without expenses or losses, but likewise without increase or income; enclosed by "nothingness" as by a boundary; not something blurry or wasted,

The means employed by the lust for power have changed, but the same volcano continues to glow, the impatience and the immoderate love demand their sacrifice: and what one formerly did "for the sake of God" one now does for the sake of money, that is to say of that which now *gives the highest feeling of power and good conscience.*

FRIEDRICH NIETZSCHE

The highest and strongest drives, when they break out passionately and drive the individual far above the average and the flats of the herd conscience, wreck the self-confidence of the community, its faith in itself, and it is as if its spine snapped.

FRIEDRICH NIETZSCHE

not something endlessly extended, but set in a definite space as a definite force, and not a space that might be "empty" here or there, but rather as force throughout . . . .

[This is] my . . . world of the eternally self-creating, the eternally self-destroying, this mystery world of the twofold voluptuous delight, my "beyond good and evil," without goal, unless the joy of the circle is itself a goal; without will, unless a ring feels good-will toward itself—do you want a *name* for this world? A *solution* for all its riddles? . . . *This world is the will to power—and nothing besides!* And you yourselves are also this will to power—and nothing besides![15]

Nietzsche claimed that late-nineteenth-century European culture was dominated by a superficially optimistic belief that scientific progress and Christian morality could subdue the will to power and thereby make life safe and meaningful for the masses. But just under the surface, Nietzsche said, lay a fatal, festering cultural sickness: modernity.

The cultural sickness that Nietzsche describes rests on unabashed, unwarranted faith: in science, in philosophy, and in Christianity. Each of these "decaying" belief systems is, Nietzsche asserts, hostile to the will to power, the will to exalt ourselves, the will to *live*. Science, for instance, reduces us to inevitable helpless effects, limited by the myth of objective reality, to whatever causal accounts of our world, our origins, and our selves science deigns to pronounce. Prolonged dominance of scientism results in self-contempt.

High and independent spirituality, the will to stand alone, even a powerful reason are experienced as dangers; everything that elevates an individual above the herd and intimidates the neighbor is henceforth called evil; and the fair, modest, submissive, conforming mentality, the mediocrity of desires attains moral designations and honors.

FRIEDRICH NIETZSCHE

The Problem of Morality

In Nietzsche's view, the same desires that attract us to science's false promise of control and objectivity attract us to such products of modern philosophy as utilitarian and Kantian ethics. (See Chapters 12 and 11.) Like science, these modernist ethical schemes reduce the great passions of *living* to thin utilitarian calculations or pinched Kantian formulae. And just as the scientist is mendacious for failing to reveal her own will to power, so too is the modern moral philosopher mendacious for being blinded to the brute fact that his philosophizing is always philosophizing from a perspective, for a *purpose*:

With a stiff seriousness that inspires laughter, all our philosophers demanded something . . . exalted, presumptuous, and solemn from themselves as soon as they approached the study of morality: they wanted to supply a *rational foundation* for morality—and every philosopher so far has believed that he has provided such a foundation. Morality itself, however, was accepted as "given." How remote from their clumsy pride was that task which they considered insignificant and left in dust and must—the task of description—although the subtlest fingers and senses can scarcely be subtle enough for it.

Just because our moral philosophers knew the facts of morality only very approximately in arbitrary extracts or in accidental epitomes—for example, as the morality of *their* environment, *their* class, *their* church, the spirit of *their* time, *their* climate and part of the world—just because they were poorly informed

One knows my demand of philosophers that they place themselves beyond good and evil . . . that they have the illusion of moral judgement beneath them.

FRIEDRICH NIETZSCHE

There are no evil thoughts except one: the refusal to think.

AYN RAND

and not even very curious about different peoples, times, and past ages—they never laid eyes on the real problems of morality; for these emerge only when we compare *many* moralities. In all "science of morals" so far one thing was *lacking,* strange as it may sound: the problem of morality itself; what was lacking was any suspicion that there was something problematic here. What the philosophers called "a rational foundation for morality" and tried to supply was, seen in the right light, merely a scholarly variation of the common *faith* in the prevalent morality; a new means of *expression* for this faith; and thus just another fact within a particular morality; indeed, in the last analysis a kind of denial that this morality might ever be considered problematic—certainly the very opposite of an examination, analysis, questioning, and vivisection of this very faith.[16]

Of every morality, Nietzsche says, "one can still always ask: what does such a claim tell us about the man who makes it? . . . In short, moralities are also merely a *sign language of the affects.*"[17] Far from expressing objective or universal truths, or even scientific facts, moral codes reflect the desires and perspectives of those who create them.

Nietzsche accuses modern Western culture of being *moralistic.* To be **moralistic** is to express commonplace moral sentiments that conflict with one's behavior and to equate moral sentimentality with virtuous living. Being moralistic is a form of hypocrisy that resembles what Freudian psychologists refer to as a *reaction formation.* **Reaction formation** is the name of the ego defense mechanism that attempts to prevent "dangerous" desires from being exposed and expressed by endorsing opposite attitudes and types of behavior as "barriers" against them. In the following passage, Nietzsche goes so far as to say that *the most distinctive feature of modern souls and modern books is moralistic mendaciousness:*

> For if a psychologist today has *good taste* (others might say, integrity) it consists in resistance to the shamefully *moralized* way of speaking which has gradually made all modern judgments of men and things slimy. One should not deceive oneself in this manner: the most distinctive feature of modern souls and modern books is not lying but their inveterate *innocence* in moralistic mendaciousness. To have to rediscover this "innocence" everywhere—this constitutes perhaps the most disgusting job among all the precarious tasks a psychologist has to tackle today.[18]

From the perspective of modern Christian morality—and for Nietzsche, all modern morality has a Christian basis—Nietzsche is an anti-moralist, or to use his more provocative term, he is "the first immoralist."[19]

In Nietzsche's view, modernity is anti-life and anti-nature, and modern, Christianized, moralities are symptoms of this *décadence,* this decay. In the following passage, Nietzsche ascribes the "error of modernity" to all of humankind (with an oblique reference to Kantianism):

> It is *not* error as error which horrifies me . . . it is the lack of nature, it is the utterly ghastly fact that *antinature* itself has received the highest honours as morality, and has hung over mankind as law, as categorical imperative! . . . To blunder to this extent, *not* as an individual, *not* as a people, but as mankind![20]

Insofar as we believe in morality we pass sentence on existence.

FRIEDRICH NIETZSCHE

moralistic
Being moralistic consists of expressing commonplace moral sentiments that conflict with one's behavior and equating moral sentimentality with virtuous living; a form of hypocrisy that resembles a reaction formation.

reaction formation
Freudian ego defense mechanism that attempts to prevent "dangerous" desires from being exposed and expressed by endorsing opposite attitudes and types of behavior as "barriers" against them.

The Problem of Generalized Accounts

At first glance, utilitarian ethics would seem to avoid the Nietzschean charge of being *anti-life*. After all, as we learned in Chapter 12, utilitarians accept an egoistic basis for their philosophy; Jeremy Bentham even hangs the principle of utility on an *egoistic hook*. But according to Nietzsche, the great Mill notwithstanding, the utilitarians sublimate the individual to the *group* (which Nietzsche sometimes refers to as the *herd*). They also manifest unwarranted faith in reason and, in Mill's case, preach altruism.

Further, according to Nietzsche, the mendacious belief that bad actions stem from curable ignorance—not evil—is as old as Socrates. In *Beyond Good and Evil*, Nietzsche links this optimistic faith in the capacity of reason to produce good behavior with utilitarian faith in science as the vehicle of social reform. He is particularly harsh toward the modern notion that through proper education and the application of scientific empiricism, society can be reformed. In the following passage, Nietzsche's contempt for this perspective is clear:

> "Nobody wants to do harm to himself, therefore all that is bad is done involuntarily. For the bad do harm to themselves: this they would not do if they knew that the bad is bad. Hence the bad are bad only because of an error; if one removes the error, one necessarily makes them—good."
>
> This type of inference smells of the *rabble* that sees nothing in bad actions but the unpleasant consequences and really judges, "it is *stupid* to do what is bad," while "good" is taken without further ado to be identical with "useful and agreeable." In the case of every moral utilitarianism one may immediately infer the same origin and follow one's nose: one will rarely go astray.[21]

For Nietzsche, the equation of "bad" with "stupid" and "ignorant" is both a result of and a contributor toward the modern decline of culture, the reduction of the threatening—but vital—passions to mere "errors." And, of course, errors are correctable. But, Nietzsche says, what modern society sees as progress—gained by adopting a "scientific" attitude toward badness—is in fact a loss of grandeur. The ideal modern citizen is tame, democratic, sheeplike, and compassionate. This view, however, is merely one *fashion in morality*:

> *Fashions in morality.*—How the overall moral judgements have shifted! The great men of antique morality, Epictetus for instance, knew nothing of the now normal glorification of thinking of others, of living for others; in the light of our moral fashion they would have to be called downright immoral, for they strove with all their might *for* their *ego* and *against* feeling with others (that is to say, with the sufferings and moral frailties of others). Perhaps they would reply to us: "If you are so boring or ugly an object to yourself, by all means think of others more than yourself! It is right you should!"[22]

Nietzsche's critique of culture centers on his deep and abiding suspicion of all attempts to generalize or universalize a code for living. Nietzsche insisted that science, modern philosophy, and all transcendental schemes turn away from life itself, from vitality, joy, depth, and moral health to the degree that they speak of

Among helpful and charitable people one almost regularly encounters that clumsy ruse which first doctors the person to be helped—as if, for example, he "deserved" help, required just their help, and would prove to be profoundly grateful for all help, faithful and submissive. With these fancies they dispose of the needy as of possessions. . . . One finds them jealous if one crosses or anticipates them when they want to help.

FRIEDRICH NIETZSCHE

If we have our own why of life, we shall get along with almost any how.

FRIEDRICH NIETZSCHE

In the last analysis, "love of the neighbor" is always something secondary, partly conventional and arbitrary-illusory in relation to fear of the neighbor.

FRIEDRICH NIETZSCHE

How much or how little is dangerous to the community, dangerous to equality, in an opinion, in a state or affect, in a will, in a talent—that now constitutes the moral perspective: here, too, fear is again the mother of morals.

FRIEDRICH NIETZSCHE

and to *all.* They sow cultural and spiritual disease *because they generalize where one must not generalize:*

> All these moralities that address themselves to the individual, for the sake of his "happiness," as one says—what are they but counsels for behavior in relation to the degree of *dangerousness* in which the individual lives with himself; recipes against his passions, his good and bad inclinations insofar as they have the will to power and want to play the master . . . they generalize where one must not generalize. All of them speak unconditionally, take themselves for unconditional, all of them flavored with more than one grain of salt. . . . All of it is, measured intellectually, worth very little and not by a long shot "science" much less "wisdom," but rather, to say it once more, three times more, prudence, prudence, prudence, mixed with stupidity, stupidity, stupidity. . . . "Morality as Timidity."[23]

So intense is modernity's assault on individual expressions of the will to power that Western society produces individuals who "side with" those who harm them. (We "forgive," we "understand," we "tolerate" and "empathize with" our abusers and enemies.)

> There is a point in the history of society when it becomes so pathologically soft and tender that among other things it sides even with those who harm it, criminals, and does this quite seriously and honestly. Punishing somehow seems unfair to it, and it is certain that imagining "punishment" and "being supposed to punish" hurts it, arouses fear in it. "Is it not enough to render him *undangerous?* Why still punish? Punishing itself is terrible." With this question, herd morality, the morality of timidity, draws its ultimate consequence. Supposing that one could altogether abolish danger, the reason for fear, this morality would be abolished, too, *eo ipso:* it would no longer be needed, it would no longer *consider itself* necessary.
>
> Whoever examines the conscience of the [citizen] today will have to pull the same imperative out of a thousand moral folds and hideouts—the imperative of herd timidity: "we want that some day there should be *nothing any more to be afraid of!*" Some day . . . is now called "progress."[24]

In Nietzsche's view, all of modernity's efforts to make scientific and moral *progress* are pointing toward a great cultural shift that heralds the next level of evolution, the end of human history and the beginning of the age of the overman. Like it or not, Nietzsche says, science and philosophy do not provide us with meaning; we create it. And like it or not, religion does not provide us with salvation: God is dead.

■ GOD IS DEAD ■

Nietzsche claimed he was the first to have "discovered" the death of God. In part, he meant that the *idea of God* has lost its full creative force, its full power. The full extent of the dethronement of God is not yet felt by the great masses, who still *believe that they believe in God.* Yet if we dig deep into our own psyches, Nietzsche prophesied, we will discover that we no longer have ultimate faith in God: Our true faith is in scientific and technological progress.

For me, then, nobility is synonymous with a life of effort, ever set on excelling oneself, in passing beyond what one is [at a given moment] to what one sets up as a duty and an obligation. In this way the noble life stands opposed to the common or inert life, which reclines statically upon itself, condemned to perpetual immobility, unless external force compels it to come out of itself.

JOSÉ ORTEGA Y GASSET

What I then got hold of, something frightful and dangerous, . . . was the problem of science itself, science considered for the first time as problematic, as questionable.

FRIEDRICH NIETZSCHE

Moreover, Nietzsche thought there is no turning back; authentic faith in God is not possible in the modern world. God is dead and we have killed him, with "progress," with "optimism," with faith in this world. Yet so deeply ingrained is the language of God, the idea of God, that we are unaware of the great spiritual shift. The news of God's death has not reached us—that is, it has not penetrated to our very bones. We worship, but falsely. Our faith is empty at bottom. And even though some of us may sense that the old religions are dead and dying, we remain unable to face the consequences of life without God.

And terrible those consequences can be. If there is no God, Nietzsche said, then all values must be revalued. In one of the most famous passages in Western philosophy, Nietzsche, the prophet of the death of God, delivered his message in the form of a parable:

> *The madman.*—Have you not heard of the madman who lit a lantern in the bright morning hours, ran to the market place, and cried incessantly: "I seek God! I seek God!"—As many of those who did not believe in God were standing around just then, he provoked much laughter. Has he got lost? asked one. Did he lose his way like a child? asked another. Or is he hiding? Is he afraid of us? Has he gone on a voyage? emigrated?—Thus they yelled and laughed.
>
> The madman jumped into their midst and pierced them with his eyes. "Whither is God?" he cried; "I will tell you. *We have killed him*—you and I. All of us are his murderers. But how did we do this? How could we drink up the sea? Who gave us the sponge to wipe away the entire horizon? What were we doing when we unchained the earth from its sun? Whither is it moving now? Whither are we moving? Away from all suns? Are we not plunging continually? Backward, sideward, forward, in all directions? Is there still any up or down? Are we not straying as through an infinite nothing? Do we not feel the breath of empty space? Has it not become colder? Is not night continually closing in on us? Do we not need to light lanterns in the morning? Do we hear nothing as yet of the noise of the gravediggers who are burying God? Do we smell nothing yet of the divine decomposition? Gods, too, decompose. God is dead. God remains dead. And we have killed him."[25]

This parable is best understood in light of Nietzsche's overall cultural critique, in which he predicted the decline of Christianity. That is, he saw the world as no longer innocent. Copernicus and Galileo had forever changed our sense of scale: The earth is a tiny, virtually invisible speck in a massive, purposeless universe. "What were we doing when we unchained the earth from its sun?" This new universe has no fixed center: "Is there still any up or down? Are we not straying as through an infinite nothing?" Darwin had forever altered our sense of ourselves as God's special creation. The new image of *merely human* beings is ignoble: We are but one species among millions struggling to survive, descendants of some primordial ooze.

What the masses think of as progress has come at a great price: the price of a way of life, the price of our vision of ourselves. It is difficult to comprehend the enormous scale of this change, this death of a worldview, Nietzsche insisted. Indeed, some of us may lack the intelligence, the courage, and the will to comprehend it.

"Faith" means not wanting to know.

FRIEDRICH NIETZSCHE

Almost two thousand years, and no new god!

FRIEDRICH NIETZSCHE

Those who claim to be hurt by words must be led to expect nothing as compensation. Otherwise, once they learn they can get something by claiming to be hurt, they will go into the business of being offended.

JONATHAN RAUCH

Nihilism as the wave of the future: The Nazis claimed Nietzsche as one of their philosophical fathers, distributing copies of *Thus Spake Zarathustra* to the Hitler Youth and placing a special copy in the Tannenberg Memorial. Although their doctrine of power and the master race often echoes Nietzschean language, no mass movement could ever reflect Nietzsche's philosophy of self-overcoming. How many overmen can you spot in this crowd?

©Associated Press

How shall we comfort ourselves, the murderers of all murderers? What was holiest and mightiest of all that the world has yet owned has bled to death under our knives: who will wipe this blood off us? What water is there for us to clean ourselves? What festivals of atonement, what sacred games shall we have to invent? Is not the greatness of this deed too great for us? Must we not ourselves become gods simply to appear worthy of it? There has never been a greater deed; and whoever is born after us—for the sake of this deed he will belong to a higher history than all history hitherto.[26]

nihilism

From Latin for "nothing"; belief that the universe lacks meaning and purpose.

According to Nietzsche, the death of God leads to nihilism. From the Latin word for "nothing," **nihilism** refers to the belief that the universe lacks objective meaning and purpose. Consequently, moral, social, and political values are *creative interpretations;* they reflect their subjective origins. Without God, there can be no objective base for values.

Nietzsche predicted that nihilism would be the wave of the future (our present). He predicted that as more and more people perceive religious values to be empty and science as having no meaning or purpose to offer us, a sense of emptiness would initially prevail: It all amounts to nothing. Life is a cosmic accident. There is no supernatural order; no divinely or rationally ordained goal. Without God, without *the* goal, what is left? Only many goals; only *this* momentary goal. Without God, we can turn only to ourselves.

In a nihilistic universe, what determines what counts? What determines which physique is beautiful? What determines whether it is better to be meek or arrogant? According to Nietzsche, the answers are always found in the particular,

subjective interests of individuals and groups. We *choose* value systems and philosophies based on our sense of power: Which interpretation gives me and my kind advantage over others?

▓ OVERMAN ▓

The death of God signals both a great calamity and a great opportunity—depending on the individual's perspective. It is a calamity to those inferior types who cannot bear to stand on their own. It is a glorious opportunity for the fearless, the brave, the overman.

The **overman** is a new "higher type" that will emerge out of the weakness and hypocrisies of the common herd. He is more than a *merely human* being. Zarathustra says the overman cannot emerge except through struggle and by abolishing the false idols of conventional morality and decadent religion.

> But my fervent will to create impels me ever again toward man; thus is the hammer impelled toward the stone, O men, in the stone there sleeps an image, the image of my images. Alas, that it must sleep in the hardest, the ugliest stone! Now my hammer rages cruelly against its prison. Pieces of rock rain from the stone; what is that to me? I want to perfect it; for a shadow came to me—the stillest and lightest of all things once came to me. The beauty of the overman came to me as a shadow. O my brothers, what are the gods to me now?
>
> Thus spoke Zarathustra.[27]

Without God to limit us, to define us, to smother us, we can finally grow "beyond man." In Nietzsche's philosophy, "man," meaning the *merely human* being, is defined in terms of God. We are created in "the image of God" and remain perpetual "children of God." When God dies, we are left without identity or purpose, in a vast universe that "just is." The same science that has given us so much has robbed us of purpose. The deeper science looks, the less it finds: molecules, atoms, electrons, quarks, energy . . . the abyss.

Nietzsche, the prophet of the next stage in human evolution, predicts that the next order is virtually a new species in terms of its psychological and spiritual differences from mere man. Having no permanent, absolute, universal identity without God, we must create identity. The overman is Nietzsche's answer to the pessimism and nihilism that follow in the wake of God's death:

> The greatest recent event—that "God is dead," that the belief in the Christian god has become unbelievable—is already beginning to cast its first shadows. . . . The event itself is far too great, too distant, too remote for the multitude's capacity for comprehension even for the tidings of it to be thought of as having *arrived* as yet. Much less may one suppose that many people know as yet *what* this event really means—and how much must collapse now that [the possibility of] faith has been undermined because it was built upon this faith [in God's existence], propped up by it, grown into it; for example, the whole of our . . . morality.[28]

overman
Nietzsche's "higher type," a more-than-human being that will emerge only by overcoming the false idols of conventional morality and religion; announced in *Thus Spake Zarathustra*.

I wonder how far Moses would have got if he'd taken a poll in Egypt? What would Jesus Christ have preached if he'd taken a poll in Israel?

HARRY S. TRUMAN

If society consisted of highly valuable individuals, it would be worthwhile to adapt to it, but generally it is dominated by weak and stupid people and thus suffocates all higher individual values.

MARIE-LOUISE VON FRANZ

Nietzsche never fully developed a picture of the overman. Of course, given that the overman is farther from mere man than we are from an ape, no *merely human* being can comprehend the overman. Nietzsche readily admitted that he is only the prophet of the higher type, adding, "But from time to time I may be granted a glance—only one glance—at something perfect, something that has attained its end, something happy, powerful, triumphant."[29]

▦ SLAVE MORALITY ▦

Though we may never fully grasp exactly what or who the overman is, we can perhaps glimpse its shadow indirectly by taking a look at the actions and beliefs of what amounts to its opposite: the slave or underman.

Underman, from the German *untermensch,* is one of the terms Nietzsche uses for the "merely human" type of person who cannot face being alone in a godless universe. Underman refuses to be an individual, does not even exist as an individual. Underman turns to the group or herd (Kierkegaard's "the crowd") for power, identity, and purpose. The inferior individual's awareness of his or her own inferiority produces envy and resentment of all "higher types" and elitist value systems.

In an effort to control their superiors, members of the herd create **slave morality**, a value system based on guilt, fear, and a distortion of the will to power in which the characteristics of the inferior type—humility, passivity, dependency—are praised as virtues, while the characteristics of the superior type—love of domination, delight in one's own talents, fearlessness—are condemned as arrogance and coldheartedness. Slave morality creates inhibitions, false ideals of equality, restrictive duties "owed" to our inferiors, and weakening of strong instincts by "bad conscience." The herd is always hostile to the individual.

In other words, slave morality tries to convince the powerful that they should protect the weak. According to Nietzsche, slave morality arose when rules conquered instincts in ancient Greece. Today, rationalistic Greek and Christian ethics are the two chief sources of slave morality in modern Western culture. Fairness, equality, moderation, "stepping aside," refusing to claim the full rights accompanying superior ability and talent, and resentment are all characteristics of slave morality.

History up to the present is a record of the withering away of a noble *master morality,* as century by century the virtues of the herd weakened Western culture. Today we even resist talking about higher types. We claim that all people are fundamentally equal. Zarathustra speaks:

> You higher men learn this from me: in the market place nobody believes in higher men. And if you want to speak there, very well! But the mob blinks: "We are all equal."
>
> "You higher men"—thus blinks the mob—"there are no higher men, we are all equal, man is man; before God we are all equal."
>
> Before God! But now this God has died. And before the mob we do not want to be equal. You higher men, go away from the market place![30]

---

underman

Nietzsche's term for the type of person who cannot face being alone in a godless universe, an inferior individual seeking safety and identity in a group or from another; characterized by resentment and hypocrisy.

slave morality

In Nietzschean philosophy, a distortion of the will to power in which the characteristics of the inferior type (underman) are praised as virtues, and the characteristics of the superior type (overman) are condemned as arrogance and coldheartedness; a morality of inhibitions, equality, restrictive duties, and "bad conscience."

An Iconoclast Looks at Education

I have never tired of calling attention to the *despiritualizing* influence of our current science-industry. The hard [servitude] to which the tremendous range of the sciences condemns every scholar today is a main reason why those with a fuller, richer, *profounder* disposition no longer find a congenial education and congenial *educators*. There is nothing of which our culture suffers more than of the superabundance of pretentious jobbers and fragments of humanity; our universities are, *against* their will, the real hothouses for this kind of withering of the instincts of the spirit. And the whole of Europe already has some idea of this—power politics deceives nobody. . . .

To call the taming of an animal its "improvement" sounds almost like a joke to our ears. Whoever knows what goes on in menageries doubts that the beasts are "improved" there. They are weakened, they are made less harmful, and through the depressive effect of fear, through pain, through wounds, and through hunger they become sickly beasts. . . .

. . . No one is any longer free to give his children a noble education: our "higher schools" are all set up for the most ambiguous mediocrity, with their teachers, curricula, and teaching aims. And everywhere an indecent haste prevails, as if something would be lost if the young man of twenty-three were not yet "finished," or if he did not yet know the answer to the "main question": *which* calling? A higher kind of human being, if I may say so, does not like "callings," precisely because he knows himself to be called. He has time, he takes time, he does not even think of "finishing": at thirty one is, in the sense of high culture, a beginner, a child. Our overcrowded secondary schools, our overworked, stupefied secondary-school teachers, are a scandal: for one to defend such conditions . . . there may perhaps be causes—reasons there are none.

Friedrich Nietzsche, *Twilight of the Idols*, in *The Portable Nietzsche*, trans. Walter Kaufmann (New York: Penguin, 1968), pp. 502, 508, 510–511.

. . . . . .

Do you think today's "marketplace" mentality discourages excellence in individuals? Using specific examples, discuss why or why not.

PHILOSOPHICAL

QUERY

Ressentiment

Slave morality originates from a deep form of psychically polluting resentment that Nietzsche always referred to with the French word **ressentiment**. In the following passage from *Toward a Genealogy of Morals,* Nietzsche distinguishes between the slave morality of the underman and the master morality of the overman:

> The slaves' revolt in morals begins with this, that *ressentiment* itself becomes creative and gives birth to values: the *ressentiment* of those who are denied the real reaction, that of the deed, and who compensate with an imaginary revenge. Whereas all noble morality begins out of a triumphant affirmation of oneself, slave morality immediately says No to what comes from outside, to what is different, to what is not oneself: and *this* No is its creative deed. This reversal of the value-positing glance—this *necessary* direction outward instead

ressentiment
French for "resentment"; term used in Nietzschean philosophy for a deep form of psychically polluting resentment that generates slave morality; the dominant emotion of the underman.

of back to oneself—is of the nature of *ressentiment:* to come into being, slave morality requires an outside world, a counterworld; physiologically speaking, it requires external stimuli in order to react at all: its action is always at bottom a reaction.[31]

In other words, slave morality is alien to true individuality. Slave morality is so opposed to the authentic individual that his or her own self-creating urges and impulses are stifled in favor of "external stimuli" that function as guide-lines from others and from the herd. Slave morality is inauthentic (phony and uncreative) because it is "always a reaction," never an originating impulse. (See Chapter 14 for more on authenticity.) Slave morality settles for the "imaginary revenge" of the afterlife: "God will punish the bad people since we are too weak to do so."

The underman fears "the other" whether in the form of the authentic indi-vidual or in the merely different. Thus, slave morality encourages conformity; national, ethnic, gender, and religious bigotry; and unthinking patriotism: "Slave morality immediately says No to what comes from outside, to what is different, to what is not oneself." The underman lacks the godlike confidence necessary for "the value-positing glance," the ability to impose one's own values without refer-ence to "external stimuli" for guidance and security.

From a healthy aesthetic perspective, underman is repulsive, characterized by weakness, evasion, hypocrisy, and grudge. Slave morality is a morality of resigna-tion, deferment, withdrawal from the full range of life, and prohibition. In reality, the underman does not reject the lusty, fateful, self-affirming, creative aspects of the human psyche because they are bad, but because the underman is too weak, sick, and corrupt to live up to them—and out of *ressentiment* wants to prevent others from living up to them as well.

The Greek philosophers went through life feeling secretly that there were far more slaves than one might think—meaning that everybody who was not a philosopher was a slave. Their pride overflowed at the thought that even the most powerful men on earth belong among their slaves.

FRIEDRICH NIETZSCHE

Great Man is always at ease; Petty Man is always on edge.

CONFUCIUS

PHILOSOPHICAL

QUERY

• • • • • •

As you might expect, Nietzsche's characterization of slave morality was and remains controversial. Do you think it is dangerous? Is it unfair to expect most people not to have some ressentiment? *Is today's tendency to see many people as "victims" a reflection of slave morality?*

To dream here perhaps of equal rights, equal training, equal claims and obligations: that is a typical sign of shallow-mindedness.

FRIEDRICH NIETZSCHE

▪ MASTER MORALITY ▪

If there are two fundamentally different types of people (underman and overman), then there must be two radically different types of morality. One universal standard cannot apply equally to the common herd and to the superior, perfected overman.

Although both types possess the *will to power,* they differ significantly in their approaches to power. For the overman, the will to power is expressed openly, honestly, and nobly through exuberant, life-affirming self-creation and self-imposition. That is, the overman creates—experiments with—a "new law tablet," a code of values that is the opposite of the weak underman's slave morality. Because the underman lacks courage and nobility, he or she must resort to appeals to a "father God," to neurotic guilt, and demands for pity (dressed up as an "obligation" to show compassion). In the herd, the will to individual power is perverted through manipulation, *ressentiment,* and indirection shaped by feelings of gross inadequacy—it is not expressed honestly and openly.

Master morality, in contrast to slave morality, is an *aesthetic-heroic* code of honor. That is, the overman looks only to himself or herself for value. And value is defined in aesthetic terms: noble–ignoble (shameful), glorious–degrading, honorable–dishonorable, refined–vulgar, and so on. In simple terms, for the overman, "good" equals "noble" and "evil" equals "vulgar."

According to Nietzsche:

> To be unable to take one's own enemies, accidents, and misdeeds seriously for long—that is the sign of strong and rich natures. . . . Such a man simply shakes off with one shrug much vermin that would have buried itself deep in others; here alone is it also possible—assuming that is possible at all on earth—that there be real "*love* of one's enemies." How much respect has a noble person for his enemies! . . . Conversely, imagine "the enemy" as conceived by a man of *ressentiment*—and here precisely is his deed, his creation: he has conceived "the evil enemy," *"the evil one"*—and indeed as the fundamental concept from which he then derives, as an after-image and counterinstance, a "good one"— himself.[32]

Whereas the overman's morality begins with his affirmation of his own beloved self, the underman's morality begins with the invention of the "evil other," the *evil one.* For the overman, "bad" is the afterimage. For the underman, "good" is the afterimage. Thus, master morality is positive in its orientation; slave morality is negative.

If Nietzsche is correct, we live in the twilight of a culture. The "horizon is free" because no new value system and vision have replaced the old dying one. Those who live through the twilight of the old beliefs will experience confusion, fear, a strong desire to hold on to idols; but they will also experience unlimited opportunities for growth. In the twilight of our idols, we are handed the opportunity to fashion our own way. It is up to us to define—to actually create—our very selves.

Zarathustra says:

> "*I teach you the overman.* Man is something that shall be overcome. What have you done to overcome him?
>
> "All beings so far have created something beyond themselves; and do you want to be the ebb of this great flood and even go back to the beasts rather than overcome man? What is the ape to man? A laughingstock or a painful embarrassment. And man shall be just that for the overman: a laughingstock or a painful embarrassment. You have made your way from worm to man, and much in you is still worm. Once you were apes, and even now, too, man is more ape than any ape. . . .
>
> "Man is a rope, tied between beast and overman—a rope over an abyss. A dangerous across, a dangerous on-the-way, a dangerous looking-back, a dangerous shuddering and stopping. . . .

I see many people die because they judge that life is not worth living. I see others paradoxically getting killed for the ideas and illusions that give them a reason for living (what is called a reason for living is also an excellent reason for dying). I therefore conclude that the meaning of life is the most urgent of questions.

ALBERT CAMUS

Inasmuch as at all times, as long as there have been human beings, there have also been herds of men (clans, communities, tribes, peoples, states, churches) and always a great many people who obeyed, compared with the small number of those commanding . . . it may fairly be assumed that the need for [herding together] is now innate in the average man. . . .

FRIEDRICH NIETZSCHE

Although Adolf Hitler, with the help of Nietzsche's sister, Elisabeth Förster-Nietzsche, tried to take advantage of Nietzsche's growing reputation by claiming that the Nazi doctrine of "Aryan supremacy" had roots in Nietzschean philosophy, there is no evidence that Hitler ever read a word of Nietzsche's philosophy. In this publicity photo, Hitler gazes "admiringly" at a bust of Nietzsche.

Stiftung Weimarer Klassik und Kunstsammlungen GJA 101/239

"I love all those who are as heavy drops, falling one by one out of the dark cloud that hangs over men; they herald the advent of lightning, and, as heralds, they perish.

"Behold, I am the herald of the lightning and a heavy drop from the cloud; but this lightning is called *overman*."[33]

The very same conditions of nihilism and value annihilation that despirit, discourage, and frighten the underman exhilarate and inspire the overman. Having overcome merely human resentment and self-loathing, overman *looks forward to being precisely what and who he (or she) is.*

■ AMOR FATI ■

In the absence of God, Nietzsche says, we must redeem ourselves with the *sacred Yes to life* expressed through **amor fati**, the love of our specific fate expressed as joyous affirmation and delight that everything is exactly as and what it is. Nihilism teaches us that there is no divine purpose or design that gives meaning and quality to our lives. Science shows us that matter follows inexorable laws. God is dead. What is left?

amor fati
Nietzsche's term meaning "the love of fate"; expressed as joyous affirmation and delight that everything is exactly as and what it is.

[I]f you ever wanted one moment twice, if ever you said: "You please me, happiness, instant, moment!" then you wanted everything to return!

FRIEDRICH NIETZSCHE

What alone can *our* teaching be?—That no one *gives* a human being his qualities: not God, not society, not his parents or ancestors, not *he himself.* . . . *No one* is accountable for existing at all, or for being constituted as he is, or for living in the circumstances and surroundings in which he lives. The fatality of nature cannot be disentangled from the fatality of all that which has been and will be. He is *not* the result of special design, a will, a purpose . . . it is absurd to want to *hand over* his nature to some purpose or other. *We* invented the concept of "purpose": in reality purpose is *lacking.* . . . One is necessary, one is a piece of fate . . . there exists nothing which could judge, measure, compare, condemn the whole. . . . *nothing exists apart from the whole.* . . . We deny God; in denying God, we deny accountability: only by doing *that* do we redeem the world.[34]

Amor fati blesses everything exactly as it is. Through *amor fati,* we realize that we exist as parts of a complex whole that can be only precisely what it is and cannot be otherwise. *Amor fati* cures us of the corruption imposed by modernity and slave morality; it restores us to innocence by redeeming us from the ancient concepts of sin and guilt before others and before God. Nietzsche says:

> My formula for greatness in a human being is *amor fati:* that one wants nothing to be other than it is, not in the future, not in the past, not in all eternity. Not merely to endure that which happens of necessity, still less to dissemble it . . . but to *love* it.[35]

■ COMMENTARY ■

Nietzsche was nothing if not authentic. And as disturbing as much of his philosophy can be, there is no escaping its power to provoke a response—often a passionate response. His assertive denial of objective meaning has influenced a whole generation of scholars and literary critics (called *new critics* and *deconstructionists*). Nietzsche's influence on postmodern scholarship cannot be overestimated. Nietzschean influences on current critical theories are found in the rejection of the possibility of unbiased (objective) interpretation, the view that all scholarship is autobiography, and unapologetic self-reference on the part of academic authors.

In the postmodern world, a world without objective value, without God, without "the truth," all that is left seems to be "my truth"—or more precisely, "my truths." Ironically, however, when nihilistic self-promotion becomes the trend and when "being an individual" becomes a consciously contrived goal, Nietzschean originality and authenticity disappear. Being "a Nietzschean" is no more possible than following someone else's orders to be free! After all, it was Nietzsche himself who insisted that "Those who understand me, understand that I can have no disciples." There is bitter (but not unexpected) irony in the notion of being "a Nietzschean."

Nietzsche's critique of contemporary culture is subtle and profound. On the whole, our culture does seem to have lost faith in the very idea of a single true religion and a common, shared value system that asserts more than sweeping generalities. Education seems to have lost any central focus and seems increasingly reduced to training without purpose or to efforts by various groups (herds?) to enforce their individual points of view (today we call them agendas). Even the current national debate over school curricula has Nietzschean roots: If there is no objective meaning, then everything is a "point of view," an expression of "diversity." If everything is a point of view, why should I have to accept your point of view or you mine? If everything is a point of view, there is no true history, no true interpretation of literature, no clear hierarchy of values.

Though it is not currently *politically correct* to suggest that we are not all equal, that some of us are entitled to more than the rest, we do not appear to believe the doctrine of equality that we preach: Each new wave of immigrants ("the evil other") generates hostility, fear, and resentment (ethnic resentment, gender resentment, class resentment). We certainly seem to be a culture searching for something, some clear, unifying set of values.

He who is afraid to look back, alas, has already done so in his own heart.

GEORGE LINVILLE

To choose what is harmful to oneself, *to be* attracted *by "disinterested" motives almost always constitutes the formula for* décadence.

FRIEDRICH NIETZSCHE

I mistrust all systematizers and I avoid them. The will to a system is a lack of integrity.

FRIEDRICH NIETZSCHE

Effect of happiness.—*The first effect of happiness is the feeling of power: this wants to* express itself, *either to us ourselves, or to other men, or to ideas or imaginary beings. The most common modes of expression are: to bestow, to mock, to destroy—all three out of a common basic drive.*

FRIEDRICH NIETZSCHE

So it is, that for us, Nietzschean questions remain: Is God dead? If so, what next? If not, whence our widespread resentments, confusions, and fears? Are we all equal in any significant sense? If not, what then? Can we bear to ask these questions? Dare we not ask them?

I leave the last word to Nietzsche, a hopeful word, expressed in 1882 as a comment entitled "For the New Year," but which speaks to the psychological possibility of renewal and affirmation of life at any moment:

> Today everyone is permitted to express his desire and dearest thoughts: so I too would like to say what I have desired of myself today and what thought was the first to cross my heart this year—what thought shall be the basis and guarantee and sweetness of all my future life! I want to learn more and more to see what is necessary in things as the beautiful in them–thus I shall become one of those who make things beautiful. *Amor fati:* may that be my love from now on! I want to wage no war against the ugly. I do not want to accuse, I do not want even to accuse the accusers. May *looking away* be my only form of negation! And, all in all: I want to be at all times hereafter only an affirmer.[36]

I want no "believers"; I think I am too sarcastic to believe in myself.

FRIEDRICH NIETZSCHE

No victor believes in chance.

FRIEDRICH NIETZSCHE

■ SUMMARY OF MAIN POINTS ■

- Nietzsche saw himself as the first to recognize a profound sickness at the core of modernity. Modernity refers to the historical period of the nineteenth and twentieth centuries and a corresponding set of cultural conditions and beliefs dominated by Enlightenment ideals, including faith in science, objective truth, and rationality.

- Influenced by Schopenhauer's pessimism, Nietzsche concluded that life itself is an irrational, purposeless striving for a pointless existence. Nietzsche insisted that life is governed by the will to power, a universal desire to control others and impose our values on them. The will to power is also the basis of the distinction between good and evil.

- Nietzschean perspectivism, the contention that every view is only one among many possible interpretations, rejects the possibility of a neutral stance or perspectiveless perspective. According to Nietzsche, art or aesthetic vision (taste) is the basis of meaning, not science, not religion, not morality, not rationality.

- Nietzsche accuses modern Western culture of being moralistic, a form of hypocrisy that resembles what Freudian psychologists refer to as a reaction formation, the name of the ego defense mechanism that attempts to prevent dangerous desires from being exposed and expressed by endorsing opposite attitudes and types of behavior as barriers against them.

- Nietzsche claimed that he discovered the death of God: The idea of God has lost its full creative force, its full power, because science and technology have usurped God's place in people's lives. The death of God leads to nihilism, the belief that the universe lacks meaning and purpose, and that moral, social, and political values are creative interpretations because without God, there is no objective base for values.

- Slave morality is a distortion of the will to power in which the characteristics of the inferior type are praised as virtues, and the characteristics of the superior type are condemned as arrogance and cold-heartedness. Slave morality creates inhibitions, false ideals of equality, and "bad conscience."

- Master morality is an aesthetic-heroic code of honor. The overman looks only to himself or herself for value defined in aesthetic terms: noble–ignoble (shameful), glorious–degrading, honorable–dishonorable, refined–vulgar, and so on; "good" equals "noble" and "evil" equals "vulgar."

- Through *amor fati* (the love of fate), the overman approaches his life with delight that everything is and eternally will be exactly as and what it is.

■ POST-READING REFLECTIONS ■

Now that you have had a chance to learn about the Anti-Philosopher, use your new knowledge to answer these questions.

1. How did pessimism influence Nietzsche's philosophy?

2. What role does the will to power play in Nietzsche's philosophy?

3. What is tragic about tragic optimism? What is optimistic? Why did Nietzsche reject ordinary optimism?

4. How did Nietzsche's personal experiences affect his philosophy of overcoming? What is to be overcome? Overcome by what?

5. How does Nietzsche's perspectivism free him as a thinker? Why does it result in a kind of anti-philosophy?

6. What are the diseases of modernity, and what is their cumulative effect on the underman? On the overman? How is it that the same conditions can nurture two such distinct types?

7. Explain what is meant by characterizing master morality as an aesthetic-heroic honor code. Why did Nietzsche prefer an "aesthetic" code to a moral code?

8. Why does Nietzsche associate *ressentiment* with the underman? How does *ressentiment* lead to the development of slave morality?

9. What is the chief quality of the overman? In what sense is this quality a result of being beyond good and evil? What can we do to become overmen? Explain.

10. What does *amor fati* mean—literally, and to Nietzsche?

 ## PHILOSOPHY INTERNET RESOURCES

Go to the Soccio Web page at **http://philosophy.wadsworth.com/ Soccio7e** for Web links, practice quizzes and tests, a pronunciation guide, and study tips.

THE TWENTIETH CENTURY

Ludwig Wittgenstein and Martin Heidegger

WHEN WE DO PHILOSOPHY WE ARE LIKE SAVAGES, PRIMITIVE PEOPLE, WHO HEAR THE EXPRESSIONS OF CIVILIZED MEN, PUT A FALSE INTERPRETATION ON THEM, AND THEN DRAW THE QUEEREST CONCLUSIONS FROM IT.

Ludwig Wittgenstein

PERHAPS THE DISTINCTION OF THIS AGE CONSISTS IN THE FACT THAT THE DIMENSION OF GRACE HAS BEEN CLOSED. PERHAPS THIS IS ITS UNIQUE DIS-GRACE.

Martin Heidegger

FOR YOUR REFLECTION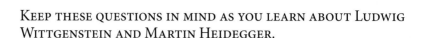

KEEP THESE QUESTIONS IN MIND AS YOU LEARN ABOUT LUDWIG
WITTGENSTEIN AND MARTIN HEIDEGGER.

1. *What is philosophical deconstruction?*
2. *What is analytic philosophy?*
3. *What is continental philosophy?*
4. *What is philosophical realism?*
5. *What makes a proposition meaningful?*
6. *What is phenomenology?*
7. *What is constructivism?*
8. *What is ontology?*
9. *What is the "they"?*
10. *What is "idle talk"?*
11. *What is the "standing-reserve"?*

FOR DEEPER CONSIDERATION

A. What is "the problem of skepticism"? How does Wittgenstein refute it? What
do you think of his refutation? Does it solve the problem? What role is left for
philosophy in Wittgenstein's refutation? Is there even a problem to be solved in
the first place? Make your case.

B. Assess Heidegger's assessment of technology. What does he mean by technology? How is that different from more common notions of technology? Most
importantly, why is Heidegger interested in technology at all? That is, what role
does he see technology playing in living authentically?

From the eighteenth century onward, philosophy has grown increasingly specialized, in part due to the influence of the university system; in part due to modern philosophers' emphasis on and development of a technical philosophical vocabulary; in part due to attempts to make philosophy systematic and precise; in part due to renewed interest in the history of philosophical arguments concerning being, reality, knowledge, truth, value, and reason.[1] By the twentieth century, diverse philosophers were struggling against or furthering what has been described as the "post-Nietzschean deconstruction of metaphysics."

As a proper noun, Deconstruction*ism* refers to the writings of Jacques Derrida (1930–2004) and to an approach to literary criticism that is not confined to philosophy. As a common noun, *deconstruction* refers to the treatment of philosophical problems as conceptual and linguistic confusions that reveal their ulterior purposes when complex claims and statements are reduced to their smallest meaningful components. That is the sense we are interested in here.

Generally understood, then, philosophical **deconstruction** includes any close textual analysis that focuses on uncovering and overcoming hitherto concealed "privileges" hidden in philosophical arguments, theories, and claims. Depending on the deconstructor, philosophical assertions that cannot be clarified are set aside or rejected as empty, meaningless, nonsensical, mystical, poetic, or inauthentic.

Philosophical "deconstructors" approach philosophy historically, not as historians per se, but as scrutinizers of the specific development and uses of particular philosophical notions and arguments as they pertain to actual, concrete, particular existence, to living in a specific here and now. Consequently, deconstructors challenge the notion that any text can have any definite meaning. Careful linguistic analysis is a common hallmark of otherwise divergent, even hostile, approaches to philosophical deconstruction.

In the loose sense of deconstruction, we can say that Hume deconstructed the self, causality, and ethics; Kant deconstructed Cartesian rationalism, dualism, and Humean skepticism; Bentham and Mill deconstructed the good; Marx deconstructed capitalism, philosophy, theology, and science; Kierkegaard deconstructed the crowd, objectivity, faith, truth, and existence.

Philosophical deconstruction has its most direct and influential expression in Nietzsche's critique of Western philosophy as just one more historically rooted expression of the will to power. "We are historians from top to bottom," Nietzsche said in *Human, All Too Human,* drawing a sharp line between anti-philosophers who deconstruct traditional philosophy and metaphysics and philosophers who "all to a man think unhistorically, as is the age-old custom with philosophers." To think unhistorically is to think objectively, universally, generally, and formally, rather than existentially and concretely.

> "Disinterested contemplation" . . . is a rank absurdity. . . . Let us, from now on, be on our guard against the hallowed philosophers' myth of a "pure, will-less, painless, timeless knower": let us beware of the tentacles of such contradictory notions as "pure reason," "absolute knowledge," "absolute intelligence."

deconstruction (philosophical)
A kind of close textual analysis focused on uncovering and overcoming "privileges" hidden in philosophic arguments and theories by taking a text apart—by de-constructing it; questions whether any text can have any definite meaning.

*For doubt can exist only
where a question exists,
a question only where
an answer exists, and
an answer only where
something can be said.*

LUDWIG WITTGENSTEIN

analytic philosophy

Influential nonliterary
approach to philosophy
that stresses logic,
testability, precision, and
clarity with antecedents
in an anglophile tradition
that includes John Locke,
David Hume, Bertrand
Russell, and Ludwig
Wittgenstein; contends that
close logical and linguistic
analyses are the only proper
methods for sorting out
philosophical confusions;
commonly contrasted with
continental philosophy.

**continental
philosophy**

Broad term referring to
philosophies associated
with European
philosophers such as
Kant, Hegel, Kierkegaard,
Marx, Nietzsche, Husserl,
and Heidegger, not a
school of philosophy
as such or single way
of doing philosophy;
includes phenomenology,
existentialism,
Deconstructionism;
commonly contrasted
with analytic philosophy.

All these concepts presuppose an eye such as no living creature can imagine, an eye required to have no direction, to abrogate its active and interpretative powers—precisely those powers that alone make seeing, *seeing something.* All seeing is essentially perspective, and so is all knowing.[2]

Against a vibrant but unstable backdrop of two world wars, fast-paced scientific advances, and changing social mores, twentieth-century philosophers questioned the very possibility of philosophy itself, asking a series of increasingly narrow and specialized questions about the future of metaphysics and the possibility of universal truth that prompted the pragmatist John Dewey (1859–1952) to declare that "despair of any integrated outlook and attitude is the chief intellectual characteristic of the twentieth century." The philosopher and novelist Iris Murdoch (1919–1999) said of twentieth-century philosophy that "There may be no deep structure," that is, no objective, independent, universal metaphysical reality "out there." Alasdair MacIntyre quipped, "Epitaph-writing has been added to the list of accredited philosophical activities."[3]

Twentieth-century philosophy is by far too diverse, too complex, too specialized, and too recent to know which—if any—among its many impressive philosophers will emerge as archetypal philosophers. As you might suspect, such divisive figures cannot be summarized without more risk than less controversial and complex philosophers can. We can minimize the risk of serious distortion, however, if our goals are modest, and they are. So here, to get a sense—and only a sense—of two influential trends in twentieth-century philosophy, are sketches of two (so far) major twentieth-century philosophers' struggles to find a unique role for philosophy in a complex, contentious, and invigorating cultural milieu. I hope they entice you to dig further—not just into their philosophies, but also into your own.

■ TWO APPROACHES TO PHILOSOPHY ■

Analytic philosophy emerged in England around 1912 when Ludwig Wittgenstein began to study philosophy with Bertrand Russell at Cambridge University. As generally understood, analytic philosophy refers to a nonliterary approach to philosophy that stresses logic, testability, precision, and clarity. Analytic philosophers do not belong to a single school of philosophy, but to a philosophical tradition that goes back to Locke and Hume.

Common to the analytic tradition is the notion that the universe consists of independent (atomic) entities, although individual philosophers disagree about whether these entities are material particles, sense data, impressions, "facts," or something else. Philosophy is restricted to analyzing complex statements and claims in order to reduce them to elemental, unanalyzable components. Logical and linguistic analyses are thought to be the only proper methods for sorting out philosophical confusions. The goal is to "do philosophy," not theology, sociology, or history.[4]

Twentieth-century philosophers often contrast analytic philosophy with what is broadly referred to as **continental philosophy**. Of course, a quick bit of linguistic analysis reveals a certain conceptual lack of symmetry: "Analytic" refers to a method, whereas "continental" refers to a locale. Be that as it may, there is, nonetheless, a useful contrast to be made. As it is currently used, the phrase "continental philosophy" came into vogue after World War II to acknowledge a growing divide between the English-speaking philosophical world and that of continental Europe, although continental philosophy as such began just before the death of Kant and includes Hegel, Schopenhauer, Kierkegaard, Marx, Nietzsche, and Martin Heidegger.[5]

Continental philosophers tend to explain things not by reducing them to simple entities but by understanding them in a broader, holistic context. Like analytic philosophy, twentieth-century continental philosophy is not a school of philosophy as such or a single way of doing philosophy, but a diverse, often inter-disciplinary approach to philosophy. Formalism, idealism, phenomenology, and existentialism are examples of continental approaches to philosophy.

■ LUDWIG WITTGENSTEIN ■

Ludwig Wittgenstein (1889–1951) has been described as a philosopher's philosopher and as a genius whose work and thinking are audacious, complicated, austere, obscure, and unsystematic. His admirers see him as a—if not the—major figure in twentieth-century philosophy. His detractors see him as a marginal, overrated character, a perplexing footnote in the history of analytic philosophy, which, these detractors insist, will itself turn out to be just a blip in the history of philosophy. Consequently, there is as yet no consensus concerning Wittgenstein's place in the history of philosophy.

And yet, in an era in which philosophers are largely unknown among the general public, Wittgenstein is famous *as a great philosopher* because, it has been suggested, he fits the general public's notions of a philosopher: eccentric, otherworldly, cryptic, and arrogant.[6]

The youngest of eight children, Ludwig Josef Wittgenstein was born on April 26, 1889, in Vienna to one of Europe's most cultured and influential families. The Wittgensteins were wealthy, artistic, brilliant, and talented.

Wittgenstein's gifts and interests were broad. As an adult, he taught himself to play the clarinet, whistled entire musical scores from memory, dabbled in architecture, taught grade school, considered becoming a monk, devoured pulp fiction, and spent hours in the front rows of the cinema watching the same movies again and again. As a child he is supposed to have made a working model of a sewing machine.

After being home-schooled in the arts, Wittgenstein was sent to a technical college in Berlin-Charlottenburg. Unhappy, he left without completing his studies and went to England. In 1908, he began studying aeronautical engineering at Manchester University but spent most of the two years he was officially registered there living on the continent. While working on a design for a propeller with jet nozzles on the tips, Wittgenstein became intrigued by the mathematics of his design. This led to a general interest in mathematics, which, in turn, led to an interest in the philosophy of pure mathematics.

When he returned to England, Wittgenstein met the logician and mathematician Gottlob Frege (1848–1925) and read Bertrand Russell's (1872–1970)

Ludwig Wittgenstein

Wittgenstein retreated to this mountain cabin when he wanted to get away from Cambridge.

©S. C. Shaffer/www.ludwigwittgenstein.org

All that which many *are babbling today, I have defined by remaining silent about it.*

LUDWIG WITTGENSTEIN

My German engineer, I think, is a fool. He thinks nothing empirical is knowable—I asked him to admit that there was not a rhinoceros in the room, but he wouldn't.

BERTRAND RUSSELL

The philosopher's treatment of a question is like the treatment of an illness.

LUDWIG WITTGENSTEIN

Principles of Mathematics. Intrigued by their new work in logic and philosophy, he took Frege's advice and in 1912 registered at Cambridge University in order to study with Russell.

From 1911 to 1913, Wittgenstein discussed the foundations of logic and philosophy with Russell and with important figures such as the philosopher G. E. Moore (1873–1958), the economist John Maynard Keynes (1883–1946), and the mathematician and philosopher Frank Ramsey (1903–1930). Retreating to Norway for months at a time, he would wrestle with philosophical and logical problems and work on solutions to them by himself.

In 1913, Wittgenstein returned to Austria. In 1914, at the start of World War I (1914–1918), he joined the Austrian army, which essentially put an end to his close relationship with Russell, who was a pacifist. In 1917, he was captured and spent the rest of the war in an Italian prison camp, where he wrote the notes and drafts of what was to become the influential *Tractatus Logico-Philosophicus,* his first book.

Although they were no longer close, Russell thought Wittgenstein's work buttressed his own, and so he helped Wittgenstein get the *Tractatus* published, first in German in 1921 and then in English in 1922. Wittgenstein accepted Russell's help, even though he was convinced that Russell did not understand what he was trying to express in the *Tractatus,* noting as early as 1919 that neither Russell nor Frege understood him.

In 1920, Wittgenstein temporarily gave up philosophy, convinced that in the *Tractatus* he had, once and for all, solved all philosophical problems. He also gave away his share of the family fortune and worked variously as a gardener in a monastery, a grade school teacher, and an architect in and around Vienna. He also contemplated becoming a monk.

By 1929, Wittgenstein was back in Cambridge, where he used the *Tractatus* to secure a Ph.D., supposedly prompting G. E. Moore, one of his examiners, to write in his report, "The *Tractatus* is a work of genius, but it otherwise satisfies the requirements for a Ph.D."[7] With a five-year fellowship to Cambridge, Wittgenstein was free to study and write, which he did with energy and intensity. His notions of philosophy and philosophical problems changed radically during this so-called middle-period as he rejected all dogmatic philosophy, including his own *Tractatus.*

During the 1930s and 1940s Wittgenstein conducted a series of lectures and seminars that became known as much for his odd behavior and apparent animosity toward his students as for his philosophy. During his seminars, Wittgenstein would struggle aloud with philosophical problems, occasionally bursting out, "I'm stupid today!" and other times sitting for long periods silently sunk in thought. In this halting way, he worked out many of the ideas that were eventually published as the *Philosophical Investigations,* his second ground breaking book—his second book, period.

The *Philosophical Investigations,* which includes sections on psychology and mathematics, reflects a deep, pervasive skepticism about philosophy's "pretensions." It signals a turn away from formal logic toward an analysis of ordinary language. By this time, the later Wittgenstein considered most philosophical problems to be nonsense (more about this below) and once jokingly and unfavorably compared the intellectual—and moral—quality of a prestigious philosophy journal to detective magazines.[8]

Wittgenstein almost published the *Philosophical Investigations* in 1945 but changed his mind, preferring instead that it be published posthumously. In addition to *Investigations,* other posthumously published writings include, in the order Wittgenstein wrote them, *Notebooks 1914–16* (1961), *The Blue and Brown Books* (1958), *Zettel* (1967, revised 1981), *Remarks on the Philosophy of Psychology* (1980), and *On Certainty* (1969).

In 1939, Wittgenstein was made a professor of philosophy at Cambridge, but World War II interfered and he worked as a hospital porter until 1944. After the war, he lectured at Cambridge but found the task distasteful. Wittgenstein resigned and moved to Ireland. In 1949, he briefly visited America and then returned to England, where he stayed with various friends in Oxford and Cambridge until his death.

Upon his return to Cambridge from America, Wittgenstein was diagnosed with prostate cancer. He spent his last days at the home of Dr. Edward Bevan and his wife, Joan. On April 28, 1951, Wittgenstein fell ill just after he and Mrs. Bevan returned from their nightly stroll. Before losing consciousness, he said to Mrs. Bevan, "Tell them I've had a wonderful life." Ludwig Wittgenstein died the next day without regaining consciousness.[9]

A few days before he died, the man who took language so seriously wrote, "God may say to me: 'I am judging you out of your own mouth. Your own actions have made you shudder with disgust when you have seen other people do them.'"[10]

I ought to be no more than a mirror, in which my reader can see his own thinking with all its deformities so that, helped in this way, he can put it right.

LUDWIG WITTGENSTEIN

It is important to note that the word "meaning" is being used illicitly if it is used to signify anything that "corresponds" to the word. This is to confound the meaning of a name with the bearer of the name. When Mr. N. N. dies, one says that the bearer of the name dies, not that the meaning dies.

LUDWIG WITTGENSTEIN

There is no defending the tradition. Systematic analytic philosophy and its Continental cousins along with their historical ancestors must be given up.

KAI NIELSEN

■ WHAT ARE YOU TALKING ABOUT? ■

The analytic tradition in philosophy began with a recognition that philosophers need to be sure they know what they are saying before they can philosophize with any confidence. Just as the epistemological turn began when Descartes recognized that the thinking thing had been taken for granted, the linguistic turn began when philosophers such as Locke began to wonder about the effects of linguistic confusions on philosophy:

> Vague and insignificant forms of speech, and abuse of language, have . . . long passed for mysteries of science; and hard or misapplied words, with little or no meaning, have [been] mistaken for deep learning. . . . They are but covers of ignorance, [and] hindrance of true knowledge.[11]

From the first, analytically oriented philosophers concentrated on clarifying our experience of experience by clarifying what we say about it—and what we can say about anything. "Saying," in this context, is different from "uttering." We utter all sorts of things that, upon reflection, do not mean much of anything. So an important, primary task of philosophy is to clear up language confusions so that we, philosophers and nonphilosophers alike, do not waste ourselves haggling over empty noises and, worse, worshiping nonsensical expressions and fighting one another over what they "really mean."

As analytic philosophy developed, it became increasingly technical—more professional than traditional philosophy; some would say, less "sloppy," less existential and personal, focusing on logic and language rather than on life. Now, of course, this is a broad characterization, and individual analytic philosophers such as Bertrand Russell took a great interest in social issues—but not technically, not professionally, not *as philosophers.*

Lastly, analytic philosophers rejected traditional, idealistic metaphysics in favor of what they took to be a hard-headed, down-to-earth **realism**, the belief that there exists an independent, objective world of things, facts, and states of affairs that are accessible to us. From this perspective, the proper task of philosophy is to identify and then to toss aside mistaken claims about reality, replacing them, when possible, with sensible—meaningful, testable—assertions identified by rigorous analysis. Things are what they are, and all we have to do is to clear up our understanding of them by learning how to talk about them in ways that do not allow language to "bewitch" our intelligence.

We cannot speak in science of a great problem.

LUDWIG WITTGENSTEIN

I may find scientific questions interesting but they never really grip me.

LUDWIG WITTGENSTEIN

realism

In philosophy, the belief that there exists an independent, objective world of things, facts, and states of affairs that are accessible to us.

PHILOSOPHICAL QUERY

• • • • • •

Has language ever "bewitched" your intelligence? Think carefully before you say no. Consider, as just three possibilities, "he changed his mind," "she is not being her true self," "God is everywhere."

The Tractatus

Wittgenstein's *Tractatus Logico-Philosophicus* is widely seen as one of the first major examples of the linguistic-analytic turn in twentieth-century philosophy. It begins with a clarion call for clarity.

> The book deals with the problems of philosophy and shows, I believe, that the reason why these problems are posed is that the logic of our language is misunderstood. The whole sense of the book might be summed up in the

following words: what can be said at all can be said clearly, and what we cannot talk about must be passed over in silence.

> Thus the aim of the book is to set a limit to thought, or rather, not to thought but to the expression of thoughts: for in order to be able to set a limit to thought, we should have to find both sides of the limit thinkable (i.e., we should have to able to think what cannot be thought).
>
> It will therefore only be in language that the limit can be set, and what lies on the other side of the limit will simply be nonsense.[12]

Although Wittgenstein himself ultimately moved beyond the *Tractatus*, it remains an important, influential, difficult work. Philosophers continue to argue about what Wittgenstein was getting at and whether or not he succeeded. Nonphilosophers also are fascinated by the little book, partly, no doubt, because of its cryptic, aphoristic style, partly, perhaps, by its odd, numerical arrangement.

The *Tractatus* consists of seven main numbered propositions and comments on those seven, arranged numerically. So, for instance,

1   is a distinct proposition
1.1   is a comment on proposition 1
1.11   is a comment on 1.1, which is itself a comment

Following common practice, extracts from the *Tractatus* will be referenced with these numbers, rather than via endnotes with page citations.

In the *Tractatus,* Wittgenstein confidently rejects earlier philosophers' attempts to grapple directly with problems of existence, knowledge, truth, and value because, he says, those so-called problems are illusory, linguistic, results of misunderstanding what language is and how it works. These bogus "philosophical problems" will—not might—disappear once their true nature is recognized.

> The truth of the thoughts that are here set forth seems to me to be unassailable and definitive. I therefore believe myself to have found, on all essential points, the final solutions of the problems.[13]

Accordingly, the *Tractatus* is Wittgenstein's attempt to *show*—not explain or prove—the underlying structure of language. What can be *said* is what can be said meaningfully. What can be said is the same as what can be *thought*—grasped, understood. What cannot be said cannot be thought, and trying to say the unsayable—as philosophers have heretofore done—amounts to trying to think the unthinkable.[14]

1   The world is all that is the case.
1.1   The world is the totality of facts, not things.
1.11   The world is determined by the facts, and by their being *all* the facts.
1.12   For the totality of facts determines what is the case, and also whatever is not the case.

Wittgenstein believed that he had set the stage to show, among other things, that complex propositions, including all the propositions we assert in ordinary, everyday language, are *meaningful* only if they are analyzable into simpler and simpler, ultimately elemental, propositions that consist only of names (not

I am not aiming at the same target as the scientists, and my way of thinking is different from theirs.

LUDWIG WITTGENSTEIN

The truth of the thoughts that are here set forth seems to me to be unassailable and definitive. I therefore believe myself to have found, on all essential points, the final solutions of the problems.

LUDWIG WITTGENSTEIN

It is like a pair of glasses on our nose through which we see whatever we look at. It never occurs to us to take them off.

LUDWIG WITTGENSTEIN

descriptions or relationships). Analysis must end in simple, unanalyzable names that refer to objects.

> 3.25   A proposition has one and only one complete analysis. . . .
> 3.26   A name cannot be dissected any further by means of a definition: it is a primitive sign. . . .

Sentences that cannot be reduced to simple symbols—primitive names—are meaningless. Objects themselves cannot be analyzed, only pictured. That there are objects, that they exist, cannot be proved, only shown. So where does all of this leave philosophy?

> 4.003   Most of the propositions and questions to be found in philosophical works are not false but nonsensical. Consequently we cannot give any answer to questions of this kind, but can only establish that they are nonsensical. Most of the propositions and questions of philosophers arise from our failure to understand the logic of our language.
> (They belong to the same class as the question whether the good is more or less identical with the beautiful.)
> And it is not surprising that the deepest problems are in fact not problems at all.

Consider, for instance, the so-called problem of skepticism about knowledge of the external world generated by Locke's egocentric predicament and the sort of withering arguments Hume made about what we can and cannot know. (See Chapter 10.) These seemingly difficult philosophical problems cannot be refuted in the conventional way because the conventional way rests on linguistic misunderstandings. The way out is to *see* that Humean skepticism is not the powerful expression of an irrefutable philosophical problem at all, but a garbled way of speaking. It is *nonsensical:*

> 6.51   Skepticism is not irrefutable, but obviously nonsensical, when it tries to raise doubts where no question can be asked.
> For doubt can exist only where a question exists, a question only where an answer exists, and an answer only where something can be said.

Does this mean that aesthetics, ethics, religion, the "problems of life," are themselves nonsensical? No, they themselves are not nonsensical, but trying to *say anything* about them is.

Then what is left for philosophers to do? Believe it or not, if philosophers do their jobs properly, they will see that all meaningful propositions fall into the bailiwick of the natural sciences and, hence, will allow science to deal with them. So much for Plato, Aristotle, Augustine, Hume, and Kant, so much for the history of traditional philosophy; so much even for Wittgenstein and the *Tractatus,* for even its propositions are senseless, meant to be discarded after they have shown the way out of traditional philosophical nonsense.

> 6.53   The correct method in philosophy would really be the following: to say nothing except what can be said, i.e., propositions of natural science—i.e.,

---

All facts are theory-laden.

N. R. HANSON

Agreement in judgments means agreement in what people do and say, not what they believe.

LUDWIG WITTGENSTEIN

(A)n unknown German appeared, speaking very little English but refusing to speak German. He . . . had acquired, by himself, a passion for the philosophy of mathematics & now has come to Cambridge on purpose to hear me.

BERTRAND RUSSELL

something that has nothing to do with philosophy—and then, whenever someone else wanted to say something metaphysical, to demonstrate to him that he had failed to give a meaning to certain signs in his propositions. Although it would not be satisfying to the other person—he would not have the feeling that we were teaching him philosophy—*this* method would be the only strictly correct one.

6.54   My propositions serve as elucidations in the following way: anyone who understands me eventually recognizes them as nonsensical, when he has used them—as steps—to climb up beyond them.

(He must, so to speak, throw away the ladder after he has climbed up it.)

He must transcend these propositions, and then he will see the world aright.

You are not alone if you sense something going on here besides philosophical analysis. Wittgenstein realized that for all its successes, science will never touch the really important problems of life. Wittgenstein, it turns out, is, like so many of his philosophical predecessors, concerned with the meaning of life. His deconstruction of traditional philosophy is not intended to leave us with nothing of value. It is, rather, an ethical and therapeutic enterprise, a way out of cloudy, empty babble, an encouragement to shut up and look. If we do, we might see the world not just aright, but afresh.

7.   What we cannot speak about we must pass over in silence.

My German friend threatens to be an infliction, he came back with me after my lecture & argued till dinner time—obstinate and perverse, but I think not stupid.

BERTRAND RUSSELL

It is very hard not to be understood by a single soul.

LUDWIG WITTGENSTEIN

. . . . . .

PHILOSOPHICAL
QUERY

Do you believe that there is anything whereof we cannot—not should *not, but* cannot—*speak? Explain.*

WITTGENSTEIN'S TURN

Following his own advice, Wittgenstein did not return to Cambridge after the war and the completion of the *Tractatus*. Instead, as we have seen, he tried to abandon philosophy, but was eventually drawn back after nearly a decade of trying other things. During his stint as a grade school teacher, he developed an interest in informal, that is, everyday—ordinary—language. Also, as part of his teacher training, he studied psychology and developed an interest in analytic psychology—one of his sisters was analyzed by Sigmund Freud (1856–1939).

The more he reflected on language uses, the more Wittgenstein became convinced that rather than solving the problems of philosophy, the *Tractatus* had succumbed to the problem it set out to combat because the claim that the only meaningful language was one in which sentences stated facts in ways that reflected the logical structure of the world was itself a metaphysical assumption, a misunderstanding of the uses—the logic—of language.

An attempt to summarize [Wittgenstein] would be neither successful nor useful. Wittgenstein compressed his thoughts to the point where further compression is impossible.

NORMAN MALCOLM

Some philosophers (or whatever you call them) suffer from what may be called "loss of problems." Then everything seems quite simple to them, no deep problems seem to exist anymore, the world becomes broad and flat and loses all depth, and what they write becomes immeasurably shallow and trivial. Russell and H. G. Wells suffer from this.

LUDWIG WITTGENSTEIN

Rather than one meaningful language, there are many different languages with many different structures and many different uses. In the *Tractatus,* Wittgenstein had said that the structure of the real world determines the structure of language. In the *Investigations,* he begins to think of words as tools and sentences as instruments. In this and his later work, he makes a turnabout and says that the structure of our language determines the structure of thought and, so, the structure of our experience. Fact-stating is only one language use (tool); there are countless others and, hence, countless other ways of experiencing the world.[15]

In the *Investigations* and other writings, Wittgenstein talks about language as we use it in ordinary life, using such expressions as "forms of life," "language games," and "family resemblances," not as once-and-for-all, fixed, logically exact relationships, but rather as certain kinds of *natural human practices.* In this light, Wittgenstein once described his own work as "one of the heirs of the subject that used to be called philosophy."[16]

"We may not advance any kind of theory," Wittgenstein says in the *Investigations,* frustrating traditional and even some analytic philosophers. In *Culture and Value,* he indicates that his unease with theorizing in philosophy is part of a broader unease, an ethical, nearly religious discomfort.

> Our civilization is characterized by the word "progress." . . . Typically it constructs. It is occupied with building an ever more complicated structure and even clarity is sought only as a means to this end, not as an end in itself. For me on the contrary clarity, perspicuity are valuable in themselves.[17]

Rather than replace mistaken philosophical theories with his own new, correct, "progressive" philosophical theory, Wittgenstein suggests that, when it succeeds, philosophy allows us to give philosophical questions—and ourselves—a rest.

> The real discovery is the one that makes me capable of stopping doing philosophy when I want to.—The one that gives philosophy peace, so that it is no longer tormented by questions which bring *itself* in question.—Instead, we now demonstrate a method by examples, and the series of examples can be broken off.—Problems are solved (difficulties eliminated), not a *single* problem.
>
> There is not a philosophical method, though there are indeed methods, like different therapies.[18]

Our task as philosophers consists not in solving grand—super—problems but in "assembling reminders for a particular purpose," the purpose of seeing how language really works.

> We must do away with all *explanation,* and description alone must take its place. And this description gets its light, that is to say its purpose—from the philosophical problems. These are, of course, not empirical problems; they are solved, rather, by looking into the workings of our language, and that in such a way as to make us realize these workings: *in despite of* an urge to misunderstand them. The problems are solved not by giving new information but by arranging what we have always known. Philosophy is a battle against the bewitchment of our intelligence by means of language.[19]

Wittgenstein is the nearest to a prophet I have ever known. He is a man who is like a tower, who stands high and unattached, leaning on no one. He has his own feet. He fears no man. . . . But other men fear him. . . . They fear his judgment. And so I feared Wittgenstein, felt responsible to him

O. K. BOUWSMA

● ● ● ● ● ●

PHILOSOPHICAL

QUERY

What do you think? Are philosophical problems really problems of language? Is philosophy a funny way of talking that appears to be more substantive than it, in fact, is? If so, why does it persist? If not, what is philosophy really about and for?

■ MARTIN HEIDEGGER ■

Depending on whom you ask, **Martin Heidegger** (1889–1976) is "one of the most significant and influential philosophers of the twentieth century" and "in all likelihood the most influential existentialist figure after Kierkegaard and Nietzsche"—or he is an untrustworthy, incoherent, lifelong Nazi sympathizer.

The impartial observer cannot help but wonder what accounts for such extreme reactions. Part of the explanation, no doubt, has to do with the divisiveness of twentieth-century philosophy, reflected, for example, in the distrust, even contempt, some analytic and continental philosophers feel for "the other way" of doing philosophy. But that sort of philosophical wrangling cannot be the whole story. Part of the explanation no doubt has to do with Heidegger's notoriously difficult language, so difficult that he has been described as a purveyor of audacious "nonsense" and "humbug and mystification," a "dismal windbag whose influence has been completely disastrous."[20]

Still, something more than philosophical disagreements seems to be going on when some analytic philosophers refuse to read any continental philosophy on the grounds that whatever "it" is, it is not philosophy and some continental philosophers respond by dismissing analytic philosophy as mere word games and sterile logic-chopping. Gauging from these most extreme reactions, it would appear that something more important than a philosophical disagreement about this argument or that theory is thought to be at stake in these extreme positions. What? For some contemporary philosophers, the future of philosophy itself is at stake. For others, human existence is at stake, not just in a physical sense, but in an existential sense. Heidegger falls into both camps.

Martin Heidegger

It is an awful thing to work under the gaze and questioning of such piercing eyes, and such discernment, knowing rubbish and gold! And one who speaks the word: "This is rubbish!"

O. K. BOUWSMA

Roots and Ground

Martin Heidegger, the eldest of three children born to Friedrich Heidegger, the sexton of the Catholic Church of St. Martin, and Johanna Kemp, the daughter of a farmer from a nearby village, was born into a lower-middle-class Catholic family on September 26, 1889, in the village of Messkirch in Baden, South Germany.

As a child, Heidegger spent a great deal of time with his mother's family on a farm that had belonged to them for hundreds of years. Except for a five-year period spent teaching at Marburg University, Heidegger lived and worked in Messkirch, Freiburg, and in a mountain cottage he built for himself in Todtnauberg in the

We need only to draw the curtain of words, to behold the fairest tree of knowledge, whose fruit is excellent, and within the reach of our hand.

GEORGE BERKELEY

"We Are Alone with No Excuses"

In 1929, **Jean-Paul-Charles-Aymard Sartre** (1905–1980) graduated from the Ecole Normale Supérieure, which accepted only the finest students, who had passed a series of competitive examinations. For the next ten years Sartre taught philosophy at various schools. During this time, he realized that an enormous gap existed between his "living, breathing" life and the values he had learned as a child and had taught to others as a professor. Conventional, academic philosophy disappointed him; its abstractions and elaborate metaphysical systems bore little or no relevance to his actual existence. Life, Sartre noted, is made up of difficult decisions and concrete experiences, but traditional philosophy, on the whole, fails to address these living issues and choices.

Sartre's philosophical disillusionment ended when he discovered Edmund Husserl and Martin Heidegger. Just as Heidegger transformed Husserl's phenomenology in a way that Husserl rejected, so, too, Sartre transformed Heidegger's fundamental ontology in a way that Heidegger disowned. Although he shared Heidegger's interest in man's fallenness, Sartre was less interested in Being, which he saw as a neutral, Parmenidean "one." Sartre's primary focus was on finding a way to exist authentically in a world without God.

Sartre was drafted into the French army in 1939 and in 1940 was captured by the Germans. He spent nine months as a prisoner of war before being released because of poor health. Sartre returned to Paris and became an influential member of the French Resistance movement. During this time he met Albert Camus (1913–1960), his only near-rival in contemporary existential influence, and the brilliant Simone de Beauvoir (1908–1986), who became Sartre's mistress and lifelong friend.

The German occupation of France drove home to Sartre the fact that evil is not a mere abstraction; it is real and concrete. He concluded that civilization and social order are a thin veneer and that at any moment "the beast" can break loose and reveal "the absurd," which most of us try to deny through rationalizations in the form of abstractions and comforting philosophical and religious beliefs. Such rationalizations are always accompanied by denial, which prevents us from recognizing evil for what it is. Sartre rejected Kierkegaard's leap of faith (Chapter 14) as a cowardly way of living and, in its

place, advocated living without illusion in a world of absolute freedom. We are, Sartre insists, what we do, not what we think, believe, or feel.

It is neither to our fault nor our merit if we lived in a time when torture was a daily fact. Chateaubriand, Oradour, the Rue des Saussaies, Dachau, and Auschwitz have all demonstrated to us that Evil is not an appearance, that knowing its cause does not dispel it, that it is not opposed to Good as a confused idea is to a clear one, that it is not the effect of passions that might be cured, of an ignorance that might be enlightened, that it can in no way be incorporated into idealistic humanism.

After the horrors of the Holocaust and the terrors wrought by the Nazis' use of science and advanced technology, a whole generation shared Sartre's nauseating vision of the absurd.

For Sartre, living with the horror and irrationality of the Nazi occupation shattered any hope for an ordered universe governed by a wise, powerful, and loving God. Science provides no certainty either; indeed, the Nazi concentration camps were "scientific" and "rationally ordered." Even nature is only another bourgeois delusion, a mental construct designed to cover up the hideous absurdity of existence. By pretending that facts dictate choices or that certain choices are "natural," we obscure our own responsibility. Like it or not, we are free to choose "the facts" or to reject them; free to "follow nature" or not, because we are free to define the facts and to define what is natural.

Sartre concluded that "being" is not enough, to merely *be* an authentic self is not possible. There is no fixed "essence" lingering behind the roles we play. We are whatever we do, the totality of our actions. *An authentic self exists as and through the choices it makes for itself, uncontrolled by the values of others.* Put another way, we do not *have* a given nature (Being); we *become* a certain kind of person. We are existentially free. There is no fixed self on which we build. When we face life alone, without God, without certainty—we experience Sartrean *forlornness*—with only absolute freedom and the chilling responsibility that accompanies it.

When we speak of forlornness . . . we mean only that God does not exist and that we have to face all the consequences of this. The existentialist is strongly opposed to a certain kind of secular ethics which would like to abolish God with the least popular expense. . . .

The existentialist, on the contrary, thinks it very distressing that God does not exist, because all possibility of finding values in a heaven of ideas disappears along with Him. . . . Nowhere is it written that the Good exists, that we must be honest, that we must not lie; because the fact is we are on a plane where there are only men. Dostoievsky said, "If God didn't exist, everything would be possible." That is the very starting point of existentialism. Indeed, everything is permissible if God does not exist, and as a result man is forlorn, because neither within him nor without does he find anything to cling to. He can't start making excuses for himself.

Most significant, in Sartre's view, is that without God there is no fixed human nature, no essence or being that infuses us. We are not governed by fixed laws: We are free, not determined. First we exist; then we choose; then we act. We fashion our essence by how we actually live our lives—without God to guide and console us.

If existence really does precede essence, there is no explaining things away by reference to a fixed and given human nature. In other words, there is no determinism, man is free, man is freedom. On the other hand, if God does not exist, we find no values or commands to turn to which legitimize our conduct. So, in the bright realm of values, we have no excuse behind us, nor justification before us. We are alone with no excuses.

The first quotation from Sartre is from *What Is Literature?*, trans. Bernard Frechtman (New York: Philosophical Library, 1949), p. 217; the second and third are from *Existentialism Is a Humanism*, trans. Bernard Frechtman, 1957, in *The Fabric of Existentialism: Philosophical and Literary Sources*, eds. Richard Gill and Ernest Sherman (Englewood Cliffs, N.J.: Prentice-Hall, 1973), p. 523 and pp. 523–524.

Black Forest. When he was fourteen, a local priest noted that Heidegger was unusually intelligent and arranged for him to attend a Jesuit grammar school in Kostanz on a church scholarship. Three years later Heidegger attended a Jesuit high school in Freiburg, where he developed an interest in Aristotle and philosophy after reading Franz Brentano's (1838–1917) *On the Manifold Meaning of Being According to Aristotle*. Brentano's book triggered Heidegger's lifelong quest for "the meaning of Being."

In 1909, with the priesthood in mind, Heidegger entered a Jesuit novitiate in Austria but was dismissed in only two weeks for health reasons. He returned to Freiburg and studied at both a Jesuit seminary and the University of Freiburg. In about 1911, Heidegger had a nervous breakdown that forced him to abandon his studies briefly. During his recuperation, he gave up the idea of the priesthood and concentrated on the study of mathematics, natural science, and philosophy. In 1913, he completed his doctorate in philosophy.

In 1914, at the outbreak of World War I, Heidegger enlisted in the German army but was almost immediately discharged due to poor health. In 1915, he was recruited as a censor with the Central Board of the Post Office at Freiburg. During this period, hoping to secure an appointment as the chair of Catholic Philosophy at the University of Freiburg, Heidegger began to write a habilitation dissertation on the Catholic philosopher Duns Scotus. Habilitation dissertations were scholarly works that, if adequate, qualified would-be professors to teach at the university. Meanwhile, Heidegger lectured on ancient and scholastic philosophy, Immanuel Kant, and Aristotle as a *privatdozent,* an unpaid lecturer. In 1916, **Edmund Husserl** (1859–1938), whose phenomenology was to play a big role in Heidegger's philosophy, began to teach at Freiburg.

Heidegger was oblivious of the torment of his Jewish friends and colleagues, but after a year of hectic propagandizing and organizing, he did notice that the Nazi higher-ups were not paying much attention to him. This sufficed to show him that he had overestimated National Socialism. . . . So he retreated to his mountain cabin and, as Safranski nicely says, traded decisiveness for imperturbability.

RICHARD RORTY

Throughout his life, Heidegger sought solace and renewal in the mountains, forests, and valleys of the Black Forest.

©Stephen Studd/Getty Images

In 1917, Heidegger married Thea Elfride Petri, a Lutheran economics student who had been attending his courses since 1915, with whom he had two sons, Jorge and Hermann. In 1918, Heidegger was recalled for active military duty and sent to Verdun, where he served as a meteorologist for the last few months of the war.

At the end of the war, Husserl convinced the university to hire Heidegger as his assistant. Soon thereafter, Heidegger's lectures and seminars began to attract a following. About this time, Heidegger announced that he was "breaking with" Catholicism, personally and philosophically: "I [quickly] gave up my theological studies and dedicated myself entirely to philosophy."[21]

As he worked with Husserl, Heidegger also broke, though less dramatically, from Husserl's way of doing phenomenology. Pursuing a new line of inquiry, Heidegger was determined to apply the phenomenological method to what he saw as a momentous spiritual crisis rooted in modernity's "forgetting" of Being.

Thinking Has Come to Life Again

After he was rejected for the chair in Catholic Philosophy at Freiburg, Heidegger secured a position as a junior professor at Marburg University in 1927. At Marburg, Heidegger knew Karl Jaspers (1883–1969), Max Scheler (1874–1928), Paul Tillich (1886–1965), and Hans-Georg Gadamer (1900–2002) and held regular discussions in theology with Rudolf Bultmann (1884–1976). Gadamer said that Heidegger's reputation as a teacher was so strong that he was able to fill classes beginning at seven o'clock in the morning. Referring to the transformative effect of Heidegger's "orality" and "word-genius," the critic George Steiner said that

> Witnesses . . . are of one voice saying that those who did not hear Martin Heidegger lecture or conduct his seminars can have only an imperfect, even distorted notion of his purpose. It is the lectures, the seminars already prior to *Sein und Zeit*, which, in Marburg in the very early 1920s, came as a shock and a revelation to colleagues and students. The "secret king of thought," as [Hannah] Arendt memorably called her master, acted through the spoken word.[22]

Hannah Arendt (1906–1975) was an eighteen-year-old Jewish student with whom a thirty-five-year-old Heidegger had a romantic and academic relationship. During World War II, Arendt's relationship with Heidegger came to a halt because of Heidegger's Nazi affiliations. It resumed, in a different form, in 1950 when Arendt renewed their friendship. Subsequently, Arendt played a major role in introducing Heidegger's work to America. In the following passage, as a mature and influential philosopher in her own right, Arendt describes Heidegger's long-ago impact as a teacher:

> The rumor about Heidegger put it quite simply: Thinking has come to life again; the cultural treasures of the past, believed to be dead, are being made to speak, in the course of which it turns out that they propose things altogether different from the familiar worn-out trivialities that they had been presumed to say. There exists a teacher; one can perhaps learn to think.[23]

Heidegger's power as a teacher stemmed, in great part, from his conviction that philosophy cannot be divorced from life. Like Kierkegaard, he believed that philosophy is grounded in living, or, more precisely, grounded in concerns about concrete human existence. Thus, philosophy cannot be divorced from the existence of the philosopher. Philosophy cannot be done in a detached relational way, but only in an existential, involved, concerned way. This belief was not an attempt to turn philosophy into biography, however. Arendt notes, for instance, that Heidegger once summarized Aristotle's life as "Aristotle was born, worked and died."

Heidegger's point is that life itself is always at stake—the way of life of the particular philosopher, to be sure, but also the life of the university. Our thinking and existing are at stake when we philosophize. Our own *being* is always—somehow—implicated.[24]

We do not know how to harmonize the contradictory tasks contemporary society imposes upon us. We can only try to reach an uncertain balance between these tasks because we have no blueprint for a conflictless and secure society.

LESZEK KOWLAKOWSKI

PHILOSOPHICAL QUERY

● ● ● ● ● ●

Have you had a truly charismatic teacher? How does a charismatic teacher differ from a merely appealing, powerful one? If so, was his or her influence positive or negative? Explain. (You might want to double-check the meaning of charismatic before deciding.)

In 1927, Heidegger published an incomplete version of *Being and Time*. He planned to develop it further but never did. Even in its incomplete form, *Being and Time* secured Heidegger's reputation as a major figure, both in Germany and internationally. In 1928, Heidegger was called back to the University of Freiburg to succeed Husserl upon the latter's retirement. Almost immediately, Heidegger distanced himself from his former advocate, for philosophical reasons, to be sure, but also, it seems, because Husserl was Jewish. From about 1930 to 1936, Heidegger reassessed this original expression of philosophy in a way that led to *die Kehre,* the turning. This "turning" was not so much a radical shift away from Heidegger's early ideas as it was a new focus on them from a different direction.

In 1933, Heidegger, an ardent Nazi supporter at the time, was named rector of the university. By 1934, his relationship with the Nazis changed, and he resigned the rectorship but retained his professorship under the watchful eye of the Gestapo. In 1944, the Nazis sent Heidegger to dig trenches along the Rhine, declaring him to be the most "expendable" member of the Freiburg faculty.

In 1945, Heidegger was forbidden to teach, and in 1946 he lost his chair in philosophy due to concerns about his Nazi affiliations. In 1949, the ban against teaching was lifted, and in 1951 Heidegger was granted emeritus status by the University of Freiburg and allowed to conduct seminars and lectures into the late 1960s.

After the war, Heidegger divided his time between Freiburg, Messkirch, and his hut in the mountains of the Black Forest. He continued to write and publish such essays and lectures as "What are Poets For?" (1946), "Letter on Humanism" (1947), "The Question Concerning Technology" (1953), "The Way to Language" (1959), "Time and Being" (1962), and "The End of Philosophy and the Task of Thinking" (1964). Much of his work focused on modernity and the history of being as he struggled to find appropriate ways to express and clarify his thinking after *die Kehre*.

During this prolific period, Heidegger was visited by Hannah Arendt, Rudolf Bultmann, and such other notable figures as the physicist Werner Heisenberg and the psychologist Ludwig Binswanger (1881–1966). He died on May 26, 1976. Martin Heidegger was buried in the Messkirch churchyard, with his nephew serving as sextant.

We cannot by philosophical analysis decide whether anything is real, but only what it means to say that it is real.

Moritz Schlick

Heidegger's Children

We can get some sense of Heidegger's impact on philosophy and other disciplines by considering some of the notable twentieth-century figures he has influenced, many of whom disagree with one another about the scope and purposes of philosophy. A partial list includes Jean-Paul Sartre and Hannah Arendt in existentialism and phenomenology; Hans-Georg Gadamer in hermeneutics; Jacques Derrida (1930–2004) in Deconstructionism; Richard Rorty (1931–2007) in pragmatism; Rudolf Bultmann and Paul Tillich (1886–1965) in theology—even Charles Taylor (b. 1931) and Stanley Cavell (b. 1926) in analytic philosophy.[25]

Despite Heidegger's significant and growing influence, troublesome matters persist. One is his infamously difficult writing style, a style so complex and arcane that it prompts some philosophers—especially analytically inclined philosophers—to dismiss Heidegger's work as irretrievably ambiguous, vague, even meaningless, an inflated pseudo-philosophy tinged with messianic religious overtones that do not square with Heidegger's purported focus on existential matters. According to such critics, Heidegger's influence is not due to the quality of his thought, but the opposite. The ambiguity and unintelligibility of Heidegger's language allows readers to make his dense prose mean whatever they wish it to mean.

Of course, as we have seen, Heidegger is not unique among philosophers when it comes to difficult writing. Kant (Chapter 11), for instance, immediately comes to mind, as do any number of other important philosophers. Difficult, so-called bad writing can be an impediment to understanding and accessibility to be sure, but does not, of itself, tell us whether a philosopher's ideas are important and worthwhile any more than simplicity and clarity, of themselves, guarantee philosophical merit.

For many philosophers, the most notorious, controversial complicating factor when it comes to Heidegger is his troubling and seemingly absolute refusal to repudiate his early affiliations with the Nazis and his utter—some say devastating—silence in regard to the Nazi death camps. This, critics note, is particularly difficult to explain away in light of Heidegger's concerns about modern technology and science—tools the Nazis used to objectify and destroy millions of people.

In 1966, Heidegger tried to justify his involvement with the Nazis in an interview entitled "Only a God Can Save Us," which was not published until after his death. There, he said that, like many others, he at first had been misled and then had been pressured by the Nazis. When asked why he deleted the dedication to his mentor Husserl from the editions of *Being and Time* published under the Nazis, Heidegger suggested that it was only sensible, given that Husserl was a Jew.

Most troubling of all to many observers was Heidegger's absolute public silence regarding the Holocaust in the 1966 interview and, so far as we know, in any of his later writings. These, however, are so voluminous that some philosophers advise us to wait and see, to which critics retort that Heidegger's public silence in the face of such an unprecedented assault on humanity cannot be mitigated by any comments buried in a mass of writings—if such comments even exist. In the following passage, George Steiner expresses the unease of those who find Heidegger's early support of National Socialism (Nazism) and subsequent silence difficult, if not impossible, to justify.

> It is an ill-kept secret that cloistered intellectuals . . . who spend their lives immersed in words, in texts, can experience with especial intensity the seductions of violent political proposals, most particularly where such violence does not touch their own person. There can be in the sensibility and outlook of the charismatic teacher, of the philosophical absolutist, more than a touch of surrogate sadism. . . .
>
> Martin Heidegger's . . . notorious address in support of Hitler's break with the League of Nations, his elegy on a nationalist thug . . . whom the Nazis made a martyr, are nauseating documents. . . .
>
> Once more: the disabling fact is Heidegger's silence after 1945. . . . the thinker of Being found nothing to say of the Holocaust and the death-camps.[26]

The case of Heidegger's Nazism has generated considerable scholarship and journalism over the years, some of it thoughtful, much of it dreadful. Most authors who have chosen to tackle the subject succumb to one of two temptations, both of which reflect a failure of moral judgment. Either they are led by indignation to dismiss Heidegger as a demonic charlatan or they arrogantly defend him without stooping to confront the serious moral concerns raised by his actions and ideas.

DAMON LINKER

Agriculture is now a motorized food industry, the same thing in its essence as the production of corpses in the gas chamber and the extermination camps, the same thing as blockades and the reduction of countries to famine, the same thing as the manufacture of hydrogen bombs.

MARTIN HEIDEGGER

Does such unease help us assess Heidegger's philosophy? When all is said and done, probably not, as Richard Rorty explains:

> A bad reason for caring [about Heidegger's Nazism] is the notion that learning about a philosopher's moral character helps one evaluate his philosophy. It does not, any more than our knowledge of Einstein's character helps us evaluate his physics. You can be a great, original, and profound artist or thinker, and also a complete bastard. . . .
>
> . . . [A]ttempts to simplify the thought of original thinkers by reducing them to moral or political attitudes should be avoided . . . [they] are of no use when dealing with authors of the complexity and originality of a Heidegger. . . . They are merely excuses for not reading them.[27]

PHILOSOPHICAL

QUERY

• • • • • •

Do you agree with Rorty that Heidegger's Nazism is irrelevant to his philosophy? Would his religious beliefs be relevant? Is the issue the same for logicians as it is for existentialists? Does it matter philosophically if a proponent of vegetarianism eats meat? When, if ever, are a philosopher's personal beliefs and habits philosophically relevant? Discuss.

■ PHENOMENOLOGY: THE SCIENCE ■ OF BEINGS

In 1919, Edmund Husserl secured a position for Heidegger as his assistant in Husserl's "phenomenological workshop," where Heidegger said he received the "step-by-step training in phenomenological 'seeing'" that was to play a vital role in the development of his own philosophy.[28]

Phenomenology is a method of philosophical analysis first developed by Husserl that uses purely descriptive statements to provide a "descriptive analysis" of consciousness in all its forms. Phenomenology focuses on concrete "experienced facts" rather than abstractions in order to reveal the "essence" of human consciousness. Borrowing from Franz Brentano's "descriptive psychology," Husserl held that consciousness is *intentional,* that is, *consciousness of something.* It is not a representation, not a subjective reflection of some private, inner state, but an experience of something that exists in its own way and in its own right.

According to Husserl, Descartes was on the right track when he said that one thing is certain and undoubtable—our own conscious awareness—and that this is the place to start if we want a solid philosophical foundation. What Descartes failed to see, Husserl said, is that consciousness is always *consciousness of something.* Consciousness—thinking—cannot exist as a Cartesian cogito, an objectless state of mind, a "thinking thing" detached from bodily experience. In theory, we might be able to distinguish between thinking (consciousness) and thoughts (objects of consciousness), but in experience, in practice, we cannot make such a distinction.

phenomenology
Method of philosophical analysis first developed by Husserl that uses purely descriptive statements to provide a "descriptive analysis" of consciousness in all its forms; focuses on concrete "experienced facts" rather than abstractions in order to reveal the "essence" of human consciousness.

"The Enthusiastic Embrace of Tyranny by Philosophers"

The tension between philosophy and politics is as old as philosophy itself. The case of Socrates—tried and executed for impiety and corrupting the youth of ancient Athens—might be the most famous example of political-philosophical conflict, but it is hardly the only one. From Anaxagoras, Aristotle, and Cicero to Averroes, Maimonides, Descartes, Spinoza, Locke, Rousseau, and Kant, history is filled with examples of philosophers persecuted at the hands of political authorities. . . .

But there is another dimension to the problematic relation between politics and philosophy—one that has showed itself more vividly in our time than in any previous era: the enthusiastic embrace of tyranny by philosophers. Throughout much of the twentieth century, and especially in the post–World War II period, intellectuals living in the free societies of the West were faced with a choice. They could offer support—however measured or qualified—for the liberal democratic order and its freedoms. Or they could reject it in favor of one of the various experiments in antiliberal and antidemocratic politics that arose throughout the course of the century. To be sure, some took the former path. But a distressingly large number of the century's most gifted minds opted, instead, for tyranny—or at least refused to acknowledge that there is a significant qualitative difference between constitutionalism and dictatorship.

What are we to make of this decision for despotism?

Damon Linker, "Philosophy and Tyranny," *First Things First: A Monthly Journal of Religion and Public Life* (Jan. 2002), p. 40.

It is at this point that Husserl thinks he has found the solution to the age-old skeptical argument that we can never be sure that objects of consciousness exist objectively, that is, independently of us. (See Chapters 9–11.) Remarkably, Husserl's solution is that *we do not need to answer* the skeptics' challenge because it is enough for human purposes that objects of consciousness exist—*as objects of consciousness*. We have no reason to get all tangled up in academic disputes about whether or not they exist in other ways too. We can investigate objects *as they appear* to us, study them and know them, without struggling with what are, after all, *unanswerable* questions.

Husserl's project was part of his overarching concern with what he and many others, including Heidegger, saw as a European crisis associated with the spread of relativism, skepticism, and the use of science to "objectivize" psychic life, the life of the spirit, and reduce the spiritual realm—which includes judging and valuing—to matter.

> To speak of the spirit as [an] annex to bodies and having its supposedly spatiotemporal being within nature is an absurdity. . . .
>
> There are all sorts of problems that stem from this naiveté, according to which objectivistic science holds what it calls the objective world to be the totality of what is, without paying any attention to the fact that no objective science can do justice to the subjectivity that achieves science.[29]

Philosophers were hired by the comfortable classes to prove that everything is all right.

OLIVER WENDELL HOLMES

For Husserl, careful, phenomenological observation—attending to the objects of consciousness without "interfering"—reveals clearly and without any ambiguity the true natures of the various modes of being. Modes of being are not inferred, not deduced; they are seen—disclosed—when we learn how to look, how to attend to reality. Being is present all around us; we do not need to look for it in some super, transcendental, Platonic level of reality. It is right here. All we have to do to see it is to look deeper and deeper into the one-and-only reality, this one. Enter Heidegger.

▓ BEING HUMAN ▓

Heidegger believed that Husserl's real insight was the recognition of a kind of thinking that is concealed by modern technological and scientific thought and that by treating phenomenology as a method, rather than a subject matter, he could reach back to the ancient Greeks and "revitalize thought and overcome the spiritual crisis of the twentieth century."[30] Husserl saw phenomenology as the science of beings (in the plural), but, according to Heidegger, it is more properly understood as the science of Being with a capital B.

Taking off from Husserl's conviction that what we see phenomenologically is what is the thing itself, Heidegger held that in our everyday experience we encounter "Being itself." This is not the Being of transcendental metaphysics, some other level of Being, but Being as it exists in the world.

In *Being and Time*, Heidegger begins his search for Being with a phenomenological study of humans, looking to see what our very nature discloses to us, or, as he puts it, what is "unconcealed." Concerned with both *human* be-ing (humanity) and with individual human beings, Heidegger develops a complex terminology to try to uncover a uniquely human way of existing that is distinct from other ways of existing as mere objects of scientific inquiry.

In that spirit, let us concentrate on getting a basic sense of Heidegger's "questioning of Being," a task he undertakes on our behalf. Anything more is beyond the scope and purposes of this survey. Given the enormity of Heidegger's writings and the complexity of the language he uses, initial forays into his philosophy run the risk of focusing so heavily on terminology that they pay short shrift to Heidegger's spirit—to the "marvel of all marvels," the fact that we exist at all, that alone among all other kinds of things that exist, human beings care about existence itself, and as such, we are the "shepherds of Being" in this world.

According to Heidegger, what makes us uniquely human is not, as so many other philosophers have suggested, detached and objective knowing. That is, we are not unique because we *think about* the world. Rather, our fundamental human condition is *concern* about our fundamental—human—condition. It is our nature to care about how we exist in the world, to care about human be-ing. Alone among all other beings, we are concerned about our fate in an alien world. Consequently, any inquiry into the nature of human nature, into the conditions of human be-ing, is, ultimately, also an inquiry into the nature of Being itself, into our ownmost existence.

Heidegger notes that we can be described from two different "levels." One is the ordinary, day-to-day level of facts. (Heidegger calls this the *ontic* level). Considered from the ordinary level of facts, we are understood in quantitative and objective ways in terms of our particular bodies, temperaments, histories, and worldviews. But that is not all there is to us. Thus, we resist and resent being "treated like an object" or being "reduced to a thing." We instinctively and intuitively recognize that treating human beings this way exclusively amounts to stripping away their humanity or humanness.

From Plato until the present, with a few notable exceptions, reason rather than emotion has been regarded as the indispensable faculty for acquiring knowledge.

ALISON M. JAGGAR

Yet the knowledge that is craved today tends to be very different from that sought by the cultivated elite of an earlier age. The present-day knowledgeable man may lack any cultivation, and the well-informed person may be but a cheerful robot. The increase of information may indeed have led, contrary to the belief of the Enlightenment, to a decrease in rationality.

LEWIS A. COSER

We are unique among beings because our nature and the fact that we exist at all is something we care about, something that matters to us. Indeed, our concern with the deeper meaning of our own existence is part of our very essence, part of who and what we are, a reflection of a deeper level of Being. Heidegger calls this the *ontological* level of Being; this is the level of our uniquely *human* way of existing in the world. At this level, we discover that unlike all other entities, our very existence (our Being) is an *issue* for us. We do not "just occur" as one entity among other entities.[31]

Ontology, recall, is the study of being. So when Heidegger says that our nature *is* ontological, he is telling us that our essence is to try to understand our essence. It is not enough for us humans to merely exist. We want to know what we are, not just in a day-to-day ordinary way—not, say, how tall we are or how well we can play the piano—but what makes us *human*. So we "question Being" and in doing so discover that we do not just react. Things just react. We, on the other hand, "comport ourselves." That is, we respond to things in accordance with our own idea of what makes us, us.

If some of this seems alien to you or meaningless or a waste of your valuable time, stop for a moment and ask yourself what it would mean to have absolutely no, none, zip, nada interest in, not to have even the dimmest flicker of concern with the "meaning" of your life in a fundamental, "philosophical," thoughtful, and reflective way.

Think about what you would lose if you were content to just exist as an organism, a set of urges, appetites, immediate goals, and conditioned responses. I bet you cannot—literally cannot—exist like that, certainly not for very long. If, somehow, you could shut off all philosophical (ontological) concerns, wouldn't you be more of an "entity" or automaton than a human being in the fullest, truest, sense? This is not to say that being human means being "a philosopher" in a technical sense or having a specific "quantifiable" and "measurable" level of intelligence. Having ontological concerns is primarily caring about how you live in a way that goes beyond exclusively pragmatic and means-to-ends ways.

As you begin to think about these things, see, too, if you can't identify "echoes of Being" in some of your ordinary conversations and reflections about life. Consider, also, the common experience of feeling as if we're "merely existing" as opposed to really, fully *living!* Isn't this sort of feeling a way of questioning our own existence? Most of us, at times of tribulation or disappointment especially, but not only then, ask: What's it all about? Is this it? Why am I here? Without knowing it, we are ontologists "questioning Being," whether or not we ever explicitly refer to Being and even if we have never heard the word *ontology*.

Today's widespread unawareness of our ontological needs is most likely a function of the fact that we commonly use the terms *exist, existing,* and *existence* to mean "merely existing," which we contrast with "being alive!" This kind of everyday linguistic confusion contributes to minimizing the force of Heidegger's concern with the "fundamental ontology of Being" (human existence).

We would do well to remind ourselves that, although we tend to be unaware of it, we are already familiar with the "interrogation of Being" even if we have never thought about it in Heidegger's terms. We are so familiar with it, in fact, that we don't always recognize what we're doing or what we most deeply care about. This is what it means to "forget" Being. Heidegger's unusual language is grounded

ontology
The study of being.

We ought to ask whether the increase of these variegated types of knowledge has made us happier or wiser, whether it has enriched or impoverished the quality of our lives, whether the increased production of intellectual knowledge necessarily had to be accompanied by an even greater increase of trivialized and trashy knowledge.

LEWIS A. COSER

I, for one, do not doubt that the sane view of the world is the true one. But is that what is always wanted, truth?

SUSAN SONTAG

in his struggle to help us recover what we have lost and forgotten. He wants to awaken us from a kind of amnesia that constitutes what he sees as the spiritual crisis of the present age, an amnesia that induces us to squander our humanity by settling for "merely existing."

What makes us human is that we, alone among beings, engage the world and wrest meaning and significance from it; in so doing we confront and engage our very selves. We are, thus, active, creative participants in our own existence. Alone among beings, we reflect on the nature of existence itself. We alone wonder what it means to *exist*.

■ WHAT IS THE MEANING OF BEING? ■

At its core, Heidegger's ambitious, therapeutic task is to remind us of what we and our culture have lost by taking existence so much for granted, lost by "forgetting" Being. What we have lost is the primordial sense of wonder that there is anything at all, the amazement that *something exists!*—that *we* exist! So Heidegger "questions Being" on our behalf. *Being and Time* begins with a quotation from Plato's *The Sophist* followed by a question from Heidegger that, together, alert us to this.

> For manifestly you have long been aware of what you mean when you use the expression "being." We, however, who used to think we understood it have now become perplexed.
>
> Do we in our time have an answer to the question of what we really mean by the word "being"? Not at all. So it is fitting that we should raise anew *the question of the meaning of Being*. But are we nowadays even perplexed at our inability to understand the expression "Being"? Not at all. So first of all we must reawaken an understanding for the meaning of this question. Our aim in the following treatise is to work out the question of the meaning of *Being* and to do so concretely.[32]

We modern men and women "forget" Being to such an extent that we are not even perplexed by it. We get "lost" in the everyday world as we become so involved in mundane affairs that we do not even wonder that we no longer wonder. All the while, Heidegger says, Being remains in the background, always ready to disclose itself. The world is imbued with "signs" and "markers" "waiting" to "point the way" for us, waiting to remind us of what it really means to be human.

The spiritual stakes here are high, especially so because we think they are not. In our fallen state, we debunk this sort of philosophical/ontological inquiry as a waste, as frivolous, impractical. "What's the big deal?" we grouse. "Everybody knows what human beings are." Knowing "what human beings are" in the ordinary, scientific, technical, taken-for-granted everybody-knows way is one thing. Knowing and caring about what is essential and authentic about being *human* is another. Equating these distinct kinds of knowing puts us at risk of diminishing ourselves by, to borrow Kant's language, treating humanity, in our own case and in that of others, as means-only and not as ends-in-ourselves. What's lost by not seeing people (ourselves and others) as people is humanity, human nature itself.

An idea which is a distortion may have a greater intellectual thrust than the truth; it may better serve the needs of the spirit, which vary.

SUSAN SONTAG

Particular questions must receive particular answers; and if the series of crises which we have lived through since the beginning of this century can teach us anything at all, it is, I think, the simple fact that there are no general standards to determine our judgments unfailingly, no general rules under which to subsume the particular cases with any degree of certainty.

HANNAH ARENDT

The "question of being," then is not about this or that being—not, say, why are there roses or stones or Doug Soccio—but why, especially, is there Being itself, and more importantly, what does it mean to be us, to be you and me, to be human. What a wondrous, amazing thing being human is, Heidegger thinks—and yet we do not seem to notice, so absorbed are we in our immediate tasks.

This is our tragedy, for to be truly and fully *human* is to be amazed in the presence of being human. This alone and uniquely makes us human, not mastering objects, not uninvolved, disengaged, objective knowledge. The special task of philosophy, as Heidegger conceives it, is to evoke the wonder and amazement that are necessary to reveal us to ourselves as *human* beings—as opposed to just beings. And because traditional metaphysics talked about Being as if it were an entity, a thing, our way back to authentic humanity requires that we "overcome" metaphysics.

> Due to the manner in which it thinks of beings, metaphysics almost seems to be, without knowing it, the barrier which keeps man from the original involvement of Being in human nature.
>
> What if the absence of this involvement and the oblivion of this absence determined the entire modern age. . . . [and] abandoned man more and more exclusively to beings, leaving him forsaken and far from any involvement of Being in his nature, while this forsakenness itself remained veiled? What if this were the case—and had been the case for a long time now? What if there were signs that this oblivion will become still more decisive in the future?[33]

[Philosophers] all to a man think unhistorically, as is the age old custom with philosophers.

FRIEDRICH NIETZSCHE

PHILOSOPHICAL QUERY

• • • • • •

Do we take Being for granted? Do you? If so, is that a symptom of a loss or evidence of cultural progress and stability? That is, does it matter if we take being human for granted in a world that, for all of its problems, is a better world than ever before? Or is it—really—better? Is the modern, technological, busy-busy world more, or less, human than it once was? Can we ever know?

■ THE ATTITUDE OF HUMANITY ■

Scientists and philosophers have long sought, and quarreled over, the distinctly "human" part of human nature, which they have variously defined as being created in God's image, rationality, tool making, the development of agriculture, the ability to use language and create symbols, DNA. We are, from the scientific-technological point of view, human animals existing alongside nonhuman animals, one kind of organism among many other organisms, one entity among many entities.

For Heidegger, however, living authentically, being human, means living with an attitude in "a" world, as opposed to "the" world. According to Heidegger, "the" world, as most of us understand it, is merely one dualistic Cartesian (Chapter 9) world among many other possible worlds. This distinctly modern worldview

I have no sympathy for the stream of European civilization and do not understand its goals, if it has any.

LUDWIG WITTGENSTEIN

dehumanizes us, de-humans us, as it were. We need only catalogue the distinctive features that make us human to see this because reflecting on what it means to be a *human* being reveals the general (fundamental) nature of humanity. When we do this, we see that:

> We are at our most human when we are concerned with our world, not "the" world, but "a" world—our world as we experience it, inhabit it, exist in it. We are at our most human when, contrary to Enlightenment notions, we are engaged rather than disinterestedly and objectively knowing. We *exist as an attitude toward a world*—not toward the single, one-and-only world, but toward our particular world. We do not *exist* as the cogito (Chapter 9) or some sort of empirical perceiver (Chapter 10) or as "disinterested rational agents" (Chapter 11).

Other beings, including nonhuman animals, respond automatically to their worlds according to their various fixed natures and the fixed natures of whatever stimulates them. We alone do not have a fixed nature that endures and persists across time like an unvarying clockwork. It is our nature to choose our existence. We cannot avoid choosing: Choosing not to choose is itself a choice. Neglecting to choose is choosing to neglect to choose. We are not things, not automatic responses to stimuli, not objects that are "just there" in "the" world. We are subjects, beings with attitudes that we call "existence."

> The question of existence never gets straightened out except through existing ·itself.[34]

We cannot interrogate rocks, plants, or animals. We can, of course, study them scientifically, but not *inquire of them* because they cannot answer. They can only react to their environment according to their fixed natures. But you and I can question ourselves about the nature of our existence by looking for the meaning of Being as it is disclosed in everyday life—and Being will respond.

Humanity Is a Relationship

Humanity cannot be separated—abstracted, understood, analyzed—in isolation from the existing individual. We do not and cannot exist as a separate "thinking thing" or as a neutral "perceiver." When we try to adopt an uninvolved, transcendental, purely rational, or neutral mode of existence, we objectify ourselves and our world, thereby losing sight of the nature of authentic (concerned) human existence. Consequently, we see ourselves not as human, but as what Heidegger calls things "present-at-hand," things next to the world the way a chair is "just there" next to a couch.[35] This sort of independent existence is "merely existing," existing without interest, concern, or engaged involvement. It is nonhuman. The difference between the way we *exist* in the human world and the way things are "just there" in the world of things is that in the human world things are not neutral, they are for us or against us, ready to fulfill some purpose, to be *of* us.

In the human world, things appear "inviting" to us, useful for our purposes, or off-putting and uncongenial to our purposes. We have dealings with the things we encounter, dealings that involve more than mere perceptual or rational cognition. The things that matter are not "just there," not just things-in-themselves, but things-for-a-purpose, things-for-my-purpose, things that *matter to us*. Descartes, Hume, Kant, and other philosophers who have struggled to find a solution to the

We have abolished the true world. What has remained? The apparent one perhaps? Oh no! With the true world abolished we have also abolished the apparent one.

FRIEDRICH NIETZSCHE

So long as man exists, philosophizing exists.

MARTIN HEIDEGGER

"problem" of things-in-themselves, the so-called problem of the external world, have forgotten what it means to *exist as a human being*. In their philosophizing—not in their living—they lost touch with humanity.

Existence, Heidegger says, is not a "property," which we sometimes have and sometimes do not have, and *without* which we could live just as well. "It is not the case that man 'is' and then has, by way of an extra, a relationship . . . towards the 'world.'"[36] Human existence *is* a relationship with the world. We exist because and to the extent that we are "in a relationship" with our world. The human way of existing (Being) in the world is not, as Heidegger repeatedly warns us, one of cold calculation or detachment, but one of involvement and concern.

Far beyond Nietzsche, Heidegger thinks, feels in categories outside good and evil.

GEORGE STEINER

- - - - - -

PHILOSOPHICAL
QUERY

Sociopaths are commonly characterized in terms of their extreme detachment from others, a radical detachment that leads some experts to suggest that sociopaths see other people as objects, things, entities, things "just there." Discuss the possibility that sociopaths are examples of entities most out of touch with humanity—with humanness. Do we want to go so far as to say that, in their inability to see others as human beings, sociopaths are themselves not human? Why or why not?

■ THE "THEY" ■

When the burdens of human concern seem too great to bear, we try to absolve ourselves from having to choose among many possibilities and seek to lose ourselves in what Heidegger calls **the "they."** The "they-self" is sometimes called our social self. Unlike our authentic self, a self of open possibilities and potentiality, the inauthentic they-self is "neat and tidy," defined by the anonymous "they." The they-self conforms to a socially contrived "nature" by living as a type rather than *existing* authentically. When we live inauthentically, we lose sight of others as others. Instead of empathetically existing with others, we see ourselves as "one-another" among an averaged aggregate, a vague, amorphous, abstracted norm: the "they." The "they" is a diminished, inauthentic way of Being in which "one speaks of oneself" from the outside.

When we hide out in the amorphous "they," we busy ourselves by taking stock of where we stand and calculating how well or poorly we are conforming to social norms, checking to see how we stack up.

> The "they" has its own ways in which to be . . . grounded in . . . *averageness*, which is an existential characteristic of the "they." The "they" in its Being, essentially makes an issue of this. Thus the "they" . . . keeps watch over everything exceptional that thrusts itself to the fore. Every kind of priority gets noiselessly suppressed. Overnight, everything that is primordial gets glossed over as something that has been well known. Everything gained by a struggle becomes just something to be manipulated. Every secret loses its force. This care of averageness reveals in turn an essential tendency of [human beings] which we call the "leveling down" of all possibilities of being. . . .

the "they"
Heidegger's name for being-with-another; an inauthentic way of avoiding anxiety by allowing an "aggregate average" to determine how we live and think; enemy of authenticity.

There are reasons, perhaps decisive, for not attempting a brief introduction to the thought of Martin Heidegger.

GEORGE STEINER

During the 2008 presidential campaign, Barack Obama declared "We are the ones we have been waiting for." Both he and his opponent John McCain routinely referred to "the American people" and spoke of "we" to huge, enthusiastic crowds. Do the "American people" actually *exist* or were Obama and McCain appealing to the *they* by engaging in what Heidegger called idle talk— chatter that "releases one from the task of genuinely understanding"?

© Adam Berry/Bloomberg News/Landov

Thus the particular [human being] in its everydayness is *disburdened* by the "they." Not only that: by this disburdening of its Being, the "they" accommodates [the particular human being] if [he or she] has any tendency to take things easily and make them easy. And because the "they" constantly accommodates . . . the "they" retains and enhances its stubborn dominion.[37]

Idle Talk

idle talk

Heidegger's name for superficial "they talk"; includes chatter, gossip, and merely verbal understanding; contrasted with conversation or dialogue.

Among the "they," there is only **idle talk**, chatter. There can be no *dialogue*. "Dialogue" occurs when we see others as others. In dialogue, each participant is concerned with understanding the other and with being understood. In idle talk, no one is concerned with genuine understanding and caring. Idle talk never rises above verbal understanding; it seeks nothing more penetrating.

> [W]hat the talk is about is understood only approximately and superficially. . . . following the route of *gossiping* and *passing the word along*. . . . Things are so because one says so. . . .
>
> The groundlessness of idle talk is no obstacle to its becoming public; instead it encourages this. . . . Idle talk . . . releases one from the task of genuinely understanding.[38]

You do not get to philosophy by reading many and multifarious philosophical books, nor by torturing yourself with solving the riddles of the universe . . . philosophy remains latent in every human existence and need not be first added to it from somewhere else.

MARTIN HEIDEGGER

In everyday life, we evade the burden of being fully human (deeply concerned) by speaking of the "they" as "one," as "everybody," as "people," as "nobody": "Everybody knows that is wrong." "People will talk if you go through with that." "One hardly knows what to say." "Nobody believes in God anymore." "The American people are fed up."

Such chatter absolves us of the responsibility of knowing whereof we speak. Idle talk lowers expectations and exalts "public opinion." Evading the task of genuinely understanding, we feel free—nay, encouraged—to spout off without bothering to understand, free to treat information as understanding. In idle talk, we do not *experience* the full majesty and mystery of the human world. Whatever we do see is dimmed so that beauty is averaged down, terror is averaged, joy, diversity, mystery—everything is averaged, made safe, put in its place. We live up—or down—to our way of talking (and attending to what is said). Our lives lack majesty and grandeur if we rarely speak of majesty and grandeur. They lack awe when we routinely describe the most trivial things as "Awesome!" It is as if Being has no meaning for us, as if existence did not exist.

You might wonder why we allow the "they" to rob us this way. We do not *allow* it. We *encourage* it as a way of evading the hard decisions about which aspects of life to put aside and which to pursue. Instead of struggling with how and what to *be*, we focus on what to *do*. We rely on the "they" to disburden us of our humanity by telling us what we are "supposed to do," by conforming to what has been predetermined for us by the "they." The "they" absolves us from the agony of deciding. No longer need we choose: One simply does whatever is normal for "people like us." We make a virtue out of conforming to the norms and expectations of an ethnic group, profession, political party, gender, or social class—we eagerly fall in step with some they-determined set of expectations, purposes, and values.

When we succumb to the dictates of the "they," our mode of Being is inauthenticity, a kind of existence dominated by and lost in "the" world, rather than being responsive to "our" world and concerned with our own Being, with our humanity. We are consumed with being with one another, absorbed by idle talk, curiosity, ambiguity. We are lost, fallen.

> "Inauthenticity" . . . is completely fascinated by the "world" and by . . . the "they."[39]

We think we know everything, but our notion of knowing is superficial, external, disengaging, phony—inauthentic. We understand nothing, really, least of all our own humanity, our "humanness." Unaware and unconcerned with existence, the they-self is tranquil and at ease, convinced that nothing more is required of it. After all, it thinks, what's the big deal about "being"? Here I am. I am human regardless of what I do or how I live. I exist without having to make such a big deal out of it.

Satisfied with trivial knowledge, with "information," the they-self is alternately indifferent to and actively discouraging of the kind of inquiry necessary for authenticity. Its attitude is distant, manipulative, and thereby indifferent to what it means to be a human being.

Metaphysics cannot be abolished like an opinion. One can by no means leave it behind as a doctrine no longer believed and represented.

MARTIN HEIDEGGER

What is meant by the talk about the end of philosophy? We understand the end of something all too easily in the negative sense as a mere stopping, as the lack of continuation, perhaps even as decline and impotence. In contrast, what we say about the end of philosophy means the completion of metaphysics.

MARTIN HEIDEGGER

PHILOSOPHICAL

QUERY

• • • • • •

Apply the notion of disburdening idle talk to today's mass media pundits and experts. Scrutinize op-ed articles, blogs—especially blogs—and television talk shows for examples of "they" talk. Be alert for different "theys": conservatives and liberals, fundamentalists and secularists, males and females, blacks, whites, and Latinos, for example. Must all such mass talk be idle? Why or why not?

Authenticity and Death

Man is not the lord of beings. Man is the shepherd of Being.

MARTIN HEIDEGGER

Authentic individuals know that they are "there" in the world, without any say in the matter, and denied a comforting, metaphysical explanation. They understand and accept that they are going to die. This is an existential (and ontological) understanding of death, not the detached, objective, "averaged" understanding of death in the abstract, but the subjective, concerned knowledge of death in our very own case.

Among all other entities, only we know that our specific existence will inevitably come to an end. Knowing this—and only knowing this—allows us to understand ourselves as a totality, a whole, an end-in-ourselves. Only we humans have the capacity to know ourselves explicitly—that is, only we have the capacity to articulate what we sometimes realize implicitly: Our existence has a beginning, and it will come to an end. We are inauthentic to the extent that we deny and suppress the fact that we are going to die. We lose touch with our humanness and get lost in discrete particularities, reducing ourselves to "a this" or "a that" only. The only way back from this fallen state is by living authentically in the full knowledge that we will die—that you and I *will* die—not in some vague, abstract way, but really, truly, finally, inescapably *die*.

> [The particular human being] does not . . . have any explicit or theoretical knowledge of the fact that it has been delivered over to its death, and that death thus belongs to Being-in-the-world. Thrownness into death reveals itself . . . in a more primordial and impressive manner in that state-of-mind which we have called "anxiety."[40]

The objective world itself, "the" world as opposed to "our" world, is indifferent to our hopes, fears, questions, and projects. It is "out there," objectified, "just there"—alien. In Heidegger's vivid description, the world "tarries alongside" of us but is not of us, nor are we of it. So, as we have seen, we try our best to suppress even the vaguest sense that, objectively, scientifically, technologically understood we are homeless, orphaned, insignificant entities, one more thing "just there" in the world of things.

Philosophy will be unable to effect any immediate change in the current state of the world. This is true not only of philosophy but of all purely human reflection and endeavor. Only a god can save us. The only possibility available to us is that by thinking and poeticizing we prepare a readiness for the appearance of a god, or for the absence of a god in [our] decline, insofar as in view of the absent god we are in a state of decline.

MARTIN HEIDEGGER

Given all the creative energy expended on not-knowing, on disappearing into the "they" and busy-ness, how do we ever come to exist as *human* beings rather than just beings? One way is by experiencing a mood that Heidegger labels "anxiety." Anxiety is directed toward nothing in particular. We experience it when we are aware of the world's indifference to us. Whereas fear alerts us to something specific—the snake in the grass, failing to pass algebra—anxiety does not focus on a specific thing. Anxiety discloses our fundamental human condition, our way of being in the world.

What threatens our sense of belonging here is not a thing or a place, but the nature of the world *as such* and the nature of human beings *as such*, rather than as things among other things that are "just there." Understood this way, anxiety is "friendly" toward us. Anxiety shows us how the world is for us and how we exist in the world. Anxiety prevents us from feeling at home in the world of mere things. More precisely, anxiety shows us that we cannot exist as authentic human beings if we feel at home in "the" world.

If we want to live authentically, we must constantly resist the temptation to escape from anxiety by diluting what we experience, by numbing it, as it were, into a be-happy-don't-worry lightness or by distracting ourselves with an infinite series of multi-tasks, projects, and undertakings that rob us of the richness of what it means to be human.

■ THE AGE OF TECHNOLOGY ■

In *The Question Concerning Technology*, Heidegger raises questions that are especially timely and interesting in this era of multi-tasking and seemingly perpetual information seeking and leveling. He begins by noting that even when we are not actively concerned with fundamental matters, Being sends us clues about ourselves that we can recognize, if we are open to them. These clues correspond to particular historical epochs or ages. They invite, but do not compel, us to recognize what it means to exist (in the fullest human sense) under the conditions of the present age. They call us to authentic existence at this particular time, the age of technology.

● ● ● ● ● ●

Compare Kierkegaard's and Nietzsche's critique of "the present age" with Heidegger's. What do these critiques have in common? How do such "existentially oriented" critiques differ from, say, Plato's critique of democracy? In regard to Kierkegaard, Nietzsche, and Heidegger, what do you think of their dis-ease about modernity? Do you share it?

PHILOSOPHICAL

QUERY

It is important to note that Heidegger's understanding of technology goes beyond the common notion of technology as neutral instruments, as tools and devices that we are free to use for whatever purposes we wish. It's not that we are wrong to think about technology in such a neutral means-to-ends way. On one level, technology is clearly "neutral." Prior to and during World War II, the Nazis, for instance, were master technologists who used the latest technology to efficiently "relocate," "eliminate," and "recycle" those they deemed unfit or undesirable. Almost as soon as that war ended, some of those same technologies were used for humane and peaceful purposes. Today, the same technology that allows students to produce sophisticated, computer-researched papers also allows for the clandestine buying, selling, copying, and taking credit for others' work. It seems obvious that, considered this way, technology is neutral, deserving neither praise nor blame for the way it is used.

Does this particular attitude toward technology disclose its essence or does it, perhaps, hide the true nature of technology from us? What is concealed or revealed when we correspondingly see ourselves, and by extension, humanity, as masters of a neutral, your-wish-is-my-command servant, a magical servant to whom we look to give us whatever we desire and save us from whatever we want to be saved from? Does the common conception of technology help us recognize

I appeal to the philosophers of all countries to unite and never again mention Heidegger or talk to another philosopher who defends Heidegger. This man was a devil. I mean, he behaved like a devil to his beloved teacher [Husserl], and he was a devilish influence in Germany.

KARL POPPER

the full extent and nature of technology's role in our day-to-day dealings and in our sense of ourselves?

Even a superficial look at the current technological age reveals that we are the benefactors of such wondrous technological marvels as iPods and iPhones; streaming video on demand; personal GPS navigators; big, thin television screens; teeny-tiny digital cameras; online classes taken at our convenience; smart vehicles that apply their brakes on our behalf; and classroom "clickers" that allow professors to get instant feedback from students. So widespread and constant is the parade of technological superstars that it is easy to forget about less glamorous, but nonetheless equally technological, aspects of our lives, forget how deeply and pervasively our lives and consciousness are imbued with such taken-for-granted technology as dental braces; indoor plumbing; central heating and air conditioning; no-wrinkle, no-stain fabrics; eyeglasses and contact lenses; hearing aids and cochlear implants; prosthetic limbs and artificial joints; ATM cards; microwave ovens; television and radio; ballpoint pens and mechanical pencils; electricity; skateboards, mountain bikes, automobiles, and motorcycles; running shoes; vaccinations; running water; multivitamins; paperback books—all technology.

Maybe we don't "forget" that these things are technology so much as we just don't think about *what it means that they are technology*. Maybe we are so comfortable with them—so dependent on them, so involved with them—that we don't really pay close attention to how pervasively technological our present way of living is. And, so, we slip into taking technology as a whole for granted, assuming that, as a rule, we are the masters of our own contrivances. But are we? Are we in "control" when we cannot stray too far from our cell phones and MP3 players, when we must make sure we have plenty of batteries, chargers, cords, and other "necessities" before we can comfortably go about our business? What kind of freedom and ease is provided by so much technology?

Are we in control when we are afraid not to take advantage of the latest technological improvements in athletic performance lest we be outperformed by those who do use them: HGH, steroids, blood doping, metal alloy bats, high-tech tennis rackets, customized alloy golf clubs, and space-age, speed-enhancing swimsuits? Are we in control if we are unable to study without background music and a laptop, incapable of talking on the phone without simultaneously checking our e-mail or surfing the Web? Are we in control when we cannot—not will not, but *cannot*—write a research paper without a computer and Internet access? In other words, are we in control when we feel lost and naked without the technological umbilical cords that link us to the "they" 24/7?

Are we in control when our lives are based on an endless series of calculations, technical assessments of advantages versus disadvantages, long- and short-range projections? What is the effect on our lives and psyches of continuously scrutinizing studies, surveys, charts, statistics, longevity tables, and BMI calculators to "figure out" if it is okay to consume caffeine, and if so, when and how much? What happens to the *human* experience of eating when I preface each meal with a careful study of its nutritional content, down to grams, ounces, micrograms, recommended daily percentages for "average" adults or "typical" diabetics or . . . ?

When we take technology and technical knowledge and mastery so much for granted, we unavoidably take ourselves and our humanness for granted because this era's default approach to the world is "calculative," focused on solving problems and organizing knowledge and accomplishing our goals scientifically, efficiently, quickly, and predictably. Without great care, we risk "doing" more and "being" less. We take existence (Being) itself for granted, overlooking what Heidegger described as "the marvel of all marvels; that what-is *is*."[41]

This taken-for-granted, crudely pragmatic, so-what attitude is a dominant feature of the present age. We modern men and women are action-oriented, "proactive" folks, prone to "getting things done" rather than dwelling on them, more interested in results than in reflecting on the nature or essence of things. To us, existence = doing, calculating, negotiating, consuming, and manipulating everything freely and as fully as possible. Even our efforts to "save the environment" are based on calculations, carbon-credits, species counts.

So fully have we embraced and absorbed technology and the kind of thinking that comes along with it that we believe that we can fix technology by coming up with better technology. If technology has polluted our atmosphere, better technology will clean it up. When our streams and waterways are dirtied, we calculate ways to filter out pollutants. We'll save water with low-flush toilets, operate our increasing cache of gadgets with solar and wind power, cut our consumption of oil by driving technologically complex and sophisticated vehicles that can "think" for themselves. We'll save trees by going to the "paperless office" and downloading e-books. We'll end killing and war by creating some technologically "smart" weapons that can disable other weapons without hurting living things and by finding alternative sources of energy so there is plenty for all. We'll "cure" philosophical anxiety with medication. And we'll "figure out" how to accomplish all of these goals without pain, at no cost to the environment or to ourselves.

> *It is the peculiar business of philosophy to ascertain and make clear the meaning of statements and questions. The chaotic state in which philosophy found itself during the greater part of its history is due to the unfortunate fact that, in the first place, it took certain questions to be real questions before carefully ascertaining whether they really made any sense.*
>
> MORITZ SCHLICK

● ● ● ● ● ●

PHILOSOPHICAL

QUERY

Take a technology inventory of your own life. Here are some obvious places to start: What role does the Internet play in your study habits, music and video consumption, social interaction, work? As a consumer, look for less-than-obvious forms of technology, from UPC code scanners to the things you buy, or want to buy. Look around your school and classroom for examples of technology. Then reflect on how technology affects how you think about life and what you want from it.

Human Resources

Occasionally, we may have a flickering sense that somehow something is amiss here, that something seems lacking in our lives. What could it be? A first temptation might be to think that we only need to figure out how to have more money, more gadgets, more freedom. But what if we are thinking about all of this in a flawed way, calculating and analyzing and looking for the *wrong kind of answer* in the wrong places and in the wrong way—and not seeing what could save us, could enrich our lives? What if we must stop thinking technologically before we can respond to what technology "wants" to reveal to us—the *truth of Being*.

Premodern technology used nature as a means in a kind of ongoing exchange. Consider the way a windmill shares the power of the wind to create energy. It relies on the wind and only works when there is wind. The windmill waits for the wind. Not so modern technology "which puts to nature the unreasonable demand that it supply energy which can be extracted and stored as such" and then calculates ways to accomplish this. Modern technological thinking treats everything as a means, a tool, a source of energy to be stored to await our beck and call. In Heidegger's language, modern technology sees everything as a "standing-reserve" of potential power to be "ordered" and "challenged" (arranged and manipulated) and stored.

> . . . a tract of land is challenged in the hauling out of coal and ore. The earth now reveals itself as a coal mining district, the soil as a mineral deposit. . . . Agriculture is now the mechanized food industry. Air is now set upon to yield nitrogen, the earth to yield ore, ore to yield uranium, for example; uranium is set upon to yield atomic energy, which can be released either for destruction or for peaceful use.[42]

Today the rhythms of nature are disrupted; we no longer wait for the wind, we create it (or its equivalent) in fuel cells and turbines and generators. Corn is "challenged" to yield ethanol, which "stands in reserve" in refineries and fuel tanks until we tap into its "stored" energy. Nothing is allowed to "arrive" or to exist as an end-in-itself. Everything serves a calculated, pragmatic purpose, is seen as a potential source of something else, as a means, an instrument, something passively waiting to be "taken."

Technologically understood, you and I are human resources. Most likely, your college or business has a Human Resources Department. You can even major in human resources management or work for a temporary employment agency that keeps human resources "ordered" by experience, training, and skill-sets, "standing in reserve" until needed.

Danger

Heidegger was [possibly] a small character, an ageing man haunted by ruse, by ambition, by certain deeply-incised "agrarian" traditions of concealment and exploitation. His acre of ground might have seen the harvest of Hell, but it was his.

GEORGE STEINER

For Heidegger, the supreme danger of our time is the transformation of the human being into something fundamentally less than human, even nonhuman. Technology itself—essentially, by its nature—transforms how we think and, thereby, how we live more than any particular technological device or practice. Thus, technology and pragmatic calculation dominate our existence and, tragically, human beings are folded into the standing-reserve.

"The essence of technology is by no means anything technological," Heidegger notes. Rather, the essence of technology is a way of looking at the world as raw material to be used. Technology is a frame of mind, a way of thinking. But it is not a frame of mind that we have chosen. It is a frame of mind shaped by the way technology sees nature itself as an instrument. Today, unlike in other eras, we literally experience the entire world as standing-reserve, and we tarry alongside of it rather than exist in it.

We do not come to this of our own accord but are thrown into a technological and scientific relationship to the world. The technological frame of mind constitutes our modern destiny. We even approach spiritual matters scientifically and technologically, conducting studies to prove or disprove the efficacy of prayer or meditation or life after death. We carbon-date pages of Scripture and bones of saints, looking for scientific answers to age-old questions. We conduct sociological and anthropological studies of religion. We conduct "placebo-controlled, double-blind" studies of spiritual practices. We scan our brains as we listen to music and poetry and as we look at paintings and sunsets to better "understand" music or poetry or art or beauty.

We measure—"order"—the cosmos itself, looking to outer space for new sources of energy to add to the ever-expanding standing-reserve. When nature as a whole is threatened by technology, we employ technology to count and record ("order") endangered species via wireless transmitters. We scientifically analyze soil and air samples, track storms via satellite, and obsessively tweak additives and supplements to enhance our food supply. We seek out new superdrugs to kill off superbugs created by older drugs crafted to kill off older bugs.

Yet in these very attempts to control the world and to come to technically "correct" understandings of the world, "the truth will withdraw," Heidegger warns. Correct, calculative, objective understanding of particulars, though not sufficient for grasping the truth of existence, is potently useful, seductive, and distracting and induces complacency. This, says Heidegger, is "the supreme danger" of technology, a danger rooted in our overall indifference to everything that is not part of the standing-reserve. So long as we are chiefly interested in things as means, as instruments, as standing-reserve, we inevitably come to a point where we take ourselves for standing-reserve. Then, ironically and monstrously,

> . . . precisely as the one so threatened, [man] exalts himself to the posture of the lord of the earth. In this way the illusion comes to prevail that everything man encounters exists only insofar as it is his construct. This illusion gives rise in turn to one final delusion: it seems as though man everywhere and always encounters only himself. . . . *In truth, however, precisely nowhere does man today any longer encounter himself, i.e., his essence.*[43]

Demanding that we ourselves produce "on call" reduces us to mere means (a danger Kant, Kierkegaard, and Nietzsche so vehemently warned against). This way of thinking hides the truth of Being from us and prevents us from existing authentically.

The technological frame of mind is, we might say, as blind to human essence as a chemical analysis of the paint applied to the Sistine Chapel is blind to the majesty of Michelangelo's frescoes. So long as we consign ourselves to a technological frame of mind, we remain hidden from ourselves. Unaware that we are hidden from ourselves, we are blindly confident that nothing can hide from us. This is an irony of tragic, and to use Heidegger's term, monstrous proportions because we no longer encounter anything but caricatures of ourselves: Our great tragedy is to be unable to recognize our great tragedy.

> [Technological reasoning] blocks the shining-forth and holding sway of truth. . . . What is dangerous is not technology. Technology is not demonic; but its essence is mysterious. The essence of technology . . . is the danger. . . .

Lacking an ethic, self-maimed in the face of the inhuman, Heidegger's ontology remains an overwhelming fragment.

GEORGE STEINER

The threat to man does not come . . . from the potentially lethal machines and apparatuses of technology. The actual threat has already afflicted man in its essence. . . . with the possibility that it could be denied to him to . . . experience the call of a more primal truth.[44]

▧ HUMANITY IS A CONVERSATION ▧

In his 1936 essay "Hölederin and the Essence of Poetry," Heidegger says, "We—mankind—are a conversation." A **conversation** is more than idle talk. A conversation is *dialogue*, progressively empathetic communication about Being. Conversation makes humanity possible

Heidegger notes that we have been taught that Aristotle defined man as the "rational animal," which we interpret as meaning that calculative reasoning is our uniquely human essence. But this is a Latin-based shift in meaning from a more poetic Greek description of humans as *zoon logon echon*: the animal with words.

It is the richer, more poetic function of language, Heidegger says, that makes *human* existence possible, that allows us to ask, What is Being? What am I? What is my essence? This is not the obvious, hence trivial, point that we need language to verbalize any question about anything. Rather, Heidegger is saying that language's "poetic" function—as distinct from its informative, technological uses—is essential to our full humanity. "The rose, the swans, the stag in the forest," are so immersed in Being, Heidegger says, that they are not amazed by it. Language (*logos*) sets us apart from them and in so doing creates a human world.[45]

These distinct functions of language reveal the contrast between merely exchanging information and having a conversation. Participants in a conversation attend to each other and to whatever they are talking about. They cannot treat each other as means-only, as "one," and still have a conversation. Nor can they half-attend, multi-tasking while scanning the Internet and chatting on the phone, cursorily grunting yea and nay while inwardly dwelling on some private, other matter. As conversation proceeds, empathy among the conversants emerges and increases by means of "mutual tuning" until what was dimly and implicitly understood is explicitly recognized.

So what? we might be tempted to ask—yet again. Why make such a big deal about something everybody already knows, namely that language is one of the defining characteristics of humans, and what's the big deal about something we commonly experience—meaningful, empathetic conversations?

But wait. Have we lost our way so quickly and easily? Isn't this kind of automatic, knee-jerk "everybody already knows" reaction an instance of idle chatter? This compulsion to always ask "so what?" is, Heidegger says, just that, a compulsion. We are just as free not to ask "so what?" as we are to ask. We are free to rise above the "they," free to rise above the compulsion, free to free ourselves from endless means-ends calculations.

The widespread temptation to ask "so what?," to mock and to trivialize poetic language, is important, Heidegger says, because we are always at risk of missing language's deeper disclosures. To say it again, with emphasis, "We—mankind— *are* a conversation." We are not a calculation, not a tool, not merely or even mostly human resources. We are also, uniquely, the stuff of which dreams and poems are

---

conversation

For Heidegger, dialogue; progressively attuned communication about Being; language function contrasted with idle talk.

The world of explanations and reasons is not the world of existence.

JEAN-PAUL SARTRE

made. All *conversations* are really one conversation, the subject of which, ultimately, essentially, down deep, is Being, is what it means to be us, what it means
to be human.

> The being of men is founded in language. But this only becomes actual in
> *conversation*. . . . Being able to hear is not a mere consequence of speaking with
> one another, on the contrary, it is rather pre-supposed in the latter process. . . .
> We are a conversation—and that means we can hear from one another. We are a
> conversation, that always means at the same time: we are a *single* conversation.[46]

Rather than dismiss Heidegger's idea of conversation as ridiculous, impractical, or obvious, let's suppose, as a thought experiment at least, that when we pay
attention, when we "attune ourselves" and "wait on Being," to use Heidegger's language, we "hear" some common chord underneath mankind's ongoing discourses
about philosophy and religion, about the meaning of life, about values, about significance, about whatever matters most in a basic, fundamental way. When we
speak, listen, and hear this way, when we engage in conversation, we experience
the quiet and peace of Being amidst the insatiable busy-ness of life.

There is no point in trying to exhaust all of the possible ways and names we
have given to whatever "it" is that we "animals with words" are trying to get in touch
with and articulate—to ourselves and to *anyone who will listen*. Surely we are not
just "exchanging information," reporting facts, or "gossiping" about the "meaning
of life," the One, or YWH, or Jehovah, Shiva, Krishna, or Zeus, Poseidon, Hera,
or Athena, or the Good, the True, and the Beautiful, about God, Allah, Nirvana,
the Great Mother. Are we not, in some way and on some level, trying to say the
unsayable and name the unnameable? Does not Genesis, the first book of Judeo-
Christian Scripture, begin as a conversation about God's *saying*—a conversation
about a primordial conversation as it were? Are we not, then, whatever else we
may be, always and fundamentally related to the *logos*?

For Heidegger, if we attune ourselves to it, the ongoing "great conversation" discloses that the continual struggle to name the unnameable is not about pointing to
what already exists, but is an "act of establishing" our humanity. For Heidegger, we
emerged in the world *as human beings* with the creative, poetic use of language, a
deep, ontological use of language that allows us to exist as more than mere entities:
When the poet "speaks the essential word," language "establishes being by means
of the word."[47]

Think about what Heidegger is suggesting. Think about the "stammer" that
runs through human history, through our individual attempts to express—
what?—our sense of something real and important, just out of reach of ordinary
language. Think, too, about this small, textbook history of philosophy as conversation about how philosophers have tried to express important things in words
and how, for the most part, they have failed to "finish the job." There always seems
to be one more "Yes, but what about *X*?"

Suppose further that failing to "finish the job" is inevitable because trying to
finish the job *is* the job. Suppose that what we—philosophers, theologians, mothers
and fathers, poets, friends and enemies, concerned human beings of all stripes—
are really doing is trying to express our essence. If so, then Heidegger may be onto
something when he says that we human beings do not "have" a history: We *are*

*The [philosophical]
tradition is in shambles.*
HILARY PUTNAM

*Logic is the essence of
philosophy.*
BERTRAND RUSSELL

our history, and our history is an ongoing conversation that alternately discloses and conceals what matters most to us. Heidegger calls it Being. Others have called it by other names: Logos, Truth, the One, God, Tao, to mention five of its most persistent and evocative names.

According to Heidegger, the disparity of names only means that we cannot name the unnameable with finality, cannot utter *the* one, true-for-all name. It does not mean that we cannot talk about Being at all. We can, we have, and we will keep trying, keep conversing because that is who and what we are. That is *how* we are.

I, for one among many, would like to think that Heidegger is right on this much at least, that despite our very real differences and disagreements, underneath or prior to our objective diversity, there exists a *human* world. It is in that spirit that I have written *Archetypes of Wisdom* as a conversation to which you and I are mutually tuned: I, by writing in my study, attuned as best I can be to the conversations of the philosophers and to you, as I empathetically imagine you to be; you, by reading this book, by talking about philosophy with your professor, friends, and family, and by good-naturedly entering into its spirit.

If the language of the preceding paragraph seems soft and ambiguous, too "poetic" for philosophy, think again. Reread Lao-tzu, Plato, Marcus Aurelius, Augustine, Hume, Kant, Kierkegaard, James, Nietzsche—poets all, as well as philosophers, in my opinion. Consider it also in the context of the kind of *conversation* that attempts to articulate who and what we are, not as particular individuals, but as *human* beings who care about more than information, gratification, and "stuff." Consider it one small utterance in the chorus of human Being.

> Poetry is not merely an ornament accompanying existence. . . . Poetry is the foundation which supports history. . . .
>
> The time is needy and therefore its poet is extremely rich.[48]

■ WITHER PHILOSOPHY? (A PUN) ■

From its inception, philosophy has been self-conscious, self-assessing, and self-correcting. Philosophers have argued about particular issues and about "meta-issues"—that is, about questions concerning what constitutes legitimate philosophy and the *philosophical* treatment of *philosophical* issues—as opposed to, say, scientific, literary, historical, or theological treatments of non-philosophical issues.

By the twentieth century, philosophers began to accuse other philosophers of not *being* philosophers. This was an altogether different kind of criticism than accusing one another of not being *good* philosophers. Existentialists contemned idealists; postmodernists contemned existentialists; analytic philosophers rejected continental philosophy and vice versa. Some philosophers, as we have seen, questioned even the possibility of philosophy. In a 1987 address to the American Philosophy Association, Kai Nielsen went so far as to say, "There is no defending the tradition. Systematic analytic philosophy and its Continental cousins along with their historical ancestors must be given up."[49]

In some ways, this is hardly surprising. Indeed, it would have been more troubling if twentieth-century Western philosophy had remained aloof from the divisiveness, the diversity, and the unease of the polarized world around it: On the one hand, the smashing of boundaries and shibboleths; on the other, the anxiety of nearly absolute personal freedom without the guiding hand of tradition. On the one hand, faith in science and obvious signs of progress; on the other, the reduction of life to biochemistry and the growing use of science in the service of destructive, partisan purposes. On the one hand, sophisticated and specialized techniques that work exceptionally well in their own domains; on the other, the inability of technique to satisfy persistent meaning-needs. On the one hand, enlightening attention to language itself and how it works; on the other, the suspicion that, at base, nothing *really means* anything.

Wittgenstein and Heidegger were sensitive to these themes and sensitive to the crisis twentieth-century philosophy faced. Each in his own way tried to "save" philosophy and, in the process, spoke at times in a prophetic, quasi-biblical poetic voice that reflected and reinforced their charismatic personalities and seriousness. Whether one, both, or neither stand(s) the test of time is not for us to know, but this much we can say with confidence: Wittgenstein and Heidegger deserve our thanks for trying to find or recover the archetypal voice of philosophy, the voice that speaks beyond the academic and the technical, the voice that speaks directly to the problems of life and the challenges of living authentically in an unsettled age.

If, at times, they stammer and seem, paradoxically, both over-simple and unnecessarily complex, perhaps it is because they are trying to say precisely what, in the end, can be heard but not spoken. If *that* (what I just said) seems nonsensical, then you may already be an analytic philosopher. If it seems—feels—as if it is *about something*, then you may be more of a continentalist. In either case, if you care at all about such things, then perhaps you are a philosopher.

Whatever that may be.

▦ Summary of Main Points ▦

- By the twentieth century, philosophers were struggling with the "post-Nietzschean deconstruction of metaphysics." Philosophical deconstruction is a kind of close textual analysis focused on uncovering and overcoming "privileges" hidden in philosophical arguments and theories—"texts."

- Analytic philosophers stress logic, testability, precision, and clarity. Common to this way of approaching philosophy is the notion that the universe consists of independent (atomic) entities, material particles, sense data, impressions, "facts," or something else. Logical and linguistic analyses are said to be the only proper methods for sorting out philosophical confusions. Continental philosophers tend to explain things not by reducing them to simple entities but by understanding them in a broader, holistic, historical context. This approach to philosophy includes formalism, idealism, phenomenology, and existentialism.

- In the *Tractatus Logico-Philosophicus*, Ludwig Wittgenstein tried to show the underlying structure of language, asserting that what can be said is what can be said meaningfully, that what can be said is the same as what can be thought, and that what cannot be said cannot be thought. Trying to say the unsayable, as earlier philosophers did, amounts to trying to think the unthinkable. According to Wittgenstein, this applies to the *Tractatus* as well, for its propositions are senseless and meant to be discarded after they have shown the way out of traditional philosophical nonsense.

- In the *Philosophical Investigations*, Wittgenstein questions his own earlier work and says that the structure of language determines the structure of thought and, therefore, the structure of our experience, not the other way around. Rather than replace mistaken philosophical theories with his own new, correct, philosophical theory, the later Wittgenstein suggests that, when it succeeds, philosophy allows us to give philosophical questions a rest.

● Martin Heidegger's unique blend of phenomenology, ontology, and existentialism grew out of his study of Edmund Husserl's phenomenology. According to Heidegger, Husserl saw phenomenology as the science of beings (in the plural), whereas it is more properly understood as the science of Being with a capital B. Toward that end, Heidegger attempted to articulate the fundamental condition of uniquely human existence.

● According to Heidegger, the fundamental human condition is concern about our unique condition, our be-ing. Thus, any inquiry into the nature of human existence, is, ultimately, an inquiry into the nature of Being. Heidegger wants to remind us of what we have lost, our primal amazement that we (humanity) exist. Unlike any other entity, we "comport" ourselves toward "the" world. We exist as human beings with an attitude toward a human world, not toward the single, detached, objective, one-and-only world.

● According to Heidegger, most philosophers have lost sight of Being because they have treated detached, calculative thinking as the defining characteristic of being human. But unless we have an attitude and a relationship toward things, we cannot understand them. We understand something only when we are involved with it and "attuned" to it.

● According to Heidegger, we exist without any explanation no matter how hard we try to make it otherwise. When the burden and anxiety of the human condition are too great to bear, we escape by losing ourselves in the "they." When we do this, our mode of being is inauthenticity, a way of being dominated by "the" world. In this condition, there can be no dialogue, only idle talk. Idle talk never rises above verbal understanding.

● In his analysis of technology, Heidegger says that calculative technological thinking sees everything as "standing-reserve," a source of energy to be stored to await our beck and call. This way of thinking transforms human beings into beings "just there," entities to be used and treated like everything else in the standing-reserve. The essence of technology is a way of looking at the world as raw material to be used. Technology is a frame of mind that we have not chosen and that characterizes and dominates our era.

● According to Heidegger, there is an important distinction between idle talk and having a conversation, between everyday language and poetic language. Participants in a conversation must be attuned to each other and to whatever they are talking about. All conversations are really one conversation, the true subject of which is humanity. For Heidegger, truly human existence emerged in the world with the creative, poetic, ontological use of language that allows us to exist as more than mere entities. Thus, human history is a single conversation about forgetting and remembering Being.

■ POST-READING REFLECTIONS ■

Now that you have had a chance to learn about Ludwig Wittgenstein and Martin Heidegger, use your new knowledge to answer these questions.

1. Why do philosophers distinguish between the "early" and "later" Wittgenstein? How do they differ?

2. How is the *Tractatus* organized? Why is it organized that way?

3. What is the significance of "saying" in the *Tractatus*?

4. How does Wittgenstein's attitude toward language as expressed in the *Tractatus* change in his later work?

5. Why are some philosophers troubled by Heidegger's attitude toward Nazism? What was his attitude? Why is this issue particularly significant given Heidegger's overriding concerns with authenticity?

6. What is the central question in Heidegger's philosophy? Why is it important?

7. What does Heidegger mean by existence? What kinds of things can exist?

8. What is the "they," and what function does it serve in dealing with the burden of being human?

9. What kind of thinking characterizes technology (the technological frame of mind), and what role does that kind of thinking play in Heidegger's critique of technology?

10. What are human resources according to Heidegger?

11. How does idle talk differ from dialogue? Is one "better" than the other? Why?

12. What does Heidegger mean by "conversation"? What role does conversation play in human history?

 ## PHILOSOPHY INTERNET RESOURCES

Go to the Soccio Web page at **http://philosophy.wadsworth.com/ Soccio7e** for Web links, practice quizzes and tests, a pronunciation guide, and study tips.

PHILOSOPHY AS A WAY OF LIFE

LET NO ONE BE SLOW TO SEEK WISDOM WHEN HE IS YOUNG,
NOR WEARY IN THE SEARCH THEREOF WHEN HE IS GROWN
OLD. FOR NO AGE IS TOO EARLY OR TOO LATE FOR THE
HEALTH OF THE SOUL. AND TO SAY THAT THE SEASON FOR
STUDYING PHILOSOPHY HAS NOT YET COME, OR THAT IT
IS PAST AND GONE, IS LIKE SAYING THAT THE SEASON FOR
HAPPINESS IS NOT YET OR THAT IT IS NOW NO MORE.

Epicurus

LEARNING OBJECTIVES

- WHAT IS PHILOSOPHICAL ADVOCACY?
- WHAT IS THE "DIFFERENT VOICE" CAROL GILLIGAN IDENTIFIES?
- WHAT IS THE ISSUE OF "REPRESENTATION" IN ACADEMIC PHILOSOPHY?
- WHO IS PETER SINGER?
- WHO IS MARTHA C. NUSSBAUM?
- WHY DOES NUSSBAUM DESCRIBE HER PHILOSOPHY AS "NEO-STOIC"?
- WHO IS PIERRE HADOT?
- WHAT DOES HADOT SEE AS THE GOAL OF THE SAGE?

FOR YOUR REFLECTION

KEEP THESE QUESTIONS IN MIND AS YOU LEARN ABOUT PHILOSOPHY
AS A WAY OF LIFE.

1. *What is philosophical advocacy?*
2. *What is the "different voice" Carol Gilligan identifies?*
3. *What is the issue of "representation" in academic philosophy?*
4. *Who is Peter Singer?*
5. *Who is Martha C. Nussbaum?*
6. *Why does Nussbaum describe her philosophy as "Neo-stoic"?*
7. *Who is Pierre Hadot?*
8. *What does Hadot see as the goal of the sage?*

FOR DEEPER CONSIDERATION

A. Some philosophers argue that "autobiographical" considerations are irrelevant when it comes to philosophy. Others are not so sure. What do they mean by autobiographical considerations, and why is this issue significant? Is this a philosophical issue or not?

B. Present and then assess Peter Singer's views regarding our obligations toward alleviating world poverty. Is he too strict? Make your case that he is or isn't.

*W*hat is the role of the philosopher in contemporary society? Do philosophers have a role to play beyond that of philosophy teachers and scholars?

Traditionally, the philosopher has been viewed as a detached observer, someone outside the mainstream of society. Beginning with the apocryphal story of Thales falling into a well, one popular stereotype of the philosopher remains the befuddled, impractical critic, the character who gives advice and asks silly riddles about God making rocks too large to lift and trees falling in empty forests—but who bakes no bread. Less benign philosophical stereotypes include that of the icy, impersonal *logic chopper*, the individual who has mastered the art of exposing contradictions and ambiguities in other people's arguments and beliefs but who has no positive, practical skills to offer. A more charitable picture of the contemporary philosopher is of the well-intentioned intellectual who asks "good questions" but who, nonetheless, fails to understand and come to grips with "practical matters."

The popular notion of the philosopher as somehow irrelevant to modern life probably owes a great deal to the importance placed on theory, argument, and, most of all, objectivity and rationality by most modern philosophers. With the notable exceptions of philosophers such as Kierkegaard, James, and Nietzsche (Chapters 14–16), most modern philosophers write in a detached, impersonal voice. Even Marx (Chapter 13) wrote in an impersonal voice when he said that the time had come for philosophers to change the world, as did Wittgenstein and Heidegger when they attempted to introduce a "therapeutic" element into philosophy.

In this last chapter, we will take a *selective look* at some contemporary philosophers I have chosen to refer to under the broad heading of *philosophical advocates*. A **philosophical advocate** is a philosopher whose work identifies, clarifies, and actively opposes a perceived injustice; philosophical advocates give philosophical credence to personal experience based on gender, ethnic background, and social status.

Although philosophical advocates are not always academically trained philosophers, they always address philosophical questions in ways that speak to present-day concerns. They raise questions about the relationships of means to ends; about the effects of technology or culture or class structure on our individual and communal well-being. Jeremy Bentham, John Stuart Mill, Karl Marx, and William James are examples of philosophical advocates who were also public philosophers (Chapters 12–15).

Public philosophers are writers or speakers whose philosophical positions are expressed in ways accessible to a broad audience. The most effective public philosophers tap into—or identify—vital philosophical issues of the day. When public philosophers also "practice what they preach," they function much like sages or prophets in their capacity to provoke individual self-assessment and collective consciousness-raising.

Philosophical advocates refuse to remain on the sidelines of the major social controversies of our time. These include, but are not limited to, issues of poverty, quality of life, cultural equality, women's rights, and gender influences. I believe

Knowledge for the sake of knowledge is, say what you will, nothing but a dismal begging of the question.

MIGUEL DE UNAMUNO

philosophical advocate
Philosopher whose work identifies, clarifies, and actively opposes a perceived injustice; philosophical advocates give philosophical credence to personal experience based on gender, ethnic background, or social status.

public philosopher
Compelling writer or speaker whose philosophical positions are expressed in ways accessible to a broad audience; public philosophers tap into— or identify—vital philosophical issues of the day.

"It Is the Age of Socrates Again"

The late historian of philosophy Will Durant believed that without wisdom, technological progress and social "success" will only confuse us and make us unhappier than before:

> Human conduct and belief are now undergoing transformations profounder and more disturbing than any since the appearance of wealth and philosophy put an end to the traditional religion of the Greeks. It is the age of Socrates again: our moral life is threatened, and our intellectual life is quickened and enlarged by the disintegration of ancient customs and beliefs. Everything is new and experimental in our ideas and our actions; nothing is established or certain any more. The rate, complexity, and variety of change in our time are without precedent . . . all forms about us are altered, from the tools that complicate our toil, to the wheels that whirl us restlessly about the earth, to the innovations in our sexual relationships, and to the hard disillusionment of our souls. . . .
>
> Our culture is superficial today, and our knowledge dangerous, because we are rich in mechanisms and poor in purposes. The balance of mind which once came of a warm religious faith is gone; science has taken from us the supernatural bases of our morality, and all the world seems consumed in a disorderly individualism that reflects the chaotic fragmentation of our character. . . . We move about the earth with unprecedented speed, but we do not know, and have not thought, where we are going, or whether we shall find any happiness there for our harassed souls. We are being destroyed by our knowledge, which has made us drunk with our power. And we shall not be saved without wisdom.

Will Durant, *The Mansions of Philosophy: A Survey of Human Life and Destiny* (Garden City, N.Y.: Simon and Schuster, 1929), pp. vii, viii, xff.

---

that any new philosophical archetypes are likely to include some form of public philosophical advocacy. I also believe that it is unwise to predict precisely who the chief exemplars of these new archetypes will be, since that determination must be made over time. Consequently, I recommend treating this last chapter as a kind of *philosophical preview of coming attractions* indicating some (but certainly not all) fertile and important areas of contemporary philosophical activity.

Contemporary philosophers disagree among themselves about whether or not it is proper for philosophers—as philosophers—to base philosophical views on *autobiography* (the philosopher's specific life circumstances) or *advocacy* ("taking sides" by promoting specific social and political positions based on the philosopher's gender, ethnic, or economic circumstances). One camp argues that philosophers should strive for detached (objective) rationality—not become personally attached to their philosophical conclusions. Another camp argues that philosophers have both *rights* and *obligations* to take personal stands on timely issues—as philosophers.

In simplified terms, we can summarize the general critique of modern (Enlightenment) philosophy as follows: With rare exceptions, Western philosophers have failed to recognize that they have personal, social, gendered, and ethnic perspectives. When philosophers do this, they overlook the fact that their philosophy reflects the special interests of only a small portion of the human community.

idiot: *originally from the Greek* idiotes, *a disparaging term for private person; one who does not participate in community affairs; one who shuns the body politic; sometimes translated as "good for nothing."*

Hans Holbein, *Venus and Cupid*, photo © AKG London

Hans Jordaens, *Minerva Visiting the Muses on Mount Helicon*, photo © Bridgeman Art Library, London

The association of rationality with masculinity is being challenged by contemporary women (and men) philosophers, reaffirming some of the earliest, most compelling archetypal representations of woman as a symbol of both wisdom (Athena, right) and love (Aphrodite, left). Many of these contemporary philosophers also challenge the association of femininity with emotions, pointing out that both men and women can be wise.

Critics of modern philosophy assert that until very recently this blindness has resulted in a separation of professional philosophy from the real-life concerns of all persons not of the typical (privileged) philosophical classes: highly educated white males. The result, it is argued, is a tradition that has systematically excluded or marginalized the voices of philosophers concerned with family matters, children's interests, and other traditionally "unphilosophical" and "private" topics.

Whether or not philosophers must have particular experiences before they can philosophize about them is a difficult and controversial issue. Must one be a woman in order to philosophize about the oppression of women? Can philosophers of one social class or ethnic group really understand the particularities of members of some other group? And if they cannot, how can they speak for people in general when they deal with ethical issues or social philosophy—or the nature of knowledge?

Such questions are difficult to answer for many reasons. In the first place, there is the problem of who can possibly judge among competing claims of unique insight. Consider, for instance, the notion that only women are qualified to philosophize about "women's issues." Must we then also argue that women cannot speak out on "men's issues"? Are we thus committed to the principle that only

We should exercise ourselves with realities, not with dialectical speculations, like a man who has devoured some textbook on harmonics, but has never put his knowledge into practice. Likewise, we must not be like those who can astonish their onlookers by their skill in syllogistic argumentation, but who, when it comes to their own lives, contradict their own teachings.

POLEMON

those who suffer a particular form of oppression are qualified to address its identification and remedy?

If we are, then does it also follow that only African American working-class women can speak to the oppression of African American working-class women—but not to the oppression of African American middle-class women or Laotian American professional women or Haitian American working-class women? Should philosophers who have not given birth and raised children philosophize about motherhood?

These are not frivolous questions; they address important and controversial issues that extend beyond philosophy into campus politics, elections, legislation, the composition of juries. Answering these sorts of questions is fraught with peril, since any answer must appeal to some foundational principle of justification, which can—in turn—be questioned.

■ THE REEMERGENCE OF OTHER VOICES ■

Modern philosophy's emphases on objectivity and personal detachment have become increasingly disturbing to growing numbers of philosophers. Converging social, political, and intellectual movements are contributing to reawakened interest in *other voices* and other approaches to doing philosophy and practicing science. Susan Bordo (Chapter 9) does not see this as a complete rejection of modern philosophy, but rather as a *complement*, a completion or enrichment:

> This is not to say that detachment, clarity, and precision will cease to have enormous value in the process of understanding. Rather, our culture needs to reconceive the status of what Descartes assigned to the shadows. Such revaluation has been a constant, although "recessive" strain in the history of philosophy since Descartes. . . . Hume's insistence that "reason is and ought to be the slave of the passions," and, perhaps most importantly, Kant's revelation that objectivity itself is the result of human structuring, opened various doors that in retrospect now appear as critical openings.
>
> Hume, for example, may now be seen as having a rightful place—along with Nietzsche . . . [and] . . . James . . . in the critical protest against the Cartesian notion that reason can and should be a "pure" realm free from contamination by emotion, instinct, will, sentiment, and value. Within this protest, we see the development both of a "naturalist" *anthropology* of the Cartesian ideals of precision, certainty, and neutrality (Nietzsche . . . and James), and a complementary *metaphysics* . . . in which "vagueness" as well as specificity, tentativeness, and valuation are honored as essential to thought.[1]

Contemporary philosophers and social scientists pose a series of interrelated questions that challenge the exclusive status of the traditional (masculinized) model of rationality as detached, objective knowing: Is there only one way of reasoning? Is objective reasoning the only or best way of knowing? To what extent, if any, are personal detachment and objectivity possible? Perhaps most important, when—if ever—are personal detachment and objectivity undesirable?

One geometry cannot be more true than another. It can only be more convenient.

HENRI POINCARÉ

Now perhaps you may think it not fitting for a woman to philosophize, just as it is not fitting for her to ride horses or speak in public. But I think that some things are peculiar to a man, some to a woman, some are common to both. . . . I say that courage and justice and wisdom are common to both.

PHINTYS OF SPARTA

Can one live in reason's kingdom . . . and still be a creature of wonder, grief, and love?

MARTHA C. NUSSBAUM

That's an excellent suggestion, Miss Triggs. Perhaps one of the men here would like to make it.

In 1982, Harvard psychologist **Carol Gilligan** (b. 1936) published her groundbreaking book *In a Different Voice: Psychological Theory and Women's Development,* a work that prompted a necessary reassessment of moral reasoning. The following passage conveys some sense of the importance and delicacy of research into the area of gender bias—and how pervasive such bias can be:

> A word, finally, about the politics and the controversy of this research. The stark fact of the all-male research sample, accepted for years as representative by psychologists studying human development, in one sense speaks for itself. That such samples were not seen long ago as problematic by women or men points to different blindnesses on the part of each sex. The fact that these samples passed the scrutiny of peer review boards, that studies of . . . moral development . . . using all-male samples were repeatedly funded and widely published in professional journals indicates that the psychological research community needs to reexamine its claims to objectivity and dispassion. If the omission of half the human population was not seen, or not seen as significant, or not spoken about as a problem (by women or men), what other omissions are not being seen? The contribution of women's thinking . . . is a different voice, a different way of speaking about relationships and about the experience of the self. The inclusion of this voice changes the map of the moral domain. Listening to girls and women, we have come to listen differently to boys and men. And we have come to think differently about human nature and the human condition, and in turn, about . . . disciplines devoted to improving human life. . . .

Carol Gilligan

The different voice I describe is characterized not by gender but by theme. Its association with women is an empirical observation, and it is primarily through women's voices that I trace its development. But this association is not absolute, and the contrasts between male and female voices . . . highlight a distinction between two modes of thought and . . . focus [on] a problem of interpretation rather than represent a generalization about either sex.[2]

Gilligan notes that excessive reliance on "rationality" results in injustice by excluding those who do not speak in the "objective voice" from full participation in philosophy, science, law, higher education—and by denying everyone access to the full range of knowledge necessary for wise choices. When we confine our standard of reasoning to the "impersonal" modern model, we fail to recognize wisdom as it is expressed in some Asian, Native American, African, and Hispanic philosophies that are not built on the objective, rationalistic model. The result is a tendency to classify wisdom philosophies as religions or mythologies rather than as "real" philosophies.

In the spring of 2008—more than a quarter of a century after Carol Gilligan called contemporary philosophers' attention to the exclusion of "other voices" from philosophy—organizers of the first meeting of the Collegium of Black Women Philosophers were able to identify only thirty full-time black women philosophy teachers in America. That's correct: thirty.[3]

Kathryn T. Gines, the black assistant professor at Vanderbilt University who founded the Collegium, points out that, "If you're a black woman, you cannot identify with the majority of the people in the profession." Jacqueline R. Scott, an associate professor of philosophy at Loyola University Chicago, expressed similar frustrations: "I spend a lot of time being the only woman and the only black person. . . . Every once in a while it hits me, and I wonder what I'm doing here." Although philosophy is academe's oldest discipline, the first Ph.D. was not awarded to a black woman until 1965, when Joyce Mitchell Cook earned her philosophy doctorate at Yale University.

When Sally Haslanger, a philosophy professor at the Massachusetts Institute of Technology, discovered that the American Philosophical Association (APA) does not keep current records of how many of its ten thousand philosophers are women (or members of other minority groups), she collected her own data from America's top twenty philosophy departments and discovered that only about 19 percent are women. Anna Stubblefield, chair of the philosophy department at Rutgers University's Newark campus and head of the APA's Committee on Blacks and Philosophy, estimated that about a hundred, or 1 percent, of the ten thousand academic philosophers in North America are black, and of those, perhaps twenty are female, while Gines put the number at twenty-nine.

Does this sort of thing matter *philosophically*, as opposed to, say, sociologically or legally? Surely it does, for, as we have seen throughout our journey together, philosophy, from its origins, has been associated with a love of wisdom. From its inception, philosophers have struggled to articulate, assess, and establish moral principles and universal standards of justice, or to show that there are no such principles. What philosophers have not done, because to do so would render them unphilosophical, is to ignore unspoken, uncritiqued epistemological assumptions and prejudicial social practices and preferences once they are pointed out, whether by social scientists, theologians, poets, protestors, or by other philosophers.

This is not to say that philosophers, as philosophers, are free from biases and always open to new questions and modes of inquiry. They are, obviously, not immune to human frailties. But philosophers, as philosophers, are expected to base their philosophical conclusions on arguments, evidence, and reasons—not on preferences pertaining to personalities, nationality, gender, religion, ethnicity, appearance.

As a truly critical and reflective discipline, philosophy cannot tolerate the systemic and persistent exclusion and suppression of philosophers based solely on social, gender, or other autobiographical considerations—nor can it include or make exceptions for individuals or ideas on those bases. And this is where the role of the contemporary philosophical advocate can get particularly tricky.

Whether it is done deliberately or not, systematically limiting the participation of "outsiders" and "minorities" in the ranks of professional, academic philosophy is clearly unreasonable because doing so deprives us of the contributions of individuals who may have insights and capacities that we lack. It is also unfair because it creates a caste system based not on talent, experience, or character, but on luck, custom, and ethnocentrism. Yet one common "fix" for the underrepresentation of certain groups in the ranks of professional philosophy may be exacerbating the very problem it seeks to redress by increasing rather than reducing the role of autobiography in philosophy. "There is a certain type of research done by black scholars that isn't accepted by the larger white academy," reports Carol M. Swain, a black professor of political science and law at Vanderbilt, who worries about what she describes as the "self-segregation" that can result by "Encouraging black people to marginalize themselves by pursuing a line of philosophy not accepted by the mainstream [and that] just reinforces the stereotype that blacks can't do philosophy the way other scholars can."

What, then, does it mean to philosophize *as a woman*, or *as a black woman*, or *as a Native American*, or *as an Italian American*, or *as a gay man*, or *as a lesbian*? And what, if any, is the limit to such categories? That is, is the category black-lesbian *philosophically* different from black-woman or black-gay-person? Whatever their social, political, and legal ramifications, such considerations also raise epistemological, moral, and philosophical questions.

. . . . . .

PHILOSOPHICAL

QUERY

Does categorizing philosophical areas of specialization along gender, ethnic, and other autobiographical lines turn "doing philosophy" into sociology or social work? Is this a philosophical question? If not, why not? If so, who is qualified to deal with it?

▪ PETER SINGER: "THE DANGEROUS ▪ PHILOSOPHER"

Peter Singer

The Australian philosopher **Peter Singer** (b. 1946) is an important professional philosopher who believes in making people uncomfortable as a way of raising moral consciousness. For more than thirty years, Singer has advocated a rigorous brand of contemporary utilitarianism (Chapter 12). Due to the potent combination of the life-and-death topics he addresses, the clarity of his prose, and the relentless quality of reasoning, Singer has become the rare philosopher whose philosophical writings and arguments are widely discussed among academic philosophers and the nonprofessional mass media.

Singer emerged as an international figure with the publication of *Animal Liberation* in 1975; in 1979 he published *Practical Ethics. Animal Liberation* has sold half a million copies, and *Practical Ethics* more than one hundred and twenty thousand copies—remarkable figures for carefully reasoned philosophy books.

By the time of his 1999 appointment as Princeton University's first professor of bioethics, Singer was already one of the most famous—and controversial—philosophers writing and speaking today. His influence is a product of a relentless application of utilitarian principles to some of the most troublesome and important issues of our era: euthanasia, abortion, suicide, poverty. Even Singer's position at Princeton is controversial. The philosophy department wanted a theoretical philosopher, not a practical (or applied) ethicist. The biology department was uneasy about appointing someone who openly opposed animal experimentation. As a result, Singer's bioethics professoriate is in the Center for Human Values. Because of protests against the university and death threats against Singer, Princeton has had to take extraordinary security precautions, carefully guarding the exact location of Singer's office and varying his routine.

Singer has long argued that euthanasia and infanticide (the killing of babies) are sometimes "necessary" given the complexities of the modern world. "It is ridiculous to pretend that old ethics still make sense when plainly they do not," Singer says in his characteristically straightforward way.[4] He also argues that a human's life is not necessarily "more sacred" than a dog's. Singer suggests that it might even be more compassionate to conduct medical experiments on permanently disabled unconscious orphans than on conscious, sentient animals. Following Bentham, Singer argues that what matters most is not whether any animal (including human animals) can reason or talk, but whether it can suffer: "The notion that human life is sacred just because it's human is medieval," Singer says, ". . . it's time to stop pretending that the world is not the way we know it to be."[5]

As if such ideas are not disturbing enough to many people, Singer challenges everyone not already living in abject poverty—and that is most of the readers of this text—with forceful arguments for giving away all income over $30,000 (a 1999 figure he accepted as the baseline for adequately supporting a typical middle-class household). Single adults could, of course, live on much less and so give away much more. Singer himself gives one-fifth of his income (including royalties from his books) to famine-relief agencies.

Discourse about philosophy is not the same thing as philosophy.

PIERRE HADOT

Discourse on virtue and they pass by in droves; whistle and dance the shimmy and you've got an audience.

DIOGENES

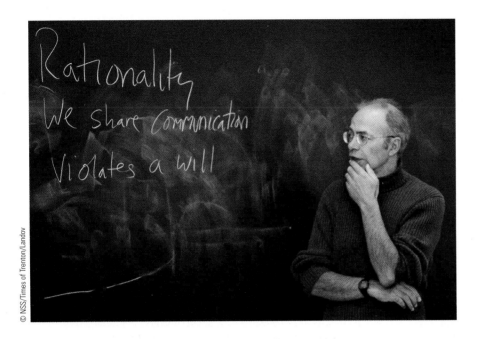

Peter Singer has devoted much of his life to questions of moral significance, including the matter of what characteristics (if any) distinguish human animals from nonhuman animals. This is dangerous stuff: "We like to distinguish ourselves from animals by saying that only humans are rational, can use language, are self-aware, or are autonomous. But . . . there are many humans who are not rational, self-aware, or autonomous, and who have no language— all humans under three months of age, for a start."

The Singer Solution to World Poverty

In "The Singer Solution to World Poverty," an article published in the *New York Times* rather than in a philosophy journal, Singer considers the hypothetical case of "Bob," who would rather see an innocent child run over by a train than throw a switch that would save the child's life by diverting the train onto the track where Bob's precious Bugatti automobile is stalled. In the hypothetical scenario, Bob, who is close to retirement age, has invested most of his savings in the Bugatti. If it is destroyed, he will not have a chance to recoup his losses. So he chooses the car over the child.

Singer then presents a series of Socratic arguments designed to challenge us to think long and hard about how (or if) we are morally different from Bob. In the passage that follows, the figure of $200 is borrowed from the work of the philosopher Peter Unger, who has calculated that approximately $200 donated to Unicef or Oxfam of America could provide enough aid to transform a sickly two-year-old into a healthy six-year-old. (This includes the costs of administrative fees.) As you read, note how deftly Singer anticipates some of the more common arguments we offer to explain why we do not give more to those in dire need. Singer writes:

> To show how practical philosophical argument can be, Unger even tells his readers that they can easily donate funds by using their credit card and calling one of these toll-free numbers: (800) 367–5437 for Unicef; [(800) 77-OXFAM] for Oxfam America. . . .
>
> Now you, too, have the information you need to save a child's life. How should you judge yourself if you don't do it? Think again about Bob and his Bugatti. . . .
>
> If you still think that it was very wrong of Bob not to throw the switch that would have diverted the train and saved the child's life, then it is hard to see how you could deny that it is also very wrong not to send money to one of the

Whatever arguments they undertake, I say that these should be undertaken for the sake of deeds. Just as a medical argument is no use unless it brings human bodies to health, so too, if someone grasps or teaches an argument as a philosopher, that argument is no use unless it conduces to the excellence of the human soul.

SENECA

Our campuses educate our citizens. Becoming an educated citizen means learning a lot of facts and mastering techniques of reasoning. But it means something more. It means learning how to be a human being capable of love and imagination.

MARTHA C. NUSSBAUM

organizations listed above. Unless, that is, there is some morally important difference between the two situations that I have overlooked.

Is it the practical uncertainties about whether aid will really reach the people who need it? Nobody who knows the world of overseas aid can doubt that such uncertainties exist. But Unger's figure of $200 to save a child's life was reached after he had made conservative assumptions about the proportion of the money donated that will actually reach its target.

One genuine difference between Bob and those who can afford to donate to overseas aid organizations but don't is that only Bob can save the child on the tracks, whereas there are hundreds of millions of people who can give $200 to overseas aid organizations. The problem is that most of them aren't doing it. Does this mean that it is all right for you not to do it? . . .

We seem to lack a sound basis for drawing a clear moral line between Bob's situation and that of any reader of this article with $200 to spare who does not donate it to an overseas aid agency. These readers seem to be acting at least as badly as Bob was acting when he chose to let the runaway train hurtle toward the unsuspecting child. In the light of this conclusion, I trust that many readers will reach for the phone and donate that $200. Perhaps you should do it before reading further.

Now that you have distinguished yourself morally from people who put their vintage cars ahead of a child's life, how about treating yourself and your partner to dinner at your favorite restaurant? But wait. The money you will spend at the restaurant could also help save the lives of children overseas! True, you weren't planning to blow $200 tonight, but if you were to give up dining out just for one month, you would easily save that amount. And what is one month's dining out, compared to a child's life? There's the rub. Since there are a lot of desperately needy children in the world, there will always be another child whose life you could save for another $200. Are you therefore obliged to keep giving until you have nothing left? At what point can you stop? . . .

In the world as it is now, I can see no escape from the conclusion that each one of us with wealth surplus to his or her essential needs should be giving most of it to help people suffering from poverty so dire as to be life-threatening. That's right: I'm saying that you shouldn't buy that new car, take that cruise, redecorate the house or get that pricey new suit. After all, a $1,000 suit could save five children's lives.

So how does my philosophy break down in dollars and cents? An American household with an income of $50,000 spends around $30,000 annually on necessities, according to the Conference Board, a nonprofit economic research organization. Therefore, for a household bringing in $50,000 a year, donations to help the world's poor should be as close as possible to $20,000. The $30,000 required for necessities holds for higher incomes as well. So a household making $100,000 could cut a yearly check for $70,000. Again, the formula is simple: whatever money you're spending on luxuries, not necessities, should be given away. . . .

When Bob first grasped the dilemma that faced him as he stood by that railway switch, he must have thought how extraordinarily unlucky he was to be placed in a situation in which he must choose between the life of an innocent child and the sacrifice of most of his savings. But he was not unlucky at all. We are all in that situation.[6]

The history of philosophy is a history of misfits; but, then, who in her right mind would have wanted to "fit in" with Caligula's court, Stalin's sadists, or Hitler's thugs? "Normal" is hardly a term of high praise.

SIR ROSS DELBERT-FETTERS

Wisdom has never been a social norm; talking about wisdom, on the other hand, seems to be.

GUISEPPE VARGASINI

Sed quis custodiet ipsos custodes? (Who will reform the reformers?)

JUVENAL

• • • • • •

Whew! Well, what do you think of Singer's reasoning? Should you save up your pizza and beer money, your latté and movie money, and send it to the poor? What principles or reasons are there—if any—for not doing so? (That is, has Singer succeeded in creating moral tension for you?)

PHILOSOPHICAL

QUERY

Without philosophy the mind is sickly.

SENECA

MARTHA C. NUSSBAUM: "LAWYER FOR HUMANITY"

The philosopher **Martha C. Nussbaum** (b. 1947) speaks for many public philosophers when she notes that too often professional intellectuals fail to use their theories and talents to improve the human condition by fighting for equality, justice, and freedom.[7] Nussbaum's background in classics and theology enriches and informs her work. Nussbaum believes that philosophers ought to be "lawyers for humanity" (a term she borrows from Seneca):

> For any view you put forward the next question has to be, "What would the world be like if this idea were actually taken up?" . . . It's what happens in the long haul that really matters. You just never know where or how your ideals will be realized.[8]

Nussbaum's conviction that philosophy should make a practical difference in our lives has both theoretical and experiential roots. Trained in philosophy and classics, Nussbaum now holds a joint appointment in divinity and law at the University of Chicago. In *Cultivating Humanity: A Classical Defense of Reform in Liberal Education*, Nussbaum comments on the experience of exclusion and expresses a contemporary version of the Stoic concept of the *cosmopolis*, or universal city.

> When I arrived at Harvard in 1969, my fellow first-year graduate students and I were taken up to the roof of the Widener Library by a well-known professor of classics. He told us how many Episcopal churches could be seen from that vantage point. As a Jew (in fact a convert from Episcopalian Christianity), I knew that my husband and I would have been forbidden to marry in Harvard's church, which had just refused to accept a Jewish wedding. As a woman I could not eat in the main dining room for the faculty club, even as a member's guest. Only a few years before, a woman would not have been able to use the undergraduate library. In 1972 I became the first female to hold the Junior Fellowship that relieved certain graduate students from teaching so that they could get on with their research. At that time I received a letter of congratulation from a prestigious classicist saying that it would be difficult to know what to call a female fellow, since "fellowess" was an awkward term. Perhaps the Greek language could solve the problem: since the masculine for "fellow" in Greek was *hetairos*, I could be called a *hetaira*. *Hetaira*, however, as I knew, is the ancient Greek word not for "fellowess" but for "courtesan."

Martha C. Nussbaum

Philosophy heals human diseases, diseases produced by false beliefs. Its arguments are to the soul as the doctor's remedies are to the body.

MARTHA C. NUSSBAUM

Today there are no more schools, and the "philosopher" is alone. How shall he find his way?

PIERRE HADOT

The association of cognitive style with gender is in itself nothing new. We find it in ancient mythology, in archetypal psychology, in philosophical and scientific writings, and in a host of enduring popular stereotypes about men and women (for example, that women are more "intuitive," men are more "logical," etc.).

SUSAN BORDO

We cannot and should not hope to produce a nation of students who can write excellent papers about Socratic arguments. . . . We can, I think, hope to produce students . . . who have examined their beliefs Socratically to some extent and who have mastered some techniques by which they can push that inquiry further, students whose moral and political beliefs are not simply a function of talk-radio or peer pressure, students who have gained the confidence that their own minds can confront the toughest questions of citizenship. To produce this independence we need to rely on philosophy.

MARTHA C. NUSSBAUM

"What is the fruit of your doctrines?" Epictetus was asked. His reply was three crisp words: "Tranquillity, Fearlessness, and Freedom." I'll never let go of that. I've moved "inside."

JAMES BOND STOCKDALE

In a setting in which exclusions and such "jokes" were routine, is it any wonder that the academic study of women's history, of literature written by women, of the sociology and politics of gender—that all of these perfectly normal and central topics were unavailable for serious study? They were just as unavailable as was (in most places) the serious academic study of Judaism, of African and of African-American cultures, of many other ethnic minorities, of many non-Western religions and cultures, of the variety and diversity of human sexuality. Exclusions of people and exclusions of their lives from the domain of knowledge went hand in hand. The exclusions seemed natural and apolitical; only the demand for inclusion seemed motivated by a "political agenda." From the rooftop of the Widener, there were many people and many lives that my colleague could not see.

We are now trying to build an academy . . . in which to be a "fellowess" need not mean being called a "courtesan," an academy in which the world will be seen to have many different types of citizen and in which we can all learn to function as citizens of that entire world.[9]

Nussbaum functions as a citizen of the world by writing about philosophical issues for the general public in *The New York Review of Books, The New Republic,* national newspapers, and other nonacademic publications. Her work generates mixed reviews, as is to be expected when any serious writer takes strong positions. The debate over the extent to which philosophy can—and should—be made accessible to a broad audience has always been contentious in American history. Nussbaum sides with those philosophers who want to extend philosophy's reach. Referring to her own privileged background (her mother's family has roots going back to the *Mayflower,* and her father was a prosperous lawyer), Nussbaum says, "a lot of my impatience with [the work of elitist philosophers] grew out of my repudiation of my own aristocratic upbringing. I don't like anything that sets itself up as an in-group or an elite."[10]

Philosophy for the Sake of Humanity

With notable exceptions, as Western philosophy developed, philosophers increasingly dismissed and distrusted subjective—private—emotional responses to philosophical problems, focusing more on the dangers inherent in subjectivity than on the cost of pursuing objectivity at all costs. Yet objectivity and detachment are as susceptible to abuse as are overreliance on emotions and indiscriminate personal responses to life's predicaments. To the extent that being *fully human* is characterized as always deferring to a universal, objective, impersonal way of knowing, the responsible person is defined as one who exhibits the capacity to think in an objective, impersonal, unemotional way.

Nussbaum challenges modern philosophy's wariness of emotions and what she sees as its correspondingly limited view of philosophy (and life) in *The Therapy of Desire* and *Upheavals of Thought: The Intelligence of Emotions,* two books that have attracted the attention of readers from inside and outside of academic circles. Building on her knowledge of Hellenistic philosophy, Nussbaum presents what she describes as a "Neo-stoic" philosophy that takes the "art of life" seriously by

© 1999 J. Shimon & J. Lindermann

When a reporter asked Martha Nussbaum if she takes philosophy "too seriously," the lawyer for humanity replied: "For any view you put forward, the next question simply has to be, 'What would the world be like if this idea were actually taken up?' It's what happens in the long haul that really matters. You just never know where or how your ideals will be realized." How might our lives change if we took our beliefs seriously enough to ask—to really ask—*What would the world be like if my beliefs were actually taken up?*

treating philosophy as more than an intellectual or academic exercise. In the following passage, note how Nussbaum opens *The Therapy of Desire* by characterizing her role as a writer and teacher of philosophy in a broad way that excludes neither reason nor feeling. Note, too, her appeal to the practical nature of ancient philosophy.

> The idea of a practical and compassionate philosophy—a philosophy that exists for the sake of human beings, in order to address their deepest needs, confront their most urgent perplexities, and bring them from misery to some greater measure of flourishing—this idea makes the study of Hellenistic ethics riveting for a philosopher who wonders what philosophy has to do with the world. The writer and teacher of philosophy is a lucky person, fortunate, as few human beings are, to spend her life expressing her most serious thoughts and feelings about the problems that have moved and fascinated her most. But this exhilarating and wonderful life is also part of the world as a whole, a world in which hunger, illiteracy, and disease are the daily lot of a large portion of the human beings who still exist, as well as the causes of death of many who do not still exist. A life of leisured self-expression is, for most of the world's people, a dream so distant that it can rarely even be formed. The contrast between these two images of human life gives rise to a question: what business does anyone have living in the happy, self-expressive world, so long as the other world exists and one is a part of it?

One answer to this question may certainly be to use some portion of one's time and material resources to support relevant types of political action and social service. On the other hand, it seems possible that philosophy itself, while remaining itself, can perform social and political functions, making a difference in the world by using its own distinctive methods and skills.

[The Epicureans and Stoics] . . . saw the philosopher as a compassionate physician whose arts could heal many pervasive types of human suffering. They practiced philosophy not as a detached intellectual technique dedicated to the display of cleverness but as an immersed and worldly art of grappling with human misery. They focused their attention, in consequence, on issues of daily and urgent human significance—the fear of death, love and sexuality, anger and aggression—issues that are sometimes avoided as embarrassingly messy and personal by the more detached varieties of philosophy. They confronted these issues as they arose in ordinary human lives, with a keen attention to the vicissitudes of those lives, and to what would be necessary and sufficient to make them better.[11]

In the final analysis, Nussbaum reminds us that although it cannot perfect human life, philosophy has unique skills to help us tell our stories in ways that can free us from at least some unhappiness and guide us toward better lives.

Here, I think, we must turn, with Seneca, to mercy and narrative—trying to respond to what has taken place without strict punishment, asking the watchful eyes of wisdom to look with narrative understanding into the complexities of another's motivation and one's own. The bold . . . attempt to purify social life of all its ills, rigorously carried through, ends by removing, as well, its finite humanity, its risk-taking loyalty, its passionate love. Abandoning the zeal for absolute perfection as inappropriate to the life of a finite being, abandoning the thirst for punishment and self-punishment that so frequently accompanies that zeal, the education I recommend looks with mercy at the ambivalent excellence and passion of a human life.[12]

PHILOSOPHY AND HUMAN DEVELOPMENT

Although much of her work focuses on problems inhibiting the flourishing and development of women around the world, Nussbaum articulates a "big" vision of philosophy that I find wholesome, compelling, and congenial because it recognizes that, for all of its inevitable human limitations and periodic setbacks, the kind of philosophy that mattered to Confucius, Socrates, Diogenes, Marcus Aurelius, Augustine, Marx, Mill, Kierkegaard, James, Nietzsche, Heidegger, and so many others still matters—at least as much now as ever.

All times are perilous. All cultures and individuals remain blind to certain of their own weaknesses and, equally often, unaware of some of their greatest strengths. Even so, collectively and individually, we persist in trying to understand our lives in particular and humanity in general, and to discern what matters most and why, and to do right by what we learn as we go. What better friend can we have in our perennial search for meaning than philosophy—richly, open-heartedly, and humanely understood? Here's Nussbaum:

> But we do not need philosophy only as a counterweight to . . . philosophical assumptions. . . . We need it to help us think through our own intuitive ideas, to criticize them, and to figure out which ones we are willing to hold on to. People do not go through life without forming views about the human good and the right, about what has value and what does not, about what choice is, about what justice and mercy and aggression and grief are. They have views about these things and they use them—not least when they enter the political arena. Often these views embed pieces of highly general theory, derived from custom, or religion, or social science. When public policies are chosen, then, they are the product of many people's intuitions and theories, some of them examined, and many of them unexamined. It seems sensible to deliberate about which theories we really want to hold onto, which intuitions are really the most deeply rooted in our moral sensibility. In the absence of such public deliberation, the most influential views are likely to be those, simply, that are held by the most powerful or rhetorically adept people. This way of proceeding, defective in itself, is especially defective when we consider the interests of the powerless, who rarely get a chance to bring their own ideas about such matters to the table.
>
> Philosophy asks for public deliberation instead of the usual contest of power. It asks us to choose the view that stands the test of argument, rather than the view that has the most prestigious backers; the view that gets all the details worked out coherently and clearly, rather than the view whose proponents shout the loudest. At its best, its conceptual fussiness is profoundly practical: only if things are worked out in all their detail will we know whether we really do have the alternative that can stand up to objection better than another, and sometimes the fatal objection to a view emerges only after considerable probing. It makes sense for public deliberation to take account of these apparently fussy debates, because this is how we think through what we have to do, see what we really want to stand for.
>
> Philosophy often fails to impress people with its relevance, and sometimes this is the fault of philosophers. Philosophy can offer good guidance to practice, I believe, only if it is responsive to experience and periodically immersed in it. . . . Philosophers . . . should be able to show that their work responds to the complexity of experience and has been shaped by a mature beings sense of that complexity. Feminists rightly demand that the theories dealing with women's lives show their understanding of women's experience of subordination and exclusion. Much of what philosophers of the past (in all traditions) have written about women, sex, and the family has not shown such understanding. Again, it is right to demand that philosophers writing about poverty show that they have some understanding of the complex interaction of agency and constraint in the lives of those concerning whom they make recommendations. Again, many traditions of thought have approached these problems with either

naïveté or callousness. The solution to these problems, however, is not to reject philosophy, or even the tradition; it is to learn from them and move forward, with an even more passionate commitment to inclusiveness, precision, and sound argument.[13]

■ PHILOSOPHY AS A WAY OF LIFE ■

It is tempting for some sophisticated Americans to dismiss the search for wisdom as a form of sophomoric naïveté and self-indulgence—or to romanticize it as the cure-all for the ills of our confused, technological, crowded society. Both views miss the true splendor and power of one important aspect of searching for wisdom: the *therapeutic* unifying function of seriously valuing such a search. One of the best ways to achieve this therapeutic effect is to make philosophical reading and reflection a regular part of our lives—as regular as exercise, recreation, and work. Without deluding ourselves or trying to become sages ourselves, we can nonetheless join the sages by living our own examined lives.

Pierre Hadot (b. 1922), Professor Emeritus of the History of Hellenistic and Roman Thought at the Collège de France, takes seriously the sage's goal that philosophy become a way of life. Hadot's *Philosophy as a Way of Life* is one of my favorite books. Although somewhat technical and scholarly, Hadot's text contains many accessible passages that capture the richness of lived philosophy, the therapeutic action of philosophy done out of love of wisdom. According to Hadot, the true philosopher:

> knows that the normal, natural state of [human beings] should be wisdom, for wisdom is nothing more than the vision of things as they are, the vision of the cosmos as it is in the light of reason, and wisdom is also nothing more than the mode of being and living that should correspond to this vision. But the philosopher also knows that this wisdom is an ideal state, almost inaccessible. For such a [lover of wisdom], daily life, as it is organized and lived by other [people], must necessarily appear abnormal, like a state of madness, unconsciousness, and ignorance of reality. . . . And it is precisely in this daily life that [lovers of wisdom] must seek to attain that way of life which is utterly foreign to the everyday world. The result is a perpetual conflict between the philosopher's effort to see things as they are from the standpoint of universal nature and the conventional vision of things underlying human society, a conflict between the life one should live and the customs and conventions of daily life. This conflict can never be totally resolved.[14]

Even though Hadot asserts that the conflict between philosophy and "the world" can never be totally resolved, he nonetheless promises what the sages have always promised: Life is better with philosophy than without it, and if wisdom is hard to define precisely, it is still worth seeking because taking wisdom seriously raises our sights and requires more of us than does abandoning the search. Whatever wisdom is or is not, we do know that technology, possessions, fame, fortune, high grades, attractive figures, and disease-free years are not enough to make life meaningful.

Pierre Hadot

Receive each moment of accumulating time as though it came about by an incredible stroke of luck.

PIERRE HADOT

"The Individual Struggles for the Possession of His Soul"

Can it be that human beings are at a dead end? Is individuality really so dependent on historical and cultural conditions? Can we accept the account of those conditions we are so "authoritatively" given? I suggest that it is not in the intrinsic interest of human beings but in these ideas and accounts that the problem lies. The staleness, the inadequacy of these repels us. To find the source of trouble we must look into our own heads. . . .

The intelligent public is . . . waiting to hear from art what it does not hear from theology, philosophy, social theory, and what it cannot hear from pure science. Out of the struggle at the center has come an immense, painful longing for a broader, more flexible, fuller, more coherent, more comprehensive account of what we human beings are, who we are, and what this life is for. At the center humankind struggles with collective powers for its freedom, the individual struggles with dehumanization for the possession of his soul.

Saul Bellow, *1976 Nobel Laureate Lecture*

As attractive and pleasing as these things can be, nothing external can make us happy if being happy means more than satisfied or pleased. In one form or another, this is the teaching of Socrates, Epicurus, Epictetus, Marcus Aurelius, Buddha, Jesus, Muhammad, Kierkegaard, our grandparents, pastors, and wiser elders. Who are we to refute the teachings of the wise? But how wise is it to accept such teachings without testing and questioning them? Hadot offers some advice:

> The trick is to maintain oneself on the level of reason, and not allow oneself to be blinded by political passions, anger, resentments, or prejudices. To be sure, there is an equilibrium—almost impossible to achieve—between the inner peace brought about by wisdom, and the passions to which the sight of the injustices, sufferings, and misery of mankind cannot help but give rise. Wisdom, however, consists in precisely such an equilibrium, and inner peace is indispensable for efficacious action.

Such is the lesson of ancient philosophy: an invitation to each human being to transform himself. Philosophy is a conversion, a transformation of one's way of being and living, and a quest for wisdom. This is not an easy matter. As Spinoza wrote at the end of the *Ethics*:

> If the way which I have pointed out as leading to this result seems exceedingly hard, it may nevertheless be discovered. It must indeed be hard, since it is so seldom found. How would it be possible, if salvation were easy to find, and could without great labour be found, that it should be neglected by almost everybody? But all excellent things are as difficult as they are rare.[15]

Hadot reminds us that part of the difficulty Spinoza recognizes is due to the very nature of the human condition:

> Everything which is "technical" in the broad sense of the term, whether we are talking about the exact sciences or the humanistic sciences, is perfectly able to be communicated by teaching or conversation. But everything that touches the domain of the existential—which is what is most important for human beings—for instance, our feeling of existence, our impressions when

Think about these and related matters day and night, by yourself and in company with someone like yourself. If you do, you will never experience anxiety, waking or sleeping, but you will live like a god among men. For a human being who lives in the midst of immortal blessings is in no way like mortal man!

EPICURUS

The medicines for the soul were discovered by the ancients—but it is our job to find out how to apply them and when. Our predecessors accomplished a lot, but not everything.

SENECA

faced by death, our perception of nature, our sensations . . . is not directly communicable. The phrases we use to describe them are conventional and banal; we realize this when we try to console someone over the loss of a loved one. That's why it often happens that a poem or a biography are more philosophical than a philosophical treatise, simply because they allow us to glimpse this unsayable in an indirect way.[16]

To Live Like a Philosopher

In *What Is Ancient Philosophy*? Hadot expresses his conviction that the ancient concept of philosophy as a practical way of life is still possible and that the rediscovery of philosophy as a way of life has a certain urgency in today's world.

> *What interests everyone, or rather, what should interest everyone, is nothing other than wisdom. The normal, natural, everyday state of human beings ought to be wisdom, but they cannot reach it.*
>
> PIERRE HADOT

Isn't there an urgent need to rediscover the ancient notion of the "philosopher"—the living, choosing philosopher without whom the notion of philosophy has no meaning? Why not define the philosopher not as a professor or a writer who develops a philosophical discourse but, in accordance with the concept which was constant in antiquity, as a person who leads a philosophical life? Shouldn't we reverse the habitual use of the word "philosopher" (which usually refers only to the theoretician) so that it applies to the person who practices philosophy, just as Christians can practice Christianity without being theorists or theologians? Do we ourselves have to construct a philosophical system before we can live philosophically? This does not mean, of course, that we needn't reflect upon our own experience, as well as that of philosophers both past and present.

Yet what does it mean to "live like a philosopher"? What is the practice of philosophy? . . .

. . . There is an abyss between fine phrases and becoming genuinely aware of oneself, truly transforming oneself. . . . Throughout the history of ancient philosophy . . . we encounter the same warnings against the danger the philosopher incurs, if he thinks his philosophical discourse can be sufficient unto itself without being linked to a philosophical life. Plato already sensed this ever-present danger when . . . he wrote: "I was afraid that I would see myself as a fine talker, incapable of resolutely undertaking an action."

> *The life of a fool is hard and worrisome. It is wholly devoured by the future.*
>
> CICERO

Another danger, the worst of all, is to believe that one can do without philosophical reflection. . . . Without such reflection, the philosophical life risks sinking into vapid banality, "respectable" feelings, or deviance. To be sure, we cannot wait until we have read Kant's *Critique of Pure Reason* in order to live as philosophers. Nevertheless, living as a philosopher also means to reflect, to reason, to conceptualize, in a rigorous, technical way. . . . The philosophical life is a never-ending quest.

Finally, and despite all the tenacious clichés which still clog philosophy manuals, we must never forget that the ancient philosophical life was always linked to the care for others, and that this demand is inherent in the philosophical life, especially when it is lived in the contemporary world. . . . The philosopher is cruelly aware of his solitude and impotence in a world which is torn between two states of unconsciousness: that which derives from the idolatry of money, and that which results in the face of the misery and suffering of billions of human beings. In such conditions, the philosopher will surely never be able to attain the absolute serenity of the sage. . . . But ancient philosophy

> *Why not define the philosopher . . . as a person who leads a philosophical life?*
>
> PIERRE HADOT

also teaches us not to resign ourselves, but to continue to act reasonably and try to live according to the norm constituted by the Idea of wisdom, whatever happens, and even if our action seems very limited to us. In the words of Marcus Aurelius: "Do not wait for Plato's Republic, but be happy if one little thing leads to progress, and reflect on the fact that what results from such a little thing is not, in fact, so very little."[17]

Soon we shall breathe our last. Meanwhile, while we live, while we are among human beings, let us cultivate humanity.

SENECA

WISDOM

QUERY

• • • • • •

Imagine Socrates, Epictetus, and Diogenes wandering through a modern bookstore. Imagine them channel-surfing or roaming the Internet. Describe a detailed scenario—including philosophical conversations and comments—in which these sages confront today's claimants to wisdom. Would they be impressed? Angry? Amused? Saddened? Generate a rational, respectful discussion of specific books, guru figures, "philosophical" belief systems. This is dangerous stuff—but it's also invigorating and important stuff. (Try using other philosophers, too.)

■ A VISION FOR YOU ■

It is too soon to tell whether or not philosophical advocacy will produce new philosophical archetypes. But we can reasonably expect that some of the topics touched on in this chapter will continue to attract serious philosophical attention. Complex questions concerning the effects of gender, ethnicity, and social climate on philosophizing are not easily answered. Indeed, some of these issues hearken back to issues raised by Socrates in his encounters with Sophists. That is why I have written *Archetypes of Wisdom* not just to convey philosophical facts and arguments, but also to evoke philosophical yearnings that most of us experience—but don't always recognize as being philosophical. I can think of no better way to say "Fare thee well" than to encourage you not to diminish, forget, or forsake the love of wisdom. Think of this last section as a personal invitation to keep company with the sages.

The untrained mind shivers with excitement at everything it hears.

HERACLITUS

I hope that in addition to any intellectual satisfaction you have found in philosophy, you have also *experienced* something special: a sense of the majesty of the human condition that is simultaneously poignant, profound, encouraging, humbling, and comforting. The special experience I am referring to evokes a longing to be a better, wiser person—not in any specific way, but in a fundamental way. This longing is the *love of wisdom*, and it triggers a "felt need" for an honest vision of the human condition and of our particular place in it.

While we're waiting to live, life passes us by.

PIERRE HADOT

Once felt, the need to see the human condition and our particular place in it "as a whole" never leaves us. The need to find meaning in a capricious, dangerous world never leaves us. Life assaults us with questions of choice, value, meaning—*philosophical* questions: issues of fairness; choices among evils; existential conditions that demand action; forced choices that, once made, obliterate all other possibilities. Highly specialized professional philosophers properly see themselves as scholars rather than as sages. Scholars and other experts abound, but sages are rare.

To be truly commercial is to do well that which should not be done at all.

GORE VIDAL

If you come to doubt whether a specific person is a prophet or not, certainty can only be reached by acquaintance with his conduct, either by personal observation, or by hearsay as a matter of common knowledge.

ABU HAMID
MUHAMMAD
AL-GHAZALI

Douglas J. Soccio

The lessons of wisdom are not new, just hard to take sometimes—and easy to forget when things are going well.

DOUGLAS J. SOCCIO

Remember that it is no chance matter that we are discussing, but how one should live.

SOCRATES

Today, with the exception of a limited number of public philosophers, the public function of the *sophos*, or sage, has been taken over by the priest, the scientist, the psychologist, and the all-too-eager celebrity guru. Every year seems to produce another celebrity guru, another blockbuster book about the soul, wisdom, metaphysics, ancient secrets, past lives, angels, wise entities, simple secrets of happiness.

Without wisdom, intelligence has no guide. When Empedocles told Xenophanes that it was impossible to find a wise man, Xenophanes is said to have replied: "Naturally, for it takes a wise man to recognize a wise man."

Passages from many philosophical masterpieces are included throughout *Archetypes of Wisdom*. Others are listed in the Bibliography of Philosophical Delights. I find myself returning again and again to a select few for consolation, encouragement, and wisdom. Of all of my favorites, I have probably read the small collection of teachings of Epictetus known as the *Enchiridion* more than any other book. I think so highly of it that I have handed out hundreds of copies to students, friends, and family members. You will recall that the handbook was originally compiled for Roman soldiers to carry on long, difficult military campaigns. We might also think of it as a handbook to carry and consult in our daily campaign against the confusions, deceptions, and distractions of modern life. So it is especially fitting that I say, "Fare thee well, philosopher" with a message from Epictetus:

> How long do you put off thinking yourself worthy of the best things, and [worthy of] never going against the definitive capacity of reason? You have received the philosophical propositions that you ought to agree to and you have agreed to them. Then what sort of teacher are you still waiting for, that you put off improving yourself until he comes? You are not a [child] anymore, but already . . . full grown. . . . If you now neglect things and are lazy and are always making delay after delay and set one day after another as the day for paying attention to yourself, then without realizing it you will make no progress but will end up a non-philosopher all through life and death. So decide now that you are worthy of living as a full-grown [human being] who is making progress, and make everything that seems best be a law you cannot go against. And if you meet with any hardship or anything pleasant or reputable or disreputable, then remember that the contest is now and the Olympic games are now and you cannot put things off any more and that your progress is made or destroyed by a single day and a single action. Socrates became fully perfect in this way. . . . You, even if you are not yet Socrates, ought to live as one wanting to be [like] Socrates.[18]

■ SUMMARY OF MAIN POINTS ■

- A philosophical advocate is a philosopher whose work identifies, clarifies, and actively opposes a perceived injustice. Philosophical advocates give philosophical credence to personal experience based on gender, ethnic background, or social status.

- Critics of modern philosophy associate the dominance of the detached philosophical specialist with modern philosophy's emphasis on philosophical arguments presented in a detached—objective—voice that deliberately minimizes the philosopher's personal qualities (social status, gender, ethnicity). Consequently, some modern and contemporary philosophers remain indifferent to the fact that their philosophy reflects the interests of only a small portion of the human community.

● Carol Gilligan's research into moral development has led her to distinguish between a traditional, masculine-oriented "voice" and a feminine-oriented "different voice" that is not confined to objective argument (or scientific evidence), but that expresses other "ways of knowing." Gilligan argues that excessive reliance on "rationality" results in injustice by excluding those who do not speak in the "objective voice" from full participation in philosophy, science, law, and higher education.

● Public philosophers are writers or speakers whose philosophical positions are expressed in ways accessible to a broad audience. The most effective public philosophers tap into—or identify—vital philosophical issues of the day. When public philosophers also "practice what they preach," they function much like sages or prophets in their capacity to provoke individual self-assessment and collective consciousness-raising.

● Peter Singer is a controversial public philosopher who believes in making people uncomfortable as a way of raising moral consciousness. Singer applies utilitarian principles to such current issues as animal rights, infanticide, euthanasia, and world poverty. Singer challenges everyone not already living in abject poverty to give away all income over $30,000. Single adults could, of course, give away much more. Singer himself gives one-fifth of his income (including royalties from his books) to famine-relief agencies.

● Martha C. Nussbaum describes public philosophers as "lawyers for humanity." Nussbaum suggests that too many professional intellectuals fail to use their theories and talents to improve the human condition by fighting for equality, justice, and freedom.

● Pierre Hadot's *Philosophy as a Way of Life* presents a distillation of his accumulated knowledge and experience as a professional scholar and lover of wisdom. Hadot takes seriously the sage's goal that philosophy become a way of life. Although Hadot asserts that the conflict between wisdom and "the world" can never be totally resolved, he believes that life is better with philosophy than without it, because taking wisdom seriously raises our sights and requires more of us than does abandoning the search.

▦ POST-READING REFLECTIONS ▦

Now that you have had a chance to learn about Philosophy as a Way of Life, use your new knowledge to answer these questions.

1. What philosophical issues are associated with the problem of advocacy?

2. What is Singer's solution to world poverty?

3. Why is Singer such a controversial philosopher?

4. Discuss the insult Martha C. Nussbaum experienced in a letter of congratulation, paying special attention to the context in which this occurred.

5. Why does Nussbaum think that we need philosophy today?

6. What is the tension Hadot sees between wisdom and "the world"?

7. What does Pierre Hadot mean when he says that our lives are better with philosophy than without it and that even wisdom is hard to define precisely?

8. What, according to Hadot, is the lesson of ancient philosophy?

9. Compare Nussbaum's and Hadot's arguments on behalf of philosophy as a way of life.

PHILOSOPHY INTERNET RESOURCES

Go to the Soccio Web page at **http://philosophy.wadsworth.com/ Soccio7e** for Web links, practice quizzes and tests, a pronunciation guide, and study tips.

NOTES

Chapter 1
Philosophy and the Search for Wisdom

1. Mary Ellen Waithe, *Introduction to the Series, A History of Women Philosophers,* vol. 1, 600 B.C.–500 A.D., ed. Mary Ellen Waithe (Dordrecht: Martinus Nijhoff, 1987), pp. IX–X.

2. James Q. Wilson, *The Moral Sense* (New York: Free Press, 1993), pp. 8–9.

Chapter 2
The Asian Sages: Lao-tzu, Confucius, and Buddha

1. Wing-Tsit Chan, *A Source Book in Chinese Philosophy* (Princeton, N.J.: Princeton University Press, 1963), p. 98.

2. See Michael C. Brannigan, *The Pulse of Wisdom,* 2nd ed. (Belmont, Calif.: Wadsworth, 2000), pp. 23–27; and Warren Matthews, *World Religions,* 3rd ed. (Belmont, Calif.: Wadsworth, 1999), p. 209.

3. Chad Hansen, "Classical Chinese Ethics," in *A Companion to Ethics,* ed. Peter Singer (Oxford: Blackwell, 1993), p. 69.

4. A. C. Graham, *Disputers of the Tao* (La Salle, Ill.: Open Court, 1989), pp. 1–4.

5. Brannigan, p. 24.

6. Graham, pp. 216–217.

7. Holmes Welch, *Taoism: The Parting of the Way* (Boston: Beacon Press, 1965), p. 2.

8. Lao-tzu, *Tao Te Ching,* in Chan, p. 136.

9. Lao-tzu, *The Wisdom of Laotse,* trans. and ed. Lin Yutang (New York: Modern Library, 1976), p. 41. Reprinted by permission of Random House, Inc.

10. Lao-tzu, *Te-Tao Ching: A New Translation Based on the Recently Discovered Mawang-tui Texts,* trans. with introduction and commentary by Robert G. Henricks (New York: Ballantine, 1989), p. 53. Reprinted by permission of Random House, Inc.

11. Graham, p. 219.

12. Ibid., p. 220.

13. Ibid., p. 221.

14. Ibid., p. 221.

15. Ibid., p. 223.

16. Lao-tzu, in Chan, p. 140.

17. After Graham, pp. 223f.

18. Graham, p. 232.

19. Ibid., p. 235.

20. Lao-tzu, in Chan, pp. 162–163.

21. *Tao te Ching,* #57, Graham, p. 233.

22. Lin Yutang, *The Wisdom of Confucius* (New York: Modern Library, 1938), p. 6.

23. Ibid., pp. 26–27.

24. Ibid., p. 29.

25. Chan, p. 17.

26. Yutang, p. 52.

27. Ibid., p. 98.

28. Chan, p. 15.

29. Confucius, *Analects,* 7:21, in Graham, p. 15.

30. Graham, p. 15.

31. Confucius, *Analects,* 6:22, in Graham, pp. 15f.

32. Graham, p. 10.

33. Confucius, *Analects,* 7:1, in Graham, p. 10.

34. Ibid., 15:31, in Graham, p. 11.

35. *The Doctrine of the Mean,* Chu Hsi arrangement, trans. Wing-Tsit Chan, in Chan, pp. 98–99. Copyright © 1963 by Princeton University Press. Reprinted by permission.

36. Ibid., pp. 98–101.

37. Graham, p. 13.

38. Ibid.

39. Ibid.

40. Confucius's disciple Yu-tzu, quoted in Graham, p. 12.

41. Chan, pp. 15f.

42. Graham, p. 19.

43. Confucius, *Analects,* 12:1, in Graham, p. 22.

44. Yutang, p. 24.

45. Ibid., pp. 19–20.

46. Confucius, *Analects,* 6:28, in Chan, p. 31.

47. *The Doctrine of the Mean,* in Chan, p. 105.

48. Confucius, *Analects,* 4:6, in Chan, p. 26.

49. The brief sketch that follows is based on Nancy Wilson Ross, *Buddhism: A Way of Life and Thought* (New York: Vintage, 1981); see also Edward Conze, *Buddhism: Its Essence and Development* (New York: Harper Torchbooks, 1965); *Stories of the Buddha: Being Selections from the Jakata,* trans. and ed. Caroline A. F. Rhys Davids (New York: Dover, 1989); Richard H. Robinson and Willard L. Johnson, *The Buddhist Religion* (Encino, Calif.: Dickenson, 1977); and Donald S. Lopez, Jr., *The Story of Buddhism* (San Francisco: HarperSanFrancisco, 2001).

50. Ross, p. 6.

51. Ibid., p. 10.

52. Ibid., p. 18.

53. Ibid.

54. Ibid., p. 33.

55. The Buddha, "The Discourse on Universal Love," in Ross, p. 32.

56. Padmasiri de Silva, "Buddhist Ethics," in *A Companion to Ethics,* ed. Peter Singer, p. 58.

57. Ibid., pp. 59–60.

58. Ibid., p. 61; and Rev. Master P.T.N.H. Jiyu-Kennett, M.O.B.C., "Basic Original Doctrines Essential to Zen," in Jiyu-Kennett, *Zen Is Eternal Life* (Mt. Shasta, Calif.: Shasta Abbey, 1987), p. 9.

59. Ross, pp. 23ff.

60. Modified from Ross, p. 24.

61. See Ross, pp. 24ff.

62. Ibid., p. 26.

63. Ibid., p. 27.

64. Ibid., pp. 26f.

65. Ibid., p. 37.

66. A. Burtt, ed., *The Teachings of the Compassionate Buddha* (New York: Mentor, 1982), pp. 202ff.

67. Ibid., pp. 34ff., 36.

68. Ibid., p. 204.

Chapter 3
The Sophist: Protagoras

1. Plato, *The Republic,* trans. H. D. P. Lee (London: Penguin, 1955), bk. 7, sec. 6.

2. Pierre Hadot, *Philosophy as a Way of Life,* trans. Arnold I. Davidson (Oxford: Blackwell, 1995), pp. 56–61.

3. Plato, Theatetus, 174A, trans. F. M. Cornford, in *The Collected Dialogues of Plato: Including the Letters* (New York: Pantheon, 1961), p. 879.

4. Hadot, p. 57.

5. Ibid.

6. Amaury de Riencourt, *Sex and Power in History* (New York: David McKay Company, 1974), pp. 97–98.

7. Heraclitus, Fragment 23, *Herakleitos and Diogenes,* trans. Guy Davenport (San Francisco: Grey Fox Press, 1979), p. 15.

8. W. T. Jones, *The Classical Mind: A History of Western Philosophy,* 2nd ed. (New York: Harcourt Brace Jovanovich, 1970), p. 16.

9. Plato, *Parmenides,* 127A, in Cornford, p. 921.

10. Jones, pp. 21–22.

11. See W. K. C. Guthrie, *The Sophists* (Cambridge: Cambridge University Press, 1971); Giovanni Reale, *A History of Ancient Philosophy,* vol. 1, *From the Origins to Socrates,* trans. John R. Catan (Albany: State University of New York Press, 1987), p. 84; Will Durant, *The Story of Civilization,* vol. 2, *The Life of Greece* (New York: Simon & Schuster, 1939); Frederick Copleston, S. J., *A History of Philosophy,* vol. 1, *Greece and Rome* (New York: Image, 1985).

12. Will Durant, *The Story of Philosophy* (New York: Simon & Schuster, 1953), p. 358.

13. Guthrie, p. 35.

14. Plato, *The Sophist,* 231D–E, in Reale, p. 149.

15. Xenophon, *Memorabilia,* trans. E. C. Marchant, in *Xenophon, Memorabilia and Oeconomics* (London: Loeb Classical Library, 1959), bk. 1, sec. 6, line 13.

16. Plato, *Theaetetus,* trans. F. M. Cornford, 151E–152A, in Reale, p. 157.

17. Ibid., 166D, in Reale, pp. 160ff.

18. Plato, *Gorgias,* trans. W. C. Helmbold (Indianapolis: Bobbs-Merrill, 1952), pp. 482–486.

19. Ibid., 457B.

Chapter 4
The Wise Man: Socrates

1. W. K. C. Guthrie, *Socrates* (Cambridge: Cambridge University Press, 1971), p. 6.

2. Plato, *Phaedo,* 60C–D, trans. Benjamin Jowett, in *The Dialogues of Plato,* 3rd ed. (Oxford: Clarendon, 1892).

3. Guthrie, p. 4.

4. Ibid.

5. Xenophon, *Symposium,* trans. E. C. Marchant (London: Loeb Classical Library, 1959), ch. 2, line 18.

6. Plato, *Gorgias,* 470E, in Giovanni Reale, *A History of Ancient Philosophy,* vol. 1, *From the Origins to Socrates,* trans. John R. Catan (Albany: State University of New York Press, 1987), p. 219.

7. Xenophon, *Symposium,* ch. 5, in Guthrie, pp. 67–68.

8. Xenophon, *Memorabilia,* bk. 1, sec. 6, line 10, in Reale, p. 216.

9. Ibid., sec. 2, lines 29–30. See also Mary Renault's novel *The Last of the Wine* (New York: New English Library, 1968), pp. 120ff.

10. Xenophon, *Memorabilia,* bk. 4, sec. 5, lines 9ff., in Reale, p. 218.

11. Plato, *Apology,* 34D, trans. Benjamin Jowett, in *The Dialogues of Plato: Phaedo,* 60A.

12. Will Durant, *The Story of Civilization,* vol. 2, *The Life of Greece* (New York: Simon & Schuster, 1939), p. 367.

13. Karl Jaspers, *Socrates, Buddha, Confucius, Jesus: The Paradigmatic Individuals,* trans. Ralph Manheim, ed. Hannah Arendt (New York: Harcourt Brace Jovanovich, 1962), p. 87.

14. Pierre Hadot, *Philosophy as a Way of Life,* trans. Arnold I. Davidson (Oxford: Blackwell, 1995), p. 147.

15. Plato, *Apology,* 17A.

16. Plato, *The Republic,* trans. H. D. P. Lee, 1955, Book I, Section 3, lines 336–339. Copyright © H. D. P. Lee 1953, 1974, 1987. Reprinted by permission of Penguin Books, U.K.

17. Reale, p. 202.

18. Plato, *Apology,* 21B–E.

19. Ibid., 20C.

20. Ibid., 22D, 23A.

21. Ibid., 29–30.

22. Plato, *Gorgias,* trans. W. C. Helmbold (Indianapolis: Bobbs-Merrill, 1952), pp. 468b–468c.

23. Plato, *Protagoras,* 345e, trans. Benjamin Jowett, rev. ed., Martin Ostwald (Indianapolis: Bobbs-Merrill, 1956), p. 49.

24. Meno, 77b–78b, trans. Benjamin Jowett in *Plato's Meno: Text and Criticism,* eds. Alexander Sesonske and Noel Fleming (Belmont, Calif.: Wadsworth, 1965), pp. 12–13.

25. Ibid., 87–89, pp. 23–25.

26. Plato, *Apology,* 40A.

27. Plato, *Phaedo,* 115Dff.

28. Ibid., 117Bff.

Chapter 5
The Philosopher-King: Plato

1. Diogenes Läertius, *Life of Plato,* trans. R. H. Hicks, in *Lives of Eminent Philosophers* (Cambridge, Mass.: Harvard University Press, 1925).

2. Plato, *Letter: VII,* 324E, trans. L. A. Post, in *Plato: The Collected Dialogues* (New York: Pantheon, 1961), p. 1575.

3. See A. W. Levi, "Ancient Philosophy: The Age of the Aristocrat," ch. 2 in *Philosophy as Social Expression* (Chicago: University of Chicago Press, 1974), for a full discussion of the influence of social class on Plato.

4. Ibid, p. 66.

5. Plato, *Letter: VII,* 325D–326B, p. 1576.

6. A. E. Taylor, *Plato: The Man and His Works* (London: Methuen, 1966), pp. 6ff.

7. Luc Brisson, "Platonism," trans. Rita Guerlac and Anne Slack, in *Greek Thought: A Guide to Classical Knowledge,* trans. under the direction of Catherine Porter, eds. Jacques Brunschwig and Geoffrey E. R. Lloyd, with the collaboration of Pierre Pellegrin (Cambridge, Mass.: Belknap Press, 2000), p. 893.

8. Christopher Janaway, "Ancient Greek Philosophy I: The Pre-Socratics and Plato," in *Philosophy: A Guide Through the Subject,* ed. A. C. Grayling (Oxford: Oxford University Press, 1995), pp. 378, 380. In the *Parmenides,* Plato revisits some of the difficult questions generated by the theory of forms.

9. Janaway, p. 378.

10. Peter A. Angeles, *Dictionary of Philosophy* (New York: Barnes & Noble, 1981), p. 124.

11. Plato, *Timaeus,* 27D–28A, trans. Benjamin Jowett, in *The Dialogues of Plato,* 3rd ed. (Oxford: Clarendon, 1892).

12. Plato, *Republic,* 506, pp. 269–270.

13. Plato, *Republic,* 510–511, pp. 276–277.

14. Plato, *Republic,* 508–509, pp. 272–273.

15. Plato, *Republic,* 511, p. 278.

16. Plato, *Republic,* 516, p. 278–281.

17. Plato, *Republic,* 516–517, p. 281–282.

18. Plato, *Republic,* bk. 1, Prelude, pp. 327–328.

19. H. D. P. Lee, Introduction to Plato, *Republic* (London: Penguin, 1955), p. 87.

20. B. A. G. Fuller, *History of Greek Philosophy,* vol. 2 (New York: Henry Holt, 1931), p. 214.

21. Plato, *Republic,* bk. 2, 363, pp. 94ff.

22. Taylor, *Plato: The Man and His Works,* p. 270.

23. Plato, *Republic,* bk. 4, 442E–443A, p. 194.

24. Ibid., bk. 8, sec. 6, p. 326.

25. Ibid., 555C, p. 327.

26. Ibid., 557, pp. 329ff.

27. Ibid., p. 330.

28. Ibid., p. 351.

29. Ibid., 561, p. 334.

30. Ibid., 563, pp. 336–337.

31. Ibid., bk. 9, 573–574, pp. 346ff.

Chapter 6

The Naturalist: Aristotle

1. In the 1970s, psychologists Daniel Levinson and G. E. Vailant identified something called a "mid-life crisis," which, they claimed, prompted major disruptions in men's lives. Since then, other psychologists, like Carol Gilligan, have pointed out that in mid-life both men and women try to establish better balance in their lives. Earlier, Erik Erikson had proposed a theory of personal development based on psychosocial stages. He coined the term *identity crisis* to characterize typical changes during adolescence. See Philip G. Zimbardo, *Psychology and Life,* 12th ed. (Glenview, Ill.: Scott, Foresman, 1988), pp. 98–99.

2. Will Durant, *The Story of Civilization,* vol. 2, *The Life of Greece* (New York: Simon & Schuster, 1966), p. 526.

3. Diogenes Laërtius, *Life of Plato,* trans. R. H. Hicks, in *Lives of Eminent Philosophers* (Cambridge, Mass.: Harvard University Press, 1925), sec. 25.

4. Samuel Enoch Stumpf, *Philosophy: History and Problems,* 4th ed. (New York: McGraw-Hill, 1989), bk. 1, p. 83.

5. Durant, *Life of Greece,* p. 525.

6. W. T. Jones, *The Classical Mind,* 2nd ed. (New York: Harcourt Brace Jovanovich, 1970), p. 219.

7. Aristotle, *Metaphysics,* bk. 7, ch. 1, 1028A10, in *The Philosophy of Aristotle,* ed. Renford Bambrough (New York: New American Library, 1963).

8. Aristotle, *Physics,* bk. 2, ch. 7, 198A20, trans. Phillip Wheelwright, in *Aristotle* (New York: Odyssey, 1951).

9. Ibid., bk.2, ch.1, 93A10.

10. Ibid., bk. 2, ch. 1, 193A36–193B6.

11. Ibid., bk. 2, ch. 7, 198A, 33–35.

12. Ibid., bk. 2, ch. 8, sec. 199b.

13. Sir David Ross, *Aristotle* (London: Methuen, 1966), p. 129.

14. Pierre Pellegrin, "Aristotle," trans. Rita Guerlac and Anne Slack, in *Greek Thought: A Guide to Classical Knowledge,* trans. under the direction of Catherine Porter, eds. Jacques Brunschwig and Geoffrey E. R. Lloyd, with the collaboration of Pierre Pellegrin (Cambridge, Mass.: Belknap Press, 2000), p. 572.

15. Aristotle, *Nicomachean Ethics,* bk. 1, 1094A, trans. J. C. Welldon, in *Philosophers Speak for Themselves,* ed. T. V. Smith (Chicago: University of Chicago Press, 1934).

16. Ibid., 1094B.

17. Ibid., 1095A.

18. Ibid., 1095B.

19. Ibid., 1096A.

20. Ibid., 1095B.

21. This treatment of *eudaimonia* is based in part on material found in Burton F. Porter, *Reasons for Living: A Basic Ethics* (New York: Macmillan, 1988), pp. 204–207.

22. Aristotle, *Nicomachean Ethics,* trans. Wheelwright, bk. 1, 1095Bff.

23. Aristotle, *Nicomachean Ethics,* 1103B30, trans. Martin Ostwald (Indianapolis: Library of Liberal Arts, 1962).

24. Ibid., 1104A13–25.

25. Ibid., 1104Aff.

26. Aristotle, *Nicomachean Ethics,* 1103A17ff., trans. W. D. Ross, in *Basic Works of Aristotle,* p. 952.

27. Ibid., 1144A6.

28. Aristotle, *Nicomachean Ethics,* trans. Ostwald, 1143B22.

29. Ibid., 1106B15.

Chapter 7

The Stoic: Epictetus and Marcus Aurelius

1. Epicurus, Fragment 221, in Giovanni Reale, *A History of Ancient Philosophy,* vol. 3, *The Systems of the Hellenistic Age,* ed. and trans. John R. Catan (Albany: State University of New York Press, 1985), p. 111.

2. Will Durant, *The Story of Civilization,* vol. 2, *The Life of Greece* (New York: Simon & Schuster, 1939), p. 645.

3. Epicurus, *Letter to Menoceceus,* trans. George D. Strodach, quoted in *Hellenistic Philosophy,* eds. Herman Shapiro and Edwin M. Curley (New York: Modern Library, 1965), p. 6.

4. Ibid., pp. 7ff.

5. Ibid., p. 8.

6. Epictetus, *Discourses,* trans. P. E. Matheson (Oxford: Clarendon, 1916), in William Sahakian and Mabel Lewis Sahakian, *Realms of Philosophy* (Cambridge, Mass.: Schenkman, 1965), p. 133.

7. Epictetus, *Discourses as Reported by Arrian, The Manual, and Fragments,* vol. 2, trans. W. A. Oldfather (Cambridge, Mass.: Harvard University Press, 1928), bk. xxii, pp. 139–149.

8. Ibid., p. 159.

9. Epictetus, *Handbook of Epictetus,* trans. Nicholas P. White (Indianapolis: Hackett, 1983), p. 13.

10. This sketch of Epictetus's life is based on Philip Hallie's entry on Epictetus in *The Encyclopedia of Philosophy,* vol. 3, eds. Paul Edwards et al. (New York: Macmillan and the Free Press, 1967), p. 1.

11. Marcus Aurelius, *Meditations,* bk. 7, sec. 54, trans. George Long, in *Plato, Epictetus, Marcus Aurelius* (Harvard Classics edition) (New York: Collier, 1937).

12. Ibid., bk. 6, sec. 2.

13. Ibid., bk. 7, sec. 58, 59.

14. From Maxwell Staniforth's entry in *Encyclopedia of Philosophy,* vol. 5, p. 156.

15. Seneca, "On Tranquility," in *The Stoic Philosophy of Seneca,* trans. Moses Hadas (New York: Norton, 1958), p. 93.

16. Epictetus, *Enchiridion,* sec. 27, trans. George Long, in *The Discourses of Epictetus with the Enchiridion and Fragments* (New York: A. L. Burt, 1929).

17. Seneca, Letter 41, in *The Stoic Philosophy of Seneca,* p. 188.

18. Ibid.

19. Marcus Aurelius, *Meditations,* bk. 7, sec. 22, 23, 25, trans. Maxwell Staniforth (Middlesex: Penguin, 1970).

20. Ibid.

21. Seneca, "On Self-Control," trans. Gunmere, in *Philosophers Speak for Themselves: Guides and Readings for Greek, Roman, and Early Christian Philosophy,* by T. V. Smith (Chicago: University of Chicago Press, 1934), pp. 623ff.

22. Epictetus, *Enchiridion,* sec. 1.

23. Ibid., sec. 4.

24. Ibid., sec. 1.

25. Ibid.

26. Ibid., sec. 30.

27. Ibid., sec. 25.

28. Seneca, "On Providence," in *The Stoic Philosophy of Seneca,* p. 37.

29. Ibid., pp. 38–39.

30. From "The World of Epictetus" by James B. Stockdale, *Atlantic Monthly,* April 1978. Used by permission of the author.

31. James Bond Stockdale, "Epictetus' Enchiridion," in *Text and Teaching: The Search for Human Excellence,* eds. Michael J. Collins and Frances J. Ambosio (Washington, D.C.: Georgetown University Press, 1991), pp. 39–42.

Chapter 8
The Scholar: Thomas Aquinas

1. Augustine, *Confessions,* trans, R. S. Pine-Coffin (Harmondsworth, England: Penguin, 1961), 2.3.

2. Paul, Epistle to the Romans, 13:13, The Revised English Bible (Oxford: Oxford University Press, and Cambridge: Cambridge University Press, 1989).

3. Ibid., 2.2.

4. Ibid., 8.5.

5. Augustine, *Letters,* New Advent (Electronic version copyright © 1997 by New Advent, Inc.), 118.21.

6. Paul, Acts of the Apostles, 17:18–34, The Revised English Bible.

7. Vernon J. Bourke, in *Aquinas' Search for Wisdom* (Milwaukee: Bruce, 1965), identifies discrepancies in many biographical sketches of Thomas Aquinas, since most are based on William of Tocco. Bourke points out that all we know for sure is that Thomas was born between 1220 and 1227. The commonly cited date of 1225 originated with Tocco and cannot be verified.

8. A. W. Levi, *Philosophy as Social Expression* (Chicago: University of Chicago Press, 1974), p. 106.

9. William of Tocco in Bourke, *Aquinas' Search for Wisdom,* p. 37.

10. See "The Age of the Saint" in Levi, *Philosophy as Social Expression.*

11. Ibid.

12. Based on Peter A. Angeles, *Dictionary of Philosophy* (New York: Barnes & Noble, 1981), p. 250.

13. Levi, *Philosophy as Social Expression,* pp. 122ff.

14. Ibid., p. 124.

15. From Thomas Aquinas's commentary on Aristotle's *Metaphysics,* quoted in Levi, *Philosophy as Social Expression,* p. 102.

16. The Five Ways are found in *Summa Theologica,* trans. the Dominican Fathers, *Basic Writings of Saint Thomas Aquinas,* ed. A. C. Pegis (New York: Random House, 1945), part 1, ques. 2, art. 3.

17. Ibid.

18. Ibid.

19. Ibid.

20. Ibid.

21. W. T. Jones, *A History of Western Philosophy: The Medieval Mind,* 2nd ed. (New York: Harcourt Brace Jovanovich, 1969), pp. 220ff.

22. Augustine, *City of God,* trans. M. Dods (Edinburgh: T. & T. Clark, 1872), xi, 26.

23. Thomas Aquinas, *Summa contra Gentiles,* trans. English Dominican Fathers (London: Bunns Oates, 1924), part 3, ques. 25.

Overview of Modern Themes

1. Quoted in William K. Hartmann, *Astronomy: The Cosmic Journey* (Belmont, Calif.: Wadsworth, 1991), p. 64.

Chapter 9

The Rationalist: René Descartes

1. René Descartes, *Discourse on Method,* trans. Elizabeth Haldane and G. R. T. Ross, in *The Philosophical Works of Descartes,* vol. 1 (Cambridge: Cambridge University Press, 1931; reprint, New York: Dover), p. 83. Reprinted by permission.

2. Ibid., p. 87.

3. Quoted in Levi, *Philosophy as Social Expression* (Chicago: University of Chicago Press, 1974), p. 185.

4. Descartes, *Rules for the Direction of the Mind,* in *Philosophical Works,* vol. 1, p. 6.

5. Ibid., pp. 9, 14.

6. Descartes, *Discourse on Method,* p. 88.

7. Ibid., pp. 81ff.

8. Descartes, *Meditation I,* in *Philosophical Works,* vol. 1, pp. 144–145.

9. Ibid., pp. 145–146.

10. Ibid., p. 148.

11. Descartes, *Meditation II,* in *Philosophical Works,* vol. 1, p. 150.

12. Ibid., pp. 151–153.

13. Descartes, *Meditation III,* in *Philosophical Works,* vol. 1, p. 159.

14. Ibid., p. 157.

15. Ibid., p. 165.

16. Ibid., p. 166.

17. Ibid., p. 163.

18. Ibid., p. 169.

19. Ibid., p. 170.

20. Ibid., pp. 170–171.

21. Descartes, *Meditation V,* in *Philosophical Works,* vol. 1, pp. 181–182.

22. Descartes, *Meditation VI,* in *Philosophical Works,* vol. 1, p. 185.

23. Ibid., p. 191.

24. Ibid., p. 195.

25. Gilbert Ryle, *The Concept of Mind* (New York: Harper & Row, 1941), p. 11.

26. Descartes, *Meditation VI,* in *Philosophical Works,* vol. 1, p. 192.

27. Amaury de Riencourt, *Sex and Power in History* (New York: David McKay, 1974), pp. 97ff.

28. Ibid., p. 99.

29. Lawrence Cahoone, ed., *From Modernism to Postmodernism: An Anthology* (Cambridge, Mass.: Blackwell, 1966), p. 638.

30. See "The Cartesian Masculinization of Thought" in Susan Bordo, *The Flight to Objectivity: Essays on Cartesianism and Culture* (Albany: State University of New York Press, 1987), pp. 97–118, in Cahoone, pp. 638–660. Notes have been deleted from all Bordo passages.

31. Ibid.

32. Ibid., p. 643.

33. Ibid., p. 645.

34. Ibid., p. 656.

Chapter 10

The Skeptic: David Hume

1. H. R. Fox Bourne, *The Life of John Locke,* vol. 1 (New York: Harper, 1876), pp. 200–201.

2. John Locke, "Epistle to the Reader" in *An Essay Concerning Human Understanding,* ed. A. C. Fraser (Oxford: Clarendon, 1894), p. 9.

3. John Locke, "The Art of Medicine," (a paper written in 1669), quoted in Fox Bourne, vol. I, p. 224, and John Locke, *An Essay Concerning Human Understanding,* bk. 4, ch. 7, sec. 11.

4. Ibid., bk. 1, ch. 3, secs. 24–25.

5. Ibid., bk. 2, ch. 11, sec. 17.

6. Ibid., bk. 2, ch. 1, sec. 2.

7. Ibid., bk. 2, ch. 23, sec. 1.

8. Ibid., sec. 2.

9. Ibid., sec. 3.

10. Ibid., sec. 5.

11. Ibid., sec. 29.

12. George Berkeley, *Three Dialogues Between Hylas and Philonous,* in *Selections,* ed. Mary W. Calkins (New York: Scribner's, 1957), pp. 268–269.

13. Ibid., pp. 238–239.

14. George Berkeley, *A Treatise Concerning the Principles of Human Knowledge,* in *The Works of George Berkeley,* vol. 1, ed. A. C. Fraser (Oxford: Clarendon, 1901), pt. 1, sec. 3.

15. Ernest C. Mossner, *Life of David Hume* (1954; reprint, Oxford: Clarendon, 1970), p. 51.

16. Thomas H. Huxley, *Hume* (New York, 1901), p. 3.

17. Mossner, p. 94.

18. Richard Watson, *The Philosopher's Diet: How to Lose Weight and Change the World* (Boston: Atlantic Monthly Press, 1985), p. 97.

19. Mossner, p. 111.

20. Ibid., p. 213.

21. Ibid., pp. 223, 318.

22. David Hume, "My Own Life," in *Dialogues Concerning Natural Religion,* ed. Henry D. Aiken (New York: Hafner, 1948), p. 239.

23. Mossner, p. 568.

24. Hume, "My Own Life," p. 239.

25. Ibid., p. 244.

26. Mossner, pp. 598–600.

27. David Hume, *An Enquiry Concerning Human Understanding,* ed. L. A. Selby-Bigge (Oxford: Clarendon, 1894), sec. 1.

28. Ibid., sec. 2.

29. Ibid.

30. David Hume, *A Treatise of Human Nature,* ed. L. A. Selby-Bigge (Oxford: Clarendon, 1896), bk. 1, pt. 4, sec. 6.

31. Ibid.

32. Ibid.

33. Hume, *Enquiry Concerning Human Understanding,* bk. 12, pt. 1.

34. Hume, *Treatise,* bk. 1, pt. 4, sec. 2.

35. Ibid.

36. Hume, *Enquiry Concerning Human Understanding,* sec. 7, pts. 1, 2.

37. Hume, *Dialogues Concerning Human Religion,* ed. Norman Kemp-Smith (Edinburgh: Nelson, 1947), pts. 2, 11. Used by permission of Thomas Nelson & Sons Limited.

38. Ibid., pts. 10, 11.

39. Ibid.

40. Ibid., bk. II, sec. III.

41. David Hume, *An Enquiry Concerning the Principles of Morals,* ed. L. A. Selby-Bigge (Oxford: Clarendon, 1894), Appendix I.

42. Ibid., sec. I.

43. Hume, *Treatise,* bk. 2, pt. 3. sec. 3.

44. Ibid., bk. 3, pt. 1. sec. 1.

45. Hume, *An Enquiry Concerning the Principles of Morals,* sec. I.

46. Hume, *Treatise,* bk. 3, pt. 1. sec. 2.

47. Hume, *An Enquiry Concerning the Principles of Morals,* Appendix II.

48. Ibid.

49. Ibid.

50. Hume, *Dialogues,* pt. 10, 11.

51. Hume, *Treatise,* bk. 1, pt. 4, sec. 7.

52. Hume, *Enquiry Concerning Human Understanding,* pt. 1.

Chapter 11
The Universalist: Immanuel Kant

1. In A. D. Lindsay, *Kant* (London: Oxford University Press, 1934), p. 2.

2. Henry Thomas and Dana Lee Thomas, *Living Biographies of Great Philosophers* (Garden City, N.Y.: Blue Ribbon, 1941), p. 191.

3. Josiah Royce, *The Spirit of Modern Philosophy* (Boston: Houghton Mifflin, 1892), p. 108.

4. Norman Kemp Smith, *Commentary to Kant's "Critique of Pure Reason"* (London: Macmillan, 1923), p. xix.

5. Immanuel Kant, preface, *Critique of Pure Reason,* 1st ed., trans. Norman Kemp Smith (London: Macmillan, 1929), p. 13.

6. Thomas and Thomas, *Living Biographies,* p. 196.

7. Friedrich Schiller, *Poems in Works* (London, 1901).

8. Immanuel Kant, *Prolegomena to Any Future Metaphysics,* trans. Lewis White Beck (Indianapolis: Liberal Arts, 1950), intro., pp. 5–6.

9. W. T. Jones, *A History of Western Philosophy: Kant and the Nineteenth Century,* rev. 2nd ed. (New York: Harcourt Brace Jovanovich, 1975), pp. 19ff.

10. Immanuel Kant, *Critique of Pure Reason,* 2nd ed., unabridged ed., trans. Norman Kemp Smith (New York: St. Martin's, 1929), pp. 41–42.

11. Ibid., p. 532.

12. Ibid., pp. 557ff.

13. Ibid., pp. 558ff.

14. Ibid., p. 559.

15. Roger Scruton, "The Rationalists and Kant," in *Philosophy: A Guide Through the Subject*, ed. A. C. Grayling (Oxford: Oxford University Press, 1995), p. 475.

16. Ibid., pp. 475–476.

17. See Immanuel Kant, *Critique of Practical Reason and Other Essays*, trans. Lewis White Beck (Chicago: University of Chicago Press, 1949), p. 8, B, ix.

18. S. Körner, *Kant* (Baltimore: Penguin, 1955), pp. 129ff.

19. Immanuel Kant, *Fundamental Principles of the Metaphysics of Morals*, trans. T. K. Abbott (London: Longmans, Green, 1927), sec. 1, p. 10.

20. Ibid., p. 16.

21. Ibid., p. 17.

22. Ibid., sec. 2, p. 36.

23. Ibid., sec. 1, p. 18.

24. Kant, *Metaphysics of Morals*, sec. 2, pp. 46–47.

25. Immanuel Kant, *Groundwork of the Metaphysics of Morals*, in H. J. Paton, trans., *Kant's Groundwork of the Metaphysics of Morals*, 3rd ed. (New York: Harper & Row Torchbook, 1964), p. 96.

26. John Rawls, *A Theory of Justice* (Cambridge, Mass.: Harvard University Press, 1971), p. 12.

27. Ibid., pp. 60–61.

28. Ibid., p. 13.

29. Susan Moller Okin, *Justice, Gender, and the Family* (New York: Basic, 1989), p. 8.

30. Ibid., p. 91.

31. Rawls, p. 12.

32. Okin, p. 91.

Chapter 12

The Utilitarian: John Stuart Mill

1. W. T. Jones, *Kant and the Nineteenth Century: A History of Western Philosophy*, rev. 2nd ed. (New York: Harcourt Brace Jovanovich, 1975), p. 162.

2. Thomas Malthus, *An Essay on the Principle of Population as It Affects the Future Improvement of Society* (London, 1798), p. 4.

3. Jeremy Bentham, *An Introduction to Principles of Morals and Legislation* (Oxford: Oxford University Press, 1823 ed.), ch. 1, sec. 1.

4. Richard Watson, *Cogito, Ergo Sum: The Life of René Descartes* (Boston: David R. Godine, 2002), p. 11.

5. Benedict de Spinoza, *The Ethics*, trans. R. H. M. Elwes (New York: Dover, 1955), proposition 37, note 1.

6. Immanuel Kant, "Duties towards Animals and Spirits," in *Lectures on Ethics*, trans. L. Infeld (New York: Harper & Row, 1963), pp. 239–240.

7. Jeremy Bentham, *An Introduction to Principles of Morals and Legislation* (New York: Hafner, 1948), p. 311n.

8. A. Bain, *John Stuart Mill* (1882; reprint, New York: Augustus M. Kelley, 1966), pp. 334f., and B. Mazlish, *James and John Stuart Mill* (New York: Basic Books, 1975), p. 66.

9. John Stuart Mill, *Autobiography*, ed. J. D. Stillinger (London: Oxford University Press, 1971), pp. 6, 9.

10. John Stuart Mill, *Autobiography* (New York: Columbia University Press, 1924), pp. 21–22.

11. Mill, *Autobiography*, ed. J. D. Stillinger, p. 20.

12. Ibid., p. 33, note 3.

13. Mazlish, pp. 201–202, and M. St. John Packe, *The Life of John Stuart Mill* (London: Stecker & Warburg, 1954), pp. 66–68.

14. Mill, *Autobiography*, ed. J. D. Stillinger, pp. 32, 33, note 3.

15. Mill, *Autobiography* (Columbia), pp. 97–98.

16. Mill, *Autobiography*, ed. J. D. Stillinger, pp. 83–84.

17. Mill, *Autobiography* (Columbia), p. 122.

18. Lewis S. Feuer, "John Stuart Mill as a Sociologist: The Unwritten Ethology," in John Stuart Mill, *On Socialism* (1879; reprint, Buffalo, N.Y.: Prometheus, 1987), p. 10.

19. Jeremy Bentham, *The Rationale of Reward*, in *The Works of Jeremy Bentham* (Edinburgh: Tait, 1838–1843), part 2, sec. 1, p. 253.

20. John Stuart Mill, *Utilitarianism*, ch. 2, "What Utilitarianism Is," in *The Utilitarians* (Garden City, N.Y.: Dolphin, 1961), p. 407.

21. Ibid., pp. 408–409.

22. Ibid., p. 409.

23. Ibid., pp. 410–411.

24. Ibid., p. 418.

25. Ibid., p. 415.

26. Ibid., pp. 412–413.

27. Ibid., pp. 414–415.

28. Ibid., pp. 415ff.

29. Ibid., p. 416.

30. Ibid., ch. 3, p. 437.

31. Mill, *Autobiography* (Columbia), p. 100.

Chapter 13

The Materialist: Karl Marx

1. Quoted in Isaiah Berlin, *Karl Marx* (New York: Oxford University Press, 1939), p. 73.

2. Condensed from "Karl Marx's Funeral," in Robert Payne, *Marx* (New York: Simon & Schuster, 1968), pp. 500–502.

3. Karl Marx, *Critique of Political Economy,* trans. N. I. Stone, in *Marx and Engels: Selected Works,* vol. 1 (Moscow: Foreign Languages Publishing, 1955), pp. 362–364.

4. In Sidney Hook, *Towards the Understanding of Karl Marx* (New York: John Day, 1932), pp. 80–81, and "Theses on Feuerbach, III," in *Karl Marx and Friedrich Engels on Religion,* ed. Reinhold Niebuhr (New York: Schocken, 1964), p. 70.

5. Karl Marx, *Economic and Philosophic Manuscripts,* trans. T. B. Bottomore, in Erich Fromm, *Marx's Concept of Man* (New York: Ungar, 1961), p. 181.

6. Karl Marx, *Critique of Political Economy,* trans. N. I. Stone (Chicago: C. H. Kerr, 1911), p. 11.

7. Karl Marx and Friedrich Engels, *Manifesto of the Communist Party,* 1888 ed., reprinted in *Introductory Readings in Philosophy,* eds. Avrum Stroll and Richard H. Popkin (New York: Holt, Rinehart & Winston, 1972), p. 412.

8. Ibid., p. 413.

9. Ibid., p. 415.

10. Ibid.

11. Ibid., p. 416.

12. Ibid., pp. 416–417.

13. Ibid., p. 418.

14. Karl Marx, *Economic and Philosophic Manuscripts* (1844), in *Writings of the Young Marx on Philosophy and Society,* eds. and trans. Loyd D. Easton and Kurt H. Guddat (Garden City, N.Y.: Anchor Doubleday, 1967), p. 290. Used by permission of Loyd D. Easton and Mrs. Kurt H. Guddat.

15. Ibid., p. 292.

16. Ibid., p. 294.

Chapter 14

The Existentialist: Søren Kierkegaard

1. Samuel Enoch Stumpf, *Philosophy: History and Problems,* 4th ed. (New York: McGraw-Hill, 1989), bk. 1, p. 475.

2. Søren Kierkegaard, *The Journals of Søren Kierkegaard,* trans. Alexander Dru (New York: Oxford University Press, 1938), p. 94.

3. Søren Kierkegaard, "Conclusion of" *The Point of View for My Work as an Author,* trans. Walter K. Lowrie (abridged), in *A Kierkegaard Anthology,* ed. Robert Bretall (New York: Modern Library, 1946), pp. 337, 339. Used by permission of Princeton University Library.

4. Kierkegaard, *Journals,* p. 4.

5. Kierkegaard, *Concluding Unscientific Postscript,* 1846 ed., trans. D. F. Swenson, L. M. Swenson, and W. K. Lowrie, in *A Kierkegaard Anthology,* p. 276, and *The Journals of Kierkegaard,* trans. and ed. Alexander Dru (London: Collins, 1958), p. 46.

6. Søren Kierkegaard, *Either/Or,* vol. 1: *Diaspsalmata,* trans. D. F. Swenson, L. M. Swenson, and W. K. Lowrie in *A Kierkegaard Anthology,* p. 33.

7. William Barrett, *Irrational Man: A Study in Existential Philosophy* (Garden City, N.Y.: Doubleday Anchor, 1958), p. 173.

8. Søren Kierkegaard, in *The Present Age,* trans. Alexander Dru, "The Individual and the Public," in *A Kierkegaard Anthology,* pp. 260–261.

9. Ibid., p. 263.

10. Kierkegaard, *The Point of View,* in Bretall, pp. 330, 332.

11. Kierkegaard, *Concluding Unscientific Postscript,* in Bretall, p. 198.

12. Søren Kierkegaard, *Kierkegaard's Concluding Unscientific Postscript,* trans. D. F. Swenson, with notes and introduction by W. Lowrie (Princeton, N.J.: Princeton University Press, 1941), p. 276.

13. David R. Law, *Kierkegaard as Negative Theologian* (Oxford: Clarendon Press, 1993), p. 115.

14. *Journals,* in Bretall, p. 11.

15. Ibid., p. 7.

16. Søren Kierkegaard, *The Point of View for My Work as an Author,* trans. W. Lowrie, ed. B. Nelson (New York: Harper & Row, 1962), p. 18.

17. *Journals,* in Bretall, p. 8.

18. Søren Kierkegaard, *Christian Discourses,* trans. Howard V. Hong and Edna H. Hong (Princeton, N.J.: Princeton University Press, 1978–2000), *Kierkegaard's Writings* vol. 17, p. 317.

19. Søren Kierkegaard, *Philosophical Fragments,* trans. Howard V. Hong and Edna H. Hong (Princeton, N.J.: Princeton University Press, 1978–2000), *Kierkegaard's Writings* vol. 7, pp. 190–191.

20. *Kierkegaard's Concluding Unscientific Postscript,* pp. 25–30.

21. David E. Cooper, "Kierkegaard," *The Blackwell Guide to Continental Philosophy,* eds. Robert C. Solomon

and David Sherman (Malden, Mass.: Blackwell, 2003), p. 54.

22. Søren Kierkegaard, *Sickness Unto Death,* trans. Walter Lowrie, in Bretall, p. 338.

23. For a discussion regarding the implication that the crowd level is also a stage on life's way, see A. Rudd, *Kierkegaard and the Limits of the Ethical* (Oxford: Blackwell, 1997), p. 24.

24. Søren Kierkegaard, *Purity of Heart (is to will one thing),* trans. D. Steered (London: Fontana, 1961), p. 54.

25. Søren Kierkegaard, *Either/Or: A Fragment of Life,* trans. David F. Swenson, Lillian Marvin Swenson, and Walter K. Lowrie, in Bretall, pp. 22–24.

26. Ibid., p. 34.

27. Søren Kierkegaard, *Either/Or,* vol. II, trans. W. Lowrie (Princeton, N.J.: Princeton University Press, 1971), p. 229.

28. Ibid., p. 164.

29. *Either/Or,* in Bretall, pp. 106–108.

30. Kierkegaard, *Journals,* pp. 181–182.

31. *Kierkegaard's Concluding Unscientific Postscript,* p. 276.

32. Søren Kierkegaard, *Fear and Trembling,* trans. Walter Lowrie, in Bretall, pp. 132–134.

33. *Kierkegaard's Concluding Unscientific Postscript,* pp. 31–32.

34. *Fear and Trembling,* in Bretall, p. 129.

35. Ibid., p. 130.

36. Søren Kierkegaard, quoted in Bruce H. Krimmse, *Encounters with Kierkegaard: A Life as Seen by His Contemporaries* (Princeton, N. J.: Princeton University Press, 1996), p. 464.

37. Ibid., pp. 471ff.

38. Ibid., p. 462.

39. *Either/Or,* in Bretall, p. 81.

Chapter 15

The Pragmatist: William James

1. G. W. Allen, *William James: A Biography* (New York: Viking, 1967), p. 134.

2. Ibid., p. 163.

3. Ibid., pp. 168–169.

4. Ralph Barton Perry, *The Thought and Character of William James* (Cambridge, Mass.: Harvard University Press, 1948), p. 386.

5. Allen, pp. 214–220.

6. Guy W. Stroh, *American Philosophy from Edwards to Dewey: An Introduction* (Princeton, N.J.: Van Nostrand, 1968), p. 123.

7. Perry, p. 300.

8. Ibid.

9. Quoted in Robert F. Davidson, *Philosophies Men Live By* (Fort Worth: Holt, Rinehart & Winston, 1971), p. 296.

10. Charles Sanders Peirce, *Collected Papers of Charles Sanders Peirce,* vol. 5, eds. Charles Hartshorne and Paul Weiss (Cambridge, Mass.: Harvard University Press, 1931–1935), pp. 276ff.

11. Ibid., pp. 284ff.

12. Ibid., pp. 272–273, 259–262.

13. William James, *The Will to Believe and Other Essays in Popular Philosophy* (1897; reprinted in *Human Immortality: Two Supposed Objections to the Doctrine,* New York: Dover, 1956), pp. 146–147.

14. Ibid., p. 177.

15. William James, *Pragmatism,* 1907 text, in *William James: Writings 1902–1910* (New York: Library of America, 1987), pp. 573ff.

16. Ibid., pp. 489, 490, 491.

17. James, *The Will to Believe,* pp. 28, 30.

18. William James, *Pragmatism* (New York: Longmans, Green, 1907), p. 58.

19. Ibid., pp. 59–64.

20. Ibid., p. 64.

21. William James, "The Dilemma of Determinism," in *The Will to Believe,* p. 150.

22. Ibid., pp. 161–163.

23. William James, "Some Problems in Philosophy," in *The Moral Equivalent of War and Other Essays,* ed. John K. Roth (New York: Harper & Row, 1971), p. 164.

24. William James, "The Dilemma of Determinism," in *The Will to Believe,* pp. 146–147.

25. James, *The Will to Believe,* p. 31.

26. Ibid., pp. 200–201.

27. William James, "Is Life Worth Living?" an address to the Harvard Young Men's Christian Association, published in *International Journal of Ethics,* October 1895, and in *The Search for Meaning in Life: Readings in Philosophy,* ed. Robert F. Davidson (New York: Holt, Rinehart & Winston, 1962), p. 61.

28. William James, "The Moral Philosopher and Moral Life," in *The Will to Believe,* pp. 211ff.

29. William James, *The Varieties of Religious Experience* (New York: Longmans, Green, 1902), pp. 525, 516–517.

30. James, *The Varieties of Religious Experience,* in *William James: Writings 1902–1910,* p. 124.

31. Ibid., p. 152.

32. William James, "A Pluralistic Mystic," cited in Dmitri Tymoczko, "The Nitrous Oxide Philosopher," *Atlantic Monthly,* May 1996, pp. 98–99.

33. Quoted in Tymoczko, p. 100.

34. James, *The Will to Believe,* pp. 202ff.

35. W. T. Jones, *Kant and the Nineteenth Century: A History of Western Philosophy,* rev. 2nd ed. (New York: Harcourt Brace Jovanovich, 1975), p. 323.

36. James, *The Will to Believe,* p. 320.

37. Ibid., pp. 18–19.

38. James, *The Varieties of Religious Experience,* p. 26.

39. Tymoczko, pp. 99–100.

40. Ibid.

Chapter 16

The Anti-Philosopher: Friedrich Nietzsche

1. Friedrich Nietzsche, *The Will to Power,* ed. Walter Kaufmann, trans. Walter Kaufmann and R. J. Hollingdale (New York: Vintage, 1967), p. 3.

2. Friedrich Nietzsche, *The Birth of Tragedy,* trans. W. A. Haussmann (New York: Russell & Russell, 1964), p. xvii.

3. Letter from Friedrich Ritschl in *The Portable Nietzsche,* trans. Walter Kaufmann (New York: Penguin, 1968), pp. 8–9.

4. R. J. Hollingdale, introduction to his translation of *Thus Spake Zarathustra* (Baltimore, Md.: Penguin, 1967), p. 26.

5. Friedrich Nietzsche, *Ecce Homo,* quoted in *Thus Spake Zarathustra,* trans. Thomas Cotton (New York: Modern Library, 1967), pp. 18–19.

6. Friedrich Nietzsche, *Ecce Homo,* in *The Portable Nietzsche,* p. 298.

7. Friedrich Nietzsche, "Attempt at a Self-Criticism," in *The Birth of Tragedy,* trans. Walter Kaufmann (New York: Vintage, 1967), sec. 3, pp. 19–20.

8. Quoted in Karl Jaspers, *Nietzsche: An Introduction to the Understanding of His Philosophical Activity* (Tucson: University of Arizona Press, 1965), p. 56.

9. Nietzsche, letter to Franz Overbeck, quoted in Jaspers, p. 87.

10. Nietzsche, "Attempt at a Self-Criticism," sec. 5, p. 23.

11. Alexander Nehamas, *Nietzsche: Life as Literature* (Cambridge, Mass.: Harvard University Press, 1985), p. 2.

12. Friedrich Nietzsche, "On Truth and Lie in an Extra-Moral Sense," in *The Portable Nietzsche,* pp. 42, 44.

13. Nietzsche, *Thus Spake Zarathustra,* "Of Self-Overcoming," pp. 136, 137, 138.

14. Philip Novak, *The Vision of Nietzsche* (Rockport, Mass.: Element, 1996), pp. 8–9.

15. Nietzsche, *The Will to Power,* sec. 1067, pp. 549–550.

16. Friedrich Nietzsche, "The Natural History of Morals," Part Five of *Beyond Good and Evil,* trans. Walter Kaufmann and R. J. Hollingdale, sec. 186, in *From Modernism to Postmodernism: An Anthology,* ed. Lawrence Cahoone (Cambridge, Mass.: Blackwell, 1966), pp. 104–105.

17. Ibid.

18. Nietzsche, *On the Genealogy of Morals,* in *On the Genealogy of Morals and Ecce Homo,* ed. Walter Kaufmann, trans. Walter Kaufmann and R. J. Hollingdale (New York: Vintage, 1969), Third Essay, sec. 19, pp. 136–137.

19. Friedrich Nietzsche, *Ecce Homo,* "Why I Am a Destiny," sec. 6, in *On the Genealogy of Morals and Ecce Homo,* p. 331.

20. Ibid., sec. 7, p. 332.

21. Nietzsche, *Beyond Good and Evil,* sec. 190, in Cahoone, p. 108.

22. Nietzsche, *Daybreak,* in Novak, sec. 131, p. 78.

23. Nietzsche, *Beyond Good and Evil,* sec. 198, in Cahoone, p. 113.

24. Ibid., sec. 201, p. 117.

25. Friedrich Nietzsche, *The Gay Science,* trans. Walter Kaufmann (New York: Vintage, 1974), bk. 3, sec. 125, p. 181.

26. Ibid.

27. Nietzsche, *Thus Spoke Zarathustra,* in *The Portable Nietzsche,* pp. 199–200.

28. Nietzsche, *The Gay Science,* sec. 343, p. 279.

29. Quoted in Jaspers, p. 162.

30. Nietzsche, *Thus Spoke Zarathustra,* in *The Portable Nietzsche,* p. 398.

31. Nietzsche, *Toward a Genealogy of Morals,* trans. Walter Kaufmann, "Good and Evil Versus Good and Bad," sec. 10, in *The Portable Nietzsche,* pp. 451–452.

32. Ibid.

33. Nietzsche, *Thus Spoke Zarathustra,* in *The Portable Nietzsche,* pp. 124–128.

34. Friedrich Nietzsche, *Twilight of the Idols,* "Four Great Errors," sec. 8, in *Twilight of the Idols* and *The Anti-Christ,* trans. R. J. Hollingdale (Middlesex: Penguin, 1968), p. 54.

35. Nietzsche, *Ecce Homo,* "Why I Am So Clever," sec. 10, p. 258.

36. Nietzsche, *The Gay Science,* sec. 276, Novak, p. 160.

Chapter 17

The Twentieth Century: Ludwig Wittgenstein and Martin Heidegger

1. See Albert William Levi, *Philosophy as Social Expression* (Chicago: University of Chicago Press, 1974), pp. 239–241.

2. Friedrich Nietzsche, *The Genealogy of Morals,* trans. F. Golffing (Garden City, N.Y.: 1956), p. 255.

3. Alasdair MacIntyre, "Philosophy: Past Conflict and Future Direction," address delivered to the Pacific Division of the American Philosophy Association, March 1987, quoted in Huston Smith, *Beyond the Postmodern Mind,* updated and revised (Wheaton, Ill., Quest Books, 1982, 1989, 2003), p. 119.

4. See W. T. Jones, *The Twentieth Century to Wittgenstein and Sartre: A History of Philosophy,* vol. 5 (San Diego: Harcourt Brace Jovanovich, 1975), pp. 88–93.

5. Robert C. Solomon, "Introduction," *The Blackwell Guide to Continental Philosophy,* eds. Robert C. Solomon and David Sherman (Malden, Mass.: Blackwell, 2003), p. 3.

6. See A. C. Grayling, *Wittgenstein: A Very Short Introduction* (Oxford: Oxford University Press, 1996), pp. 1 and 134.

7. Ibid., p. 11.

8. Jaakko Hintikka, *On Wittgenstein* (Belmont, Calif.: Wadsworth, 2000), p. i.

9. Ray Monk, *Wittgenstein: The Duty of Genius* (New York: Penguin, 1990), p. 579.

10. Ibid., p. 580.

11. John Locke, "Epistle to the Reader" in *An Essay Concerning Human Understanding,* ed. A. C. Fraser (Oxford: Clarendon Press, 1894).

12. Ludwig Wittgenstein, *Tractatus Logico-Philosophicus,* trans. D. F. Pears and B. F. McGuinness (London: Routledge and Kegan Paul, 1961), p. 3.

13. Ibid.

14. Grayling, p. 18.

15. See Hans Sluga, "Introduction," *The Cambridge Companion to Wittgenstein,* pp. 16–17, and Bryan Magee's interview with John Searle in *The Great Philosophers: An Introduction to Western Philosophy* (Oxford: Oxford University Press: 1988), pp. 326–327.

16. Ludwig Wittgenstein, The *Blue and Brown Books* (Oxford: Blackwell, 1960), p. 28.

17. Ludwig Wittgenstein, *Culture and Value,* ed. G. G. von Wright, trans. P. Winch (Oxford: Blackwell, 1980), pp. 6–10 and 79.

18. *Philosophical Investigations,* par. 133.

19. Ibid., par. 109.

20. Jeff Malpas, "Martin Heidegger," *The Blackwell Guide to Modern Philosophy,* eds. Robert C. Solomon and David Sherman (Malden, Mass.: Blackwell, 2003), p. 143; Richard Gill and Ernest Sherman, *The Fabric of Existentialism: Philosophical and Literary Sources,* eds. Richard Gill and Ernest Sherman (Englewood Cliffs, N.J., 1973), pp. 415–416; Simon Blackburn, "Enquivering," *The New Republic* (Oct. 30, 2000), p. 43; A. J. Ayer cited in *L'Espresso* (Rome), May 25, 1980, p. 199; Paul Edwards, *Heidegger on Death: A Critical Evaluation* (La Salle, Ill.: Hegeler, 1979), p. v.

21. Martin Heidegger, "My Way to Phenomenology," in *On Being and Time,* trans. J. Stambaugh (New York: Harper & Row, 1972), p. 75.

22. George Steiner, "Introduction—Heidegger: In 1991," in *Martin Heidegger* (Chicago: University of Chicago Press, 1989), p. xv.

23. Hannah Arendt, "Martin Heidegger at Eighty," trans. A. Hofstadter, in *Heidegger and Modern Philosophy,* ed. M. Murray (New Haven, Conn.: Yale University Press, 1971), p. 295.

24. Malpas, pp. 146–147.

25. Malpas, pp. 143–161; and Gill and Sherman, pp. 415–416.

26. Steiner, pp. xxvi–xxviii.

27. Richard Rorty, "Heidegger et la Nazisme," in *The New Republic,* April 11, 1988, pp. 32–33.

28. Heidegger, "My Way to Phenomenology," p. 78.

29. Edmund Husserl, "Philosophy and the Crisis of European Man," trans. Q. Lauer, in *Phenomenology and the Crisis of Philosophy* (New York: Harper & Row, 1965), p. 184f.

30. Patricia Altenbernd Johnson, *On Heidegger* (Belmont, Calif.: Wadsworth, 2000), p. 5.

31. Martin Heidegger, *Being and Time,* trans. J. Macquarrie and E. Robinson (New York: Harper & Row, 1962), p. 32.

32. Ibid., p. 19.

33. Martin Heidegger, "The Way Back into the Ground of Metaphysics," in *Existentialism from Dostoevsky to Sartre,* trans. Walter Kaufmann (New York: Meridian, 1957), pp. 209ff.

34. *Being and Time,* pp. 32–33.

35. Ibid., pp. 79f.

36. Ibid., pp. 83–84.

37. Ibid., pp. 163–165.

38. Ibid., pp. 212–213.

39. Ibid., pp. 219–220.

40. Ibid., pp. 294–295.

41. Martin Heidegger, "Postscript to *What Is Metaphysics?*" in *Existence and Being*, ed. Werner Brock (Chicago: Henry Regnery, 1949), p. 355.

42. Martin Heidegger, *The Question Concerning Technology*, trans. William Lovitt, in *Basic Writings*, ed. David Farrell Krell (New York: Harper & Row, 1977), p. 296.

43. Ibid., p. 308.

44. Ibid., p. 309.

45. See Jones, pp. 326–328.

46. Martin Heidegger, *Existence and Being,* intro. W. Brock (London: Vision, 1949), p. 301.

47. Ibid., p. 304.

48. Ibid., pp. 306, 314.

49. Kai Nielsen, "Philosophy: Past Conflict and Future Direction," an address delivered to the Pacific Division of the American Philosophical Association, March 1987.

Chapter 18
Philosophy as a Way of Life

1. Susan Bordo, "The Cartesian Masculinization of Thought" in *From Modernism to Postmodernism: An Anthology*, ed. Lawrence Cahoone (Cambridge, Mass.: Blackwell, 1966), pp. 656–657.

2. Carol Gilligan, *Mapping the Moral Domain: A Contribution of Women's Thinking to Psychological Theory and Education*, eds. Carol Gilligan, Janie Victoria Ward, and Jill McLean Taylor, with Betty Baridge (Cambridge, Mass.: Center for the Study of Gender Education and Human Development, distributed by Harvard University Press, 1988), p. v; Carol Gilligan, *In a Different Voice: Psychological Theory and Women's Development* (Cambridge, Mass.: Harvard University Press, 1982), pp. 1–2.

3. This material is based on Robin Wilson's article "Black Women Seek a Role in Philosophy," *The Chronicle of Higher Education* (September 28, 2007), vol. 54, issue 5, p. B4.

4. Michael Specter, "The Dangerous Philosopher," *New Yorker*, September 6, 1999, p. 46.

5. Ibid.

6. Peter Singer, "The Singer Solution to World Poverty," *New York Times*, September 5, 1999.

7. This sketch is based on Robert Boynton's article, "Who Needs Philosophy?" *New York Times Magazine*, November 12, 1999.

8. Ibid.

9. Martha C. Nussbaum, *Cultivating Humanity: A Classical Defense of Reform in Liberal Education* (Cambridge, Mass.: Harvard University Press, 1997), pp. 6–7.

10. Quoted by Boynton.

11. Martha C. Nussbaum, *The Therapy of Desire: Theory and Practice in Hellenistic Ethics* (Princeton, N. J.: Princeton University Press, 1994), pp. 3–4.

12. Ibid., p. 510.

13. Martha C. Nussbaum, *Women and Human Development: The Capabilities Approach* (New York, N.Y.: Cambridge University Press, 2000), pp. 299–301.

14. Pierre Hadot, *Philosophy as a Way of Life*, trans. Arnold I. Davidson (Oxford: Blackwell, 1995), p. 58.

15. Ibid., p. 274.

16. Ibid., p. 285.

17. Pierre Hadot, *What Is Ancient Philosophy?* trans. Michael Chase (Cambridge, Mass.: Harvard University Press, 2002), pp. 275–281.

18. Epictetus, *Handbook of Epictetus*, trans. Nicholas P. White (Indianapolis: Hackett, 1983), pp. 28ff.

GLOSSARY

This Glossary contains all of the terms defined in the margins of the text (and a few additional key terms). Chapter and page number notations for margin definitions are indicated in parentheses. Consult the index for terms and concepts not listed here.

absolute idealism, see *idealism (absolute or Hegelian)*

aesthetics Branch of philosophy that studies all forms of art.

alienated life Unconscious, unspontaneous, and unfulfilled life; deprived of fundamental conditions necessary for self-actualization. (Ch. 13, p. 384)

alienation According to Marx, condition of workers separated from the products of their labor; primarily an objective state, but can also refer to not feeling "at one" with the product of labor. (Ch. 13, p. 382)

altruism From Latin for "other"; the capacity to promote the welfare of others; opposed to egoism. (Ch. 12, p. 355)

amor fati Nietzsche's term meaning "the love of fate"; expressed as joyous affirmation and delight that everything is exactly as and what it is. (Ch. 16, p. 476)

amoral, see *nonmoral*

analytic philosophy Influential nonliterary approach to philosophy that stresses logic, testability, precision, and clarity with antecedents in an anglophile tradition that includes John Locke, David Hume, Bertrand Russell, and Ludwig Wittgenstein; contends that close logical and linguistic analyses are thought to be the only proper methods for sorting out philosophical confusions; commonly contrasted with continental philosophy. (Ch. 17, p. 484)

anti-philosopher A radical critic of the techniques and doctrines of modern science and philosophy. The anti-philosopher disputes the possibility of objectivity and universality and rejects the absolute authority of reason; anti-philosophers also reject the possibility of a *neutral stance* or *perspectiveless perspective*. (Ch. 16, p. 462)

a posteriori knowledge Empirical knowledge derived from sense experience and not regarded as universal because the conditions under which it is acquired change, perceivers vary, and factual relationships change. (Ch. 9, p. 255)

a priori ideas, see *innate ideas*

a priori knowledge Derived from reason without reference to sense experience. Examples include "All triangles contain 180°" and "Every event has a cause." (Ch. 9, p. 255)

archetypal (paradigmatic) individual A special class of teachers, philosophers, and religious figures whose nature becomes a standard by which a culture judges the "ideal" human being; a rare human being whose very nature represents something elemental about the human condition. (Ch. 4, p. 92)

archetype Basic image that represents our conception of the essence of a certain type of person; according to psychologist C. G. Jung, some of the images have been shared by the whole human race from the earliest times. (Ch. 1, p. 6)

archetype (philosophical) A philosopher who represents an original or influential point of view in a way that significantly affects philosophers and nonphilosophers: cynic, saint, pessimist, optimist, atheist, rationalist, idealist, and so on. (Ch. 1, p. 6)

argument from design, see *teleological argument*

argument from gradation Argument for the existence of God based on the idea that being progresses from inanimate objects to increasingly complex animated creatures, culminating in a qualitatively unique God; Aristotelian argument that forms the basis for the fourth of Aquinas's Five Ways. (Ch. 8, p. 228)

argument from motion Attempt to prove the existence of God based on the reasoning that to avoid an infinite regress, there must be an Unmoved Mover capable of imparting motion to all other things; Aristotelian argument that forms the basis for the first of Thomas Aquinas's Five Ways. (Ch. 8, p. 225)

argument from necessity Argument for the existence of God based on the idea that if nothing had ever existed, nothing would always exist; therefore, there is something whose existence is necessary (an eternal something); Aristotelian argument that forms the basis for the third of Aquinas's Five Ways. (Ch. 8, p. 227)

ascetic Individual who turns away from pleasure and severely limits all sensual appetites in order to achieve salvation or peace of mind. (Ch. 2, p. 41)

atomism Early Greek philosophy developed by Leucippus and Democritus and later refined by Epicurus and Lucretius; materialistic view that the universe consists entirely of empty space and ultimately simple entities that combine to form objects. (Ch. 3, p. 67)

atoms From the Greek *atomos,* meaning "indivisible," "having no parts," or "uncuttable"; minute material particles; the ultimate material constituents of all things. Atoms have such properties as size, shape, position, arrangement (combination), and motion, but lack qualities like color, taste, temperature, or smell. (Ch. 3, p. 68)

authenticity Subjective condition of an individual living honestly and courageously in the moment, refusing to make excuses, and not relying on groups or institutions for meaning and purpose; for Heidegger, living in and with the "understanding" of our death. (Ch. 14, p. 397; Ch. 17, p. 510)

axiology Branch of philosophy that studies values in general.

barbarian From a rude "bar-bar" noise used to mock dialects considered crude by the ancient Athenians; originally referred to other cultures considered "less than human" or uncivilized. (Ch. 3, p. 60)

belief Conviction or trust that a claim is true; an individual's subjective mental state; distinct from knowledge. (Ch.1, p. 13)

belief (mere) A conviction that something is true for which the only evidence is the sincerity of the believer. (Ch. 1, p. 14)

bodhisattva An enlightened being who voluntarily postpones his own nirvana in order to help all other conscious life-forms find "supreme release"; not a savior. (Ch. 2, p. 43)

bourgeoisie All those who do not produce anything, yet who own and control the means of production. (Ch. 13, p. 373)

bundle theory of the self Humean theory that there is no fixed self, but that the self is merely a "bundle of perceptions"; a self is merely a habitual way of discussing certain perceptions. (Ch. 10, p. 294)

capitalism Economic system in which the means of production and distribution are all (or mostly) privately owned and operated for profit under fully competitive conditions; tends to be accompanied by concentration of wealth and growth of great corporations. (Ch. 13, p. 377)

categorical imperative According to Kant, a command that is universally binding on all rational creatures; the ultimate foundation of all moral law: "Act as if the maxim of thy action were to become a universal law of nature." (Ch. 11, p. 329)

character From the Greek *charakter,* a word derived from *charassein,* "to make sharp" or "to engrave," character refers to the sum total of a person's traits, including behavior, habits, likes and dislikes, capacities, potentials, and so on; a key element of Aristotelian ethics and psychology, meaning the overall (generally fixed) nature or tone of a person's habits. (Ch. 6, p. 174)

chun-tzu Literally, "the lord's son"; originally the sovereign himself or a "cultivated gentleman"; Confucian morally superior man; a great or noble soul. (Ch. 2, p. 38)

chung-yung Literally, "centrality and universality," the Golden Mean of Confucius, consisting of moderation and normality; universal moral law; also equilibrium or harmony. (Ch. 2, p. 35)

Cogito, ergo sum Latin for "I think, therefore I am." (Ch. 9, p. 260)

coherence theory of truth Truth test in which new or unclear ideas are evaluated in terms of rational or logical consistency and in relation to already established truths. (Ch. 9, p. 249)

continental philosophy Broad term referring to philosophies associated with European philosophers such as Kant, Hegel, Kierkegaard, Marx, Nietzsche, Husserl, and Heidegger; not a school of philosophy as such or single way of doing philosophy; includes phenomenology, existentialism, Deconstructionism; commonly contrasted with analytic philosophy. (Ch. 17, p. 484)

conversation For Heidegger, dialogue; progressively attuned communication about Being; language function contrasted with idle talk. (Ch. 17, p. 516)

co-opt In Marxian social analysis, co-option occurs when workers identify with the economic system that oppresses them by confusing the remote possibility of accumulating wealth with their actual living and working conditions; being co-opted also refers to anyone who is somehow convinced to further interests that are to her or his ultimate disadvantage. (Ch. 13, p. 381)

correspondence (copy or representation) theory of truth Truth test that holds that an idea (or belief or thought) is true if whatever it refers to actually exists (corresponds to a fact). (Ch. 10, p. 280)

cosmological argument From the Greek word *kosmos,* meaning "world," "universe," or "orderly structure"; argument for the existence of God that because it is impossible for any natural thing to be the complete and sufficient source of its own existence, there must be an Uncaused Cause capable of imparting existence to all other things; Aristotelian argument that forms the basis for the second of Aquinas's Five Ways. (Ch. 8, p. 226)

cosmology From the Greek word *kosmos*, meaning "world," "universe," or "orderly structure," the study of the universe as an ordered system or cosmos. (Ch. 3, p. 65)

cosmos Greek term for "ordered whole"; first used by the Pythagoreans to characterize the universe as an ordered whole consisting of harmonies of contrasting elements. (Ch. 3, p. 64)

critical philosophy Kant's term for his effort to assess the nature and limits of "pure reason," unadulterated by experience, in order to identify the actual relationship of the mind to knowledge. (Ch. 11, p. 319)

Cynic Individual who lives an austere, unconventional life based on Cynic doctrine. (Ch. 7, p. 187)

Cynicism Philosophy based on the belief that the very essence of civilization is corrupt and that civilization destroys individuals by making them soft and subject to the whims of fortune. (Ch. 7, p. 187)

Cyrenaic hedonism, see *hedonism (Cyrenaic)*

deconstruction (philosophical) A kind of close textual analysis focused on uncovering and overcoming "privileges" hidden in philosophic arguments and theories by taking a text apart—by de-constructing it; questions whether any text can have any definite meaning. (Ch. 17, p. 483)

determinism Belief that everything that happens must happen exactly the way it does because all matter is governed by cause and effect and follows laws of nature. (Ch. 15, p. 437)

dialectic (Hegelian) According to Hegel, a three-step pattern in which an original idea, known as a thesis, struggles with a contrary idea, known as an antithesis, to produce a new synthesis that combines elements of both. (Ch. 13, p. 368)

dialectic (Socratic), see *Socratic method*

dialectical process (Hegelian) Internally governed evolutionary cycle in which progress occurs as the result of a struggle between two opposing conditions. (Ch. 13, p. 372)

dualism Any philosophical position that divides existence into two completely distinct, independent, unique substances. (Ch. 9, p. 266)

dualism (epistemological) The view that knowing consists of two distinct aspects: the knower and the known. (Ch. 10, p. 283)

economic As used by Marx, the complete array of social relationships and arrangements that constitutes a particular social order. (Ch. 13, p. 376)

Efficient Cause The triggering cause that initiates activity; the substance by which a change is brought about;

close to the contemporary meaning of cause; third of Aristotle's Four Causes. (Ch. 6, p. 163)

egocentric predicament Problem generated by epistemological dualism: If all knowledge comes in the form of my own ideas, how can I verify the existence of anything external to them? (Ch. 10, p. 283)

egoism Belief that self-interest is or ought to be the basis of all deliberate action; psychological egoists deny that altruism is even possible.

Eightfold Path Buddha's prescription for rooting out suffering: (1) right understanding; (2) right purpose; (3) right speech; (4) right conduct; (5) right livelihood; (6) right effort; (7) right mindfulness; (8) right meditation. (Ch. 2, p. 48)

empirical criterion of meaning Meaningful ideas are those that can be traced back to sense experience (impressions); beliefs that cannot be reduced to sense experience are not "ideas" at all, but meaningless utterances. (Ch. 10, p. 293)

empiricism Belief that all knowledge is ultimately derived from the senses (experience) and that all ideas can be traced to sense data. (Ch. 10, p. 278)

entelechy From the Greek for "having its end within itself"; according to Aristotle, an inner urge that drives all things to blossom into their own unique selves; inner order or design that governs all natural processes. (Ch. 6, p. 163)

epistemological dualism see *dualism (epistemological)*

epistemology Branch of philosophy that studies the nature and possibility of knowledge. (Ch. 10, p. 278)

esse est percipi Latin for Berkeley's belief that "to be is to be perceived." (Ch. 10, p. 287)

ethical hedonism, see *hedonism (ethical)*

ethics Branch of philosophy concerned with the good life and with moral value and moral reasoning.

ethnocentrism From Greek roots meaning "the race is the center"; belief that the customs and beliefs of one's own culture are inherently superior to all others. (Ch. 3, p. 59)

eudaimonia Often translated as "happiness"; term Aristotle used to refer to fully realized existence; state of being fully aware, vital, alert. (Ch. 6, p. 169; see also Ch. 13, p. 383)

existentialism Term used to refer to any philosophy that emphasizes fundamental questions of meaning and choice as they affect existing individuals; existential themes include choice, freedom, identity, alienation, inauthenticity, despair, and awareness of our own mortality. (Ch. 14, p. 391)

fallacy of anachronism Error in reasoning that results from uncritically and rigidly applying contemporary values to past practices and ideas. (Overview of Classical Themes, p. 19)

Final Cause That for which an activity or process takes place; a thing's very reason for being (*raison d'être*); fourth of Aristotle's Four Causes. (Ch. 6, p. 163)

forces of production In philosophical Marxism, the forces of production are factories, equipment, technology, knowledge, and skill; a part of the substructure of society. (Ch. 13, p. 376)

forlornness Jean-Paul Sartre's term for his belief that we face life alone, without God, without certainty, with only absolute freedom and the responsibility that accompanies it. (Ch. 17, p. 494f.)

form (Aristotle) From the Greek word for essence (*ousia*), that which is in matter and makes a thing what it is; can be abstracted from matter but cannot exist independently of matter. (Ch. 6, p. 158)

Formal Cause The shape, or form, into which matter is changed; second of Aristotle's Four Causes. (Ch. 6, p. 162)

forms see *Platonic Forms*

Four Noble Truths Foundation of Buddha's teachings: (1) to exist is to suffer; (2) self-centeredness is the chief cause of human suffering; (3) the cause of suffering can be understood and rooted out; (4) suffering can be alleviated by following the Eightfold Path. (Ch. 2, p. 47)

functionalist theory of morality Moral position that right and wrong can be understood only in terms of their effect on anything's natural function; each kind of thing has a natural purpose (function). (Ch. 5, p. 142)

hedonism From the Greek root for "pleasure"; general term for any philosophy that asserts that pleasure = good and pain = evil (bad). (Ch. 7, p. 182)

hedonism (Cyrenaic) Philosophy that advocates the unreflective pursuit of intense, immediate pleasure; makes no qualitative distinctions among pleasures. (Ch. 7, p. 183)

hedonism (ethical) The belief that although it is possible to deliberately avoid pleasure or choose pain, it is morally wrong to do so. (Ch. 12, p. 344)

hedonism (psychological) The belief that all decisions are based on considerations of pleasure and pain because it is psychologically impossible for human beings to do otherwise. (Ch. 12, p. 344)

hsiao-jen Small or vulgar man; in Confucian philosophy, the opposite of the *chun-tzu;* a petty and base individual. (Ch. 2, p. 38)

humanism Name given to any philosophy that emphasizes human welfare and dignity; belief that human intelligence and effort are capable of improving conditions in the here and now. (Ch. 2, p. 35)

hypothetical imperatives Propositions that tell us what to do under specific, variable conditions. (Ch. 11, p. 328)

idealism (absolute or Hegelian) Term used to identify Hegel's particular form of German idealism; a monistic philosophy that is based on an all-encompassing Absolute Spirit that is self-actualizing into perfection; Reality (Absolute Mind or Absolute Spirit) is independent of any individual's mind; not to be confused with Berkeleian idealism (immaterialism), in which objective reality is said to exist in the individual's mind. (Ch. 13, p. 368)

idealism (immaterialism) Belief that only ideas (mental states) exist; the material world is a fiction—it does not exist. (Ch. 10, p. 285)

idealism (Kantian) Theory that knowledge is the result of the interaction between the mind and sensation and is structured by regulative ideas called categories; also known as *Kantian formalism* and *transcendental idealism.* (Ch. 11, p. 316)

idle talk Heidegger's name for superficial "they talk"; includes chatter, gossip, and merely verbal understanding; contrasted with conversation or dialogue. (Ch. 17, p. 508)

immoral Morally wrong, bad, or not right; a moral value judgment or prescriptive claim. (Ch. 11, p. 311)

inauthenticity Condition that results when the nature and needs of the individual are ignored, denied, and obscured or sacrificed for institutions, abstractions, or groups. (Ch. 14, p. 396)

inductive reasoning Reasoning pattern that proceeds from the particular to the general or from "some" to "all" and results in generalized rules or principles established with degrees of probability. (Ch. 10, p. 297)

innate ideas (*a priori* ideas) Truths that are not derived from observation or experiment; characterized as being certain, deductive, universally true, and independent of all experience. (Ch. 9, p. 249; see also Ch. 10, p. 280)

instrumental theory of morality Moral position that right and wrong must be determined by the consequences of acts; right and wrong viewed as means (instruments) for getting something else. (Ch. 5, p. 141)

intellectualism Term used to refer to the claim that behavior is always controlled by beliefs about what is good and the means to that good. (Ch. 4, p. 109)

irony Communication on at least two levels, a literal or obvious level and a hidden or real level; favored by Socrates as a technique for keeping his listeners alert and involved. (Ch. 4, p. 96)

jen General human virtue; translated as human, humane, humanitarian, humanity, and benevolence; can mean both humankind and kindness; also a man or woman who is truly himself or herself; a "real person." (Ch. 2, p. 39)

justice (Platonic) Excellence of function for the whole; in a just society each individual performs his or her natural function according to class; in a just individual, reason rules the spirit and the appetites. (Ch. 5, p. 144)

Kantian formalism, see *idealism (Kantian)*

Kantian idealism, see *idealism (Kantian)*

karma From the Pali *kamma;* according to Buddhist tradition, the law of moral causation (moral cause and effect); it includes past and present actions and is not to be confused with fate or predestination; good or bad karma results from our own actions. (Ch. 2, p. 46)

knowledge True belief. (Ch. 1, p. 13)

knowledge (practical) The skills needed to do things like play the piano, use a band saw, remove a tumor, or bake a cake. (Ch. 1, p. 13)

knowledge (theoretical) The accurate compilation and assessment of factual and systematic relationships. (Ch. 1, p. 13)

knowledge, see *a posteriori knowledge*

knowledge, see *a priori knowledge*

law of contradiction Rule of inference that says no statement can be both true and false at the same time and under the same conditions; sometimes known as the law of noncontradiction. (Ch. 8, p. 215)

law of noncontradiction, see *law of contradiction*

li Literally, "ceremony"; encompasses rites, customs, and conventions ranging from ritual sacrifices honoring one's ancestors to everyday etiquette and good manners. (Ch. 2, p. 37)

logic Branch of philosophy that studies the rules of correct reasoning.

logos One of the richest and most complex terms in ancient philosophy; associated meanings include: "intelligence," "speech," "discourse," "thought," "reason," "word," "meaning"; the root of "log" (record), "logo," "logic," and the "ology" suffix found in terms like *sociology* and *physiology*. According to Heraclitus, the rule according to which all things are accomplished and the law found in all things. (Ch. 3, p. 64)

Logos **(Stoic)** According to Stoic doctrine, World Reason, also referred to as Cosmic Mind, God, Zeus, Nature, Providence, Cosmic Meaning, and Fate; force that governs the universe; also see Chapter 3. (Ch. 7, p. 193)

master morality In Nietzschean philosophy, the *aesthetic* honor code of the overman; morality that looks only to the authentic individual (overman) for values that transcend the slave's good–evil dichotomy with glorious–degrading, honorable–dishonorable, refined–vulgar, and so on; "good" equals "noble" and "evil" equals "vulgar." (Ch. 16, p. 475)

Material Cause The material (substance) from which a thing comes, and in which change occurs; first of Aristotle's Four Causes. (Ch. 6, p. 161)

materialism (or behaviorism, mechanism, reductionism) Belief that everything is composed of matter (and energy) and can be explained by physical laws, that all human activity can be understood as the natural behavior of matter according to mechanical laws, and that thinking is merely a complex form of behaving: The body is a fleshy machine. (Ch. 9, p. 266)

materialism (Marxian) Form of social determinism based on a reciprocal relationship between individuals and their environment; distinguished from strict materialism and hard determinism. (Ch. 13, p. 375)

matter (Aristotle) From the Greek *hyle*, the common material stuff found in a variety of things; it has no distinct characteristics until some form is imparted to it or until the form inherent in a thing becomes actualized. (Ch. 6, p. 159)

mean From the Latin *medius*, the midpoint between two other points; for Aristotle, moral virtue was characterized as a mean between too little (deficiency) and too much (excess). (Ch. 6, p. 175)

means of production In philosophical Marxism, the means of production include natural resources such as water, coal, land, and so forth; a part of the substructure of society. (Ch. 13, p. 376)

mere belief, see *belief (mere)*

metaphysics Branch of philosophy that addresses the problem of what is real.

methodic doubt Cartesian strategy of deliberately doubting everything it is possible to doubt in the least degree so that what remains will be known with absolute certainty. (Ch. 9, p. 254)

modernity The historical period of nineteenth- and twentieth-century nation states and a corresponding set of cultural conditions and beliefs dominated by Enlightenment ideals, including faith in science, objective truth, and rationality; expectations of inevitable progress;

political democracy; capitalism; urbanization; mass literacy; mass media; mass culture; anti-traditionalism; large-scale industrial enterprise; individualism; and secularization. (Ch. 16, p. 453)

monism General name for the belief that everything consists of only one, ultimate, unique substance such as matter or spirit. (Ch. 9, p. 266)

moral From the Latin *moralis,* meaning "custom," "manner," or "conduct"; refers to what people consider good or bad, right or wrong; used descriptively as a contrast to *amoral* or *nonmoral* and prescriptively as a contrast to *immoral.* (Ch. 11, p. 311)

moral realism Pragmatic social philosophy unfettered by moral considerations; expressed in the formula "might makes right." (Ch. 3, p. 78)

moralistic Being moralistic consists of expressing commonplace moral sentiments that conflict with one's behavior and equating moral sentimentality with virtuous living; a form of hypocrisy that resembles a reaction formation. (Ch. 16, p. 466)

mystification Use of cloudy abstractions to create elaborate metaphysical systems that distract us from concrete material reality. (Ch. 13, p. 374)

naturalism Belief that reality consists of the natural world; denial of the existence of a separate supernatural order of reality; belief that nature follows orderly, discoverable laws. (Ch. 6, p. 156)

Nietzschean perspectivism The contention that every view is only one among many possible interpretations, including, especially, Nietzschean perspectivism, which itself is just one interpretation among many interpretations. (Ch. 16, p. 461)

nihilism From Latin for "nothing"; belief that the universe lacks meaning and purpose. (Ch. 16, p. 470)

nirvana Annihilation of the ego; a state of emptiness or "no-thing-ness"; a state of bliss; "pure consciousness" that leads to release from suffering while remaining conscious. (Ch. 2, p. 43)

nonmoral (amoral) Not pertaining to moral; a value-neutral descriptive claim or classification. (Ch. 11, p. 311)

noumenal reality Kant's term for reality as it is, independent of our perceptions; what is commonly called "objective reality." (Ch. 11, p. 319)

ontological argument An attempt to prove the existence of God either by referring to the meaning of the word *God* when it is understood a certain way or by referring to the purportedly unique quality of the concept of God. (Ch. 9, p. 264)

ontology The study of being. (Ch. 3, p. 65; Ch. 17, p. 503)

original position John Rawls's imaginary setting in which we can identify the fundamental principles of justice from an objective, impartial perspective, as rational agents, rather than as "interested parties"; similar to the "state of nature" in the social contract theories of Thomas Hobbes, Jean-Jacques Rousseau, and John Locke. (Ch. 11, p. 333)

overman Nietzsche's "higher type," a more-than-human being that will emerge only by overcoming the false idols of conventional morality and religion; announced in *Thus Spake Zarathustra.* (Ch. 16, p. 471)

paradigmatic individual, see *archetypal individual*

perspectivism, see *Nietzschean perspectivism*

pessimism Schopenhauer's theory that life is disappointing and that for every satisfied desire, new desires emerge; our only hope is detachment and withdrawal. Ch. 16, p. 455)

phenomenal reality Kant's term for the world as we experience it. (Ch. 11, p. 319)

phenomenology Method of philosophical analysis first developed by Husserl that uses purely descriptive statements to provide a "descriptive analysis" of consciousness in all its forms; focuses on concrete "experienced facts" rather than abstractions in order to reveal the "essence" of human consciousness. (Ch. 17, p. 500)

philophaster A pretender or dabbler in philosophy. (FYI)

philosophical advocate Philosopher whose work identifies, clarifies, and actively opposes a perceived injustice; philosophical advocates give philosophical credence to personal experience based on gender, ethnic background, or social status. (Ch. 18, p. 525)

philosophical archetype, see *archetype (philosophical)*

philosophy From Greek roots meaning "the love of wisdom." (Ch. 1, p. 3)

philosophy (political) Branch of philosophy concerned with the state and issues of sovereignty.

philosophy (social) Branch of philosophy concerned with social institutions and relations.

Platonic Forms Independently existing, nonspatial, nontemporal "somethings" ("kinds," "types," or "sorts") known only through thought and that cannot be known through the senses; independently existing objects of thought; that which makes a particular thing uniquely and essentially what it is. (Ch. 5, p. 128)

Platonic virtue, see *virtue (Platonic)*

plenitude, see *principle of plenitude*

pluralism The belief that there exist many realities or substances. (Ch. 9, p. 266)

practical imperative (or principle of dignity) Kant's formulation of the categorical imperative based on the concept of dignity: "Act in such a way that you always treat humanity, whether in your own person or in the person of another, never simply as a means but always at the same time as an end." (Ch. 11, p. 332)

practical knowledge, see *knowledge (practical)*

practical reason, see *reason (practical)*

pragmatic paradox Pragmatism works only if we believe that our ideas are true according to nonpragmatic criteria. (Ch. 15, p. 447)

pragmatism From the Greek for "deed"; belief that ideas have meaning or truth value to the extent that they produce practical results and effectively further our aims; empirically based philosophy that defines knowledge and truth in terms of practical consequences. (Ch. 3, p. 74; see also Ch. 15, p. 423)

primary qualities According to Locke, objective sensible qualities that exist independently of any perceiver; shape, size, location, and motion are examples of primary qualities. (Ch. 10, p. 283)

principle of dignity, see *practical imperative*

principle of plenitude The name given by American historian of ideas Arthur O. Lovejoy (1873–1962) to the metaphysical principle that, given infinity, any real possibility must occur (at least once). (Ch. 8, p. 228)

principle of sufficient reason The principle that nothing happens without a reason; consequently, no adequate theory or explanation can contain any brute, crude, unexplained facts. First specifically encountered in the work of the medieval philosopher Peter Abelard (1079–1142), it is usually associated with the rationalist philosopher Gottfried Wilhelm Leibniz (1646–1716), who used it in his famous "best of all possible worlds" argument. (Ch.,8, p. 228)

principle of utility, see *utility (principle of)*

principles of reason (or rules of inference) Principles (such as the law of contradiction) that define the limits of rationality by their very structure and that cannot be rationally refuted since we rely on them in order to reason. (Ch. 8, p. 215)

problem of evil If God can prevent the suffering of the innocent, yet chooses not to, He is not good. If God chooses to prevent the suffering, but cannot, He is not omnipotent. If God cannot recognize the suffering of the innocent, He is not wise. (Ch. 8, p. 233)

proletariat All those whose labor produces goods and provides essential services, yet who do not own the means of production. (Ch. 13, p. 373)

psyche Greek for "soul"; in today's terms, combination of mind and soul, including capacity for reflective thinking. (Ch. 3, p. 64; see also Ch. 4, p. 102)

psychological hedonism, see *hedonism (psychological)*

public philosopher Compelling writer or speaker whose philosophical positions are expressed in ways accessible to a broad audience; public philosophers tap into—or identify—vital philosophical issues of the day. (Ch. 18, p. 525)

qualities, see *primary qualities* and *secondary qualities*

rational discourse The interplay of carefully argued ideas; the use of reason to order, clarify, and identify reality and truth according to agreed upon standards of verification. (Ch. 3, p. 63)

rationalism An epistemological position in which reason is said to be the primary source of all knowledge, superior to sense evidence. Rationalists argue that only reason can distinguish reality from illusion and give meaning to experience. (Ch. 9, p. 249)

reaction formation Freudian ego defense mechanism that attempts to prevent "dangerous" desires from being exposed and expressed by endorsing opposite attitudes and types of behavior as "barriers" against them. (Ch. 16, p. 466)

realism In philosophy, the belief that there exists an independent, objective world of things, facts, and states of affairs that are accessible to us. (Ch. 17, p. 488)

reality (noumenal), see *noumenal reality*

reality (phenomenal), see *phenomenal reality*

reason (practical) According to Kant, moral function of reason that produces religious feelings and intuitions based on knowledge of moral conduct. (Ch. 11, p. 323)

reason (theoretical) According to Kant, a function of reason confined to the empirical, phenomenal world. (Ch. 11, p. 323)

reductio ad absurdum From the Latin for "reduce to absurdity"; form of argument that refutes an opponent's position by showing that accepting it leads to absurd, unacceptable, or contradictory conclusions because (1) accepting it leads to a logical contradiction, or (2) it leads to a logical conclusion that is somehow obviously ridiculous because it offends either our reason or common sense. (Ch. 3, p. 67)

regulative ideas (transcendental ideas) In Kantian philosophy, a special class of transcendental ideas that bridges the gap between the phenomenal and noumenal worlds: the ideas of self, cosmos (totality), and God. (Ch. 11, p. 320)

relationships of production In philosophical Marxism, relationships of production consist of who does what, who owns what, and how this affects members of both groups; a part of the substructure of society. (Ch. 13, p. 376)

relativism Belief that knowledge is determined by specific qualities of the observer, including age, ethnicity, gender, cultural conditioning. (Ch. 1, p. 11; see also Ch. 3, p. 72)

ressentiment French for "resentment"; term used in Nietzschean philosophy for a deep form of psychically polluting resentment that generates slave morality; the dominant emotion of the underman. (Ch. 16, p. 473)

rules of inference, see *principles of reason*

sage Archetypal figure who combines religious inspiration and extraordinary insight into the human condition; the English word *sage* is derived from the Latin *sapiens,* meaning "wise." (Ch. 2, p. 23)

Scholasticism Christian philosophy dominating medieval Europe from about 1000 to 1300 that stressed logical and linguistic analysis of texts and arguments in order to produce a systematic statement and defense of Christian beliefs. (Ch. 8, p. 222)

scientism The belief that the methods of the natural sciences apply to all areas of knowledge, and that only they can overcome the vagaries of prescientific superstition, religion, and metaphysics. (Ch. 16, p. 463)

secondary qualities According to Locke, subjective qualities whose existence depends on a perceiver; color, sound, taste, and texture are examples of secondary qualities. (Ch. 10, p. 283)

self-fulfilling prophecy A belief that affects events in such a way that it causes itself to come true; an example is the student who does poorly on an exam because she expects to fail it. (Ch. 15, p. 447)

skeptic From the Greek *skeptesthai,* "to consider or examine"; a person who demands clear, observable, undoubtable evidence before accepting any knowledge claim as true. (Ch. 10, p. 277)

slave morality In Nietzschean philosophy, a distortion of the will to power in which the characteristics of the inferior type (underman) are praised as virtues, and

the characteristics of the superior type (overman) are condemned as arrogance and coldheartedness; a morality of inhibitions, equality, restrictive duties, and "bad conscience." (Ch. 16, p. 472)

Socratic dialectic, Socratic method Question-and-answer technique used by Socrates to draw truth out of his pupils, often by means of achieving a clearer, more precise definition of a key term or concept. (Ch. 4, p. 95)

sophistry The teachings and practices of the original Sophists; modern usage refers to subtle, plausible, but fallacious reasoning used to persuade rather than discover truth.

Sophists In fifth century B.C.E., teachers of rhetoric (who were paid); relativists who taught that might makes right, truth is a matter of appearance and convention, and power is the ultimate value. (Ch. 3, p. 70)

sophos Sage or wise man; term applied to the first philosophers; from the Greek word for "wise." (Ch. 3, p. 61)

sophrosyne Wisdom as moderation; hitting the mark; quality of finding the mean between excess and deficiency. (Ch. 6, p. 173)

species-life Fully human life lived productively and consciously; not alienated. (Ch. 13, p. 384)

Stoic Individual who attempts to live according to Stoic doctrine. (Ch. 7, p. 181)

Stoicism Philosophy that counsels self-control, detachment, and acceptance of one's fate as identified by the objective use of reason. (Ch. 7, p. 181)

substructure of society In philosophical Marxism, the material substructure or base of society determines the nature of all social relationships, as well as religions, art, philosophies, literature, science, and government. (Ch. 13, p. 376)

sufficient reason, see *principle of sufficient reason*

superstructure of society According to philosophical Marxism, the superstructure of a culture consists of the ideas and institutions (religious beliefs, educational systems, philosophies, the arts, and such) compatible with and produced by the material substructure of the society. (Ch. 13, p. 377)

surplus value Term Marx used to refer to the capital accumulated by owners; the result of keeping prices higher than the costs of production at the expense of workers. (Ch. 13, p. 377)

tabula rasa Latin expression for a "clean slate," used by John Locke to challenge the possibility of innate ideas by characterizing the mind at birth as a blank tablet or clean slate. (Ch. 10, p. 281)

Tao Literally "way" or "path," Tao (or Dao) is variously translated as the source of all existence, the principle of all things, the way or path of the universe or the moral law; key concept in Confucian and Taoist philosophy. (Ch. 2, p. 23)

te Traditionally, moral neutral virtue; potency, the power to affect others without using physical force; expanded by Confucius to mean the capacity to act according to Tao and to bring others to Tao. (Ch. 2, p. 37)

techne From the Greek for "art," "skill," "craft," "technique," "trade," "system," or "method of doing some thing"; root of English words such as technique, technical, and technology; term Socrates used when he asserted that virtue (*arete*) is knowledge or wisdom (*techne*). (Ch. 4, p. 109)

teleological argument Also called the argument from design, this widely known argument for the existence of God claims that the universe manifests order and purpose that can only be the result of a conscious intelligence (God); Aristotelian argument that forms the basis for the fifth of Aquinas's Five Ways and the basis of William Paley's watchmaker argument. (Ch. 8, p. 230)

teleological thinking Way of explaining things in terms of their ultimate goals; understanding things functionally in terms of the relationship of the parts to the whole. (Ch. 6, p. 168)

the "they" Heidegger's name for Being-with-another; an inauthentic way of avoiding anxiety by allowing an "aggregate average" to determine how we live and think; enemy of authenticity. (Ch. 17, p. 507)

theology From the Greek *theos* (God) and *logos* (study of); "talking about God" or "the study or science of God." (Ch. 8, p. 214)

theoretical reason, see *reason (theoretical)*

thought experiment A way of using our imaginations to test a hypothesis; we think rather than field-test a hypothesis, using reasoned imagination to provide the necessary conditions for the experiment, and carefully reasoning out the most likely consequences according to our hypothesis. (Ch. 11, p. 333)

tragic optimism According to Nietzsche, the sense of joy and vitality that accompanies the superior individual's clear-sighted imposition of his own freely chosen values on a meaningless world. (Ch. 16, p. 457)

transcendental idealism, see *idealism (Kantian)*

transcendental ideas, see *regulative ideas*

tyranny Form of government in which all power rests in a single individual, known as the tyrant. (Ch. 5, p. 148)

underman Nietzsche's term for the type of person who cannot face being alone in a godless universe, an inferior individual seeking safety and identity in a group or from another; characterized by resentment and hypocrisy. (Ch. 16, p. 472)

utility (principle of) Always act to promote the greatest happiness for the greatest number. (Ch. 12, p. 345)

utopia Term for a perfect or ideal society derived from Sir Thomas More's 1516 novel of the same name; the word was created from the Greek root meaning "nowhere." (Ch. 5, p. 144)

veil of ignorance John Rawls's mechanism for imaginatively entering into the original position by avoiding all personal considerations in the process of determining principles of justice; the veil of ignorance is a problem-solving device that prevents us from knowing our social status, what property we own, what we like and don't like, how intelligent we are, what our talents and strengths are, and so on. (Ch. 11, p. 333)

virtue From the Greek *arete*, meaning "that at which something excels," or "excellence of function." (Ch. 4, p. 108)

virtue (Platonic) Excellence of function. (Ch. 5, p. 143)

will to power Nietzsche's term for what he thought is a universal desire to control others and impose our values on them. (Ch. 16, p. 456)

willed ignorance An attitude of indifference to the possibility of error or enlightenment that holds on to beliefs regardless of the facts. (Ch. 1, p. 14)

wisdom Fundamental understanding of reality as it relates to living a good life; reasonable and practical, focusing on the true circumstances and character of each individual; good judgment about complex situations involving reflection, insight, and a plausible conception of the human condition. (Ch. 1, p. 13)

wu wei Literally, "not to act"; in the *Tao te Ching*, a warning against unnatural or demanding action. (Ch. 2, p. 31)

yang In Ancient Chinese metaphysics, strong, positive, light, and constructive natural force or principle; linked with yin. (Ch. 2, p. 23)

yin In Ancient Chinese metaphysics, weak, negative, dark, and destructive natural force or principle; linked with yang. (Ch. 2, p. 23)

BIBLIOGRAPHY OF PHILOSOPHICAL DELIGHTS

Here is a small sampling of some especially well-written, interesting, and engaging books that complement the material covered in Archetypes of Wisdom, *7th edition. They are some of my favorite philosophical and philosophy books. What is the difference? "Philosophical books" do not have to be written by philosophers, nor do they have to present technical, scholarly philosophical arguments. Rather, philosophical books, as I see them, express, nurture, and encourage philosophical themes. They flow from and touch upon our "meaning needs," our innate curiosities about what matters and why. Not only can they be valuable in a philosophically technical way, they are also practically—that is,* humanly—*valuable. To borrow from Heidegger, they are part of the elemental human conversation. As such, most of them are "good reads."*

With only a few exceptions, this list does not duplicate the main philosophical sources cited in the text since these are fully annotated in the Notes section.

GENERAL SOURCES

Blackburn, Simon. *The Oxford Dictionary of Philosophy,* 2nd ed. Oxford: Oxford University Press, 2007. This witty and authoritative philosophical dictionary includes excellent cross-references.

Craig, Edward. *The Shorter Routledge Encyclopedia of Philosophy.* New York: Routledge, 2005. Here's a handy one-volume desk reference culled from the ten-volume *Routledge Encyclopedia of Philosophy.*

Edwards, Paul, ed. in chief. *The Encyclopedia of Philosophy.* New York: Macmillan & the Free Press, 1967. Two versions of this indispensable source are available: the regular edition of eight separate volumes and a four-volume "student edition" that contains exactly the same material.

Honderich, Ted, ed. *The Oxford Companion to Philosophy,* 2nd ed. Oxford: Oxford University Press, 2005. Checking in at a massive 1,076 pages, Honderich's text is one of the most thorough single-volume reference books available—nearly an encyclopedia.

Chapter 1

Philosophy and the Search for Wisdom

Gaarder, Jostein. *Sophie's World.* New York: Farrar, Straus and Giroux, 1994. Paulette Møller's excellent translation of Gaarder's clever story of an eighteen-year-old girl's intriguing introduction to philosophy is highly recommended.

Needleman, Jacob. *The Heart of Philosophy.* New York: Knopf, 1982. Needleman's adventures teaching philosophy through dialogue to high school students and their parents produced intriguing ideas about education, society, and the need for philosophy.

Rand, Ayn. *Philosophy: Who Needs It?* Ayn Rand Library, vol. 1. New York: Signet, 1982. Rand ranks as one of the few best-selling philosophical writers of the twentieth century. In this collection of essays, she argues for her own objectivist philosophy. Even when her argument is weak, her confrontational style raises questions about the value of philosophy rarely asked in popular literature.

OVERVIEW OF CLASSICAL THEMES

Cook, Elizabeth. *Achilles.* New York: Macmillan, 2003. I can't resist recommending this tiny, short (107 pages) retelling of Homer's *Iliad* in poetic, contemporary English. It is a haunting, moving evocation of mythic themes and human longing—superb!

Hadot, Pierre. *What Is Ancient Philosophy?* Translated by Michael Chase. Cambridge, Mass.: Harvard University Press, 2002. Don't be misled by the title; this is a magnificent book—technically informative, evocatively written, and generous in its view of philosophy and the human condition.

Homer. *Iliad and Odyssey.* I'm partial to the Robert Fagels translations of these compelling epics, but almost any of the many inexpensive, widely available versions is well-worth reading. If you've never read Homer, don't deprive yourself of "conversing" with one of the most profound voices in Western history.

Chapter 2
The Asian Sages: Lao-tzu, Confucius, and Buddha

Bankei. *The Unborn.* Translated by Norman Waddell. San Francisco: North Point Press, 1984. Delightful collections of talks and sermons by a seventeenth-century Japanese sage. Bankei's wisdom is funny, profound, and relevant. An excellent introduction to Buddhism without technical language.

Benares, Camden. *Zen Without Zen Masters.* Berkeley, Calif.: And/Or Press, 1977. Bizarre collection of Buddhist-like tales, most with punch lines. A kind of stand-up comedy approach to philosophy.

Confucius. *The Wisdom of Confucius.* Translated and edited by Lin Yutang. New York: Modern Library, 1938. An elegant and especially readable treatment of Confucius's *Analects* along with engaging stories and Lin Yutang's helpful commentaries.

Emerson, Ralph Waldo, and Lao-tzu. *The Tao of Emerson: The Wisdom of the Tao te Ching as Found in the Words of Ralph Waldo Emerson.* Edited by Richard Grossman. New York: Modern Library, 2007. This is a creative, engaging pairing of two popular philosophical writers whose words, although separated by 2,500 years and two radically distinct cultures, often echo each other. Goodman positions passages from Lao-tzu and Emerson on facing pages as a way of testing Emerson's assertion that "all philosophy, East and West, has the same centerpiece." What do you think? Or should I ask, how does your psyche answer?

Lao-tzu. *The Wisdom of Laotse.* Translated and edited by Lin Yutang. New York: Modern Library, 1948. This is one of my favorite books. It's a modestly priced little hardback containing excellent translations of both Lao-tzu and Chuang-tzu. Wise and witty.

Maugham, W. Somerset. *The Razor's Edge.* New York: Penguin, 1979. A classic of spiritual discovery.

Pirsig, Robert. *Zen and the Art of Motorcycle Maintenance: An Inquiry into Values.* New York: Morrow, 1974. A remarkably moving book that works on many levels. It's about motorcycles, parenthood, traveling, mental breakdowns, values, Plato, Buddhism, courage, loneliness, and wisdom.

Chapter 3
The Sophist: Protagoras

Davenport, Guy. *7 Greeks.* New York: New Directions, 1995. The late Guy Davenport is one of my favorite translator's of ancient Greek poetry. This colorful and sophisticated collection includes five poets and two philosophers. These lusty and poignant fragments reveal a complex, beautiful, and disturbing culture.

Grant, Michael. *The Classical Greeks.* New York: Scribner's, 1989. This nicely written history of classical Greece often reads like a novel. Good index, useful for selective research.

Guthrie, W. K. C. *The Sophists.* Cambridge: Cambridge University Press, 1971. Thorough, major source of general information. Best read in conjunction with a general history of the period.

Henry, Jules. *Culture Against Man.* New York: Vintage, 1963. The section on advertising as a philosophical system, though dated in its examples, is a stinging indictment of modern sophistry.

Chapter 4
The Wise Man: Socrates

Guthrie, W. K. C. *Socrates.* Cambridge: Cambridge University Press, 1971. Comprehensive survey of Socrates' life and philosophy. Sophisticated reading level, but valuable source for research papers.

Jaspers, Karl. *Socrates, Buddha, Confucius, Jesus: The Paradigmatic Individuals.* Edited by Hannah Arendt. Translated by Ralph Manheim. New York: Harcourt Brace Jovanovich, 1962. This excerpt from Jaspers's history of philosophy presents his fascinating notion of the paradigmatic individual. Worth tracking down for those interested in wise people.

Stone, I. F. *The Trial of Socrates.* Toronto: Little, Brown, 1988. Valuable as an alternative view of Socrates and as an example of a first-rate mind driven by wonder. Working outside the academic establishment, Stone, like Joseph Campbell, reminds us of the virtues of curiosity and independence.

Chapter 5
The Philosopher-King: Plato

Levi, A. W. *Philosophy as Social Expression.* Chicago: University of Chicago Press, 1974. See Chapter 2, "Ancient Philosophy: The Age of the Aristocrat," for a full discussion of the influence of social class on Plato.

Taylor, A. E. *Plato: The Man and His Work.* London: Methuen, 1966. Scholarly and sometimes difficult, but useful for research papers.

Chapter 6
The Naturalist: Aristotle

Andrews, Lewis M. *To Thine Own Self Be True: The Re-birth of Values in the New Ethical Theory.* New York: Doubleday/Anchor, 1987. Intriguing blend of philosophy and psychology. Andrews's ethical therapy is based on universal moral principles derived from Plato and Aristotle.

MacIntyre, Alasdair. *After Virtue.* Notre Dame, Ind.: University of Notre Dame Press, 1981. MacIntyre argues that virtues are necessary for society and human development. An impressive assessment of excellence and community.

Merton, Thomas. *New Seeds of Contemplation.* New York: New Directions, 1961. This is one of Merton's best, a rare combination of literature, philosophy, psychology, and Catholic theology. A gem.

Chapter 7
The Stoic: Epictetus and Marcus Aurelius

Epictetus. *Handbook of Epictetus.* Translated by Nicholas P. White. Indianapolis: Hackett, 1983. First-rate translation, inexpensive edition.

Frankl, Viktor E. *Man's Search for Meaning: An Introduction to Logotherapy.* New York: Pocket, 1963. A modern classic. Frankl's account of his concentration camp experiences is harrowing, and the conversion of those experiences into a form of philosophical therapy is inspiring. If I had my way, this would be required reading for just about everyone.

Hadot, Pierre. *The Inner Citadel: The Meditations of Marcus Aurelius.* Translated by Michael Chase. Cambridge, Mass.: Harvard University Press, 1998. Hadot is one of my very favorite contemporary philosophical writers, and this extended meditation on Marcus's *Meditations* is simply magnificent. It is scholarly, to be sure, but is also deep, rich, and profoundly affecting.

Lasch, Christopher. *The Culture of Narcissism: American Life in an Age of Diminishing Expectations.* New York: Norton, 1979. Interesting, troubling analysis of contemporary culture by a social historian.

Lin Yutang. *The Importance of Living.* New York: Morrow, 1937, 1965. A genuinely delightful book that raises questions about what's important and what's not. Some dated passages, but much of this is elegant, pleasant—everything a hedonist looks for. William Morrow's 1996 hardcover edition of this gem is itself appropriately elegant. An excellent edition.

Lippmann, Walter. *A Preface to Morals.* 1929. Reprint. New Brunswick, N.J.: Transaction, 1982. Though dated, the opening and closing chapters present a stirring Stoic analysis of American culture.

Marcus Aurelius. *The Essential Marcus Aurelius.* Translated by Jacob Needleman and John Piazza. New York: Tarcher/Penguin, 2008. This compact, truncated new translation of the heart of the *Meditations* boasts Needleman's magnificent introduction, a rare attempt to articulate precisely why and how Marcus's notes to himself act on our souls.

Marcus Aurelius. *Meditations.* Translated by Gregory Hays. New York: Modern Library, 2002. Stoicism seems to be enjoying a mini-revival, and Hays's new translation of the *Meditations* includes a first-rate introduction; this attractive edition makes a great gift. A number of inexpensive editions of George Long's elegant Victorian translation are widely available as well. Truly timeless.

Seneca. *The Stoic Philosophy of Seneca.* Translated by Moses Hadas. New York: Norton, 1958. This excellent translation is still available as a paperback reprint. Seneca's letters remain edifying.

Stockdale, Jim. *Thoughts of a Philosophical Fighter Pilot.* Stanford, Calif.: Hoover Institution Press, 1995. An inspiring and accessible collection of essays, articles, lectures, and speeches focusing on the human capacity for meeting adversity with courage, dignity, and wisdom; Stockdale was the Epictetus of our time.

Chapter 8

The Scholar: Thomas Aquinas

Armstrong, Karen. *A History of God: The 4,000-Year Quest of Judaism, Christianity, and Islam.* New York: Ballantine, 1993. Written by a former Roman Catholic nun, this comparative history of Western monotheism is also a profoundly moving search for a sense of God that "works for us in the empirical age."

Augustine. *Confessions.* Translated by R. S. Pine-Coffin. Middlesex, England: Penguin, 1961. The first "autobiography" as such. You'll be surprised how contemporary Augustine sounds in this honest, introspective blend of philosophy and journal writing.

Dawkins, Richard. *The God Delusion.* New York: Houghton Mifflin, 2008. Dawkins's entry into the "religious wars" of the early twenty-first century derides Aquinas's proofs for God's existence as "fatuous" and religion itself as "nonsense." Contrast this tone—independent of any arguments—with that of Thomas Merton and C. S. Lewis to see how much religion and philosophy still matter.

Hitchens, Christopher. *God Is Not Great: How Religion Poisons Everything.* New York: Twelve Books/ Hachette, 2007. This pungent indictment of religion— Hitchens describes religious education as "child abuse"—is deliberately provocative and disturbing. It's also biased. But it raises a foundational question: If religion is as foolish and harmful as Hitchens claims, what accounts for its persistence?

Kaufmann, Walter. *The Faith of a Heretic.* New York: New American Library, 1978. A wholly different kind of critique of theology from those of Dawkins and Hitchens. Intense, to be sure, yet reasonable rather than mostly polemical.

Lewis, C. S. *Mere Christianity.* New York: Macmillan, 1976. One of the most popular examples of contemporary apologetics. Lewis attempts to construct a rational argument for Christianity. Quite interesting and persuasive to many.

Russell, Bertrand. *Why I Am Not a Christian, and Other Essays on Religion and Related Subjects.* New York: Simon & Schuster, 1957. Russell's tightly argued but clear account of his objections to Christianity. Intelligent atheism at its best. (For an interesting take on cultural changes, compare Russell to Dawkins and Hitchens.)

Chapter 9

The Rationalist: René Descartes

Descartes, René. *Objections and Replies to Descartes' Meditations,* in *The Philosophical Works of Descartes,* vol. 2. Translated by Elizabeth S. Haldane and G. R. T. Ross. Cambridge: Cambridge University Press, 1968. This witty exchange of letters between Descartes and Hobbes (and others) is philosophically important and has the added virtue of showing us philosophy in action.

Jaggar, Alison M, and Susan R. Bordo, eds. *Gender/ Body/Knowledge: Feminist Reconstructions of Being and Knowing.* New Brunswick, N.J.: Rutgers University Press, 1989. Sophisticated anthology of feminist analyses of epistemological and metaphysical issues.

Ryle, Gilbert. *The Concept of Mind.* New York: Barnes & Noble, 1949. Important work in the analytic tradition. Quite readable introduction to early analytic method.

Watson, Richard. *Cogito Ergo Sum: The Life of René Descartes.* Boston: Godine, 2002. Hold on to your hats! Watson's written a quirky (in a good sense), witty biography that manages to be both scholarly and entertaining.

Chapter 10
The Skeptic: David Hume

Annas, Julia, and Jonathan Barnes. *The Modes of Scepticism: Ancient Texts and Modern Interpretations.* Cambridge: Cambridge University Press, 1985. First-rate contemporary look at skepticism.

Hallie, Phillip P. "Classical Scepticism—A Polemical Introduction." In *Sextus Empiricus, Selections from the Major Writings on Scepticism, Man, & God.* Edited by Phillip P. Hallie. Translated by Sanford G. Etheridge. Indianapolis: Hackett, 1985. Lucid commentary on classical skepticism.

Russell, Bertrand. *Our Knowledge of the External World.* Chicago: Open Court, 1915. First-rate assessment of some fundamental epistemological problems.

Santayana, George. *Scepticism and Animal Faith.* 1923. Reprint. New York: Dover, 1955. Santayana's challenge to skepticism is an excellent example of precise thinking presented in nontechnical terms. Very well written.

Watson, Richard. *The Philosopher's Diet: How to Lose Weight and Change the World.* Boston: Atlantic Monthly Press, 1985. Watson talks about diets, exercise, philosophy, and David Hume in a powerful, witty, surprisingly effective manner. This is a delightful book you'll want to reread. A refreshing change of pace.

Chapter 11
The Universalist: Immanuel Kant

Campbell, Jeremy. *The Liar's Tale: A History of Falsehood.* New York: Norton, 2002. An intriguing look at the possibility that not only is deception unavoidable but also downright valuable and necessary for human well-being; chock-full of examples.

Okin, Susan Moller. *Justice, Gender, and the Family.* New York: Basic, 1989. Disturbing (in a valuable way) challenge to John Rawls's influential theory of justice and the possibility of gender-free rationality. Excellent discussion of "original position" reasoning.

Stout, Martha. *The Sociopath Next Door.* New York: Broadway, 2005. What would life be like with absolutely no conscience, no moral sense, no empathy whatsoever? Would it be glorious and successful, as some of the most radical Sophists suggested? Stout, a clinical psychologist, thinks not, going so far as to say that conscience makes us fully human. A chilling and worthwhile survey of what social scientists have been saying about morality.

Chapter 12
The Utilitarian: John Stuart Mill

Capaldi, Nicholas. *John Stuart Mill: A Biography.* Cambridge: Cambridge University Press, 2004. "The two most important factors about the life of John Stuart Mill were that he was the son of James Mill and that he fell in love with Harriet Taylor." To the dismay of some philosophers, Capaldi's intellectual biography of Mill is more sympathetic to Mrs. Taylor than other assessments of Mill's life are. It is also rich in engaging anecdotes and analysis of Mill's place in Victorian culture and the evolution of his thought. The result is thought-provoking and moving.

Mill, John Stuart. *Autobiography.* New York: Columbia University Press, 1924. A classic autobiography, readable, and, I think, commendable for its brevity and modesty—which, considering Mill's gifts and accomplishments, is particularly enlightening in this era of the pervasive, bloated memoir.

Reeves, Richard. *John Stuart Mill: Victorian Firebrand.* New York: Overlook, 2008. Reeves's new biography of Mill puts the philosopher's ideas and life together in an engaging way that diminishes neither the personal nor the philosophical.

Chapter 13
The Materialist: Karl Marx

Berlin, Isaiah. *Karl Marx: His Life and Environment,* 4th ed. Oxford: Oxford University Press, 1978. A superb brief (256 pages) biography. Berlin's characterizations of Marx's ideas are clear, and his portrait of the man is sympathetic without going overboard. Here's an example of fair and balanced treatment of a philosopher with whom one (in this case Berlin) disagrees. That in itself is a lesson for these hyper-partisan times.

Fromm, Erich. *The Art of Loving.* 1956. Reprint. New York: Perennial Library, 1974. Another good book with a potentially misleading title. This is not a self-help book; it's much more. The chapter on the disintegration of love is a fine humanistic analysis of modern capitalism that raises worthwhile questions half a century after it was written.

Marcuse, Herbert. *One-Dimensional Man: Studies in the Ideology of Advanced Industrial Society.* Boston: Beacon, 1964. Critique of modern capitalism's "flattening effect" on our psyches.

Wheen, Francis. *Karl Marx: A Life.* New York: Norton, 2001. More personal (biographical) than philosophical, this is an "odd" biography of an "odd" man. Nonetheless, and perhaps because of this, it is unsettling but entertaining. Good as a change of pace, but not so good if you're looking to dig deeper in Marx's ideas.

Chapter 14
The Existentialist: Søren Kierkegaard

Barrett, William. *Irrational Man: A Study in Existential Philosophy.* Garden City, N.Y.: Doubleday/Anchor, 1962. This impressive analysis of the 1960s intellectual and social scene is still widely read and discussed.

Camus, Albert. *The Stranger.* Translated by Matthew Ward. New York: Vintage, 1989. "Maman died today. Or maybe yesterday. I don't know. I got a telegram from the home: 'Mother deceased. Funeral tomorrow. Faithfully yours.' That doesn't mean anything. Maybe it was yesterday." Thus begins one of the most intriguing, disturbing "existential novels" of the twentieth century. The book is small; its wallop is not.

Garff, Joakim. *Søren Kierkegaard: A Biography.* Translated by Bruce H. Kimmse. Princeton, N.J.: Princeton University Press, 2005. I think Kierkegaard would have gotten a kick out of Garff's beautifully written search for the self-created individual hiding behind Kierkegaard's fictional personae, particularly since this is not a philosophical analysis as such. It is a life story—or is that "a life's" stories, one of many?

Chapter 15
The Pragmatist: William James

James, William. *William James: Writings 1902–1910.* New York: Literary Classics of the United States, Library of America—vol. 38, 1987. Excellent edition, though both Collier and Dover have inexpensive paperback editions available of *The Will to Believe* and *Varieties of Religious Experience.*

Richardson, Robert D. *Emerson: The Mind on Fire.* Berkeley: University of California Press, 1995. Although not a philosopher in the academic, technical sense, the "sage of Concord" expressed spiritual, literary, social, and philosophical interests in such compelling ways that he became one of the most influential and—gasp—popular intellectuals of his era. He's still widely read today, and this biography provides an exciting and moving background to James's life and work.

Richardson, Robert D. *William James: In the Maelstrom of American Modernism.* New York: Mariner/Houghton Mifflin, 2007. This big-hearted biography of what Richardson calls James's "matchless incandescent spirit" is chock-full of quotations and anecdotes, such as the time a friend tried to praise James by comparing him to St. Paul and Isaiah to which James retorted, "Why drag in Saint Paul and Isaiah?"

Chapter 16
The Anti-Philosopher: Friedrich Nietzsche

Hollingdale, R. J. *Nietzsche: The Man and His Philosophy,* Revised. Cambridge: University of Cambridge, 1999. More than a biography, this updated edition of one of the most humane and accessible treatments of Nietzsche includes excellent translations of key passages, illuminating notes, and a fascinating new appendix that discusses some of the more recent Nietzsche scholarship.

Kaufmann, Walter. *Without Guilt and Justice: From Decidophobia to Autonomy.* New York: Delta, 1973. Kaufmann's attempt to construct a Nietzschean ethic is easy to read and guaranteed to get you thinking about contemporary values. His assessment of the various strategies of "decidophobia" (fear of making decisions) is especially effective.

MacIntyre, Ben. *Forgotten Fatherland: The Search for Elisabeth Nietzsche.* New York: Farrar, Straus and Giroux, 1992. This fascinating account of efforts to establish a "New Germany" in South America raises disturbing questions about ways that Nietzsche's sister distorted her brother's reputation.

Nietzsche, Friedrich. *The Portable Nietzsche.* Edited and translated by Walter Kaufmann. New York: Penguin, 1968. A "best buy," this handy collection includes Kaufmann's helpful comments.

Safranski, Rüdiger. *Nietzsche: A Philosophical Biography.* New York: Norton, 2002. In the words of one reviewer, "a graceful and elegant book"; Safranski delivers on his subtitle by commingling Nietzsche's life and philosophy in a way that illuminates both.

Solomon, Robert, and Kathleen M. Higgins. *What Nietzsche Really Said.* New York: Schocken, 2000. I suspect that Nietzsche would have been simpatico with this exuberant, nose-tweaking, error-busting romp through his life and ideas, perhaps all the more so because Solomon and Higgins are respected philosophers who deflate thirty common misconceptions about the bogeyman along the way.

Chapter 17

The Twentieth Century: Ludwig Wittgenstein and Martin Heidegger

Arendt, Hannah. *Responsibility and Judgment.* Edited with an introduction by Jerome Kohn. New York: Schocken, 2003. Accessible introduction to Arendt's attempts to come to grips with the problematic relationship between philosophy and politics or between thinking and acting. A collection of previously unpublished writings triggered by widespread misunderstandings of her notion of the "banality of evil" first articulated in her controversial book *Eichmann in Jerusalem.*

Barison, David, and Daniel Ross. *The Ister.* Brooklyn, N.Y.: First Run/Icarus Films, 2004. This intriguing film uses a journey from the mouth of the Danube upstream to its source in the Black Forest as a background for a conversation among three philosophers (Philippe Lacoue-Labarthe, Jean-Luc Nancy, Bernard Stiegler) and a filmmaker (Hans-Jürgen Syberberg) about Heidegger's life, work, and historical place. The title comes from a course Heidegger gave on Hölderin's poem "The Ister."

Edmonds, David, and John Eidinow. *Wittgenstein's Poker: The Story of a Ten-Minute Argument Between Two Great Philosophers.* New York: HarperCollins, 2001. This look at a legendary, disputed argument between Ludwig Wittgenstein and Karl Popper makes for a fascinating blend of philosophy and story-telling. Bracing, informed, and entertaining. Works on many levels.

Grayling, A. C. *Wittgenstein: A Very Short Introduction.* Oxford: Oxford University Press, 2001. Weighing in at 137 pages, Grayling's look at the later Wittgenstein lives up to the Very Short Introductions series hype as a "stimulating way in to a new subject."

Magee, Bryan. *Confessions of a Philosopher: A Personal Journey Through Western Philosophy; From Plato to Popper.* New York: Modern Library, 1999. Magee chronicles his development as a philosopher as he discovers and reacts to the Presocratics, Schopenhauer, Nietzsche, Russell, and Wittgenstein. A contemporary philosophical memoir that is as personally interesting as it is intellectually engaging.

McGinn, Colin. *The Making of a Philosopher: My Journey Through Twentieth-Century Philosophy.* New York: HarperCollins, 2002. Well-written, funny, intelligent memoir that truly does describe the making of a twentieth-century philosopher. McGinn's descriptions of fellow philosophers and their thinking are crisp and elegant. His stories about famous and not-so-famous thinkers are engaging, warm, and philosophically interesting.

Monk, Ray. *Ludwig Wittgenstein: The Duty of Genius.* New York: Penguin, 1991. Philosophically interesting and personally moving account of one of the most fascinating figures in recent philosophy. Engrossing.

Smith, Huston. *Beyond the Postmodern Mind: The Place of Meaning in a Global Civilization.* Wheaton, Ill.: Quest, 2003. Smith's reflections on what he sees as a "crisis" of meaning that affects philosophy, religion, and science. Smith raises important questions and provides captivating, if somewhat skewed, overviews of postmodern philosophy. Thought-provoking take on modernity from a philosopher of religion.

Solomon, Robert C., and David Sherman, eds. *The Blackwell Guide to Continental Philosophy.* Malden, Mass.: Blackwell, 2003. Excellent introductory essays on continental philosophers from Hegel to Derrida and related trends in contemporary philosophy. Good starting point for serious readers.

Steiner, George. *Martin Heidegger: With a New Introduction.* Chicago: University of Chicago Press, 1991. Engaging, learned, and idiosyncratic overview of Heidegger's thinking. The introduction is particularly interesting in light of the rest of the book—so stinging in its assessment of Heidegger's character that some critics dismiss it as an *ad hominem* attack. Decide for yourself.

Wolin, Richard. *Heidegger's Children: Hannah Arendt, Karl Löwith, Hans Jonas, and Herbert Marcuse.* Princeton, N.J.: Princeton University Press, 2003. Wolin uses four of Heidegger's most famous students as a springboard for an examination of the relationship between philosophy and history. Itself a controversial book about an ongoing, contentious issue that extends beyond academic philosophy.

Wolin, Richard. *The Seduction of Unreason: The Intellectual Romance with Fascism from Nietzsche to Postmodernism.* Princeton, N.J.: Princeton University Press, 2004. Difficult, tough-minded critique of postmodernism that asks why—and how—it is that philosophers can be seduced by tyranny and fascism. Disturbing yet important questions here.

Chapter 18

Philosophy as a Way of Life

Davies, Robertson. *The Cunning Man.* New York: Penguin, 1994. A truly magnificent novel, Davies's last book presents a fine account of the journey from intelligence to wisdom; the fictional Jonathan Hullah is warm, wise, and kind. The sort of book you can't wait to finish but don't want to end.

Hadot, Pierre. *Philosophy as a Way of Life.* Translated by Arnold I. Davidson. Oxford: Blackwell, 1995. Hadot's book deserves wider attention than it has received. This valedictory statement by one of our era's premier intellectuals combines the scholarly authority of a lifetime with passion, spiritual depth, and superlative philosophical taste. I recommend it without qualification. A "must read" for anyone even remotely interested in the sophos.

Hadot, Pierre. *The Veil of Isis: An Essay on the History of the Idea of Nature.* Translated by Michael Chase. Cambridge, Mass.: Harvard University Press, 2006. This elegant, sophisticated, and moving inquiry is the result of Hadot's twenty-five-year meditation on Heraclitus's statement "Nature loves to hide." Rather than choosing between the extreme positions of technologically "stripping" nature or mystically idolizing it by demonizing technology, Hadot invites us to treat nature as art and art as nature.

Marinoff, Lou. *Therapy for the Sane: How Philosophy Can Change Your Life.* New York: Bloomsbury, 2003. Here's an unusual collection of case studies from Marinoff's "philosophical counseling" practice, which Marinoff describes as the application of useful philosophical ideas to the concrete problems of living or "advanced common sense." Not all philosophers agree with or accept the possibility of uniquely "philosophical" counseling. This accessible book is a good place to start if you are intrigued by—or uneasy with—the notion that philosophers can and should practice therapy.

Nussbaum, Martha C. *Frontiers of Justice: Disability, Nationality, Species Membership.* Cambridge, Mass.: Harvard University Press, 2006. This extension of Nussbaum's "capabilities approach" to social justice focuses on three unsolved problems, with attention to Kant, Marx, Rawls, and Singer among others: doing justice to people with physical and mental impairments; extending justice to people throughout the world; facing up to matters of justice for nonhuman animals.

Nussbaum, Martha C. *The Therapy of Desire.* Princeton, N.J.: Princeton University Press, 1994. I like this book for many reasons, but most of all because of the way it makes a contemporary case for the Hellenistic philosophers—and for their unshakable faith in philosophy's therapeutic virtues.

Nussbaum, Martha C. *Upheavals of Thought: The Intelligence of Emotions.* Cambridge: Cambridge University Press, 2001. An enormous book that covers such diverse fields as philosophy, anthropology, psychology, and literature; compelling yet difficult, personal yet technical; well worth the effort to work through.

Singer, Peter. *Writings on an Ethical Life.* New York: HarperCollins, 2000. Here's a handy one-volume introduction to one of today's most controversial and influential public philosophers; it contains excerpts from some of Singer's best work.

INDEX OF MARGIN QUOTES

INDEX